13th Linguistic Annotation Workshop 2019 (LAW XIII)

Florence, Italy
1 August 2019

ISBN: 978-1-5108-9100-5

LAW XIII

The 13th Linguistic Annotation Workshop

Proceedings of the Workshop

August 1, 2019
Florence, Italy

©2019 The Association for Computational Linguistics

Order copies of this and other ACL proceedings from:

Association for Computational Linguistics (ACL)
209 N. Eighth Street
Stroudsburg, PA 18360
USA
Tel: +1-570-476-8006
Fax: +1-570-476-0860
acl@aclweb.org

ISBN 978-1-950737-38-3

Introduction to the Workshop

The Linguistic Annotation Workshop (LAW) is organized annually by the Association for Computational Linguistics' Special Interest Group for Annotation (ACL SIGANN). It provides a forum to facilitate the exchange and propagation of research results concerned with the annotation, manipulation, and exploitation of corpora; work towards harmonisation and interoperability from the perspective of the increasingly large number of tools and frameworks for annotated language resources; and work towards a consensus on all issues crucial to the advancement of the field of corpus annotation. These proceedings include papers that were presented at LAW XIII, held in conjunction with the annual meeting of the Association for Computational Linguistics (ACL) in Florence, Italy, on August 1, 2019.

The series is now in its thirteenth year. The first workshop took place in 2007 at the ACL in Prague. Since then, the LAW has been held every year, consistently drawing substantial participation (both in terms of paper/poster submissions and participation in the actual workshop) providing evidence that the LAW's overall focus continues to be an important area of interest in the field.

This year's LAW has received 52 submissions, out of which 28 papers have been accepted to be presented at the workshop, 10 as talks and 18 as posters. In addition to oral and poster paper presentations, LAW XIII also features an invited talk by Rebecca Passonneau and a discussion session.

Our thanks go to SIGANN, our organizing committee, for its continuing organization of the LAW workshops, and to the ACL 2019 workshop chairs for their support. Also, we thank Jet Hoek, the LAW XIII publications chair, for her invaluable help with these proceedings. Most of all, we would like to thank all the authors for submitting their papers to the workshop, and our program committee members for their dedication and their thoughtful reviews.

Special Theme: Marking of information quality in discourse

This special theme considers the marking of information quality in discourse, i.e., annotations that mark how the speaker/writer expresses assessments. These assessments may be explicit and/or implicit in discourse, and may reflect positions, beliefs, opinions, appraisals and/or assessments about written or spoken propositions, for example, how a politician shows in discourse the degree of truthfulness in one of his/her electoral promises, or how a reporter shows his/her degree of belief in what the politician stated. This might include the annotation of devices such as hedges ("Donald claims that the crowd size, if you can really trust him to measure it, was enormous."), committed belief ("The winners of the contest will be announced tomorrow.") or attitudes ("It is with great sadness that we have learnt about the death of 6 people in the accident.").

Annemarie Friedrich and Deniz Zeyrek
Workshop chairs

Organizers:

Annemarie Friedrich, Bosch Research
Deniz Zeyrek, Middle East Technical University, Ankara

Publications chair:

Jet Hoek, The University of Edinburgh

Invited Speaker:

Rebecca Passonneau, Penn State University

Organizing Committee:

Stefanie Dipper, Ruhr University Bochum
Annemarie Friedrich, Bosch Research
Chu-Ren Huang, The Hong Kong Polytechnic University
Nancy Ide, Vassar College
Lori Levin, Carnegie Mellon University
Adam Meyers, New York University
Antonio Pareja-Lora, Universidad Complutense de Madrid / ATLAS, UNED
Massimo Poesio, Queen Mary University of London
Sameer Pradhan, Boulder Learning, Inc.
Ines Rehbein, Leibniz Science Campus, Institute for German Language and Heidelberg University
Manfred Stede, University of Potsdam
Katrin Tomanek, Google
Fei Xia, University of Washington
Heike Zinsmeister, University of Hamburg

Program Committee:

Adam Meyers, New York University
Alexis Palmer, University of North Texas
Amir Zeldes, Georgetown University
Amália Mendes, University of Lisbon
Andrea Horbach, University of Duisburg-Essen
Ann Bies, Linguistic Data Consortium
Anna Nedoluzhko, Charles University Prague
Antonio Pareja-Lora, Universidad Complutense de Madrid
Archna Bhatia, Florida Institute for Human and Machine Cognition
Arndt Riester, University of Stuttgart
Bonnie Webber, The University of Edinburgh
Caroline Sporleder, University of Göttingen
Chloé Braud, Loria
Christian Chiarcos, Goethe University Frankfurt
Djamé Seddah, University Paris-Sorbonne
Ellen Dodge, International Computer Science Institute
Els Lefever, Ghent University

Emmanuele Chersoni, The Hong Kong Polytechnic University
Éva Mújdricza-Maydt, Heidelberg University
Federico Fancellu, Samsung Artificial Intelligence Center
Fei Xia, University of Washington
Heike Zinsmeister, Hamburg University
Ines Rehbein, Leibniz Science Campus, Institute for German Language and Heidelberg University
Jena D. Hwang, Institute for Human & Machine Cognition
Jinghang Gu, Soochow University
Jiři Mírovský, Charles University Prague
John Lee, City University of Hong Kong
Jonathan Dunn, University of Canterbury
Kathryn Conger, University of Colorado Boulder
Kemal Oflazer, Carnegie Mellon University in Qatar
Kilian Evang, University of Düsseldorf
Kim Gerdes, University Paris-Sorbonne
Kristen Wright-Bettner, University of Colorado Boulder
Lilja Øvrelid, University of Oslo
Lori Levin, Carnegie Mellon University
Maciej Ogrodniczuk, Institute of Computer Science, Polish Academy of Sciences
Manfred Stede, University of Potsdam
Marie-Catherine de Marneffe, The Ohio State University
Massimo Poesio, Queen Mary University of London
Michael Wiegand, Heidelberg University
Michael Roth, University of Stuttgart
Mingyu WAN, City University of Hong Kong
Miriam R.L. Petruck, International Computer Science Institute
Nancy Ide, Vassar College
Nathan Schneider, Georgetown University
Nianwen Xue, Brandeis University
Nicoletta Calzolari, Italian National Research Council
Omri Abend, The Hebrew University of Jerusalem
Özlem Çetinoğlu, University of Stuttgart
Pablo Picasso Feliciano de Faria, University of Campinas
Phillippe Muller, IRIT, Université de Toulouse
Reut Tsarfaty, Open University of Israel
Ron Artstein, USC Institute for Creative Technologies
Sandra Kübler, Indiana University
Simon Ostermann, Saarland University
Stefanie Dipper, Ruhr University Bochum
Susan Windisch Brown, University of Colorado Boulder
Tim O'Gorman, University of Colorado Boulder
Udo Hahn, University of Jena

Table of Contents

Conference Program

Thursday 1 August 2019

Breakfast is served from 7.30am to 9.00am.

08:30–10:00   Session 1

08:30–08:45   *Introduction by workshop chairs*

08:45–09:45   *Invited talk: Rebecca Passonneau*

09:45–10:00   *Crowdsourced Hedge Term Disambiguation*
Morgan Ulinski and Julia Hirschberg

10:00–11:00   Poster session 1
Coffee is served from 10.30-11.00

11:00–12:15   Session 2

11:00–11:20   *WiRe57 : A Fine-Grained Benchmark for Open Information Extraction*
William Lechelle, Fabrizio Gotti and Phillippe Langlais

11:20–11:40   *Crowdsourcing Discourse Relation Annotations by a Two-Step Connective Insertion Task*
Frances Yung, Vera Demberg and Merel Scholman

11:40–12:00   *Annotating and Analyzing the Interactions between Meaning Relations*
Darina Gold, Venelin Kovatchev and Torsten Zesch

12:00–12:15   *CCGweb: a New Annotation Tool and a First Quadrilingual CCG Treebank*
Kilian Evang, Lasha Abzianidze and Johan Bos

12:15–14:00   *Lunch break*

Thursday 1 August 2019 (continued)

14:00–15:00   Session 3

14:00–14:20   *The Making of the Litkey Corpus, a Richly Annotated Longitudinal Corpus of German Texts Written by Primary School Children*
Ronja Laarmann-Quante, Stefanie Dipper and Eva Belke

14:20–14:40   *The Materials Science Procedural Text Corpus: Annotating Materials Synthesis Procedures with Shallow Semantic Structures*
Sheshera Mysore, Zachary Jensen, Edward Kim, Kevin Huang, Haw-Shiuan Chang, Emma Strubell, Jeffrey Flanigan, Andrew McCallum and Elsa Olivetti

14:40–14:55   *Tagging Modality in Oceanic Languages of Melanesia*
Annika Tjuka, Lena Weißmann and Kilu von Prince

15:00–16:00   Poster session 2
Coffee & snacks are served from 15.30-16.00

16:00–16:40   Session 4

16:00–16:20   *Harmonizing Different Lemmatization Strategies for Building a Knowledge Base of Linguistic Resources for Latin*
Francesco Mambrini and Marco Passarotti

16:20–16:40   *Assessing Back-Translation as a Corpus Generation Strategy for Non-English Tasks: A Study in Reading Comprehension and Word Sense Disambiguation*
Fabricio Monsalve, Kervy Rivas Rojas, Marco Antonio Sobrevilla Cabezudo and Arturo Oncevay

16:40–17:40   Discussion / Panel Session

Poster session 1 *(10.00-11.00)*

Poster session 2 *(15.00-16.00)*

Crowdsourced Hedge Term Disambiguation

Morgan Ulinski and **Julia Hirschberg**
Department of Computer Science
Columbia University
New York, NY, USA
{mulinski,julia}@cs.columbia.edu

Abstract

We address the issue of acquiring quality annotations of *hedging* words and phrases, linguistic phenomenona in which words, sounds, or other constructions are used to express ambiguity or uncertainty. Due to the limited availability of existing corpora annotated for hedging, linguists and other language scientists have been constrained as to the extent they can study this phenomenon. In this paper, we introduce a new method of acquiring hedging annotations via crowdsourcing, based on reformulating the task of labeling hedges as a simple word sense disambiguation task. We also introduce a new hedging corpus we have constructed by applying this method, a collection of forum posts annotated using Amazon Mechanical Turk. We found that the crowdsourced judgments we obtained had an inter-annotator agreement of 92.89% (Fleiss' Kappa=0.751) and, when comparing a subset of these annotations to an expert-annotated gold standard, an accuracy of 96.65%.

1 Introduction

Hedging refers to the use of words, sounds, or constructions that add ambiguity or uncertainty to spoken or written language. Hedging can indicate a speaker's lack of commitment to what they are saying or an attempt to distance themselves from the proposition they are communicating. Identifying hedging behavior in conversational speech and text can also reveal information about social and power relations between conversants. Additionally, since hedging can be indicative of a lack of speaker commitment, identifying hedging is of interest to the information extraction community, to determine the extent to which statements have been believed by the writer or speaker.

A major challenge in identifying hedges is that many hedge words and phrases are ambiguous.

For example, in (1a), *appear* is used as a hedge word, but not in (1b).

(1) a. The problem **appears** to be a bug in the software.

    b. A man suddenly **appeared** in the doorway.

Currently there are few corpora annotated for hedging, and these are available in a limited number of genres. In particular, there is currently no corpus of *informal* language annotated with hedge behavior. Acquiring expert annotations on text in other genres can be time consuming and may be cost prohibitive, which is an impediment to exploring how hedging can help with applications based on text in other genres. To address these issues, we have developed a method of acquiring hedge annotations through crowdsourcing, by framing the hedge identification task as a simple word sense disambiguation problem. In this paper, we describe this method and also our use of Amazon Mechanical Turk to construct a corpus of forum posts labeled with hedge information.

In Section 2, we discuss related work. In Section 3, we describe how we constructed our dictionary of hedge terms and created the *hedge* and *non-hedge* definitions for each. Section 4 describes the crowdsourcing task in more detail and discusses the resulting corpus. We conclude in Section 5.

2 Related Work

Currently, there is limited material available for studying hedging. The CoNLL-2010 shared task on learning to detect hedges (Farkas et al., 2010) used the BioScope corpus (Vincze et al., 2008) of biomedical abstracts and articles and a Wikipedia corpus annotated for "*weasel words*". Because of the domain-specific nature of these corpora,

Proceedings of the 13th Linguistic Annotation Workshop, pages 1–5
Florence, Italy, August 1, 2019. ©2019 Association for Computational Linguistics

they can be difficult to apply to other text genres, such as social media or blogs. Additionally, the Wikipedia definition of a *weasel word* is slightly different than that of a *hedge*. Weasel words include language referring to personal opinions and subjectivity (e.g. *excellent, best*) in addition to uncertainty and lack of speaker commitment. Thus, it may be difficult to use the Wikipedia corpus to study hedging as a phenomenon that is distinct from subjectivity. Both the BioScope corpus and the Wikipedia corpus were annotated by experts and/or trained linguists; as with any annotation task, acquiring new expert-annotated data can be time- and cost-prohibitive. Our work differs from these in that we annotate a corpus of documents containing more informal language —a collection of forum posts. Additionally, rather than relying on the availability of trained linguists to annotate the corpus, our work explores how we can use crowdsourcing to obtain hedge annotations.

To facilitate annotation by non-experts, we frame the annotation task as a word sense disambiguation problem rather than asking directly about hedging. Note that there is a precedent for reformulating hedge detection in this way: as a follow-up to the CoNLL-2010 hedge classification task, Velldal (2011) described a new approach to classification in which hedge detection was viewed as a simple disambiguation task, restricted to words that have previously been observed as hedge cues. Velldal transformed the CoNLL data for the binary classification task by defining the dictionary of potential hedge terms as any tokens that appeared as hedge cues in the training data; all unlabeled instances of these terms were assumed to be non-hedge usages. A classifier trained using this approach was found to outperform the systems presented at CoNLL-2010, which relied on standard methods of token-by-token or sentence-level classification. Our work extends the word sense disambiguation approach to the problem of obtaining hedging annotations on new corpora.

Crowdsourcing has been successfully used in the past for collecting annotations for word sense disambiguation. Chklovski and Mihalcea (2002) had users select the WordNet sense that most closely matched the definition of a word as used in a given sentence. Likewise, Akkaya et al. (2010) used Amazon Mechanical Turk (AMT) to annotate Subjectivity Word Sense Disambiguation (SWSD), a coarse-grained word sense disambiguation task. In a much easier task, Snow et al. (2008) had users select from among three different senses of the word *president*. Our work follows these examples by presenting hedging and non-hedging definitions and asking users to choose between them.

3 Hedging Dictionary

We compiled a dictionary of 117 potential hedge words and phrases. We began with the hedge terms identified during the CoNLL-2010 shared task (Farkas et al., 2010), along with synonyms of these terms. This list was further expanded and edited through consultation with the LDC and other linguists, to ensure representation of hedge terms from more informal text.

The full list of hedge words and phrases in our dictionary is shown in Table 1. This hedging dictionary is divided into *relational* and *propositional* hedges. As described in Prokofieva and Hirschberg (2014), relational hedges have to do

Relational Hedges
according to, appear, arguably, assume, believe, consider, could, doubt, estimate, expect, feel, find, guess, hear, I mean, I would say, imagine, impression, in my mind, in my opinion, in my understanding, in my view, know, likely, look like, looks like, may, maybe, might, my thinking, my understanding, necessarily, perhaps, possibly, presumably, probably, read, say, seem, seemingly, should, sound like, sounds like, speculate, suggest, suppose, sure, tend, think, understand, unlikely, unsure

Propositional Hedges
a bit, a bunch, a couple, a few, a little, a whole bunch, about, allegedly, among others, and all that, and so forth, and so on, and suchlike, apparently, approximately, around, at least, basic, basically, completely, et cetera, etc, fair, fairly, for the most part, frequently, general, generally, in a way, in part, in some ways, kind of, kinda, largely, like, mainly, more or less, most, mostly, much, occasionally, often, partial, partially, partly, possible, practically, pretty, pretty much, probable, rarely, rather, really, relatively, rough, roughly, seldom, several, something or other, sort of, to a certain extent, to some extent, totally, usually, virtually

Table 1: List of (potential) hedge words and phrases

Hedge Term	Hedge Definition	Non-Hedge Definition
about	• almost; approximately ("There are <u>about</u> 10 million packages in transit right now.")	• on the subject of; concerning ("We need to talk <u>about</u> Mark.") • located in a particular area ("He is <u>about</u> the house.") • on the verge of ("He was <u>about</u> to leave.")
practically	• virtually; almost; nearly ("Their provisions were <u>practically</u> gone." "It has rained <u>practically</u> every day.")	• in a practical manner; realistically; sensibly ("<u>Practically</u> speaking, the plan is not very promising." "He purchased as many items as he could <u>practically</u> afford.")
suppose	• to believe or assume as true ("It is generally <u>supposed</u> that his death was an accident.") • to think or hold as an opinion ("I <u>suppose</u> the package will arrive next week.")	• to be expected or designed; to be required or permitted ("The machine is <u>supposed</u> to make noise." "I'm <u>supposed</u> to call if I'm going to be late.")
think	• to have an opinion, belief, or idea about someone or something ("I <u>think</u> it's an important issue." "John doesn't <u>think</u> he will win the election.") • to have as a plan or intention ("I <u>thought</u> that I would go.")	• to use one's mind actively to form ideas ("<u>Think</u> carefully before you begin." "I didn't <u>think</u> of the solution in time.") • to direct one's mind toward something or someone ("I was <u>thinking</u> about you.")

Table 2: Example definitions from our hedging dictionary

with the speaker's relation to the propositional content, while propositional hedges are those that introduce uncertainty into the propositional content itself. The examples in (2) demonstrate relational and propositional hedges.

(2) a. I **think** the ball is blue.

    b. The ball is **sort of** blue.

In (2a), *think* is a relational hedge. In (2b), *sort of* is a propositional hedge.

For each hedge term in our dictionary, we created definitions for the hedging and non-hedging usages of the term, including examples for each case. We attempted to keep these definitions as simple as possible while still providing enough direction for workers completing the AMT task. These definitions were revised as we tested the AMT task with real-world users and received feedback pointing out ambiguities or other problems with the definitions. We did find that some words were too complicated or that the differences in senses was too nuanced to reduce definitions to short hedge and non-hedge definitions: in par-

ticular, *hear*, *read*, and *say* were identified as such. For example, the sentences in (3) differ only slightly, but *hear* is being used a hedge in the first and not in the second:

(3) a. I **heard** that there was an arrest.

    b. I **heard** about the arrest.

For these words, it might be more effective to develop a separate AMT task that provides a more comprehensive set of definitions and examples rather than trying to reduce them to a simple binary choice. Another option would be to ask AMT workers more directly about how the speaker is using a term: e.g. whether the usage reflects uncertainty or lack of commitment to a proposition.

Table 2 shows some examples of hedging and non-hedging definitions. The complete dictionary of hedge terms, definitions, and examples is available from the authors upon request. Note that for 34 entries in our dictionary, the *non-hedge* definition is simply "Other". These are cases where the word or phrase is generally unambiguous except for extremely rare instances (generally, typos

Instructions

1. Read the sentence and answer the question based on the selected word.
2. Select the definition and example pair that most closely matches the meaning of the selected word as it is used in that sentence.
3. If one of the answers is 'Other', select it only if the alternative option doesn't apply at all.
4. Please answer carefully. Each HIT may contain one or more questions to which we know the correct answer; if you answer these incorrectly, we will reject the HIT. **If you have questions or feel your work was rejected unfairly, please contact us.**

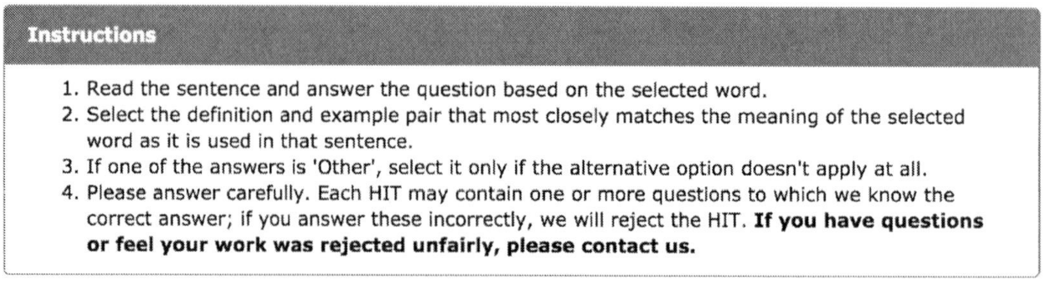

Figure 1: Instructions for Amazon Mechanical Turk Task

4. It seems a bit silly now but I was **fairly** young when we met and this seemed to so important to me.

Is the meaning of the word *fairly* closer to:

- justly or honestly, impartially ("The judge decided fairly.")

- to quite a high degree ("I was fairly certain she had nothing to do with it.")
- somewhat ("This judgment passed down fairly recently.")

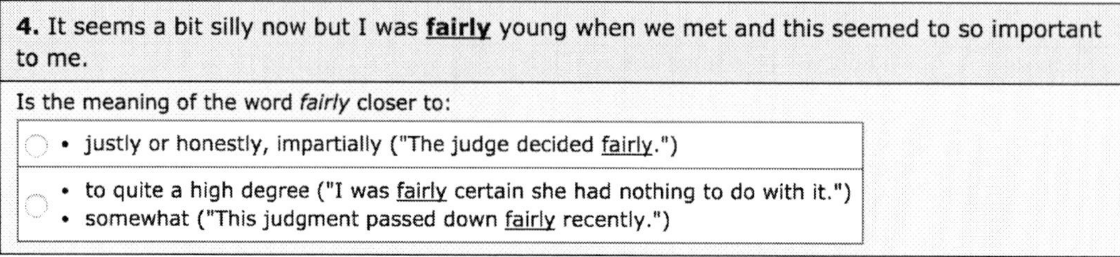

Figure 2: Example of AMT word sense disambiguation task

or other errors).

4 Corpus Annotation

We began with a collection of discussion forum posts from the 2014 Deft Committed Belief Corpora (Release No. LDC2014E55, LDC2014E106, and LDC2014E125). These posts were originally collected for the DARPA BOLT program and were selected according to a variety of criteria, including that the posts should contain primarily informal discussion and that the main focus of the threads should be discussion of dynamic events or personal anecdotes (Garland et al., 2012).

We located all instances of the hedges from our dictionary in these corpora and presented each of these instances as a potential hedge to workers on AMT. The hedge term was shown as a highlighted word or phrase within a sentence; below this sentence, we displayed definitions and examples of the hedging and non-hedging uses of the term. We asked workers which definition they felt most closely matched the meaning of the word highlighted in the sentence. To avoid bias based on the placement of the choices, we varied the order in which the hedging and non-hedging definitions appeared. Each Human Intelligence Task (HIT) asked for judgments on 10 sentences, with one being a gold-standard check judgment. If the worker failed to answer the check judgment correctly, we discarded their data and republished the HIT. We obtained 5 judgments for every potential hedge word and picked the majority vote as the label for that instance. Figure 1 shows the instructions given to workers. An example of the task for the word *fairly* is shown in Figure 2.

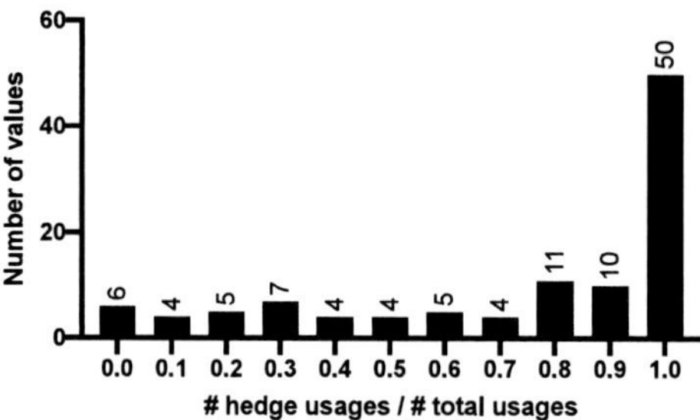

Figure 3: Distribution of proportion of hedge usages out of all occurrences of each term.

The resulting corpus has a total of 20,683 annotated potential hedge terms, although the data set is very unbalanced, with some hedge terms appearing many more times than others. For example, *about* appears 2,124 times but *in some ways*, *et cetera*, and *to a certain extent* each appear only once. The number of hedge usages vs. non-hedge usages for each term also varied. Figure 3 shows the distribution of the proportion of times a term was used a hedge out of all occurrences of that term. Overall agreement among the AMT workers was 92.89%, with Fleiss' Kappa equal to 0.751.

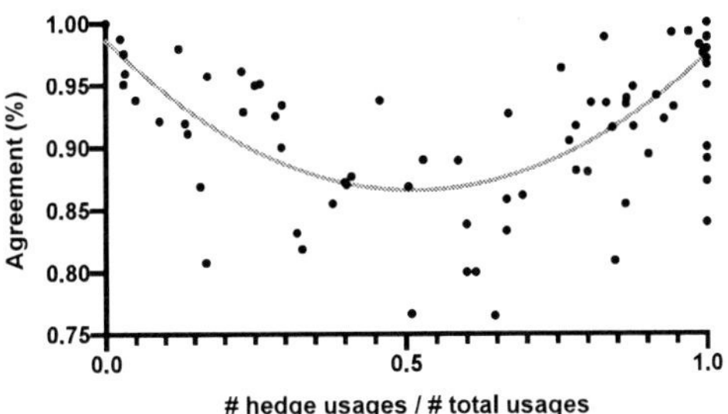

Figure 4: Plot of agreement vs. proportion of hedge usages out of total occurrences for each term.

The agreement varied depending on the hedge term. Figure 4 shows a scatterplot of the agreement percentage vs. how often each term is used a hedge. As one might expect, the general trend shows that agreement is higher for terms that are almost always used as hedges (or as non-hedges) than for the more ambiguous terms.

To get a sense of the quality of the crowdsourced judgments, we annotated a subset of the corpus ourselves. This subset was constructed by randomly selecting two instances for each hedge term. Each instance received two judgments, one by each of the two authors of this paper. As one would expect, inter-annotator agreement was higher, 94.73% overall, with Cohen's Kappa equal to 0.857. For most hedge terms, agreement was 100%; however, 11 hedge terms had an agreement of 50%. We adjudicated the questions for which we disagreed to create a single gold standard answer. We then compared our gold standard answers for this subset to the majority vote judgments obtained from AMT workers for the same questions. The crowdsourced majority vote judgment differed from the gold standard on only 7 questions, for an overall accuracy of 96.65%.

5 Summary

We have described a new method of using crowdsourcing to annotate a corpus with hedging information, by framing the hedge detection task as a word sense disambiguation problem. We have used this method to annotate a corpus of forum posts, which we hope to make generally available through the LDC. We have shown that annotations obtained using this method can in fact be very accurate; when comparing the crowdsourced judgments to an expert-annotated subset of the corpus, we obtained an accuracy of 96.65%.

Acknowledgments

This paper is based upon work supported by the DARPA DEFT program. The views expressed here are those of the author(s) and do not reflect the official policy or position of the Department of Defense or the U.S. Government.

References

Cem Akkaya, Alexander Conrad, Janyce Wiebe, and Rada Mihalcea. 2010. Amazon Mechanical Turk for Subjectivity Word Sense Disambiguation. In *Proceedings of the NAACL HLT 2010 Workshop on Creating Speech and Language Data with Amazon's Mechanical Turk*, pages 195–203, Los Angeles. Association for Computational Linguistics.

Timothy Chklovski and Rada Mihalcea. 2002. Building a Sense Tagged Corpus with Open Mind Word Expert. In *Proceedings of the ACL-02 Workshop on Word Sense Disambiguation: Recent Successes and Future Directions*, pages 116–122. Association for Computational Linguistics.

Richárd Farkas, Veronika Vincze, György Móra, János Csirik, and György Szarvas. 2010. The CoNLL-2010 Shared Task: Learning to Detect Hedges and their Scope in Natural Language Text. In *Proceedings of the Fourteenth Conference on Computational Natural Language Learning*, pages 1–12, Uppsala, Sweden. Association for Computational Linguistics.

Jennifer Garland, Stephanie Strassel, Safa Ismael, Zhiyi Song, and Haejoong Lee. 2012. Linguistic resources for genre-independent language technologies: User-generated content in BOLT. In *@NLP Can u Tag #user_generated_content ?! Via Lrec-Conf.Org (NLP4UGC 2012)*.

Anna Prokofieva and Julia Hirschberg. 2014. Hedging and speaker commitment. In *Proceedings of the 5th International Workshop on Emotion, Social Signals, Sentiment & Linked Open Data*, pages 10–13, Reykjavik, Iceland.

Rion Snow, Brendan O'Connor, Daniel Jurafsky, and Andrew Ng. 2008. Cheap and Fast – But is it Good? Evaluating Non-Expert Annotations for Natural Language Tasks. In *Proceedings of the 2008 Conference on Empirical Methods in Natural Language Processing*, pages 254–263, Honolulu, Hawaii. Association for Computational Linguistics.

Erik Velldal. 2011. Predicting speculation: A simple disambiguation approach to hedge detection in biomedical literature. *Journal of Biomedical Semantics*, 2(5):S7.

Veronika Vincze, György Szarvas, Richárd Farkas, György Móra, and János Csirik. 2008. The BioScope corpus: Biomedical texts annotated for uncertainty, negation and their scopes. *BMC Bioinformatics*, 9(11):S9.

WiRe57 : A Fine-Grained Benchmark for Open Information Extraction

William Léchelle, Fabrizio Gotti, Philippe Langlais
RALI, University of Montreal
{lechellw, gottif, felipe} @iro.umontreal.ca

Abstract

We build a reference for the task of Open Information Extraction, on five documents. We tentatively resolve a number of issues that arise, including coreference and granularity, and we take steps toward addressing inference, a significant problem. We seek to better pinpoint the requirements for the task. We produce our annotation guidelines specifying what is correct to extract and what is not. In turn, we use this reference to score existing Open IE systems. We address the nontrivial problem of evaluating the extractions produced by systems against the reference tuples, and share our evaluation script. Among seven compared extractors, we find the MinIE system to perform best.

1 Introduction

Open Information Extraction systems, starting with TextRunner (Yates et al., 2007), seek to extract all relational tuples expressed in text, without being bound to an anticipated list of predicates. Such systems have been used recently for relation extraction (Soderland et al., 2013), question-answering (Fader et al., 2014), and for building domain-targeted knowledge bases (Mishra et al., 2017), among others.

Subsequent extractors (ReVerb, Ollie, ClausIE, OpenIE 4, etc.) have sought to improve yield and precision, i.e. the number of facts extracted from a given corpus, and the proportion of those facts that is deemed correct.

Nonetheless, the task definition is underspecified, and, to the best of our knowledge, there is no gold standard. Most evaluations require somewhat subjective and inconsistent judgment calls to be made about extracted tuples being acceptable or not. The most recent automatic benchmark of Stanovsky and Dagan (2016) has some shortcomings that we propose to tackle here, regarding the theory underlining the task definition as well as the evaluation procedure.

We manually performed the task of Open Information Extraction on 5 short documents, elaborating tentative guidelines for the task, and resulting in a ground truth reference of 347 tuples. We evaluate against our benchmark the available OIE engines up to MinIE, with a fine-grained token-level evaluation. We distribute our resource and annotation guidelines, along with the evaluation script.[1]

2 Related Work

For their evaluation, typically, developers of Open IE systems pool the output of various systems on a given corpus. They label a sample of produced tuples as correct or incorrect, with the general guideline that an extraction is correct if it is implied by the sentence. Thus, Mausam et al. (2012) write: *"Two annotators tagged the extractions as correct if the sentence asserted or implied that the relation was true."* Del Corro and Gemulla (2013) propose: *"We also asked labelers to be liberal with respect to coreference or entity resolution; e.g., a proposition such as ('he' ; 'has' ; 'office'), or any unlemmatized version thereof, is treated as correct."* Saha et al. (2017): *"We sample a random testset of 2,000 sentences [. . .] Two annotators with NLP experience annotate each extraction for correctness."* Gashteovski et al. (2017): *"A triple is labeled as correct if it is entailed by its corresponding clause."* Then, precision and yield are used as performance metrics. Without a reference, recall is naturally impossible to measure.

We define a reference *a priori*. This allows for automatic scoring of systems' outputs, which greatly diminishes subjectivity from the process of labelling facts "for correctness". Above all, it is meant to help researchers agree on what the task

---

[1] https://github.com/rali-udem/WiRe57

Proceedings of the 13th Linguistic Annotation Workshop, pages 6–15
Florence, Italy, August 1, 2019. ©2019 Association for Computational Linguistics

precisely entails. Therefore, it allows to measure a true recall (albeit on a small corpus).

The complexity of our guidelines is indicative of all that is swept under the carpet when "annotating for correctness". As a matter of fact, when closely examining other references for OIE, many extracted tuples eventually labelled as "good" have more or less important issues. Some really dubious cases are hard to gauge and their labelling is ultimately subjective. To showcase the devilishly difficult judgment calls that this implies, compare the following two extractions. "*'The opportunity is significant and I hope we can take the opportunity to move forward,' he said referring to his coming trip to Britain.*" yields (*his ; has ; coming trip*), and "*[...], the companies included CNN, but not its parent, AOL Time Warner*" yields (*its ; has ; parent*). Are the extractions implied by the sentence ? In (Del Corro and Gemulla, 2013), the annotator approved the latter, and rejected the former. The extraction (*he ; said ; The opportunity is significant referring to his coming trip to Britain*) was also deemed correct, despite the composed second argument.

Some other tasks for which OIE output is used, such as Open QA (Fader et al., 2014), TAC-KBP (Soderland et al., 2013), or textual similarity and reading comprehension as in (Stanovsky et al., 2015) — could in principle be used to compare extractors' performance, but only give a very coarse-grained signal, mostly unaffected by the tuning of systems.

A promising method is that explored by Mishra et al. (2017) for the Aristo KB.[2] Aristo is a science-focused KB extracted from a high-quality 7M-sentence corpus. The authors preprocessed a smaller, similarly science-related, independent corpus of 1.2M sentences, into a "Reference KB" of 4147 facts, validated by Turkers. Assuming that these 4147 facts are representative of the science domain as a whole, they measured comprehensiveness (recall) over this domain by measuring coverage on the Reference KB.

2.1 ORE benchmark

Mesquita et al. (2013) compare more or less deep 'parsers', including the OIE systems Ollie and Re-Verb, on the germane task of Open Relation Extraction (ORE), between named entities. They build a benchmark of 662 binary relations over 1100 sentences from 3 sources (the Web, the New York Times and the Penn Treebank). They label an additional 222 NYT sentences with as many n-ary relations, and 12,000 with automatic annotations.

Besides the named entity arguments, their annotations consist of one mandatory trigger word (indicating the relation), surrounded by a window of allowed tokens. To compare OIE with ORE systems, they have to replace the target entities by salient arguments (*Asia* and *Europe*) which are easy to recognize. They discuss some of the challenges that arise from divergent annotation styles and evaluation methods.

While the tasks are similar, restraining arguments to be named entities limits IE to capturing only the most salient relations expressed in the text. Allowing for any NP to be an argument, we extract 6 facts per sentence on average in the benchmark presented here, compared to 0.6 in the ORE dataset. We also annotate some relations that do not have a trigger in the sentence (such as (*Paris ; [is in] ; France*) from "*Chilly Gonzales lived in Paris, France*").

2.2 QA-SRL OIE benchmark

Stanovsky and Dagan (2016) build a large benchmark for OIE, by automatically processing the QA-SRL dataset (He et al., 2015). Precisely, for each predicate annotated in QA-SRL, they generate one tuple expressing each element of the Cartesian product of answers to the questions about this predicate.

For instance, QA-SRL lists five questions asked about the sentence "*Investors are appealing to the SEC not to limit their access to information about stock purchases and sales by corporate insiders*" : "*who are <u>appealing</u> to something ?*", "*who are someone <u>appealing</u> to ?*", "*what are someone appealing ?*", "*what might not <u>limit</u> something ?*" and "*what might not someone <u>limit</u> ?*", with one answer per question. This generates the reference tuples (*Investors ; appealing ; not to limit their access to information about stock purchases and sales by corporate insiders ; to the SEC*) and (*the SEC ; might not limit ; their access to information about stock purchases and sales by corporate insiders*).

Their dataset is comprised of 10,359 tuples over 3200 sentences (from the Wall Street Journal and Wikipedia), and is available for download.[3]

While this work makes a big step in the right direction, there are a few important issues with this benchmark.

First, a major strength of the dataset is its intended and partly achieved completeness, but we do not find it to be a suitably comprehensive reference against which to measure systems' recall. This might be because the QA-SRL dataset doesn't lend itself well to exhaustiveness in the realm of Open IE, partly because it is restricted to explicit predicates. For instance, the sentence *"However, Paul Johanson, Monsanto's director of plant sciences, said the company's chemical spray overcomes these problems and is 'gentle on the female organ'."* contains two predicates, generating the extractions (*Paul Johanson ; said ; the company's chemical spray overcomes these problems and is "gentle on the female organ."*) and (*the company's chemical spray ; overcomes ; these problems*). Yet, that omits the (in our view useful) extractions (*the company's chemical spray ; is ; "gentle on the female organ"*), and (*Paul Johanson ; is ; Monsanto's director of plant sciences*).

Another issue is that some words not found in the original sentence were quietly added by the SRL-to-QA process, retained in the QA-to-OIE transformation, and become part of the reference. In the example above, it is unclear how the second predicate *"might not limit"* is extracted from the sentence. At the very least, the fact that these words are foreign to the original sentence should be made explicit. Further, although in this particular case adding the modal is a good way of expressing the information, its repeated use by QA-SRL to produce questions waters down the expressed facts in the end. For instance, the uninformative triple (*a manufacturer ; might get ; something*) is generated from the sentence *"...and if a manufacturer is clearly trying to get something out of it ..."*, with the same added *"might"*.

Last, the scoring procedure is not robust. Using the code made available by the authors[4], we were able to get top results with a dummy extractor.

This is because the scorer doesn't penalize extractions for being too long, nor for misplacing parts of the relation in the object slot or vice versa. Therefore, if $w_0w_1...w_n$ is an input sentence, a

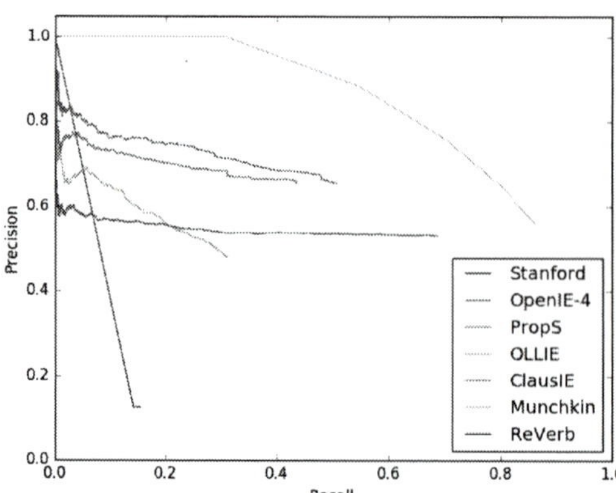

Figure 1: Performance metrics must take span precision into account. The 25-line long Munchkin script returns variations of the full sentence (with decreasing confidence) and is not penalized by the evaluation script of the latest benchmark (Stanovsky and Dagan, 2016). Its superior performance is artificially inflated.

trivial system that "extracts" $(w_0; w_1; w_2...w_n)$, $(w_0; w_1w_2; w_3...w_n)$, etc., will be given an unfairly great score. We implemented that program (dubbed Munchkin) which predictably performed well above other genuine extraction systems, as pictured in Figure 1.

2.3 RelVis benchmarking toolkit

Schneider et al. (2017) evaluate four systems (ClausIE, OpenIE 4, Stanford Open IE and PredPatt) against the two datasets mentioned above.[5] They use two methods to match predicted and reference tuples : "containment" and "relaxed containment". These methods mean that the predicted tuple must include the reference tuple, and that inclusion must happen for each argument, in the non-relaxed case. In the relaxed case, the boundaries between parts of a tuple are ignored. Like that of Stanovsky and Dagan (2016), this scoring procedure doesn't penalize systems for returning overlong spans.

2.4 Scoring

To compare facts with a reference, most authors require matching tuples to have the same number of arguments and to share the grammatical head words of each part, e.g. Angeli and Manning (2013) and the article of Stanovsky and Da-

---

[4]https://github.com/gabrielStanovsky/ oie-benchmark — the scoring function was updated since its description in the article. We believe the published function suffers from similar issues.

[5]Their code is announced but not available as of this writing — https://github.com/schmaR/relvis

gan (2016). In their updated GitHub repository, Stanovsky and Dagan (2016) instead use lexical match : more than half of the words of a predicted tuple must match the reference for it to be correct.

In contrast with these works and (Schneider et al., 2017), our scorer penalizes verbosity by measuring precision at the token level. We penalize the omission of parts of a reference tuple by gradually diminishing recall (at the token level), instead of a sharp all-or-nothing criterion.

Mesquita et al. (2013) annotate relations as one mandatory target plus some optional complementary words, and treat arguments (named entities) in an ad-hoc fashion for OIE systems.

3 WiRe57

Open IE bears some similarity to the task of Semantic Role Labelling, as explored in (Christensen et al., 2011; Mesquita et al., 2013), and as demonstrated by SRLIE, a component of OpenIE 4.

In effect extracted tuples are akin to simplified PropBank[6] or FrameNet[7] frames, and our annotations were inspired by those projects. Still, with a focus on extracting new relations at scale, optional arguments such as Propbank's modifiers (ArgM) are *discouraged* in OIE. Another major difference is the vocabulary of predicates being open to any relational phrase, rather than belonging to a closed curated list such as VerbNet. Within reason, OIE seeks to extract rich and precise relations phrases.

Phenomenon	N	%
All tuples	343	100
Anaphora	196	57
Contains inferred words	186	54
Hallucinated parts	135	39
Binary relations	254	74
n-ary, $n = 3$	72	21
n-ary, $n = 4$	16	5
n-ary, $n = 5$	1	0.3
Inferred words	347/2597	13.4

Table 1: Frequencies of various phenomena in WiRe57.

3.1 Annotation process

A small corpus of 57 sentences taken from the beginning of 5 documents in English was used as the

source text from which to extract tuples. Three documents are Wikipedia articles (Chilly Gonzales, the EM algorithm, and Tokyo) and two are newswire articles (taken from Reuters, hence the Wi-Re name).

Two annotators (authors of this paper) first independently extracted tuples from the documents, based on a first version of the annotation guidelines which quickly proved insufficient to reach any significant agreement. The two sets of annotations were then merged, and the guidelines rectified along the way in order to resolve the issues that arose. After merging, a quick test on a few additional sentences from a different document showed a much improved agreement, more than half of extractions matching exactly and the remaining missing a few details. The guidelines are detailed in the next sections.

3.2 Annotation principles

In keeping with past literature, our guiding principles for the annotation were as follows.

The first, obvious purpose of extracted information is to be **informative**. Fader et al. (2011) mention how extracting (*Faust ; made ; a deal*) instead of the correct (*Faust ; made a deal with ; the devil*) would be pointless. Further, anaphoric mentions being so ubiquitous and being void of meaning outside the context of their original sentence, we resolve anaphora in our extractions.

Moreover and following (Stanovsky and Dagan, 2016), extracted tuples should each be **minimal**, in the sense that they should convey the smallest standalone piece of information, though that piece must be completely expressed. Thus, some facts must be extracted as n-ary relations.[8] The MinIE system in particular addresses this issue and "minimizes its extractions by identifying and removing parts that are considered overly specific".

The annotation shall be **exhaustive**, in the sense of capturing as much of the information expressed in the text as possible. This is to measure absolute recall for a system, a notoriously difficult evaluation metric for Open IE.

This in turn raises the issue of **inference**: some information is merely suggested by the text, rather than explicitly expressed, and should not be annotated. Light inference, in the form of reformulation, is helpful to make use of the information ex-

---

[6]`propbank.github.io` – (Kingsbury and Palmer, 2002)

[7]`framenet.icsi.berkeley.edu` – (Ruppenhofer et al., 2005)

[8]Some systems — namely CSD-IE (Bast and Haussmann, 2013) and NestIE (Bhutani et al., 2016) — explore nesting extractions, but we didn't adopt this strategy.

tracted, but full-fledged inference should be processed by a dedicated program, and is not part of the Open IE task. Because the concept of "light inference" is subjective, we propose in the guidelines a few examples and counterexamples that delineate the limits between the two classes.

Other authors mention this issue. From (Wu and Weld, 2010) : "The extractor should produce one triple for every relation stated explicitly in the text, but is not required to infer implicit facts." Stanovsky and Dagan (2016) say: "an Open IE extractor should produce the tuple (*John; managed to open; the door*) but is not required to produce the extraction (*John; opened; the door*)". In our resource we do also annotate (*John; [opened]; the door*), marking the reworded relation as inferred (which in turn makes it optional to find when scoring).

His parents are Ashkenazi Jews who had to flee from Hungary during World War II.

Extract the tuples

REVERB

His parents | are | Ashkenazi Jews | 0,78
Ashkenazi Jews | had to flee from | Hungary | 0,58

OLLIE

Ashkenazi Jews | had during | World War II | 0,78

MINIE

His | has | parents
parents | are | Ashkenazi Jews
Ashkenazi Jews | had to flee from Hungary during | World War II
Ashkenazi Jews | had to flee from | Hungary

OPENIE

His parents | are | Ashkenazi Jews

Figure 2: Example output of evaluated OIE systems, on sentence CH 7. This cropped screenshot is of a in-house web application that allows us to submit any sentence for tuple extraction and to visualize the results.

3.3 Annotation guidelines[9]

Extracted tuples should reflect all meaningful relationships found in the source text. Typically, this means that there are multiple tuples for a given sentence. A number of times, two arguments are connected in a sentence but the relation that links them is implicit (e.g. *Paris, France ; the North Atlantic Treaty Organization (NATO) ; the Nature paper* or *the Turing paper*, etc.). In this case, we

---

[9]We share at https://github.com/rali-udem/WiRe57 our annotation guidelines. We present its major points here.

Sentence CH 7 – "*His parents are Ashkenazi Jews who had to flee from Hungary during World War II.*"

Annotations
– (His/(Chilly Gonzales's) parents ; are ; Ashkenazi Jews)
– (His/(Chilly Gonzales's) parents ; are ; Jews)
– (His/(Chilly Gonzales's) parents ; had to flee from ; Hungary ; during World War II)
– (His/(Chilly Gonzales's) parents ; [fled] from ; Hungary ; during World War II)
– ([Chilly Gonzales] ; [has] ; parents)

Sentence EM 5 – "*They pointed out that the method had been 'proposed many times in special circumstances' by earlier authors.*"

Annotations
– (They/(Arthur Dempster, Nan Laird, and Donald Rubin) ; pointed out that ; (the method)/(The EM algorithm) had been "proposed many times in special circumstances" by earlier authors)
– ((the method)/(The EM algorithm) ; had been proposed by; earlier authors ; in special circumstances) [attributed]
– (earlier authors ; proposed ; (the method)/(The EM algorithm) ; in special circumstances) [attributed]

Sentence FI 2 – "*A police statement did not name the man in the boot, but in effect indicated the traveler was State Secretary Samuli Virtanen, who is also the deputy to Foreign Minister Timo Soini.*"

Annotations
– (A police/(Finnish police) statement ; did not name ; (the man in the boot)/(Samuli Virtanen))
– ((the man in the boot)/(Samuli Virtanen) ; was ; Samuli Virtanen) [attributed]
– ((the traveler)/(Samuli Virtanen) ; was ; Samuli Virtanen) [attributed]
– (Samuli Virtanen ; [is] ; State Secretary)
– (Samuli Virtanen ; is ; the deputy to Foreign Minister Timo Soini)
– (Samuli Virtanen ; is ; [a] deputy)
– (Timo Soini ; [is] ; Foreign Minister)
– (Timo Soini ; [has] ; [a] deputy)

Sentence CE 4 – "*The International Monetary Fund, for example, saw 2017 global growth at 3.4 percent with advanced economies advancing 1.8 percent.*"

Annotations
– (The International Monetary Fund ; saw ; 2017 global growth ; at 3.4 percent)
– (The International Monetary Fund ; saw ; advanced economies ; advancing 1.8 percent ; [in] 2017)
– (2017 global growth ; [was] ; 3.4 percent)
– (advanced economies ; [advanced] ; 1.8 percent ; [in] 2017) [attributed]

Figure 3: Sample annotations from WiRe57, from four of the documents. Reformulated words are enclosed in [brackets] and coreference information is indicated with forward slashes and parentheses.

annotate a somewhat arbitrary relationship (such as *is in, stands for, published in* and *published by* respectively), the tokens of which are thus inferred. This is the case for 39% of our tuples.

Some OIE systems similarly attempt to hallucinate some or part of relations. Notably, ClausIE wrongly extracts (*New Delhi ; is ; India*), and MinIE gets right (*Paris ; is in ; France*). Ollie adds some "be" auxiliaries to otherwise nominal relations, as in *Barack Obama, former president of the United States, [. . .]*, which OpenIE 4 also infers. Yet, we acknowledge that most work in Open IE rely on explicit predicate tokens as in (Mesquita et al., 2013), and don't try to elicit relations further. At scoring time, systems are not penalized for not finding inferred words, or not finding inferred relations. If the whole predicate of a tuple is inferred, a predicted tuple is scored on its token overlap with the arguments only.

We suggest "platinum" annotations, including inferred words, to be a very high standard for extractors, while the gold standard for the task, recall-wise, is based only on words found in the original sentences.

Noun phrases can be rich in elements of information. To solve the problem of finding the granularity level to use when including argument NPs, we extract two tuples, one as generic as possible and the other as specific as possible, for the same relation. Adjectives and other elements of meaning that can be easily separated from the noun phrase to create other tuples are so split. Only elements that cannot be separated become part of the most specific noun phrase.

For instance, the sentence *"Solo Piano is a great album of classical piano compositions"* would yield 3 tuples : the split adjective (*Solo Piano ; is ; great*), the generic (*Solo Piano ; is ; [an] album*) and the specific (*Solo Piano ; is ; [an] album of classical piano compositions*).

When predicates contain nouns or other elements (e.g. *Tokyo is the capital of Japan.*), we annotate the richer relationship (*Tokyo ; is the capital of ; Japan*) rather than the more basic (*Tokyo ; is ; the capital of Japan*). This allows tuple relations to be more meaningful, and more easily compared, clustered, and aggregated with other relations. This also is in line with ReVerb.

Like ClausIE and other extractors since, we split conjunctions : *"Andrea lived in both Poland and Italy"* yields both (*Andrea ; lived in ; Poland*) and (*Andrea ; lived in ; Italy*).

3.4 Resource

A sample of annotations is pictured in Figure 3. The occurring frequency of various phenomena is presented in Table 1. Our resource is comprised of 343 relational facts (or tuples), three quarters of them binary relations. One in five have three arguments, sometimes "two objects" as in (*This performance ; has made ; some economists ; optimistic*) or more frequently a complement as in (*His parents ; had to flee ; from Hungary ; during World War II*). Five percent of them have four arguments or more : for instance (*Tokyo ; ranked ; third ; in the International Financial Centres Development IndexEdit ; twice*) and (*The International Monetary Fund ; saw ; advanced economies ; advancing 1.8 percent ; [in] 2017*).

We found (and resolved) anaphoric phrases in more than half the tuples, as in (*Emperor Meiji ; moved ; his/(Emperor Meiji's) seat ; to (the city)/Tokyo ; from the old capital of Kyoto ; in 1868*). The released dataset contains the raw and anaphora-resolved argument spans.

When solely extracting words from the sentence would not yield clear factual tuples, we reworded or adapted the text into more explicit statements. In this case, we explicitly marked the changed (or added) words as inferred (they are bracketed in Figure 3). For instance in sentence CE 4, the relation "[advanced]" was reformulated from the sentence word "*advancing*", and the word [in] was added before "2017". In the resource, each token is accompanied by its index in the sentence if it comes from it, or the "inferred" mark. Inferred words represent 13% of the lot but affect 54% of the tuples.

3.5 Inter-annotator agreement

	# tokens	1↔2	1↔R	2↔R
Sentence 1	24	84.4	90.6	93.8
Sentence 2	19	98.7	98.7	100
Sentence 3	33	78.0	90.9	85.6
Average		**85.2**	**92.8**	**91.9**

Table 2: **Inter-annotator agreement.** Percentage of agreement on the labelling of each sentence token as belonging to 4 classes. Each annotator's original production differs only slightly from the agreed-on result (columns 1↔R and 2↔R), and the disagreement between both annotators is slightly larger (column 1↔2). The average is computed token-wise.

As mentioned in section 3.1, a qualitatively high agreement was reached after the merging of preliminary annotations and deliberation over the guidelines' items. After the guidelines were fully settled, three additional sentences from one of the documents were annotated by two annotators (1 and 2) in order to *quantitatively* measure inter-annotator agreement. Afterward, annotation discrepancies were resolved in cases of disagreement to produce a merged reference (R). Here, we report the agreement between the two original annotations ($1 \leftrightarrow 2$), and between each original annotation and the merged reference ($1 \leftrightarrow R$ and $2 \leftrightarrow R$).

Comparing triples can become quite tricky for many reasons, including missing complements, overlapping spans, etc. We therefore resorted to another scheme, where we reframe the annotation task as taking each annotated token and classifying it as either belonging or not belonging to each of 4 classes (subject, relation, object, or complementary argument). These classifications can be trivially derived from the triples produced beforehand. For instance, a triple $(t_1\ t_2; t_3; t_4\ t_5)$ implies that the annotator classified tokens t_1 and t_2 as belonging to the subject class. It then becomes possible to measure an agreement percentage on the full binary labelling grid (obtained automatically from the long-form annotations). We believe the resulting figures (shown in Table 2) aptly reflect the level of overall agreement between the annotators, despite the minimal sample size. We measure an overall inter-annotator agreement ($1 \leftrightarrow 2$) of 85.2% for the three sentences.

Qualitatively, one annotator steered close to the sentence syntax, sometimes missing some of the meaning obscured by long-winded formulations. The other annotator tended to be overly specific, including some non essential complements, and making longer-ranged inferences that fall out of the scope of this task. Some possessive and passive constructions were also overlooked.

4 Evaluation of Existing Systems

4.1 Scorer

An important step when measuring extractors' performances is the scoring process. Matching a system's output to a reference is not trivial. As detailed in Section 2.2, because it didn't penalize overlong extractions, we could game the basic evaluation method of the QA-SRL OIE benchmark with a trivial extractor.

Our scorer computes precision and recall of a system's predicted tuples at the token level. Precision is, briefly put, the proportion of extracted words that are found in the reference. Recall is the proportion of reference words found in the systems' predictions.

More formally, let $G = \{g_1, g_2, \ldots, g_N\}$ be the gold tuples, and $T_{\text{sys}} = \{t_1, t_2, \ldots, t_n\}$ a system's extractions. We denote the parts of a tuple $t = (t^{a_1}; t^r; t^{a_2}; t^{a_3}; \ldots) = (t^{p_k})_{k \in [1,6]}$, where p_1 is the first argument, p_2 is the relation, etc., up to p_6 the fifth argument when it exists (no reference tuple contains more than 5 arguments). Let $t_i^p \cap g_j^p$ be the subset of words shared by parts t_i^p and g_j^p, where parts are considered as bags of words. The length of a tuple is the sum of lengths of its parts, i.e. $|t_i| = |t_i^{a_1}| + |t_i^r| + |t_i^{a_2}| + |t_i^{a_3}| + \cdots = \sum_k |t_i^{p_k}|$.

A predicted tuple t_i may match a reference tuple g_j from the same sentence if they share at least one word from each of the relation, first and second arguments, that is iff (w_{a_1}, w_r, w_{a_2}) exist such that $w_1 \in g_j^{a_1} \cap t_i^{a_1}$, $w_r \in g_j^r \cap t_i^r$ and $w_2 \in g_j^{a_2} \cap t_i^{a_2}$.

For all tuple pairs that may match, we have the matching scores:

$$\text{precision}(t_i, g_j) = \frac{\sum_k |t_i^{p_k} \cap g_j^{p_k}|}{|t_i|}$$

$$\text{recall}(t_i, g_j) = \frac{\sum_k |t_i^{p_k} \cap g_j^{p_k}|}{|g_j|}$$

$$F_1 = \frac{2\,p\,r}{p + r}.$$

We match predicted tuples with reference ones by greedily removing from the potential match pool the pair with maximum F_1 score, until no remaining tuples match. Let $m(.)$ be the matching function such that t_i matches with $g_{m(i)}$ (and conversely $t_{m(j)}$ matches g_j), assuming that $|t_i \cap g_{m(i)}| = 0$ if there is no match for t_i.

Hence, the overall performance metrics of an extractor are its token-weighted precision and recall over all tuples, i.e.

$$\text{precision}_{\text{sys}} = \frac{\sum_i^n \left(\sum_k |t_i^{p_k} \cap g_{m(i)}^{p_k}| \right)}{\sum_i^n |t_i|}$$

$$\text{recall}_{\text{sys}} = \frac{\sum_j^N \left(\sum_k |t_{m(j)}^{p_k} \cap g_j^{p_k}| \right)}{\sum_j^N |g_j|}$$

$$F_{1\text{sys}} = \frac{2\,p_{\text{sys}}\,r_{\text{sys}}}{p_{\text{sys}} + r_{\text{sys}}}.$$

To avoid penalizing systems for not finding them, neither the words annotated as inferred, nor

	Extractions	Matches	Exact matches	Prec. of matches	Recall of matches	Prec.	Recall	F1
ReVerb (Fader et al., 2011)	79	54	13	.83	.77	**.569**	.121	.200
Ollie (Mausam et al., 2012)	145	74	8	.73	.81	.347	.175	.239
ClausIE (Del Corro and Gemulla, 2013)	223	121	**24**	.74	.84	.401	.298	.342
Stanford (Angeli et al., 2015)	371	99	2	.79	.65	.210	.188	.198
OpenIE 4 (Mausam, 2016)	101	74	5	.68	.84	.501	.182	.267
PropS (Stanovsky et al., 2016)	184	69	0	.59	.80	.222	.162	.187
MinIE (Gashteovski et al., 2017)	252	**134**	10	.75	.83	.400	**.323**	**.358**

Table 3: Performance of available OpenIE systems (in chronological order) on our reference. Precision and recall are computed at the token level. Systems with lower precision of matches are penalized for producing overlong tuples. High precision and recall of matches overall show that our matching function (one shared word in each of the first three parts) works correctly. Inferred words are required for exact matches.

the coreference information are used in this evaluation (g_j is the non-resolved version of the tuple, and inferred words are not included in recall denominators). Future work can look into evaluating OIE systems that mean to resolve anaphoras.

4.2 Results

In order to experiment with the 7 systems used in this paper, we bundled them as a web service. A client application need only submit a sentence and a list of OIE system names to perform extraction. All tuples are in turn served as uniform JSON objects, no matter the OIE system used. This facilitates the development of clients, shielded from the various tuple formats, coding languages, and other quirks of the OIE systems. It also allowed us to visualize the tuples using a web application (see Figure 2). Moreover, because the various extractors run as servers, they load their respective resources only once, when the service is launched, and are then always quick to respond to a given extraction task (a few seconds). Otherwise, the user would have had to wait a few minutes for the resources to load each time when querying the extractors.

While creating such a framework is a significant effort, it ultimately saved us a lot of time when writing the clients. It also provided a common frame of reference for all collaborators in our lab. Typically, we used the default configuration for each OIE system, but we tweaked the available flags in order to favor exhaustiveness, when such flags were present and properly documented. When additional information did not fit into a traditional tuple (arg1; rel; arg2), e.g. MinIE's quantities, we resorted to simple schemes to faithfully cast that information into a tuple.

Table 3 details the performance of available OIE

systems against our reference. MinIE produces a large number of correct tuples, and performs best, especially recall-wise. The conservative choices made by ReVerb achieve a relatively high precision, though it lacks in comprehensiveness. Ollie improves recall over ReVerb, and Open IE 4 improves precision over Ollie. Stanford Open IE produces a very large number of tuples, hindering its precision (it is possible that limiting its verboseness through configuration would improve this).

5 Conclusion

In this paper, we set out to create additional resources useful to researchers in Open Information Extraction. We distribute these resources freely.

Primarily, we provide a manually crafted, tentative reference for the task. It consists of 343 manually extracted facts, including some implicit relations, over 57 sentences. A quarter of them are n-ary relations and coreference information is included in over half of them. We believe that such a benchmark is valuable because it offers a common frame of reference allowing OIE systems to be tested and compared fairly, a task we carried out on 7 OIE systems. This also entailed the creation of a scoring algorithm and program, which we release along with the data. We assess the ReVerb, Ollie, ClausIE, Stanford Open IE, OpenIE 4, PropS, and MinIE systems against our reference, using a fine-grained token-level scorer. We find the MinIE system to perform best.

Naturally, such an annotation effort requires one to attempt to "pin down" the task of OIE by confronting real-life data. We provide guidelines that propose such a definition. While by no means definitive or exhaustive, these guidelines have at least the merit of being sufficiently clear to yield an annotated dataset with a reasonable inter-annotator agreement. At the same time, we believe they are not too overwrought, and rather invite further contributions by other researchers. The thorniest issues are the fine line between useful reformulation of information to a canonical form and ill-advised inference, and how to trim and annotate complex noun-phrase arguments. These difficulties can affect the manual annotation process, and, interestingly, are also likely to arise when building OIE systems, which is the ultimate goal in this research field after all.

References

Gabor Angeli and Christopher D. Manning. 2013. Philosophers are mortal: Inferring the truth of unseen facts. In *Proceedings of the Seventeenth Conference on Computational Natural Language Learning, CoNLL 2013, Sofia, Bulgaria, August 8-9, 2013*, pages 133–142. ACL.

Gabor Angeli, Melvin Johnson Premkumar, and Christopher D. Manning. 2015. Leveraging linguistic structure for open domain information extraction. In *ACL*.

Hannah Bast and Elmar Haussmann. 2013. Open information extraction via contextual sentence decomposition. In *Semantic Computing (ICSC), 2013 IEEE Seventh International Conference on*, pages 154–159. IEEE.

Nikita Bhutani, H V Jagadish, and Dragomir Radev. 2016. Nested propositions in open information extraction. In *Proceedings of the 2016 Conference on Empirical Methods in Natural Language Processing*, pages 55–64. Association for Computational Linguistics.

Janara Christensen, Mausam, Stephen Soderland, and Oren Etzioni. 2011. An analysis of open information extraction based on semantic role labeling. In *Proceedings of the Sixth International Conference on Knowledge Capture*, K-CAP '11, pages 113–120, New York, NY, USA. ACM.

Luciano Del Corro and Rainer Gemulla. 2013. Clausie: Clause-based open information extraction. In *Proceedings of the 22Nd International Conference on World Wide Web*, WWW '13, pages 355–366, Republic and Canton of Geneva, Switzerland. International World Wide Web Conferences Steering Committee.

Anthony Fader, Stephen Soderland, and Oren Etzioni. 2011. Identifying relations for open information extraction. In *Proceedings of the Conference on Empirical Methods in Natural Language Processing*, EMNLP '11, pages 1535–1545, Stroudsburg, PA, USA. Association for Computational Linguistics.

Anthony Fader, Luke Zettlemoyer, and Oren Etzioni. 2014. Open question answering over curated and extracted knowledge bases. In *Proceedings of the 20th ACM SIGKDD International Conference on Knowledge Discovery and Data Mining*, KDD '14, pages 1156–1165, New York, NY, USA. ACM.

Kiril Gashteovski, Rainer Gemulla, and Luciano Del Corro. 2017. Minie: Minimizing facts in open information extraction. In *Proceedings of the 2017 Conference on Empirical Methods in Natural Language Processing*, pages 2630–2640. Association for Computational Linguistics.

Luheng He, Mike Lewis, and Luke Zettlemoyer. 2015. Question-answer driven semantic role labeling: Using natural language to annotate natural language. In *Proceedings of the 2015 Conference on Empirical Methods in Natural Language Processing*, pages 643–653. Association for Computational Linguistics.

Paul Kingsbury and Martha Palmer. 2002. From treebank to propbank. In *Language Resources and Evaluation*.

Mausam, Michael Schmitz, Robert Bart, Stephen Soderland, and Oren Etzioni. 2012. Open language learning for information extraction. In *Proceedings of Conference on Empirical Methods in Natural Language Processing and Computational Natural Language Learning (EMNLP-CONLL)*.

Mausam Mausam. 2016. Open information extraction systems and downstream applications. In *Proceedings of the Twenty-Fifth International Joint Conference on Artificial Intelligence*, IJCAI'16, pages 4074–4077. AAAI Press.

Filipe Mesquita, Jordan Schmidek, and Denilson Barbosa. 2013. Effectiveness and efficiency of open relation extraction. In *Proceedings of the 2013 Conference on Empirical Methods in Natural Language Processing*, pages 447–457. Association for Computational Linguistics.

Bhavana Dalvi Mishra, Niket Tandon, and Peter Clark. 2017. Domain-targeted, high precision knowledge extraction. *TACL*, 5:233–246.

Josef Ruppenhofer, Michael Ellsworth, Miriam R. L. Petruck, Christopher R. Johnson, and Jan Scheffczyk. 2005. FrameNet II: Extended theory and practice. Technical report, ICSI.

Swarnadeep Saha, Harinder Pal, and Mausam. 2017. Bootstrapping for numerical open IE. In *Proceedings of the 55th Annual Meeting of the Association for Computational Linguistics, ACL 2017, Vancouver, Canada, July 30 - August 4, Volume 2: Short Papers*, pages 317–323. Association for Computational Linguistics.

Rudolf Schneider, Tom Oberhauser, Tobias Klatt, Felix A. Gers, and Alexander Löser. 2017. Analysing errors of open information extraction systems. In

Proceedings of the First Workshop on Building Linguistically Generalizable NLP Systems, pages 11–18. Association for Computational Linguistics.

Stephen Soderland, John Gilmer, Robert Bart, Oren Etzioni, and Daniel S. Weld. 2013. Open information extraction to KBP relations in 3 hours. In *Proceedings of the Sixth Text Analysis Conference, TAC 2013, Gaithersburg, Maryland, USA, November 18-19, 2013*. NIST.

Gabriel Stanovsky and Ido Dagan. 2016. Creating a large benchmark for open information extraction. In *Proceedings of the 2016 Conference on Empirical Methods in Natural Language Processing (EMNLP)*, Austin, Texas. Association for Computational Linguistics.

Gabriel Stanovsky, Ido Dagan, and Mausam. 2015. Open ie as an intermediate structure for semantic tasks. In *Proceedings of the 53rd Annual Meeting of the Association for Computational Linguistics and the 7th International Joint Conference on Natural Language Processing (Volume 2: Short Papers)*, pages 303–308, Beijing, China. Association for Computational Linguistics.

Gabriel Stanovsky, Jessica Ficler, Ido Dagan, and Yoav Goldberg. 2016. Getting more out of syntax with props. *CoRR*, abs/1603.01648.

Fei Wu and Daniel S. Weld. 2010. Open information extraction using wikipedia. In *Proceedings of the 48th Annual Meeting of the Association for Computational Linguistics*, ACL '10, pages 118–127, Stroudsburg, PA, USA. Association for Computational Linguistics.

Alexander Yates, Michael Cafarella, Michele Banko, Oren Etzioni, Matthew Broadhead, and Stephen Soderland. 2007. Textrunner: Open information extraction on the web. In *Proceedings of Human Language Technologies: The Annual Conference of the North American Chapter of the Association for Computational Linguistics: Demonstrations*, NAACL-Demonstrations '07, pages 25–26, Stroudsburg, PA, USA. Association for Computational Linguistics.

Crowdsourcing Discourse Relation Annotations
by a Two-Step Connective Insertion Task

Frances Yung[†], **Merel C.J. Scholman**[†] and **Vera Demberg**[†,‡]
[†]Dept. of Language Science and Technology
[‡]Dept. of Mathematics and Computer Science, Saarland University
Saarland Informatic Campus, 66123 Saarbrücken, Germany
`[frances|m.c.j.scholman|vera]@coli.uni-saarland.de`

Abstract

The perspective of being able to crowd-source coherence relations bears the promise of acquiring annotations for new texts quickly, which could then increase the size and variety of discourse-annotated corpora. It would also open the avenue to answering new research questions: Collecting annotations from a larger number of individuals per instance would allow to investigate the distribution of inferred relations, and to study individual differences in coherence relation interpretation.

However, annotating coherence relations with untrained workers is not trivial. We here propose a novel two-step annotation procedure, which extends an earlier method by Scholman and Demberg (2017a). In our approach, coherence relation labels are inferred from connectives that workers insert into the text.

We show that the proposed method leads to replicable coherence annotations, and analyse the agreement between the obtained relation labels and annotations from PDTB and RST-DT on the same texts.

1 Introduction

Implicit coherence relations are connections between text segments that are not overtly marked. Annotating implicit coherence relations using crowd-sourcing is methodologically challenging, because assigning coherence relation labels as used in popular discourse frameworks like the Penn Discourse Treebank style (PDTB, Prasad et al., 2008, 2018) or the Rhetorical Structure Theory (RST, Mann and Thompson, 1988; Carlson et al., 2003) requires linguistic knowledge and substantial training. It is thus not possible to obtain high quality annotations of coherence relation labels from untrained crowd workers (Kawahara et al., 2014; Kishimoto et al., 2018).

A more promising method for obtaining discourse annotations through crowd-sourcing is to ask workers to insert discourse connectives (Rohde et al., 2016; Scholman and Demberg, 2017a). However, this method so far has only been used in settings where it was sufficient to give workers a small set of connectives to choose from, and not in broad-coverage coherence relation annotation. For example, Rohde et al. (2016) focused on identifying cases where several coherence relations may hold between two segments. They provided participants with relations that were already marked with a discourse adverbial, and asked them to additionally insert a conjunction out of a list of six highly frequent connectives (*and, but, so, because, before, or*).

Highly frequent connectives are often ambiguous, for instance, the insertion of *but* does not allow us to infer whether the relation is a contrast or a concession relation. When we want to do fine-grained relation annotation, providing only general connectives is thus not sufficient. Scholman and Demberg (2017a) addressed this problem by restricting the types of relations that could occur in their experiment. They selected six types of coherence relations from the overlapping part of the PDTB2.0 and RST-DT corpora, and re-annotated them using crowd-sourced annotators. Workers in this study could choose from a list of connectives which distinguish unambiguously between the six relation types of interest. For example, instead of the connective *but*, they provided a choice between *nevertheless* and *by contrast*.

However, for annotating text more generally, we need to provide connectives that can capture all types of relations, and on top of that make sure that the insertions can help us to disambiguate between coherence relations. This poses the problem that the list of connectives that participants should choose from would be come unwieldily large – it's unlikely that participants would be very capable of choosing one connective to insert from a list of 50

Proceedings of the 13th Linguistic Annotation Workshop, pages 16–25
Florence, Italy, August 1, 2019. ©2019 Association for Computational Linguistics

connectives.

In this work, we therefore propose a new annotation procedure which builds on the method of Scholman and Demberg (2017a). Our contributions in this paper consist of:

- a novel two-step procedure for eliciting discourse connective insertions from naïve workers;

- a demonstration that the generalized method is comparable in reliability of annotations to the original more restricted crowd-sourcing method proposed by (Scholman and Demberg, 2017a);

- a "connective bank" consisting of 800 entries including traditional connectives as well as variations of connectives and alternative lexicalizations;

- an analysis comparing the obtained coherence labels to labels from professionally annotated discourse treebanks. Our analysis shows that crowd-sourcing captures a mixture of characteristics from PDTB 3.0 and RST-DT annotations.

The data collected in this study, including the crowdsourced annotations of 447 implicit discourse relations and a *connective bank* of 800 connective phrases, is freely available for the community.[1]

2 Background

Crowd-sourcing is an increasing popular alternative to professional annotation of linguistic materials because of time efficiency. However, classification of discourse relations is not a trivial task. This is especially true for implicit relations, where explicit connectives are missing. Detailed guidelines and extensive training are used in traditional annotation by experts.

Kawahara et al. (2014) presented a first attempt to crowd-source discourse relation annotation. The workers first decided whether text spans were connected by a relation, and then assigned one out of seven sense labels in case a relation was identified. The proposal is appealing in terms of time efficiency, but the quality is questionable because evaluation was not carried out. Kishimoto

et al. (2018) later re-annotated a portion of the relations by trained annotators, and found that the quality of the annotation from crowd-sourcing was not satisfactory. They argued that the naïve workers did not completely understand the definition of relation senses and the task was too demanding.

Following the success of analyzing multiple coherence interpretation based on connective insertions by crowd workers (Rohde et al., 2016), Scholman and Demberg (2017a) proposed to use a connective insertion task as a more intuitive alternative to the annotation of coherence relation labels, when working with untrained annotators.

In their experiment, workers are asked to "drag-and-drop" one out of eight unambiguous connectives into the blank between two text spans to express the discourse relation holding between them.[2]

Scholman and Demberg (2017a) evaluated the annotation method by re-annotating a portion of the WSJ text for which professional coherence relation annotations (PDTB, RST-DT) are also available. The majority of the crowd-sourced labels converged with the label of PDTB, showing that the method is reliable, at least in this simplified setting where the set of possible discourse relations is limited and given.

Furthermore, replicability and robustness of the crowd-sourced annotation was demonstrated by replicating the crowd-sourced annotation on the same coherence relations without providing the participants with extra contexts. The resulting connective distributions of the two experiments closely agreed with each other, showing that the annotation is replicable even when contexts are absent.

However, the method used by Scholman and Demberg (2017a) also presents some shortcomings: firstly, it doesn't easily scale up to distinguish between the full set of coherence relations that can occur in a text, and secondly, prompting workers to choose among a set of given connectives might affect their interpretation of the coherence relation[3]. For example, workers might have refrained from inserting an unambiguous but rather heavy-handed connective like "as an illustration" if the text doesn't sound "natural" after

---

[1] https://git.sfb1102.uni-saarland.de/francesyung/2-step-crowdsourced-discourse-annotation

[2] The connectives are *because, as a result, in addition, even though, nevertheless, by contrast, as an illustration* and *more specifically*.

[3] Although workers were also allowed to type other phrases, such manual inputs were rare.

inserting the connective.

We here propose a two-step design which allows the workers to mark each relation by a free insertion step followed by a customized disambiguation step.

3 Method

3.1 Annotation task design

In the first step, workers are shown a short text passage containing a blank between two text segments. They are asked to type in a connective that they think best expresses the relation between the textual arguments. They are also given the option to type *nothing* if they think no phrase possibly fits between the segments.

We expected that freely inserted connectives chosen by workers might often be ambiguous, such that we would not be able to infer a specific coherence relation label from these free insertions. We therefore include a second step, where participants are presented with a list of at most 10 connectives that disambiguate the connective phrase they chose to insert in the first step. The selection of the connectives is determined dynamically from their choice in the first step. They are then asked to drag and drop the phrase that best expresses the relation holding between the text segments. They can choose the *none of these* option if they think none of the given options fit.

For example, the worker had typed *however* in the first step, and this connective can mark ARG1-AS-DENIER, ARG2-AS-DENIER, and CONTRAST, the connectives *even though, despite this* and *on the contrary* will be given as a choice to the worker in the second step. If the first free insertion is already an unambiguous connective, the second step is skipped, and the worker proceeds to the next task.

In order to allow us to determine what connectives should be shown in the second step, we constructed a connective bank containing a collection of connective phrases and their (multiple) senses. We also created a list of unambiguous connective phrases for each of the coherence relations that we distinguish.

In some cases, the insertion in the first step did not match any of the entries in our connective bank (see Section 3.2). This might happen because of typos, insertions that are not actually connective phrases, or which are new connective phrases that are not yet contained in our connective bank. We

observed during the development of our method that this happens particularly frequently in cases where none of the frequent connectives seem to fit the text well. We therefore created a list of ten connectives that typically fit such cases well. This default list is presented to workers when we do not recognize their insertion from the first step, or if they typed *nothing*. This list of default connectives includes *accordingly, actually, as you can see, essentially, evidently, in other words, in summary, on top of that, specifically,* and *to provide some background information*.

3.2 Connective bank

Based on existing discourse resources, we constructed a bank of discourse connecting phrases and manually annotated the possible senses of each phrase. The set of labels is adapted from the sense hierarchy of PDTB3; it is shown in Table 2[4].

We tested the coverage of the connective bank in a number of pretests with a separate group of crowd workers, using materials from PDTB, as well as transcripts of TED talks, in order to capture the possible connectives used by the naïve workers. The free insertions collected from the pretests were manually classified as to whether they are connective phrases. The identified connectives are furthermore labelled with discourse senses and added to the connective bank.

The final version of our connective bank contains 800 entries, which include typical discourse connectives (e.g. *because*), variation of connectives (e.g. *largely because*), combination of connectives (e.g. *and because*) and "alternative lexicalization" (e.g. *the reason is that*).[5] The bank can be expanded with the new free insertions collected after each round of annotation.

The list given in Step 2 contains connectives that mark the relation senses that we want to distinguish as unambiguously as possible. We determined these connectives with the help of Knott (1996)'s connective hierarchy. The complete list is shown in Table 2.

---

[4]We cover each Level-3 sense in PDTB 3.0, except the 4 speech-act relations, because the speech-act relations are rare and cannot be distinguished with their non-speech-act versions by means of the inserted connective. In addition, we included two extra relations: PRESENTATIONAL and BACK-GROUND

[5]We also find a lot of frequent typos among the insertions in the first step, such as "becuase". These typos are also stored as variants in the connective bank, but are not counted towards the 800 entries.

3.3 Aggregation of annotation

From each worker, we thus typically collect one freely inserted label and one forced choice label. In order to determine the coherence relation label, we retrieve the potential relation senses of both the freely inserted and the forced choice connectives from the connective bank, and calculate the intersection of the relation senses they can mark. The exact algorithm is shown in the Appendix.

Each worker assigns either a single or multiple senses to a relation. If the intersection set contains one sense, the relation is resolved to a single unambiguous sense. If the worker chooses an ambiguous phrase in the first step and "none of these" in the second step, then the relation is annotated with the multiple senses of the ambiguous phrase.[6]

It can however happen that participants type a phrase we do not know (and cannot interpret, e.g. because it is not a connective), or choose to insert *nothing* in the first step, and then choose *none of these* in the second step. In these cases, which are rare (3% of the annotation), we remove the data from further analysis.

The multiple annotations collected from multiple workers for each item are aggregated to a sense distribution per item. If a worker assigned more than one sense to the item, the count is equally split among the multiple senses.

We conducted two annotation experiments to evaluate the methodology and reliability of the proposed method.

4 Experiment 1

The objective of this experiment is to confirm the proposed task design and compare it with the forced-choice design proposed by Scholman and Demberg (2017a).

4.1 Materials

Experiment 1 used the same set of items as in Scholman and Demberg (2017a). These are 234 items of six types of explicit and implicit relations chosen from the PDTB[7], which are also annotated in RST-DT.

In the PDTB, each of these items consists of two consecutive text segments connected by a dis-course connective, which is either present in the original text (explicit relation) or inserted by the PDTB annotators (implicit relation). An example of each is shown below.

1. *Some automotive programs have been delayed,* **while** they haven't been canceled. [wsj_0628: explicit relation= ARG1-AS-DENIER]

2. *The explosions began when a seal blew out.* **As a result,** dozens of workers were injured. [wsj_1320: implicit relation= RESULT]

In the experiment, workers see the text segments and are asked to insert a connective phrase.

For the CAUSE, CONJUNCTION, CONCESSION and CONTRAST relations that are contained in this experiment, both PDTB and RST-DT annotations agreed with one another. The INSTANTIATION and LEVEL-OF-DETAIL items were however selected such that RST-DT annotations do not always agree with PDTB annotations (see Scholman and Demberg (2017a) for more details). Therefore, these two types of relations are expected to be more ambiguous. The number of instances per relation is given in the subgraph titles in Figure 2. The items are divided into 12 sense-balanced batches.

Following the experimental design in (Scholman and Demberg, 2017a), we conducted two versions of this experiment – one with context and the other without, where context is defined by the window of two sentences before and one sentence after the text spans linked by the coherence relation.

4.2 Procedure

Each set of items was divided into 12 batches, and each batch of 17-20 questions was annotated by 12 workers.

In total, 380 workers were recruited and each of them completed one or more batches, but never the same batch in two conditions. Workers who inserted less than three different phrases in step one, or selected "none of these" in step two in more than 60% of their responses were screened and their annotations were examined and, if necessary, replaced by annotations of newly recruited workers.

The task was implemented by LingoTurk (Pusse et al., 2016) and the workers were recruited through Prolific.[8] They were awarded with 2.2

---

[6]Scholman and Demberg (2017a) allowed insertion of multiple connectives, but they found that workers seldom do so, possibly due to increased workload.

[7]We used the same items but the updated sense labels from PDTB3.

[8]https://prolific.ac

British pounds on average for each batch of annotation.

4.3 Results

We first analyzed the free and forced insertions collected in each step of the two-step approach, and then compared the annotations with those of Scholman and Demberg (2017a).

The results showed that the proposed two-step free-choice annotation method successfully scaled the connective insertion task to a procedure for crowd-sourcing discourse annotation.

4.3.1 Connective insertion in Steps 1 and 2

First we tested whether the proposed method worked as it was intended. On one hand, if workers mostly inserted an unambiguous connective in the first step, the second step would not be necessary. On the other hand, if the workers often inserted ambiguous connectives in the first step but failed to choose any connectives in the second step, the 2-step operation failed in labeling the relation with a precise sense.

The experiment results demonstrated that the proposed method is flexible and useful. Table 1 shows the proportion of connectives inserted by the workers in each step of the experiment.

Step 1	free insertion			
	unamb.	ambiguous	unknown	nothing
	23%	64%	9%	4%

Step 2	skip	customized		default		
	unamb.	unamb.	amb.	unamb.	amb.	none
	23%	58%	6%	6%	4%	3%

Table 1: Proportions of insertion normalized per step. The proportion of the unambiguous connective in Step 1 is carried over to Step 2.

In the first step, workers freely typed a connectives between the two text segments. Most (87%) of the connectives were identified in our connective bank, and the majority (64%) of them were ambiguous.

Table 2 lists the most common connective phrases the workers typed in Step 1. Naïve workers tended to insert common connectives that are usually ambiguous, such as *and, as* and *but*. The unambiguous connecting phrases, such as *simultaneously*, are uncommon expressions that people do not intuitively produce.

relation sense to be labelled	most common free insertion in Step 1	connective for disambiguation in Step 2
CAUSE		
reason	because	for the reason that
result	and	as a result
negative result*	-	that's why it is impossible that
reason-belief	because	considering that
result-belief	so	so I think
CONCESSION		
arg1-as-denier	but	even though
arg2-as-denier	however	despite this,
CONTRAST		
contrast	however	on the contrary
CONJUNCTION		
conjunction	and	in addition in conjunction with this
INSTANTIATION		
arg1-as-instance*	-	this example illustrates that
arg2-as-instan.	for example	as an example
LEVEL-OF-DETAIL		
arg1-as-detail	actually	in general
arg2-as-detail	specifically	in more detail, specifically
OTHERS		
synchronous	as	simultaneously
precedence	and	afterwards
succession	previously	previously
arg1-as-cond.	in this case	in this case
arg2-as-cond.	where	if
arg1-as-neg.cond.*	-	if not
arg2-as-neg.cond.*	-	unless
arg1-as-goal	through	for that purpose
arg2-as-goal	in order to	in order to
arg1-as-manner	by doing so	by doing so
arg2-as-manner	by	by means of
arg1-as-subst	-	rather than, instead of
arg2-as-subst	but	instead
disjunction*	-	and/or
equivalence	*nothing*	in other words, that is to say
arg1-as-except.*	-	other than that
arg2-as-except.	but	except
similarity	as	in a similar manner
background	*nothing*	to provide some background information
presentational	*nothing*	as you can see

Table 2: The list of 33 discourse relations to be annotated by the two-step connective insertion task and the most common phrase workers typed in Step 1 alongside the unambiguous connective defined in the connective bank for the identification of relation in Step 2. Relations marked by * (6 in total) are defined but never annotated by the workers. BACKGROUND and PRESENTATIONAL are two additional senses that are not from the PDTB3 taxonomy.

However, people were still able to use these uncommon expressions when they were prompted to do so in the second step. The majority of the ambiguous connectives in the first step were disambiguated to a single sense in the second step. For example, *however* was readily distinguished between the ARG2-AS-DENIER and CONTRAST senses; and *and* was disambiguated between PRECEDENCE, RESULT and CONJUNCTION.

A manual check of the responses inserted as free text revealed that 9% of the insertions in this first step were not actually connectives. This is not surprising, given that untrained workers may not know the concept of discourse connectives and could insert non-connective phrases depending on context, such as *unfortunately*, or *they think*. Also, workers preferred not to insert any phrases in 4% of the instances. This is also expected because some discourse relations, e.g. CONJUNCTIONS, are often implicit.

Nonetheless, workers were able to choose a connective from the default options suggested to them for most of the unknown/nothing cases. This shows that our default list of connectives successfully helped the untrained workers to express discourse relations that were not obvious to them.

Overall, the two-step approach resolved the workers' insertions to a single label in 87% of the cases and 27 types of sense labels were collected (See Table 2). This is encouraging because untrained workers would not have been able to carry out such fine-grained classification in one step.

4.3.2 Comparison between forced and free insertions

Next, we compared the methodology of the proposed two-step free-choice task with the one-step forced-choice task of Scholman and Demberg (2017a). We wanted to see if workers' identification of the discourse relation was biased to the set of options available to them and whether contexts were necessary for workers to infer the relations.

The overall distributions of the annotated senses under different annotation conditions are shown in Figure 1.

It can be seen that the relative distribution of the senses was maintained across different approaches, suggesting that the 2-step setup successfully replicates the results obtained from the force-choice method. However, the distributions were statistically different across the two methods be-

cause 12% of the annotated sense did not belong to the 6 original classes of relations. This is expected because the workers were free to assign any relations instead of from a predefined list.

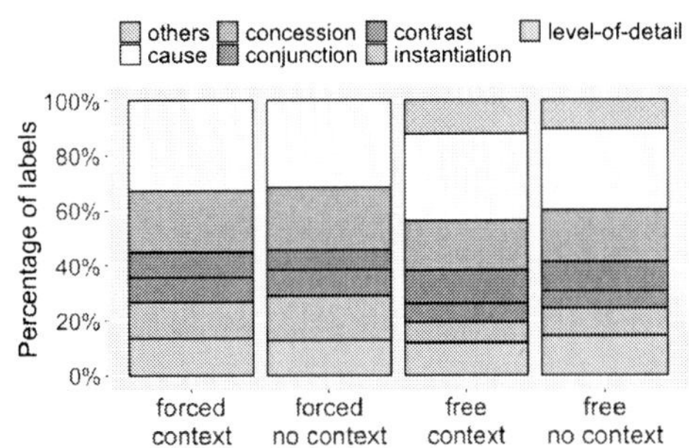

Figure 1: Label distribution per annotation condition of the S&D set

Another finding was that the distributions between the *no context* and *context* conditions were similar. Pearson's χ^2 tests showed a significant difference in the distribution of senses between the two conditions for the original CAUSE ($p = .0478$) and LEVEL-OF-DETAIL ($p = .0159$) items but no significant difference for the other items (CONCESSION: $p = .991$, CONJUNCTION: $p = .258$, CONTRAST: $p = .975$, INSTANTIATION: $p = .232$).

This result partially replicates the finding in Scholman and Demberg (2017a) that contexts offer limited help in this set of items.

4.3.3 Comparison with reference annotation

To assess the quality of the annotations collected by the proposed method, we compared the collected labels with the original expert label per item.

We selected the majority label of each item based on the aggregated distribution for comparison. If an item had more than one majority label, one of them was selected randomly.[9]

Figure 2 shows the distribution of the crowdsourced labels, grouped by their original PDTB label. Only the results under the *context* conditions are shown because the results under the *without context* condition are similar. It can be seen that the distribution mostly replicated the distribution obtained in Scholman and Demberg (2017a),

---

[9]We also tried aggregation by an annotation model (Dawid and Skene, 1979; Passonneau and Carpenter, 2014), but the predicted labels were mostly the same as the majority label.

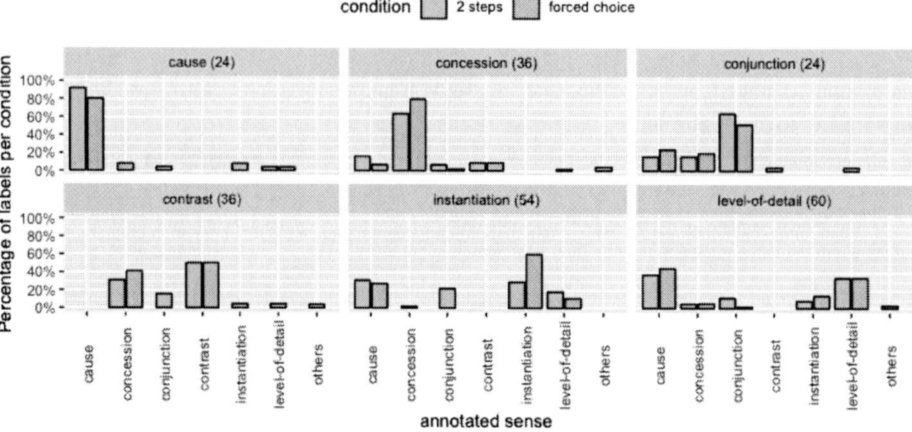

Figure 2: (Experiment 1 results) Distribution of majority sense of the items annotated by the **2 steps** approach in comparison with the **forced choice** approach under the *context* condition. Results are grouped by the original PDTB relation (titles of subgraphs). The item count of each group of relations are bracketed.

except for the INSTANTIATION items. For these items, workers tended to choose CONJUNCTION rather than INSTANTIATION in the two-step task comparing to the forced choice task.

It is known that INSTANTIATION relations have an additive function and thus often coexist with CONJUNCTIONS (Scholman and Demberg, 2017b). However, the labelling of CONJUNCTION could have been suppressed in the forced choice setting, because the single connective that was provided for CONJUNCTIONS was *in addition*, and this phrase may not fit in certain contexts.

Comparing with PDTB annotation, it can be observed that the distributions converged and diverged following the manipulation on the agreement between PDTB and RSTDT.

For example, the crowd-sourced labels converged on the CAUSE sense for the CAUSE items, which were selected if they had high cross-framework agreement. On the other hand, the crowd-sourced labels diverged to a number of senses for the LEVEL-OF-DETAIL items, which were selected if they had low cross-framework agreement.

In addition, CONTRAST items were often annotated as CONCESSION, which is not surprising because the two types of relations are easily confused even for expert annotators. In fact, the overall sense distribution of CONTRAST and CONCESSION reversed when the sense labels were updated from PDTB2 to PDTB3.

In sum, the results of Experiment 1 validated the flexibility and potential of the two-step design and showed that it can be used to obtain similarly reliable annotation as in the oracle forced-choice setting. We conducted another experiment to evaluate the performance of the approach in practical annotation.

5 Experiment 2

The items used in Experiment 1 were chosen such that RST-DT annotations for the same text spans were comparable to the PDTB annotations (for CONTRAST, CONCESSION, CAUSE AND CONJUNCTION). This means that the items were not entirely representative of a real-life annotation setting (i.e., the relations might have been easier to annotate). We therefore conducted another experiment using items that were selected without this constraint.

5.1 Materials

We selected a set of 215 items from the overlapping section of PDTB and RST-DT. We only chose relations where the argument spans were the same in PDTB and RST-DT and the second argument immediately follows the first argument. For comparability to the previous experiment, we restricted the selection to the same six sense classes. Items already tested in Experiment 1 were excluded. The distribution of relation labels in this new set provides a reference of the natural distribution of these six types of coherence relations. The items were randomly divided to 12 batches

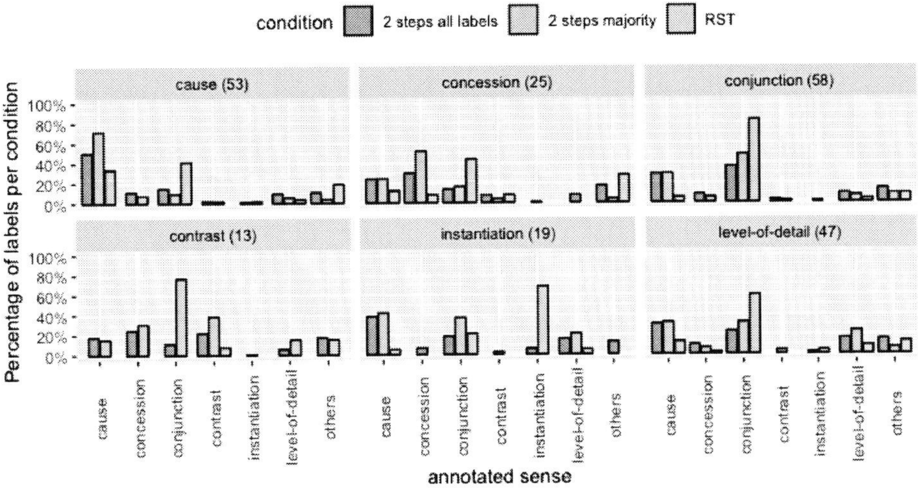

Figure 3: (Experiment 2 results) Distribution of all sense labels (**2 step all labels**) and the majority sense (**2 step majority**) of the items annotated by the *2 steps* approach under the *context* condition in comparison with annotation of RSTDT (**RST**). Results are grouped by the original PDTB relation (titles of subgraphs). The item count of each group of relations are bracketed.

(instead of being sense-balanced). This resembles a situation in which the proposed method is applied to annotate new items. The rest of the experimental set up was the same as in Experiment 1.

5.2 Results

Figure 3 shows the distribution of all the crowd-sourced labels as well as the majority labels collected for each group of relations as annotated in PDTB. Distribution of the RST-DT labels are also shown for comparison. The relation definitions of PDTB and RST-DT do not directly map with each other. In order to compare the annotations of both resources with the crowdsourced labels, we converted the RST labels to PDTB labels according to the Unifying Dimensions interlingua (Demberg et al., 2017).

The results showed that the distributions of the crowd-sourced labels overlapped with both PDTB and RST-DT annotations, except for INSTANTIATIONS (see discussion). The annotations of PDTB and RST-DT largely differ for this more representative selection.

Table 3 shows the agreement of the crowd-sourced labels with PDTB, compared with the agreement between the PDTB and RST-DT labels. It can be seen that the labels crowdsourced by the proposed method had higher overall agreement with PDTB comparing with RST-DT labels.

This experiment showed that expert annotation

PDTB3	2 steps		RST-DT	
	Prec.	Recall	Prec.	Recall
cause	.44	.71	.58	.34
concession	.48	.52	.67	.06
conjunction	.47	.47	.39	.83
contrast	.63	.38	.33	.08
instantiation	.0	.0	.56	.47
level-of-detail	.46	.23	.44	.09
overall	.44	.44	.40	.40

Table 3: Agreement of the majority crowd-sourced and RST-DT labels with the PDTB3 labels and the label distribution of the random set.

of discourse relations cannot be represented by a single label and the annotation crowdsourced by the two-step method captured the characteristics of both resources.

6 Discussion

The results demonstrated that the multiple readings of discourse relations were reproduced across the two annotation conditions, even though there was not always agreement with professional annotations. While Scholman and Demberg (2017a) had already reported the reproduction of label distributions under the with and without context conditions, we found that the distributions are also reproduced when free insertion of connectives is allowed. This is stronger evidence that the limited labels collected by traditional annotations might not be sufficient to reflect the multiple reading of discourse relations, while a distribution of labels collected by multiple annotation is more informative.

However, we also identified potential problems: our naïve workers seem to have under-labelled INSTANTIATION relations, especially in Experiment 2. On top of the fact that INSTANTIATIONS are difficult in general, a closer look shows that these items mostly contain quotations, and it is difficult to distinguish whether the relation is between the previous argument and the content of the quote, or the fact that someone said something. This could be the source of confusion for the crowd workers, which deserves to be addressed more specifically in future research.

Another challenge is the causal preference bias (Sanders, 2005). Although we expected that over-interpretation would be reduced in the *free* insertion approach compared with *forced* selection from an available list, we observed an over-interpretation of CAUSE relations. CAUSE relations may be over-labelled because readers readily infer causality during text processing: Scholman (2019) shows that readers infer causal relations readily when not processing the text very deeply. Since the materials we used came from outdated news journal texts from the US, they were likely to be hard to understand for the workers who mostly come from the UK, and the causality bias could hence be particularly prominent in our study. A future study on a different text type would be informative in this respect.

In terms of methodology, we also plan to extend the method to make better use of the connectives provided during the free insertion step. For example, if a worker types *and* in the first step and chooses *so* in the second step, the current algorithm would simply combine the two insertions to a CAUSE relation by taking the intersection of senses. However, there is a chance that the forced choice was prompted by the given options, and that the inference of the relation was thus strengthened by the task. A more dynamic approach should take into account the pragmatic choice of *and* over other alternatives, in order to determine whether the worker inferred a causal relation in the first place.

Lastly, the current method assumes that all dis-course relations can be made explicit – in our experiments, we only used items where a connective phrase originally existed or can possibly be inserted. However, it is not always possible to insert a connective. For example, there are no explicit markers for ENTITY RELATIONS. Furthermore, there is also the possibility that the two consecutive segments are *unrelated*. The current method has to be extended to identify these cases for practical annotations.

7 Conclusion

We propose a two-step procedure to convert the challenging task of fine-grained implicit discourse relation annotation to an intuitive task that naïve crowd workers can manage. The method can be directly applied to annotate coherence relations in other languages, and crowdsourcing is a time efficient alternative. On top of the discourse annotation, the methodology also allows creation of large connective banks in other languages.

The results from the current studies also indicate that the discourse relation annotations are more representative when they can be characterized by sense distributions. Automatic discourse relation classification is a bottleneck task, and resources annotated with sense distributions allow more informative evaluation by ranking.

We plan to carry out large scale annotation using the two-step approach to build discourse annotated resources in a variety of data.

Acknowledgments

This research was funded by the German Research Foundation (DFG) as part of SFB 1102 Information Density and Linguistic Encoding

References

Lynn Carlson, Daniel Marcu, and Mary Ellen Okurowski. 2003. Building a discourse-tagged corpus in the framework of Rhetorical Structure Theory. In *Current and new directions in discourse and dialogue*, pages 85–112. Springer.

Alexander Philip Dawid and Allan M Skene. 1979. Maximum likelihood estimation of observer error-rates using the em algorithm. *Journal of the Royal Statistical Society: Series C (Applied Statistics)*, 28(1):20–28.

Vera Demberg, Fatemeh Torabi Asr, and Merel C.J. Scholman. 2017. How compatible are our discourse annotations? Insights from mapping RST-

DT and PDTB annotations. *arXiv preprint arXiv:1704.08893*.

Daisuke Kawahara, Yuichiro Machida, Tomohide Shibata, Sadao Kurohashi, Hayato Kobayashi, and Manabu Sassano. 2014. Rapid development of a corpus with discourse annotations using two-stage crowdsourcing. In *Proceedings of the 25th International Conference on Computational Linguistics*, pages 269–278.

Yudai Kishimoto, Shinnosuke Sawada, Yugo Murawaki, Daisuke Kawahara, and Sadao Kurohashi. 2018. Improving crowdsourcing-based annotation of japanese discourse relations. In *Proceedings of the 11th Language Resources and Evaluation Conference*.

Alastair Knott. 1996. *A Data-Driven Methodology for Motivating a Set of Coherence Relations*. Ph.D. thesis, University of Edinburgh.

William C Mann and Sandra A Thompson. 1988. Rhetorical structure theory: Toward a functional theory of text organization. *Text-Interdisciplinary Journal for the Study of Discourse*, 8(3):243–281.

Rebecca J Passonneau and Bob Carpenter. 2014. The benefits of a model of annotation. *Transactions of the Association for Computational Linguistics*, 2:311–326.

Rashmi Prasad, Nikhil Dinesh, Alan Lee, Eleni Miltsakaki, Livio Robaldo, Aravind K Joshi, and Bonnie L Webber. 2008. The Penn Discourse Treebank 2.0. In *Proceedings of the 6th Language Resources and Evaluation Conference*.

Rashmi Prasad, Bonnie Webber, and Alan Lee. 2018. Discourse annotation in the PDTB: The next generation. In *Proceedings of the 14th Joint ACL-ISO Workshop on Interoperable Semantic Annotation*, pages 87–97.

Florian Pusse, Asad Sayeed, and Vera Demberg. 2016. Lingoturk: managing crowdsourced tasks for psycholinguistics. In *Proceedings of the Conference of the North American Chapter of the Association for Computational Linguistics: Demonstrations*, pages 57–61.

Hannah Rohde, Anna Dickinson, Nathan Schneider, Christopher NL Clark, Annie Louis, and Bonnie Webber. 2016. Filling in the blanks in understanding discourse adverbials: Consistency, conflict, and context-dependence in a crowdsourced elicitation task. In *Proceedings of the 10th Linguistic Annotation Workshop*, pages 49–58.

Ted Sanders. 2005. Coherence, causality and cognitive complexity in discourse. In *Proceedings of the First International Symposium on the exploration and modelling of meaning*, pages 105–114. University of Toulouse-le-Mirail Toulouse.

Merel C.J. Scholman. 2019. *Coherence relations in discourse and cognition: comparing approaches, annotations and interpretations*. Ph.D. thesis, University of Saarland.

Merel C.J. Scholman and Vera Demberg. 2017a. Crowdsourcing discourse interpretations: On the influence of context and the reliability of a connective insertion task. In *Proceedings of the 11th Linguistic Annotation Workshop*, pages 24–33.

Merel C.J. Scholman and Vera Demberg. 2017b. Examples and specifications that prove a point: Identifying elaborative and argumentative discourse relations. *Dialogue & Discourse*, 8(2):56–83.

A Appendix: Algorithm for the combination of inserted connectives

for each insertion pair **do**
    if free insertion $\in$ connective bank **then**
        $R1 \leftarrow$ sense(s) of free insertion
    else
        manual check
        if free insertion is connective **then**
            added to connective bank
            manual sense annotation
            $R1 \leftarrow$ sense(s) of free insertion
        else
            $R1 \leftarrow \emptyset$
        end if
    end if
    if forced insertion $=$ *none of these* **then**
        $R2 \leftarrow \emptyset$
    else
        $R2 \leftarrow$ sense(s) of forced insertion
    end if
    $S \leftarrow R1 \cap R2$
end for

Annotating and analyzing the interactions between meaning relations

Darina Gold[1*], Venelin Kovatchev[23*], Torsten Zesch[1]
[1]Language Technology Lab, University of Duisburg-Essen, Germany
[2]Language and Computation Center, Universitat de Barcelona, Spain
[3]Institute of Complex Systems, Universitat de Barcelona, Spain
`{darina.gold,torsten.zesch}@uni-due.de`
`vkovatchev@ub.edu`
[*]Both authors contributed equally to this work

Abstract

Pairs of sentences, phrases, or other text pieces can hold semantic relations such as paraphrasing, textual entailment, contradiction, specificity, and semantic similarity. These relations are usually studied in isolation and no dataset exists where they can be compared empirically. Here we present a corpus annotated with these relations and the analysis of these results. The corpus contains 520 sentence pairs, annotated with these relations. We measure the annotation reliability of each individual relation and we examine their interactions and correlations. Among the unexpected results revealed by our analysis is that the traditionally considered direct relationship between paraphrasing and bi-directional entailment does not hold in our data.

1 Introduction

Meaning relations refer to the way in which two sentences can be connected, e.g. if they express approximately the same content, they are considered paraphrases. Other meaning relations we focus on here are textual entailment and contradiction[1] (Dagan et al., 2005), and specificity.

Meaning relations have applications in many NLP tasks, e.g. recognition of textual entailment is used for summarization (Lloret et al., 2008) or machine translation evaluation (Padó et al., 2009), and paraphrase identification is used in summarization (Harabagiu and Lacatusu, 2010).

The complex nature of the meaning relations makes it difficult to come up with a precise and widely accepted definition for each of them. Also, there is a difference between theoretical definitions and definitions adopted in practical tasks. In this paper, we follow the approach taken in pre-

vious annotation tasks and we give the annotators generic and practically oriented instructions.

Paraphrases are differently worded texts with approximately the same content (Bhagat and Hovy, 2013; De Beaugrande and Dressler, 1981). The relation is symmetric. In the following example, (a) and (b) are paraphrases.

(a) *Education is equal for all children.*

(b) *All children get the same education.*

Textual Entailment is a directional relation between pieces of text in which the information of the *Text* entails the information of the *Hypothesis* (Dagan et al., 2005). In the following example, Text (t) entails Hypothesis (h):

(t) *All children get the same education.*

(h) *Education exists.*

Specificity is a relation between phrases in which one phrase is more precise and the other more vague. Specificity is mostly regarded between noun phrases (Cruse, 1977; Enç, 1991; Farkas, 2002). However, there has also been work on specificity on the sentence level (Louis and Nenkova, 2012). In the following example, (c) is more specific than (d) as it gives information on who does not get good education:

(c) *Girls do not get good education.*

(d) *Some children do not get good education.*

Semantic Similarity between texts is not a meaning relation in itself, but rather a gradation of meaning similarity. It has often been used as a proxy for the other relations in applications such as summarization (Lloret et al., 2008), plagiarism detection (Alzahrani and Salim, 2010; Bär et al., 2012), machine translation (Padó et al.,

---

[1]Mostly, contradiction is regarded as one of the relations within an entailment annotation.

Proceedings of the 13th Linguistic Annotation Workshop, pages 26–36
Florence, Italy, August 1, 2019. ©2019 Association for Computational Linguistics

2009), question answering (Harabagiu and Hickl, 2006), and natural language generation (Agirre et al., 2013). We use it in this paper to quantify the strength of relationship on a continuous scale. Given two linguistic expressions, semantic text similarity measures the degree of semantic equivalence (Agirre et al., 2013). For example, (a) and (b) have a semantic similarity score of 5 (on a scale from 0-5 as used in the SemEval STS task) (Agirre et al., 2013, 2014).

Interaction between Relations Despite the interactions and close connection of these meaning relations, to our knowledge, there exists neither an empirical analysis of the connection between them nor a corpus enabling it. We bridge this gap by creating and analyzing a corpus of sentence pairs annotated with all discussed meaning relations.

Our analysis finds that previously made assumptions on some relations (e.g. paraphrasing being bi-directional entailment (Madnani and Dorr, 2010; Androutsopoulos and Malakasiotis, 2010; Sukhareva et al., 2016)) are not necessarily right in a practical setting. Furthermore, we explore the interactions of the meaning relation of specificity, which has not been extensively studied from an empirical point of view. We find that it can be found in pairs on all levels of semantic relatedness and does not correlate with entailment.

2 Related Work

To our knowledge, there is no other work where the discussed meaning relations have been annotated separately on the same data, enabling an unbiased analysis of the interactions between them. There are corpora annotated with multiple semantic phenomena, including meaning relations.

2.1 Interactions between relations

There has been some work on the interaction between some of the discussed meaning relations, especially on the relation between entailment and paraphrasing, and also on how semantic similarity is connected to the other relations.

Interaction between entailment and paraphrases According to Madnani and Dorr (2010); Androutsopoulos and Malakasiotis (2010), bi-directional entailment can be seen as paraphrasing. Furthermore, according to Androutsopoulos and Malakasiotis (2010) both entailment and paraphrasing are intended to capture human intuition. Kovatchev et al. (2018) emphasize the similarity between linguistic phenomena underlying paraphrasing and entailment. There has been practical work on using paraphrasing to solve entailment (Bosma and Callison-Burch, 2006).

Interaction between entailment and specificity Specificity was involved in rules for the recognition of textual entailment (Bobrow et al., 2007).

Interaction with semantic similarity Cer et al. (2017) argue that to find paraphrases or entailment, some level of semantic similarity must be given. Furthermore, Cer et al. (2017) state that although semantic similarity includes both entailment and paraphrasing, it is different, as it has a gradation and not a binary measure of the semantic overlap. Based on their corpus, Marelli et al. (2014) state that paraphrases, entailment, and contradiction have a high similarity score; paraphrases having the highest and contradiction the lowest of them. There also was practical work using the interaction between semantic similarity and entailment: Yokote et al. (2011) and Castillo and Cardenas (2010) used semantic similarity to solve entailment.

2.2 Corpora with multiple semantic layers

There are several works describing the creation, annotation, and subsequent analysis of corpora with multiple parallel phenomena.

MASC The annotation of corpora with multiple phenomena in parallel has been most notably explored within the Manually Annotated Sub-Corpus (MASC) project[2] — It is a large-scale, multi-genre corpus manually annotated with multiple semantic layers, including Word-Net senses(Miller, 1998), Penn Treebank Syntax (Marcus et al., 1993), and opinions. The multiple layers enable analyses between several phenomena.

SICK is a corpus of around 10,000 sentence pairs that were annotated with semantic similarity and entailment in parallel (Marelli et al., 2014). As it is the corpus that is the most similar to our work, we will compare some of our annotation decisions and results with theirs.

Sukhareva et al. (2016) annotated subclasses of entailment, including *paraphrase, forward, revert,* and *null* on propositions extracted from doc-

---

[2]http://www.anc.org/MASC/About.html

Getting a high educational degree is important for finding a good job, especially in big cities.
In many countries, girls are less likely to get a good school education.
Going to school socializes kids through constant interaction with others.
One important part of modern education is technology, if not the most important.
Modern assistants such Cortana, Alexa, or Siri make our everyday life easier by giving quicker access to information.
New technologies lead to asocial behavior by e.g. depriving us from face-to-face social interaction.
Being able to use modern technologies is obligatory for finding a good job.
Self-driving cars are safer than humans as they don't drink.
Machines are good in strategic games such as chess and Go.
Machines are good in communicating with people.
Learning a second language is beneficial in life.
Speaking more than one language helps in finding a good job.
Christian clergymen learn Latin to read the bible.

Table 1: List of given source sentences

uments on educational topics that were paired according to semantic overlap. Hence, they implicitly regarded paraphrases as a kind of entailment.

3 Corpus Creation

To analyze the interactions between semantic relations, a corpus annotated with all relations in parallel is needed. Hence, we develop a new corpus-creation methodology which ensures all relations of interest to be present. First, we create a pool of potentially related sentences. Second, based on the pool of sentences, we create sentence pairs that contain all relations of interest with sufficient frequency. This contrasts existing corpora on meaning relations that are tailored towards one relation only. Finally, we take a portion of the corpus and annotate all relations via crowdsourcing. This part of our methodology differs significantly from the approach taken in the SICK corpus (Marelli et al., 2014). They don't create new corpora, but rather re-annotate pre-existing corpora, which does not allow them to control for the overall similarity between the pairs.

3.1 Sentence Pool

In the first step, the authors create 13 sentences, henceforth *source sentences*, shown in Table 1. The sentences are on three topics: *education, technology*, and *language*. We choose sentences that can be understood by a competent speaker without any domain-specific knowledge and which due to their complexity potentially give rise to a variety of lexically differing sentences in the next step. Then, a group of 15 people, further on called *sentence generators*, is asked to generate *true* and *false* sentences that vary lexically from the source sentence.[3] Overall, 780 sentences are generated. The 13 *source sentences* are not considered in the further procedure.

For creating the *true* sentences, we ask each sentence generator to create two sentences that are true and for the *false* sentences, two sentences that are false given one source sentence. This way of generating a sentence pool is similar to that of the textual entailment SNLI corpus (Bowman et al., 2015), where the generators were asked to create true and false captions for given images. The following are exemplary true and false sentences created from one source sentence.

> Source: *Getting a high educational degree is important for finding a good job, especially in big cities.*

> True: *Good education helps to get a good job.*

> False: *There are no good or bad jobs.*

3.2 Pair Generation

We combine individual sentences from the sentence pool into pairs, as meaning relations are present between pairs and not individual sentences. To obtain a corpus that contains all discussed meaning relation with sufficient frequency, we use four pair combinations: 1) a pair of two sentences that are true given the same source sentence — *true-true*; 2) a pair of two sentences that are false given the same source sentence — *false-false*; 3) a pair of one sentence that is true and one sentence that is false given the same source sentence — *true-false*; 4) a pair of randomly matched sentences from the whole sentence pool and all source sentences — *random*.

---

[3] The full instructions given to the sentence generators is included with the corpus data.

From the 780 sentences in the sentence pool, we created a corpus of 11,310 pairs, with a pair distribution as follows: 5,655 (50%) *true-true*; 2,262 (20%) *false-false*, 2,262 (20%) *true-false*, and 1,131 (10%) *random*. We include all possible 5,655 *true-true* combinations of 30 true sentences for each of the 13 source sentences. For *false-false*, *true-false*, and *random* we downsample the full set of pairs to obtain the desired number, keeping an equal number of samples per source sentence. We chose this distribution because we are mainly interested in paraphrases and entailment, as well as their relation to specificity. We hypothesize that pairs of sentences that are both true have the highest potential to contain these relations.

From the 11,310 pairs, we randomly selected 520 (5%) for annotation, with the same 50-20-20-10 distribution as the full corpus. We select an equal number of pairs from each source sentence. We hypothesize that length strongly correlates with specificity, as there is potentially more information in a longer sentence that in a shorter one. Hence, for half of the pairs, we made sure that the difference in length between the two sentences is not more than 1 token.

3.3 Relation Annotation

We annotate all the relations in the corpus of 520 sentence pairs using Amazon Turk. We select 10 crowdworkers per task, as this gives us the possibility to measure how well the tasks has been understood overall, but especially how easy or difficult individual pairs are in the annotation of a specific relation. In the SICK corpus, the same platform and number of annotators were used.

We chose to annotate the relations separately to avoid biasing the crowdworkers who might learn heuristic shortcuts when seeing the same relations together too often. We launched the tasks consecutively to have the annotations as independent as possible. This differs from the SICK corpus annotation setting, where entailment, contradiction, and semantic similarity were annotated together.

The complex nature of the meaning relations makes it difficult to come up with a precise and widely accepted definition and annotation instructions for each of them. This problem has already been emphasized in previous annotation tasks and theoretical settings (Bhagat and Hovy, 2013). The standard approach in most of the existing paraphrasing and entailment datasets is to use a more

generic and less strict definitions. For example, pairs annotated as "paraphrases" in MRPC (Dolan et al., 2004) can have "obvious differences in information content". This "relatively loose definition of semantic equivalence" is adopted in most empirically oriented paraphrasing corpora.

We take the same approach towards the task of annotating semantic relations: we provide the annotators with simplified guidelines, as well as with few positive and negative examples. In this way, we believe that annotation is more generic, reproducible, and applicable to any kind of data. It also relies more on the intuitions of a competent speaker than on understanding complex linguistic concepts. Prior to the full annotation, we performed several pilot studies on a sample of the corpus in order to improve instructions and examples given to the annotators. In the following, we will shortly outline the instructions for each task.

Paraphrasing In Paraphrasing (PP), we ask the crowdworkers whether the two sentences have approximately the same meaning or not, which is similar to the definition of Bhagat and Hovy (2013) and De Beaugrande and Dressler (1981).

Textual Entailment In Textual Entailment (TE), we ask whether the first sentence makes the second sentence true. Similar to RTE Tasks (Dagan et al., 2005) - (Bentivogli et al., 2011), we only annotate for forward entailment (FTE). Hence, we use the pairs twice: in the order we ask for all other tasks and in reversed order, to get the entailment for both directions. Backward Entailment is referred to as *BTE*. If a pair contains only backward or forward entailment, it is uni-directional (UTE). If a pair contains both forward and backward entailment, it is bi-directional (BiTE). Our annotation instructions and the way we interpret directionality is similar to other crowdworking tasks for textual entailment (Marelli et al., 2014; Bowman et al., 2015).

Contradiction In Contradiction (Cont), we ask the annotators whether the sentences contradict each other. Here, our instructions are different from the typical approach in RTE (Dagan et al., 2005), where contradiction is often understood as the absence of entailment.

Specificity In Specificity (Spec), we ask whether the first sentence is more specific than the second. To annotate specificity in a comparative way is new [4]. Like in textual entailment, we pose

---

[4] Louis and Nenkova (2012) labelled individual sentences

the task only in one direction. If the originally first sentence is more specific, it is forward specificity (FSpec), whereas if the originally second sentence is more specific than the first, it is backward specificity (BSpec).

Semantic Similarity For semantic similarity (Sim), we do not only ask whether the pair is related, but rate the similarity on a scale 0-5. Unlike previous studies (Agirre et al., 2014), we decided not to provide explicit definitions for every point on the scale.

Annotation Quality To ensure the quality of the annotations, we include 10 control pairs, which are hand-picked and slightly modified pairs from the original corpus, in each task.[5] We discard workers who perform bad on the control pairs. [6]

3.4 Final Corpus

For each sentence pair, we get 10 annotations for each relation, namely paraphrasing, entailment, contradiction, specificity, and semantic similarity. Each sentence pair is assigned a binary label for each relation, except for similarity. We decide that if the majority (at least 60% of the annotators) voted for a relation, it gets the label for this relation.

Table 8 shows exemplary annotation outputs of sentence pairs taken from our corpus. For instance, sentence pair #4 contains two relations: forward entailment and forward specificity. This means that it has uni-directional entailment and the first sentence is more specific than the second. The semantic similarity of this pair is 2.7.

Inter-annotator agreement We evaluate the agreement on each task separately. For semantic similarity, we determine the average similarity score and the standard deviation for each pair. We also calculate the Pearson correlation between each annotator and the average score for their pairs. We report the average correlation, as suggested by SemEval (Agirre et al., 2014) and SICK.

For all nominal classification tasks we determine the majority vote and calculate the % of agreement between the annotators. This is the same measure used in the SICK corpus. Follow-

ing the approach used with semantic similarity, we also calculated Cohen's *kappa* between each annotator and the majority vote for their pairs. We report the average *kappa* for each task.[7]

Table 2 shows the overall inter-annotator agreement for the binary tasks. We report: 1) the average %-agreement for the whole corpus; 2) the average κ score; 3) the average %-agreement for the pairs where the majority label is *"yes"*; 4) the average %-agreement for the pairs where the majority label is *"no"*; 5) the average % agreement between the annotators and the expert-provided "control labels" on the control questions.

	%	κ	%✓	%✗	control
PP	.87	.67	.83	.90	.98
TE	.83	.61	.75	.89	.89
Cont	.94	.71	.84	.95	.95
Spec	.80	.56	.81	.82	.89

Table 2: Inter-annotator agreement for binary relations
✓denotes a relation being there
✗denotes a relation not being there

The overall agreement for all tasks is between .80 - .94, which is quite good given the difficulty of the tasks. Contradiction has the highest agreement with .94. It is followed by the paraphrase relation, which has an agreement of .87. The agreements of the entailment and specificity relations are slightly lower, which reflects that the tasks are more complex. SICK report agreement of .84 on entailment, which is consistent with our result.

The agreement is higher on the control questions than on the rest of the corpus. We consider it the upper boundary of agreement. The agreement on the individual binary classes shows that, except for the specificity relation, annotators have a higher agreement on the absence of relation.

	50%	60%	70%	80%	90%	100%
PP	.11	.12	.13	.20	.24	.20
TE	.17	.19	.17	.16	.19	.10
Cont	.04	.07	.18	.23	.23	.25
Spec	.22	.18	.21	.13	.13	.12

Table 3: Distribution of Inter-annotator agreement

Table 3 shows the distribution of agreement for the different relations. We take all pairs for which at least 50% of the annotators found the relation

---

as *specific*, *general*, or *cannot decide*.

[5]The control pairs are also available online at `https://github.com/MeDarina/meaning_relations_interaction`

[6]Only 2 annotators were discarded across all tasks. To have an equal number of annotations for each task, we reannotated these cases with other crowdworkers.

[7]We are aware that κ does not fit the restrictions of our task very well and also that it is usually not averaged. However, we wanted to report a chance corrected measure, which is non-trivial in a crowd-sourcing setting, where each pair is annotated by a different set of annotators.

and shows what percentage of these pairs have inter-annotator agreement of 50%, 60%, 70%, 80%, 90%, and 100%. We can observe that, with the exception of contradiction, the distribution of agreement is relatively equal. For our initial corpus analysis, we discarded the pairs with 50% agreement and we only considered pairs where the majority (60% or more) of the annotators voted for the relation. However, the choice of agreement threshold an empirical question and the threshold can be adjusted based on particular objectives and research needs.

The average standard deviation for semantic similarity is 1.05. SICK report average deviation of .76, which is comparable to our result, considering that they use a 5 point scale (1-5), and we use a 6 point one (0-5). Pearson's r between annotators and the average similarity score is 0.69 which is statistically significant at $\alpha = 0.05$.

Distribution of meaning relations Table 4 shows that all meaning relations are represented in our dataset. We have 160 paraphrase pairs, 195 textual entailment pairs, 68 contradiction pairs, and 381 specificity pairs. There is only a small number of contradictions, but this was already anticipated by the different pairings. The distribution is similar to Marelli et al. (2014) in that the set is slightly leaning towards entailment[8]. Furthermore, the distribution of uni- and bi-directional entailment with our and the SICK corpus are similar: they are nearly equally represented.[9]

Distribution of meaning relations with different generation pairings Table 4 shows the distribution of meaning relations and the average similarity score in the differently generated sentence pairings. In the true/true pairs, we have the highest percentage of paraphrase (49%), entailment (60%), and specificity (79%). In the false/false pairs, all relations of interest are present: paraphrases (27%), entailment (36%), and specificity (72%). Unlike in true/true pairs, false/false ones include contradictions (10%). True/false pairs contain the highest percentage of contradiction (85%). There were also few entailment and paraphrase relations in true/false pairs. In the random

---

[8]As opposed to contradiction. However, as contradiction and entailment were annotated exclusively, it is not directly comparable.

[9]In SICK 53% of the entailment is uni-directional and 46% are bi-directional, whereas we have 44% uni-directional and 55% bi-directional.

	all	T/T	F/F	T/F	rand.
PP	31%	49%	27%	2%	6%
TE	38%	60%	36%	2%	2%
Cont.	13%	0%	10 %	56%	0%
Spec	73%	79%	72%	66%	63%
∅Sim	2.27	2.90	2.39	1.32	0.77

Table 4: Distribution of meaning relations within different pair generation patterns

pairs, there were only few relations of any kind. The proportion of specificity is high in all pairs.

This different distribution of phenomena based on the source sentences can be used in further corpus creation when determining the best way to combine sentences in pairs. In our corpus, the balanced distribution of phenomena we obtain justifies our pairing choice of 50-20-20-10.

Lexical overlap within sentence pairs As discussed by Joao et al. (2007), a potential flaw of most existing relation corpora is the high lexical overlap between the pairs. They show that simple lexical overlap metrics pose a competitive baseline for paraphrase identification. Due to our creation procedure, we reduce this problem. In Table 5, we quantified it by calculating unigram and bigram BLEU score between the two texts in each pair for our corpus, MRPC and SNLI, which are the two most used corpora for paraphrasing and textual entailment. The BLEU score is much lower for our corpus that for MRPC and SNLI.

	MRPC	SNLI	Our corpus
unigram	61	24	18
bigram	50	12	6

Table 5: Comparison of BLEU scores between the sentence pairs in different corpora

Relations and Negation Our corpus also contains multiple instances of relations that involve negations and also double negations. Those examples could pose difficulties to automatic systems and could be of interest to researchers that study the interaction between inference and negation. Pairs #1, #2, and #9 in Table 8 are examples for pairs containing negation in our corpus.

4 Interactions between relations

We analyze the interactions between the relations in our corpus in two ways. First, we calculate the correlation between the binary relations and the interaction between them and similarity. Second, we analyze the overlap between the different binary relations and discuss interesting examples.

4.1 Correlations between relations

We calculate correlations between the binary relations using the Pearson correlation. For the correlations of the binary relations with semantic similarity, we discuss the average similarity and the similarity score scales of each binary relation.

4.1.1 Correlation of binary meaning relations

In Table 6, we show the Pearson correlation between the meaning relations. For entailment, we show the correlation for uni-directional (UTE), bi-directional (BTE), and any-directional (TE).

Paraphrases and any-directional entailment are highly similar with a correlation of .75. Paraphrases have a much higher correlation with bi-directional entailment (.70) than with uni-directional entailment (.20). Prototypical examples of pairs that are both paraphrases and textual entailment are pairs #1 and #2 in Table 8. Furthermore, both paraphrases and entailment have a negative correlation with contradiction, which is expected and confirms the quality of our data.

Specificity does not have any strong correlation with any of the other relations, showing that it is independent of those in our corpus.

	TE	UTE	BiTE	Cont	Spec	∅ Sim
PP	.75	.20	.70	-.25	-.01	3.77
TE		.57	.66	-.30	-.01	3.59
UTE			-.23	-.17	-.04	3.21
BiTE				-.20	-.01	3.89
Cont					-.09	1.45
Spec						2.27

Table 6: Correlation between all relations

4.1.2 Binary relations and semantic similarity

We look at the average similarity for each relation (see Table 6) and show boxplots between relation labels and similarity ratings (see Figure 1). Table 6 shows that bi-directional entailment has the highest average similarity, followed by paraphrasing, while contradiction has the lowest.

Figure 1 shows plots of the semantic similarity for all pairs where each relation is present and all pairs where it is absent. The paraphrase pairs have much higher similarity scores than the non-paraphrase pairs. The same observation can be made for entailment. The contradiction pairs have a low similarity score, whereas the non-contradiction pairs do not have a clear tendency with respect to similarity score. In contrast to the other relations, pairs with and without specificity do not have any consistent similarity score.

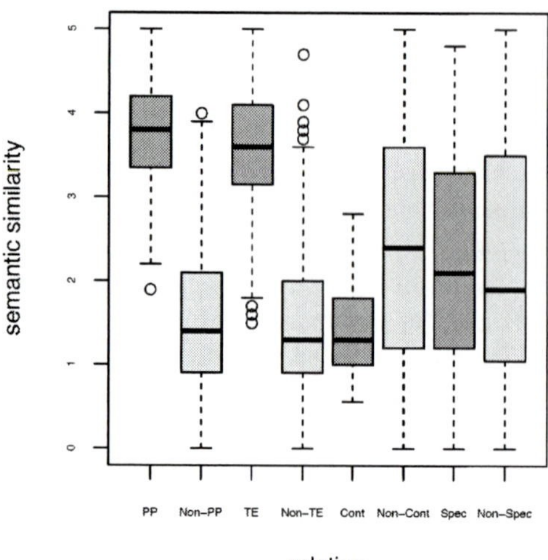

Figure 1: Similarity scores of sentences annotated with different relations

4.2 Overlap of relation labels

Table 7 shows the overlap between the different binary labels. Unlike Pearson correlation, the overlap is asymmetric - the % of paraphrases that are also entailment (UTE in PP) is different from the % of entailment pairs that are also paraphrases (PP in UTE). Using the overlap measure, we can identify interesting interactions between phenomena and take a closer look at some examples.

	PP	UTE	BiTE	Contra	Spec
In PP		28 %	64 %	0	73 %
In UTE	52 %		-	0	73 %
In BiTE	94 %	-		0	72 %
In Contra	0	0	0		63 %
In Spec	30 %	17 %	21 %	11 %	

Table 7: Distribution of overlap within relations

4.2.1 Entailment and paraphrasing overlap

In a more theoretical setting, bi-directional entailment is often defined as being paraphrases (Madnani and Dorr, 2010; Androutsopoulos and Malakasiotis, 2010; Sukhareva et al., 2016). This

#	Sentence 1	Sentence 2	PP	FTE	BTE	Cont	FSpec	BSpec	Sim
1	The importance of technology in modern education is overrated.	Technology is not mandatory to improve education	✓	✓	✓				2.8
2	Machines cannot interact with humans.	No machine can communicate with a person.	✓	✓	✓				4.9
3	The modern assistants make finding data slower.	Today's information flow is greatly facilitated by digital assistants.				✓		✓	1.9
4	The bible is in Hebrew.	Bible is not in Latin.		✓			✓		2.7
5	All around the world, girls have higher chance of getting a good school education.	Girls get a good school education everywhere.	✓					✓	4.7
6	Reading the Bible requires studying Latin.	The Bible is written in Latin.		✓	✓			✓	3.6
7	Speaking more than one language can be useful.	Languages are beneficial in life.	✓	✓	✓			✓	4.4
8	You can find a good job if you only speak one language.	People who speak more than one language could only land pretty bad jobs.			✓				2.3
9	All Christian priests need to study Persian, as the Bible is written in Ancient Greek.	Christian clergymen don't read the bible.						✓	0.9
10	School makes students anti-social.	School usually prevents children from socializing properly.	✓	✓	✓			✓	3.9

Table 8: Annotations of sentence pairs on all meaning relations taken from our corpus

implies that paraphrases equal bi-directional entailment. In our corpus, we can see that only 64% of the paraphrases are also annotated as bi-directional entailment. An example of a pair that is annotated both as paraphrase and as bi-directional entailment is pair #10 in Table 8. However, in the corpus we also found that 28 % of the paraphrases are only uni-directional entailment, while in 8% annotators did not find any entailment. An example of a pair where our annotators found paraphrasing, but not entailment is sentence pair #5 in Table 8. The agreement on the paraphrasing for this pair was 80%, the agreement on (lack of) forward and backward entailment was 80% and 70% respectively. Although the information in both sentences is nearly identical, there is no entailment, as "having a higher chance of getting smth" does not entail "getting smth" and vice versa.

If we look at the opposite direction of the overlap, we can see that 52% of the uni-directional and 94% of the bi-directional entailment pairs are also paraphrases. This finding confirms the statement that bi-directional entailment is paraphrasing (but not vice versa).

There is also a small portion (6%) of bi-directional entailments that were not annotated as paraphrases. An example of this is pair #6 in Table 8. Although both sentences make each other

true, they do not have the same content.

Neither paraphrasing nor entailment had any overlap with contradiction, which further verifies our annotation scheme and quality.

These findings are partly due to the more "relaxed" definition of paraphrasing adopted here. Our definition is consistent with other authors that work on paraphrasing and the task of paraphrase identification, so we argue that our findings are valid with respect to the practical applications of paraphrasing and entailment and their interactions.

4.2.2 Overlap with specificity

Specificity has a nearly equal overlap within all the other relations. In the pairs annotated with paraphrase or entailment, 73% are also annotated with specificity. The high number of pairs that are in a paraphrase relation, but also have a difference in specificity is interesting, as it seems more natural for paraphrases to be on the same specificity level. One example of this is pair #7 in Table 8. Although they are paraphrases (with 100% agreement), the first one is more specific, as it 1) specifies the ability of speaking a language and 2) says "more than one language".

There are also 27% of uni-directional entailment relation pairs that are not in any specificity relation. One example of this is pair #8 in Table 8.

Although the pair contains uni-directional entailment (backward entailment), none of the sentences is more specific than the other.

If we look at the other direction of the overlap, we can observe that in 62% of the cases involving difference in specificity, there is no uni-directional nor bi-directional entailment. An example of such a relation pair is pair #9 in Table 8. The two sentences are on the same topic and thus can be compared on their specificity. The first sentence is clearly more specific, as it gives information on what needs to be learned and where the Bible was written, whereas the second one just gives an information on what Christian clergymen do. These findings indicate that entailment is not specificity.

4.3 Discussion

Our methodology for generating text pairs has proven successful in creating a corpus that contains all relations of interest. By selecting different sentence pairings, we have obtained a balance between the relations that best suit our needs.

The inter-annotator agreement was good for all relations. The resulting corpus can be used to study individual relations and their interactions. It should be emphasized that our findings strongly depend on our decisions concerning the annotations setup, the guidelines in particular. When examining the interactions between the different relations, we found several interesting tendencies.

Findings on the interaction between entailment and paraphrases We showed that paraphrases and any-directional entailment had a high correlation, high overlap, and a similarly high semantic similarity. Almost all bi-directional entailment pairs are paraphrases. However, only 64% of the paraphrases are bi-directional entailment, indicating that paraphrasing is the more general phenomena, at least in practical tasks.

Findings on specificity With respect to specificity, we found that it does not correlate with other relations, showing that it is independent of those in our corpus. It also shows no clear trend on the similarity scale and no correlation with the difference in word length between the sentences. This indicates that specificity cannot be automatically predicted using the other meaning relations and requires further study.

In the examples that we discuss, we focus on interesting cases, which are complicated and unexpected (ex.: paraphrases that are not entailment or entailment pairs that do not differ in specificity). However, the full corpus also contains many conventional and non-controversial examples.

5 Conclusion and Further Work

In this paper, we made an empirical, corpus-based study on interactions between various semantic relations. We provided empirical evidence that supports or rejects previously hypothesized connections in practical settings. We release a new corpus that contains all relations of interest and the corpus creation methodology to the community. The corpus can be used to further study relation interactions or as a more challenging dataset for detecting the different relations automatically[10].

Some of our most important findings are:

1) there is a strong correlation between paraphrasing and entailment and most paraphrases include at least uni-directional entailment;

2) paraphrases and bi-directional entailment are not equivalent in practical settings;

3) specificity relation does not correlate strongly with the other relations and requires further study;

4) contradictions (in our dataset) are perceived as dis-similar.

As a future work, we plan to: 1) study the specificity relation in a different setting; 2) use a linguistic annotation to determine more fine-grained distinctions between the relations; 3) and annotate the rest of the 11,000 sentences in a semi-automated way.

Acknowledgements

We would like to thank Tobias Horsmann and Michael Wojatzki and the anonymous reviewers for their suggestions and comments. Furthermore, we would like to thank the sentence generators for their time and creativity. This work has been partially funded by Deutsche Forschungsgemeinschaft within the project ASSURE. This work has been partially funded by Spanish Ministery of Economy Project TIN2015-71147-C2-2, by the CLiC research group (2017 SGR 341), and by the APIF grant of the second author.

---

[10]The full corpus, the annotation guidelines, and the control examples can be found at `https://github.com/MeDarina/meaning_relations_interaction`

References

Eneko Agirre, Carmen Banea, Claire Cardie, Daniel Cer, Mona Diab, Aitor Gonzalez-Agirre, Weiwei Guo, Rada Mihalcea, German Rigau, and Janyce Wiebe. 2014. Semeval-2014 task 10: Multilingual semantic textual similarity. In *Proceedings of the 8th international workshop on semantic evaluation (SemEval 2014)*. pages 81–91.

Eneko Agirre, Daniel Cer, Mona Diab, Aitor Gonzalez-Agirre, and Weiwei Guo. 2013. * SEM 2013 shared task: Semantic textual similarity. In *Second Joint Conference on Lexical and Computational Semantics (* SEM), Volume 1: Proceedings of the Main Conference and the Shared Task: Semantic Textual Similarity*. volume 1, pages 32–43.

Salha Alzahrani and Naomie Salim. 2010. Fuzzy semantic-based string similarity for extrinsic plagiarism detection. *Braschler and Harman* 1176:1–8.

Ion Androutsopoulos and Prodromos Malakasiotis. 2010. A survey of paraphrasing and textual entailment methods. *Journal of Artificial Intelligence Research* 38:135–187.

Daniel Bär, Torsten Zesch, and Iryna Gurevych. 2012. Text reuse detection using a composition of text similarity measures. *Proceedings of COLING 2012* pages 167–184.

Luisa Bentivogli, Peter Clark, Ido Dagan, and Danilo Giampiccolo. 2011. The Seventh PASCAL Recognizing Textual Entailment Challenge. In *TAC*.

Rahul Bhagat and Eduard Hovy. 2013. What Is a Paraphrase? *Computational Linguistics* 39(3):463–472.

Daniel Bobrow, Dick Crouch, Tracy Halloway King, Cleo Condoravdi, Lauri Karttunen, Rowan Nairn, Valeria de Paiva, and Annie Zaenen. 2007. Precision-focused textual inference. In *Proceedings of the ACL-PASCAL Workshop on Textual Entailment and Paraphrasing*. pages 16–21.

Wauter Bosma and Chris Callison-Burch. 2006. Paraphrase substitution for recognizing textual entailment. In *Workshop of the Cross-Language Evaluation Forum for European Languages*. Springer, pages 502–509.

Samuel R Bowman, Gabor Angeli, Christopher Potts, and Christopher D Manning. 2015. A large annotated corpus for learning natural language inference. In *Proceedings of the 2015 Conference on Empirical Methods in Natural Language Processing*. pages 632–642.

Julio J. Castillo and Marina E. Cardenas. 2010. Using sentence semantic similarity based on WordNet in recognizing textual entailment. In *Ibero-American Conference on Artificial Intelligence*. Springer, pages 366–375.

Daniel Cer, Mona Diab, Eneko Agirre, Inigo Lopez-Gazpio, and Lucia Specia. 2017. Semeval-2017 task 1: Semantic textual similarity multilingual and crosslingual focused evaluation. In *Proceedings of the 11th International Workshop on Semantic Evaluation (SemEval-2017)*. pages 1–14.

D. Alan Cruse. 1977. The pragmatics of lexical specificity. *Journal of linguistics* 13(2):153–164.

Ido Dagan, Oren Glickman, and Bernardo Magnini. 2005. The pascal recognising textual entailment challenge. In *Machine Learning Challenges Workshop*. Springer, pages 177–190.

Robert De Beaugrande and Wolfgang U Dressler. 1981. *Introduction to text linguistics*. Routledge.

Bill Dolan, Chris Quirk, and Chris Brockett. 2004. Unsupervised construction of large paraphrase corpora: Exploiting massively parallel news sources. In *Proceedings of the 20th international conference on Computational Linguistics*. Association for Computational Linguistics, page 350.

Mürvet Enç. 1991. The semantics of specificity. *Linguistic inquiry* pages 1–25.

Donka F. Farkas. 2002. Specificity distinctions. *Journal of semantics* 19(3):213–243.

Sanda Harabagiu and Andrew Hickl. 2006. Methods for using textual entailment in open-domain question answering. In *Proceedings of the 21st International Conference on Computational Linguistics and the 44th annual meeting of the Association for Computational Linguistics*. Association for Computational Linguistics, pages 905–912.

Sanda Harabagiu and Finley Lacatusu. 2010. Using topic themes for multi-document summarization. *ACM Transactions on Information Systems (TOIS)* 28(3):13.

Cordeiro Joao, Dias Gaël, and Brazdil Pavel. 2007. New functions for unsupervised asymmetrical paraphrase detection. *Journal of Software* 2(4):12–23.

Venelin Kovatchev, M. Antónia Martì, and Maria Salamo. 2018. ETPC - A Paraphrase Identification Corpus Annotated with Extended Paraphrase Typology and Negation. In *Proceedings of the Eleventh International Conference on Language Resources and Evaluation (LREC 2018)*. European Language Resources Association (ELRA), Miyazaki, Japan.

Elena Lloret, Oscar Ferrández, Rafael Munoz, and Manuel Palomar. 2008. A Text Summarization Approach under the Influence of Textual Entailment. In *NLPCS*. pages 22–31.

Annie Louis and Ani Nenkova. 2012. A corpus of general and specific sentences from news. In *LREC*. pages 1818–1821.

Nitin Madnani and Bonnie J Dorr. 2010. Generating phrasal and sentential paraphrases: A survey of data-driven methods. *Computational Linguistics* 36(3):341–387.

Mitchell Marcus, Beatrice Santorini, and Mary Ann Marcinkiewicz. 1993. Building a large annotated corpus of English: The Penn Treebank .

Marco Marelli, Stefano Menini, Marco Baroni, Luisa Bentivogli, Raffaella Bernardi, Roberto Zamparelli, et al. 2014. A SICK cure for the evaluation of compositional distributional semantic models. In *LREC*. pages 216–223.

George Miller. 1998. *WordNet: An electronic lexical database*. MIT press.

Sebastian Padó, Michel Galley, Dan Jurafsky, and Christopher D Manning. 2009. Textual entailment features for machine translation evaluation. In *Proceedings of the Fourth Workshop on Statistical Machine Translation*. Association for Computational Linguistics, pages 37–41.

Maria Sukhareva, Judith Eckle-Kohler, Ivan Habernal, and Iryna Gurevych. 2016. Crowdsourcing a Large Dataset of Domain-Specific Context-Sensitive Semantic Verb Relations. In *LREC*.

Ken-ichi Yokote, Shohei Tanaka, and Mitsuru Ishizuka. 2011. Effects of Using Simple Semantic Similarity on Textual Entailment Recognition. In *TAC*.

CCGweb: a New Annotation Tool
and a First Quadrilingual CCG Treebank

Kilian Evang
University of Düsseldorf
Germany
evang@hhu.de

Lasha Abzianidze
University of Groningen
The Netherlands
l.abzianidze@rug.nl

Johan Bos
University of Groningen
The Netherlands
johan.bos@rug.nl

Abstract

We present the first open-source graphical annotation tool for combinatory categorial grammar (CCG), and the first set of detailed guidelines for syntactic annotation with CCG, for four languages: English, German, Italian, and Dutch. We also release a parallel pilot CCG treebank based on these guidelines, with 4x100 adjudicated sentences, 10K single-annotator fully corrected sentences, and 82K single-annotator partially corrected sentences.

1 Introduction

Combinatory Categorial Grammar (CCG; Steedman, 2000) is a grammar formalism distinguished by its transparent syntax-semantics interface and its elegant handling of coordination. It is a popular tool in semantic parsing, and treebank creation efforts have been made for Turkish (Çakıcı, 2005), German (Hockenmaier, 2006), English (Hockenmaier and Steedman, 2007), Italian (Bos et al., 2009), Chinese (Tse and Curran, 2010), Arabic (Boxwell and Brew, 2010), Japanese (Uematsu et al., 2013), and Hindi (Ambati et al., 2018). However, all of these treebanks were not directly annotated according to the CCG formalism, but automatically converted from phrase structure or dependency treebanks, which is an error-prone process. Direct annotation in CCG has so far mostly been limited to small datasets for seeding or testing semantic parsers (e.g., Artzi et al., 2015), and no graphical annotation interface is available to support such efforts, making the annotation process difficult to scale. The only exceptions we are aware of are the Groningen Meaning Bank (Bos et al., 2017) and the Parallel Meaning Bank (Abzianidze et al., 2017), two annotation efforts which use a graphical user interface for annotating sentences with CCG derivations and other annotation layers, and which have produced CCG treebanks for English, German, Italian, and Dutch. However, these efforts are focused on semantics and have not released explicit guidelines for syntactic annotation. Their annotation tool is limited in that annotators only have control over lexical categories, not larger constituents. Even though CCG is a lexicalized formalism, where most decisions can be made on the lexical level, there is no full control over attachment phenomena in the lexicon. Moreover, these annotation tools are not open-source and cannot easily be deployed to support other annotation efforts.

In this paper, we present an open-source, lightweight, easy-to-use graphical annotation tool that employs a statistical parser to create initial CCG derivations for sentences, and allows annotators to correct these annotations via *lexical category constraints* and *span constraints*. Together, these constraints make it possible to effect (almost) all annotation decisions consistent with the principles of CCG. We also present a pilot study for multilingual CCG annotation, in which a parallel corpus of 4x100 sentences (in English, German, Italian, and Dutch) was annotated by two annotators per sentence, a detailed annotation manual was created, and adjudication was performed to create a final version. We publicly release the manual, the annotation tool, and the adjudicated data. Our release also includes an additional $> 10\,\mathrm{K}$ derivations, each manually corrected by a single annotator, and an additional $> 82\,\mathrm{K}$ sentences, each partially corrected by a single annotator.

2 An Annotation Tool for CCG

Our annotation tool CCGweb[1] is Web-based, implemented in Python, PHP, and JavaScript, and should be easy to deploy on any recent Linux dis-

---

[1] https://github.com/texttheater/ccgweb

Proceedings of the 13th Linguistic Annotation Workshop, pages 37–42
Florence, Italy, August 1, 2019. ©2019 Association for Computational Linguistics

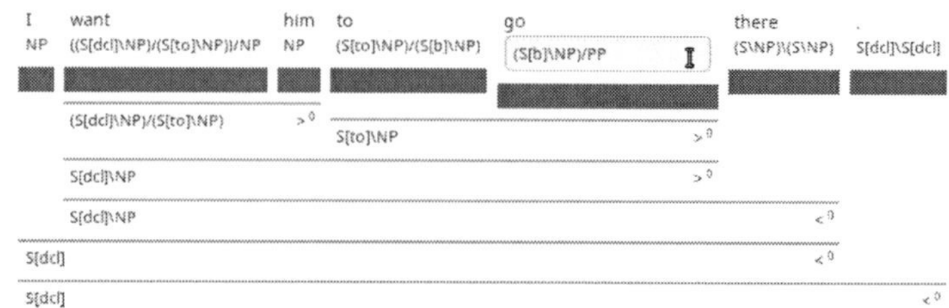

Figure 1: Correcting a lexical category.

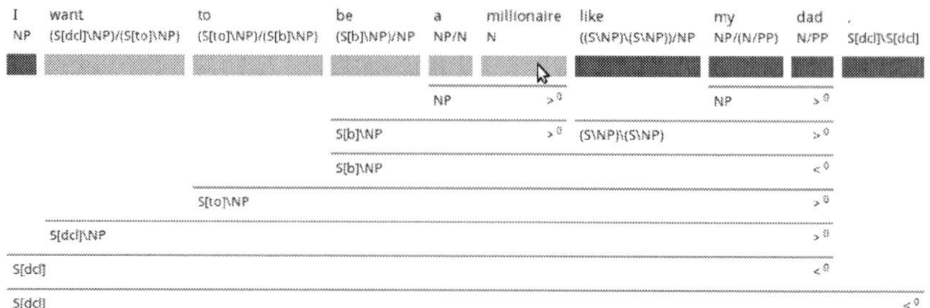

Figure 2: Correcting attachments by selecting a span that need to form a constituent.

tribution. It has two main views: the home page shows the list of sentences an annotator is assigned to annotate. Those already done are marked as "marked correct". Clicking on a sentence takes the annotator to the sentence view. Annotators can also enter arbitrary sentences to annotate, e.g., for experimenting or for producing illustrations.

Dynamic Annotation Annotation follows an approach called *dynamic annotation* (Oepen et al., 2002) or *human-aided machine annotation* (Bos et al., 2017), in which sentences are automatically analyzed, annotators impose *constraints* to rule out undesired analyses, sentences are then reanalyzed subject to the constraints, and the process is repeated until only the desired analysis remains. The current system is backed by the EasyCCG parser (Lewis and Steedman, 2014), slightly modified to allow for incorporating constraints, and other CCG parsers could be plugged in with similar modifications.

What You See Is What You Get Derivations are rendered in the same graphical format that is used in the literature, representing nodes as horizontal lines placed underneath their children. Annotators directly interact with this graphical representation when annotating, following the WYSIWYG (what you see is what you get) principle.

Lexical Category Constraints As an example of editing, consider Figure 1. Suppose that the

parser has analyzed *there* as an adjunct with category $(S \backslash NP) \backslash (S \backslash NP)$, but we wish to analyze it as an argument to the verb *go* with category PP. As a result, the category of the verb also has to change, *viz.* from $S[b] \backslash NP$ to $(S[b] \backslash NP) / PP$. To do this, the annotator clicks on the category and changes it, as shown in the figure. When they hit enter or click somewhere else, the sentence is automatically parsed again in the background, this time with the *lexical category constraint* that *go* has category $(S[b] \backslash NP) / PP$. In many cases, the parser will directly find the desired parse, with *there* being a PP, and the annotator only has to check it, not make another edit.

Span Constraints Although constraining lexical categories is often enough to determine the entire CCG derivation (cf. Bangalore and Joshi, 1999; Lewis and Steedman, 2014), this is not *always* the case. For example, consider the sentence *I want to be a millionaire like my dad.* Assuming that *like my dad* is a verb phrase modifier (category $(S \backslash NP) \backslash (S \backslash NP)$), it could attach to either *to be* or *want*, giving very different meanings (cf. Zimmer, 2013). We therefore implemented one other type of edit operation/constraint: *span constraints*. By simply clicking and dragging across a span of tokens as shown in Figure 2, annotators can constrain this span to be a constituent in the resulting parse.

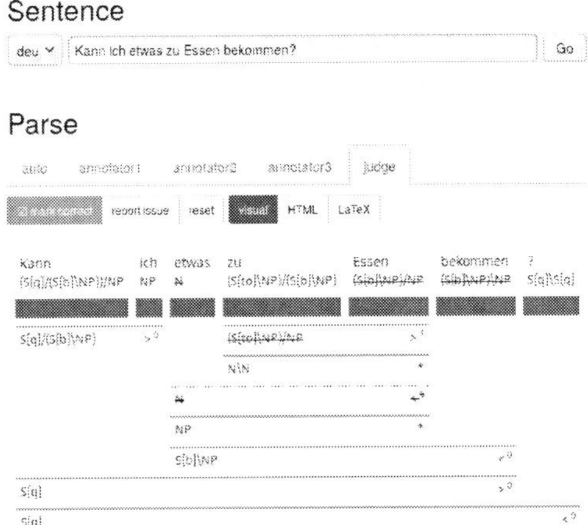

Figure 3: The judge user sees all annotators' versions and a diff view where categories with disagreements are struck through and spans with disagreements are dotted.

Additional Features Our tool offers annotators some additional convenient features. When unsure about some annotation decision, they can click the "report issue" button to open a discussion thread in an external forum, such as a GitHub issue tracker. To erase all constraints and restart annotation from the parser's original analysis, an annotator can click the "reset" button. And the buttons "HTML" and "LaTeX" provide code that can be copied and pasted to use the current derivation as an illustration on a web page or in a paper.

Adjudication Support Once two or more annotators have annotated a sentence, disagreements need to be discovered, and a final, authoritative version has to be created. Our tool supports this adjudication process through the special user account judge. This user can see the derivations of other annotators in a tabbed interface as shown in Figure 3. In order to enable the judge to easily spot disagreements, categories that annotators disagree on are struck through, and constituents that annotators disagree on are dashed.

3 A Quadrilingual Pilot CCG Treebank

To test the viability of creating multilingual CCG treebanks by direct annotation, we conducted an annotation experiment on 110 short sentences from the Tatoeba corpus (Tatoeba, 2019), each in four translations (English, German, Italian, and Dutch). The main annotation guideline was to copy the annotation style of CCGrebank (Honni-

bal et al., 2010), a CCG treebank adapted from CCGbank (Hockenmaier and Steedman, 2007), which is in turn based on the Penn Treebank (Marcus et al., 1993). Since CCGrebank only covers English and lacks some constructions observed in our corpus, an annotation manual with more specific instructions was needed. We initially annotated ten sentences in four languages and discussed disagreements. The results were recorded in an initial annotation manual, and the initial annotations were discarded. Each of the remaining 4x100 sentences was then annotated independently by at least two of the authors.

Table 1 (upper part) shows the number of non-overlapping category and span constraints that each annotator created on average per sentence before marking the sentence as correct. Annotated sentences were manually classified by the first author into four classes: (0) sentences without any disagreements, (1) sentences with only trivial violations of the annotation guidelines (e.g., concerning attachment of punctuation or underspecifying modifier features), (2) sentences with only apparent oversights, such as giving a determiner a pronoun category, (3) sentences with more intricate disagreements which required additional guidelines to resolve. Table 1 (upper part) shows the distribution of disagreement classes, and Table 2 shows examples of class (3). The first author adjudicated all disagreements and updated the annotation manual accordingly. We release the manual and the full adjudicated dataset.[2]

To make the resource more useful (e.g., for training parsers), we also include in the release the syntactic CCG derivations created so far in the Parallel Meaning Bank (Abzianidze et al., 2017). These do not follow the annotation guidelines in detail due to their focus on semantics, nor have they been adjudicated, but instead corrected by a single annotator. However, they are much greater in number. For an even greater number, we also release *partially corrected* derivations, meaning that the annotator made at least one change to the automatically created derivation. Table 1 (lower part) shows statistics of this additional data.

4 Conclusions and Future Work

We have presented the first open-source graphical annotation tool for combinatory categorial grammar. Its features include dynamic annotation via

---

[2] https://ccgweb.phil.hhu.de/

	English	German	Italian	Dutch
adjudicated sentences	100	100	100	100
∅ length	6.8	8.1	6.6	7.5
∅ category constraints per annotator	1.8	2.7	2.6	2.5
∅ span constraints per annotator	1.1	1.1	1.2	1.1
by disagreement (0) none	10	32	27	34
(1) trivial	45	17	16	12
(2) oversight	1	7	4	8
(3) intricate	44	44	53	46
single annotator, fully corrected	7 182	1 703	941	868
∅ length	6.4	5.7	5.4	5.9
single annotator, partially corrected	74 769	4 331	2 652	1 130
∅ length	8.6	7.4	6.9	7.4

Table 1: Corpus statistics and disagreements

Language	Disagreement
English	Argument or adjunct? Take$_{((S[b]\backslash NP)/PP)/NP}$ a taxi$_{PP/NP}$ to the hotel . Take$_{(S[b]\backslash NP)/NP}$ a taxi$_{(S\backslash NP)\backslash(S\backslash NP)}$ to the hotel .
	Clausal argument or adjunct? Can I have something$_{NP/(S[to]\backslash NP)}$ to$_{(S[to]\backslash NP)/(S[b]\backslash NP)}$ eat$_{S[b]\backslash NP}$? Can I have something$_{N}$ to$_{(S[to]\backslash NP)/(S[b]\backslash NP)}$ eat$_{(S[b]\backslash NP)/NP}$?
	Modification of copula or adjective? My mother is always$_{(S[adj]\backslash NP)/(S[adj]\backslash NP)}$ busy . My mother is always$_{(S\backslash NP)\backslash(S\backslash NP)}$ busy .
German	Treatment of quoted speech Sag$_{(S[b]\backslash NP)/NP}$ nur ja$_{N}$ oder$_{(N\backslash N)/N}$ nein$_{N}$. Sag$_{(S[b]\backslash NP)/S[intj]}$ nur ja$_{S[intj]}$ oder$_{(S[intj]\backslash S[intj])/S[intj]}$ nein$_{S[intj]}$.
	Analysis of *wh*-questions Wer$_{S[wq]/(S[dcl]\backslash NP)}$ hat$_{(S[dcl]\backslash NP)/(S[pt]\backslash NP)}$ diesen Brief geschrieben ? Wer$_{S[wq]/(S[q]\backslash NP)}$ hat$_{(S[q]\backslash NP)/(S[pt]\backslash NP)}$ diesen Brief geschrieben ?
	Scope of negation Rufen Sie mich nicht$_{(S/S)/(S/S)}$ mehr an ! Rufen Sie mich nicht$_{S\backslash S}$ mehr an !
Italian	Analysis of *wh*-questions Ci potete$_{S[q]/(S[b]\backslash NP)}$ aiutare ?$_{S[q]\backslash S[q]}$ Ci potete$_{S[dcl]/(S[b]\backslash NP)}$ aiutare ?$_{S[q]\backslash S[dcl]}$
	Category ambiguity in parts of multiword expressions Sono tre anni che Tom è andato$_{((S[pt]\backslash NP)/PP)/NP}$ via$_{N}$ da Boston . Sono tre anni che Tom è andato$_{((S[pt]\backslash NP)/PP)/PR}$ via$_{PR}$ da Boston .
	di: preposition or complementizer? Gli ho chiesto$_{((S[pt]\backslash NP)\backslash NP)/PP}$ di$_{PP/(S[b]\backslash NP)}$ farlo . Gli ho chiesto$_{((S[pt]\backslash NP)\backslash NP)/(S[to]\backslash NP)}$ di$_{(S[to]\backslash NP)/(S[b]\backslash NP)}$ farlo .
Dutch	Argument or adjunct? Een eekhoorntje verstopte$_{((S[dcl]\backslash NP)/PP)/NP}$ zich tussen$_{PP/NP}$ de takken . Een eekhoorntje verstopte$_{(S[dcl]\backslash NP)/NP}$ zich tussen$_{((S\backslash NP)\backslash(S\backslash NP))/NP}$ de takken .
	Participles in attributive use Windows is het meest$_{(N/N)/(N/N)}$ gebruikte$_{N/N}$ besturingssysteem in de wereld . Windows is het meest$_{(N/N)/(S[pss]\backslash NP)}$ gebruikte$_{S[pss]\backslash NP}$ besturingssysteem in de wereld .
	met: nominal or verbal argument? Hij is gestopt met$_{PP/NP}$ roken$_{N}$. Hij is gestopt met$_{PP/S[b]\backslash NP}$ roken$_{S[b]\backslash NP}$.

Table 2: Examples of intricate disagreements

lexical label constraints and span constraints, adjudication support, and various conveniences.

We have used this tool to create the first published CCG resource that comes with an explicit annotation manual for syntax and has been created by direct annotation, rather than conversion from a non-CCG treebank. It is multilingual, currently including English, German, Italian, and Dutch, and aims for cross-lingually consistent annotation guidelines.

For future work, we envision more extensive direct annotation of multilingual data with CCG derivations, and putting them to use for evaluating unsupervised and distantly supervised CCG parsers. We would also like to investigate the use of our tool as an interactive aid in teaching CCG.

Acknowledgments

The work of the first author was funded by the Consolidator Grant "TreeGraSP" of the European Research Council (ERC). The work of the second and third author was funded by the NWO-VICI grant "Lost in Translation – Found in Meaning" (288-89-003)". We would like to thank the three anonymous reviewers for their valuable comments.

References

Lasha Abzianidze, Johannes Bjerva, Kilian Evang, Hessel Haagsma, Rik van Noord, Pierre Ludmann, Duc-Duy Nguyen, and Johan Bos. 2017. The Parallel Meaning Bank: Towards a multilingual corpus of translations annotated with compositional meaning representations. In *Proceedings of the 15th Conference of the European Chapter of the Association for Computational Linguistics: Volume 2, Short Papers*, pages 242–247. Association for Computational Linguistics.

Bharat Ram Ambati, Tejaswini Deoskar, and Mark Steedman. 2018. Hindi CCGbank: A CCG treebank from the Hindi dependency treebank. *Language Resources and Evaluation*, 52(1):67–100.

Yoav Artzi, Kenton Lee, and Luke Zettlemoyer. 2015. Broad-coverage CCG semantic parsing with AMR. In *Proceedings of the 2015 Conference on Empirical Methods in Natural Language Processing*, pages 1699–1710. Association for Computational Linguistics.

Srinivas Bangalore and Aravind K. Joshi. 1999. Supertagging: An approach to almost parsing. *Computational Linguistics, Volume 25, Number 2, June 1999*.

Johan Bos, Valerio Basile, Kilian Evang, Noortje J. Venhuizen, and Johannes Bjerva. 2017. The Groningen Meaning Bank. In Nancy Ide and James Pustejovsky, editors, *Handbook of Linguistic Annotation*, pages 463–496. Springer Netherlands, Dordrecht.

Johan Bos, Cristina Bosco, and Alessandro Mazzei. 2009. Converting a dependency treebank to a categorial grammar treebank for Italian. In *Eight international workshop on treebanks and linguistic theories (TLT8)*, pages 27–38. Educatt.

Stephen A. Boxwell and Chris Brew. 2010. A pilot Arabic CCGbank. In *Proceedings of the Seventh conference on International Language Resources and Evaluation (LREC'10)*. European Languages Resources Association (ELRA).

Julia Hockenmaier. 2006. Creating a CCGbank and a wide-coverage CCG lexicon for German. In *Proceedings of the 21st International Conference on Computational Linguistics and 44th Annual Meeting of the Association for Computational Linguistics*, pages 505–512. Association for Computational Linguistics.

Julia Hockenmaier and Mark Steedman. 2007. CCGbank: A corpus of CCG derivations and dependency structures extracted from the Penn Treebank. *Computational Linguistics, Volume 33, Number 3, September 2007*.

Matthew Honnibal, James R. Curran, and Johan Bos. 2010. Rebanking CCGbank for improved NP interpretation. In *Proceedings of the 48th Annual Meeting of the Association for Computational Linguistics*, pages 207–215. Association for Computational Linguistics.

Mike Lewis and Mark Steedman. 2014. A* CCG parsing with a supertag-factored model. In *Proceedings of the 2014 Conference on Empirical Methods in Natural Language Processing (EMNLP)*, pages 990–1000. Association for Computational Linguistics.

Mitchell P. Marcus, Beatrice Santorini, and Mary Ann Marcinkiewicz. 1993. Building a large annotated corpus of English: The Penn Treebank. *Computational Linguistics, Volume 19, Number 2, June 1993, Special Issue on Using Large Corpora: II*.

Stephan Oepen, Kristina Toutanova, Stuart Shieber, Christopher Manning, Dan Flickinger, and Thorsten Brants. 2002. The LinGO Redwoods Treebank: Motivation and preliminary applications. In *COLING 2002: The 17th International Conference on Computational Linguistics: Project Notes*.

Mark Steedman. 2000. *The syntactic process*. MIT press Cambridge, MA.

Tatoeba. 2019. Tatoeba: Collection of sentences and translations. https://tatoeba.org/. Accessed: 2019-04-08.

Daniel Tse and James R. Curran. 2010. Chinese CCG-bank: extracting CCG derivations from the Penn Chinese Treebank. In *Proceedings of the 23rd International Conference on Computational Linguistics (Coling 2010)*, pages 1083–1091. Coling 2010 Organizing Committee.

Sumire Uematsu, Takuya Matsuzaki, Hiroki Hanaoka, Yusuke Miyao, and Hideki Mima. 2013. Integrating multiple dependency corpora for inducing wide-coverage Japanese CCG resources. In *Proceedings of the 51st Annual Meeting of the Association for Computational Linguistics (Volume 1: Long Papers)*, pages 1042–1051. Association for Computational Linguistics.

Ben Zimmer. 2013. Attachment ambiguity in "Frazz". http://languagelog.ldc.upenn.edu/nll/?p=4566.

Ruken Çakıcı. 2005. Automatic induction of a CCG grammar for Turkish. In *Proceedings of the ACL Student Research Workshop*, pages 73–78, Ann Arbor, Michigan. Association for Computational Linguistics.

The making of the Litkey Corpus, a richly annotated longitudinal corpus of German texts written by primary school children

Ronja Laarmann-Quante　　**Stefanie Dipper**　　**Eva Belke**
Department of Linguistics
Fakultät für Philologie
Ruhr-Universität Bochum
`laarmann-quante|dipper|belke@linguistics.rub.de`

Abstract

To date, corpus and computational linguistic work on written language acquisition has mostly dealt with second language learners who have usually already mastered orthography acquisition in their first language. In this paper, we present the Litkey Corpus, a richly-annotated longitudinal corpus of written texts produced by primary school children in Germany from grades 2 to 4. The paper focuses on the (semi-)automatic annotation procedure at various linguistic levels, which include POS tags, features of the word-internal structure (phonemes, syllables, morphemes) and key orthographic features of the target words as well as a categorization of spelling errors. Comprehensive evaluations show that high accuracy was achieved on all levels, making the Litkey Corpus a useful resource for corpus-based research on literacy acquisition of German primary school children and for developing NLP tools for educational purposes. The corpus is freely available under `https://www.linguistics.rub.de/litkeycorpus/`.

1　Introduction[1]

Language acquisition in modern societies not only concerns learning to understand and produce oral utterances but also how to read and write. Becoming literate in a language is a complex process, and it usually takes years of instruction for learners to master the stylistics of standard written language. At the beginning, learners (of alphabetical languages) first have to learn how to spell the words of their language. This is a non-trivial task because the mapping between spoken sounds and written characters is rarely one-to-one.

Most computational and corpus-based work on written language acquisition has been on L2

data, in particular data from adult learners, e.g. Reznicek et al. (2012). Usually these learners are already literate in their first language so that the concept of mapping sounds to characters, and vice versa, is not new to them, and the focus of research is on identifying (and correcting) grammatical rather than spelling errors (cf., e.g., the shared tasks on grammatical error correction, Ng et al., 2013, 2014).

Considerably less research has been done on data from children who, for the first time in their life, learn to read and write—be it in their first language or, for multilingual children, often in their second language. For German, there are some annotated corpora of primary school children's texts: the Osnabrücker Bildergeschichtenkorpus by Thelen (2000, 2010), the Karlsruhe Children's Text Corpus (Berkling et al., 2014; Lavalley et al., 2015), and the H1 and H2 Corpora by Berkling (2016, 2018). All of these corpora provide a target hypothesis for each erroneous spelling, specifying the intended wordform as perceived by the annotator. Except for the Osnabrücker Bildergeschichtenkorpus, the target forms also correct grammatical errors, making it difficult to distinguish between spelling and grammatical competence of the children.

This paper presents the annotation and evaluation of the Litkey Corpus, a longitudinal corpus of written texts in German from children in primary school between grades 2 to 4. The corpus includes a target hypothesis that corrects for spelling errors only and is richly annotated with linguistic information that relates to spelling and orthography. For example, the word-internal structure (phonemes, syllables and morphemes) and key orthographic features of the target words are provided as well as error tags characterizing the spelling errors in the texts. The paper explains in detail how the corpus was annotated and presents

---

[1] All URLs provided in this article were checked on May 31st, 2019.

43

Proceedings of the 13th Linguistic Annotation Workshop, pages 43–55
Florence, Italy, August 1, 2019. ©2019 Association for Computational Linguistics

an evaluation of the annotation quality. For further information about the composition of the corpus, including rich metadata about the children that provided the texts, see Laarmann-Quante et al. (to appear(b)). The detailed annotation guidelines can be found in Laarmann-Quante et al. (to appear(a)).

The paper is structured as follows. Sec. 2 provides a short introduction to relevant principles of German orthography. Sec. 3 presents the annotation layers, semi-automatic procedures and annotation quality in detail, followed by a conclusion in Sec. 4.

2 German Orthography

Following Eisenberg (2006), the basis of German word spelling is formed by correspondences between phonemes and graphemes (PGC mappings) such as /l/ ↔ <l>[2]. These default mappings are frequently overwritten by (i) syllabic, (ii) morphological and/or (iii) morpho-syntactic principles.

(i) For example, the word *fallen* (['falən], '(to) fall') would be spelled *<falen> according to the default PGC mappings (see Laarmann-Quante et al., to appear(b), for a detailed description of this example). However, one of the syllabic principles requires that the letter that represents a single consonant phoneme between a short stressed and a reduced vowel is doubled, hence the correct spelling is <fallen>.

(ii) According to the principle of morpheme constancy, the spelling of a reference form (which is usually a disyllabic word form like *fallen*) is retained in all other morphologically related word forms. This is why also monosyllabic inflected forms such as <fallt> (['falt],'(you.PL) fall'), <fällt> (['fɛlt], '(he/she/it) falls'), or the derived noun <Fall> (['fal], '(the) fall') are spelled with <ll>. Another case of morpheme constancy can be seen in the grapheme <ä> in <fällt> : According to the PGC mappings, the [ɛ] would be spelled <e>, yielding *<fellt>. The grapheme <ä> contains a visual clue to the morphological relationship between <fällt> and <fallen>/<fallt>/<Fall> in spite of its different pronunciation.

(iii) Finally, a prominent morpho-syntactic spelling principle is the capitalization of nuclei of

---

#Children	251 (8–11 years; grades 2–4; 63% multilingual)
#Elicitations (avg.)	7.7 ± 2.1 texts/child
#Texts	1,922
#Tokens / #Types	212,505 / 6,364

Table 1: Basic information on the Litkey Corpus

noun phrases. This is why the noun <Fall> '(the) fall' is not spelled *<fall>.

3 Annotations and Annotation Procedures

The Litkey Corpus is based on a set of texts (manuscripts) collected by Frieg (2014) from 2010–2012. The texts were written by primary school children, who were asked to write down short picture stories, featuring Lea (a girl), Lars (a boy), and Dodo (a dog). Table 1 presents basic statistics on the subset of texts that is used in the Litkey Corpus.

In the context of the Litkey project, the manuscripts were manually transcribed and annotated with a target hypothesis. To assess the quality of these steps, we measured inter-annotator agreement (IAA) among four annotators on a set of ten texts. Across all texts, IAA was high for both the transcription (95.8%, Fleiss' $\kappa = .98$) and the target forms (90.78%). For more details, see Laarmann-Quante et al. (2017).

Based on the target forms, linguistic and error-related information was annotated automatically. This section presents details about the annotations and annotation procedures.

3.1 POS tagging

While there are numerous POS taggers for German, it is well known that performance of state-of-the-art taggers on non-standard data is considerably lower than on standard data, such as newspaper texts (e.g., Giesbrecht and Evert, 2009). Hence we opted for training a specialized POS tagger, which we would then apply to our data, using the STTS tagset (Schiller et al., 1999). A short description of all tags with example words from the Litkey Corpus can be found in Table 7 in the Appendix.

Creating training data As there are no POS-annotated corpora of children's text available, we first created training data. To this end, we extracted the grammatical target hypotheses of

---

[2]Graphemes are marked with <>, phonemes with / / and phones with [ ]. Orthographically incorrect spellings are marked with *.

the Osnabrücker Bildergeschichtenkorpus (Thelen, 2000, 2010) and H1 Corpus (Berkling, 2016) (see Sec. 1). These corpora are rather similar to our corpus. For instance, they also include grammatically ill-formed texts without proper sentence boundary marking.

We enriched the texts semi-automatically with POS tags as follows: The data was first tagged independently by two taggers, the TreeTagger (Schmid, 1995) using the standard German model and the Stanford POS Tagger (Toutanova et al., 2003) using the 'hgc' model. For words on which the taggers did not agree, the final tag was chosen manually or semi-automatically by identifying areas in which one of the taggers consistently produced better results. For instance, the TreeTagger performed better than the Stanford Tagger in distinguishing between articles and pronouns (in particular PDS, PIS—i.e., demonstrative and indefinite pronouns).

We manually evaluated a random sample of 10% of the texts from the Osnabrücker Bildergeschichtenkorpus and 7% from the H1 Corpus (one text per class per test date), which showed an overall POS error rate of 2.5% after processing as described above.[3]

To further improve the quality of the training data, we reviewed unusual tag sequences, such as determiner–determiner, and corrected them manually. A second evaluation on another random sample of the same size, which did not include any of the texts from the previous sample, showed a considerable decrease of the error rate to 1.2%, so approximately one tag in a hundred in the training data is expected to be incorrect.

Training We next trained the Stanford POS Tagger on the training data, using its bidirectional architecture. That is, the tagger considers the previous and the following word as well as one or two previous and following tags to determine the correct tag for a given word. The tagger model was trained to be case-sensitive. This implies that it can take advantage of letter case information, for instance when tagging nouns and proper nouns, which are capitalized in German. This tagger was used to automatically tag the entire Litkey Corpus

without any manual correction.

Test set The test set—which we use for evaluating all automatic annotations (POS, graphemes, morphemes, etc.)—consists of 20 texts chosen randomly from our corpus. The sample amounts to 1,795 target tokens (477 types). Among these, 1,623 target tokens contain at least one alphabetical character (458 types). Average length of target tokens with at least one alphabetical character is 4.4 ± 1.9 characters.

Evaluation The gold standard was constructed by one human annotator who tagged all of the tokens manually. Difficult or unclear cases, which constituted less than 1% of the data, were discussed with two other project members.

The tagger achieved an overall accuracy of 92.81%. This is below state-of-the-art results for standard German, which range from 95-98% (Giesbrecht and Evert, 2009). However, applying standard taggers to nonstandard web data results in accuracies in the range of 90–94%, and our tagger's performance is within this range. Given that we trained our model on nonstandard data, one could have expected a better outcome; however, it has to be taken into account that our training base was rather small ($< 110{,}000$ tokens, which corresponds to approximately 10% of the TIGER Corpus used by Giesbrecht and Evert, 2009).[4]

POS categories which turned out difficult for the tagger include PTKVZ (verb particles, 35% recall), ITJ (interjections, 61%), VVINF (infinitives, 67%), PAV (pronominal adverbs, 80%), XY (nonwords, 80%). PTKVZ marks separated verb particles and is notorious for being confounded with adverbs. In addition, our data shows that PTKVZ is confounded with ADJD (adjectives) and APPR (prepositions), probably because many of our texts do not have reliable markers of sentence boundaries. In the Litkey Corpus, XY-words include syntactically unclear cases, like in (1): *um* could be a separated verb particle but cannot cooccur with *runtergefallen*, so the gold standard (G) tags it as XY, whereas the tagger (system, S) decided for KOUI.

---

[3]The most frequent errors were confusions of noun vs. proper name, finite verb vs. infinitive, adverbial or predicative adjective vs. adverb, and coordinating conjunction vs. adverb. Also, no relative pronoun was detected correctly due to missing commas in the children's texts (commas are usually strong indicators of such pronouns in German).

[4]An idea for future work could be to merge the TIGER Corpus with our nonstandard learner data for training. This kind of procedure has succesfully been applied to texts from computer-mediated communication, see Horbach et al. (2014). Also, the impact of sentence boundary detection would be an interesting further point of study. We thank the reviewers for these suggestions.

Analysis	Description
fröhlich	Original input
fr'2:.lIC	Phonemes with stress marks (') and syllable boundaries (.) in SAMPA notation (Wells, 1997)
fröh lich	Morphemes (space-separated)
ADJ SFX	Morpheme tags (adjective stem and suffix)

Table 2: BAS' G2P analysis for *fröhlich* 'happy'

(1)

	Fast	hat	der	Turm	um	runtergefallen
	almost	has	the	tower	?	down_fallen
S:	ADV	VAFIN	ART	NN	KOUI	XY
G:	ADV	VAFIN	ART	NN	XY	VVPP

'The tower has almost fallen down'

3.2 Word-internal structure

For each target word (type), we obtained information on the word-internal structure from the web service G2P of the Bavarian Archive of Speech Signals (BAS) (Reichel, 2012; Reichel and Kisler, 2014).[5] Table 2 shows the (reformatted) output of the G2P web service for the word *fröhlich* 'happy'.[6]

The following paragraphs explain how we processed G2P's output in the Litkey Corpus. For evaluating these word-internal analyses, the test set of 1,623 tokens with at least one alphabetical character was used (458 types).

3.2.1 Phonemes and PCUs

We aligned the characters of our target forms with G2P phonemes, to form phoneme-corresponding units (PCUs).[7] How this was achieved automatically is described in detail in Laarmann-Quante

---

[5] https://clarin.phonetik.uni-muenchen.de/BASWebServices/interface/Grapheme2Phoneme.
The following parameters were set: "lng":"deu-DE", "syl":"yes", "stress":"yes", "iform": "list", "oform":"exttab", "featset":"extended".

[6] The original G2P output also provides POS tags. However, for efficiency reasons, we used the G2P web service to analyze individual words (types) rather than word sequences. As a result, the web service's analysis of POS tags was not informed by a word's phrasal or sentential context, which is why we expected our own tagger to outperform the web-service's tagger and decided to ignore G2P's POS tags.
Similarly, G2P provides an alignment of phonemes and graphemes. However, the tool often had problems aligning words with <x>/[ks] or <z>/[ts], so we did not use it.

[7] G2P provides a phoneme analysis for all words but we decided to exclude some types of words like abbreviations from receiving a phoneme annotation in the Litkey Corpus. For details, see Laarmann-Quante et al. (to appear(b)).

(2016). In summary, we first statistically determined a 1:1 (or 1:0, 0:1) mapping of phonemes and characters based on cost-weighted Levenshtein distance[8], see (2).

(2)

Characters	f	r	ö	h	l	i	c	h
Phonemes	f	r	2	:	l	I		C

Next, we applied hand-coded rules to merge those characters which together correspond to one phoneme, and those phonemes which together correspond to one grapheme. An example is given in (3); here, merged PCUs are <öh> ≈ /2:/ and <ch> ≈ /C/.

(3)

Characters	f	r	öh	l	i	ch
Phonemes	f	r	2:	l	I	C

We evaluated the accuracy of the PCUs on our test set. Two independent raters, who reconciled cases of disagreement in subsequent discussions, judged for each PCU whether the PCU was correctly aligned ("c") or false ("f"). Cases where the G2P phoneme was incorrect were also marked as false ("f"). We also marked missing ("m"), or superfluous ("s") phonemes. When in doubt about a pronunciation, the Duden pronunciation dictionary (Mangold, 2005) was used as a reference. IAA was 97.7%, Cohen's κ = .70.[9] Example (4a) provides cases of incorrect alignments in the word *Angst* 'fear', (4b) shows a missing phoneme and an incorrect G2P phoneme in the analysis of the proper name *Lars*.

(4) a.

Chars		A	n	g	s	t
G2P		?	a	N	s	t
Gold	?	a		N	s	t
Raters	m	f	f	f	c	c

b.

Chars	L	a	r	s
G2P	l	a		S
Gold	l	a	r	s
Raters	c	c	m	f

Table 3 displays the result of the PCU/phoneme evaluation (see second column): 96.19% of the PCUs are correct, i.e., the aligned G2P and gold

---

[8] Using a script created by Marcel Bollmann, https://github.com/mbollmann/levenshtein/.

[9] The R package irr was used for computing agreement, https://CRAN.R-project.org/package=irr.

phonemes are identical. At the word level, 90.33% of the tokens and 94.04% of the types receive a completely correct PCU/phoneme analysis.[10]

We went through all incorrect cases again and decided which errors are due to incorrect alignments (all cases of "f" in (4a)) and which ones are due to incorrect G2P phonemes ("f" in (4b) and all cases of "m" and "s").[11] It turned out that incorrect alignments ("false boundary") are only a minor problem. Similarly, missing or superfluous units play virtually no role.

After the evaluation, we decided to further improve the quality of the phoneme annotations in our corpus by manually correcting the G2P phoneme analyses for all target types in the entire corpus.[12] In total, 1,184 of 6,340 types underwent a correction in that step.

3.2.2 Graphemes

We identified multi-letter graphemes automatically based on PCUs as follows: Whenever one of the sequences <ie>, <qu>, <ch>, or <sch> was found within a PCU, we considered it a single grapheme, as in *Flasche* 'bottle', see (5a). Otherwise we split it into several graphemes, as in *bisschen* 'a little', see (5b). The evaluation showed that grapheme identification was almost perfect: in just two cases, a grapheme was analyzed incorrectly.[13]

(5) a.

Graphemes	F	l	a	sch	e
Phonemes	f	l	a	S	@

b.

Graphemes	b	i	ss	ch	e	n
Phonemes	b	I	s	C	@	n

3.2.3 Syllables

For each word (type), the G2P web service marks the syllable boundaries and assigns exactly one stressed syllable (see Table 2). G2P records these

features at the phoneme level. In the Litkey Corpus, we moved these features to the level of the target characters so that we are able to make statements about a character's position in a syllable. This is particularly relevant for ambisyllabic consonants: In syllable joints, an ambisyllabic phoneme belongs to the coda of the first and the onset of the second syllable at the same time, e.g., /t/ in *Ratte* ([rat@], 'rat'). At the grapheme level, an ambisyllabic phoneme usually corresponds to a doubled consonant (e.g., <tt>) or another consonant pair (such as <ck>, <tz>, or <ng>). In these cases, the orthographic syllable boundary is placed between these consonants (<Rat.te> 'rat', <Jac.ke> 'jacket').[14]

The G2P phoneme representation only distinguishes between (one) stressed syllable vs. unstressed syllables in a word. We introduced a third category, reduced, using the following heuristics: each syllable with a G2P stress mark is classified as stressed, each syllable that has [@] or [6] as its nucleus is a reduced syllable, and the rest is classified as unstressed.

We evaluated syllable boundaries and syllable types (stressed, unstressed, reduced) in the same way as PCUs (see above). IAA was 97.3%, Cohen's $\kappa = .79$. Overall system accuracy is 91.84% (see Table 3, third column), and word-level accuracy is 93.04% (tokens) and 87.16% (types).[15] Compared to PCUs/phonemes, labeling was easier for syllables as there are only three types to choose between. Incorrect boundaries, which make up two thirds of the errors, are either wrong in the G2P output from the start or the G2P boundaries had been correct initially but were spoilt by mapping them from the phoneme to the character level.

As in the case of phonemes, we made some efforts after the evaluation to further improve the annotations. We made minor adjustments to the syllable scripts and manually corrected all syllable boundary and stress marks in the G2P output for all target types in our corpus.

---

[10] The difference between the token and type level can be explained by the fact that some high-frequency words in the corpus were analyzed incorrectly, such as *Lars*, see (4b).

[11] Some cases of "m" and "s" could alternatively be analyzed as follow-up errors of an incorrect alignment, as in (4a).

[12] Some rare cases of homographs with differing pronunciations would have required knowledge of the actual context, which we did not have in the correction step since we considered types instead of tokens. In such cases, the most common usage was chosen for the annotation. An example is *so*, which can be read (in IPA) as [zo:] ('this way') or [zɔ] (interjection similar in meaning to 'right!') and was annotated as [zo:].

[13] This was due to a bug in the script, which has been fixed.

[14] An exception are the multi-letter graphemes <ch> and <sch>: they can correspond either to a syllable-initial phoneme, as in *Suche* ([zu:.x@] 'search', or to an ambisyllabic phoneme, as in *Sache* ([zax@] 'thing'). Here, we placed the boundaries always in front of the respective grapheme: <Su.che>, <Sa.che>.

[15] In 96.24% of the word tokens (94.72% of types), at least one syllable was analyzed correctly.

Linguistic Unit	PCUs/Phonemes	Syllables	Morphemes
Total number	6,690	2,378	2,278
Correct	96.19%	91.84%	82.88%
False	2.44%	8.07%	13.56%
among them: false boundary [a]	6.13%	67.19%	25.89%
among them: false label [a]	95.09%	34.38%	82.52%
Missing	1.38%	0.08%	3.56%
Superfluous[b]	$< 0.01\%$	$< 0.01\%$	$< 0.01\%$
Correct word tokens (1623)	90.33%	93.04%	85.21%
Correct word types (436)[c,d]	94.04%	87.16%	–

Table 3: Evaluation of the analysis of a word's internal structure based on the BAS web service G2P

[a] The figures for false boundary and false label do not add up to 100% because both the boundary and the label can be wrong at the same time.

[b] The proportion of superfluous elements was calculated as $\frac{\#superfluous}{\#gold\text{-}phonemes}$. Note that there could be more than 100% superfluous elements, and there is no upper bound.

[c] Letter case is usually irrelevant for phoneme and syllable annotation, so word types are case-insensitive here.

[d] Since certain morpheme categories are context-dependent, they cannot be evaluated on word types but only on word tokens.

3.2.4 Morphemes

Morphemes can be either stems or affixes, and are tagged accordingly (see Table 2). While suffix morphemes are always unambiguous (just like phonemes, PCUs, and syllables), certain stem morphemes can only be determined in the phrasal or sentential context. For example, the stem d- may be an article (ART) or a demonstrative pronoun (PD) depending on the context, see (6). In the examples, morphemes are separated by hyphens, and corresponding glosses and morpheme tags are marked in the same way.

(6) a. Original: der   Lars lacht
         Morphemes: d-er   Lars lach-t
                       the-NOM.SG.M Lars laugh-3SG
         Morph. tags: ART-INFL   NN V-INFL
                       'Lars laughs'

   b. Original: der   lacht
         Morphemes: d-er   lach-t
                       that-NOM.SG.M laugh-3SG
         Morph. tags: PD-INFL   V-INFL
                       'That one laughs'

For efficiency reasons, we used G2P to analyze the morphemes of word types, i.e., G2P's analyses were not informed by a word's phrase or sentence contexts (also see Footnote 6). To integrate this information in the annotations, we fed the analysis of our POS tagger into the morpheme analysis: whenever a word consisted of one stem morpheme only, or one stem morpheme followed by an INFL-morpheme, the word's POS tag was used to derive the tag for the stem morpheme.

This fixed certain errors introduced by G2P. For instance, for a verb whose stem coincides with an existing noun stem, G2P often analyzed the stem as a noun, as in (7): the verb stem *wein-* is also a noun stem, *Wein* ('wine'). Looking at the POS tag, VVFIN, it becomes clear that it is the verb stem in this case.

(7)   Original: weint 'cries'
      Morphemes: wein-t
                     cry-3SG
      G2P analysis: N-INFL
      corrected: V-INFL
      POS tag: VVFIN

For words with two morphemes one of which has the type INFL, we found that replacing the G2P stem morpheme tag based on the POS information of the full word form yielded an overall improvement in accuracy of 2.9 percentage points for morphemes and 3.7 percentage points for tokens. However, some instances were negatively affected by this procedure, e.g. verb stems that are derived from a noun via conversion, such as *teil-t* 'shares', which is derived from *Teil* 'part'.

We evaluated the automatic morpheme analysis on the test set in the same way as the PCUs presented above. The raters used the online grammar canoonet[16] as a reference when they were in doubt about a word's morphological structure. IAA was 89.9%, Cohen's $\kappa = .66$.

---

[16] http://canoo.net/.

Table 3 (fourth column) shows that 82.88% of the morphemes and 85.21% of the tokens are analyzed correctly by the system (in 90.02% of the tokens at least one morpheme has been identified correctly in terms of label and boundaries). Similarly to PCUs, selecting the label was more error-prone than establishing the morpheme boundaries.

The most problematic tags, which have a recall below 75%, are ITJ (interjections, 47.6%), SFX (suffixes, 50.0%), PRFX (prefixes, 64.5%), and INFL (inflection, 74.7%). It is noteworthy, however, that confusions of tags are mainly found within categories for stems (e.g., nouns vs. verbs) or affixes (e.g., INFL vs. SFX) rather than across categories.

This time, we did not correct the morpheme analyses manually after the evaluation, in contrast to phonemes and syllables, because some morphemes are context-dependent and a correction would have required that we assess each morpheme in context.

3.3 Key orthographic features

The focus of the Litkey project is on analyzing orthographic errors. To this end, we developed a scheme of fine-grained spelling categories (see Laarmann-Quante et al., to appear(a), for a detailed presentation). These categories are annotated at the PCUs and specify detailed orthographic properties of the respective PCU in its context. For instance, the PCU <öh> ≈ /2:/ in (3) is annotated with the spelling category Vlong_single_h, which specifies that the letter <h> marks a (preceding) single vowel as long. The spelling categories are purely descriptive and are intended to highlight locations where errors are likely to occur.

On top of the highly specific spelling categories, we define more general key orthographic features (KOFs), which encode important spelling-related properties of the word (see Sec. 2) and are inspired by categories as they are used in teaching contexts. Table 6 in the Appendix provides a list of all KOFs (for more details, see Laarmann-Quante et al., to appear(b)).

Technically, all KOFs are derived from the fine-grained spelling categories. Some KOFs match some spelling categories exactly. For example, if final devoicing is a spelling category on a given word (category final_devoice), this word is assigned the KOF devoice_final. In some cases, however, KOFs are not purely descriptive (in contrast to the fine-grained spelling categories) but relate the PCUs to the spelling principles. For instance, the spelling categories for doubled consonants within a morpheme only describe the context, e.g., Cdouble_interV specifies that the doubled consonants occur between vowels; Cdouble_beforeC means that it occurs before another consonant.

The corresponding KOFs, in contrast, distinguish between those doubled consonants that arise from a syllabic principle (see Sec. 2) and those which do not. For instance, *alle* (['al@], 'all') is an example of consonant doubling due to syllabic constraints (KOF: doubleC_syl), namely because there is a single consonant letter between a short stressed and an unstressed vowel. In *allein* ([a'laIn], 'alone'), the doubled consonant is between an unstressed and a stressed vowel, which is a marked stress pattern. Here, the doubling cannot be explained synchronically (hence, KOF: doubleC_other). So in order to determine automatically which kind of consonant doubling is present, information about a word's syllable and morpheme structure is necessary.

We evaluated the automatic analysis of KOFs based on 427 types from our test set (excluding words marked as ungrammatical or unidentifiable). Five independent raters judged for each word and each KOF whether the word features this KOF, possibly more than once. For example, the word *Staubsauger* ([StaUpsaUg6], 'vacuum cleaner') contains three instances of the KOF graph_comb (<St>, <au>, <au>), and one instance each of devoice_final (<b>) and r_voc (<er>). Together the raters agreed on a gold standard, using the pronunciation Duden (Mangold, 2005) as a reference.

The evaluation results in Table 4 specify correct ("c"), missing ("m") and superfluous ("s") KOFs and provide precision and recall scores for each KOF. While most features were determined automatically with high accuracy, the detection of doubleC_other was problematic. Three types of doubleC_other were annotated incorrectly as doubleC_syl (e.g., *Uff* 'Phew!', *Bumm* 'Boom!'). This happened mainly because the evaluation was type based, i.e., without context information, causing the tagger to assign incorrect POS tags in some places. This resulted in incorrect morpheme analyses, which are one of the criteria for distinguish-

KOF	c	m	s	Prec	Rec
graph_comb	104	1	0	1.00	0.99
graph_marked	26	2	0	1.00	0.93
ie	28	0	0	1.00	1.00
schwa_silent	40	4	0	1.00	0.91
doubleC_syl	71	7	3	0.96	0.91
doubleC_other	4	3	6	0.40	0.57
doubleV	3	0	0	1.00	1.00
h_length	12	0	0	1.00	1.00
h_sep	10	0	2	0.83	1.00
r_voc	100	0	7	0.93	1.00
devoice_final	72	4	3	0.96	0.95
g_spirant	4	0	2	0.67	1.00
morph_bound	1	0	0	1.00	1.00

Table 4: Evaluation results of key orthographic features; "c": correct, "m": missing, "s": superfluous

KOF error	count
other	293
doubleC_syl	63
hyp	29
ie	18
graph_marked	17
r_voc	12
devoice_final	9
h_sep	8
h_length	8
doubleC_other	7
graph_comb	5
doubleV	3
g_spirant	2
morph_bound	1

Table 5: KOF errors occurring in the test set (based on the gold standard)

ing doubleC_syl from doubleC_other. For annotating the corpus, though, the POS tagger can make use of the context, and the KOF annotations of these types are mostly correct. On the other hand, six types were annotated as doubleC_other instead of doubleC_syl due to minor errors in the processing pipeline, which have been fixed in the meantime.

3.4 KOF errors

Apart from the key orthographic features that a target word contains, the Litkey Corpus also shows which KOFs are violated in a child's spelling. Take the word *annehmen*, which contains the two KOFs morph_bound (<nn>) and h_length (<eh>). If the word was misspelled as *<anehmen>, the error would violate the KOF morph_bound; *<annemen>, by contrast, would pertain to KOF h_length. Any other error, e.g., *<Annehmen>, would not affect a KOF.

Like the KOFs, KOF errors are derived from the more fine-grained spelling categories. We evaluated the automatic annotation of KOF errors on 317 types from our test set. A type consisted of a pair of original and target spelling. Three human annotators established the gold standard in that they determined the KOF error categories that applied to a misspelling. The position of the error in a word was not annotated. 115 words contained more than one error, resulting in 475 errors in total. An example annotation is given in (8). The KOF error category "other" indicates that there was one other error which did not pertain to a KOF (in this case, the incorrect capitalization).

(8)   orig   Felt
          target   fällt
          KOF errors   doubleC_syl,graph_marked,other

Table 5 shows the distribution of KOF error categories in the test set. The majority of errors falls under "other", which subsumes all errors not pertaining to a KOF. The KOFs were chosen to reflect instances of syllabic spelling principles and morpheme constancy, where the correct spelling deviates from default phoneme-grapheme mappings. The category "other" includes some highly frequent errors pertaining to morpho-syntax such as capitalization as well as violations of regular phoneme-grapheme mappings (e.g. *<brcht> for *<bricht> '(it) breaks').

For the evaluation, the automatically generated set of KOF errors for a word was compared to the manually created one. When the two did not match completely, the automatic annotation was considered incorrect. Since in this evaluation we did not mark the position of individual errors, the system categories could not be mapped onto the gold categories. Hence, an analysis of which categories were missed or confused by the automatic script was not possible. In total, 281 (88.6%) orig-target pairs were analyzed correctly and 36 incorrectly. Of these, 23 contained words with more than one KOF error in the gold standard, which shows that these pose a particular challenge to the automatic analysis.

4 Conclusion and Outlook

This paper presents annotations and annotation procedures for the Litkey Corpus, a longitudinal corpus of written texts produced by German primary school children. Besides categorization of spelling errors, the annotations include information on POS, the word-internal structure (phonemes, syllables, morphemes), and key orthographic features of the target words. Evaluations of all annotations show high accuracy, so that we believe that the corpus can serve as a reliable resource for research on literacy acquisition and for the development of NLP tools in educational contexts. Using the corpus, research questions that have so far only been addressed using experimental methods (i.e., with small, pre-selected sets of materials), can now be addressed on a larger scale and based on spellings that were produced spontaneously rather than spellings that were produced on dictation. In addition, the corpus allows for longitudinal studies of spelling acquisition, which is particularly helpful for studies on the role of implicit learning in spelling acquisition. Here, the question is to what extent cues that are not taught at school can influence the acquisition of word spellings. Such cues are likely to be of a statistical nature, such as bigram frequencies or syllable frequencies or orthographic consistency. Experimental studies (e.g., de Bree et al., 2018; Treiman and Wolter, 2018) suggest that implicit cues have a substantial impact on the acquisition of vowel spellings and double consonant spellings.

The Litkey Corpus is available via the website `https://www.linguistics.rub.de/ litkeycorpus/` under the Creative Commons Attribution-ShareAlike 4.0 license (CC BY-SA 4.0). It comes in different formats, including a custom-made XML format (see Laarmann-Quante et al., 2016) and a tabular format including information on types and tokens, respectively, and their annotations (see Laarmann-Quante et al., to appear(b)). The corpus can also be searched via the corpus search tool ANNIS (Krause and Zeldes, 2016). For future work, we plan to enrich the corpus with annotations on grammatical errors as well.

Acknowledgments

This research is part of the project *Literacy as the key to social participation: Psycholinguistic perspectives on orthography instruction and literacy acquisition* funded by the Volkswagen Foundation as part of the research initiative "Key Issues for Research and Society" (grant no. I/89 479). We would also like to thank the anonymous reviewers for their helpful comments.

References

Kay Berkling. 2016. Corpus for children's writing with enhanced output for specific spelling patterns (2nd and 3rd grade). In *Proceedings of the Tenth International Conference on Language Resources and Evaluation (LREC 2016)*, pages 3200–3206.

Kay Berkling. 2018. A 2nd longitudinal corpus for children's writing with enhanced output for specific spelling patterns. In *Proceedings of the Eleventh International Conference on Language Resources and Evaluation (LREC 2018)*, pages 2262–2268.

Kay Berkling, Johanna Fay, Masood Ghayoomi, Katrin Heinz, Rémi Lavalley, Ludwig Linhuber, and Sebastian Stüker. 2014. A database of freely written texts of German school students for the purpose of automatic spelling error classification. In *Proceedings of the Ninth International Conference on Language Resources and Evaluation (LREC 2014)*, pages 1212–1217.

Elise de Bree, Jan Geelhoed, and Madelon van den Boer. 2018. Overruled! Implicit cues rather than an orthographic rule determine Dutch children's vowel spelling. *Learning and Instruction*, 56:30–41.

Peter Eisenberg. 2006. *Das Wort*, 3rd edition, volume 1 of *Grundriss der deutschen Grammatik*. J.B. Metzler, Stuttgart.

Hendrike Frieg. 2014. *Sprachförderung im Regelunterricht der Grundschule: Eine Evaluation der Generativen Textproduktion*. Ph.D. thesis, Ruhr-Universität Bochum.

Eugenie Giesbrecht and Stefan Evert. 2009. Is part-of-speech tagging a solved task? An evaluation of POS taggers for the German web as corpus. In *Proceedings of the fifth Web as Corpus workshop (WAC5)*, pages 27–35.

Andrea Horbach, Diana Steffen, Stefan Thater, and Manfred Pinkal. 2014. Improving the performance of standard part-of-speech taggers for computer-mediated communication. In *KONVENS 2014*, pages 171–177.

Thomas Krause and Amir Zeldes. 2016. ANNIS3: A new architecture for generic corpus query and visualization. *Digital Scholarship in the Humanities*, 31(1):118–139.

Ronja Laarmann-Quante. 2016. Automating multi-level annotations of orthographic properties of German words and children's spelling errors. In *Proceedings of the 2nd Language Teaching, Learning and Technology Workshop (LTLT)*, pages 14–22.

Ronja Laarmann-Quante, Anna Ehlert, Katrin Ortmann, Doreen Scholz, Carina Betken, Lukas Knichel, Simon Masloch, and Stefanie Dipper. to appear(a). *The Litkey spelling error annotation scheme: Guidelines for the annotation of orthographic errors in German texts*. Bochumer Linguistische Arbeitsberichte (BLA).

Ronja Laarmann-Quante, Lukas Knichel, Stefanie Dipper, and Carina Betken. 2016. Annotating spelling errors in German texts produced by primary school children. In *Proceedings of the 10th Linguistic Annotation Workshop held in conjunction with ACL 2016 (LAW-X 2016)*, pages 32–42.

Ronja Laarmann-Quante, Katrin Ortmann, Anna Ehlert, Simon Masloch, Doreen Scholz, Eva Belke, and Stefanie Dipper. to appear(b). The Litkey Corpus: A richly annotated longitudinal corpus of German texts written by primary school children. *Behavior Research Methods*.

Ronja Laarmann-Quante, Katrin Ortmann, Anna Ehlert, Maurice Vogel, and Stefanie Dipper. 2017. Annotating orthographic target hypotheses in a German L1 learner corpus. In *Proceedings of the 12th Workshop on Innovative Use of NLP for Building Educational Applications (BEA)*, pages 444–456.

Rémi Lavalley, Kay Berkling, and Sebastian Stüker. 2015. Preparing children's writing database for automated processing. In *Workshop on L1 Teaching, Learning and Technology (L1TLT)*, pages 9–15.

Max Mangold. 2005. *Duden (Band 6). Das Aussprachewörterbuch*, 6th edition. Dudenverlag, Mannheim.

Hwee Tou Ng, Siew Mei Wu, Ted Briscoe, Christian Hadiwinoto, Raymond Hendy Susanto, and Christopher Bryant. 2014. The CoNLL-2014 shared task on grammatical error correction. In *Proceedings of the Eighteenth Conference on Computational Natural Language Learning: Shared Task*, pages 1–14.

Hwee Tou Ng, Siew Mei Wu, Yuanbin Wu, Christian Hadiwinoto, and Joel Tetreault. 2013. The CoNLL-2013 shared task on grammatical error correction. In *Proceedings of the Seventeenth Conference on Computational Natural Language Learning: Shared Task*, pages 1–12. Association for Computational Linguistics.

Uwe D. Reichel. 2012. PermA and Balloon: Tools for string alignment and text processing. In *INTERSPEECH*.

Uwe D. Reichel and Thomas Kisler. 2014. Language-independent grapheme-phoneme conversion and word stress assignment as a web service. In R. Hoffmann, editor, *Elektronische Sprachverarbeitung: Studientexte zur Sprachkommunikation 71*, pages 42–49. TUDpress.

Marc Reznicek, Anke Ludeling, Cedric Krummes, Franziska Schwantuschke, Maik Walter, Karin Schmidt, Hagen Hirschmann, and Torsten Andreas. 2012. Das Falko-Handbuch. Korpusaufbau und Annotationen Version 2.01. Berlin, Germany.

Anne Schiller, Simone Teufel, Christine Stöckert, and Christine Thielen. 1999. Guidelines für das Tagging deutscher Textcorpora mit STTS. Universities of Stuttgart and Tübingen.

Helmut Schmid. 1995. Improvements in part-of-speech tagging with an application to German. In *Proceedings of the ACL SIGDAT-Workshop*.

Tobias Thelen. 2000. Osnabrücker Bildergeschichtenkorpus: Version 1.0.0.

Tobias Thelen. 2010. *Automatische Analyse orthographischer Leistungen von Schreibanfängern*. Ph.D. thesis, Universität Osnabrück.

Kristina Toutanova, Dan Klein, Christopher D. Manning, and Yoram Singer. 2003. Feature-rich part-of-speech tagging with a cyclic dependency network. In *Proceedings of the 2003 Conference of the North American Chapter of the Association for Computational Linguistics on Human Language Technology - NAACL '03*, pages 173–180. Association for Computational Linguistics.

Rebecca Treiman and Sloane Wolter. 2018. Phonological and graphotactic influences on spellers' decisions about consonant doubling. *Memory & Cognition*, 46(4):614–624.

John C. Wells. 1997. SAMPA computer readable phonetic alphabet. In Dafydd Gibbon, Roger Moore, and Richard Winski, editors, *Handbook of standards and resources for spoken language systems*. Mouton de Gruyter, Berlin, New York.

Appendix

KOF	Princ	Description	Examples
graph_comb	–	Grapheme combinations: Graphemes for phoneme combinations that could be spelled by combining the individual graphemes but that have an idiosyncratic spelling (e.g., <qu> for [kv], <eu> for [OY]).	<sp>, <st>, <ei>, <ai>, <eu>, <äu>, <au>, <qu>
graph_marked	PG	Marked graphemes: Graphemes for which other graphemes would be available by default (e.g., <ai> is a marked grapheme for [aI], which is spelled <ei>, by default).	<ai>, <äu>, <ä>, <y>, <c> (except in <ch>, <sch>, <ck>), <chs>, <ks>, <dt>, <th>, <v>, <ph>, <ts>
ie	PG	<ie>: A special grapheme in that it is the only multi-letter grapheme for a tense vowel /i/; the lax counterpart, /I/, is mapped onto <i>. All other pairs of tense and lax vowels (e.g., /y/–/Y/) are mapped onto the same single-letter grapheme by default.	<ie>
schwa_silent	SL	Silent schwa: In reduced syllables [@] is often not audible in words ending with /@m/, /@n/, and /@l/. Irrespective of this, the spelling of all reduced syllables including a silent schwa always includes an <e>.	*Hasen* 'rabbits'
doubleC_syl	SL	Double consonant spellings: In disyllabic words with the default German stress pattern (trochee: stressed-unstressed, typically stressed-reduced), doubled consonants indicate to the reader the laxness/shortness of the first vowel; doubleC_syl is also annotated in word forms for which morpheme constancy requires that the double consonant spelling is carried forth from a reference form.	*fallen/fällt* '(to) fall/(s/he) falls'
doubleC_other	–	Other double consonants: Consonant doublings which can neither be explained via the word's syllabic structure, nor morpheme constancy, nor a morpheme boundary.	*dann* 'then', *jetzt* 'now'
doubleV	SL	Double vowels: Indicate the length of tense vowels in stressed syllables.	*Seelen* 'souls'
h_length	SL	Vowel-lengthening <h>: Indicates the length of tense vowels in stressed syllables.	*Kehlen* 'throats'
h_sep	SL	Syllable-separating <h>: Indicates separate syllables in the spelling of words that include two adjacent vowels belonging to different syllables; h_sep is also annotated in word forms for which morpheme constancy requires that the syllable-separating <h> is carried forth from a reference form.	*drohen, droht* '(to) threaten, (s/he) threatens'
r_voc	SL	Vocalic r: When it occurs after a vowel in stressed syllables, <r> is pronounced [6]. In reduced syllables, <r> frequently co-occurs with <e> in <er>, which is pronounced [6].	*dort* 'there', *Winter* 'winter'
devoice_final	MO	Final devoicing: Word forms that are pronounced with final devoicing are not spelled phonographically but with the grapheme for the voiced consonant to signal the morphological relation between the stem and multisyllabic inflected forms.	*Hund, Hunde* 'dog, dogs'
g_spirant	MO	g_spirantization: A special case of final devoicing is spirantization of final /g/ to /ç/ and /x/, respectively. Following Eisenberg (2006)'s overview, it is obligatory after /I/, but not after /a/. There, /g/ may alternatively be pronounced /k/.	*winzig* 'tiny', *Tag* 'day'
morph_bound	MO	Morpheme boundaries: Morphologically complex words that include the same consonant at the end of one morpheme and at the beginning of the next include a double consonant spelling, with one of the consonants pertaining to the first and the other to the second morpheme, even though articulatorily speakers typically produce only one phoneme.	*annehmen* 'take on'

Table 6: List of key orthographic features (KOF), along with the spelling principles (Princ) they relate to as well as a description and relevant graphemes or examples. The spelling principles are: PG: nondefault phonographic mappings; SL: syllabic principles; MO: morpheme constancy.

POS	Explanation	Examples
ADJA	attributive adjective	das kaputte Fenster ('the broken window'); ein süßer Hund ('a cute dog')
ADJD	adverbial or predicative adjective	Dodo kommt schnell ('Dodo arrives quickly'); Er war schnell ('He was quick')
ADV	adverb	schon ('already'); bald ('soon'); doch ('however'/'yet')
APPR	preposition; circumposition (left)	auf dem Bürgersteig ('on the sidewalk'); ohne Lars ('without Lars')
APPRART	preposition with an article	am Ende ('at_the end'); im Teich ('in_the pond')
APPO	postposition	ein Jahr lang ('for a year')
APZR	circumposition (right)	[no instances in the Litkey Corpus]
ART	definite and indefinite article	der/die/das ('the'); ein/eine ('a'/'an')
CARD	cardinal number	16; drei ('three')
FM	foreign material	the; happy
ITJ	interjection	hm; oh
KOUI	subordinating conjunction with "zu" and infinitive	um alles zu notieren ('in order to note everything'); anstatt zu ('instead of')
KOUS	subordinating conjunction with a sentence	weil ('because'); ob ('if'); damit ('so')
KON	coordinating conjunction	und ('and'); oder ('or'); aber ('but')
KOKOM	comparative conjunction	als ('than')
NN	noun	Hund ('dog'); Freund ('friend')
NE	proper name	Lea; Schiller
PDS	substituting demonstrative pronoun	Ist das dieser hier? ('Is it this one here?')
PDAT	attributive demonstrative pronoun	in diesem Moment ('in this moment'); dieser Hund ('this dog')
PIS	substituting indefinite pronoun	jemand ('someone'), keiner ('nobody')
PIAT	attributive indefinite pronoun without determiner	kein Anruf ('no call'); irgendein Tier ('some animal')
PIDAT	attributive indefinite pronoun with determiner	die anderen Kinder ('the other kids'); ein paar Tage ('a few days')
PPER	irreflexive personal pronoun	ich ('I'); er ('he'); ihm ('him'); mich ('me')
PPOSS	substituting possessive pronoun	meins ('mine'); deiner ('yours')
PPOSAT	attributive possessive pronoun	meine Mutter ('my mother'); dein Hund ('your dog')
PRELS	substituting relative pronoun	das Eis; das ('the ice that'); der Mann; der ('the man who')
PRELAT	attributive relative pronoun	[no instances in the Litkey Corpus]
PRF	reflexive personal pronoun	sich ('oneself'); einander ('each other'); dich ('you'); mir ('me')

PWS	substituting interrogative pronoun	was ('what'); wer ('who')
PWAT	attributive interrogative pronoun	welche Nummer ('which number'); auf welcher Straße ('on which street')
PWAV	adverbial interrogative or relative pronoun	warum ('why'); wo ('where'); wann ('when')
PAV	pronominal adverb	dafür ('for that'); dabei ('thereby'); deswegen ('therefore'); trotzdem ('nevertheless')
PTKZU	"zu" before infinitve	zu rollen ('to roll'); zu sehen ('to see')
PTKNEG	particle of negation	nicht ('not')
PTKVZ	separated verb-addition	Lars ruft an ('Lars calls'); Sie hängt Bilder auf ('She hangs up pictures')
PTKANT	particle of response	ja ('yes'); nein ('no'); danke ('thanks'); bitte ('please')
PTKA	particle belonging to adjectives or adverbs	zu schnell ('too fast')
TRUNC	first part of a composition	[no instances in the Litkey Corpus]
VVFIN	finite verb; full	Lars ruft ('Lars shouts'); Dodo bellte ('Dodo barked');
VVIMP	imperative; full	Guck! ('Look!'); Gib! ('Give!')
VVINF	infinitive; full	passieren ('(to) happen'); kaufen ('(to) buy')
VVIZU	infinitive with "zu"; full	aufzureißen ('to rip open'); auszuleeren ('to empty out')
VVPP	perfect participle	geschrieben ('written'); gefunden ('found')
VAFIN	finite verb; auxiliary	du bist ('you are'); Lars hat ('Lars has')
VAIMP	imperative; auxiliary	sei leise! ('be quiet!')
VAINF	infinitve; auxiliary	wo er sein könnte ('where he could be'); weil er die Knochen haben will ('because he wants to have the bones')
VAPP	perfect participle; auxiliary	Dodo ist aggressiv geworden ('Dodo has become aggressive'); da hat Dodo was zu Fressen gehabt ('then Dodo has had something to eat')
VMFIN	finite verb; modal	wer darf Dodo mit in die Schule nehmen ('who is allowed to take Dodo to school'); sie wollte gerade gehen ('she wanted to go right now')
VMINF	infinitive; modal	wollen ('want (to)')
VMPP	perfect participle; modal	[no instances in the Litkey Corpus]
XY	non-word; including special symbols	C. Ronaldo; Hr. ('Mr.'); aules** [unreadable fragment]
$,	comma	,
$.	punctuation at the end of a sentence	. ? !! ; :
$(	other punctuation; sentence-internal	" ( )

Table 7: STTS tagset (Schiller et al., 1999) used for POS tagging. Examples are taken from the Litkey Corpus. The word in question is marked in red.

The Materials Science Procedural Text Corpus: Annotating Materials Synthesis Procedures with Shallow Semantic Structures

Sheshera Mysore[1*]   Zach Jensen[2*]   Edward Kim[2]   Kevin Huang[2]
Haw-Shiuan Chang[1]   Emma Strubell[1]   Jeffrey Flanigan[1]
Andrew McCallum[1]   Elsa Olivetti[2]

[1]College of Information and Computer Sciences
University of Massachusetts Amherst
{smysore, hschang, strubell, jflanigan, mccallum}@cs.umass.edu

[2]Department of Materials Science and Engineering
Massachusetts Institute of Technology
{zjensen, edwardk, kjhuang, elsao}@mit.edu

Abstract

Materials science literature contains millions of materials synthesis procedures described in unstructured natural language text. Large-scale analysis of these synthesis procedures would facilitate deeper scientific understanding of materials synthesis and enable automated synthesis planning. Such analysis requires extracting structured representations of synthesis procedures from the raw text as a first step. To facilitate the training and evaluation of synthesis extraction models, we introduce a dataset of 230 synthesis procedures annotated by domain experts with labeled graphs that express the semantics of the synthesis sentences. The nodes in this graph are synthesis operations and their typed arguments, and labeled edges specify relations between the nodes. We describe this new resource in detail and highlight some specific challenges to annotating scientific text with shallow semantic structure. We make the corpus available to the community to promote further research and development of scientific information extraction systems.

1 Introduction

Systematically reducing the time and effort required to synthesize novel materials remains one of the grand challenges in materials science. Massive knowledge bases which tabulate known chemical reactions for *organic* chemistry (Lawson et al., 2014) have accelerated data-driven synthesis planning and related analyses (Segler et al., 2018; Coley et al., 2017). Automated synthesis planning for organic molecules has recently achieved human-level

In a typical procedure for the synthesis of β-MnO$_2$ nanowires, **2.5** **mL** of **50** **wt%** **Mn(NO$_3$)$_2$** **solution** was diluted to **25.0** **ml**, and **ozone** was fed into the bottom of the **solution** for **30** **min** under vigorous stirring. With the indraught of **ozone**, **black solid** appeared gradually and the **clear solution** turned into **black slurry** finally. Then the **suspension** was transferred into an **autoclave** of **48.0** **ml**, sealed and maintained at **200°C** for **8** **h**. After this, the **autoclave** was cooled to **room temperature** naturally. The resulting **solid products** were washed with **water**, and dried at **120°C** for **8** **h**. The obtained products were collected for the following characterization.

Figure 1: Example synthesis procedure text from a materials journal article (Dong et al., 2009). Bold red indicates the operations (predicates) involved in the synthesis; **bold black** indicates arguments; underlines demarcate entity boundaries.

planning performance using massive organic reaction knowledge bases as training data (Segler et al., 2018). There are, however, currently no comprehensive knowledge bases which systematically document the methods by which *inorganic* materials are synthesized (Kim et al., 2017a,b). Despite efforts to standardize the reporting of chemical and materials science data (Murray-Rust and Rzepa, 1999), inorganic materials synthesis procedures continue to reside as natural language descriptions in the text of journal articles. Figure 1 presents an example of such a synthesis procedure. To achieve similar success for inorganic synthesis as has been achieved for organic materials, we must develop new techniques for automatically extracting structured representations of materials synthesis procedures from the unstructured narrative in scientific papers (Kim et al., 2017b).

To facilitate the development and evaluation of

*Equal contribution

Proceedings of the 13th Linguistic Annotation Workshop, pages 56–64
Florence, Italy, August 1, 2019. ©2019 Association for Computational Linguistics

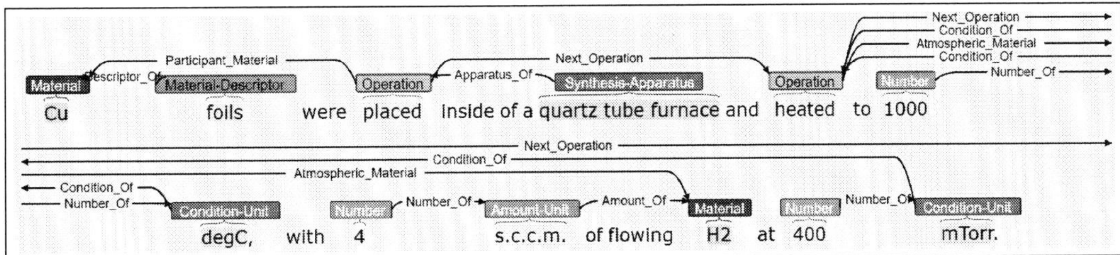

Figure 2: An example annotated sentence. Shallow semantic structures generally consist of verbal predicates and arguments of these predicates as nodes and labeled edges between predicate and argument nodes, example. Heated(*Condition_of*: degC, *Atmospheric_Material*: H2, *Condition_of*: mTorr). We also label relations between argument entities and non-predicate entities, for example. *Descriptor_of*(Cu, foils) and relations between predicates, for example. *Next_Operation*(placed, heated).

machine learning models for automatic extraction of materials syntheses from text, in this work we present a new dataset of synthesis procedures annotated with semantic structure by domain experts in materials science. We annotate each step in a synthesis with a structured frame-semantic representation, with all the steps in a synthesis making up a Directed Acyclic Graph (DAG). The types of nodes in the graph include synthesis operations (i.e. predicates), and the materials, conditions, apparatus and other entities participating in each synthesis step. Labeled edges represent relationships between entities, for example *Condition_of* or *Next_Operation*. Our dataset consists of 230 synthesis procedures annotated with these structures. An example sentence level annotation is given in Fig. 2. We make the corpus available to the community to promote further research and development of scientific information extraction systems for procedural text.[1]

2 Description of the Annotated Dataset

Here we describe the manner in which synthesis procedures were chosen for annotation (§2.1), present a description of the structures we annotate (§2.2), summarize key statistics of the dataset (§2.3), highlight specific annotation decisions (§2.4) and present inter-annotator agreements (§2.5). All annotations were performed by three materials scientists using the BRAT[2] annotation tool (Stenetorp et al., 2012).

2.1 Selecting Synthesis Procedures for Annotation

The 230 synthesis procedures annotated were selected from our database of 2.5 million publications describing materials synthesis. The database was built from agreements with major scientific publication companies. Synthesis procedure text were obtained by first parsing the HTML text of the full publications, then automatically identifying candidate synthesis paragraphs using a trained classifier. This paragraph classifier was trained on a set of manually labeled paragraph examples and has a F1 score of 90.2 on a held out test set.[3] The paragraphs selected by the classifier were manually verified as containing complete, valid materials synthesis procedures by domain experts. While a given synthesis procedure is most often a single paragraph, there are cases where it spans multiple paragraphs, we consider all the paragraphs to be a single synthesis procedure. All the semantic structures were then manually annotated in these selected synthesis procedures. Fig 1 depicts an example paragraph containing a synthesis procedure. In selecting a synthesis procedure for annotation, a small number of valid synthesis procedures ($\sim 20\%$) are ignored; this is done for the synthesis procedures which are not amenable to annotation from a sentence-level frame-semantic view of synthesis steps, or ones in which most entities in the synthesis do not agree with our definitions of operations and argument entities (see §2.4 for further discussion).

2.2 Structures Annotated

An annotated graph consists of nodes denoting the participants of synthesis steps and edges denoting relationships between the participants in the synthesis. Operation nodes define the main structure of the graph and the arguments for each operation include different materials, conditions and appara-

---

[1]Public dataset: https://bit.ly/2WLCbyh
[2]http://brat.nlplab.org/

[3]The labeled data for this classifier is *not* part of the data release associated with this paper due to licensing restrictions from publishers.

Entity type	Count
Material	4843
Number	4095
Operation	3786
Amount-Unit	1659
Condition-Unit	1621
Material-Descriptor	1430
Condition-Misc	535
Synthesis-Apparatus	490
Nonrecipe-Material	475
Brand	348

(a)

Operation-argument relations	*Recipe-target, Solvent-material, Atmospheric-material, Recipe-precursor, Participant-material, Apparatus-of Condition-of*
Non-operation entity relations	*Descriptor-of, Number-of, Amount-of, Apparatus-attr-of, Brand-of, Coref-of,*
Operation-Operation relations	*Next-operation*

(b)

Table 1: Entity types and relation labels annotated in our dataset. The table (a) depicts the 10 most frequent of the 21 entity types defined in our dataset, and the table (b) highlights the 14 relation labels among entities possible in our dataset.

tus. For annotating the text describing a synthesis procedure, we define a set of span-level labels that identify the operations and typed arguments in the text, i.e. the nodes of the graph. We also define a set of relationships between text spans, which label the edges of the synthesis graph. We detail these two kinds of labels next.

Span-level Labels: Each span is a sequence of tokens or characters which form one entity mention (for example. "quartz tube furnace"). Entity mentions are associated with *entity types* which specify a category/kind for the entity mention. Our dataset defines a total of 21 entity types, with the least frequent entity type occuring 32 times. The 10 most frequent entity types defined for our dataset are listed in Table 1a. We describe a notable subset of the entity types in more detail below alongside examples of their occurrence in text. In examples, the text underlined is the span to be annotated.

Material: Materials that are used in the synthesis of the target. For example: Cr_2O_3, Strontium carbonate, $BaTiO_3$, Li_2CO_3, Water, Ethanol.

Nonrecipe-Material: Chemically specified materials that are not used in the synthesis of the synthesis target. For example: "$BaTiO_3$ powder (Ba/Ti=0.999)", "Li_2CO_3 was used as the Li source", "Si/Al ratio was 5".

Operation: Discrete actions physically performed by the researcher or discrete process steps taken to synthesize the target.

Material-Descriptor: Describes a material's structure, shape, form, type, role, etc. and must be directly or nearly adjacent to the material it describes. Does not include

amounts, concentrations, or purities of materials. For example: $CaCu_3Ti_4O_{12}$ compound, Copper ion, GaAs nanowires, Anatase TiO_2, Deionized water.

Meta: A canonical name to specify a particular overall synthesis method used for synthesis. For example: "Graphite oxide was prepared by oxidation of graphite powder according to the modified Hummers' method". "Bi2S3 nanorods with orthorhombic structure were prepared through the hydrothermal method". "Graphene oxide (GO) was prepared from graphite powder by the Staudenmaier method."

Amount-Unit: These describe absolute amounts, concentrations, purities, ratios, flow rates and so on. For example: mg, mL, M, %.

Condition-Unit: These describe the units of measurement for intangible conditions under which operations are performed. For ex: °C, K, sec, RPM, mW.

Condition-Misc: Qualitative descriptions of conditions. For example: Room temperature, Dropwise, Naturally, Vacuum.

Synthesis Apparatus: Equipment used to perform an operation involved in the synthesis.

Characterization-Apparatus: Equipment used to characterize a materials properties.

Relation Labels: We define a set of relationships between entity mentions, which label the edges of the synthesis graph. A subset of these relations describe direct relationships between operations and their arguments, others describe re-

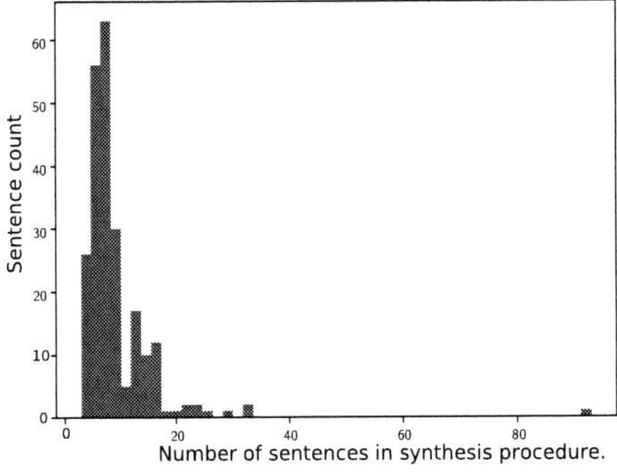

(a) Sentences per synthesis document.

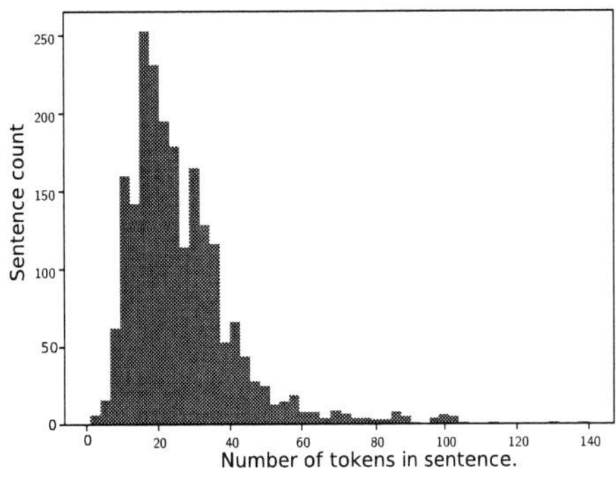

(b) Tokens per sentence.

Figure 3: Sentences count statistics of the corpus; On average a synthesis procedure contains 9 sentences, each of which contain 26 tokens on average.

lationships between argument mentions, and the *Next-Operation* relation describes relationships between operations so as to step towards annotating full recipe graphs. The different relation labels we define are tabulated in Table 1b, a subset of these are defined below:

Recipe-target: Indicates a material assigned to an operation which is the target of the synthesis procedure.

Participant-material: A material that is part of a particular synthesis step.

Recipe-precursor: Indicates a material which is the source of an element for the target material used in a specific synthesis operation.

Apparatus-of: Denotes an apparatus to be used in a synthesis operation.

Condition-of: Denotes a reaction condition for a synthesis operation.

Coref-of: Intended to capture coreferent mentions of entities presented by abbreviations, text in parenthesis and so on. For example: "Air (O_2/N_2 mixture gases)" and "He were supplied to the porous support side ...". "Air" is coreferent with O_2 and N_2.

Amount-of: Links a number entity to the corresponding unit of measurement.

Next-operation: A relation intended to denote the true synthesis order of the synthesis steps; the relation is also intended to implicitly denote the flow of intermediate materials in the synthesis. However, in this first release of the data, as a placeholder for future annotations, *Next-Operation* is used simply used to indicate the next operation in text order rather than in true synthesis order.

We refer readers to our annotation guidelines for definitions of the complete set of entity type and relation labels in the dataset.

2.3 Dataset Statistics

Some key statistics of the dataset such as number of documents, tokens, entities and unique operations are listed in Table 2 and Fig. 3. In reporting these statistics we perform tokenization and sentence segmentation using the ChemDataExtractor package (Swain and Cole, 2016).[4]

2.4 Annotation Decisions

Next we highlight specific points of contention in creating the current set of annotations.

What constitutes an operation?: While our definition of the `Operation` entity type specifies only actions performed by a lab researcher to be valid operations, there are cases where our annotations diverge from this definition. This happens in the following cases:

- Cases where an operation isn't explicitly performed by the researcher. For example: "After this, the autoclave was `cooled` to room temperature naturally".
- Cases with nested verb structures. For example: "white precipitate which was `harvested` by `centrifugation` ...".

In the current set of annotations, we allow experts to decide when a particular candidate operation

---

[4] `https://pypi.org/project/ChemDataExtractor/1.2.2/`

Item	Count
Synthesis procedures	230
Sentences	2113
Tokens	56510
Entity mentions	20849
Entities	4883
Unique operations	409
Entity types (Table 1a)	21
Relation types (Table 1b)	14
Avg. sentence length (Fig. 3b)	26
Avg. sentences/synthesis proc (Fig. 3a)	9

Table 2: Various dataset statistics. Additional details provided in referred figures. To determine unique operations, `Operation` entity mentions are lemmatized with the WordNet lemmatizer and the unique lemmas are counted.

should be considered valid and when it can be omitted. As our inter-annotator agreements will demonstrate, experts tend to agree often on what should be considered an operation. The question of what constitutes an operation is analogous to the notion of what constitutes an "event" in the broader NLP literature as highlighted by Mostafazadeh et al. (2016).

Argument state and argument re-use: Annotation of semantic structures often allow for argument spans to have multiple parents (Surdeanu et al., 2008; Banarescu et al., 2013; Oepen et al., 2015). For example in Figure 2, the material "Cu" could be considered an argument of the operations "placed" and "heated". Allowing for arguments to have multiple parents however runs into complications when the operation causes the state of a material to change (incidentally, this is not the case in the example we highlight above). When a materials state changes due to a specific operation, considering the same text span to be the argument of a different operation would not be chemically valid. For example, in the sentence:

> After that, the mixed solution was aged at 60 degC for 48 h, followed by heating at 900 degC for 2 h with a heating rate of 5 degC min-1 in an N2 atmosphere.

"solution" is labeled as *Participant-material* for "aged", but it isnt considered a *Participant-material* to "heating" since aging caused it to be a different material. Similarly, in:

> 1.6632 g lithium acetate was dissolved into 26 mL of ethanol-water mixture

(12:1 in volume) and slowly dropped into the above suspension.

"lithium acetate" is only labeled as *Participant-material* for "dissolved" and not for "dropped" whose sole argument is "suspension". This clearly highlights an instance of a material entirely absent from the text being the true argument of an operation. Therefore the current set of annotations does not allow for arguments to have multiple parents. Further, the tracking of state itself is also complicated by the difficulty in being able to write down precise states at a meaningful level of granularity for all possible materials, this is further complicated by the ambiguity presented by under-specified materials in synthesis text, for example in the sentence:

> With the indraught of ozone, black solid appeared gradually and the clear solution turned into black slurry finally.

Most of the entities, "black solid", "clear solution" and "black slurry" are chemically under-specified, with precise specification even unnecessary for describing the synthesis procedure.

Relations across sentences: Often, in synthesis procedures, a given synthesis step is described across multiple sentences. In these cases it would be meaningful to allow for relationships between operation-argument entities which are in different sentences. For the sake of simplicity and to stick more closely to a sentence level shallow semantic annotation, our current iteration of the annotations has avoided this annotation, however a very small number of instances of cross-sentence relations do exist ($< 1\%$ of all relations in the dataset). Examples of this type are as follows:

> First, sulfuric acid and nitric acid were mixed well by stirring 15 min in an ice bath, and then graphite powder was dispersed into the solution. After 15 min, potassium chlorate was added into the system - very slowly to prevent strong reaction during the oxidation process.

> Oxygen with 20 sccm flow rate and argon with 40 sccm flow rate were used as the sputtering gas. Growth temperature was 400 degC and the RF power was 90 W.

Here "min" and "dispersed" are related by a *Condition_Of* relation. Similarly, "degC" and "W",

Entity type	Fleiss' Kappa
Material	0.916
Number	0.971
Operation	0.859
Amount-Unit	0.967
Condition-Unit	0.985
Material-Descriptor	0.638
Condition-Misc	0.784
Synthesis-Apparatus	0.860
Nonrecipe-Material	0.371
Brand	0.862

(a)

Annotation	Fleiss' Kappa
Span-level labels	0.861
Relation labels	0.941

(b)

Table 3: Annotator agreements in our dataset. The table (a) depicts the percent agreements on 10 most frequent of the 21 entity types defined in our dataset, and the table (b) denotes overall agreements on the different annotations in our dataset.

both are annotated with *Condition_Of* relations to "used". Annotations of this kind were created when annotators deemed such an annotation absolutely necessary. Synthesis procedures which required annotation primarily of cross-sentence relations were ignored.

2.5 Inter-annotator Agreement

Next we report a host of inter-annotator agreements for the different levels of semantic annotation in our dataset. The agreements we report are based on a collection of 5 synthesis procedures which were annotated separately by all three expert annotators. All the numbers we report are Fleiss' Kappa scores for the 3 expert annotators.

Span-level Labels: Agreements on span level labels correspond to the agreement on entity type labels assigned to individual tokens. We observe the overall agreement on the token level labels to be 0.861. A break down of this agreement by the entity type is presented in Table 3a. As this indicates, there seems to be high agreement on labels which have clear definitions; namely. Number, Amount-Unit. Labels which by definition are a lot more ambiguous, however, have a lower agreement. The two entity types Material-Descriptor and Nonrecipe-Material see the lowest agree-

ments. We believe these to be inherently more subjective entity types. In the case of Material-Descriptor it is often that some annotators may consider the descriptor and the adjacent material to be Material in its own right, for example: "Deionized Water" may be considered as a material in its own right or "deionized" may be considered to be a descriptor. In the case of Nonrecipe-Material, a similarly harder decision needs to be made by the annotator, since these are materials which aren't involved in the synthesis but are still mentioned in the text for completeness information. Often it is up to the interpretation of the annotator to decide whether a material is indeed involved in the synthesis leading to the low agreement on this entity type.

Relation Labels: Agreement on relation labels were computed for the set of cases where a pair of annotators agreed on the token level annotations, this happens 66% of the time in our repeated annotations. For a pair of entities, if both annotators indicate the same relation type the annotators are considered to be in agreement. For relation labels we observe a agreement score of 0.941. Since we only consider cases where the token labels are in agreement, we believe that it is likely that when annotators agree on the token level annotations they also tend to agree on the relation level labels.

3 Related Work

Shallow semantic parsing in NLP: Prior work in the NLP community has defined and annotated semantic structures for text. These structured representations often seek to generalize about sentence level predicate-argument structure, abstracting away from the surface nuances of natural language and representing its semantics (Abend and Rappoport, 2017). A large body of work has created these resources for non-scientific text, as done in PropBank (Palmer et al., 2005; Surdeanu et al., 2008), FrameNet (Fillmore and Baker, 2010), AMR (Banarescu et al., 2013), semantic dependencies (Oepen et al., 2015) and ACE event schemas (Doddington et al., 2004). The GENIA project has defined event structures for biomedical data (Kim et al., 2003) while Garg et al. (2016) extended the AMR framework to biomedical text. Closer still to the work presented here, Mori et al. (2014) have annotated cooking recipes with sentence and discourse level semantic relations. There has also been an interest in labeling scientific wetlab protocol text, with semantic structures and to facilitate training supervised models for the extraction of these structures (Kulkarni et al., 2018). Kulkarni et al. make use of an altered version of the EXACT2 ontology, created for the annotation of biomedical procedural text (Soldatova et al., 2014). The dataset presented here can be viewed to fit within the theme of sentence level semantics for procedural text, specifically tailored to materials science synthesis.

Materials Science & Chemistry: Prior work in the materials science community have shown that manual extraction and subsequent text mining can be an effective approach to analysis of synthesis routes for specific compounds and classes of materials (Raccuglia et al., 2016; Ghadbeigi et al., 2015); these approaches however have been limited by scale due to the manual extraction step. There has also been strong a consensus that comprehensively extracting the knowledge contained within written inorganic materials syntheses is a key step towards reducing the overall discovery and development time for novel materials (Butler et al., 2018). We believe that the dataset we release fills an important gap in the existing work on extraction of inorganic materials synthesis procedures, by allowing exploration into extraction at a scale not attempted before. Parallel with this work, work by Kim et al. (2018) and Tamari et al. (2019) adopt the dataset released here to aid extraction of structured representations from synthesis procedures and with Kim et al. presenting early experiments in synthesis planning from extracted synthesis.

The focus of existing datasets and resources in the materials science community, has been on materials structures and properties knowledge bases (Jain et al., 2013), rather than reactions and synthesis. In pursuit of more scalable methods for materials synthesis data extraction, Young et al. (2018) have made use of automated methods for extracting specific categories of materials synthesis parameters, while Mysore et al. (2017) and Kim et al. (2017a) have both presented preliminary methodological explorations for automated extraction of elements of a synthesis graph from materials science literature. However, these lines of work have not presented general purpose annotated data with which to train information extraction models for extraction of structured synthesis representations at scale, the focus of this work.

4 Conclusion and Future Directions

In this work we present a shallow semantic parsing dataset consisting of 230 synthesis procedures. The dataset was annotated by domain experts in materials science. We also highlight specific difficulties in the annotation process and present agreement metrics on the different levels of our annotation. We believe the dataset will enable the development of robust supervised entity tagging models and is suitable for evaluating models trained to extract shallow semantic structures. This is evidenced by the adoption of the dataset by work contemporaneous with this work (Kim et al., 2018; Tamari et al., 2019).

Future work in the development of this dataset could involve methods for the scaling up of the annotation process, perhaps by adapting the guidelines to enable annotation by non-experts at some stages of the annotation process. Further, we also plan to quantitatively establish the limits of our annotation schema for the kinds of information it isn't able to capture. We also plan to add additional layers of annotation, including: co-reference relations between synthesis steps, states of argument entities, and linking annotated entities to entries in materials science knowledge bases such as The Materials Project.[5]

5 Acknowledgements

The authors would like to acknowledge funding from the National Science Foundation Award 1534340/1534341 DMREF and support from the Office of Naval Research (ONR) under Contract No. N00014-16-1-2432. Early work was collaborative under the Dept. of Energys Basic Energy Science Program through the Materials Project under Grant No. EDCBEE.

References

Omri Abend and Ari Rappoport. 2017. The state of the art in semantic representation. In *ACL*.

Laura Banarescu, Claire Bonial, Shu Cai, Madalina Georgescu, Kira Griffitt, Ulf Hermjakob, Kevin Knight, Philipp Koehn, Martha Palmer, and Nathan Schneider. 2013. Abstract meaning representation for sembanking. In *Proceedings of the 7th Linguistic Annotation Workshop and Interoperability with Discourse*.

---

[5] https://materialsproject.org/

Keith T Butler, Daniel W Davies, Hugh Cartwright, Olexandr Isayev, and Aron Walsh. 2018. Machine learning for molecular and materials science. *Nature*.

Connor W Coley, Regina Barzilay, Tommi S Jaakkola, William H Green, and Klavs F Jensen. 2017. Prediction of organic reaction outcomes using machine learning. *ACS central science*.

George R Doddington, Alexis Mitchell, Mark A Przybocki, Lance A Ramshaw, Stephanie Strassel, and Ralph M Weischedel. 2004. The automatic content extraction (ace) program-tasks, data, and evaluation. In *LREC*.

Yuming Dong, Hongxiao Yang, Kun He, Shaoqing Song, and Aimin Zhang. 2009. β-mno 2 nanowires: a novel ozonation catalyst for water treatment. *Applied Catalysis B: Environmental*.

Charles J Fillmore and Collin Baker. 2010. A frames approach to semantic analysis. In *The Oxford handbook of linguistic analysis*.

Sahil Garg, Aram Galstyan, Ulf Hermjakob, and Daniel Marcu. 2016. Extracting biomolecular interactions using semantic parsing of biomedical text. In *Thirtieth AAAI Conference on Artificial Intelligence*.

Leila Ghadbeigi, Jaye K Harada, Bethany R Lettiere, and Taylor D Sparks. 2015. Performance and resource considerations of li-ion battery electrode materials. *Energy & Environmental Science*.

Anubhav Jain, Shyue Ping Ong, Geoffroy Hautier, Wei Chen, William Davidson Richards, Stephen Dacek, Shreyas Cholia, Dan Gunter, David Skinner, Gerbrand Ceder, et al. 2013. Commentary: The materials project: A materials genome approach to accelerating materials innovation. *Apl Materials*.

Edward Kim, Kevin Huang, Adam Saunders, Andrew McCallum, Gerbrand Ceder, and Elsa Olivetti. 2017a. Materials synthesis insights from scientific literature via text extraction and machine learning. *Chemistry of Materials*.

Edward Kim, Kevin Huang, Alex Tomala, Sara Matthews, Emma Strubell, Adam Saunders, Andrew McCallum, and Elsa Olivetti. 2017b. Machine-learned and codified synthesis parameters of oxide materials. *Scientific Data*.

Edward Kim, Zach Jensen, Alexander van Grootel, Kevin Huang, Matthew Staib, Sheshera Mysore, Haw-Shiuan Chang, Emma Strubell, Andrew McCallum, Stefanie Jegelka, et al. 2018. Inorganic materials synthesis planning with literature-trained neural networks. *arXiv preprint arXiv:1901.00032*.

J-D Kim, Tomoko Ohta, Yuka Tateisi, and Junichi Tsujii. 2003. Genia corpusa semantically annotated corpus for bio-textmining. *Bioinformatics*.

Chaitanya Kulkarni, Wei Xu, Alan Ritter, and Raghu Machiraju. 2018. An annotated corpus for machine reading of instructions in wet lab protocols. *NAACL*.

Alexander J Lawson, Jürgen Swienty-Busch, Thibault Géoui, and David Evans. 2014. The making of reaxystowards unobstructed access to relevant chemistry information. In *The Future of the History of Chemical Information*.

Shinsuke Mori, Hirokuni Maeta, Yoko Yamakata, and Tetsuro Sasada. 2014. Flow graph corpus from recipe texts. In *LREC*, pages 2370–2377.

Nasrin Mostafazadeh, Alyson Grealish, Nathanael Chambers, James Allen, and Lucy Vanderwende. 2016. Caters: Causal and temporal relation scheme for semantic annotation of event structures. In *Proceedings of the Fourth Workshop on Events*, pages 51–61.

Peter Murray-Rust and Henry S Rzepa. 1999. Chemical markup, xml, and the worldwide web. 1. basic principles. *Journal of Chemical Information and Computer Sciences*.

Sheshera Mysore, Edward Kim, Emma Strubell, Ao Liu, Haw-Shiuan Chang, Srikrishna Kompella, Kevin Huang, Andrew McCallum, and Elsa Olivetti. 2017. Automatically extracting action graphs from materials science synthesis procedures. *Workshop on Machine Learning for Molecules and Materials at NIPS*.

Stephan Oepen, Marco Kuhlmann, Yusuke Miyao, Daniel Zeman, Silvie Cinková, Dan Flickinger, Jan Hajic, and Zdenka Urešová. 2015. Semeval 2015 task 18: Broad-coverage semantic dependency parsing. *SemEval-2015*, page 915.

Martha Palmer, Paul Kingsbury, and Daniel Gildea. 2005. The Proposition Bank: An Annotated Corpus of Semantic Roles. *Computational Linguistics*.

Paul Raccuglia, Katherine C Elbert, Philip DF Adler, Casey Falk, Malia B Wenny, Aurelio Mollo, Matthias Zeller, Sorelle A Friedler, Joshua Schrier, and Alexander J Norquist. 2016. Machine-learning-assisted materials discovery using failed experiments. *Nature*.

Marwin HS Segler, Mike Preuss, and Mark P Waller. 2018. Planning chemical syntheses with deep neural networks and symbolic ai. *Nature*.

Larisa N Soldatova, Daniel Nadis, Ross D King, Piyali S Basu, Emma Haddi, Véronique Baumlé, Nigel J Saunders, Wolfgang Marwan, and Brian B Rudkin. 2014. Exact2: the semantics of biomedical protocols. *BMC bioinformatics*.

Pontus Stenetorp, Sampo Pyysalo, Goran Topi, Tomoko Ohta, Sophia Ananiadou, and Jun'ichi Tsujii. 2012. BRAT: A web-based tool for NLP-assisted text annotation.

Mihai Surdeanu, Richard Johansson, Adam Meyers, Lluís Màrquez, and Joakim Nivre. 2008. The conll-2008 shared task on joint parsing of syntactic and semantic dependencies. In *Proceedings of the Twelfth Conference on Computational Natural Language Learning*, pages 159–177. Association for Computational Linguistics.

Matthew C Swain and Jacqueline M Cole. 2016. Chemdataextractor: a toolkit for automated extraction of chemical information from the scientific literature. *Journal of chemical information and modeling*, 56(10):1894–1904.

Ronen Tamari, Hiroyuki Shindo, Dafna Shahaf, and Yuji Matsumoto. 2019. Playing by the book: An interactive game approach for action graph extraction from text. In *Workshop on Extracting Structured Knowledge from Scientific Publications at NAACL 2019*.

Steven R Young, Artem Maksov, Maxim Ziatdinov, Ye Cao, Matthew Burch, Janakiraman Balachandran, Linglong Li, Suhas Somnath, Robert M Patton, Sergei V Kalinin, et al. 2018. Data mining for better material synthesis: The case of pulsed laser deposition of complex oxides. *Journal of Applied Physics*.

Tagging modality in Oceanic languages of Melanesia

Annika Tjuka
Humboldt-Universität zu Berlin
tjukanni@hu-berlin.de

Lena Weißmann
Freie Universität Berlin
lena.weissmann@fu-berlin.de

Kilu von Prince
Humboldt-Universität zu Berlin
kilu.von.prince@hu-berlin.de

Abstract

Primary data from small, low-resource languages of Oceania have only recently become available through language documentation. In our study, we explore corpus data of five Oceanic languages of Melanesia which are known to be mood-prominent (in the sense of Bhat, 1999). In order to find out more about tense, aspect, modality, and polarity, we tagged these categories in a subset of our corpora. For the category of modality, we developed a novel tag set (MelaTAMP, 2017), which categorizes clauses into *factual, possible*, and *counterfactual*. Based on an analysis of the inter-annotator consistency, we argue that our tag set for the modal domain is efficient for our subject languages and might be useful for other languages and purposes.

1 Introduction

Our understanding of the Oceanic languages of Melanesia has so far been based mostly on descriptive accounts rather than primary data, since no documentation existed until recently. For some of these languages, high-quality corpora have now become available, but their exploration is still in its infancy.

In our MelaTAMP research project, we carry out a comparative, corpus-based study on tense, aspect, and modality (TAM) categories in seven Oceanic languages: Daakaka, Dalkalaen, Daakie, Mavea, Nafsan, Saliba-Logea, North Ambrym (cf. MelaTAMP, 2017). Speaker populations range from about 30 (Mavea) to around 6000 (Nafsan). TAM-related meanings are often expressed obligatorily within the verbal complex, sometimes in more than one place. Thus, Mavea has three preverbal slots for expressing TAM values; in addition, some subject-agreement markers also express the difference between realis and irrealis modalities and reduplication can be used to express pluractionality (see Table 1). By contrast,

Saliba-Logea only uses optional particles to express TAM-related meanings.

In this paper, we discuss our tag set and its application in a subset of texts in the corpora of five languages: Daakaka, Dalkalaen, Mavea, Nafsan, and Saliba-Logea. The focus of our paper is on the process of tagging modality.

Previous studies which tag modality in corpora have focused on differentiating between modal flavours such as deontic and epistemic, and modal forces such as necessity and possibility. Thus, the sentence in (1-a) expresses an epistemic possibility while (1-b) conveys a deontic necessity.

(1) a. *Naomi might be a surgeon.*
     b. *Martha must hand in her assignment tomorrow.*

These distinctions are notoriously difficult to tag, with coarse-grained ontologies yielding better results than more fine-grained ones (Rubinstein et al., 2013). Most approaches focus on modal auxiliaries such as *must*, and modal adverbs such as *probably* (Cui and Chi, 2013; Quaresma et al., 2014).

In the languages of our project, however, modal auxiliaries and adverbs are rare, and do not play the same role in expressing modality as they do in many European languages. Instead, verb moods, such as *realis* and *irrealis*, are largely responsible for the modal interpretation of a clause. These expressions are usually under-specified for modal force and flavour. Instead of modal forces and flavours, we therefore differentiate three modal categories based on a branching-times framework (von Prince, 2019), which is explained in section 3.2.

The ontology of our modal tag set was primarily motivated by theoretical concerns and preliminary experiences with the driving factors in Oceanic TAM systems. The targets of our tags were individual clauses, regardless of the presence of spe-

Proceedings of the 13th Linguistic Annotation Workshop, pages 65–70
Florence, Italy, August 1, 2019. ©2019 Association for Computational Linguistics

SBJ.AGR	COND	NEG	IT/INCPT	NUM	IMPF	REDUP-	**Verb**	ADV	TR	OBJ
i-, …	*mo-*	*sopo-*	*me-/pete-*	*r-/tol-*	*l(o)-*				*=i*	*=a/*NP

Table 1: The verbal complex in Mavea (Guérin, 2011).

cific modality-related expressions. Their TAM values were tagged according to their temporal-modal reference, irrespective of the presence of specific TAM markers (e. g., in *Emma wants [to eat ice cream]*, the infinitive complement clause would be tagged to refer to the (relative) possible future).

The analysis of inter-annotator consistency in the tagging process shows that our modal categories are reasonably easy to assign based on the translations into English. This suggests that the same ontology might be useful for other purposes and languages as well.

2 Data

The data of our study consists of a series of narrative and explanatory texts in corpora of five Oceanic languages. These corpora are the result of language documentation and are richly annotated, with morpheme-by-morpheme glosses, part-of-speech tags, translations into English, as well as metadata on speakers, text genre, and the circumstances of the recording. In addition, we enriched parts of the corpora with our own tag set for TAM values. For optimal facilities for searching and analysis, we imported all corpora to the AN-NIS platform (Krause and Zeldes, 2016). We used Druskat (2018) to import them from their native SIL Toolbox format.

The corpora of the MelaTAMP project are held and versioned in a git repository (MelaTAMP, 2017). The repository itself is private and currently only accessible by members of the project team. Published versions of each corpus are available from various archives: von Prince (2013a,b); Krifka (2013); Guérin (2006); Thieberger (2006); Franjieh (2013); Margetts et al. (2017).

3 The Tag Set

3.1 Overview

In an initial stage of exploration, we identified comparable texts across the corpora (see Table 2). Each of the selected 26 texts was segmented into annotation units, which often correspond to a single sentence. These units were further segmented into clause-based subdivisions for TAM annotation (1953 clauses in total). Each clause was annotated for clause type, temporal reference, modal reference, aspect, and polarity. Our tag set which consisted of five categories with 21 tags is displayed in Table 3. Compared to some previous approaches, our ontology of clause types is richer than, e. g., Leech and Weisser (2003), but far less fine-grained than Twitchell and Nunamaker (2004); our tag set for tense is less fine-grained than, e. g., Zymla (2017). These differences are mostly due to different goals and data. We concentrated on those categories that were most likely to determine differential TAM marking in our subject languages. The tag set for clauses should be applicable for similar purposes to other languages. The tag sets for temporal and aspectual reference would have to be more fine-grained to accommodate graded tense systems, highly differentiated aspect systems, and similar.

3.2 The Modal Tag Set

We found that, for our subject languages, the distinction which is most useful and basic to the TAM systems is the distinction between *realis* and *irrealis*, as is often the case in Oceanic (compare Lichtenberk, 2016). At the same time, irrealis is a very large modal domain that is often subdivided by more specific markers. This can be modeled by the approach of von Prince (2019), which shows that a branching-times framework can be used to generate three different modal domains: the possible (future), the actual (past and present), and the counterfactual (past, present and future). This differs crucially from previous approaches to modality which were based on a binary distinction, without the option to exclusively quantify over counterfactual indices. It is this theoretical innovation which allows for a tag set that is more informative than a mere realis/irrealis distinction, without relying on the often elusive distinctions between modal flavors.

Given the assumptions in von Prince (2019), the three domains are defined as follows:

- The actual present i_0 and the actual past (predecessors of i_0).

Language	#Texts	#Tokens	#Texts taggged	#Clauses taggged
Daakaka	119	68k	5	143
Dalkalaen	114	34k	6	724
Mavea	61	45k	3	639
Nafsan	110	65k	6	364
Saliba-Logea	214	150k*	6	159
Total	618	362k	26	2029

Table 2: Corpora included in this study; *of the 150k tokens in this corpus, about 70k are fully annotated.

Category	Name	Tags
Clause type	clause	assertion, question, directive; embedded: proposition, conditional, e.question, temporal, adverbial, attributive
Temporal domain	time	past, future, present
Modal domain	mood	factual, counterfactual, possible
Aspectual domain	event	bounded, ongoing, repeated, stative
Polarity	polarity	positive, negative

Table 3: Tag set of the MelaTAMP project (MelaTAMP, 2017).

- The counterfactual past, present, and future: indices that are neither predecessors nor successors of i_0.
- The possible future(s): successors of i_0.

Figure 1 illustrates the three domains of modality.

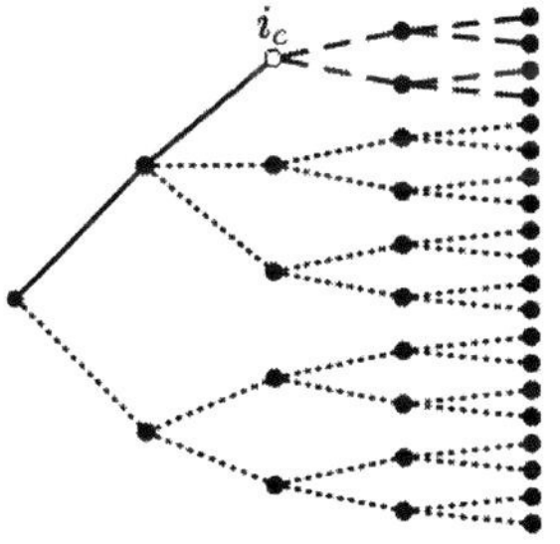

Figure 1: The three domains of the factual (solid line), the counterfactual (dotted lines), and the possible future (dashed lines). Vertically aligned indices are here taken to be simultaneous.

For the purposes of our tag set, we make a three-way distinction which builds on those domains, but is not entirely identical to them. The three values that we use are `factual`, `counterfactual`, and `possible`: the tags `factual` (*it rained*) and `counterfactual` (*she should have run faster*, *winning would have been hard*) coincide with the corresponding domains. The tag `possible` comprises several domains, depending on the temporal reference of the clause: the possible future (*it will rain*) and quantification over both the actual and the counterfactual domain (*it may have rained*).

Tagging was mainly based on the English translations of the texts although in some cases, the glosses were considered as well, when translations were unclear. Each clause was tagged manually by two annotators: Annika Tjuka and Lena Weißmann. There were no discontinuous clauses. The sentence in (2) was tagged as follows:

(2) *tenem   iya Gesila   stoli-na*
     that.DIST 3SG Place.Name story-3SG.POSS
     "that's the story of Gesila"   (Saliba-Logea: Gesila_01BC_0265)

- clause: `assertion`
- time: `present`
- mood: `factual`
- event: `stative`
- polarity: `positive`

After a text was tagged by the two annotators independently, the tags of both versions were compared by one of the annotators and the inconsistencies were noted in a table and discussed. If the decision for either one of the tags was clear, the correct tag was inserted in the final document. Many early sources of disagreement were clarified by guidelines in the documentation of the tag set (MelaTAMP, 2017). In doubtful cases, the tags were discussed with the principal investigator of the project: Kilu von Prince. The inter-annotator agreement was calculated on the basis of the inconsistencies in each tag which were detected through the initial comparison.

In addition to corpus work, we and our collaborators also carried out field work in Vanuatu to elicit modal-temporal contexts that were rarely attested in the corpora. We report on this work in von Prince et al. (2018).

4 Analysis of Inter-Annotator Consistency

A total number of 9765 tags in 1953 clauses (five tags per clause) were assigned by the two annotators. In 817 tags, inconsistencies between the annotation of the annotators were present. Figure 2 illustrates the inter-annotator consistency and inconsistency in each category of the tag set.

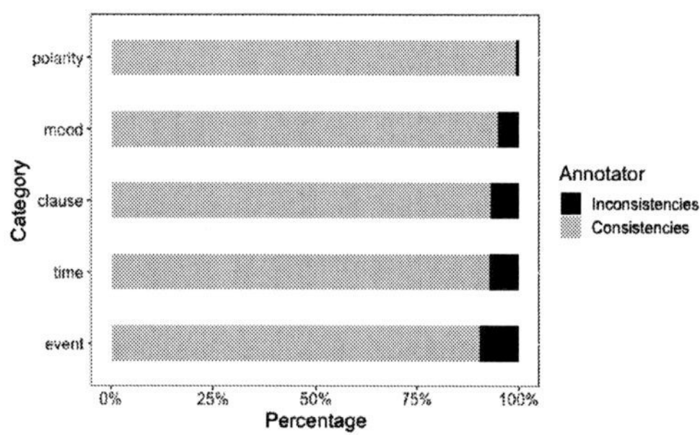

Figure 2: Percentages of inter-annotator consistencies (light) and inconsistencies (dark) in each TAM category of the tag set.

The graph shows that the percentages of inconsistencies between the categories differ. Mismatches are especially prone to arise in the event category. This category has the lowest inter-annotator agreement with $\alpha = 0.79$.[1] In contrast, the polarity category had the lowest inconsistency percentage with 0.82%. The α score in this category is $\alpha = 0.91$.

The analysis of each tag in the mood category reveals differences between the percentage of inconsistencies, as illustrated in Figure 3.

The 12.7% of the inter-annotator inconsistency in the possible tag is based on 496 clauses which are tagged as possible. Most of these inconsistencies result from mismatches in tagging

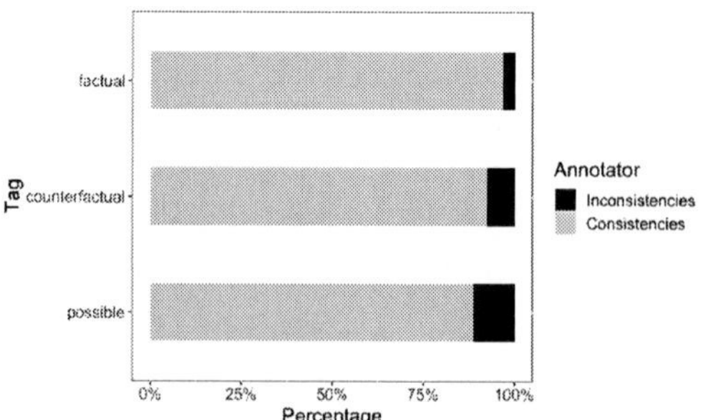

Figure 3: Percentages of inter-annotator consistencies (light) and inconsistencies (dark) in each tag of the mood category.

temporal sentences, see (3). Thus, in the following example, it is hard to tell whether the sentence implies that the agents did reach their destination or whether it only implies that they were headed there:

(3)   *...panpan na   ra=pak   nagis*
    until   PURP 3D.RS=to point
    "[they went] until they got to the [next] point"   (Nafsan: 036.017)

Among the small number of clauses which had the counterfactual tag (37 clauses), there were 8.11% inconsistencies. In general, counterfactual sentences are rare and are not easy to detect. A prominent context for counterfactual modality is false-belief-reports (compare Van Linden and Verstraete, 2008), as the embedded clause in example (4); or conditional clauses referring to situations in the past that did not occur, as the two clauses in example (5).

(4)   *ru=mroki   [na   ruk=fan   sol tete*
    3PL.RS=think COMP 3PL.IR=go get some
    mane emrom st]o.
    money inside shop
    "they thought [someone had taken money from inside the shop]."   (Nafsan: 030.048)

(5)   *[taba lahi   ya   mwamwayauma]*
    IRR   yesterday 1SG.SBJ quick-to.SP
    [kabo ya   kai]
    then 1SG.SBJ eat
    "If I **had hurriedly come here** yesterday then I **would have eaten**." (Saliba: Boneyawa_05BC_0020)

The factual tag is the most consistent tag in the mood category with 3.17% inconsistencies in 1481 clauses. The tag is based on the factual do-

---

[1]The Krippendorff's alpha coefficient measures the statistical agreement between two annotators (Krippendorff, 1980).

main of the branching-times framework and was assigned to clauses expressing the actual present and past, as in (6).

(6)   *mwe   liye an   bosi*
     REAL take 3S.POSS copra.chisel
     "He took his copra chisel." (Daakaka: 0139)

The evaluation of the mood category results in an α score of $\alpha = 0.85$ which can be considered acceptable (cf. Carletta, 1996). This result reveals how efficient the tag set in this category seems to be.

5 Discussion

In this paper, we explored the tagging of TAM categories in corpora of five Oceanic languages with a focus on the modal domain. Selected texts were divided into clause-based annotation units which were then tagged by two annotators based on the previously established tag set. The two versions of the tagged texts were then compared manually in order to identify and resolve mismatches in certain cases. The results of the inter-annotator consistency show that our tag set works especially well in the mood category.

In comparison to more fine-grained distinctions, e.g., as proposed in Rubinstein et al. (2013), the differentiation between the tags `factual`, `counterfactual`, and `possible` seems to be less prone to inter-annotator inconsistencies. Their basic score of $\alpha = 0.49$ in the Modality Type (Rubinstein et al., 2013) was much lower than our overall result ($\alpha = 0.85$). Only when they collapsed priority types (i.e., bouletic, teleological, bouletic/teleological, deontic, and priority) and non-priority types (i.e., epistemic, circumstantial, ability, epistemic/circumstantial, ability/circumstantial), they achieved an α score of 0.89. This indicates that the distinction in more than three levels results in an unreliable annotation compared to a coarse-grained approach.

Our methodology also differs from previous approaches to tagging modality in that we did not identify a specific target set of expressions to label – such as modal auxiliaries and adverbs – but tagged all clauses within a selected set of texts. We believe that this approach is particularly useful for languages that rely more on verb moods such as irrealis and subjunctive, as opposed to lexical expressions such as auxiliaries, for the expression of modality. Depending on the languages and the goals of tagging modality, our tag set may therefore be an interesting alternative to other models.

6 Conclusion

We presented a novel approach for tagging the modal domain in mood-prominent languages (cf. Bhat, 1999) which contributes to a more stable inter-annotator consistency. The overall tag set that we used to annotate the TAM categories exhibits a high percentage of inter-annotator consistency throughout different categories. In addition, our modal tag set has been proven useful for our purposes and provides an alternative to previous distinctions based on modal flavours.

Acknowledgments

We would like to thank three anonymous reviewers for their valuable feedback and suggestions. And we would like to thank the DFG (German Research Foundation) for funding this research (MelaTAMP project, 273640553).

References

D. N. S. Bhat. 1999. *The Prominence of Tense, Aspects, and Mood*. John Benjamins.

Jean Carletta. 1996. Assessing agreement on classification tasks: the kappa statistic. *Computational linguistics*, 22(2):249–254.

Xiaomeng Cui and Ting Chi. 2013. Annotating Modal Expressions in the Chinese Treebank Yanyan.

Stephan Druskat. 2018. ToolboxTextModules (Version 1.1.0).

Michael Franjieh. 2013. *A documentation of North Ambrym, a language of Vanuatu*. SOAS, ELAR., London.

Valérie Guérin. 2006. *Documentation of Mavea*. SOAS, ELAR, London.

Valérie Guérin. 2011. *A grammar of Mav̌ea: An Oceanic language of Vanuatu*. University of Hawai'i Press, Honolulu.

Thomas Krause and Amir Zeldes. 2016. ANNIS3: A new architecture for generic corpus query and visualization. *Digital Scholarship in the Humanities*, 31(1):118–139.

Manfred Krifka. 2013. *Daakie, The Language Archive*. MPI for Psycholinguistics, Nijmegen.

Klaus Krippendorff. 1980. *Content analysis: An introduction to its methodology*. Sage publications.

Geoffrey Leech and Martin Weisser. 2003. Generic speech act annotation for task-oriented dialogues. In *Proceedings of the Corpus Linguistics 2003 conference*, volume 16, Lancaster. Lancaster University.

Frantisek Lichtenberk. 2016. Modality and Mood in Oceanic. In Jan Nuyts and Johan van der Auwera, editors, *The Oxford Handbook of Mood and Modality*, chapter 14, pages 330–361. Oxford University Press, Oxford.

An Van Linden and Jean-Christophe Verstraete. 2008. The nature and origins of counterfactuality in simple clauses: Cross-linguistic evidence. *Journal of Pragmatics*, 40:1865–1895.

Anna Margetts, Andrew Margetts, and Carmen Dawuda. 2017. *Saliba/Logea, The Language Archive*. MPI for Psycholinguistics, Nijmegen.

MelaTAMP. 2017. Primary data repository – MelaTAMP. `https://wikis.hu-berlin.de/melatamp`.

Kilu von Prince. 2019. Counterfactuality and past. *Linguistics and Philosophy*.

Kilu von Prince. 2013a. *Daakaka, The Language Archive*. MPI for Psycholinguistics, Nijmegen.

Kilu von Prince. 2013b. *Dalkalaen, The Language Archive*. MPI for Psycholinguistics, Nijmegen.

Kilu von Prince, Ana Krajinović, Manfred Krifka, Valérie Guérin, and Michael Franjieh. 2018. Mapping Irreality: Storyboards for Eliciting TAM contexts. In *Proceedings of Linguistic Evidence 2018*.

Paulo Quaresma, Amália Mendes, Iris Hendrickx, and Teresa Gonçalves. 2014. Tagging and Labelling Portuguese Modal Verbs. In J. Baptista, N. Mamede, S. Candeias, I. Paraboni, T.A.S. Pardo, and M.G. Volpe Nunes, editors, *Computational Processing of the Portuguese Language*, volume 8775 of *PROPOR 2014. Lecture Notes in Computer Science*, pages 70–81. Springer, Cham.

Aynat Rubinstein, Hillary Harner, Elizabeth Krawczyk, Daniel Simonson, Graham Katz, and Paul Portner. 2013. Toward fine-grained annotation of modality in text. In *Proceedings of IWCS 10, WAMM*, Potsdam.

Nick Thieberger. 2006. *Dictionary and texts in South Efate*. Digital collection managed by PARADISEC.

Douglas P. Twitchell and Jay F. Nunamaker. 2004. Speech act profiling: A probabilistic method for analyzing persistent conversations and their participants. In *37th Annual Hawaii International Conference on System Sciences, 2004. Proceedings of the*, volume 37, pages 1713–1722.

Mark-Matthias Zymla. 2017. Comprehensive annotation of cross-linguistic variation in tense and aspect categories. In *12th International Conference on Computational Semantics*.

Harmonizing Different Lemmatization Strategies for Building a Knowledge Base of Linguistic Resources for Latin

Francesco Mambrini, Marco Passarotti

CIRCSE Research Centre

Università Cattolica del Sacro Cuore

Largo Gemelli, 1 - 20123 Milan, Italy

{francesco.mambrini}{marco.passarotti}@unicatt.it

Abstract

The interoperability between lemmatized corpora of Latin and other resources that use the lemma as indexing key is hampered by the multiple lemmatization strategies that different projects adopt. In this paper we discuss how we tackle the challenges raised by harmonizing different lemmatization criteria in a project that aims to connect linguistic resources for Latin using the Linked Data paradigm. The paper introduces the architecture supporting an open-ended, lemma-based Knowledge Base, built to make textual and lexical resources for Latin interoperable. Particularly, the paper describes the inclusion into the Knowledge Base of its lexical basis, of a word formation lexicon and of a lemmatized and syntactically annotated corpus.

1 Introduction

In spite of the growth in the quantity and coverage of linguistic resources for several languages, the greatest part of these resources are still not interoperable. Lack of interoperability is an issue that severely limits their potential for exploitation and use. Indeed, linking linguistic resources to one another would maximize their contribution to, and use in linguistic analysis at multiple levels, be those lexical, morphological, syntactic, semantic or pragmatic.

Interlinking the tremendous wealth of linguistic (meta)data accumulated in more than half a century of Computational Linguistics and empirical study of language is one of the main challenges of the present time (Chiarcos et al., 2012, p. 1). However, the task is not straightforward, in particular on account of the existence of several different formalisms (e.g. various annotation schemas) or different conceptual models (e.g. different PoS tagsets) that each project may use to represent linguistic data and which are often incompatible between systems (van Erp, 2012, p. 58).

Part-of-Speech (PoS) tagging and lemmatization are key annotation tasks that are often performed to produce empirical data for research on linguist problems, to train stochastic Natural Language Processing (NLP) tools or to support the automatic processing of higher annotation levels (like, for instance, syntactic parsing). Especially for highly inflected languages (like Latin), harmonization of lemmatization and PoS tagging strategies could already promote joint exploitation, querying and interlinking of several available resources (see Section 2). Instead, annotated corpora as well as lexical resources and NLP tools show frequent problems of mismatch (see Section 3.1).

In this paper we discuss how we tackle the challenges raised by harmonizing different lemmatization criteria in the *LiLa: Linking Latin* project, which aims to make resources for Latin interoperable.[1] To this aim, the LiLa project builds a Knowledge Base of linguistic resources based on the Linked Data paradigm, i.e. a collection of several data sets described using the same vocabulary and linked together.[2] In the LiLa Knowledge Base (henceforth LiLa), lemmas are used as a pivotal node in a dense network of linguistic information, making lexical resources, NLP tools and annotated (at least, lemmatized and PoS-tagged) corpora interact. To this end, it is crucial to harmonize the different lemmatization strategies adopted so far in the currently available linguistic resources for Latin.

The LiLa project responds to the growing need in the fields of Classics, Humanities Computing and Computational Linguistics to create an inter-

---

[1] https://lila-erc.eu

[2] See Tim Berners-Lee's note at https://www.w3.org/DesignIssues/LinkedData.html.

Proceedings of the 13th Linguistic Annotation Workshop, pages 71–80

Florence, Italy, August 1, 2019. ©2019 Association for Computational Linguistics

operable ecosystem of resources and NLP tools for Latin. In particular, the work of harmonization of lemmatizations for Latin is motivated by two main reasons that make Latin an optimal use case: (a) the diachrony and diversity of the language present complex challenges for NLP, especially with regard to the portability of the tools across different eras, genres and domains; (b) an interconnected network of the numerous linguistic resources currently available for Latin would greatly support a large and diverse community made of historians, philologists, archaeologists and literary scholars, whose research work is strictly bound to the empirical evidence provided (also) by textual data.

This paper discusses the results of a first attempt to: (a) create and organize a collection of lemmas that would serve as a "hub" point for different resources; (b) link one annotated corpus of Latin texts to it, by solving the different harmonization problems. After providing a brief summary of the linguistic resources currently available for Latin (Section 2), we describe the LiLa Knowledge Base, particularly discussing the harmonization process of the different annotation strategies concerning lemmatization for Latin (Section 3). The inclusion into the Knowledge Base of its fundamental lexical basis, of a word formation lexicon and of a syntactically annotated corpus (a dependency treebank) is described and evaluated in Section 4. Finally, Section 5 discusses a number of open challenges to be addressed by the LiLa project in the near future.

2 Linguistic Resources for Latin

A huge amount of Latin texts is currently available in digital format. Among the most prominent providers and collections of digital texts in Latin are the *Perseus Digital Library* at Tufts University in Boston, MA,[3] the *Open Greek and Latin* project in Leipzig, Germany,[4] the *Laboratoire d'Analyse Statistique des Langues Anciennes* (LASLA) in Liège, Belgium,[5] the *Patrologia Latina* database,[6] the digital archive of Latin poetry *Musisque Deoque*,[7] the collection of Medieval Italian Latinity *ALIM*,[8] and the *Monumenta Germaniae Histor-*

ica.[9]

Despite such a large availability, only a few Latin texts are currently enhanced with linguistic annotation, while most of them still lack any linguistic tagging at all. In particular, three treebanks are currently available for Latin, all featuring also a version included in the *Universal Dependencies* (UD) collection.[10] These are the *Index Thomisticus* Treebank (IT-TB) (Passarotti, 2009), based on the works of Thomas Aquinas, the *Latin Dependency Treebank* (LDT) (Bamman and Crane, 2011), including texts of the Classical era, and the PROIEL corpus (*Pragmatic Resources in Old Indo-European Languages*), which features the syntactic annotation of the oldest extant versions of the New Testament in Indo-European languages and Latin texts of both the Classical and Late eras (Haug and Jøhndal, 2008). The size of these treebanks is presently around 350,000 annotated words for the IT-TB, 55,000 for the LDT and 200,000 for the Latin section of the PROIEL corpus.

In regards to Latin digital lexical resources, many Latin dictionaries and lexica are today available in digital format. Some of the most important are the Lewis-Short dictionary available at Perseus, the *Thesaurus Linguae Latinae* by the Bayerische Akademie der Wissenschaften in Munich,[11] and the *Neulateinische Wortliste* by Johann Ramminger.[12]

The availability of Latin treebanks made it possible to induce subcategorization lexica from the IT-TB (*IT-VaLex*) (McGillivray and Passarotti, 2009) and from the LDT (*VaLex*) (McGillivray, 2013). *Latin Vallex* is a recently created lexical resource for Latin consisting in a semantic-based valency lexicon built in conjunction with the semantic and pragmatic annotation of the IT-TB and the LDT (Passarotti et al., 2016). Presently, *Latin Vallex* includes around 1,350 lexical entries.

The *Latin WordNet* (LWN) (Minozzi, 2010) was built in the context of the *MultiWordNet* project (Pianta et al., 2002), whose aim was to build a number of semantic networks for specific languages aligned with the synsets of the Princeton WordNet (PWN) (Fellbaum, 2012). The language-specific synsets were built by importing

[3]http://www.perseus.tufts.edu/hopper/
[4]https://www.dh.uni-leipzig.de/wo/ projects/open-greek-and-latin-project/
[5]http://web.philo.ulg.ac.be/lasla/
[6]http://pld.chadwyck.com/
[7]http://www.mqdq.it/
[8]http://www.alim.dfll.univr.it/

[9]http://www.dmgh.de/
[10]https://universaldependencies.org/
[11]http://www.thesaurus.badw.de/
[12]http://www.lrz-muenchen.de/ ~ramminger/

the semantic relations among the synsets for English provided by the PWN. At the moment, the LWN includes 8,973 synsets and 9,124 lemmas.

The recently built *Word Formation Latin* (WFL) lexicon (Litta et al., 2016) describes the Latin lexicon in terms of derivational morphology, by connecting lemmas via word formation rules.[13] For instance, the noun *amator*, "lover" is connected to the verb *amo*, "to love" via a rule that derives nouns from verbs by adding the agentive/instrumental suffix *-tor*.

The LiLa project wants to maximize the use of these (and other) resources for Latin by making them interoperable, thus allowing to run queries across linked and distributed resources, for instance making it possible to search in the three Latin treebanks all the occurrences of verbs featuring a specific (a) dependency relation (source: treebanks), (b) prefix (source: WFL) and (c) valency frame (source: Latin Vallex), and (d) belonging to a particular WordNet synset (source: LWN).

3 The LiLa Knowledge Base

In this section we present the first steps undertaken in order to structure the information of the Latin linguistic resources (and, then, NLP tools) in a centralized architecture representing the backbone of the LiLa Knowledge Base.

In order to achieve interoperability between distributed resources and tools, LiLa makes use of a set of Semantic Web and Linked Data standards and practices. These include ontologies to describe linguistic annotation (*OLiA*, Chiarcos and Sukhareva (2015)), corpus annotation (*NLP Interchange Format* (NIF), Hellmann et al. (2013); *CoNLL-RDF*, Chiarcos and Fäth (2017)) and lexical resources (*Lemon*, Buitelaar et al. (2011); *Ontolex*[14]). Furthermore, following Bird and Liberman (2001), the *Resource Description Framework* (RDF) (Lassila et al., 1998) is used to encode graph-based data structures to represent linguistic annotations in terms of triples: (1) a predicate-property (a relation; in graph terms: a labeled edge) that connects (2) a subject (a resource; in graph terms: a labeled node) with (3) its object (another resource, or a literal, e.g. a string). The SPARQL language is used to query the data recorded in the form of RDF triples

(Prud'Hommeaux et al., 2008).

By applying the principles of Linked Data to linguistic resources, "it is possible to follow links between existing resources to find other, related data and exploit network effects" (Chiarcos et al., 2013, p. iii). The *Linguistic Linked Open Data cloud* (LLOD) is a good example of a set of linked linguistic resources.[15]

Publishing linguistic resources using Linked Data allows existing resources to be connected, thereby creating a web of linguistic data, which supports complex querying across different and distributed resources. Consequently, Linked Data is at the core of recent research efforts in linguistics, like the *Open Linguistic Working Group* (OLWG).[16] Moreover, applying the Linked Data paradigm to linguistic data enables to connect linguistics to other disciplines and, ultimately, to the world. As a matter of fact, Linked Data has achieved success in a wide variety of domains, like geography (Goodwin et al., 2008), biomedicine (Ashburner et al., 2000) and government data.[17]

3.1 Linking Through Lemmatization

Like for many languages, modern and early-modern Latin dictionaries index each lexical entry using a canonical form known as the lemma. Selecting the canonical forms is a fundamental annotation step, which tends to follow a standardized series of conventions (e.g. the form in nominative singular for nouns, or the first person of present tense for verbs). Thesauri, including the most modern ones like the LWN, organize the lexicon by collecting all related entries, and use the canonical form to index them; so, for instance, the synset n#07202206 of the LWN, glossed as "a female human offspring", includes the nouns with lemmas: *filia*, "daughter", *nata*, "daughter" and *puella*, "girl". Similarly, other resources, like word formation based or valency lexica, use lemmas to group together entries that share certain features, like derivative morphemes or valency arguments.

Lemmas are also used to enable lexical search in corpora, given the very rich inflectional morphology of Latin; a regular Latin verb, for instance, can have up to 130 forms (not including the nominal inflection of the participles or gerundives), with

---

[13]https://github.com/CIRCSE/WFL
[14]https://www.w3.org/community/ontolex/
[15]http://linguistic-lod.org/llod-cloud
[16]http://linguistics.okfn.org
[17]https://data.gov.uk/

varying endings and, at times, different stems. Although the task of lemmatization is far from trivial just because of such rich morphology, the most accurate lemmatizers of Latin achieve an accuracy up to 95.30 (Eger et al., 2015). However, such quite high rate for automatic lemmatization of Latin must be considered carefully. Indeed, performances of stochastic NLP tools depend heavily on the training set which their models are built on, thus decreasing when they are applied to out-of-domain texts. This problem is particularly hard when Latin is concerned, because Latin texts show an enormous diversity resulting from (a) a wide time span (covering more than two millennia), (b) a large variety of genres (ranging from literary to philosophical, historical and documentary texts) and (c) a diatopic spread all over Europe (and beyond).

LiLa is highly lexically-based, grounding on a simple, but effective assumption that allows a good balance between feasibility and granularity: textual resources are made of (occurrences of) words, lexical resources describe properties of words, and NLP tools process words. Particularly, the level of lemma is considered the ideal interface between the lexical resources (dictionaries, thesauri and lexica), annotated corpora and NLP tools that lemmatize their input text. For this reason, we have identified the collection of canonical forms of Latin as the core of LiLa. Interoperability can be achieved by linking all entries in lexical resources and corpus tokens that refer to the same lemma.

The task of building and organizing a repository of canonical forms that may serve as a hub in this architecture is, however, complicated by the fact that different corpora, lexica or tools for Latin may adopt different strategies to solve conceptual and linguistic challenges posed by lemmatization. These include:

- different citation forms for the same word, resulting from alternation in (a) the graphical representation (*voluptas* vs. *uoluptas*, "satisfaction"), (b) the spelling (*sulphur* vs. *sulfur*, "brimstone"), (c) the ending (*diameter* vs. *diametros* vs. *diametrus*, "diameter") or (d) the paradigmatic slot representing the lemma (*sequor*, "to follow", first person singular of the passive/deponent present indicative vs. *sequo*, first person singular of the active present indicative);

- the existence of homographic lemmas, like *occido* (*occīdo* < *ob* + *caedo*, "to strike down") vs. *occido* (*occĭdo* < *ob* + *cado*, "to fall down");

- ambiguity in choosing the lemma: certain forms, such as participles or deadjectival adverbs, can be considered either part of the inflectional paradigm of verbs or adjectives, or independent lemmas provided with an autonomous entry in lexical resources;

- polythematic words, for which missing forms are taken from other stems, like *melior* used as comparative of *bonus* (see En. "good" and "better").

When dealing with homographs, corpora may choose to index the different entries, but most of the times the string of the lemma is not disambiguated. Participles can either be lemmatized always under the main verb, or have a dedicated participial lemma, which in turn may be used systematically or only when the participle has grown into an autonomous lexical item (e.g. *doctus*, "learned", morphologically the past participle of *doceo*, "to teach"). Deadjectival adverbs (e.g. *aequaliter*, "evenly" from *aequalis*, "equal") or peculiar forms such as comparatives (both regular and irregular) are sometimes subsumed under the (positive degree of the) adjective, or given a self-standing lemma.

3.2 Lemmas and Forms. Towards an Ontology of Latin Canonical Forms

Given the challenges and the degree of variation raised by different lemmatization strategies for Latin, our approach in LiLa is to be as descriptive and inclusive as possible: our aim is rather to collect as many word forms as may be used for lemmatization and attempt to model their relations. In order to do that, LiLa builds upon a series of ontologies for lexical resources to describe the word forms used in lemmatization, and use the *Web Ontology Language* (OWL) (McGuinness et al., 2004) in order to model the relations between them.

Building upon the Ontolex ontology, we define a Lemma as a Form of a word. In this way, lexical resources compiled using the Ontolex or Lemon formalism can already be connected to our collection. Forms have one or more written representations and are linked to one or more PoS. PoS are linked to the appropriate OLiA concepts, and we plan to represent the most widespread tagsets used in Latin PoS-tagging via dedicated OLiA ontologies.

Relations between the lemma and the other forms of the same word are defined horizontally, i.e. via direct relations between forms. Although the architecture is ready to accommodate all the inflected forms of a lexical item that are either attested in a text or morphologically possible, we are currently populating it only with those forms that are potentially used as lemmas, to create the collection of canonical forms representing the core of LiLa. The fundamental list of Latin lemmas used in the Knowledge Base is taken from the one provided by the Latin morphological analyzer Lemlat (Passarotti et al., 2017).[18] In particular, following the practice of Lemlat, we define a special subclass of lemmas, called "hypolemmas", to harmonize different strategies for the lemmatization of participles. Hypolemmas are defined as forms of the inflectional paradigm of a word that may be used in annotated corpora or by NLP tools to lemmatize certain forms instead of the main lemma. Namely, these are the nominal inflected forms of verbal paradigms (participles, gerunds, gerundives, supines). Currently, we generated hypolemmas for all the canonical forms of present, future and perfect participles of all verbs in Lemlat, and connected them with their main (verbal) lemma via a subclass of the property "Form variant" defined by the Lemon ontology.[19] Thus, for instance, the present participle *subsistens*, "taking a stand" is hypolemma of the main lemma *subsisto*, "to take a stand". The same subclass is used also for alternative paradigmatic slots representing the lemma.

Alternations in spelling and ending are managed as different written representations of the same lemma, while systematic graphical variations (e.g. *u/v*) are preprocessed automatically.

4 Populating the LiLa Knowledge Base

In this section we present the current status of the LiLa Knowledge Base obtained by (a) including the lemma collection taken from Lemlat and (b) linking one lexical resource and one treebank, using the principles discussed in the previous Sec-

tion.

The data and resources currently linked in LiLa are stored in a triple store using the Jena framework;[20] the Fuseki component exposes the data as SPARQL end-point accessible over HTTP.[21]

4.1 The Lemma Collection

As mentioned, our database of canonical forms is built on top on the lemma collection used by Lemlat. Lemlat relies on a lexical basis resulting from the collation of three Latin dictionaries (Georges and Georges, 1913–1918; Glare, 1982; Gradenwitz, 1904) for a total of 40,014 lexical entries and 43,432 lemmas, as more than one lemma can be included in one lexical entry. This lexical basis was recently enlarged by adding most of the *Onomasticon* (26,415 lemmas out of 28,178) provided by the 5th edition of the Forcellini dictionary (Budassi and Passarotti, 2016) and the entries from a large reference glossary for Medieval Latin, namely the *Glossarium Mediae et Infimae Latinitatis* (du Cange et al., 1883–1887; Cecchini et al., 2018).

In Lemlat, lemmas are annotated with up to two PoS tags expressed using the Universal PoS tagset adopted in UD (Petrov et al., 2011), as well as with other information such as the grammatical gender for nouns and the inflectional class for verbs, adjectives and nouns. While the linking between the Universal PoS tags and OLiA is already in place, the process of aligning the other morphological features is in progress.

4.2 Lexical Resources. The Word Formation Latin Lexicon

The WFL lexicon is strictly bound to Lemlat, as it enhances its lexical basis with information on derivational morphology.

The information provided by WFL can be readily linked to the lemma collection of LiLa. In the Knowledge Base, each Lemma is connected to a series of Morphemes, including at least a Lexical Base, and possibly Prefixes and Suffixes. This conceptualization yields a network representation of the morphological derivation of Latin words, where lemmas belonging to the same word formation family are linked to the same Lexical Base, which in LiLa is not assigned any written representation and functions just as a connector of the

---

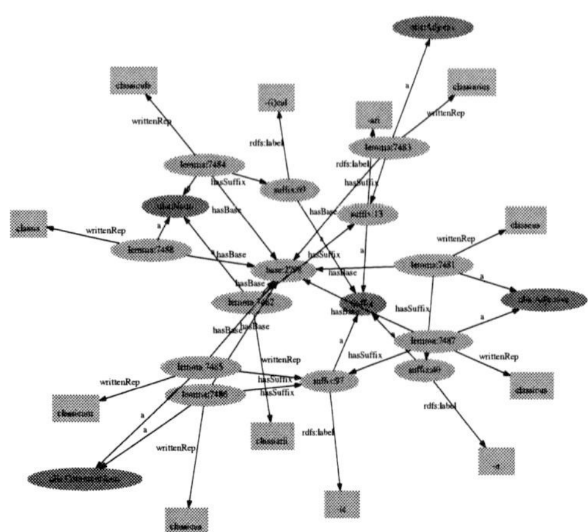

Figure 1: The word formation family including *classis* and *classicus*, with lemmas and suffixes.

lemmas of the same family; words derived with the same affixe(s) can also be readily retrieved.

Figure 1 shows a word formation family, i.e. a set of lemmas connected to a common lexical base. The family includes, among others, lemmas like noun *classis*, "class/division", and adjective *classicus*, "of the fleet/classic", the latter being derived with suffix *-ic*. By following the links to suffix 97, labelled "-ic", it would be possible to retrieve all the other lemmas that are formed with that morpheme, like for instance *ethicus*, "ethic".

4.3 Textual Resources. The PROIEL Treebank

Lemmatized Latin corpora, regardless of genre, date or provenance, are already fit to be linked to LiLa. As a preliminary experiment, we integrated one of the largest and most diverse annotated corpora of Latin, the PROIEL treebank, focusing on the version distributed in UD release 2.3. With the help of the CoNLL-RDF application, we generated an RDF graph out of the treebank, where the main nodes are the corpus tokens and sentences, as defined in NIF. Most annotations recorded in the corpus file are expressed as data attributes (strings) of the nodes, while some information (PoS, syntactic annotation) is recorded as edges between nodes.

Figure 2 gives a (simplified) representation of the nodes and relations attached to a single token in our architecture. The word *inferni* ("hell", genitive singular) from Jerome's *Vulgate* (*Revelation*

1.18) is part of sentence `proiel:s17835_0`[22] and is governed in the UD tree by the word `proiel:s17835_4` (see the attribute HEAD) via the UD relation "conj" ("conjunct"; EDGE).[23]

Although LiLa is a lexically-based resource, it integrates information about sentences if they are available in the original corpus, i.e. if the corpus, as treebanks are, is split into sentences. In this way, users have the opportunity to use also the sentence boundaries as context information for their research.

The word shares the same string in the LEMMA attribute with the written representation of one Lemma object in LiLa (`lemma:20369`; written representation: *infernus*); the two nodes point also to the same PoS concept from the OLiA ontology (CommonNoun). In this case, the token can be straightforwardly and unambiguously matched to the lemma, so that all the lexical information (currently, the links to derivational morphemes) attached to it becomes retrievable.

The figure reproduces three other lemmas that are attached to the same lexical base with id `639` (*infernalis*, "nether" and *inferiae*, "sacrifices to the dead") and the same suffix (*arcanus*, "hidden, secret") of our target word *infernus*. *Arcanus* is in fact built from the stem of *arca* ("coffin", not reported in the Figure, but retrievable following the edges) via the same suffix *-n* that produces *infernus* from *inferus* ("lower"). All this information is taken from the WFL lexicon; the image illustrates how the network of connections in LiLa can be leveraged to move from the level of lexicon to corpora and vice versa, in order to extract complex linguistic information from distributed resources. Note, therefore, that Figure 2 incorporates the type of information represented in Figure 1, although only a part of the dense network of connections can be displayed here.

4.4 Evaluation of Lemma Matching

Table 1 reports the results of our matching between the strings used in PROIEL to lemmatize the tokens and the Lemma objects in LiLa.

The PROIEL UD 2.3 corpus includes 18,400 sentences and 199,958 tokens; in total, the corpus uses 8,536 different strings (i.e. lemmas) to lemmatize them. 5,806 out of these, corresponding

---

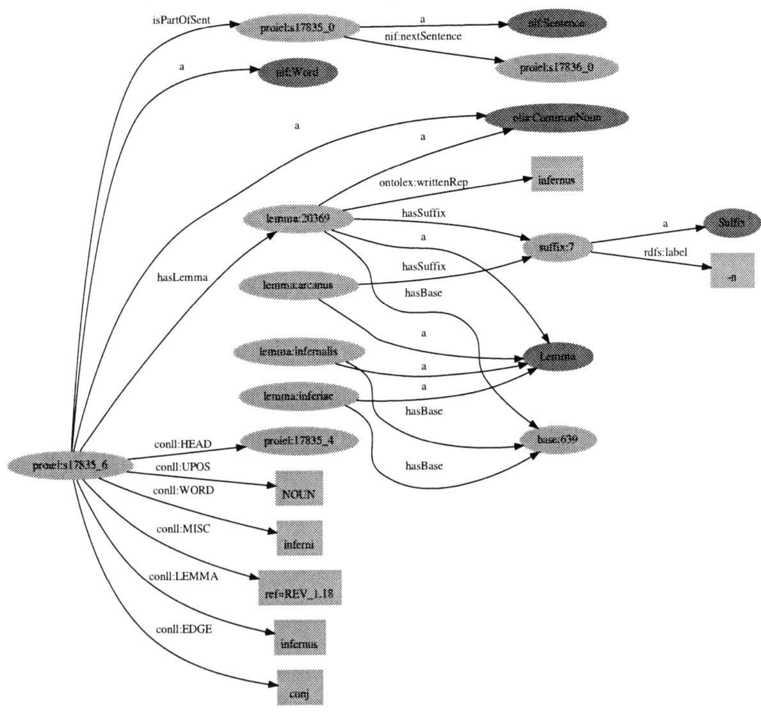

Figure 2: A token from the PROIEL UD 2.3 treebank linked to the LiLa Knowledge Base.

Type of Match	Nr. Tokens	Nr. Lemmas
String match	162,998	5,806
PoS disambig.	6,262	209
Hypolemmas	1,026	152
Onomasticon	7,252	974
Multiple matches	11,865	242
No match	10,555	1,164

Table 1: Matching scores between corpus tokens and Lemmas in the LiLa Knowledge Base.

to 162,998 tokens (81.52%), were matched unambiguously to a lemma in LiLa through a simple string comparison between the written representation of the lemma in the Knowledge Base and the PROIEL string.[24]

For 6,262 additional tokens, a single match was obtained by using the PoS tag to disambiguate between possible candidates. This is the case of the match illustrated in Figure 2, as the string *infernus*

---

[24]It might be the case that simple string comparison leads to wrong connections. This can happen when a lemma provided by a corpus is not present in the lexical basis of LiLa and it is homographic to one of the lemmas there included. However, we have not found such a case so far in our data.

can point either to an adjective ("lower") or, as it is for the token in the Figure, to a noun ("hell"). Simple match and PoS-driven disambiguation cover together 84.64% of the PROIEL tokens.

This workflow of using PoS tags to disambiguate the greedy match of simple-string comparison is more productive than comparing tuples of string and PoS tag from the onset. For the use of tagsets of different granularity or strategy might result in loss of connection even for tokens that could be unambiguously matched. For instance, the lemma *ille* (demonstrative "that"), which occurs with a frequency of 109.62 per 10k words in PROIEL, can be matched to a single Lemma using string comparison. However, while the Lemma is tagged only as an Adjective in our collection, it is annotated as Determiner in 445 cases (vs. Adjective 1,747) in PROIEL. Those 445 tokens would not be matched if we used the tuple comparison.

After PoS-driven disambiguation, 11,865 tokens (about 6% of the total) remain associated with more than one Lemma in LiLa (with a maximum of 4 links for 5 tokens). In several cases, this is due to actual ambiguity: some high-frequency lemmas admit multiple interpretations, even after PoS-driven disambiguation. For instance, the string *dico* (120.86 per 10k tokens in PROIEL) can be matched to two different entries with PoS Verb (one corresponding to a verb with infinitive *dicere*, "to say", the other with infinitive *dicare*, "to dedicate"), as does *tempus* (14.60 per 10k), which can be reduced to two different nouns with the same inflection (one meaning "time", the other "temple").

In the case of *omnis*, "all/every" (87.42 per 10k tokens), the multiple links point to an error in the Knowledge Base inherited from the Lemlat database: the lemma was wrongly duplicated and one of the entries must be deleted. Mismatches or multiple matches can thus provide a useful testbed to diagnose problems in the architecture.

Although the lemma collection of LiLa does not currently include the named entites of the Forcellini's Onomasticon provided by Lemlat, 7,252 proper names in PROIEL can be matched unambiguously to one entry in the Forcellini dictionary (see Section 5).

Unresolved mismatches (10,555 tokens) are due to different factors. Tokenization of the enclitic -*que*, "and" in PROIEL produces a lemma which is very frequent (86.97 per 10k words), but not yet present in LiLa (as Lemlat presupposes a different tokenization). Deadjectival adverbs (e.g. *vehementer*, "violently") are treated as lemmas in PROIEL, but reduced to their base adjective by Lemlat (e.g. *vehemens*, "violent"), so that no lemma like *vehementer* exists yet in LiLa. Deadjectival adverbs used as lemmas cover about 1,300 tokens in PROIEL. Named entities missing in the Onomasticon (e.g. *Iudaei*, "the Jewish people"), strings written with diacritics in PROIEL (e.g. *appr(eh)endo*, "to seize", corresponding to two written representations: *apprehendo* and *apprendo*), numerals and non-Latin expressions (e.g. the string: "Greek expression", used to lemmatize Greek words) also affect the matching.

5 Conclusions and Future Work

In this paper, we have introduced the fundamental components (and their relations) of a Knowledge Base, called LiLa, built to make linguistic resources for Latin interoperable according to the Linked Data paradigm.

As LiLa is highly lexically-based, we have discussed some issues concerning the repository of Latin lemmas that we have included so far therin, particularly focusing on some challenges raised by lemmatization. Indeed, one of the main tasks of LiLa is harmonizing between different strategies of linguistic annotation, namely lemmatization and PoS tagging, which currently still affects the interoperability between different annotated corpora (not only for Latin). Furthermore, we have described the inclusion in the Knowledge Base of a lexical resource (WFL) and of a treebank (PROIEL).

The LiLa project started in June 2018 and has a duration of five years. Thus, there are several open issues to address. Some of the most urgent and related to this paper are mentioned in what follows.

Given the central role played by the object Lemma in the Knowledge Base, one challenge of the project is building an efficient strategy for automatic PoS tagging and lemmatization of the (many) corpora of Latin texts still missing this level of linguistic annotation. Indeed, if connecting raw textual data to LiLa still remains possible (limiting interoperability at the level of tokens), the real added value results from exploiting the connecting power of the Lemma object in the Knowledge Base. We are now testing the already available tools and trained models on Latin texts of different eras and genres, to evaluate how much the application of these tools and models to out-of-domain texts affects their accuracy.

As mentioned, since Lemlat lemmatizes deadjectival adverbs under the adjective they are derived from, these are missing from the list of lemmas we populated LiLa with so far. However, generating all morphologically possible deadjectival adverbs from Lemlat is straightforward. Once generated, these will be included in the Knowledge Base as lemmas.

In the near future, we also plan to extend the lemma collection of LiLa with the lemmas provided by the Onomasticon of the Forcellini dictionary, as well with those by the du Cange glossary. Another short time goal is including the LWN as a key resource to support semantic-based search.

Our hope is that LiLa will help to foster the exploitation and accessibility of linguistic resources for Latin, enlarging the number of their users and impacting the diverse scholarly community concerned. Thanks to its open-ended nature, LiLa aims to become the main venue where publishing linguistic resources and, more generally, digital objects concerning the Latin cultural heritage.

Acknowledgments

We gratefully acknowledge the support of the project *LiLa* (*Linking Latin. Building a Knowledge Base of Linguistic Resources for Latin*). This project has received funding from the European Research Council (ERC) under the European Union's Horizon 2020 research and innovation programme - Grant Agreement No 769994.

References

Michael Ashburner, Catherine A Ball, Judith A Blake, David Botstein, Heather Butler, J Michael Cherry, Allan P Davis, Kara Dolinski, Selina S Dwight, Janan T Eppig, et al. 2000. Gene ontology: tool for the unification of biology. *Nature genetics*, 25(1):25.

David Bamman and Gregory Crane. 2011. The ancient greek and latin dependency treebanks. In *Language technology for cultural heritage*, pages 79–98. Springer.

Steven Bird and Mark Liberman. 2001. A formal framework for linguistic annotation. *Speech communication*, 33(1-2):23–60.

Marco Budassi and Marco Passarotti. 2016. Nomen omen. Enhancing the Latin morphological analyser Lemlat with an onomasticon. In *Proceedings of the 10th SIGHUM Workshop on Language Technology for Cultural Heritage, Social Sciences, and Humanities (LaTeCH)*, pages 90–94, Berlin, Germany. Association for Computational Linguistics.

Paul Buitelaar, Philipp Cimiano, John McCrae, Elena Montiel-Ponsoda, and Thierry Declerck. 2011. Ontology lexicalisation: The lemon perspective. In *Proceedings of the Workshops. 9th International Conference on Terminology and Artificial Intelligence*, pages 33–36.

Flavio Cecchini, Marco Passarotti, Paolo Ruffolo, Marinella Testori, Lia Draetta, Martina Fieromonte, Annarita Liano, Costanza Marini, and Giovanni Piantanida. 2018. Enhancing the latin morphological analyser lemlat with a medieval latin glossary. In *Proceedings of the Fifth Italian Conference on Computational Linguistics (CLiC-it 2018). 10-12 December 2018, Torino*, pages 87–92.

Christian Chiarcos, Philipp Cimiano, Thierry Declerck, and John P McCrae. 2013. Linguistic linked open data (llod). introduction and overview. In *Proceedings of the 2nd Workshop on Linked Data in Linguistics (LDL-2013): Representing and linking lexicons, terminologies and other language data*, pages i–xi.

Christian Chiarcos and Christian Fäth. 2017. CoNLL-RDF: Linked Corpora Done in an NLP-Friendly Way. In *Language, Data, and Knowledge*, pages 74–88, Cham. Springer International Publishing.

Christian Chiarcos, Sebastian Hellmann, and Sebastian Nordhoff. 2012. Introduction and overview. In *Linked Data in Linguistics*, pages 1–12. Springer.

Christian Chiarcos and Maria Sukhareva. 2015. OLiA - Ontologies of Linguistic Annotation. *Semantic Web Journal*, 6(4):379–386.

Charles du Fresne du Cange, Bénédictins de Saint-Maur, Pierre Carpentier, Louis Henschel, and Léopold Favre. 1883–1887. *Glossarium mediae et infimae latinitatis*. Niort, France.

Steffen Eger, Tim vor der Brück, and Alexander Mehler. 2015. Lexicon-assisted tagging and lemmatization in latin: A comparison of six taggers and two lemmatization methods. In *Proceedings of the 9th SIGHUM Workshop on Language Technology for Cultural Heritage, Social Sciences, and Humanities (LaTeCH)*, pages 105–113.

Marieke van Erp. 2012. Reusing linguistic resources: Tasks and goals for a linked data approach. In *Linked Data in Linguistics*, pages 57–64. Springer.

Christiane Fellbaum. 2012. Wordnet. *The Encyclopedia of Applied Linguistics*.

Karl Ernst Georges and Heinrich Georges. 1913–1918. *Ausführliches lateinisch-deutsches Handwörterbuch*. Hahn, Hannover, Germany.

Peter GW Glare. 1982. *Oxford Latin dictionary*. Clarendon Press. Oxford University Press, Oxford, UK.

John Goodwin, Catherine Dolbear, and Glen Hart. 2008. Geographical linked data: The administrative geography of great britain on the semantic web. *Transactions in GIS*, 12:19–30.

Otto Gradenwitz. 1904. *Laterculi Vocum Latinarum: voces Latinas et a fronte et a tergo ordinandas*. Hirzel, Leipzig, Germany.

Dag TT Haug and Marius Jøhndal. 2008. Creating a parallel treebank of the old indo-european bible translations. In *Proceedings of the Second Workshop on Language Technology for Cultural Heritage Data (LaTeCH 2008)*, pages 27–34.

Sebastian Hellmann, Jens Lehmann, Sören Auer, and Martin Brümmer. 2013. Integrating NLP using Linked Data. In *12th International Semantic Web Conference, Sydney, Australia, October 21-25, 2013*.

Ora Lassila, Ralph R. Swick, World Wide, and Web Consortium. 1998. Resource description framework (rdf) model and syntax specification.

Eleonora Litta, Marco Passarotti, and Chris Culy. 2016. Formatio formosa est. building a word formation lexicon for latin. In *Proceedings of the third italian conference on computational linguistics (clic–it 2016)*, pages 185–189.

Barbara McGillivray. 2013. *Methods in Latin computational linguistics*. Brill.

Barbara McGillivray and Marco Passarotti. 2009. The development of the "index thomisticus" treebank valency lexicon. In *Proceedings of the EACL 2009 Workshop on Language Technology and Resources for Cultural Heritage, Social Sciences, Humanities, and Education (LaTeCH–SHELT&R 2009)*, pages 43–50.

Deborah L McGuinness, Frank Van Harmelen, et al. 2004. Owl web ontology language overview. *W3C recommendation*, 10(10):2004.

Stefano Minozzi. 2010. The latin wordnet project. In *Latin Linguistics Today. Latin Linguistics Today. Akten des 15. Internationalen Kolloquiums zur Lateinischen Linguistik*, pages 707–716.

Marco Passarotti. 2009. Theory and practice of corpus annotation in the index thomisticus treebank. *Lexis*, 27(A):5–23.

Marco Passarotti, Marco Budassi, Eleonora Litta, and Paolo Ruffolo. 2017. The lemlat 3.0 package for morphological analysis of latin. In *Proceedings of the NoDaLiDa 2017 Workshop on Processing Historical Language*, 133, pages 24–31. Linköping University Electronic Press.

Marco Passarotti, Berta González Saavedra, and Christophe Onambele. 2016. Latin vallex. a treebank-based semantic valency lexicon for latin. In *LREC*.

Slav Petrov, Dipanjan Das, and Ryan McDonald. 2011. A universal part-of-speech tagset. *arXiv preprint arXiv:1104.2086*.

Emanuele Pianta, Luisa Bentivogli, and Christian Girardi. 2002. Multiwordnet: developing an aligned multilingual database. In *First international conference on global WordNet*, pages 293–302.

Eric Prud'Hommeaux, Andy Seaborne, et al. 2008. Sparql query language for rdf. w3c. *Internet: https://www.w3.org/TR/rdf-sparql-query/[Accessed on February 27th, 2019]*.

Assessing Back-Translation as a Corpus Generation Strategy for non-English Tasks: A Study in Reading Comprehension and Word Sense Disambiguation

Fabricio Monsalve[✠][∗] **Kervy Rivas-Rojas**[✠][∗]
Marco Antonio Sobrevilla Cabezudo[♣] **Arturo Oncevay**[◇♠]

[✠] Artificial Intelligence Research Group, Pontificia Universidad Católica del Perú
[♣] Instituto de Ciências Matemáticas e de Computação, Universidade de São Paulo
[♠] School of Informatics, University of Edinburgh
f.monsalve@pucp.edu.pe, k.rivas@pucp.pe

Abstract

Corpora curated by experts have sustained Natural Language Processing mainly in English, but the expensiveness of corpora creation is a barrier for the development in further languages. Thus, we propose a corpus generation strategy that only requires a machine translation system between English and the target language in both directions, where we filter the best translations by computing automatic translation metrics and the task performance score. By studying Reading Comprehension in Spanish and Word Sense Disambiguation in Portuguese, we identified that a more quality-oriented metric has high potential in the corpora selection without degrading the task performance. We conclude that it is possible to systematise the building of quality corpora using machine translation and automatic metrics, besides some prior effort to clean and process the data.

1 Introduction

Available data has allowed a steady improvement in Natural Language Processing (NLP) tasks for English. Nevertheless, English is not the broadest native language spoken in the world. According to Ethnologue (Simons and Fenning, 2019), English ranks third, behind Chinese (Mandarin) and Spanish, and is only one of the approximately 7000 currently spoken languages. The relevance of English as the academically universal language has allowed its growth in computational linguistic resources. Even in languages with a large number of speakers, such as Spanish, it is difficult to find specific NLP tools that match the quality and performance as in English. If we want to replicate the development of state-of-the-art models for other languages, we would need large and high-quality

corpora analogous to the English ones, and their creation cost would be prohibitive.

In this context, there is a very compelling tool that has reached several languages in commercial systems: Machine Translation (MT). However, it is worth noting that MT works for language-pairs, and therefore, most of the commercial MT tools have obtained excellent results mostly with English as the source or target language. Thus, we still need English in search of robust NLP tools, but at least there is potential for obtaining new data for new languages using high-quality MT systems. As other studies have been focusing on (see §2), we can translate task-specific corpora from English to other languages to leverage an NLP tool without the need of experts in the target language.

Under those circumstances, the next question arises: how can we guarantee the quality of the new corpus by using automatic translations and without recurring to manual validation? Previous work used quality estimation metrics from machine translation, mostly BLEU (Papineni et al., 2002), by applying back-translation and performing the quality evaluation in English. However, we are concerned about the deficiency of using only BLEU as a measurement of a correct translation (Callison-Burch et al., 2006) or text generation in general (Novikova et al., 2017), and currently there are other proposed metrics to cover the correlation gap between BLEU and a human assessment (Denkowski and Lavie, 2014; Fomicheva et al., 2016, among others). Therefore, we believe there is space for improvement in the quality assessment of a back-translation application to the generation of new corpora.

Our study and contribution are not focused in obtaining state-of-the-art results for new languages, but to obtain a new quality corpus that could be used to build state-of-the-art models, such as deep neural networks (Sutskever et al.,

---

[∗]Equal contribution

Proceedings of the 13th Linguistic Annotation Workshop, pages 81–89
Florence, Italy, August 1, 2019. ©2019 Association for Computational Linguistics

2014), in new languages. However, we also managed to surpass previous methods on the target languages in monolingual scenarios.

More details about related works are described in §2. Then, we present our methodology for corpus generation in §3, where we also introduce our case studies in Word Sense Disambiguation for Portuguese and Reading Comprehension for Spanish. Furthermore, §4 contains an extrinsic evaluation of the corpora in their respective task. Also, we make publicly available specific code and guidelines to build the new corpora from the original sources[1]. The obtained results enlightens a potential systematisation of new corpora generation for many language-related tasks and opens further work on generalisation and truly low-resource settings.

2 Background

Several strategies have been applied to build corpora for different tasks in non-English languages and, thus, to reduce the manual work. Mainly, Machine Translation-based approaches had succeeded in obtaining annotated corpora. A key point to highlight is that results from this approach depend on the availability of an MT system, the quality of the acquired translations, and the precision of the alignments between the two languages (English and non-English).

Jabaian et al. (2011) focused on applying a Phrase-based MT (PBMT) system to deal with the language portability of dialogue systems, whereas Klinger and Cimiano (2015) focused on using PBMT and some quality estimation measures to select the best translations which make up the corpus for the task of Sentiment Analysis. Also, Koehn et al. (2018) reports other works related to corpora selection but for a shared task of parallel corpora filtering, to train better machine translation with fewer noisy data.

Furthermore, back-translation strategies have emerged to improve the quality of corpus in a target language (a non-English language). Misu et al. (2012) used back-translation results to verify whether the translation keeps the semantic meaning of the original sentence in a Spoken Language Understanding System, and they also disregarded BLEU as a good quality measure. Besides, Gaspers et al. (2018) considered metrics from alignments, machine translation and language model as a measure of MT quality, independent of the Natural Language Understanding tasks and, thus, select the best sentences to incorporate into the corpus. Finally, Asai et al. (2018) explored Neural MT models to build a Reading Comprehension model for Japanese and French using English as a source. They consider back-translation as their baseline, and they build a multi-lingual model to assess the task. Our motivation differs from them, as we want to generate large quality corpora that help to build monolingual systems, which can achieve great state-of-the-art results, alike for English.

Previous studies show that translating, automatically measuring the translation, and selecting the best samples are not entirely innovative procedures. However, we want to achieve a systematisation for this procedure and look for general-purpose steps disregarding the NLP task and the language. Next section develops our idea.

3 Methodology

We introduce our strategy on back-translation and automatic assessment in a general overview. Then, we extend details specifically for our two case studies: Word Sense Disambiguation and Reading Comprehension. The procedure for the corpus generation and the evaluation (§4) is summarised in Figure 1.

3.1 Back-Translation Strategy

Our goal, similar to previous studies (Misu et al., 2012; Gaspers et al., 2018), is to choose the best translations from an automatically translated corpus to train a robust NLP model. For the following description, we consider English as our source language, whereas the target language could be anyone with an MT system available in both directions with English.

If we take a corpus for any task in English NLP and translate it to a new language, we are not going to be able to measure the translation quality in the target language itself due to the lack of a reference translation. Therefore, we automatically translate the text back to English (back-translation[2]) to measure if the semantic information of the source is retained after the process of two automatic translations. For that purpose, we consider that only

---

[1] https://github.com/iapucp/backcorp

[2] The term has been proposed by Sennrich et al. (2016) in MT, to provide monolingual training data by automatically translate a target sentence into the source language.

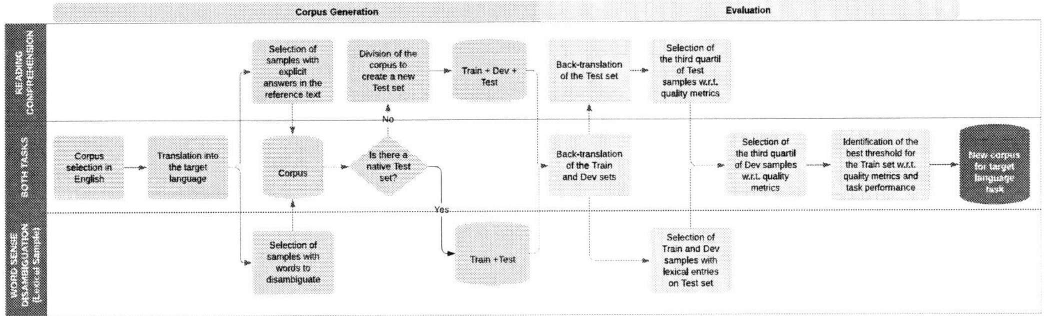

Figure 1: Work-flow of the back-translation strategy with automatic assessment for the generation of corpora for tasks in new languages. We divide general and task-specific steps, as well as the corpus processing and quality evaluation procedures.

BLEU is not a sufficient metric; thus, we attempt the comparison with different approaches.

3.2 Automatic Quality Assessment

Given an automatic translation metric, we can compute the score between the source references and the back-translation. We differentiate our work from Misu et al. (2012) by using general metrics, and not task-related ones, to assess quality in the selected translations. However, for this study, we constrained the experiment in the comparison of two word-based/n-gram coverage metrics[3]. We want to evaluate if there is a difference between a baseline metric and one with a higher correlation with human assessment in translation. For the former, we combine BLEU (Papineni et al., 2002) and ROUGE (Lin, 2004) in an F-score (F_{B+R})[4], whereas we use the last version of Meteor Universal ($M.U.$) (Denkowski and Lavie, 2014) for the latter.

At this point, we hypothesise as follows: by using one of the metrics mentioned previously, we could extract a good quality corpus if we identify a threshold in the distribution of the translation scores that obtains the best performance score given a test for an extrinsic task related to the corpus. Furthermore, as an extrinsic evaluation, we are going to compare the threshold-based extrac-

tion with a random choice of the same corpus size.

3.2.1 Train Set Filtering w.r.t. Metrics

The primary goal is to identify where should be located the best threshold to filter out bad-quality translations. Besides, we can explore whether the quality is more relevant than the potentially-noisy large number of samples to train a model.

Thus, we split the training set in progressive cuts, ranging from top-20% to 70%. We rank the training samples concerning three criteria: F_{B+R}, $M.U.$ and a random seed. Therefore, we are going to have several trained models for each cut and criteria to extrinsically measure the quality of the corpus from the performance task.

3.2.2 Development Set Processing

As we want to generate large corpora able to be processed by complex learning algorithms, we require a development (dev) set for our experiments. There is a possibility to filter the development set similar to the train set, but we want to constraint the variable of corpus selection only to the threshold of the train set. However, it is relevant to guarantee high-quality content, so we decided to constrain its content with potentially good translations only regarding our quality metrics:

1. We compute the metrics F_{B+R} and $M.U.$ for all the samples in the development set.
2. For each metric, we obtain the third quartile and intersect both sub-sets.

3.3 NLP Tasks and Target Languages

We tested our methodology on two tasks and two languages: Reading Comprehension for Spanish and Word Sense Disambiguation for Portuguese. Both languages are ranked within the top-ten languages with more first-native speakers (Simons

---

[3]We also tried to distinguish back-translation quality by using pre-trained English document vectors, but the distribution of the scores was not of much use because the $std(\sigma)$ was very small and the mean score was near 1

[4]For this decision, we consider that BLEU and ROUGE complement each other as precision and recall but for measuring overlapping n-grams. Also, we analysed the distribution of the metrics using the formula $\alpha * BLEU + (1 - \alpha) * ROUGE$, $\alpha \in [0.1, 0.9]$ and found that both of them reached the best F-score when $\alpha = 0.5$, so both had the same importance in the experiment.

	train	dev	test
SQuAD 1.1 (en)	88,013	10,570	-
SQuAD→es	62,893	6,995	-
SQuAD→es(w/test)	57,232	6,303	6,353

Table 1: Corpus size for Reading Comprehension. SQuAD 1.1 (en) is translated into Spanish (es), questions without explicit answers are dropped, and the corpus is split to generate a new test.

	dev	test
Original	6,303	6,353
Filtered	1,045	$Q1 \rightarrow 1,956$
		$Q2 \rightarrow 1,087$
		$Q3 \rightarrow 409$

Table 2: Size of development and test sets for the evaluation of Reading Comprehension in Spanish

and Fenning, 2019), and they are regularly studied in specific NLP research communities (Portugal, Spain and Latin-America). There are many core NLP tools for both languages, such as morphological analysis, POS-tagging, syntax dependency parsing, word sense disambiguation, among others. However, their performance is not at the same level as their English counterparts, and it is less probable to identify more complex NLP tools such as reading comprehension. There is an exception for machine translation although, as we can find commercial MT systems for both languages to translate from and into English.

3.3.1 Reading Comprehension (es)

In reading comprehension, the fundamental goal is to identify the position of an answer in a reference text given a question. The Stanford Question Answering Dataset (SQuAD; Rajpurkar et al., 2016) is the most famous corpus to evaluate new methods, with more than 80,000 question-answer pairs extracted from Wikipedia documents, but only available in English.

There is not a corpus with the same properties in Spanish. Previous Question-Answering (QA) challenges in Spanish, mainly hosted by the CLEF initiative, consider the extraction of text references from the web before the identification of the answer itself[5]. The most similar datasets were presented in the Question Answering for Machine Reading Evaluation tasks (QA4MRE; Peñas et al., 2013), but they were relatively small and the corpora require additional steps to be entirely similar to the SQuAD task. Nonetheless, the datasets could be processed for future experiments as testing sets directly built in the target language (es).

Therefore, we applied the back-translation strategy to generate a new Reading Comprehension corpus for Spanish. We only use the train and development sub-datasets from the English SQuAD,

as the test is not available. Thus, we extract a sample from the train and development to generate a new test for our experiments. Then, we translate the corpus to Spanish and back to English using the Google Translate API[6], and drop the questions that lost their exact answers in the reference. In other words, we do not preserve the samples where the translated answer is not exactly contained in the translated reference. See Table 1 for corpus size details.

In the construction of the dataset, we have already disregarded low-quality translations to preserve the nature of the task (we need an explicit answer in the reference text). Thus, we expect a great difficulty to surpass the proposed random baseline in the selection of the best translation, as there would mostly be high-quality translations to choose. Therefore, there is a must to accompany this study with a different task, to drive more general conclusions from the experimentation.

Furthermore, we must assume that the extracted test set contains high and low-quality translations, as a random seed split it. Thus, we divide our test into quartiles for evaluation purposes with a metric based on F_{B+R} and $M.U.$. We followed a similar process as in the filtering of the development set (see §3.2.2). Table 2 shows the filtered size of the dev set, as well of the different partitions of the test w.r.t. to the quality metrics.

3.3.2 Word Sense Disambiguation (pt)

The ambiguity arises from a linguistic problem that occurs in the language, because a word may assume different meanings depending on the specific context where it is used. In that sense, Word sense disambiguation (WSD) is the task that aims to determine the correct sense of a word given a specific context using a pre-specified sense-repository (Agirre and Edmonds, 2007).

For WSD, there is a considerable amount of English language data; however, they are not avail-

[5]Restricted access: http://catalog.elra.info/en-us/repository/browse/ELRA-E0038/

[6]https://cloud.google.com/translate/

corpus	number of sentences
OMSTI	813,798
SemCor	37,176
Senseval-2	242
Senseval-3	352
SemEval-07	135
SemEval-13	306
SemEval-15	1,138
Total	852,147

Table 3: Corpus size details for the Unified Evaluation Framework or UEF (en)

	train
UEF (en)	852,147
UEF en→pt (partial trans.)	73,784
UEF en→pt (after filtering)	14,376

Table 4: Corpus size for Word Sense Disambiguation. The Unified Evaluation Framework or UEF (en) is partially translated into Portuguese (pt), and then we only preserved the samples with one-to-one alignments of ambiguous words.

able data or comparable data (in terms of size) in other languages, such as Portuguese. Thus, we decide to apply back-translation to generate new corpora. Nevertheless, there is a specific problem, as the disambiguation corpus in English may be found in different versions of Wordnet. To overcome this issue, we use the Unified Evaluation Framework (UEF) of Raganato et al. (2017)[7], which includes an standardised corpora aligned with Wordnet 3.0 (Miller, 1995). See Table 3 for corpus size details about the corpora.

In Portuguese, there is an annotated and native WSD corpus: the CSTNews (Cardoso et al., 2011). This is a multi-document corpus composed of 140 news texts (in Brazilian Portuguese) and grouped by 50 collections. The texts in any collection belong to the same topic. Besides, there was an extended annotation for several verbs (Cabezudo et al., 2015), using WordNet 3.0 as sense-repository. In total, there are 5,082 annotated verb instances with 844 different verbs and 1,047 synsets (senses).

Because the CSTNews corpus is a curated corpus in Portuguese, it is convenient to use it as test data, and we do not need to generate a new test set similar to the Reading Comprehension case. So, all the translated sentences from UEF could be used as training and development sets. However, there is an additional consideration for this task if we want to perform an external evaluation later.

To obtain the final set of sentences for the corpus, we follow a two-step procedure. Firstly, we used the Yandex API[8] to partially translate the texts into Portuguese[9]. We decide to use this API

due to its provision of word alignments. Secondly, we deal with the alignments between English and Portuguese sentences, as we were only interested in the sentences with one-to-one word alignments for the words to disambiguate. Then, we disregard the samples with many-to-many relationships between ambiguous words, as it could carry some mistakes in the task. Corpus size is detailed in Table 4. Finally, we apply the procedure describe in §3.2.2, generating 10,592 sentences in the training set and 3,784 sentences in the development set.

4 Extrinsic Automatic Evaluation

We evaluate each generated corpus by measuring the task performance in a specific test set for the target language. We restrict our experiments in monolingual setups to control the identification of potential results.

4.1 Reading Comprehension (es)

With the newly translated corpus, we can evaluate more complex data-driven algorithms, such as deep neural networks. Thus, we adopt the method from Chen et al. (2017)[10] into Spanish, by using pre-trained language-specific models to perform named-entity recognition and part-of-speech tagging from spaCy[11], as well as pre-trained GloVe (Pennington et al., 2014) Spanish word vectors from the Spanish Billion Corpus (Cardellino, 2016). The basic network architecture was not changed and is a sequence-to-sequence with a hidden layer size of 128 and 300-dimensional embedding. We only updated parts of pre-processing modules to work for Spanish.

Following the train set filtering described in §3.2.1, we trained a QA model for each segment of the data and each criterion. We validated the

[7] http://lcl.uniroma1.it/wsdeval/

[8] https://tech.yandex.com/translate/

[9] Due to computational reasons, we were not able to translate all sentences for the corpus. To easier the task, we prepare a list of the most polysemic verbs annotated by

Cabezudo et al. (2015). With the list, we filter out entries that did not contain the expected verbs.

[10] https://github.com/hitvoice/DrQA

[11] https://spacy.io/

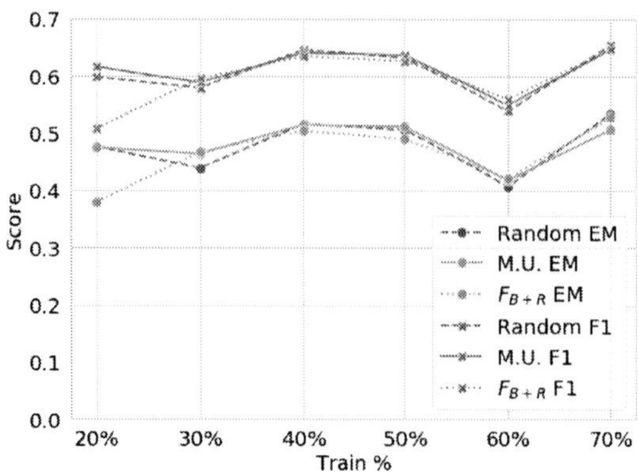

Figure 2: Reading comprehension (es): Exact Match (EM) and F1-score ($F1$) on the development set for each partition of the training set

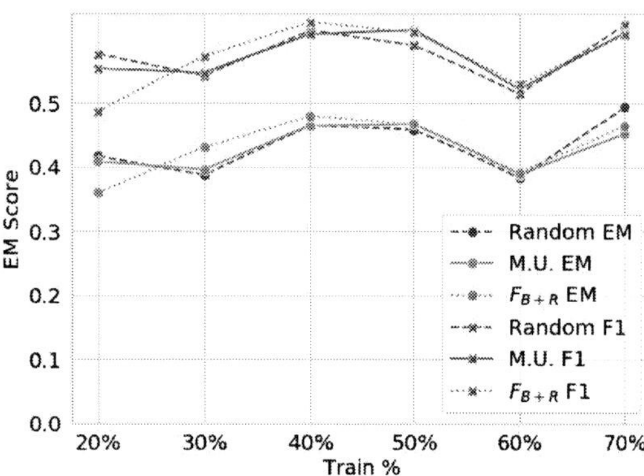

Figure 3: Reading comprehension (es): Exact Match (EM) and F1-score ($F1$) on the 3rd quartile of the test set for each partition of the training set

| Question Type | Full Test | | | | #Q |
| | (Vicedo et al., 2004) | | Our model | | |
	EM	F1	EM	F1	
Date	0.2721	0.4185	0.4545	0.5933	452
Number	0.5421	0.6377	0.4332	0.5754	404
Other	0.1376	0.1966	0.4316	0.5841	4,119
Not Recognized					1,378
Total	0.1429	0.1976	0.4347	0.5846	6,353
Test Q1					
Date	0.2436	0.3913	0.5513	0.7014	78
Number	0.4875	0.6038	0.6	0.6992	80
Other	0.1528	0.2059	0.4425	0.5956	687
Not Recognized					242
Total	0.1499	0.2026	0.4453	0.5894	1,087
Test Q2					
Date	0.2436	0.3913	0.5513	0.7014	78
Number	0.4875	0.6038	0.6	0.6992	80
Other	0.1528	0.2059	0.4425	0.5956	687
Not Recognized					242
Total	0.1499	0.2026	0.4453	0.5894	1087
Test Q3					
Date	0.3462	0.4559	0.5	0.6224	26
Number	0.4571	0.559	0.6857	0.7742	35
Other	0.1556	0.2299	0.4319	0.5962	257
Not Recognized					91
Total	0.1589	0.2212	0.4645	0.607	409

Table 5: Reading Comprehension (es): Results from our model trained with the selected threshold versus the method of Vicedo et al. (2004) in all test partitions

results against the development and test sets specified previously. The evaluation metrics for the experiments were Exact Match (EM) and F1-score ($F1$). The former one is the percentage of predicted answers that exactly match the original answer, whereas the latter one is the average overlap between the predicted and original answers. The results for both dev and test are shown in Figures 2 and 3, respectively. We use the filtered test partition with the highest quartile.

In both figures, we can observe that there is not a vast difference between any of the metrics and the random selection throughout all the partitions. We expected the previous outcome, as our processed corpus has already been filtered to preserve only the questions with an explicit and exact answer in the reference texts.

We carried out a complementary analysis, where we compared a neural method versus a non-data-driven method. One of the few methods implemented for monolingual reading comprehension in Spanish proposes a straightforward pipeline (Vicedo et al., 2004). They extract keywords from the question, search the web for related passages and identify a potential answer from them. They used the set of 200 questions from the CLEF 2003 Spanish monolingual QA evaluation task (Magnini et al., 2004), which lacks context because of the nature of the challenge. We reproduce the second half of the pipeline, assuming that we already have a related passage to look for the answer.

For this experiment, we selected the model that achieved the highest F1-score in the development set: the top 40% of the training set arranged by the $M.U.$ score (see Figure 2). Results are shown in Table 5, where we observe a difference between the neural and non-neural model, as the former take advantage of the newly generated corpus.

4.2 Word Sense Disambiguation (pt)

After the translation and filtering of the UEF corpus (see §3.3.2 for details about training and de-

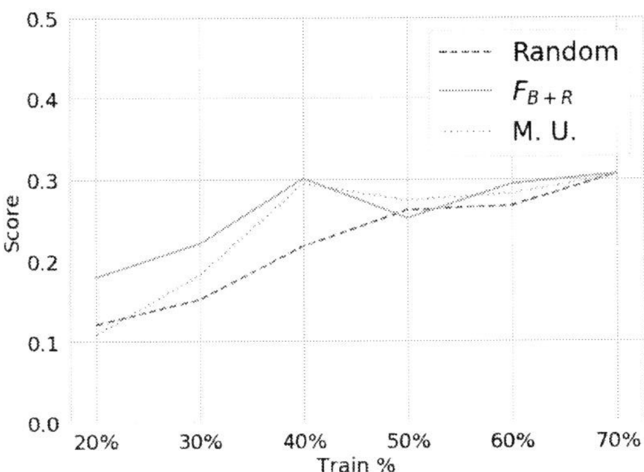

Figure 4: WSD (pt): F1-score on the Development set for each partition of the training set

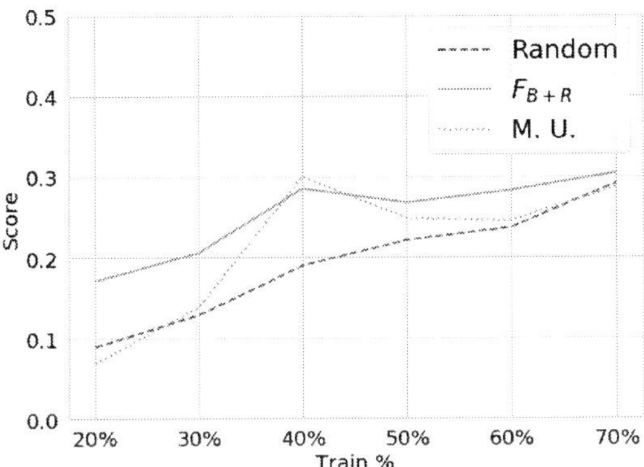

Figure 5: WSD (pt): F1-score on the Test set for each partition of the training set

velopment sets), we proceeded to train the WSD models. Due to the effectiveness of neural networks on several tasks, it was decided to use a Sequence-to-Sequence architecture with an attention mechanism, like the one proposed by Bahdanau et al. (2014). This architecture has been previously used by Raganato et al. (2017). The proposed architecture contains a hidden size of 256 and an embedding size of 300 units. Also, we consider training embeddings from scratch.

Following the training set filtering described in §3.2.1, we trained a different model for each partition of the train data and each criterion. Besides, we used F-score as the validation metric with the formulation of the precision and recall like in Cabezudo and Pardo (2017). The results achieved in the development and test sets are shown in Figure 4 and Figure 5, respectively.

Figure 4 shows that the F_{B+R}- and $M.U.$-based filters produce better results (in term of F-score)

Verb	MFS	Lesk	Our method
ser ("to be")	88.11	69.32	64.18
ter ("to have")	75.82	62.75	62.50
fazer ("to do")	31.62	11.11	21.56
apresentar ("to present")	50.00	36.11	50.00
chegar ("to arrive")	29.09	23.64	21.73
receber ("to receive")	61.11	42.86	36.84
ficar ("to stay")	11.27	8.45	0.00
registrar ("to register")	3.85	7.69	0.00
deixar ("to leave")	19.61	13.73	8.33
cair ("to fall")	17.39	17.39	20.00
passar ("to pass")	38.30	23.40	16.67
fechar ("to close")	36.84	5.26	0.00
colocar ("to put")	63.16	31.58	62.50
encontrar ("to find")	12.50	4.17	30.00
levar ("to take")	9.09	3.03	12.50
vir ("to come")	30.00	30.00	25.00
estabelecer ("to establish")	8.33	16.67	25.00
marcar ("to mark")	0.00	9.09	0.00
dar ("to give")	13.21	9.43	9.09
tratar ("to treat")	11.11	22.22	50.00
Precision	30.52	22.39	46.44

Table 6: Results for the Lexical sample task in WSD

than the Random criterion in the development set. However, the difference between both F_{B+R} and $M.U.$ and random becomes shorter by each part. Given the results, we can observe the best F-score at the 70% partition of the training set.

Nevertheless, due to our primary goal is to build a high-quality corpus, we consider the portion at 40% of the training set better than the one at 70%, as the latter could contain low-quality translations. Moreover, we select the sentences from the 40% partition provided by the F_{B+R} criterion instead of the $M.U.$, because the latter shows less stability in its results.

Besides, Figure 5 is useful to confirm that there is a peak in the validation at the 40% partition of the training data for the two metrics. For that reason, we decided to fix the 40% portion of the data as our definite high-quality corpus.

Finally, we perform a comparison using our selected corpus (at the 40% thresh by F_{B+R}) against WSD methods for Brazilian Portuguese in the Lexical Sample task (Cabezudo and Pardo, 2017). Lexical Sample consists of evaluating the 20 most polysemous words in the corpus. Specifically, we compare our results with Most Frequent Sense Heuristic (MFS), which is a strong baseline, and an adaptation of the Lesk algorithm (Lesk, 1986), a knowledge-based method and the best algorithm reported in this work. To analyse the percentage of correctness of the WSD methods on the selected verbs, we only calculate the precision and not the F1-score. Results are presented in Table 6, where we can see that our method outperforms both MFS Heuristic and Lesk, although not for all the verbs.

5 Conclusions and Future Work

We present a study of back-translation and automatic quality evaluation as a corpus generation strategy. Our further goal is to systematise the use of these methods towards a robust and general-purpose corpus generation for new languages. The analysis of several thresholds for corpus filtering and its posterior extrinsic evaluation shows that this strategy is feasible, and it only requires a machine translation system paired with English plus particular processing steps regarding the nature of the target task, but not of the specific language.

We plan to extend the experimentation using less-robust MT systems. Thus, we might assess how far this strategy could work for low-resource languages without commercial MT, as well as to analyse whether the quality-oriented metrics can perform accordingly. There is also potential work in complementing the back-translation strategy with cross-lingual embeddings, supervised or unsupervised, to increase the quality in the corpus generation. Furthermore, an exhaustive exploration could be performed, by including more automatic evaluation metrics as well as additional languages and tasks to draw more general insights.

Acknowledgments

This project has received funding from the European Union's Horizon 2020 research and innovation programme under grant agreement No. 825299. Besides, we acknowledge the support of the NVIDIA Corporation with the donation of the Titan Xp GPU used for this study. Finally, the first author is granted by the "Programa de apoyo al desarrollo de tesis de licenciatura" (Support programme of undergraduate thesis development, PADET 2018, PUCP).

References

Eneko Agirre and Philip Edmonds. 2007. *Word Sense Disambiguation: Algorithms and Applications*, 1st edition. Springer Publishing Company.

Akari Asai, Akiko Eriguchi, Kazuma Hashimoto, and Yoshimasa Tsuruoka. 2018. Multilingual extractive reading comprehension by runtime machine translation. *CoRR*, abs/1809.03275v2.

Dzmitry Bahdanau, Kyunghyun Cho, and Yoshua Bengio. 2014. Neural machine translation by jointly learning to align and translate. *CoRR*, abs/1409.0473v7.

Marco A. Sobrevilla Cabezudo, Erick Maziero, Jackson Souza, Márcio Dias, Paula Christina Cardoso, Pedro Paulo Balage Filho, Verônica Agostini, Fernando Antônio Nóbrega, Cláudia de Barros, Ariani Di Felippo, and Thiago Alexandre Pardo. 2015. Anotação de sentidos de verbos em textos jornalísticos do corpus CSTNews. *Revista de Estudos da Linguagem*, 23(3):797–832.

Marco A. Sobrevilla Cabezudo and Thiago A. Salgueiro Pardo. 2017. Exploring classical and linguistically enriched knowledge-based methods for sense disambiguation of verbs in Brazilian Portuguese news texts. *Procesamiento del Lenguaje Natural*, 59(0):83–90.

Chris Callison-Burch, Miles Osborne, and Philipp Koehn. 2006. Re-evaluation the role of BLEU in machine translation research. In *11th Conference of the European Chapter of the Association for Computational Linguistics*.

Cristian Cardellino. 2016. Spanish Billion Words Corpus and Embeddings.

Paula C. F. Cardoso, Erick G. Maziero, Maria L. C. Jorge, Eloize M. R. Seno, Ariani Di Felippo, Lucia H. M. Rino, Maria G. V. Nunes, and Thiago A. S. Pardo. 2011. CSTNews - a discourse-annotated corpus for single and multi-document summarization of news texts in Brazilian Portuguese. In *Proceedings of the 3rd RST Brazilian Meeting*, pages 88–105, Cuiab MT, Brazil. Sociedade Brasileira de Computao.

Danqi Chen, Adam Fisch, Jason Weston, and Antoine Bordes. 2017. Reading Wikipedia to answer open-domain questions. In *Proceedings of the 55th Annual Meeting of the Association for Computational Linguistics (Volume 1: Long Papers)*, pages 1870–1879, Vancouver, Canada. Association for Computational Linguistics.

Michael Denkowski and Alon Lavie. 2014. Meteor universal: Language specific translation evaluation for any target language. In *Proceedings of the Ninth Workshop on Statistical Machine Translation*, pages 376–380, Baltimore, Maryland, USA. Association for Computational Linguistics.

Marina Fomicheva, Núria Bel, Lucia Specia, Iria da Cunha, and Anton Malinovskiy. 2016. CobaltF: A fluent metric for MT evaluation. In *Proceedings of the First Conference on Machine Translation*, pages 483–490, Berlin, Germany. Association for Computational Linguistics.

Judith Gaspers, Penny Karanasou, and Rajen Chatterjee. 2018. Selecting machine-translated data for quick bootstrapping of a natural language understanding system. In *Proceedings of the 2018 Conference of the North American Chapter of the Association for Computational Linguistics: Human Language Technologies, Volume 3 (Industry Papers)*, pages 137–144, New Orleans - Louisiana. Association for Computational Linguistics.

Bassam Jabaian, Laurent Besacier, and Fabrice Lefvre. 2011. Combination of stochastic understanding and machine translation systems for language portability of dialogue systems. In *2011 IEEE International Conference on Acoustics, Speech and Signal Processing (ICASSP)*, pages 5612–5615.

Roman Klinger and Philipp Cimiano. 2015. Instance selection improves cross-lingual model training for fine-grained sentiment analysis. In *Proceedings of the Nineteenth Conference on Computational Natural Language Learning*, pages 153–163, Beijing, China. Association for Computational Linguistics.

Philipp Koehn, Huda Khayrallah, Kenneth Heafield, and Mikel L. Forcada. 2018. Findings of the WMT 2018 shared task on parallel corpus filtering. In *Proceedings of the Third Conference on Machine Translation: Shared Task Papers*, pages 726–739, Belgium, Brussels. Association for Computational Linguistics.

Michael Lesk. 1986. Automatic sense disambiguation using machine readable dictionaries: how to tell a pine cone from an ice cream cone. In *Proceedings of the 5th Annual International Conference on Systems Documentation*, pages 24–26.

Chin-Yew Lin. 2004. ROUGE: A package for automatic evaluation of summaries. In *Text Summarization Branches Out: Proceedings of the ACL-04 Workshop*, pages 74–81, Barcelona, Spain. Association for Computational Linguistics.

Bernardo Magnini, Simone Romagnoli, Alessandro Vallin, Jesús Herrera, Anselmo Peñas, Víctor Peinado, Felisa Verdejo, and Maarten de Rijke. 2004. The multiple language question answering track at CLEF 2003. In *Comparative Evaluation of Multilingual Information Access Systems*, pages 471–486, Berlin, Heidelberg. Springer Berlin Heidelberg.

George A. Miller. 1995. Wordnet: A lexical database for english. *Commun. ACM*, 38(11):39–41.

Teruhisa Misu, Etsuo Mizukami, Hideki Kashioka, Satoshi Nakamura, and Haizhou Li. 2012. A bootstrapping approach for SLU portability to a new language by inducting unannotated user queries. In *2012 IEEE International Conference on Acoustics, Speech and Signal Processing (ICASSP)*, pages 4961–4964.

Jekaterina Novikova, Ondřej Dušek, Amanda Cercas Curry, and Verena Rieser. 2017. Why we need new evaluation metrics for NLG. In *Proceedings of the 2017 Conference on Empirical Methods in Natural Language Processing*, pages 2241–2252, Copenhagen, Denmark. Association for Computational Linguistics.

Kishore Papineni, Salim Roukos, Todd Ward, and Wei-Jing Zhu. 2002. BLEU: A method for automatic evaluation of machine translation. In *Proceedings of the 40th Annual Meeting on Association for Computational Linguistics*, ACL '02, pages 311–318, Stroudsburg, PA, USA. Association for Computational Linguistics.

Anselmo Peñas, Eduard Hovy, Pamela Forner, Álvaro Rodrigo, Richard Sutcliffe, and Roser Morante. 2013. QA4MRE 2011-2013: Overview of question answering for machine reading evaluation. In *Information Access Evaluation. Multilinguality, Multimodality, and Visualization*, pages 303–320, Berlin, Heidelberg. Springer Berlin Heidelberg.

Jeffrey Pennington, Richard Socher, and Christopher Manning. 2014. Glove: Global vectors for word representation. In *Proceedings of the 2014 Conference on Empirical Methods in Natural Language Processing (EMNLP)*, pages 1532–1543, Doha, Qatar. Association for Computational Linguistics.

Alessandro Raganato, Jose Camacho-Collados, and Roberto Navigli. 2017. Word sense disambiguation: A unified evaluation framework and empirical comparison. In *Proceedings of the 15th Conference of the European Chapter of the Association for Computational Linguistics: Volume 1, Long Papers*, pages 99–110, Valencia, Spain. Association for Computational Linguistics.

Pranav Rajpurkar, Jian Zhang, Konstantin Lopyrev, and Percy Liang. 2016. SQuAD: 100,000+ questions for machine comprehension of text. In *Proceedings of the 2016 Conference on Empirical Methods in Natural Language Processing*, pages 2383–2392, Austin, Texas. Association for Computational Linguistics.

Rico Sennrich, Barry Haddow, and Alexandra Birch. 2016. Improving neural machine translation models with monolingual data. In *Proceedings of the 54th Annual Meeting of the Association for Computational Linguistics (Volume 1: Long Papers)*, pages 86–96, Berlin, Germany. Association for Computational Linguistics.

Gary F. Simons and Charles D. Fenning, editors. 2019. *Ethnologue: Languages of the World. Twenty-second edition*. Dallas Texas: SIL international. Online version: http://www.ethnologue.com.

Ilya Sutskever, Oriol Vinyals, and Quoc V Le. 2014. Sequence to sequence learning with neural networks. In *Advances in Neural Information Processing Systems 27*, pages 3104–3112. Curran Associates, Inc.

José L. Vicedo, Ruben Izquierdo, Fernando Llopis, and Rafael Muñoz. 2004. Question answering in Spanish. In *Comparative Evaluation of Multilingual Information Access Systems*, pages 541–548, Berlin, Heidelberg. Springer Berlin Heidelberg.

A Framework for Annotating 'Related Works' to Support Feedback to Novice Writers

Arlene Casey
School of Informatics
University of Edinburgh
Edinburgh, UK
a.j.casey@sms.ed.ac.uk

Bonnie Webber
School of Informatics
University of Edinburgh
Edinburgh, UK
bonnie@inf.ed.ac.uk

Dorota Głowacka
Dept. of Computer Science
University of Helsinki
Helsinki, Finland
glowacka@cs.helsinki.fi

Abstract

Understanding what is expected of academic writing can be difficult for novice writers to assimilate, and recent years have seen several automated tools become available to support academic writing. Our work presents a framework for annotating features of the *Related Work* section of academic writing, that supports writer feedback.

1 Introduction

Learning the skill of academic writing is critical for post-graduate students to be successful, yet many struggle to master the standard of quality expected of them (Aitchison et al., 2012; Paltridge and Starfield, 2007). Beyond the surface characteristics of grammar and spelling, students must grasp aspects of style and content structure expected within their discipline. Automated recognition of content features in academic writing has become a popular approach to assist students in recent years. Previous work has focused on identifying rhetoric intentions, such as those described by Swales (1981) that can be found in an Introduction (Cotos and Pendar, 2016; Anthony and V. Lashkia, 2003) or in PhD summaries (Feltrim et al., 2006). Other approaches have focused on identifying argument components and relations and how these relate to essay scores (Ghosh et al., 2016). The one aspect that these approaches have in common is the need for annotated data based on task-orientated annotation schemes. Our focus is on building an annotation schema which can help writers recognise appropriate intentions in writing their *Related Work* section, and indicate when these are missing.

Annotating intention in academic writing is challenging as the language and author intentions differ across the typical sections found in a paper (Introduction, Methods, Results, Discussion) and within disciplines (Hyland, 2015). We focus on one section of scientific text that has, for the most part, been ignored in the past — the *Related Work* section.

Currently no annotation schema specifically focuses on *Related Work*. There are schemas that capture some, but not all, elements of intentions we seek, such as those that consider citation function (Teufel et al., 2006a; Angrosh et al., 2012) or argument zones reflecting rhetoric intentions (Teufel, 1999; Teufel et al., 2009). However, these are designed for different purposes, such as understanding citation relations, summarisation or information extraction (e.g gene relations, knowledge claims). Thus, they also have labels that are irrelevant to *Related Work*, e.g. 'Conclusion', which may make the annotation task more difficult. Since previous work has shown that annotation schemes benefit from being designed for their specific goal (Guo et al., 2010), we propose a specific annotation framework to support automated writing feedback on *Related Work*.

This paper describes our framework for annotating the discourse of *Related Work* in such a way that it supports feedback on writing. The framework reflects qualities that both theory and experiments have shown to be important. We discuss how these qualities have motivated our design along with those existing schemes that are most closely related to ours. We report results that show reliable annotation for this framework. Future work will investigate the degree to which such annotation can be automated.

2 Background

Our aim is to help authors recognise rhetorical intentions that are present in their writing and highlight those that are missing, using these intentions

90

Proceedings of the 13th Linguistic Annotation Workshop, pages 90–99
Florence, Italy, August 1, 2019. ©2019 Association for Computational Linguistics

to form our feedback to writers. Argument structures are key in allowing an author to convey and provide a persuasive message, which forms the author intention. Swales (1981) was one of the first to recognise author intentions, calling them *rhetorical moves*, a strategy employed by a writer to strengthen the persuasive appeal or stage of an argument. This section discusses work on developing annotation schemes related to identifying rhetoric intentions in scientific publications and writing analytic tools. We highlight some of the challenges others have found when working with intentions in scientific publications and how this relates to our goal of writing feedback. Section 3 provides more detail how schemas directly map to our annotation design. Subsequent sections describe the dataset we have used (Section 4), the annotation process and results (Sections 5–6), and our plans to develop the work further (Section 7).

2.1 Understanding Author Intent in Scientific Discourse

Argument Zoning (AZ) (Teufel, 1999) was one of the first author intention schemas to provide reliability studies of their annotations and to fully automate these. AZ marks zones that identify knowledge claims indicating who these knowledge claims belong to, in addition to providing categories for relationships between the authors or existing works. Teufel et al. (2009) extended the AZ schema from 7 to 15 categories. This extension allowed the authors to then apply their schema to the domain of life sciences in addition to their original domain of Computational Linguistics. The AZ scheme has also been successfully adapted in other domains, e.g. biology (Mizuta and Collier, 2004). The requirement to adapt the schema to new domains supports the idea that different styles of writing across domains may influence recognising intention in writing and our choice to focus on only one domain.

Whilst the AZ scheme has proven very successful, it has been applied to capturing intentions across entire documents. The schema was designed to support tasks of summarisation and to improve information access. For a section such as *Related Work*, which is rarely used in summarisation or information access, this means that its meaningful author intentions may be labelled too generically to be useful or not at all. Nevertheless, AZ has been shown to be successful

for feedback on abstracts and summaries of PhD's (Feltrim et al., 2006). As one of the intended goals of the AZ schema is summarisation, it is not surprising that the schema works well for this type of writing feedback.

Understanding the motivation or function of a citation can help determine an author's intention (Teufel et al., 2006a). Work is not meant to be cited simply because it is on the same topic as the citing work. Rather, cited works should be ones that have implications for the author's study (Maxwell, 2006). The development of citation schemas, with corresponding annotations, has been a subject of research for several decades (Weinstock, 1971; Oppenheim and Renn, 1978; Teufel et al., 2006a; Angrosh et al., 2012). However, many of the early citation studies are based on small samples, and do not include reliability studies as annotation is done by the author only. Such weak annotation methodology could lead to unforeseen difficulties when it comes to practical implementation of these schemas. There is agreement that determining the relationship of the cited work to that of the author(s) can be difficult, and that this subjective nature makes it hard to operationalise (Teufel, 1999; Swales, 1990). Often context is linguistically unmarked, which can make judgements about the relationship of the cited work more difficult to make (Teufel, 1999). We believe that novice writers struggle to provide citations that go beyond lists or brief description, and this leads to what Teufel calls "linguistically unmarked context". We also believe the reader's experience has a role to play in interpretation, with experts in the field not requiring as many linguistic clues to relevance as a novice reader may require.

Our work differs from most other citation frameworks in that determining whether the author made the citation relevant in context to their own work is more important than the recognition of the citation function. For example, highlighting that there is a gap in a cited work is not our primary focus. We want to capture that a gap is highlighted but also further ensure it is made relevant to the authors' own work e.g. they state what they do that is different to fill the gap. Identifying neutral or linguistically unmarked citations is important as they indicate an opportunity for feedback that the writing may need revision to clarify relevance.

Some work specifically looks at developing

annotation frameworks which are more directly linked to the Toulmin model of argumentation (Toulmin, 2003) to represent argument structures in a research article. These annotation schemas represent arguments as claims and premises with some including relations of support and attack (Stab and Gurevych, 2014). Whilst this structure has been shown to work well in a persuasive essay scenario, it would not support the types of intentions discussed in the next section that are relevant to *Related Work*.

2.2 Writing Analytics Tools

Using rhetoric intentions to provide writers with feedback has been successful in academic writing. Mover (Anthony and V. Lashkia, 2003), Research Writer Tutor (RWT) (Cotos and Pendar, 2016) and ACAWriter (Abel, 2018) are three tools based on Swales CARS model (Swales, 1990). The first two tools carry out annotation based on their interpretation of the CARS model — the first on the *Abstract* and the second on the *Introduction*. Unfortunately, little information is provided on the annotation process. There are indications that the RWT is intended to be used as a University tool, so perhaps propriety concerns are behind restricting the availability of information or annotated datasets. However, as the CARS model is designed for the *Introduction*, this makes it likely any schemas would be only partially relevant to identifying content expected in *Related Work*.

Whilst previous works motivate our approach, no other work provides a match for the fine-grained author intentions that allow informative writing feedback for *Related Work*. It is known that annotation schemas benefit from being task-orientated (Guo et al., 2010). Hence, we see a need to develop an annotation schema for recognising author intentions in *Related Work* sections that meet the goal of writer feedback.

3 Annotation Schema for *Related Work*

Domain Disciplines differ in their writing conventions for academic papers. As a result, linguistic constructs and content can differ across disciplines (Hyland, 2015). Not all disciplines have a specific *Related Work* section – some include literature material in the *Introduction* or disperse it throughout other sections. Due to these challenges, we focus on the discipline of Computational Linguistics, where *Related Work* sections are more readily found.

Annotation unit We have chosen the sentence as our unit of annotation. Many other works mentioned in the background section, such as those based on AZ, use sentence as an annotation unit. We acknowledge that using a sentence could introduce challenges – for example, a given sentence could potentially serve two functions that may be better captured at clause level. For our purposes of providing feedback, we believe the sentence as an annotation unit will be the most meaningful. One reason for this is that in the next stage of our work (providing feedback), we will need to look at several sentences together to determine relevance, as citation relevance has been shown to require to look beyond just the citing sentence (Teufel et al., 2006a).

3.1 The Annotation Schema

We first consider what qualities should be present in the *Related Work* section of a paper in Computational Linguistics and then we discuss how we map these into our annotation schema.

Identifying Qualities in a Related Work Section We base our *Related Work* qualities on key tasks that Kamler and Thomson (2006, p. 28) indicate a survey of related work should accomplish.

- ***Background*** This information has an important goal of helping the author to locate their work in the field, showing they understand their field and its history through indicating seminal works and other relevant research fields. They may provide some evidence through citation to what they are saying.

- ***Cited Works*** From more generally identifying the field, the author should demonstrate specifically (i) which works, methods or ideas are most pertinent to their work; (ii) how these works have influenced and motivated what they do; and (iii) if and how the current work builds on or uses these methods.

- ***Gap*** In addition to demonstrating what works are most pertinent to their work, the author should also make clear what the gap is, what areas or applications have not yet been addressed in existing work. This can be done when citing specific work or it could be indicated as a gap in the field when discussing background.

Literature Quality	Sentence Label	Description
Background	BG-DESC-NE	Description of the state of the field, describing/listing known methods or common knowledge. No evidence i.e. citation is not included
	BG-DESC-EP	Description of the state of the field, describing/listing known methods or common knowledge. Evidence provided i.e.citation included
	BG-EVAL-P	Author highlights a positive aspect in the field
Cited Work	CW-DESC	Describes cited work, this could be specific details, or very high level details or nothing more than a reference for further information
	CW-COMP	Cited work compared to another cited work
	CW-EVAL-P	Positive aspect highlighted of cited work
	A-CW-BUILD	Author's work uses/builds on (adapts/modifies) cited work
	A-CW-SIM	Author's work is similar to cited work
Gap	CW-EVAL-SC	Shortcoming, problem or gap about the cited work is highlighted
	BG-EVAL-SC	Author highlights a shortcoming, problem or gap in the field
Author Contribution	A-DIFF	Author states their work is different with no detail
	A-DESC	Author describes their work with no linguistic marking to other's work or being different
	A-GAP	Author specifically says they address a gap or highlights the novelty of their work
	A-CW-DIFF	Author's highlights how their work is different to cited work
Additional Labels	OTHER	Sentence does not fit under any other label
	OCR	Sentence has OCR problems and annotator cannot understand
	TEXT	Sentence provides information about what will be discussed in the next section

Table 1: Annotation Labels

- ***Contribution*** Having exposed a gap, the author should indicate their contribution to address this gap and highlight what makes their work different or novel.

3.2 Mapping Qualities to the Annotation Schema

Looking just at label names, it can seem like our labels (Table 1) are direct replications of other schemas. However, on closer inspection of how authors' apply these labels, we often find discrepancies that would not work for our purpose. Table 2 provides a discussion of comparisons and similarities of our label schema to those that are most closely related (Fisas et al., 2015, 2016; Teufel, 1999; Teufel et al., 2006b; Angrosh et al., 2012; Teufel et al., 2009). One contributing factor as to why existing labels do not adequately support our goals is that they are designed to look across the whole of a document. As a result, they seek either very general or much finer grained labelling than we require. For example, Fisas et al. (2016) distinguishes between an author using methods, using data or using tools from another cited work. This finer grained approach is not relevant or needed to provide feedback in a *Related Work* section, we only need to know that the author used the cited work.

3.3 Qualities and their corresponding labels

Background These types of sentences describe the state of the field, common knowledge, or describe/list known methods. We ask our annotators to identify two types of background sentences — (i) with citations i.e. evidence provided – BG-DESC-EP and these citations are not part of the syntax of the sentence. (ii) Background sentences without evidence i.e. no citations – BG-DESC-NE. Part of the reason for this distinction is that novice writers make a limited use of citation types (Thompson and Tribble, 2001). We also include a background label that relates to when an author says something positive or highlights a strength in the field/general – BG-EVAL-P.

Cited Works To provide informative feedback, we need to establish the relevance of a cited work to the author's work or if this cited work is perfunctory in nature. Firstly, we provide a label that accounts for description of a cited work – CW-DESC. Our other labels account for contrasting the author's work to cited work saying: (i) it is similar – A-CW-SIM; (ii) the author uses/builds on or adapts/modifies the cited work – A-CW-BUILD. Teufel et al. (2006b) describes a category CoCoXY that contrasts two pieces of cited work, and highlights that this is often not annotated in the literature as most works put comparisons to author's work and a cited work together. This dis-

Quality/Our Labels	Related Works	Comparison
Background		
BG-DESC-NE BG-DESC-EP	(Teufel, 1999) (Liakata et al., 2012) (Angrosh et al., 2012) (Fisas et al., 2015)	All the related works use a label of 'Background' but they do not distinguish between those that have citation evidence or not. There are some discrepancies in what these capture to ours for e.g in Angrosh this is used for *sentences that provide background or introduction.* Fisas in addition to sentences that state common ground includes sentences of previous related work in their background category. The reason for their more general approach could be attributed to these other works capturing labels across the whole article.
BG-EVAL-P	-	We did not find evidence of other works looking for strengths in background sentences.
Cited Works		
CW-DESC	(Teufel et al., 2006b) (Angrosh et al., 2012) (Fisas et al., 2016)	Teufel and Fisas have a category 'Neutral' which is directly related to our category of CW-DESC. These are used like our label for descriptions of a cited work. Fisas differs slightly in that they also include in this category *references for more information* or *comments on common practices* which we would put in one of our 'Background' sentence labels. Teufel also allows this label to be used for an *unlisted citation function* or *not enough evidence to put in any other category.* In our case these would go into the *OTHER* label. Angrosh provides two labels 'RWD_CS' – *a sentence describing a citation occurring in that sentence,* 'RWD' – *a sentences describing a related work where the citation does not occur in that sentence.* Our one label covers both Angrosh's labels.
A-CW-SIM	(Teufel et al., 2006b) (Fisas et al., 2016)	Both Fisas with a label of 'Comparison-similarity' and Teufel with a label of 'PSim' have categories that label sentences with *authors work is similar to the cited work.*
A-CW-BUILD	(Teufel et al., 2006b) (Fisas et al., 2016)	Fisas and Tuefel have labels which align with our category of A-CW-BUILD. However, they break this into finer detail than we feel is necessary for our goal. Fisas has four labels for using another cited work: 'Use-method, 'Use-Data', 'Use-Tool', 'Use-other' and three labels for authors work based on a cited work, 'Basis-previous own work', 'Basis Others work', 'Basis -future work'. Teufel has three labels: 'PBas', *uses cited work as basis,* 'PUse', *author uses tools/algorithms/data/definition,* 'PModi', *author adapts or modifies tools/algorithms/data.* This finer grained approach supports the goal of these authors as they look across a whole document but is not necessary for our goal of writer feedback.
CW-COMP	(Teufel et al., 2006b)	Teufel includes a category CoCoXY which contrasts two pieces of cited work as our sentence label does.
CW-EVAL-P	(Angrosh et al., 2012) (Fisas et al., 2016)	Angrosh has two labels that represent what we capture here RWS_CS and RWS. The first of these labels mentions a positive (strength) in a citation sentence and in the second a positive (strength) is mentioned but the citation is not present in that sentence. Fisas also has this label 'CRITICISM-Strength'.
Gap		
CW-EVAL-SC	(Fisas et al., 2016)(Teufel et al., 2006b) (Angrosh et al., 2012)	Our evaluation category for cited works relates directly to Tuefel's category of 'Weak' - *weakness of cited approach* and Fisas's 'Criticism-weakness'. Angrosh labels this as 'RWSC' - *sentence noting the shortcomings in the related work citation.*
BG-EVAL-SC	(Teufel et al., 2009)	Tuefel's work is the only evidence of where we can find a similarity to our label of a shortcoming in the field although her label 'GAP_WEAK' - *lack of solution in field, problem with other solutions* covers a shortcoming in both the field and a cited work.
Contribution		
A-GAP	(Fisas et al., 2016)(Teufel et al., 2009)	This has similarities to Fisas's 'Novelties', although their label is not exclusive to the author's approach and could include other cited work. Teufel's category of 'NOV-ADV' is for sentences claiming a novelty or advantage of the author's own approach
A-CW-DIFF	(Fisas et al., 2016)	Our category of author and cited work comparison, A-CW-D, directly relates to the category of Fisas of 'Comparison-difference'.
A-DESC	(Teufel et al., 2009)	We could not find a schema that labels sentences just as author description. Other works such as Tuefel have several labels which in part fall under this category such as :'OWN_MTHD, OWN_FAIL,OWN_RES,OWN_CONC, AIM'. These are very specific and likely not to occur very often in a Related Work.
TXT	(Teufel, 1999)	In her original AZ schema Teufel includes a label of TEXT that is the same as our label.

Table 2: Label Schema Comparison

tinction of comparing two works rather than the author's work and a cited work is important for recognising how an author makes citations relevant. Therefore, we incorporate this category into our schema as – CW-COMP. Additionally, we include a label for an author highlighting a positive or strength of a cited work – C-EVAL-P.

Gap Locating a gap in academic writing often takes the approach of highlighting weaknesses or areas not addressed in others' work or in the field in general. We also want to identify when a gap or shortcoming is highlighted in the field in general. We add two categories: (i) BG-EVAL-SC for a background sentence highlighting a gap/weakness in the field; (ii) CW-EVAL-SC, where an author highlights a shortcoming, problem or gap about a specific cited work.

Author Contribution Here, we want to capture if the author specifically identifies how they will address a gap. This is done by authors when they specifically say their work is novel, new or describe how they address a gap with the label – A-GAP. Our label A-CW-DIFF applies when an author compares their work directly with a cited work, saying it is different and how it is different. We also capture where an author describes their own work – A-DESC. This type of description may not linguistically identify that the author has made a contribution but the explanation may describe this novelty or difference to others' work. Here, it could be expected that a reader's experience may allow them to interpret this as a contribution but we instruct our annotators only to mark it as contribution if it is linguistically marked. The identification of this type of sentence is less common in other schemas.

3.4 Learning from Pilot Annotations

Initially, a preliminary annotation study was conducted that highlighted a problem when considering author differences. There were many occurrences of an author sentence which just indicated "our work is different", giving no details why or how. The annotators pointed out that these were not very informative sentences and quite different to when the author actually provides details of why their work is different. The extra label, A-DIFF, was added to account for this.

In addition, there were some sentences which had OCR problems, so a category was created for this, along with a category for TEXT. TEXT indicates where an author says "In the next section we will discuss". This type of category was in the original AZ schema, but we thought it unlikely to arise in a *Related Work* section. However, it was highlighted in the pilot annotations. A category of OTHER was also added as there were some sentences the annotators could not assign to a label.

4 Dataset

Initial experiments were carried out on a pre-annotated dataset (Schäfer et al., 2012) consisting of 266 published scientific papers from the ACL anthology (Bird et al., 2008). The dataset was extracted from PDF by commercial OCR software, sentence-tokenised and then manually annotated, using MMAX2 (Müller and Strube, 2006). Papers were annotated for co-reference to cited papers and to the authors' own work. All the papers were 6 to 8 pages long. This is important, as short-conference papers (4 pages) would have considerably shorter *Related Work* sections. Initially, we processed the full data set, and then only those papers with *Related Work* sections were extracted. This resulted in a data set of 113 papers. Our final dataset comprised of the 95 *Related Work* sections that remained after we removed papers with OCR problems.

Authors do not always signal the relevance of a paper in its citing sentence: often it will come in the next or subsequent sentence. Although we are only assigning a label to a sentence, in future work it will be necessary to look at all sentences related to a citation to determine what feedback to give. This was our reason for choosing a dataset that was already marked for co-references to citations.

5 Annotation Process

5.1 Annotators

Both our annotators were PhD students in Computational Linguistics, in the final stages of their degree programs. Because knowledge possessed by researchers in a field can (in some instances) be used to overcome a lack of explicit linguistic marking, PhD students were preferable over domain experts in terms of bringing some, but not a lot of, knowledge to the task. This fact was acknowledged by Teufel et al. (2009) who instruct their annotators to only use rhetorical linguistic knowledge but point out how difficult it is for domain experts not to use their knowledge when annotating.

One annotator annotated the whole corpus and the other just over half the corpus (i.e., 53 *Related Work* sections).

5.2 Annotator Task

The *Related Work* sections were given to each annotator in an Excel file. Each row represented a sentence, with fields corresponding to document id, sentence id, the original sentence, and the sentence with citation and co-references marked. In the following field, the annotator entered a label from the pre-populated list provided. The final field was for comments, or for indicating any annotations they were not sure about.

5.3 Annotator Support

The annotators were given 9 pages of guidelines which contained examples and suggested workflow to decide on an annotation label. Initially, the annotators met to discuss the guidelines and ensure their understanding. They trained on the same 10 *Related Work* sections and compared their results discussing any difference.

6 Annotation Results

6.1 Corpus Analysis

The annotated corpus includes 95 *Related Works* sections and a total of 1,806 sentences. Double annotation was done for 53 *Related Works* and 955 sentences. The size of our dataset is comparable to others who have studied scientific publications in annotation. Fisas et al. (2015) studied a corpus of 40 documents, Teufel et al. (2009) studied 90 papers, Feltrim et al. (2006) 52 abstracts, and Anthony and V. Lashkia (2003) 100 abstracts.

Our results focus on the part of the corpus that double annotation was completed on to show the inter-annotator agreement and highlight the challenges.

6.2 Measuring Inter Annotator Agreement

We use Cohen's k (Cohen, 1960) to measure our annotator agreement, correcting for chance agreement. The formula is:

$$K = \frac{P_o - P_e}{1 - P_e},\qquad(1)$$

where P_o is observed and P_e is expected agreement. The range of Kappa can be between -1 and

	CW-DIFF	DESC	DIFF	GAP
CW-DIFF	69	8	5	7
DESC	1	44	0	1
DIFF	-	-	2	-
GAP	5	6	2	23

Table 3: Author Label Agreement Matrix. The letter A (Author) at the beginning of each entry was omitted for the sake of clarity.

1, where 0 means agreement is only expected by chance. A value of 0.8 is considered good agreement.

Kappa measures are widely used in annotation agreement in scientific publications in schemes that have been successful in automated classification based on their annotations (Teufel et al., 2009; Liakata et al., 2012; Fisas et al., 2016). In general, work on author intentions that uses Kappa agreement reports agreement in a range of 0.65-0.78 (Teufel et al., 2006a; Fisas et al., 2015; Teufel et al., 2009) with Liakata et al. (2012) being much lower at 0.55.

Teufel et al. (2009) points out that Kappa treats agreement in rare categories as surprising and rewards these more than frequent categories. Although she sees this as an advantage because scientific publications often have these rare categories, others see this as misleading and criticise that chance-corrected measures do this when applied to unbalanced data-sets. Hence, others often report raw agreement (Kirschner et al., 2015). Our data does have rare categories and so we report the raw agreement in addition to the Kappa agreement.

6.2.1 Inter-annotator Agreement

The inter-annotator agreement (IAA) was 0.77 (N = 955, n = 53, K = 2). Raw agreement was 80.1%. These results demonstrate good agreement and are comparable to similar studies mentioned earlier.

Out of the 955 sentences doubly annotated, the annotators agreed on 764. Based on the agreed sentences, the most frequent category was CW-DESC (32.5%), followed by the background categories BG-DESC-EP (12.2%) and BG-DESC-EP (10.9%). Following this were the author categories A-CW-DIFF (9%), A-CW-SIM (8.8%), A-DESC (5.8%) and A-GAP (3%). In the next section, we discuss some of the difficulties the annotators had with A-COMP-DIFF versus A-GAP/A-DESC. CW-EVAL-SC was surprisingly infrequent

	BG-DESC-EP	BG-DESC-NE	CW-DESC
BG-DESC-EP	83	10	16
BG-DESC-NE	2	93	6
CW-DESC	6	5	248

Table 4: Cited Work and Background Label Agreement Matrix

at 3.9% and CW-COMP at 2.23%. OCR and OTHER were both at 1.3%. All the remaining categories constituted less then 1% of sentences and interestingly all of these had good agreement. OCR will not occur in our writing feedback as we will not be processing text from PDF. However, OTHER or TEXT could happen, although these were rare categories with TEXT having 13 sentences in agreement and OTHER 10 sentences in agreement. TEXT was almost in perfect agreement, while OTHER was used more frequently by one annotator.

6.3 Sources of Disagreement

There were two main sources of disagreement between the annotators: one was in agreeing the labels about the author's work, and the other was in distinguishing between background sentences and those that pertained to specific citations.

In particular, the annotators noticed that when an author spoke about how their work was different to someone else's, they often broke this down over several sentences. The guidelines instructed the annotators to only mark what was linguistically indicated but they were unsure if this meant in the text in general or in that particular sentence. This led to annotators disagreeing on A-COMP-DIFF and A-GAP/A-DESC, as can be seen in Table 3. Our annotation guidelines need to be reviewed with some very specific examples that incorporate these scenarios with clear instructions on how to take linguistic markings into account. This will be a challenge for automated classification of our labels and writing feedback. We need to consider carefully how this lexical information can be captured.

In disagreement about background sentences compared to citation sentences, seen in Table 4, one annotator highlighted that some sentences talked about two specific citations and they labelled these as BG-DESC-EP, while the other annotator labelled them as CW-DESC. After discussion, it was suggested that including examples of this kind in the annotation guidelines would have

helped.

Annotators also noted that a sentence may belong to two labels. For example, a sentence may say something positive about a cited work but then highlight a shortcoming. In the guidelines we instruct the annotator to choose the author based labels over cited work labels in this instance. We acknowledged in choosing the sentence as the annotating unit this could occur, and we think this will prove challenging in automating the labelling.

There were two *Related Work* sections that included references to systems by their names, e.g. Moses or U-SVM. The annotators struggled with both of these as they were only given the *Related Work*. If they had the full paper, they thought they would better ascertain if the author was referring to something that was their own work or another person's. One annotator questioned whether these types of *Related Work* were more likely to come at the end of a paper once a reader was familiar with these terms. Neither annotator thought the guidelines could be updated as in this instance it would have been better to have access to the full paper. Again, this is going to be a challenging area for any automated system, especially if it only takes a submission of the *Related Work* section into account. The system will have no way of knowing if phrases of this kind relate to the author's work. It also raises a point that although we have chosen one discipline to work with, *Related Work* sections can still be written in different styles. Prior to this comment, we had not considered if order within a document impacted the style of the *Related Work*. However, it should still fulfil the qualities expected.

6.4 Annotating the Remaining Sentences

Following a discussion between the annotators on labels that were not in agreement, some changes were made. A small number of the disagreements were genuine mistakes with an annotator selecting the wrong label but most were about the differences in A-COMP-DIFF versus A-GAP/A-DESC, and between CW-DESC and the Background categories. This resulted in an increase in agreement to 0.85 and raw agreement to 87.3%. Part of the reason for this discussion and alignment was to ensure that the annotator who had completed the full corpus was confident about their decisions. They reviewed the remaining sentences following the discussion. The labels from the annotator who completed all sentences will be used as the standard for the full corpus to develop our automated system in the future.

7 Conclusions and Future Work

We have developed a new annotation schema designed to capture author intentions in *Related Work* sections. Our annotation scheme focuses on qualities that should be present in a *Related Work* section and that will support writing feedback. Our schema has 14 categories that will be used in feedback. We report good agreement in our annotation, which is comparable to other annotation experiments within our field. Our experiments help us to refine our annotation guidelines for any future annotation activities and make us aware of challenges we may encounter when trying to automate the classification of the labels within our schema for feedback.

In future work we plan to use our annotated corpus in supervised machine learning to automate the classification of our labels. Work is currently underway to determine features that will best represent the schema labels, taking into account the challenges our annotators raised. This classification model will be an important part of our automated writing system. However, this classifier will treat sentences as individual components, and we need to put these sentences into context to provide meaningful feedback. Future work will involve experiments to investigate how context can be derived from combining the individual labels to provide feedback that adequately reflects the writing.

References

Kitto Kirsty Knight Simon Buckingham Shum Simon Abel, Sophie. 2018. Designing personalised, automated feedback to develop students research writing skills. In *Proceedings of 2018 Australasian Society for Computers in Learning in Tertiary Education*, pages 15–24.

Claire Aitchison, Janice Catterall, Pauline Ross, and Shelley Burgin. 2012. 'Tough love and tears': learning doctoral writing in the sciences. *Higher Education Research & Development*, 31(4):435–447.

M A Angrosh, Stephen Cranefield, and Nigel Stanger. 2012. Context identification of sentences in research articles: Towards developing intelligent tools for the research community. *Natural Language Engineering*, 19(04):481–515.

Laurence Anthony and George V. Lashkia. 2003. Mover: A Machine Learning Tool to Assist in the Reading and Writing of Technical Papers. *Professional Communication, IEEE Transactions on*, 46:185 – 193.

Steven Bird, Robert Dale, Bonnie Dorr, Bryan Gibson, Mark Joseph, Min-Yen Kan, Dongwon Lee, Brett Powley, Dragomir Radev, and Yee Fan Tan. 2008. The ACL Anthology Reference Corpus: A Reference Dataset for Bibliographic Research in Computational Linguistics. In *LREC 2008*.

Jacob Cohen. 1960. A coefficient of agreement for nominal scales. *Educational and psychological measurement*, 20(1):37–46.

Elena Cotos and Nick Pendar. 2016. Discourse classification into rhetorical functions for awe feedback. *calico journal*, 33(1):92–116.

Valéria D Feltrim, Simone Teufel, Maria Graças V das Nunes, and Sandra M Aluísio. 2006. Argumentative zoning applied to critiquing novices scientific abstracts. In *Computing Attitude and Affect in Text: Theory and Applications*, pages 233–246. Springer.

Beatríz Fisas, Francesco Ronzano, and Horacio Saggion. 2016. A multi-layered annotated corpus of scientific papers. In *LREC 2016*.

Beatriz Fisas, Horacio Saggion, and Francesco Ronzano. 2015. On the discoursive structure of computer graphics research papers. In *Proceedings of the 9th linguistic annotation workshop*, pages 42–51, Denver, Colorado, USA. Association for Computational Linguistics.

Debanjan Ghosh, Aquila Khanam, Yubo Han, and Smaranda Muresan. 2016. Coarse-grained argumentation features for scoring persuasive essays. In *Proceedings of the 54th Annual Meeting of the Association for Computational Linguistics (Volume 2: Short Papers)*, pages 549–554, Berlin, Germany. Association for Computational Linguistics.

Yufan Guo, Anna Korhonen, Maria Liakata, Ilona Silins, Lin Sun, and Ulla Stenius. 2010. *Identifying the Information Structure of Scientific Abstracts: An Investigation of Three Different Schemes*. Association for Computational Linguistics, Uppsala, Sweden.

Ken Hyland. 2015. Genre, discipline and identity. *Journal of English for Academic Purposes*, 19(C):32–43.

Barbara Kamler and Pat Thomson. 2006. *Helping doctoral students write: Pedagogies for supervision*. Routledge.

Christian Kirschner, Judith Eckle-Kohler, and Iryna Gurevych. 2015. Linking the thoughts: Analysis of argumentation structures in scientific publications. pages 1–11.

Maria Liakata, Shyamasree Saha, Simon Dobnik, Colin Batchelor, and Dietrich Rebholz-Schuhmann. 2012. Automatic recognition of conceptualization zones in scientific articles and two life science applications. *Bioinformatics*, 28(7):991–1000.

Joseph A. Maxwell. 2006. Literature Reviews of, and for, Educational Research: A Commentary on Boote and Beile's "Scholars Before Researchers". *Educational Researcher*, 35(9):28–31.

Yoko Mizuta and Nigel Collier. 2004. Zone identification in biology articles as a basis for information extraction. In *Proceedings of the international joint workshop on natural language processing in biomedicine and its applications*, pages 29–35. Association for Computational Linguistics.

Christoph Müller and Michael Strube. 2006. Multilevel annotation of linguistic data with MMAX2. In Sabine Braun, Kurt Kohn, and Joybrato Mukherjee, editors, *Corpus Technology and Language Pedagogy: New Resources, New Tools, New Methods*, pages 197–214. Peter Lang, Frankfurt a.M., Germany.

Charles Oppenheim and Susan P Renn. 1978. Highly cited old papers and the reasons why they continue to be cited. *Journal of the American Society for Information Science*, 29(5):225–231.

Brian Paltridge and Sue Starfield. 2007. *Thesis and Dissertation Writing in a Second Language*. Routledge.

Ulrich Schäfer, Christian Spurk, and Jörg Steffen. 2012. A Fully Coreference-annotated Corpus of Scholarly Papers from the ACL Anthology. In *Proceedings of COLING 2012: Posters*, pages 1059–1070, Mumbai, India. The COLING 2012 Organizing Committee.

Christian Stab and Iryna Gurevych. 2014. Identifying argumentative discourse structures in persuasive essays. In *Proceedings of the 2014 Conference on Empirical Methods in Natural Language Processing (EMNLP)*, pages 46–56, Doha, Qatar. Association for Computational Linguistics.

J. Swales. 1981. Aspects of article introductions. *Language Studies Unit*.

J.M. Swales. 1990. *Genre Analysis: English in academic and research settings*. Cambridge University Press.

Simone Teufel. 1999. *Argumentative zoning: Information extraction from scientific text*. Ph.D. thesis, University of Edinburgh.

Simone Teufel, Advaith Siddharthan, and Colin Batchelor. 2009. Towards domain-independent argumentative zoning: Evidence from chemistry and computational linguistics. In *Proceedings of the 2009 Conference on Empirical Methods in Natural Language Processing*, pages 1493–1502, Singapore. Association for Computational Linguistics.

Simone Teufel, Advaith Siddharthan, and Dan Tidhar. 2006a. An annotation scheme for citation function. In *Proceedings of the 7th SIGdial Workshop on Discourse and Dialogue*, pages 80–87, Sydney, Australia. Association for Computational Linguistics.

Simone Teufel, Advaith Siddharthan, and Dan Tidhar. 2006b. Automatic classification of citation function. In *Proceedings of the 2006 Conference on Empirical Methods in Natural Language Processing*, pages 103–110, Sydney, Australia. Association for Computational Linguistics.

Paul Thompson and Chris Tribble. 2001. Looking at Citations: Using Corpora in English for Academic Purposes. *Language Learning Technology*, 5(3):91 – 105.

Stephen E Toulmin. 2003. *The Uses of Argument*. Cambridge University Press.

Melvin Weinstock. 1971. Citation indexes. encyclopedia of library and information science. volume 5. eds. a. kent & h. lancour.

An Online Annotation Assistant for Argument Schemes

John Lawrence   **Jacky Visser**   **Chris Reed**

Centre for Argument Technology
University of Dundee, UK
`j.lawrence/j.visser/c.a.reed@dundee.ac.uk`

Abstract

Understanding the inferential principles underpinning an argument is essential to the proper interpretation and evaluation of persuasive discourse. Argument schemes capture the conventional patterns of reasoning appealed to in persuasion. The empirical study of these patterns relies on the availability of data about the actual use of argumentation in communicative practice. Annotated corpora of argument schemes, however, are scarce, small, and unrepresentative. Aiming to address this issue, we present one step in the development of improved datasets by integrating the Argument Scheme Key – a novel annotation method based on one of the most popular typologies of argument schemes – into the widely used OVA software for argument analysis.

1 Introduction

In argumentative discourse, a speaker or writer intends to convince their audience of a contested point of view (van Eemeren et al., 2014). To convince their audience, an appeal is made to reasoning, either in direct conversation (such as a courtroom discussion), or in indirect or monological settings (such as a political speech). The argumentative quality of such discourse can be evaluated from various perspectives. In the current paper, we focus on the argumentative quality in terms of the acceptability of the reasoning appealed to in the arguments – thus disregarding, e.g., the rhetorical effectiveness, another dimension of the quality of argumentative discourse.

Consider Hillary Clinton's argument in Example (1) – taken from the US2016 annotated corpus of television debates in the lead-up to the 2016 US presidential elections (Visser et al., 2019a). Anticipating that her first asserted proposition might not be outright acceptable to the entire audience, she provides a reason in support. By defending her policy proposal by comparing the dangers of potential terrorists flying to the dangers of them buying guns, Clinton's argument relies on a conventionalised reasoning pattern: that comparable situations should be dealt with similarly.

(1)   Hillary Clinton: *And we finally need to pass a prohibition on anyone who's on the terrorist watch list from being able to buy a gun in our country. If you're too dangerous to fly, you are too dangerous to buy a gun.*

Evaluating an argument begins by identifying the reasoning pattern it is based on. These common reasoning patterns are conceptualised within the field of argumentation theory as 'argument schemes' (Section 2). While corpus-linguistic approaches have gained traction in the study of argumentation – partly motivated by the rise of 'argument mining' (Stede and Schneider, 2018) – these have generally focused on aspects of argumentative discourse other than argument schemes (such as the use of rhetorical figures of speech (Harris and Di Marco, 2017)). The empirical study of argument schemes would greatly benefit from quantitative data in the form of annotated text corpora. Existing corpora annotated with argument schemes, however, tend to be based on restricted typologies, be of limited size, or suffer from poor validation (Section 3).

In the current paper, we aim to support the annotation of argument schemes by combining a recently developed annotation method for one of the leading typologies of argument schemes (Section 4) and a popular online software tool for annotating argumentative discourse, OVA (Section 5). The standard version of OVA, and other software for manual argument annotation, such as Araucaria (Reed and Rowe, 2004), Rationale

Proceedings of the 13th Linguistic Annotation Workshop, pages 100–107
Florence, Italy, August 1, 2019. ©2019 Association for Computational Linguistics

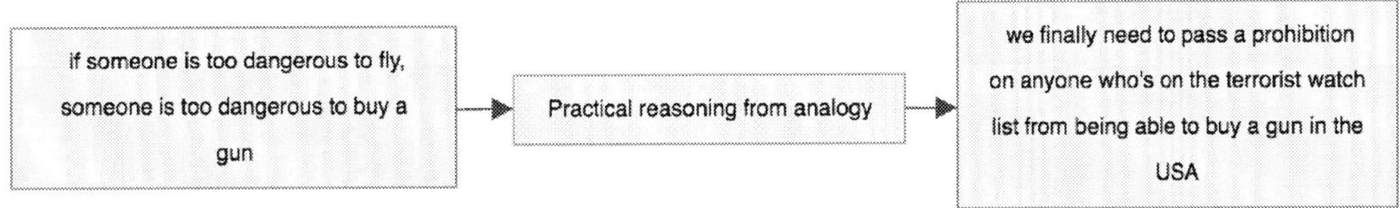

Figure 1: OVA visualisation of the *practical reasoning from analogy* scheme in Example (1).

(van Gelder, 2007), and Carneades (Gordon et al., 2007) allow the analyst to label arguments with a particular scheme, but they do not offer support to the analyst in the actual scheme selection, which is what our OVA extension is aimed at.

2 Argument Schemes

Argument schemes are theoretical abstractions of the conventional patterns of reasoning appealed to in persuasive communication, substantiating the inferential relation between premise(s) and conclusion. The defeasibility of the schemes sets them apart from the strict reasoning patterns of classical formal logic (e.g., Modus Ponens). The type of argument scheme determines its evaluation criteria, commonly expressed as *critical questions* – owing to the dialectical origins of the notion (van Eemeren and Garssen, 2019). Adequately arguing for a standpoint implies both that the premise(s) of the argument should be acceptable, and that the argumentative connection between the premise(s) and the conclusion can withstand the critical questioning.

Since their introduction (Hastings, 1963; Perelman and Olbrechts-Tyteca, 1969; van Eemeren et al., 1978), argument schemes have become a central topic in argumentation studies, leading to a variety of typologies, e.g., by Schellens (1985), Kienpointner (1992), van Eemeren and Grootendorst (1992), and Walton (1996). The latter has found particular uptake in computation-oriented approaches (Rahwan and Simari, 2009; Baroni et al., 2018), and is the starting point for the annotation tool we currently present.

Walton's typology comprises a great variety of schemes, conventionally occurring in argumentative practices ranging from colloquial discussion to legal adjudication (Walton et al., 2008). Many of the schemes are commonly distinguished in dialectical or informal-logical approaches to argumentation (e.g. *argument from sign* and *argument from cause to effect*). Others, however, are more exotic or highly specialised (e.g. *argument from*

arbitrariness of a verbal classification), are closer to modes of persuasion in a rhetorical perspective on argumentation (e.g. *ethotic argument*), or would in other approaches be considered fallacies (e.g. *generic ad hominem*). The list also includes composite schemes that combine aspects from various schemes into one (e.g. *practical reasoning from analogy* combining *practical reasoning* and *argument from analogy*).

3 Annotating Argument Schemes

The annotation of argument schemes comprises the classification of the inferential relations between premises and conclusions of arguments in accordance with a particular typology. Figure 1 shows a diagrammatic visualisation of the argument of Example (1) with in the middle the classification of the argument scheme as an instance of *practical reasoning from analogy*. While we start from Walton's typology, alternative approaches are also employed for scheme identification: Green (2015) presents ten custom argument schemes for genetics research articles, Musi et al. (2016) explore annotation guidelines on the basis of the Argumentum Model of Topics (Rigotti and Greco, 2019), and Visser et al. (2019b) annotate argument schemes on the basis of the Periodic Table of Arguments (Wagemans, 2016).

Existing annotations on the basis of Walton's typology tend to use a restricted set of scheme types, and struggle to obtain replicable results. For example, Duschl (2007) initially adopts a selection of nine argument schemes described by Walton (1996), for his annotation of transcribed middle-school student interviews about science fair projects. Later, however, he collapses several schemes into four more general classes no longer directly related to particular scheme types. This deviation from Walton's typology appears to be motivated by the need to improve annotation agreement. The validation of the annotation method does not account for chance agreement, by only providing percentage-agreement scores (in-

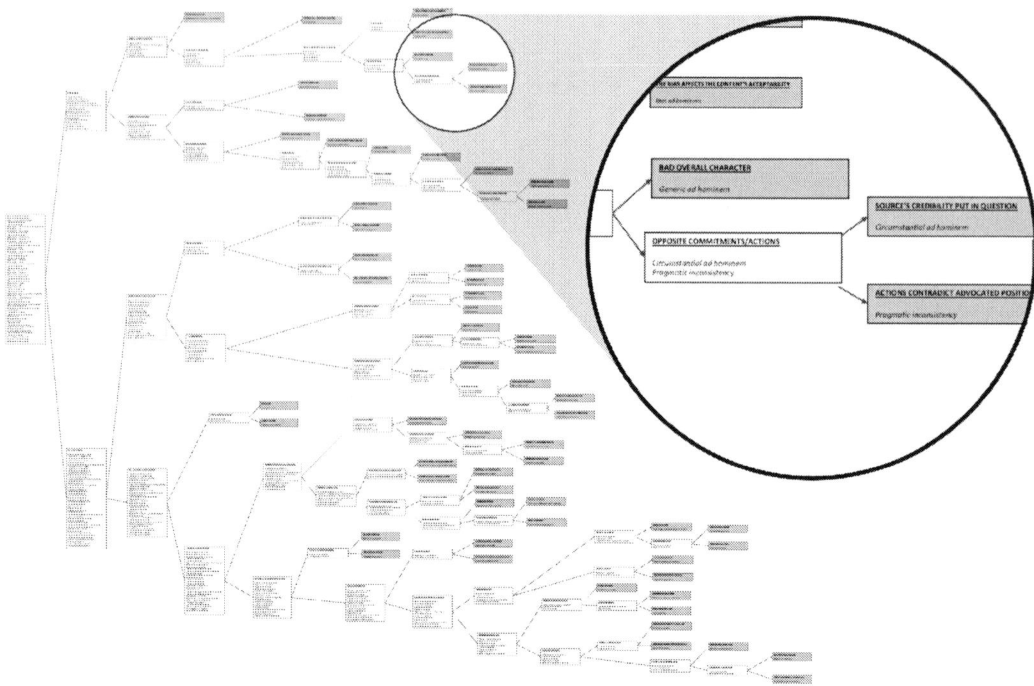

Figure 2: A binary taxonomic tree representation of the ASK

stead of resorting to, e.g., a κ or α metric. Out of a total of 17 texts, the inter-annotator agreement is reported on two as 90% and 84%. No detail is provided on the sampling method.

Similarly, Song et al. (2014) base their annotation on a modification of Walton's typology, settling on a restricted set of three more general schemes: *policy*, *causal*, and *sample* – resulting in Cohen's κ scores for inter-annotator agreement ranging from 0.364 to 0.848. Anthony and Kim (2015) employ a bespoke set of nine coding labels modified from the categories used by Duschl (2007) and nine schemes described in a textbook by Walton (2006). They do not measure any inter-annotator agreement, opting for a fully open collaborative annotation without any testing of the reliability of the methods.

4   The Argument Scheme Key (ASK)

Visser et al. (2018) aim to develop an annotation procedure that stays close to Walton's original typology, while facilitating the reliable annotation of a broad range of argument schemes. The resulting method is reported to yield an inter-annotator agreement of 0.723 (in terms of Cohen's (1960) κ) on a 10.2% random sample. The main principle guiding the annotation is the clustering of argument schemes on the basis of intuitively clear features recognisable for annotators. Due to the strong reliance on the distinctive properties of arguments that are characteristic for a particular scheme, the annotation procedure bears a striking resemblance to methods for biological taxonomy – the identification of organisms in the various subfields of biology (see, e.g., Voss (1952); Pankhurst (1978)). Drawing on the biological analogue and building on the guidelines used by Visser et al. (2018), we developed a taxonomic key for the identification of argument schemes in accordance with Walton's typology: the Argument Scheme Key – or ASK.

The ASK (reproduced in Appendix A) is a dichotomous identification key that leads the analyst through a series of disjunctive choices based on the distinctive features of a 'species' of argument scheme to the particular type. Starting from the distinction between source-based and other arguments, each further choice in the key leads to either a particular argument scheme or to a further distinction. The distinctive characteristics are numbered, listing between brackets the number of any not directly preceding previous characteristic that led to this particular point in the key.

In annotating Example (1), an analyst using the ASK follows a sequence of numbered characteristics to identify the argument as an instance of *practical reasoning from analogy*: 1. Argument does not depend on a source's opinion or character; 17(1). Conclusion is about a course of action; 18. Argument hinges on another motivation for the action [other than its outcome]; 19. Course of action is compared to a similar or alternative action; 21(19). Action is directly compared to another.

The ASK dichotomous identification key can be thought of as a linear textual rendering of a binary taxonomic tree. Figure 2 visualises the decision procedure as such a tree, with each leaf representing an argument scheme label, and all internal nodes showing clusters of schemes that share particular characteristic properties. For each of the numbered binary decision points in the ASK, the tree representation branches into two, thus leading the annotator from the full set of schemes, through their binary choices, to one (and only one) leaf – i.e. an argument scheme classification.

5 The ASK Assistant in the OVA Tool for Argument Annotation

The Online Visualisation of Argument (OVA) tool (Janier et al., 2014) is a web browser based application (http://ova.arg.tech) used by over 3,000 individuals in 38 countries, to analyse and annotate the argumentative structure of natural language text, in contexts ranging from online discussions (Lawrence et al., 2017) to election debates (Visser et al., 2019a). OVA builds on the Argument Interchange Format (AIF) (Chesñevar et al., 2006), an ontology for representing argument analyses compliant with Sematic Web and Linked Data standards, and available in a variety of 'reifications' in languages including JSON, RDF, and Prolog. The software offers import and export of AIF resources from AIFdb (Lawrence et al., 2012), the largest openly available collection of analysed argument, containing over 1.8m words and 170,000 claims in more than 15,000 AIF argument maps.

AIF analyses are graphs comprising nodes of information (I-nodes), and instances of schemes (S-nodes); with sub-types of S-nodes representing the application of rules of inference (RA-nodes), and rules of conflict (CA-nodes). An analysis in OVA begins with segmentation by selecting spans of text corresponding to propositions or Argumen-

tative Discourse Units (Peldszus and Stede, 2013), and adding these to the canvas as I-nodes. Pairs of I-nodes can then be connected, through RA- or CA-nodes to form structures like that of Figure 1. Complex argumentation structures (Groarke et al., 1997; Snoeck Henkemans, 1992) can, in turn, be formed by connecting an I-node to an existing S-node, or by chaining the connections.

Whilst the original version of OVA allows for a user to label any RA-node as an instance of an argument scheme from Walton's typology by selecting from a dropdown list, in this work, we have introduced the option for users to be guided through this process using the ASK. In order to achieve this, the ASK is first converted into JSON , a fragment of which is shown in Listing 1 (we have also made the full JSON representation available online[1] for download and integration into other argumentation tools). Each branching point in the ASK has two options, which are represented by their text, and a result – where the result can either be a scheme name ("resulttype": "scheme") or a pointer to another branching point ("resulttype": "branch").

Listing 1: A fragment of the ASK in JSON

```
{"id": "existing-character",
 "options": [
     {
         "text": "Argument relies on
         the source's good character",
         "result": "Ethotic argument",
         "resulttype": "scheme"
     },{
         "text": "Argument relies on
         bad character",
         "result": "negative-character",
         "resulttype": "branch"
     }
 ]
}
```

When a user elects to use the ASK to help them select an argument scheme, they are presented with a series of modal dialogue boxes similar to that shown in Figure 3. At each stage, the user selects one of the options and is then either presented with the next dialogue box, or they reach a scheme classification which they can choose to accept and apply. An ordered list of user selections at each stage is recorded so that they can step back through the options if they wish to correct an earlier choice.

---

[1] http://arg.tech/~john/waltonkey.json

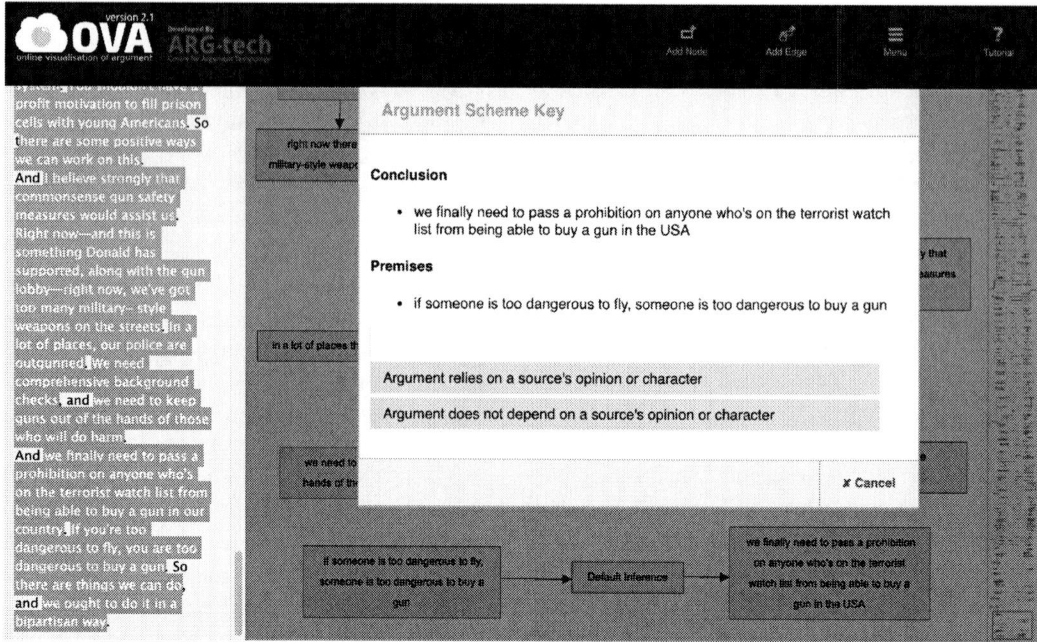

Figure 3: Using the ASK in OVA to annotate the argument scheme used by Clinton in Example (1)

6 Conclusion

Identifying the scheme an argument is based on is an important part of evaluating the argumentative quality of discourse. The availability of large, reliable, and representative datasets is essential both to the empirical study of the use of argument schemes in argumentative practice, and to the development of automated classifiers and argument mining techniques. Existing annotated corpora, however, such as those used by Feng and Hirst (2011), and Lawrence and Reed (2015), for the automatic classification of argument schemes, are not validated, of limited size, or do not represent a broad range of scheme types.

Aiming to improve the availability of high-quality argument scheme corpora, the online annotation assistant we present here combines a novel annotation method for Walton's typology, with the widely used OVA software for argument analysis. The Argument Scheme Key (ASK) module is available for annotators in OVA at `http://ova.arg.tech`. This work constitutes an intermediate step in the development of automated classifiers, utilising the uniquely identifying characteristics of the ASK. Future work will explore the accuracy and robustness of manual annotations by experts, non-experts, and crowd-sourcing (Musi et al., 2016) using the ASK module in OVA.

Acknowledgments

This research was supported by the Engineering and Physical Sciences Research Council (EPSRC) in the United Kingdom under grant EP/N014871/1.

References

Robert Anthony and Mijung Kim. 2015. Challenges and remedies for identifying and classifying argumentation schemes. *Argumentation*, 29(1):81–113.

Pietro Baroni, Dov Gabbay, Massimiliano Giacomin, and Leendert Van der Torre. 2018. *Handbook of formal argumentation, Vol. 1*. College Publications.

Carlos Chesñevar, Sanjay Modgil, Iyad Rahwan, Chris Reed, Guillermo Simari, Matthew South, Gerard Vreeswijk, Steven Willmott, et al. 2006. Towards an argument interchange format. *The Knowledge Engineering Review*, 21(04):293–316.

Jacob Cohen. 1960. A coefficient of agreement for nominal scales. *Educational and Psychological Measurement*, 20(1):37–46.

Richard A Duschl. 2007. Quality argumentation and epistemic criteria. In *Argumentation in science education*, pages 159–175. Springer.

F. H. van Eemeren, B. Garssen, E. C. W. Krabbe, A. F. Snoeck Henkemans, B. Verheij, and J. H. M. Wagemans. 2014. *Handbook of argumentation theory*. Springer.

F. H. van Eemeren and R. Grootendorst. 1992. *Argumentation, communication, and fallacies: A pragma-dialectical perspective.* Lawrence Erlbaum Associates.

F. H. van Eemeren, R. Grootendorst, and T. Kruiger. 1978. *Argumentatietheorie [Argumentation theory].* Het Spectrum.

Frans H. van Eemeren and Bart Garssen. 2019. Argument schemes: Extending the pragma-dialectical approach. In *Proceedings of the 9th Conference of the International Society for the Study of Argumentation (ISSA)*, pages 308–318, Amsterdam, The Netherlands. Sic Sat.

Vanessa Wei Feng and Graeme Hirst. 2011. Classifying arguments by scheme. In *Proceedings of the 49th Annual Meeting of the ACL: Human Language Technologies-Volume 1*, pages 987–996. ACL.

Tim van Gelder. 2007. The rationale for rationale. *Law, probability and risk*, 6(1-4):23–42.

Thomas F Gordon, Henry Prakken, and Douglas Walton. 2007. The carneades model of argument and burden of proof. *Artificial Intelligence*, 171(10):875–896.

Nancy Green. 2015. Identifying argumentation schemes in genetics research articles. In *Proceedings of the 2nd Workshop on Argumentation Mining*, pages 12–21, Denver, CO. ACL.

Leo Groarke, Christopher Tindale, and Linda Fisher. 1997. *Good reasoning matters! : a constructive approach to critical thinking.* Oxford University Press, Toronto.

Randy Allen Harris and Chrysanne Di Marco. 2017. Rhetorical figures, arguments, computation. *Argument and Computation*, 8(3):211–231.

Arthur C Hastings. 1963. *A Reformulation of the Modes of Reasoning in Argumentation.* Ph.D. thesis, Northwestern University.

Mathilde Janier, John Lawrence, and Chris Reed. 2014. OVA+: An argument analysis interface. In *Proceedings of the Fifth International Conference on Computational Models of Argument (COMMA 2014)*, pages 463–464, Pitlochry. IOS Press.

M. Kienpointner. 1992. *Alltagslogik. Struktur and Funktion von Argumentationsmustern [Everyday logic. Structure and functions of specimens of argumentation].* Fromman-Holzboog.

John Lawrence, Floris Bex, Chris Reed, and Mark Snaith. 2012. AIFdb: Infrastructure for the argument web. In *Proceedings of the Fourth COMMA*, pages 515–516.

John Lawrence, Joonsuk Park, Katarzyna Budzynska, Claire Cardie, Barbara Konat, and Chris Reed. 2017. Using argumentative structure to interpret debates in online deliberative democracy and erulemaking. *ACM Transactions on Internet Technology (TOIT)*, 17(3):25.

John Lawrence and Chris Reed. 2015. Combining argument mining techniques. In *Proceedings of the 2nd Workshop on Argumentation Mining*, pages 127–136, Denver, CO. ACL.

Elena Musi, Debanjan Ghosh, and Smaranda Muresan. 2016. Towards feasible guidelines for the annotation of argument schemes. In *Proceedings of the 3rd Workshop on Argumentation Mining*, Berlin. ACL.

R. J. Pankhurst. 1978. *Biological identification.* London: Edward Arnold.

Andreas Peldszus and Manfred Stede. 2013. From argument diagrams to argumentation mining in texts: A survey. *International Journal of Cognitive Informatics and Natural Intelligence (IJCINI)*, 7(1):1–31.

Chaïm Perelman and Lucie Olbrechts-Tyteca. 1969. *The New Rhetoric: A Treatise on Argumentation.* University of Notre Dame Press.

I. Rahwan and G. R. Simari. 2009. *Argumentation in artificial intelligence.* Springer.

Chris Reed and Glenn Rowe. 2004. Araucaria: Software for argument analysis, diagramming and representation. *International Journal on Artificial Intelligence Tools*, 13(4):961–980.

Eddo Rigotti and Sara Greco. 2019. *Inference in Argumentation: A Topics-Based Approach to Argument Schemes.* Springer.

P. J. Schellens. 1985. *Redelijke argumenten. Een onderzoek naar normen voor kritische lezers [Reasonable arguments. A study of norms for critical readers].* Foris.

A. F. Snoeck Henkemans. 1992. *Analyzing complex argumentation.* SicSat.

Yi Song, Michael Heilman, Beata Beigman Klebanov, and Paul Deane. 2014. Applying argumentation schemes for essay scoring. In *Proceedings of the First Workshop on Argumentation Mining*, pages 69–78. Association for Computational Linguistics.

Manfred Stede and Jodi Schneider. 2018. *Argumentation Mining.* Morgan and Claypool Publishers.

Jacky Visser, Barbara Konat, Rory Duthie, Marcin Koszowy, Katarzyna Budzynska, and Chris Reed. 2019a. Argumentation in the 2016 US presidential elections: annotated corpora of television debates and social media reaction. *Language Resources and Evaluation.*

Jacky Visser, John Lawrence, Jean Wagemans, and Chris Reed. 2018. Revisiting Computational Models of Argument Schemes: Classification, Annotation, Comparison. In *Proceedings of the 7th International Conference on Computational Models of*

Argument (COMMA 2018), Warsaw, Poland. IOS Press.

Jacky Visser, John Lawrence, Jean Wagemans, and Chris Reed. 2019b. An annotated corpus of argument schemes in us election debates. In *Proceedings of the 9th Conference of the International Society for the Study of Argumentation (ISSA)*, pages 1101–1111, Amsterdam, The Netherlands. Sic Sat.

E. G. Voss. 1952. The history of keys and phylogenetic trees in systematic biology. *Journal of the Science Laboratories, Denison University*, 43(1):1–25.

Jean H. M. Wagemans. 2016. Constructing a Periodic Table of Arguments. In *Argumentation, Objectivity, and Bias: Proceedings of the 11th International Conference of the Ontario Society for the Study of Argumentation (OSSA)*, pages 1–12. OSSA.

D. Walton, C. Reed, and F. Macagno. 2008. *Argumentation Schemes*. Cambridge University Press.

Douglas Walton. 1996. *Argumentation schemes for presumptive reasoning*. Lawrence Erlbaum Associates, Mahwah, New Jersey.

Douglas Walton. 2006. *Fundamentals of critical argumentation*. Cambridge University Press.

A ASK: Argument Scheme Key

1. Argument relies on a source's opinion or character . . . . 2.
  – Argument does not depend on a source's opinion or character . . . . 17.
2. Argument is about the source's character . . . . 3.
  – Argument is about the source's opinion . . . . 9.
3. Argument establishes the source's character . . . .
  . . . .*Argumentation from interaction of act and person*
  – Argument refers to the source's existing character . . . . 4.
4. Argument relies on the source's good character . . . . .
  . . . . *Ethotic argument*
  – Argument relies on bad character . . . . 5.
5. Source is biased . . . . 6.
  – Argument is not related to bias . . . . 7.
6. Source does not take both sides into account . . . .
  . . . . *Argument from bias*
  – Source's opinion is not acceptable . . . .
  . . . . *Bias ad hominem*
7 (5). Source is of bad overall character . . . .
  . . . . *Generic ad hominem*
  – The source's actions are not compatible with their commitments . . . . 8.
8. Source's actions contradict the advocated position . . .
  . . . . *Pragmatic inconsistency*
  – Source is not credible due to inconsistent commitments . . . . *Circumstantial ad hominem*
9 (2). Argument establishes a source's opinion . . . . 10.
  – Argument is based on an existing opinion . . . . . 11.
10. Commitment at issue is consistent with existing commitments . . . . *Argument from commitment*
  – Commitment at issue is not consistent with existing commitments . . . .
  . . . . *Argument from inconsistent commitment*
11 (9). Source is a general group of people . . . .
  . . . . *Argument from popular opinion*

– Source is a specific individual . . . . 12.
12. Source is an expert in the subject domain . . . .
  . . . . *Argument from expert opinion*
  – Source's credibility is not based on domain knowledge . . . . 13.
13. Source is a witness . . . .
  . . . . *Argument from witness testimony*
  – Source is not a witness . . . . 14.
14. Argument is based on the source's memories . . . . . .
  . . . . *Argument from memory*
  – Argument does not explicitly refer to memories . . . .
  . . . . 15.
15. Argument is based on the source's visual perception
  . . . . *Argument from perception*
  – Argument does not explicitly refer to perception . . . .
  . . . . 16.
16. Conclusion is about a course of action . . . .
  . . . . *Two-person practical reasoning*
  – Argument is not action-oriented . . . .
  . . . . *Argument from position to know*
17 (1). Conclusion is about a course of action . . . . . 18.
  – Conclusion is not specifically action-oriented . . . 32.
18. Argument focuses on the outcome of an action . . . 22.
  – Argument hinges on another motivation for the action
  . . . . 19.
19. Course of action follows an established practice . . . .
  . . . . 20.
  – Course of action is compared to a similar or alternative action . . . . 21.
20. Course of action is explicitly regulated . . . .
  . . . . *Argument from rules*
  – Course of action follows general practices . . . .
  . . . . *Argument from popular practice*
21 (19). Action is best alternative on the basis of prior commitments . . . . *Argument from sunk costs*
  – Action is directly compared to another . . . .
  . . . . *Practical reasoning from analogy*
22 (18). Conclusion promotes a positive outcome . . . 23.
  – Conclusion prevents a negative outcome . . . . . . 26.
23. Course of action assists someone else . . . . 24.
  – Course of action does not offer help . . . . 25.
24. Course of action relieves suffering . . . .
  . . . . *Argument from distress*
  – Argument does not mention suffering . . . .
  . . . . *Argument from need for help*
25 (23). Course of action promotes a goal . . . .
  . . . . *Argument from (positive) consequences*
  – Course of action is not related to an explicit goal . . . .
  . . . . *Practical reasoning*
26 (22). Conclusion is in favour of a course of action . . . .
  . . . . 27.
  – Conclusion is against a course of action . . . . . . 29.
27. Course of action is already ongoing . . . .
  . . . . *Argument from waste*
  – Action is still to commence . . . . 28.
28. Action is motivated by fear . . . .
  . . . . *Argument from fear appeal*
  – Argument is not about a fearful situation . . . .
  . . . . *Pragmatic argument from alternatives*
29 (26). Chain of events would lead to bad outcome . . . .
  . . . . *Slippery slope argument*
  – Action's direct outcome is bad . . . . 30.
30. Performing action would lead to punishment . . . . . .
  . . . . *Argument from threat*
  – Argument is not related to specific threat . . . . . 31.
31. Action would lead to dangerous situation . . . .
  . . . . *Argument from danger appeal*
  – Action would lead to other bad consequences . . . . .
  . . . . *Argument from (negative) consequences*
32 (17). Argument explicitly mentions values . . . . . 33.

Annotating formulaic sequences in spoken Slovenian:
structure, function and relevance

Kaja Dobrovoljc

Jozef Stefan Institute, Ljubljana, Slovenia

University of Ljubljana, Slovenia

`kaja.dobrovoljc@ijs.si`

Abstract

This paper presents the identification of formulaic sequences in the reference corpus of spoken Slovenian and their annotation in terms of syntactic structure, pragmatic function and lexicographic relevance. The annotation campaign, specific in terms of setting, subjectivity and the multifunctionality of items under investigation, resulted in a preliminary lexicon of formulaic sequences in spoken Slovenian with immediate potential for future explorations in formulaic language research. This is especially relevant for the notable number of identified multi-word expressions with discourse-structuring and stance-marking functions, which have often been overlooked by traditional phraseology research.

1 Introduction

There has been an extensive body of research on the formulaic nature of language in the last three decades (Wray, 2013) exposing the large number of multi-word combinations that speakers seem to process as single vocabulary units (Sinclair, 1991; Wray). In addition to the most commonly studied groups of multi-word expressions, such as idioms (e.g. *break a leg*) and collocations (e.g. *heavy rain*), corpus-driven research (Biber, 2009; Conklin and Schmitt, 2012) has shown that formulaic status can also be attributed to frequently recurring sequences of words (variously termed formulaic sequences or lexical bundles), which are not necessarily structurally or semantically complete (e.g. *this means that*).

Although there is a general consensus on the need to systematically identify and formalize formulaic sequences, both for native and non-native speakers of a language (Simpson-Vlach and Ellis, 2010; Brooke et al., 2015), there has been less discussion on the optimal approach to their linguistic description and (sub)categorization. In addition,

few studies that do involve some kind of quantification of formulaic sequences by syntactic, semantic or other properties, rarely report on the methodological issues related to the categorization itself.

To provide insight on the nature of formulaic language in (spoken) Slovenian, and the methodological aspects related to its linguistic categorization in general, this paper presents the annotation of formulaic sequences in the reference corpus of spoken Slovenian in terms of syntactic structure, pragmatic function and semantic relevance. After a short presentation of the corpus (Section 2) and the formulaic sequence extraction (Section 3), we present the annotation workflow and the guidelines in Section 4. Given several distinct aspects of this annotation campaign, a detailed analysis of inter-annotator disagreements is given in Section 5, followed by the presentation and discussion of the resulting list of annotated sequences in Section 6.

2 GOS corpus

GOS is the reference corpus of spoken Slovenian including approximately 120 hours (1 million tokens) of spontaneous speech in different everyday situations in public (radio and TV shows, school lessons and lectures) and non-public settings (meetings, consultations, services, private conversations).

The recordings, balanced for communication channels, situations and speaker demographics, have been manually transcribed in both pronunciation-based and standardized spelling (Verdonik et al., 2013). In this research, version 1.0 of the GOS corpus was used, freely available for download from the CLARIN.SI repository (Zwitter Vitez et al., 2013).[1]

---

[1]For GOS corpus browsing and listening see also the on-

Proceedings of the 13th Linguistic Annotation Workshop, pages 108–112

Florence, Italy, August 1, 2019. ©2019 Association for Computational Linguistics

3 Identification of formulaic sequences

3.1 N-gram extraction

To generate the list of formulaic sequences in GOS corpus, the LIST extraction tool (Krsnik et al., 2019) was used to extract all n-grams of length 2-5 tokens (words with normalized spelling) occurring above the frequency threshold of 20 occurrences per million. In addition to frequency counts, the tool also calculates the strength of association between words in a given n-gram, using three effect-size measures (Dice coeeficient, point-wise mutual information, and cubic mutual information) and two significance measures (t-score, simple log-likelihood), extended for multi-word combinations (Ramisch et al., 2010), as well.

3.2 N-gram ranking

There is no uniform consensus on the optimal method for measuring formulaicity in a language, with methods ranging from raw frequency counts to specific association measures (Biber, 2009; Gries, 2012), producing only partially overlapping recommendations of the most salient multi-word units in a language (Evert, 2009), including Slovenian (Dobrovoljc, 2017). Instead of opting for a single method, we narrowed the initial list of frequently recurring n-grams to the union of top-1,000 candidates ranked by each of the six methods (frequency, Dice, t-score, LL, MI, MI^3). This amounted to the final list of 2,374 formulaic sequences for subsequent annotation (Table 1).

Length	No. of types	Example
2-gram	1,808	*ja ja*
3-gram	504	*se mi zdi*
4-gram	53	*glede na to da*
5-gram	9	*osem nič osem nič nič*
Total	2,374	

Table 1: Number of identified formulaic sequences in GOS by length. (English translations from top to bottom: "yes yes", "it seems", "given the fact that", "eight zero eight zero zero".)

4 Annotation of formulaic sequences

The list of formulaic sequences has been split into multicolumn spreadsheets containing the sequences, slots for predefined labels and the hyperlinks to the corresponding concordances in GOS.

Each spreadsheet was manually annotated by two independent annotators (trained native speakers) based on the guidelines summarized below, with disagreements adjudicated by an expert third annotator.

4.1 Syntactic structure

In terms of syntactic structure, the sequences have been categorized into structurally complete and incomplete sequences. Structurally complete are the sequences that can be attributed a specific syntactic role in a utterance. This includes complete utterances or phrases (e.g. *to je res* "that's true", *no no* "well well"), sentence elements, such as predicates (*boš videl* "you-will see"), predicate arguments (*glava družine* "head of the family") and adjuncts (*pol ure* "half an hour"), as well as modifiers (*bolj ali manj* "more or less"), multi-word conjunctions (*zaradi tega ker* "given the fact that"), and connectives (*tako da* "so that").

Incomplete sequences, on the other hand, include fragments of the above constructions (*da bi se* "that they", *minute čez* "minutes past"), including speech-specific sequences involving fillers (*eee in eee* "uhm and uhm"), discourse markers (*ja tako da* "yes so") and repetitions (*kaj kaj* "what what").

4.2 Pragmatic function

In terms of pragmatic function, the guidelines followed previous influential functional taxonomies (Simpson-Vlach and Ellis, 2010; Biber et al., 2004), in which formulaic sequences are divided into referential expressions that reference physical or abstract entities and their properties (e.g. *to je bilo* "that was", *v skladu z* "in line with", *uradni list št.* "official gazette no.ʻ"), stance expressions that express attitudes or assessments of certainty (e.g. *na nek način* "in a way", *se mi zdi* "I think", *naj bi bil* "is supposed to", *ja ne vem* "well I don't know"), and discourse organizers that contribute to textual and interactional coherence (e.g. *kar pomeni da* "which means that", *to se pravi* "that is to say", *tako da je* "so that is", *ja ja ja* "yes yes yes").

4.3 Lexicographic relevance

In order to determine which formulaic sequences are potentially relevant for inclusion in future dictionaries and similar lexical resources for Slovenian, the annotators were asked to label the sequence in terms of its semantic relevance, i.e.

line concordancer at `www.korpus-gos.net`.

whether the sequence is a multi-word expression they would expect to find in a general dictionary intended for both native and non-native speakers of Slovenian. Specifically, they were instructed to identify multi-word expressions as opposed to free word combinations, ranging from collocations (*na internetu* "on the Internet") to fixed multi-word units with denominative (*javni sektor* "public sector"), syntactic (*kljub temu da* "despite the fact that"), or pragmatic functions (*tako rekoč* "so to speak", *dame in gospodje* "ladies and gentlemen"), regardless of semantic transparency.

4.4 Disambiguation

Only one label was allowed per category. In case of ambiguity, the annotators were advised to inspect a random sample of the concordances provided and decide for the most frequently occurring structural or functional interpretation, i.e. a primary interpretation for the given string. For semantic relevance, on the other hand, the annotators were instructed to label a sequence as relevant regardless of the frequency of this particular usage.

5 Inter-annotator agreement

On average, the two annotators agreed on 81.6% of categorization decisions, with disagreements distributed similarly across different n-gram lengths. This confirms the relatively high level of subjectivity involved in this annotation task, specific not just in terms of categories (intuitive interpretations of abstract classes), but also in terms of items under investigations (highly ambiguous and multifunctional), and the annotation setting itself (lack of immediate context, simple guidelines).

As expected, best inter-annotator agreement was observed for syntactic structure (86% absolute agreement, Cohen's Kappa 0.66), where annotators mostly disagreed on the structure of sequences occurring as both syntactically complete and incomplete units with similar frequency distribution (e.g. *veš kaj* "you know what"). Other frequent groups with structure disagreement include predicates with transitive verbs (*bom rekel* "I-will say"), numerals (*deset tisoč* "ten thousand"), repetitions (*dobro dobro* "good good"), fragments of prepositional phrases (*današnji dan* "(on) this day"), as well as strings of discourse connectives (*in s tem* "and thus"), and clause stems (*kar pomeni* "which means").

For pragmatic function, the moderate inter-

annotator agreement (81% agreement, Cohen's Kappa 0.54) was mostly due to disagreement on the referential or discourse-organizing role of specific groups of sequences, such as sentence fragments containing discourse particles and connectives (*zato je* "so is", *eee mi* "uhm us"), anaphors (*na ta način* "in this way"), and words with metadiscursive meaning (*govorimo o* "we-are-talking about", *v nadaljevanju* "in the continuation"). Similarly, expressions with competing referential and stance-marking interpretations include sequences with modal verbs and adverbs (*morati* "have to", *lahko* "can"), verbs of reasoning (*vedeti* "know", *misliti* "think") and the conditional auxiliary *bi* "would".

The lowest agreement was observed for semantic relevance (78% agreement, Cohen's Kappa 0.43), where the annotators disagreed on the relevance of semantically bleach multi-word units, such as discourse particles (*bi rekel* "say"), interjections (*a ja* "oh really", *daj no* "come on") and general extenders (*ali kaj* "or what"); modified connectives (*tudi če* "even if", *takrat ko* "exactly when"); institutionalized matrix clauses (*kar pomeni da* "which means that", *predlagam da* "I suggest that"), as well as collocations involving numerals (*petnajst minut* "fifteen minutes"), deictics (*vse to* "all this", *z drugimi* "with others") and auxiliary verbs (*bomo naredili* "we-will do").

For all three categories, the competing annotations were resolved by an expert third annotator. However, given the high level of ambiguity and subjectivity inherent to the annotation task, the information on the degree of inter-annotator agreement for each decision has been preserved in the final data release.[2]

6 List of annotated sequences

In general, the distribution of specific annotation labels in the resulting list of formulaic sequences (summarized in Table 2) confirms previous empirical observations that formulaic sequences mostly consist of structurally incomplete n-grams (72.2%) with referential function (72.0%) that do not correspond to traditional dictionary-relevant multi-word expressions (74.6%). Specifically, 50.6% of sequences (1,201) have been labelled with this exact combination of characteris-

---

[2]The resulting list and annotation guidelines will be freely available for download through the CLARIN.SI repository in accordance with the project deliverable timeline. Project website: http://slovnica.ijs.si/

tics, among which sentence fragments (*da je* "that is", *je to* "is this", *ki je v* "which is in") prevail.

Category	Label	N
structure	complete	661
	incomplete	1,713
function	referential	1,709
	stance	306
	discourse	359
relevance	yes	604
	no	1,770
Total		2,374

Table 2: Number of annotated formulaic sequences in GOS by type.

Nevertheless, the annotated list reveals several other groups of formulaic language in spoken Slovenian with potential relevance for further linguistic inquiries and applications. From the point of syntactic structure, the structurally complete sequences (27.8%) include a diverse set of constructions, ranging from sentence elements, such as predicates (*smo rekli* "we-have said"), and adjuncts (*v Sloveniji* "in Slovenia", *dve leti* "two years"), to various types of modifiers (*še en* "another") and sentence-peripheral multi-word expressions. This last group also corresponds to the function-related findings that show a notable share of formulaic sequences with discourse-organizing (15.1%, e.g. *tako da* "so that", *na primer* "for example", *a ne* "right", *dobro jutro* "good morning") and stance-marking functions (12.9%, e.g. *se mi zdi* "it seems", *mislim da* "I think", *po svoje* "in a way"), confirming the importance of discourse structuring, interaction management and speaker mitigation in speech.

In line with the observations above, the subset of sequences recognized as dictionary-relevant (25.4%) includes a heterogeneous set of speech-specific multi-word expressions, such as formulaic replies and questions (*kaj še* "what else" *točno to* "exactly", *kaj pa jaz vem* "what do I know"), expressions of politeness (*hvala lepa* "thank you very much"), temporal expressions (*na začetku* "in the beginning", *še zmeraj* "still", *do zdaj* "until now"), intensifiers (*zelo zelo* "very very", *še bolj* "even more"), discourse-structuring devices (*pri tem* "in doing so", *prav tako* "as well"), hedging expressions (*ne vem* "I don't know", *v bistvu* "actually"), colloquial expressions (*na hitro* "quickly", *ful dobro* "awesome"), as well as other

expressions related to event-specific topics (*na televiziji* "on TV", *predsednik vlade* "prime minister", *v letošnji sezoni* "this season"). Although the large majority of dictionary-relevant sequences consists of syntactically complete units, some incomplete structures have also been marked as relevant, such as multi-word prepositions (*ne glede na* "regardless of"), verbs and phrases with typical prepositions (*govorimo o* "talk about", *pride do* "come to", *hvala lepa za* "thanks for", *priložnost za* "a chance to") and discourse-structuring sentence stems (*to pomeni da* "this means that", *če pogledamo* "if we look at").

7 Conclusion

This paper presented the identification of the most frequent and statistically prominent word n-grams in the reference spoken corpus of Slovenian and their annotation in terms of syntactic structure, pragmatic function and lexicographic relevance. The annotation campaign resulted in a preliminary lexicon of formulaic sequences in (spoken) Slovenian with a high potential for future explorations in both theoretical and applied formulaic language research.

In particular in relation to the latter, our research represents an important addition to existing corpus-based collections of multi-word units in Slovenian (Gantar et al., 2016; Kosem et al., 2018; Ljubešić et al., 2015), which predominantly focus on units with propositional meaning. The large number of formulaic expressions with discourse-organizing and stance-marking functions identified in this research, however, confirms the need for future investigations of non-propositional multi-word expressions, as well.

In doing so, we plan to extend our work to the identification and annotation of formulaic sequences in written texts, drawing on the findings and observations presented above. In addition to the immediate benefits to lexicography, language teaching and natural language processing, an exhaustive inventory of formulaic sequences in Slovenian will also enable further research on methods for their identification and categorization. This also includes a comparison with manual formulaic sequence identification in corpora, bringing insight to issues related to instance-level annotation, as well.

Acknowledgments

The author acknowledges the financial support from the Slovenian Research Agency through the research core funding no. P6-0411 (*Language resources and technologies for Slovene language*) and the research project no. J6-8256 (*New grammar of contemporary standard Slovene: sources and methods*).

References

Douglas Biber. 2009. A corpus-driven approach to formulaic language in English: Multi-word patterns in speech and writing. *International Journal of Corpus Linguistics*, 14(3):275–311.

Douglas Biber, Susan Conrad, and Viviana Cortes. 2004. If you look at ...: Lexical Bundles in University Teaching and Textbooks. *Applied Linguistics*, 25(3):371–405.

Julian Brooke, Adam Hammond, David Jacob, Vivian Tsang, Graeme Hirst, and Fraser Shein. 2015. Building a lexicon of formulaic language for language learners. In *Proceedings of the 11th Workshop on Multiword Expressions*, pages 96–104, Denver, Colorado. Association for Computational Linguistics.

Kathy Conklin and Norbert Schmitt. 2012. The Processing of Formulaic Language. *Annual Review of Applied Linguistics*, 32:45–61.

Kaja Dobrovoljc. 2017. Multi-word discourse markers and their corpus-driven identification. *International journal of corpus linguistics*, 22(4):551–582.

Stefan Evert. 2009. Corpora and collocations. In *Corpus Linguistics. An International Handbook*, volume 1, pages 1212–1248.

Polona Gantar, Iztok Kosem, and Simon Krek. 2016. Discovering Automated Lexicography: The Case of the Slovene Lexical Database. *International Journal of Lexicography*, 29(2):200–225.

Stefan Th Gries. 2012. Frequencies, probabilities, and association measures in usage-/exemplar-based linguistics: some necessary clarification. *Studies in Language*, 11(3):477–510.

Iztok Kosem, Simon Krek, Polona Gantar, Špela Arhar Holdt, Jaka Čibej, and Cyprian Laskowski. 2018. Collocations Dictionary of Modern Slovene. In *Proceedings of the XVIII EURALEX International Congress: Lexicography in Global Contexts*, pages 989–997.

Luka Krsnik, Špela Arhar Holdt, Jaka Čibej, Kaja Dobrovoljc, Aleksander Ključevšek, Simon Krek, and Marko Robnik-Šikonja. 2019. Corpus extraction tool LIST 1.0. Slovenian language resource repository CLARIN.SI.

Nikola Ljubešić, Kaja Dobrovoljc, and Darja Fišer. 2015. *MWELex – MWE Lexica of Croatian, Slovene and Serbian Extracted from Parsed Corpora. *Informatica*, 39(3):293–300.

Carlos Ramisch, Aline Villavicencio, and Christian Boitet. 2010. Multiword expressions in the wild?: The mwetoolkit comes in handy. In *Proceedings of the 23rd International Conference on Computational Linguistics: Demonstrations*, COLING '10, pages 57–60, Stroudsburg, PA, USA. Association for Computational Linguistics.

Rita Simpson-Vlach and Nick C. Ellis. 2010. An Academic Formulas List: New Methods in Phraseology Research. *Applied Linguistics*, 31(4):487–512.

John Sinclair. 1991. *Corpus, concordance, collocation*. Oxford University Press, Oxford.

Darinka Verdonik, Iztok Kosem, Ana Zwitter Vitez, Simon Krek, and Marko Stabej. 2013. Compilation, transcription and usage of a reference speech corpus: the case of the Slovene corpus GOS. *Language Resources and Evaluation*, 47(4):1031–1048.

Alison Wray. *Formulaic Language and the Lexicon*. Cambridge University Press.

Alison Wray. 2013. Formulaic Language. *Language Teaching*, 46(3):316–334.

Ana Zwitter Vitez, Jana Zemljarič Miklavčič, Simon Krek, Marko Stabej, and Tomaž Erjavec. 2013. Spoken corpus Gos 1.0. Slovenian language resource repository CLARIN.SI.

Annotating Information Structure in Italian: Characteristics and Cross-Linguistic Applicability of a QUD-Based Approach

Kordula De Kuthy
SFB 833
University of Tübingen
dekuthy@uni-tuebingen.de

Lisa Brunetti
Université de Paris,
LLF, CNRS
lisa.brunetti@
linguist.univ-paris-diderot.fr

Marta Berardi
SFB 833
University of Tübingen
mberardi@sfs.uni-tuebingen.de

Abstract

We present a discourse annotation study, in which an annotation method based on *Questions under Discussion (QuD)* is applied to Italian data. The results of our inter-annotator agreement analysis show that the QUD-based approach, originally spelled out for English and German, can successfully be transferred cross-linguistically, supporting good agreement for the annotation of central information structure notions such as *focus* and non-at-issueness. Our annotation and inter-annotator agreement study on Italian authentic data confirms the cross-linguistic applicability of the QuD-based approach.

1 Introduction

In this paper, we present a discourse annotation study of Italian data, which uses the annotation scheme and discourse-analytic method, the *QUD-tree* framework, developed in **?**, **?** and **?**. Its purpose is the cross-linguistic analysis of *information structure* and *discourse structure* of textual data. On the theoretical side, the QUD framework has been applied to a number of different languages, such as German, English and French in (**?**), and various Austronesian languages as discussed in **?** and **?**. On the applied side, **?** showed that the QUD based method supports the successful annotation of discourse structure and information structure in German and English spoken language data. Here we want to broaden the crosslinguistic scope of the QUD framework and apply it to another Romance language, Italian. We will explore both the QUD annotation and the information structure annotation including all information structure labels that are part of the annotation scheme proposed in **?**, such as *focus, background, contrastive topic, nai* and *topic*. Topic is regarded as a notoriously difficult label in agreement studies (cf. **??**). While the results of our study show that the question-based

annotation method supports the successful annotation of discourse structure and of information structure, in particular focus, we will also discuss, using the example of topic, some shortcomings of the QUD based annotation method.

2 The QUD framework

The QUD framwork introduced in **?** presents an explicit method for the reconstruction of QUDs which are usually only discussed as an abstract theoretical term. The center of the QUD framework is a compact representation format for QUD trees, in which the textual assertions (A) represent the terminal nodes of a discourse tree (preserving the linear order of the text from left to right) while (implicit or explicit) QUDs (Q) form the non-terminal nodes. An abstract QUD tree is shown in Figure 1.

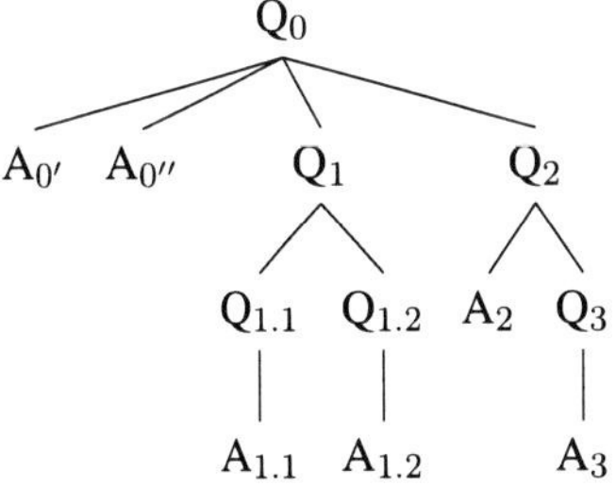

Figure 1: QUD tree

The QUD-tree framework as spelled out in **?** can be applied to any kind of written or spoken discourse or conversation. It is not language-specific and can, in principle, be used in order to investigate data from any language. While the exact analysis procedure is described at great length within the guidelines document (**?**), we just briefly introduce some basic principles here.

Proceedings of the 13th Linguistic Annotation Workshop, pages 113–123
Florence, Italy, August 1, 2019. ©2019 Association for Computational Linguistics

2.1 Segmentation

Raw texts are segmented into atomic assertions. Apart from orthographic sentence boundaries, segmentation also applies at (1) (information-structurally relevant) coordinations and (2) before (optional) syntactic adjuncts. (Obligatory) sentential arguments (3) are not split off.

(1) A_4: Ho   appena terminato un romanzo
    I-have just   finished   a   novel
    'I just finished a novel'
    $A_{4'}$: e   sono già   al lavoro su un nuovo progetto.
    and am   already at work   on a   new   project
    'and I'm already working on a new project.'

(2) $A_{7''}$: Di recente ho   ripreso   a leggere i
    of recently I-have re-started to read   the
    romanzi di formazione,
    novels   of coming-of-age
    $A_{7'''}$: senza mai tralasciare la narrativa
    without ever neglecting the contemproray
    contemporanea e   i   romance.
    fiction   and the romance'

(3) $A_{25'}$:[[Alek]$_T$ [è frutto della mia fantasia]$_F$],
    Alex   is result of-the my   imagination
    $A_{25''}$:[[nasce   in relazione a Dave]$_F$] ,
    he-is-born in relation   to Dave
    A_{26}:[[ho voluto che]$_{NAI}$ fosse ["forte" ma non
    I-have wanted that   he-was strong   but not
    "invincibile"]$_F$].
    invincible

2.2 QUD principles

The actual identification of a QUD for each assertion is guided by a number of explicit principles adapted from the formal literature on information structure (????), cf. ?:

Q-A-CONGRUENCE: QUDs must be answerable by the assertion(s) that they immediately dominate.

Q-GIVENNESS: Implicit QUDs can only consist of given (or, at least, highly salient) material.

MAXIMIZE-Q-ANAPHORICITY: Implicit QUDs should contain as much given (or salient) material as possible.

Example (4) shows that from these principles we can derive QUD Q_{32} for assertion A_{32} in the context of A_{31}, whereas any of the questions in (5), used in place of Q_{32}, would violate at least one of the QUD constraints in the same context.

(4) A_{31}:   Anche tra   i bilingui precoci che
    even   among the early   bilinguals who
    parlano due lingue   quasi mai le due
    speak   two languages almost never the two

lingue   sono del tutto equivalenti,
languages are   completely equivalent
'Even among the early bilinguals who speak two languages, the two languages are almost never completely equivalent,'
Q_{32}:   {What about the two languages instead?}
> A_{32}:   and [[normalmente]$_{NAI}$ [[ogni lingua]$_T$ [si
and usually   each language itself
sviluppa in un contesto specifico]$_F$]$\sim$
develops in a   context specific
'and usually each language develops in a specific context.'

(5) a. {What about speaking two languages?}
                    (#Q-A-CONGRUENCE)
    b. {What about the specific context?}
                    (#Q-GIVENNESS)
    c. {What happens next?}
           (#MAXIMIZE-Q-ANAPHORICITY)

Two or more assertions are defined as parallel if and only if they share some semantically identical content and represent partial answers to the same QUD, see Example (6), where the semantically shared content is *Alek* (omitted in the second assertion).

PARALLELISM: The background of a QUD with two or more parallel answers consists of the (semantically) common material of the answers.

(6) Q_{25}:   {What about the connection with reality in Alek?}
    > $A_{25'}$: [[Alek]$_T$ [è frutto   della mia
    Alek   is the result of-the my
    fantasia]$_F$] ,
    imagination
    > $A_{25''}$: [[nasce in relazione a Dave]$_F$] ,
    is-born in relation   to Dave

The resulting tree structure is shown in Figure 2.

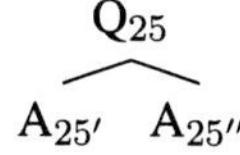

Figure 2: Two coordinated (parallel) assertions.

3 QUDs and information structure

The basis of our annotation approach is an alternative-based definition of information structural categories, in line with e.g. ?, ?, ?, ? or ?. The Table in 1 shows the definitions for the information structure categories as introduced in ?. These are the basis for the labels used in our annotation study.

(7) Q_7:   {Cosa ti   piace leggere?}
    what you like to-read

Category (Label)	Definition
Focus domain ($\sim$)	Part of an assertion that has the same background as the current QUD and that contains a focus
Focus (F)	Constituent that answers the current QUD
Background (BG)	Material mentioned in the current QUD
Contrastive topic (CT)	Material backgrounded w.r.t. the current QUD and focal w.r.t. a super-question
Topic (T)	Distinguished discourse referent identifying what the sentence is about
Non-at-issue material (NAI)	Optional material w.r.t. the current QUD

Table 1: Information structure: Label inventory

> 'What do you like to read?'
> A_7: [[Di recente]$_{NAI}$ [[ho ripreso a
> *of recently   I-have re-started to*
> leggere]$_{BG}$ [i romanzi di formazione]$_F$]$\sim$
> *read   the novels of coming-of-age*
> 'I recently started to read the novels of coming-of-age.'

(7) is an example demonstrating the assignment of information-structure labels in the context of a QUD (in curly brackets). Note that the indentation ($>$) of A_7 in the textual representation marks subordination in the discourse tree, as shown in Figure 2. The focus is *i romanzi di formazione* 'coming-of-age novels', which is labelled [ ]$_F$ and constitutes the answer to the QUD Q_7. The background is linguistic content that is mentioned in this QUD. The question is about what books the interviewee reads or likes to read, so *ho ripreso a leggere* 'I've restarted to read' (labelled [ ]$_{BG}$) is clearly recoverable from the QUD. Focus and background together form the focus domain, labelled [ ]$\sim$. The sentence initial phrase *Di recente* 'recently' is not relevant to answer the QUD Q_7, which would still receive an answer without it, therefore it is labelled [ ]$_{NAI}$.

An example of the label Topic T is given in (8).

(8) Q_{32}: Come puoi riassumere ai   tuoi
how   can-you summarize to-the your
lettori questo romanzo?
readers this   novel
'How can you summarize this novel to your readers?' [...]
> A_{32}: [[Senza Etichette]$_T$ [è la storia di Dave]$_F$]$\sim$,
Senza   Etichette   is the story of Dave

In A_{32}, the clause initial phrase *Senza etichette*, the novel's title, is part of the background (in fact, it is the only background in that utterance) because it is mentioned in Q_{32}. Since it is a referential expression, it is marked [ ]$_T$.

In (9), an example of a contrastive topic (CT) is given.

(9) Q_{10}:   Se dovessi esprimere tre desideri?
if   you-had to-express three wishes
[...]
> $Q_{10.1}$ {What is your first wish?}
>> $A_{10.1}$: quindi [[il primo]$_{CT}$ sarebbe: [la
so   the first-one   would-be the
libertà e la felicità di mio
freedom and the happiness of my
figlio]$_F$]$\sim$;
son
> $Q_{10.2}$:   {What is your second wish?}
>> $A_{10.2}$: [[il secondo]$_{CT}$ è [riuscire a
the second   is to-succeed to
emozionare quanti più lettori
touch   as-much more readers
possibile]$_F$]$\sim$,
as-possible

The (explicit) question Q_{10} asks the interviewee to tell three wishes. The speaker answers by uttering three different assertions each about one wish. Clearly, *il primo* 'the first (wish)' in $A_{10.1}$ and *il secondo* 'the second (wish)' in $A_{10.2}$ are members of the alternative set mentioned in Q_{10} (*tre desideri* 'three wishes').

4 Evaluation: Discourse structure

In the present annotation study based on the above described QUD framework, our goal is to show that the discourse annotation in terms of QUDs can be applied reliably to naturally occurring data - in this particular case, Italian data. We conducted an empirical study, in which annotators followed the QUD guidelines described in **?** to annotate two Italian blog interviews.

For the QUD-based annotation we use the tool *TreeAnno* introduced by **?**, which enables the analyst to semi-automatically segment texts, systematically enhance them with implicit *Questions under Discussion (QUDs)*, and transform the data into a discourse tree called *QUD tree*, as described in ?.

4.1 Evaluation setup

Two trained annotators (and also native speakers of Italian) analyzed and annotated two short Italian blog interviews downloaded from the internet [1]. The first blog interview consists of 95 text segments, the second one of 113 segments. The QUD discourse tree for Blog 1 resulting from the first annotator is shown in Figure 3, the other three discourse trees are included in the Appendix.

4.2 Method and results

For the comparison of the two annotated documents, we follow the method described in ?. The basic idea is that for the comparison of two QUD annotations one needs to calculate an inter-annotator agreement score that takes into account, for every segment and every possible span of segments, whether a QUD is present or not. In order to compute a κ statistics (?) based on our QUD annotations, ? propose to follow the method described in ?, which was developed for measuring agreement in the labelling of rhetorical structure categories in texts. The method is based on the idea of mapping the hierarchical structure of a discourse tree onto sets of units (i.e. text segments) that are a matrix or chart filled with categorical values. In our case, the values are whether there exists a (Q)uestion spanning the respective segments – start to end – or (n)ot).

A κ statistics can then be computed between two charts that represent two different QUD annotations for the same text, more precisely between the two resulting sets of possible spans of segments.[2] For our two annotated documents we calculated κ values for the annotation charts derived from our QUD annotations, based on the above described method. For the text *Italian Blog 1,* consisting of 95 segments, we calculated the κ statistics based on 4,256 items (i.e. possible spans of segments), for *Italian Blog 2* with 113 segments based on 6,187 items. The results are shown in Table 2.

Text	Segments	Spans	κ
Italian Blog 1	95	4,256	.61
Italian Blog 2	113	6,187	.51

Table 2: Kappa values for QUD-annotated Italian dialogues

The values show moderate agreement between the annotator pairs. For Blog 1, the κ value is at .61, which is substantially higher than what (?) report for the QUD annotations of their German and English texts: their κ values are around .5. For our Blog 2, the κ value is at .51, which is thus very similar to the scores reported in (?) for texts of similar length. Our two annotated Italian texts are relatively short, only around 100 sentences each, so it is perhaps too early to interpret the results, in particular since this is a rather complex task. However, since the results are comparable to those reported in (?), we take this as a further proof that the QUD-based annotation of discourse can successfully be applied cross-linguistically.

5 Evaluation: Information structure

The second major issue we are interested in is to evaluate the reliability of information-structure annotation based on the previous identification of QUDs.

5.1 Evaluation setup

For the evaluation of the information structural annotation, the same two Italian blog texts were annotated by the same two trained annotators, who still followed the guidelines of Riester et al. 2018). We aimed at annotating all five categories that are mentioned in ?: focus (F), background (BG), non-at-issue material (NAI), contrastive topic (CT) and topic (T). Focus domain labels ($\sim$) were not annotated, since each text segment (assertion) already corresponds to one focus domain. The annotators based their annotations on the previously performed QUD analysis in the TreeAnno tool. As an annotation tool for the token-based information-structure annotation, WebAnno (?) was chosen. Figure 4 shows a screenshot of the information-structure annotation of the beginning of *Blog 1*.

5.2 Method and results

As agreement measure for the evaluation of the information structure annotation, we calculated κ values on the annotated texts based on tokens,

---

[1] Blog 1 URL: `http://purl.org/info-struc/Italian-blog-1`, Blog 2 URL: `http://purl.org/info-struc/Italian-blog-2`

[2] Generally, for n segments contained in a document, the number of possible text spans is $\frac{n \times (n+1)}{2}$.

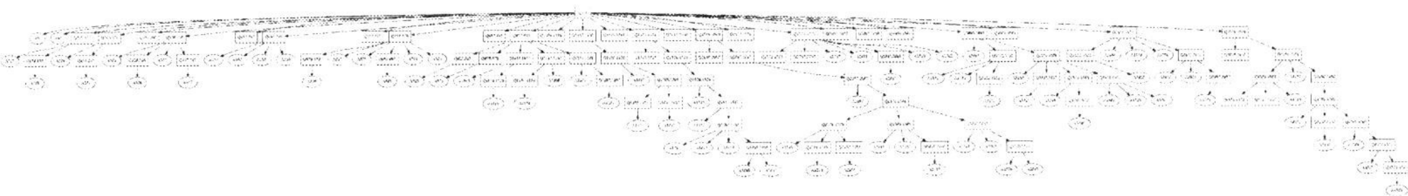

Figure 3: A QUD tree analyses for Italian Blog 1

Text	Label	Tokens	κ
Italian Blog 1	all	847	.70
	F		.72
	BG		.21
	CT		.85
	NAI		.53
	T		.45
Italian Blog 2	all	1243	.58
	F		.51
	BG		.1
	CT		.1
	NAI		.62
	T		.35

Table 3: Kappa for information structure annotation

following previous work (**???**). In addition to the specifications in **?**, in particular the QUD-to-information-structure mapping from Table 1, we defined a number of heuristic (but potentially debatable) rules in order to prevent disagreement due to theoretically unclear issues, such as:

- Discourse connectors (*but, and, although, because, therefore* etc.) at the beginning of discourse segments are not annotated.

- Punctuation: Quotation marks around an expression, commas within and at the right edge of an expression are part of the markable. Periods, colons, semicolons, exclamation marks are not.

Results are shown in Table 3, divided into scores for all labels taken together, and individual scores for each of the four labels.

The results are rather heterogeneous in both texts but overall they show that the QUD-based method does contribute to a successful annotation of information structure in Italian for a range of labels. For the first text Blog 1, the overall agreement score for all annotated categories taken together is at .7, which shows substantial agreement,

the score for focus annotation alone being at .72. The agreements scores for the second blog are overall lower, but with .58 for the overall agreement and .51 with agreement for focus they are still at a relatively high level and still comparable to the scores that (**?**) report for the annotation of German and English data (which are at around .65). The category NAI, the classification of non-at-issue material, also received reasonable agreement scores at .53 in Blog 1 and .62 for Blog 2. The agreement scores for the other three categories, BG and CT, differ a lot between the two texts. In Blog 1, the score for contrastive topic is very high with .85, in Blog 2 the score .1 shows that there was hardly any agreement between the two annotators. This might be due to the fact that there were only very few cases for which the label CT was used. In Blog 1, the label CT was used for 9 and 12 tokens in the two annotations, in Blog 2 it was assigned to 13 and 14 tokens (out of 1243 tokens). The case is similar with respect to background: in the two annotated documents, the label BG was only assigned for around 40 tokens in Blog 1 and 30 tokens in Blog 2. This means that, if the annotators disagreed in only one token when assigning the label CT or BG, this had a much greater impact on the agreement scores for these labels than in the cases of disagreement for assigning focus labels. The category topic (T) received relatively low agreement scores at .45 and .35, but still at a level which other studies report for categories like focus (cf. **?** report a κ of .44 for focus). In the following section we will qualitatively evaluate why the annotation scheme seems to better support the successful annotation of a category like focus, whereas there seems to be much more disagreement when annotating topic.

6 Qualitative Evaluation: The Case of Topics

In the question-based definitions of our information structure labels, the focus corresponds to those parts of an assertion that answer the current QUD. Especially in case of overt questions, but with implicit QUDs, the annotators agree on focus.

The definition of topic in the QUD framework, however, is the only one that does not take the current QUD into account. As remarked by **?**, while potentially all referential expressions inside the background could be labelled as topic, one might argue that not all referential expressions inside the background are actually aboutness topics. But unfortunately, the QUD method is not meant to single out the best topic candidate. And **?** do not provide any rules that help to distinguish between better and worse topic candidates. The only cue that is given through the current QUD is that all focal expressions are excluded as topic candidates.

A typical topic expression in Italian would be a clitic left or right dislocated phrase (see *quel libro* below), but no dislocation was present in our data, probably due to the fact that a blog interview is less interactive than an spoken conversation, and these construction are typically used in interaction.

(10) a. Quel libro, l'ho   dato a Giorgio.
    that book it I-have given to Giorgio

   b. L'ho   dato a Giorgio, quel libro.
    it I-have given to Giorgio that book

Clitic personal pronouns, such as *le* in A_2 in (11), are also typical candidates for (continuing) topics.

(11) A_1: Abbiamo fatto quattro chiacchiere con Maria Verdiana Rigoglioso per parlare di *Senza Etichette*, il romanzo che ha pubblicato con Libromania.
    'We had a chat with Maria Verdiana Rigoglioso to talk about *Senza Etichette*, the novel she published with Libromania.'
   Q_2: {What did you do with her exactly?}

> A_2:[[Le]$_T$ [abbiamo fatto un po' di domande]$_F$]
   to-her we-have made a little of questions
   'We asked her a few questions'
> Q_3:{What for? }
> A_3:[per [conoscere retroscena e   curiosità del
   to   know   ins-and-outs and trivia   of-the
   romanzo]$_F$].
   novel
   'to get to know the background and trivia of the novel.'

What about cases where the topic is neither a dislocated expression, nor a clitic? Our annotation method should be able to single out such cases, but this is not always true. The example above nicely illustrates a case where our annotators disagreed about labelling a given referential expression as topic: the PP *del romanzo* in A_3, which is already introduced in the previous sentence, A_1. One annotator chose to nevertheless include it in the focus and label A_3 as an all-focus assertion. The other annotator, while annotating a similar QUD, chose to label the PP as a topic. Indeed, strictly speaking, this given PP should then also be part of the QUD ("What for, with respect to the novel?").

(12) Q_3: What for with respect to the novel?
   > A_3:[per [conoscere retroscena e   curiosità]$_F$
    to   know   ins-and-outs and trivia
   [del   romanzo]$_T$] .
    of-the novel

It may be observed that the PP *del romanzo* is embedded inside the verb's direct object NP. Our assumption is that informational categories are defined and identified solely by pragmatic means, in particular by the QUD-related properties given in Table 1. Despite such an assumption, we may suppose that it was the syntactically embedded position of *del romanzo* that led one annotator to consider it as part of the focus, or more precisely, the fact that the focus (*retroscena e curiosità*) did not form a constituent on its own without the PP *del romanzo*. The relationship between the given-new structure and the syntactic structure has not been discussed by **?**, but it is something that might be worth addressing in the future. Of course, if the syntactic position of the topic must be invoked to complete the picture and arrive at its identification, then we expect different levels of complexity in the task of annotating aboutness topics depending on the language.

In other cases, the topic was well identified by both annotators, such as *le due lingue* in (13).

(13)A₁: [Spesso]_NAI [si pensa]_NAI [che sia
often   one thinks   that is
bilingue solo [chi è   stato esposto a due
bilingual only who has been exposed to two
lingue   fin   dalla tenera infanzia]_F]
languages since earliest   infancy
'It is often thought that only those who have
been exposed to two languages since child-
hood are bilingual.'

Q₁.₁: {One thinks that bilinguals are those who do
what, with such two languages?}

> A₁.₁: e   [[parla]_F [le due lingue]_T [in modo
and speaks   the two languages in way
perfetto e   equivalente]_F].
perfect and equivalent
'and speak the two languages in a perfect and
equivalent way.'

In this example syntax does not help to identify
the topic status of the direct object *le due lingue*.
Such expression is mentioned in A₁ as part of the
focus, but instead of being promoted to topic in
the subsequent utterance by some syntactic device
for topic shift (such as left dislocation, cf. **?**), it
is left in situ. One reason for the speaker's choice
may be the fact that the topic expression is inside
a free relative, a construction that seems to be incompatible with dislocations, as the unacceptabil-
ity of examples below shows:

(14)a. ??Chi l'italiano, lo conosce sa   bene dove
who the italian it knows   knows well where
sta l'errore.
is the mistake

b. ??Ho   dato un bel voto a chi   il primo
I-have given a good note to whom the first
esercizio, lo ha   fatto bene.
exercice   it they-have done well

Since *due lingue* is mentioned in the previous
sentence, the context tells us that this expression
is clearly background. Since it's a referential expression, it has all that is required to be identified
as topic. Note that a clitic pronoun might have
been acceptable here (see example (15)), but this
option is not chosen by the speaker/writer.

(15)A₁.₁: e   [[le]_T [parla]_F [in modo perfetto e
and them speaks in way   perfect and
equivalente]_F].
equivalent

The mechanism of identifying parallel structures (multiple answers to the same question) is
a strategy that our annotation tool provides to help
recognizing 'hidden' topics.

(16)A₅₃: I   genitori dovrebbero lasciare spazio
the parents should   leave   space

al   bambino o bambina che
to-the boy   or girl   which
c'è   in loro
there is in them
'Parents should leave room for the child in
them'

Q₅₄: {To do what?}
> A₅₄: [[per giocare con i   figli]_F] ,
to   play   with their children
> Q₅₅: {Parents should experience languages in
what way?}
>> A₅₅′: [dovrebbero [soprattutto]_NAI vivere [le
they-should above-all   live   the
lingue]_T [come esperienza]_F]
languages as   experience
'they should above all live languages as an
experience'
>> A₅₅″: e   [[non come performance da
and not as   performance to
misurare]_F] .
measure
'and not as a performance to be measured.'

Clearly, the fact that *le lingue* (which again oc-
cupies a canonical post-verbal position in A₅₅′) is
elided in A₅₅″, shows that it represents shared material between A₅₅′ and A₅₅″, and therefore is part
of the background.

Cases of topic shift were easily recognized by
the two annotators. One example is given below in (17). The referent *la mamma che parla
la lingua minoritaria per crescere i suoi bambini
bilingui* is introduced in the overt question Q₂₄.₁
and then it continues as topic in the answer A₂₄.₁.
Then the topic changes and becomes *i bambini* in
A₂₅. In A₂₆, the topic changes back to *la mamma
madrelingua*.

(17)Q₂₄.₁: La mamma che parla la lingua
the mother   who speaks the minority
minoritaria per crescere i   suoi
language   to raise   the her
bambini bilingui, cosa fa?
bilingual children, what she-does
'The mother who speaks the minority language to raise her bilingual children what
does she do?'
> A₂₄.₁: [[Parla   la propria lingua   ai
she-speaks the her-own language to-the
figli.]_F]
children'
'She speaks her own language to her children.'
> Q₂₅: {What do the children do?}
>> A₂₅: Solo che [molto spesso]_NAI [[i
only that very   often   the
bambini]_T [pur capendola
children   even understanding-her
perfettamente]_NAI [non parlano
perfectly   not speak
attivamente la sua lingua]_F]
actively   the her language
'It's just that very often children, even

though they understand her perfectly, don't
actively speak her language.'

$\gg$ Q$_{26}$:   {What can the mother do then?}
$\ggg$ A$_{26}$:   Ecco quindi che [[la mamma
                  there then   that the mother
                  madrelingua]$_T$ può [cominciare ad usare
                  mothertongue can start   to use
                  la   creatività]$_F$]
                  the creativity
                  'This is where mother-tongue mother can
                  begin to use her creativity.'

The fact that the topic is a preverbal subject also helped the annotators to recognize it. As discussed in (**?**), preverbal subjects are typical sentence topics, and our two annotators agreed more often when the topic was in that position. The so-called hidden topics were more challenging.

And even if an expression was correctly included within the background, the two annotators still had to decide for every referential item that was part of the background whether to label it as a topic or not. Not surprisingly, they sometimes agreed, as in (13), and they sometimes picked different elements. Since there are several characteristics of the text and the preceding discourse that have to be taken into account for the identification of possible topics, we hypothesise that this category will probably always be annotated with less accuracy than the other information structure categories such as focus or non-at-issue material.

7   Conclusion

We have presented a novel method for the annotation of information structure which achieves good inter-annotator scores. In particular the agreement scores for focus are much higher than the results reported in other similar annotation studies on naturally occurring data (cf. **?**). The method is based on the reconstruction of QUDs, from which the annotation of IS categories is then derived. The results of our inter-annotator agreement analysis show that the QUD-based approach, originally spelled out for English and German, can successfully be transferred cross-linguistically, supporting good agreement for the annotation of central information structure notions such as *focus* and non-at-issueness, with *(contrastive) topic* and *background* showing lower levels of agreement for some texts due to underrepresentation of those information structural categories in some of the data analysed. Thanks to the QUD-based method, attention was drawn to some interesting aspects of Italian information structure, and in particular of

Italian topics. Some difficulties of topic identification were shown to be reduced by the adopted annotation procedure. We believe that the discussion of the problems occurring with the labelling of topics in Italian not only contributes to the analysis of topics in Romance languages, but also helps to refine the QUD annotation procedure in general, so that future annotators are more aware of problematic cases which will hopefully lead to even more reliable annotations.

A   Appendices

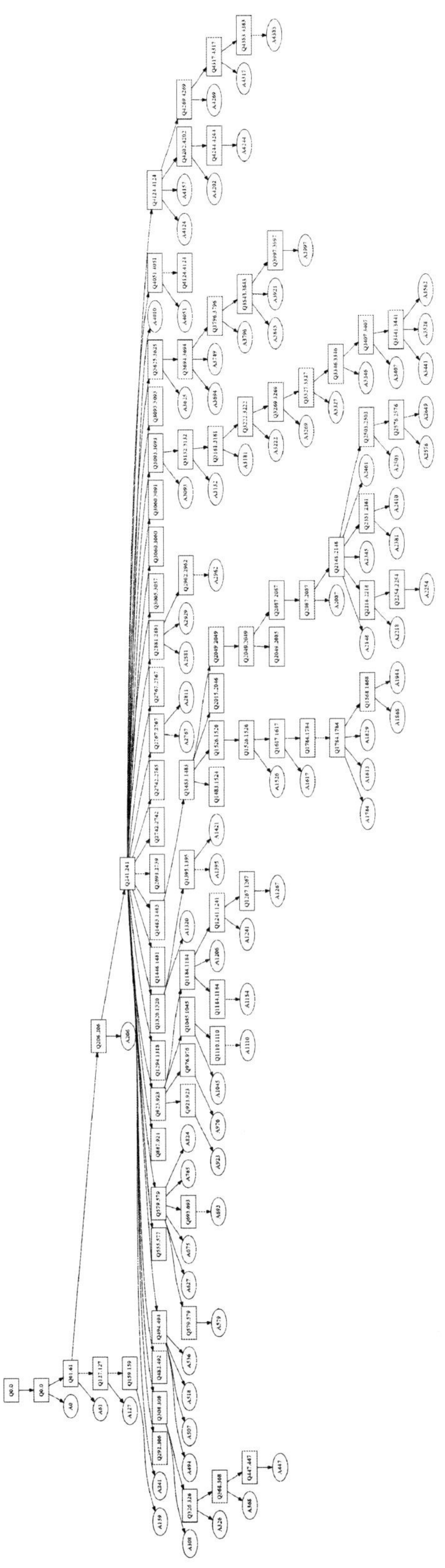

Figure 5: A QUD tree analyses for Italian Blog 1 (Second Annotator)

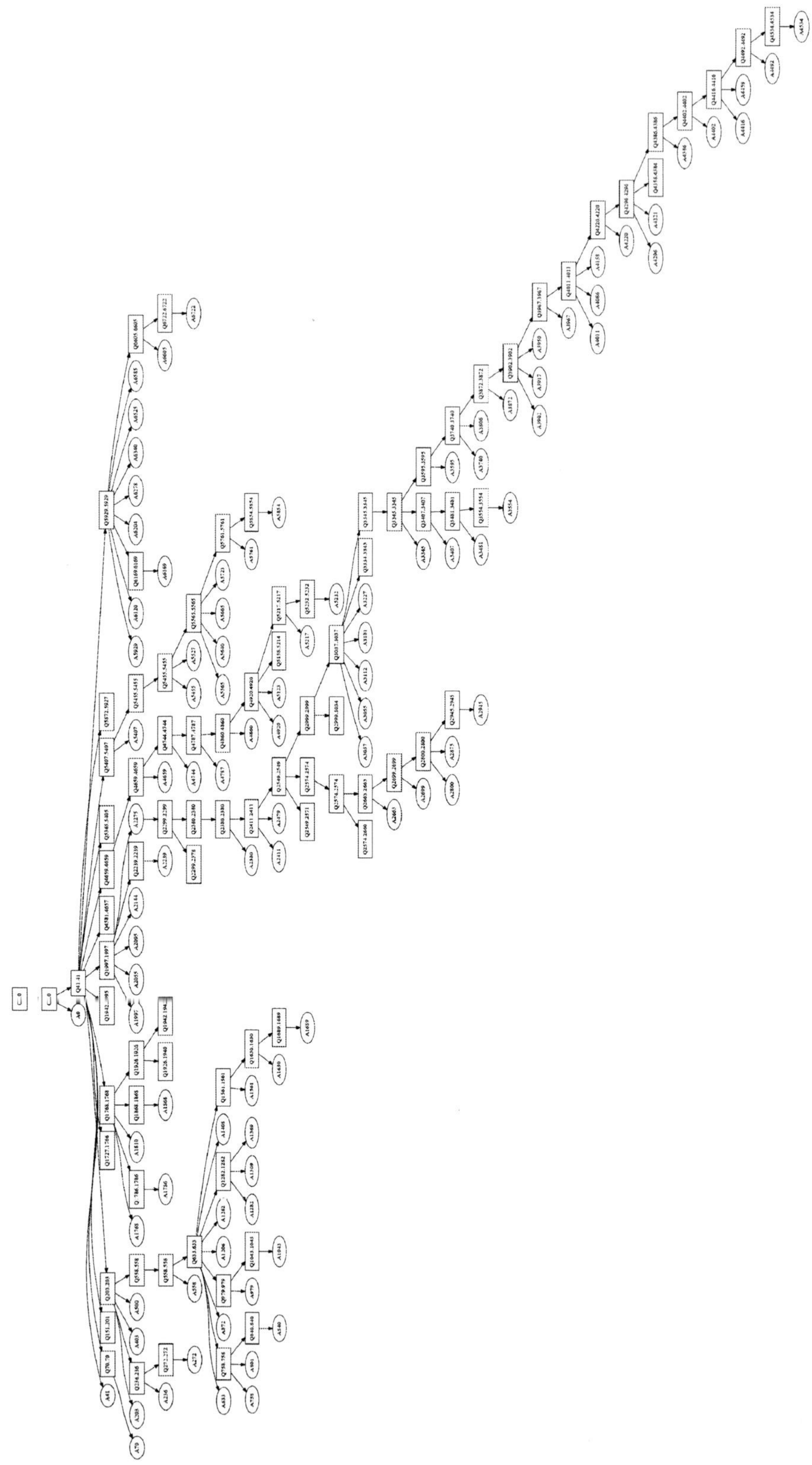

Figure 6: A QUD tree analyses for Italian Blog 2 (First Annotator)

122

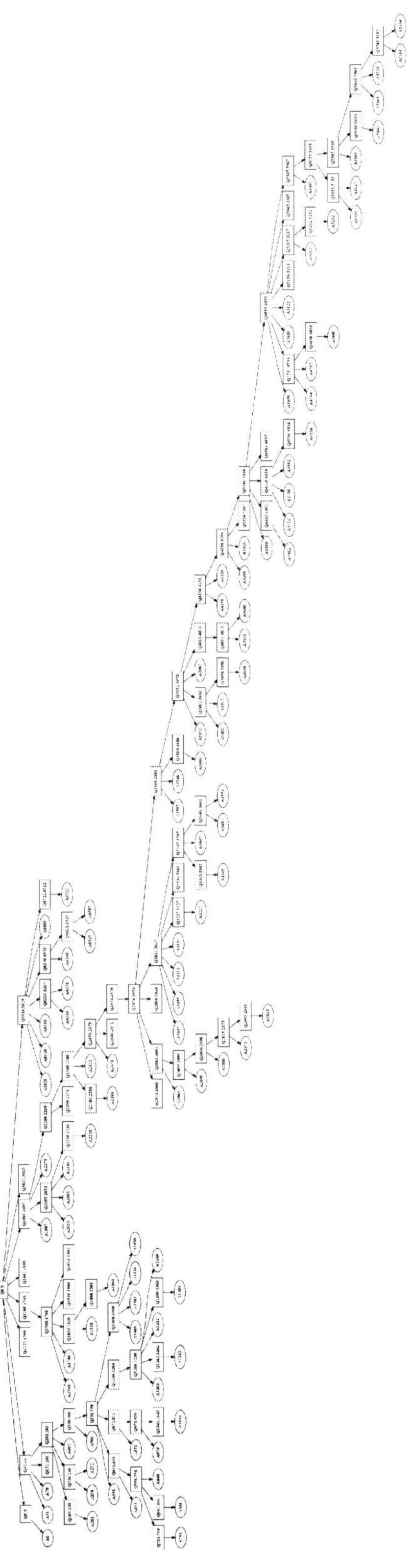

Figure 7: A QUD tree analyses for Italian Blog 2 (Second Annotator)

DEFT: A corpus for definition extraction in free- and semi-structured text

Sasha Spala[1], Nicholas A Miller[1], Yiming Yang[2*], Franck Dernoncourt[3], Carl Dockhorn[1]

[1]Adobe Inc.
345 Park Ave.
San Jose, CA
`{sspala,`
`nimiller,`
`cdockhorn}`
`@adobe.com`

[2]University of California, San Diego
9500 Gilman Dr.
La Jolla, CA
`yiy001`
`@eng.ucsd.edu`

[3]Adobe Research
345 Park Ave.
San Jose, CA
`dernonco`
`@adobe.com`

Abstract

Definition extraction has been a popular topic in NLP research for well more than a decade, but has been historically limited to well-defined, structured, and narrow conditions. In reality, natural language is messy, and messy data requires both complex solutions and data that reflects that reality. In this paper, we present a robust English corpus and annotation schema that allows us to explore the less straightforward examples of term-definition structures in free and semi-structured text.

1 Introduction

As the computational linguistics community moves further towards comprehensive natural language understanding, it has become increasingly clear that our methods need to consider scenarios that match a complex linguistic reality. In the case of term-definition pairs, that means exploring how explicit in-text definitions and glosses work in free and semi-structured text, especially those whose term-definition pair span crosses a sentence boundary and those lacking explicit definition phrases. In this paper we present a new corpus of natural language term-definition pairs, as well as a novel schema that can be generally applied for a wide range of domains.

2 Related Work

Most related work on definition extraction has relied on the idea that definitions can be captured by common "definitor" verb phrases like "means", "refers to", and "is". Early work in the field incorporated rule-based methods that extracted sentences that met this narrow standard (JL Clavens, 2001; Cui and Chua, 2004, 2005; Fahmi and Bouma, 2006; Zhang and Jiang, 2009). While predictable and easily applied, these models subsequently failed to extract sentences that

---

lack these explicit markers. In an effort to expand on the type of phrases used to extract definitions, Cui et al. (2007) used soft pattern matching in a modified HMM (PHMM). More recent work from Espinosa Anke and Schockaert (2018) makes use of a neural approach, which reached state-of-the-art performance on the word class lattices (WCL) datasets (Navigli et al., 2010). Even so, these methods require both term and definition to appear in the same sentence and for terms to appear before definitions.

Hypernym detection, a related field, has also garnered interest for quite some time (see e.g., Hearst (1992); Snow et al. (2005); Ritter et al. (2009); Shwartz et al. (2017)). Because many hypernym glosses follow the pattern *X, such as Y* or *X is a (type of) Y*, this work contains a subset of cases considered for definition extraction. Navigli and Velardi (2010) demonstrated the use of word class lattices for *both* hypernym detection and definition extraction, and Yin and Roth (2018) proved the effectiveness of including definitions in the training of hypernym detection models.

Most work on definition extraction has been applied solely to English datasets, including the WCL dataset mentioned above (Navigli et al., 2010), the ukWaC dataset (Ferraresi et al., 2008), a large crawled dataset of the .uk domain name, and the W00 dataset, a small, expertly annotated corpus introduced by Jin et al. (2013). There does exist a smaller effort for multilingual explorations, including German (Storrer and Wellinghoff, 2006), Portuguese (Del Gaudio and Branco, 2007), and Slavic (Przepiórkowski et al., 2007), as well as some language-independent approaches (Del Gaudio and Branco, 2009). The vast majority of these approaches are for unstructured text, typically scraped from online sources, as in the ukWaC dataset, though some interest has been given specifically for semi-structured text in legal contracts (see e.g. Curtotti and McCreath

---

**Work was completed while individual was employed at Adobe Research.*

Proceedings of the 13th Linguistic Annotation Workshop, pages 124–131
Florence, Italy, August 1, 2019. ©2019 Association for Computational Linguistics

Dataset	# of positive annotations	Size (in sentences)
WCL	1,871	4,718
W00	731	2,185
DEFT	**11,004**	**23,746**

Table 1: Definition extraction datasets

(2010) and Winkels and Hoekstra (2012)).

While variations of the *X is a Y* form are indeed common definition sentence structures, they do not capture a wide range of definition structures that appear in both free and semi-structured text. In particular, they typically constrain the environment in which we find these definitions. We see this in cases like the WCL dataset, of which a portion of the data was extracted by taking the first sentences of randomly sampled Wikipedia articles, as well as in much of the legal domain research, which often consider only the definitions which appear in explicitly-identified glossary sections'. Our proposed Definition Extraction from Texts (DEFT) corpus aims to alleviate this problem by providing complex, human-annotated data across a variety of topics and among both free (textbook) and semi-structured (legal document) language.

3 Corpus

The DEFT corpus[1] consists of annotated content from two different data sources: 1) 2,443 sentences (5,324,430 tokens) from various 2017 SEC contract filings from the publicly available US Securities and Exchange Commission EDGAR (SEC) database, and 2) 21,303 sentences (409,253 tokens) from the `https://cnx.org/` open source textbooks (by various authors, licensed under CC BY 4.0) including topics in biology, history, physics, psychology, economics, sociology, and government. 22% of SEC sentences contain definitions and 28% of textbook sentences contain definitions. Our entire corpus, including both datasets, is significantly larger and more complex than any existing definition extraction dataset (see Table 1).

During annotation, we found that roughly 50% of term-definition pairs appeared across sentence boundaries or with an otherwise complex struc-

---

[1]`https://github.com/adobe-research/`
`deft_corpus`

ture (e.g., containing secondary information, containing ambiguous references to previously stated terms or definitions) whereby the relationship between a term and definition requires more deduction than finding a definition verb phrase.

Our annotation schema is outlined in Table 2 and Table 3. Terms, alias terms, referential terms, and ordered terms are always annotated as a complete NP, including any determiner that may appear with the noun. Where possible, definitions, secondary definitions, referential definitions, and ordered definitions consume the entire clause(s) in which they appear. Qualifiers, which were added to handle date, location, and condition nuances in legal language, are also annotated at the clause level. Terms may not exist without either a matching alias term or definition.

With the exception of the qualifier tag, which appears only in the SEC data, the schema is applied generally across both datasets.

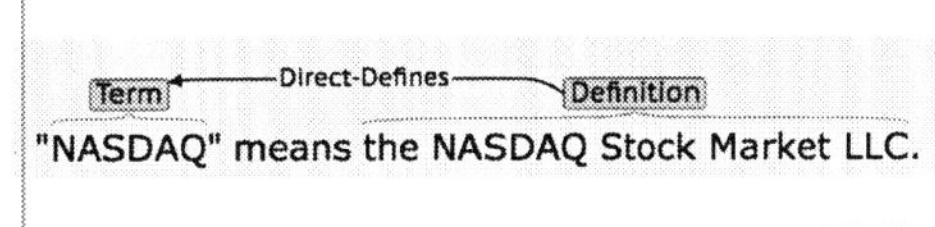

Figure 1: A typical definition within the "Definitions" section of a legal contract.

3.1 Annotation Schema

As mentioned above (see Section 2), previous work has focused primarily on term-definition pairs that appear in the same sentence. Navigli et al. (2010) used a formalized schema from Storrer and Wellinghoff (2006), which identifies a *definiendum*, *definitor*, *definiens*, and *rest* field for each term-definition pair. Curtotti and McCreath (2010) use "definition clauses", drawing on definitions in a legal sense - that is, those which appear in a formal definition or glossary section and which do not cross sentence boundaries. These definition clauses typically encompass an entire sentence; the matching term either appears in context (within the natural language of the definition clause) or with some formatting (e.g. bold, italic, heading-like) to indicate its relationship with the definition clause.

Our schema expands on these strategies to account for a wider variety of term-definition structures. Because of the sweeping variety of "definition-like" verb phrases (e.g. *means, is, defines*, etc.), and the apparent lack thereof in some

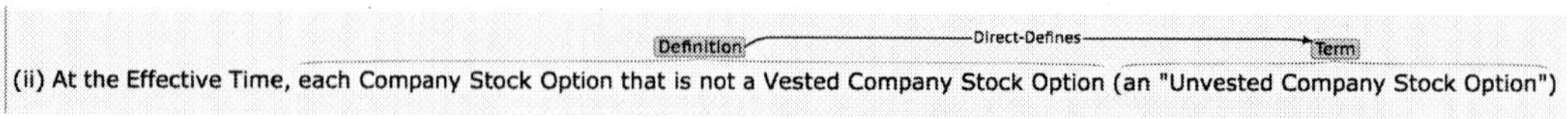

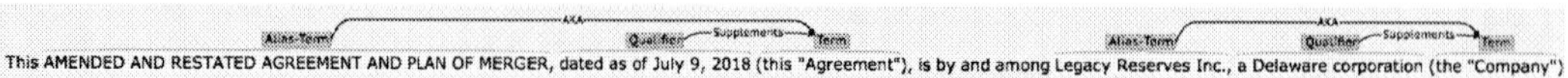

Figure 2: A typical "gloss" in the body of a contract, where a term is identified by enclosing parentheses and quotations which separate it from its definition.

Figure 3: A typical preamble of a contract in the SEC filings, with qualifiers that clarify the date, location, or condition in which the term appears.

cases (see e.g. Figs 2, 3, 7), we are most interested in identifying terms and definitions, but not necessarily the verb phrases which may or may not connect the two.

Annotators were instructed to identify definitions that had an explicitly mentioned referring term. Definitions may span entire sentences, or may be a single clause-level or smaller NP. In our schema, definitions are not merely general descriptions of a term, but refer clearly back to the term they define, and can define *only* the term. If it does not already appear as such, the term and chosen definition sequence can be typically rephrased as *X is a Y*. Definitions do *not* include definitors, words that introduce restrictive or non-restrictive clauses (such as *that, who, which*), or narratives. Definitions must also be apparent from the explicitly written text available to the annotator. Our guidelines avoid "implicit" definitions, or definitions that require external understanding of the topic to parse. If a definition crosses a sentence boundary, the sequence (in some cases, a full sentence) following the boundary identified as definition-like is labelled as a secondary definition.

3.2 Contract Data

As mentioned above, the corpus consists of 2443 sentences from SEC contract filings. These sentences are often long, with several term-definition pairs appearing within one sentence. While it is well known that many contracts contain "definition sections", glossaries, or definition clauses (Curtotti and McCreath, 2010; Curtotti and Sridharan, 2013), our annotation efforts revealed that in reality, definitions appear throughout the entire contract. Because of the nature of this spread, our annotators were instructed to annotate entire legal documents, not just the labeled "definition" sections as in Fig 1. Often, glosses outside definition

sections are identified by a term that appears in quotations and bounded by parentheses, separating it from the inline text (see Fig 2). Occasionally, the inline definitions use referential terms or definitions to indirectly define primary terms, though this is a rare case ($< 1\%$ of tags).

As mentioned above, the SEC data includes the qualifier tag, which is often found qualifying terms or alias terms in contract preambles, as seen in Fig 3. These preambles commonly contain terms with matching alias terms, but no explicit definition. It is also important to note that terms in these preambles are typically *not* the longer, expanded acronym, or more formal representation (as they may be in the textbook data, by nature of how the textbooks' style refers to those terms), but rather the acronym or otherwise shortened form of the term, as this is how they are referred to throughout the rest of the document. Here we see an interesting divergence between the two domains: In textbooks the goal may be to educate the reader of the term, and thus often uses the more formalized representation, but in contracts the goal is usually clarity, brevity, and adherence to legal code.

3.3 Textbook Data

In the textbook data, three-sentence context windows were sampled from sentences that contained a bold n-gram (a strong signal in educational texts indicating a formally defined term) with a context sentence on either side of the sentence with those bold token(s). Consistent with previous research (Cui et al., 2007; Degorski and Przepiorkowski, 2008; Curtotti and McCreath, 2010; Navigli et al., 2010) definitions do in fact appear in the *X is a Y* form, with a clear "definitor". However, many textbook examples also lack this explicit trigger, and instead implicitly define the relationship between the term and definition, either by a referential term or referential definition, or through the

Tag Name	Description
Term	A primary term
Alias Term	A secondary, less common name for the primary term. Links to a term tag.
Ordered Term	Multiple terms that have matching sets of definitions which cannot be separated from each other without creating an non-contiguous sequence of tokens. E.g. *x and y represent positive and negative versions of the definition, respectively*
Referential Term	An NP reference to a previously mentioned term tag. Typically *this/that/these + NP*
Definition	A primary definition of a term. May not exist without a matching term.
Secondary Definition	Supplemental information that may qualify as a definition sentence or phrase, but crosses a sentence boundary.
Ordered Definition	Multiple definitions that have matching sets of terms which cannot be separated from each other. See Ordered Term.
Referential Definition	NP reference to a previously mentioned definition tag. See Referential Term.
Qualifier	A specific date, location, or condition under which the definition holds

Table 2: Tag schema

Relation Name	Description
Direct-defines	Links definition to term.
Indirect-defines	Links definition to referential term or term to referential definition.
Refers-to	Links referential term to term or referential definition to definition.
AKA	Links alias term to term.
Supplements	Links secondary definition to definition.

Table 3: Relation schema

```
2267.
So too did the appointment of Clay as secretary of state.
<START> John C. Calhoun labeled the whole affair a "corrupt bargain" ([link]).<END>.
Everywhere, Jackson supporters vowed revenge against the anti-majoritarian result of 1824.
```

Figure 4: An excerpt from the extracted textbook sentences without a term-definition pair.

implication of the syntactic structure (see e.g., Fig 7). It is important to note that, as seen in Fig 6, the *X is a Y* form (or some variant thereof) may still appear between the referential term or definition and the primary term or definition, especially when the relationship between the primary term and primary definition crosses a sentence boundary.

Though we may not have captured all examples of term-definition pairs in textbooks, this did allow us to regularly and implicitly, without active annotator tagging, identify examples which may appear to be definitions at a surface level, but in fact, do not meet our schema criteria for a definition. In particular, because of the constraints of our schema and the unclear ground truth definition of people and places, our annotation excludes these cases. With the exception of definitions including the formal title of an individual or the physical composition of a location (see, e.g. Fig 4, Fig 5), they are not included in the corpus. All three-sentence windows that appear in the dataset without any labels are considered false positives, as they do contain bold tokens, but either do not have distinguishable definitions or provide auxiliary information not integral to the ground truth definition of the term, as in the case of people and places.

4 Annotation Process

The data in this corpus was annotated by a total of five annotators using the brat annotation framework (Pontus Stenetorp and Tsujii, 2012). A group of three annotators labeled data from the textbook corpus and another group of three annotators labeled the contract data, with one anno-

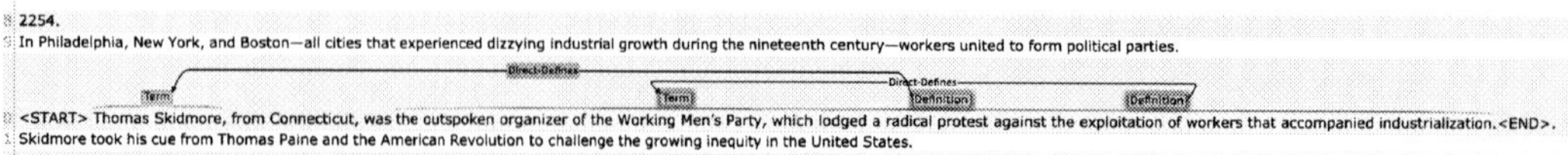

Figure 5: A person labeled as a term with a qualifying definition.

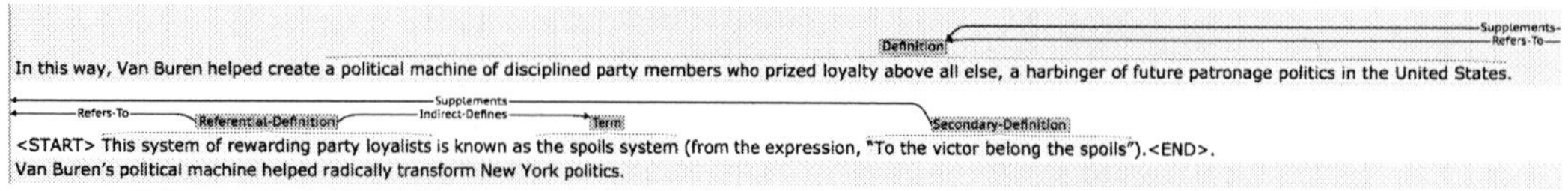

Figure 6: A cross-sentence term-definition pair, where the definition appears before the statement of the term and additional definition information is provided in the form of a secondary definition.

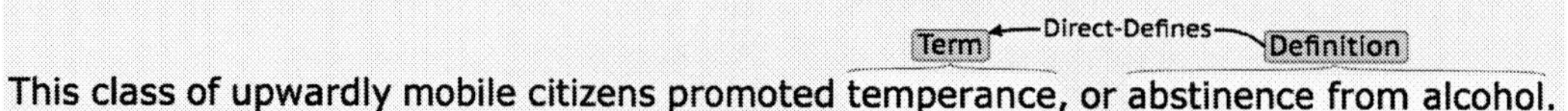

Figure 7: A term-definition pair where the term is implied to be related to the definition by way of clausal separation.

tator having also labeled the textbook data. The development of the annotation schema followed the MAMA cycle (Pustejovsky and Stubbs, 2013), with an emphasis on providing the most pragmatic annotation process while still capturing the most accurate representations of generalized definition structures. Annotators were trained before beginning annotation on the textbook data, then again before beginning annotation on the contract data.

4.1 Inter-annotator Agreement

Inter-annotator agreement (IAA) is measured using a modified version of Krippendorff's alpha (Krippendorff, 2011) with the MASI distance metric (Passonneau, 2006) in order to account for and score partial sequential overlaps of text:

$$\delta(c, k) = \begin{cases} MASI(c, k), & \text{if } c = k \\ 1, & \text{otherwise} \end{cases}$$

Where $c = k$ and the text spans match exactly, the MASI distance is 0.

IAA was calculated after every training period, with a final annotator agreement score of $\alpha_{term} = 0.80$ and $\alpha_{definition} = 0.50$ for the textbook corpus and $\alpha_{term} = 0.85$ and $\alpha_{definition} = 0.54$ for the contract corpus. We believe these IAA scores match the reality of human performance on such a complicated task. After training time, each sentence in the corpus was labeled by one annotator. For the textbook annotation, each annotator was assigned a list of three-sentence passages randomly distributed from every textbook topic. For the contract annotation, each annotator was assigned a set of a set of whole contracts to annotate.

4.2 Annotation Challenges

Though our annotation schema is intended to apply to cross-domain definition extraction, there are still certain linguistic differences between the two data sources. In particular, the goals of different document types and formats seems to instruct the use of definitions in their contexts. We briefly discussed a symptom of this in section 3.2, where the primary term takes different levels of formality depending on the intent of the document: in contracts, it is typically the simplified, abbreviated form, and in textbooks it is typically the expanded or formalized representation. We believe the same influence drives the appearance of the qualifier construct in contracts. Legal documents, by necessity, must state the conditions under which a trait, event, or system is true. This often presents as a relevant date (before, after, or on which the terms apply) or location (such as a country or state under which the terms apply). Textbooks, on the other hand, do not require this level of specificity; though they may state similar facts, such as the date or location of an event, this information is arguably not crucial to the understanding of the core definition. While we may argue for either including or excluding these textbook counterparts, the DEFT corpus does not label them. Our annotation process favors maintaining the most basic definition of the term without compromising

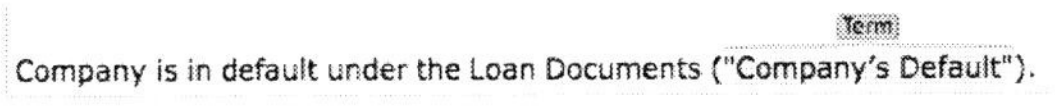

Figure 8: An example where the definition is implied from the legal "force" of the contract.

necessary information. Legal contracts also occasionally "define" terms implicitly by the legal "force" of the document. In Fig 8, "Company's Default" is an event that happens when the company's Loan Documents default. However, this does not directly define what a default is, only the implied conditions under which it happens. From the formatting of the sentence, it is clear that the author intends for "Company's Default" to be a term. "Company's Default" is indeed referred to by name later in the same document. However, it is assumed that the reader has enough knowledge of the process of defaulting that they may infer what the Company's Default means in this context.

Textbooks have similarly difficult terms: people and places, briefly discussed in section 3.3. These terms appear bold, implying the same author intent as the parenthesized terms in the legal contracts. However, the definition of these terms remain vague: is a person defined by their most well-known achievement (especially in historical contexts)? Are they defined by where they were born or died? Are places defined by their most common use? Perhaps their location within a larger geographical structure? In many cases, the way in which these examples are "defined" in the text depends on the context in which they are presented; A history textbook detailing the contributions of a major political figure may "define" that individual by their successes or failures, depending on the perspective of the textbook or the context of the broader section of the document that particular example appears in. Again, this reflects the intent of the document or section as a whole. With the exception of an individual's title and the physical composition of a location (especially in a scientific context), we determine these cases to be out of scope for our current research. As mentioned in Section 3.1, definitions must be able to refer to the term *only*, meaning that most general descriptions of locations or individuals do not qualify as definitions under our schema with one exception: A specific physical descriptor of a location, or a statement of an individual's title. These specific examples both qualify as definitions as they do *not*

require external knowledge of the term or concept, and can be directly connected back to their respective terms.

5 Conclusion

We believe that the DEFT corpus, as the largest existing corpus with the express purpose of definition extraction in a wide range of contexts, will be a major contribution to the field. In the process of creating and revising the annotation schema, we have unpacked significant nuances in the linguistic structures and requirements of definitions in a variety of contexts. As a significant increase in size and granularity of past definition extraction corpora, the DEFT corpus will be particularly useful from both corpus linguistics and computational linguistics perspectives. We believe that in addition to the existing annotated textbook and contract data, our schema could be applied to other forms of un- and semi-structured documents. The DEFT corpus and its annotation schema are an expansion on the existing assumptions of simple, hypernym-like, definition syntax, and offer a new perspective for the next generation of definition extraction models.

6 Acknowledgements and Licensing

We would like to acknowledge the contributions of our annotation team, Lucino Chiafullo, Micaela Kaplan, Roger LaCroix, Molly Moran and Jennifer Pei-Hsuan Lee, without which we would not have the annotated data we have today.

The entire dataset of textbook sentences with annotations is available for use under the CC BY-NA-SA 4.0 license. A sample of annotations of 50 documents from the SEC contracts is available for use under the CC BY-NA-SA 4.0 license.

References

Hang Cui, Min-Yen Kan, and Tat-Seng Chua. 2007. Soft pattern matching models for definitional question answering. *ACM Trans. Inf. Syst.*, 25(2).

Kan M.Y. Cui, H. and T.S. Chua. 2004. Unsupervised learning of soft patterns for generating definitions from online news. In *Proceedings of WWW*, 90-99.

Kan M.Y. Cui, H. and T.S. Chua. 2005. Generic soft pattern models for definitional question answering. In *Proceedings of the 28th Annual International ACM SIGIR Conference on Research and Development in Information Retrieval*.

McCreath Eric Curtotti, Michael and Srinivas Sridharan. 2013. Software tools for the visualization of definition networks in legal contracts. In *Proceedings of the 14th International Conference on Artificial Intelligence and the Law*.

Michael Curtotti and Eric McCreath. 2010. Corpus based classification of text in australian contracts. In *Proceedings of the Australasian Language Technology Association Workshop 2010*.

Micha Marcinczuk Degorski, ukasz and Adam Przepiorkowski. 2008. Definition extraciton using a sequential combination of baseline grammars and machine learning classifiers. In *Proceedings of the Sixth International Conference on Language Resources and Evaluation (LREC 2008)*.

Rosa Del Gaudio and Antonio Branco. 2007. Automatic extraction of definitions in portuguese: A rulebased approach. In *Proceedings of the TeMa Workshop*.

Rosa Del Gaudio and António Branco. 2009. Language independent system for definition extraction: First results using learning algorithms. In *Proceedings of the 1st Workshop on Definition Extraction*, WDE '09, pages 33–39, Stroudsburg, PA, USA. Association for Computational Linguistics.

Luis Espinosa Anke and Steven Schockaert. 2018. Syntactically aware neural architectures for definition extraction. In *Proceedings of the 2018 Conference of the North American Chapter of the Association for Computational Linguistics: Human Language Technologies, Volume 2 (Short Papers)*, pages 378–385. Association for Computational Linguistics.

Ismail Fahmi and Gosse Bouma. 2006. Learning to identify definitions using syntactic features. In *Proceedings of the EACL 2006 workshop on Learning Structured Information in Natural Language Applications*.

Adriano Ferraresi, Eros Zanchetta, Silvia Bernardini, and Marco Baroni. 2008. Introducing and evaluating ukwac, a very large web-derived corpus of english.

Marti A. Hearst. 1992. Automatic acquisition of hyponyms from large text corpora. In *Proceedings of the 14th Conference on Computational Linguistics - Volume 2*, COLING '92, pages 539–545, Stroudsburg, PA, USA. Association for Computational Linguistics.

Yiping Jin, Min-Yen Kan, Jun-Ping Ng, and Xiangnan He. 2013. Mining scientific terms and their definitions: A study of the acl anthology. In *Proceedings of the 2013 Conference on Empirical Methods in Natural Language Processing*, pages 780–790. Association for Computational Linguistics.

S Muresan JL Clavens. 2001. Evaluation of the definder system for fully automatic glossary construction. In *Proceedings of the AMIA Symposium*, pages 324–328.

Klaus Krippendorff. 2011. Computing Krippendorff's alpha-reliability.

Roberto Navigli and Paola Velardi. 2010. Learning word-class lattices for definition and hypernym extraction. In *Proceedings of the 48th Annual Meeting of the Association for Computational Linguistics*, ACL '10, pages 1318–1327, Stroudsburg, PA, USA. Association for Computational Linguistics.

Roberto Navigli, Paola Velardi, and Juana Ruiz-Martnez. 2010. An annotated dataset for extracting definitions and hypernyms from the web. In *Proceedings of the International Conference on Language Resources and Evaluation, LREC 2010*.

Rebecca Passonneau. 2006. Measuring agreement on set-valued items (masi) for semantic and pragmatic annotation.

Goran Topi Tomoko Ohta Sophia Ananiadou Pontus Stenetorp, Sampo Pyysalo and Jun'ichi Tsujii. 2012. brat: a web-based tool for nlp-assisted text annotation. In *Proceedings of the Demonstrations Session at EACL 2012*.

Adam Przepiórkowski, Degórski, Beata Wójtowicz, Miroslav Spousta, Vladislav Kuboň, Kiril Simov, Petya Osenova, and Lothar Lemnitzer. 2007. Towards the automatic extraction of definitions in slavic. In *Proceedings of the Workshop on Balto-Slavonic Natural Language Processing: Information Extraction and Enabling Technologies*, ACL '07, pages 43–50, Stroudsburg, PA, USA. Association for Computational Linguistics.

James Pustejovsky and Amber Stubbs. 2013. *Natural Language Annotation for Machine Learning*. O'Reilly Media, Inc.

Alan Ritter, Stephen Soderland, and Oren Etzioni. 2009. What is this, anyway: Automatic hypernym discovery. pages 88–93.

Vered Shwartz, Enrico Santus, and Dominik Schlechtweg. 2017. Hypernyms under siege: Linguistically-motivated artillery for hypernymy detection. In *Proceedings of the 15th Conference of the European Chapter of the Association for Computational Linguistics: Volume 1, Long Papers*, pages 65–75, Valencia, Spain. Association for Computational Linguistics.

Rion Snow, Daniel Jurafsky, and Andrew Y. Ng. 2005. Learning syntactic patterns for automatic hypernym discovery. In L. K. Saul, Y. Weiss, and L. Bottou, editors, *Advances in Neural Information Processing Systems 17*, pages 1297–1304. MIT Press.

Angelika Storrer and Sandra Wellinghoff. 2006. Automated detection and annotation of term definitions in german text corpora. In *Proceedings of the Conference on Language Resources and Evaluation (LREC)*.

R. Winkels and R. Hoekstra. 2012. Automatic extraction of legal concepts and definitions. In *Legal Knowledge and Information Systems: JURIX 2012: the twenty-fifth annual conference*.

Wenpeng Yin and Dan Roth. 2018. Term definitions help hypernymy detection. In *Proceedings of the Seventh Joint Conference on Lexical and Computational Semantics*, pages 203–213, New Orleans, Louisiana. Association for Computational Linguistics.

ChunXia Zhang and Peng Jiang. 2009. Automatic extraction of definitions. In *Proceedings of the 2nd IEEE International Conference on Computer Science and Information Technology*.

Explaining Simple Natural Language Inference

Aikaterini-Lida Kalouli
University of Konstanz
first.last@uni-konstanz.de

Annebeth Buis
University of Colorado Boulder
anne.buis@colorado.edu

Livy Real
University of São Paulo
livyreal@gmail.com

Martha Palmer
University of Colorado Boulder
martha.palmer@colorado.edu

Valeria de Paiva
University of Birmingham
valeria.depaiva@gmail.com

Abstract

The vast amount of research introducing new corpora and techniques for (semi-)automatically annotating corpora shows the important role that datasets play in today's research, especially in the machine learning community. This rapid development raises concerns about the quality of the datasets created and consequently of the models trained, as recently discussed with respect to the Natural Language Inference (NLI) task. In this work we conduct an annotation experiment based on a small subset of the SICK corpus. The experiment reveals several problems in the annotation guidelines, and various challenges of the NLI task itself. Our quantitative evaluation of the experiment allows us to assign our empirical observations to specific linguistic phenomena and leads us to recommendations for future annotation tasks, for NLI and possibly for other tasks.

1 Introduction

In the era of big data and deep learning there is an increasing need for large annotated corpora that can be used as training and evaluation data for (semi-)supervised methods. This can be seen by the vast amount of work introducing new datasets and techniques for (semi-)automatically annotating corpora. Different NLP tasks require different kinds of datasets and annotations and provide us with different challenges. One task that has lately gained much attention in the community is the task of Natural Language Inference (NLI). NLI, also known as Recognizing Textual Entailment (RTE) (Dagan et al., 2006), is the task of defining the semantic relation between a premise text p and a conclusion text c. p can a) entail, b) contradict or c) be neutral to c. The premise p is taken to entail conclusion c when a human reading p would infer that c is most probably true (Dagan et al., 2006).

This notion of "human reading" assumes human common sense and common background knowledge. This means that a successful automatic NLI system is a suitable evaluation measure for real natural language understanding, as discussed by Condoravdi et al. (2003) and others. It is also a necessary step towards reasoning as more recently discussed by Goldberg and Hirst (2017) and Nangia et al. (2017) who say that solving NLI perfectly means achieving human level understanding of language. Thus, there is an increasing effort to design high-performing NLI systems, which in turn leads to the creation of massive learning corpora. Early datasets, like FraCas (Consortium et al., 1996) or the seven RTE challenges (Dagan et al., 2006; Bar-Haim et al., 2006; Giampiccolo et al., 2007; Dagan et al., 2010; Bentivogli et al., 2009b,a, 2011), contained a few hundred hand-annotated pairs. More recent sets have exploded from some thousand pairs (e.g., SICK, Marelli et al., 2014b) to some hundred thousand examples: SciTail (Khot et al., 2018), SNLI (Bowman et al., 2015), Multi-NLI (Williams et al., 2018). The latter two have been vastly used to train learning algorithms and achieve high performance. However, it was recently shown that this high performance can drop significantly by slightly modifying the training process (Poliak et al., 2017; Glockner et al., 2018). It was also shown that such training sets contain annotation artifacts that bias the learning (Gururangan et al., 2018; Naik et al., 2018). Other recent work (Kalouli et al., 2017b,a, 2018) discussed problematic annotations of the SICK corpus (Marelli et al., 2014b) and attempted to improve the annotations. All this work leads to the conclusion that corpus construction, including the annotation process, is much more important than what is often assumed and that bad corpora can falsely deliver promising results.

In this paper we take a closer look at the work

Proceedings of the 13th Linguistic Annotation Workshop, pages 132–143
Florence, Italy, August 1, 2019. ©2019 Association for Computational Linguistics

by Kalouli et al. (2017b,a) and attempt to build on the two conclusions that arise from their work. The first conclusion is that the guidelines for the NLI annotation task need be improved, as it seems clear that human annotators often have opposing perspectives when annotating for inference. This can result in faulty and illogical annotations. The second conclusion concerns the annotation procedure: having an inference label is not enough; knowing *why* a human subject decides that an inference is an entailment or a contradiction is useful information that we should also be collecting, if we want to make sure that the corpus created adheres to the guidelines given. Specifically, in this work we discuss an experiment, realized at the University of Colorado Boulder (CU), which attempts to address both these issues: provide uncontroversial, clear guidelines and give the annotators the chance to justify their decisions. Our goal is to evaluate the guidelines based on the resulting agreement rates and gain insights into the NLI annotation task by collecting the annotators' comments on the annotations. Thus, in the current work we make three contributions: Firstly, we discover which linguistic phenomena are hard for humans to annotate and show that these do not always coincide with what is assumed to be difficult for automatic systems. Then, we propose aspects of NLI and of the annotation task itself that should be taken into account when designing future NLI corpora and annotation guidelines. Thirdly, we show that it is essential to include a justification method in similar annotation tasks as a suitable way of checking the guidelines and improving the training and evaluation processes of automatic systems towards explainable AI.

2   Background: the SICK corpus

To achieve these goals, we look at the SICK corpus (Marelli et al., 2014b). SICK is an English corpus of almost 10,000 pairs, annotated for their degree of similarity and for the inference relation between the sentences of each pair. The corpus was created from captions of pictures talking about daily activities and non-abstract entities. It was also further simplified in terms of the linguistic phenomena included, e.g. named entities and temporal phenomena were removed. Annotators were not given strict definitions as guidelines but instead one example for each type of label. They were also not told that the sentences came from

pictures. This creation process caused much confusion as discussed in the original paper but also in Kalouli et al. (2017b,a). In particular, the process did not resolve event and entity coreference issues so that a pair like *A woman is carrying a bag* and *A woman is not carrying a bag* ended up labelled as neutral, instead of as a contradiction. This weakness was specifically targeted in the later corpora SNLI and Multi-NLI. In these corpora, in an attempt to provide premise examples grounded in specific scenarios, the annotators were given the freedom to write themselves a conclusion sentence for a given premise and they were informed that the premises come from captions of pictures.

3   The CU experiment

Our experiment was undertaken with the help of 12 Computer Science and Linguistics graduate students in a Computational Linguistics seminar. These annotators were not under the pressure of making hasty judgements for money and had a much smaller number of pairs to work with than an average 'Mechanical Turker'. The goal was to provide the students with clear, uncontroversial guidelines and ask them to annotate a small part of SICK. They were also asked to justify their decisions, in order for us to see whether the given guidelines solved some of the problems discussed in relevant literature (e.g. Marelli et al. (2014b); Bowman et al. (2015); Kalouli et al. (2017b,a)) and whether we could gain additional insights from the students' justifications. Apart from the inference relation and the justification, the students were also asked to give a score from 0-10 for what we would like to call "computational feasibility", i.e. their estimation of the likelihood of an automatic system getting the inference right.

The guidelines   The guidelines for the CU experiment gave a detailed definition of NLI/RTE by using common literature definitions. The annotators were asked to imagine sentence *A* as a caption of a picture, describing whatever is on that picture – following the creators of SNLI and MultiNLI to deal with coreference issues. For each judgment, they were instructed to consider only the inference relation from *A* to *B* and not vice versa. They were also instructed to assume that sentence *A* represents everything they know about the world of the picture; *A* represents the truth based on which they have to judge sentence *B*. If *A* is talking about *a man in red pants walking* and *B* is also talking about *a man in red pants running*, they were told to assume that both sentences are talking about the same man and event. The guidelines also provided detailed examples of each inference relation, along with the kinds of justifications expected. Finally, special remarks were made for corner cases or cases that had already been shown in Kalouli et al. (2017b,a) to cause confusion. For example, they were told to ignore differences in determiners[1] and to use common-sense for matters that might seem subjective, e.g. *a huge stick* contradicts *a small stick*, even if a huge stick for a child might be a normal size stick for an adult, etc.

The annotation process For the current experiment, a total of 224 pairs was randomly chosen from SICK. The pairs were annotated for their inference relation in both directions, resulting in a total of 448 judgments. Each direction was annotated *separately* by 3 annotators. The annotators had to provide an inference label (*E, C, N* for entailment, contradiction, neutrality, or, if they could not decide at all, *DN* for "don't know"), a justification for their choice and the "computational feasibility" score discussed above. They could also note whether something was ungrammatical or nonsensical or if they had additional comments.[2] A set of 24 pairs (48 judgements) was given to all annotators at the beginning of the process for calibration. The annotators were instructed to use the same four labels described above (E, C, N, DN). In this set the three inference relations were almost equally represented: 16 entailments, 14 contradictions and 18 neutrals. For the set there was 75.8% overall inter-annotator agreement (IAA) with Cohen's κ at 0.68 ("allowing tentative conclusions" according to Carletta (1996)).[3] More concretely, there was 80% IAA for contradiction, 93% for entailment and 63% for neutrals. These agreement rates gave the preliminary impression that the guidelines were satisfactory.

4 Preliminary Observations

After collecting all annotations, we first calculated their IAA to compare it to the calibration set. Indeed, the overall average IAA was 73.25% with κ 64.25, comparable to the calibration set. κ is a standard metric in any similar task and here the high Kappa means that our guidelines work well enough to propose them for future tasks and allow us to make the annotated set available for further purposes. However, we decided to look deeper into the annotated data and examine whether this metric is indeed sufficient to ensure reliable annotations. After all, the goal of this work is to examine the annotation process in detail, especially observing the usefulness and need for the justifications we asked from the annotators. This goal was reinforced by our further finding that the annotations provided by our annotators were different from the original SICK annotations in 17% of the annotated cases! Assuming that our annotators are more reliable due to their training and better "working" conditions, this finding raises questions about the quality of the original SICK corpus, as already discussed by Kalouli et al. (2017a).

Detailed analysis of the data revealed different kinds of justifications. Firstly, there were the expected, less-informative justifications of the kind "no relation" or "sentences mean the same thing". Though allowed, such justifications do not offer a lot of insight into the annotation. Secondly, there were justifications describing the relation between the sentences and thus explaining the decision. For example, for the pair *A = A person is brushing a cat. B = Nobody is brushing a cat*, we got the justifications: "cat cannot be both brushed and not brushed", "cannot both brush and not brush a cat" and "someone != no one". Such justifications were the expected ones and what we hoped for when integrating the justification annotation.

Thirdly, the justifications and the annotations themselves indicated that there was much confusion about when a pair should be a contradiction or neutral. Annotators considered as contradiction pairs in which sentence *B* had nothing to do with *A*. In an attempt to find some relation between the sentences and without paying attention to the fact that contradictions can be defined only when entities/events are coreferent, the annotators found many contradictions. For example, the pair *A = Two sumo ringers are fighting. B = A man is riding a water toy in the water* was labeled as contradiction, with the justification "the subjects and activities are completely different". However, in what we considered clear guidelines, we had stated that "*A* represents everything you

---

[1]This "forced" equivalence of the determiners is suitable for this restricted annotation scenario, but would be unnatural for other contexts, e.g. consecutive sentences in a text.

[2]The guidelines and the re-annotated subcorpus are available under `https://github.com/kkalouli/SICK-processing`

[3]Label "DN" was also included for computing κ.

know about the world of the picture, *A* represents the truth based on which you have to judge sentence *B*" and that therefore in such an example, sentence *B* cannot be judged given *A*, hence the pair should be neutral. This observation is very interesting because it seems to concern other NLI corpora as well, e.g. in SNLI we find pairs like *A = A young boy in a field of flowers carrying a ball. B = dog in pool* also marked as contradiction, although it is clear that there is no coreference and thus it should be neutral. Conversely, we found many cases where there was an obvious coreference and contradictory events/entities but the annotators attempted to think of scenarios where both things could still co-occur. The pair, *A = A girl is getting a tattoo removed from her hand. B = A girl is getting a tattoo on her hand*, was correctly judged by two annotators as contradiction because "getting a tattoo contradicts tattoo removal" but the third one thought of it as neutral because "could be getting both at the same time".

Another more important observation was that the same pair had different agreement rates depending on its direction. Recall that the pairs were given in both directions but separately from each other. An example is the calibration pair *A = A light brown dog is sprinting in the water. B = A light brown dog is running in the water.* This direction of the pair (A → B) was unanimously annotated as entailment by 12 annotators. However, the opposite direction B → A got an agreement of 25% entailment and 75% neutrality. Here, some annotators gave justifications like "running and sprinting are kind of the same for every day situations" while others, following dictionaries more carefully, assumed that while sprinting is a kind of running, running does not entail sprinting. Only one direction of the pair is thus uncontroversial. This raises questions of whether one direction is indeed harder than the other and whether such directionality effects should be considered in the design and evaluation of NLI annotation tasks. To the best of our knowledge, this has so far not been taken into account for such datasets.

This observation is closely related to another: pairs involving what we would call "loose definitions/loose human inference" are also more prone to disagreements. Looking at the calibration pair *A = A white dog is standing on a hill covered by grass. B = A dog is standing on the side of a mountain*, the annotators have to decide whether *hill covered by grass* is the same as *mountain* and since definitions tend to be loose and subjective, such pairs get bad IAA (25% E, 33% C, 41% N). Interestingly, the opposite direction gets a slightly better agreement (17% C, 83% N), which again brings up the issue of directionality described above. Another good example is *A = A man is talking on the phone. B = A man is making a phone call.* Here, one annotator marked it as neutral as "talking on the phone does not entail that the man initiated the call", another marked it as contradiction because "making a phone call is an action that precludes talking on the phone", while the third one considered it an entailment because "talking on implies phone call". For tasks like NLI and for certain domains, we might need this kind of looseness that would allow the pair to be an entailment even though "talking on the phone" does not logically entail "making a phone call" (assuming that "making a phone call" contains the concept of in fact *initiating* the call, "talking on the phone" does not entail "initiating the call" and thus it also does not logically entail "making a phone call" (modus tollens)). But then, how do we define such corner cases? Could the annotation guidelines ever exactly *define* the concept of common sense, so that such cases are treated uniformly?

Another preliminary observation was the correlation of high "computational feasibility" scores (CF scores) with highly unambiguous pairs. The CF score was introduced in the annotation to check whether the annotators thought it was likely for an NLI system to get the inference label right. Since the score relied more on the annotators' intuition and less on objective annotation guidelines, we observed that the given answers varied widely with poor agreement. However, general observations can be made: high scores (above 8) were mainly given to pairs with direct, clear-cut negations like *A = Nobody is holding a hedgehog. B = Someone is holding a hedgehog.* or to entailments with only differences in determiners, such as *A = The person is peeling an onion. B = A person is peeling an onion.* or to entailment pairs with only one-word-difference, e.g. *A = A child in orange is playing outdoors with a snowball. B = A kid in orange is playing outside with a snowball*, where child = kid is an easy lexical entailment. These observations are not surprising: Kalouli et al. (2018) discuss such cases that can be easily solved solely based on WordNet (Fellbaum, 1998) and heuristics.

5 The experiment on the experiment

The previous observations lead us to two important conclusions: for one, the justifications the annotators provided were crucial to make us understand what was being annotated and what aspects of the guidelines were still unclear. Thus, if we are interested in annotated data that enables us to confirm the quality of the annotation task, similar justification fields are needed. Furthermore, the guidelines need to address aspects that can be controversial, e.g. they need to state explicitly and a priori that contradictions can occur if and only if coreference can be established. Such improvements will be discussed further in Section 6.1. The second conclusion is even more crucial: what if the previous observations are not merely random but can indeed be classified in phenomena and observed in other NLI data? While we know that many linguistic phenomena impose challenges for automatically detecting the inference relation between a pair of sentences, it is unclear which phenomena are also difficult for a human to annotate. For example, the passive/active voice distinction is a phenomenon that always receives attention when dealing with inference relations. However, this kind of phenomenon seems very easy for humans. On the other hand, dealing with loose definitions or coreference seems difficult even for humans. Since such phenomena repeatedly appeared in the justifications of the annotators, we decided to verify if the sentences that had lower agreement actually showed exactly these phenomena. We conjecture that these phenomena are measurable quantities that need to be considered in all future annotation tasks. If so, there should be a measurable correlation among the phenomena and the low IAA, so that these phenomena lead to statistically worse agreements. To investigate these questions, we conducted a second experiment based on the CU experiment: based on our observations of Section 4 and the previous literature on SICK, we defined six distinct categories according to which we ourselves meta-annotated all 224 pairs. Although this meta-annotation took place after making our preliminary observations on the data, the validity of this annotation is not influenced in any significant way: our preliminary observations were only that; observations and no real analysis of the data, also not an informal one. It was exactly this question that we seek to answer by this second experiment: can these abstract observations be quantified and analyzed in a formal way?

Specific Annotation Precisely, we meta-annotated the pairs for *coreference, directionality, loose definitions, atomicity, negation* and *quantification* phenomena. For the feature *coreference*, we marked whether a pair contains events or entities that are hard to assume coreferent (we annotated True for hard coreference and False for easy coreference). Coreference difficulty could lead to the first phenomenon described above; not being able to decide whether something is coreferent and thus contradictory, or neutral. In the category *directionality*, we marked for each pair direction whether this direction was harder, easier or equally difficult to annotate as the opposite direction. In the *loose definition* category, we checked whether the pair contains concepts that are "loose", subjective or vague to define (annotated as True) or not (annotated as False). The next category was inspired by the previous work of Kalouli et al. (2017a) on SICK: *atomicity* concerns the question of whether a sentence contains only one predicate-argument structure or more. This relates to the observation by Kalouli et al. (2017b) that marking the inference relation, and especially making events and entities coreferent, is easier to do when the pair only contains atomic sentences, i.e. sentences with one main verb. In non-atomic sentences, all parts of the sentence should be able to be made coreferent with the other sentence, something that often proves a challenge, especially if the other sentence is atomic. An example is the pair A = *The singer is playing the guitar at an acoustic concert for a woman. B = A person is playing a guitar and singing.* A is atomic but B is not (*playing and singing*), so that the question arises whether the *person singing* can be coreferent with the *singer*. We annotate each sentence of each pair with True or False, depending on whether they are atomic or not. *Negation* also contains the labels True or False: here we mark if each sentence of the pair contains a negation of any kind (verbal, pronominal, etc.). We do a similar task for *quantifiers*: we mark whether each sentence contains a quantifier or not.[4] We added these last two categories to quantitatively test our impression that negation and quantifiers also cause more annotation problems, just as coreference, loose definitions, etc.

---

[4] *a* is taken to be a determiner and not a quantifier

Phenomenon	IAA		CF score	
	True	**False**	**True**	**False**
A_is_atomic	72.06	79.41	6.81	6.68
B_is_atomic	72.60	76.81	6.83	6.59
A_is_negated	**88.88**	**71.46**	**7.66**	**6.68**
B_is_negated	**90.47**	**71.27**	**7.51**	**6.7**
A_has_quant	79.67	72.60	7.03	6.76
B_has_quant	80.48	72.50	7.05	6.75
hard_coref	**62.45**	**77.27**	**6.22**	**6.99**
loose_def	**59.60**	**77.19**	6.2	6.95

Directionality			
Measure	**Easier**	**Harder**	**Equal**
IAA	**81.18**	**58.33**	**74.90**
CF score	6.57	6.58	6.88

Table 1: Overview of the average IAA (%) and CF score (1-10) for each condition of our experiment.

Results The overall goal of these meta-annotations was to check if the presence of these phenomena correlates with low IAA and low CF scores. In other words, we wanted to test whether the IAA and CF scores are statistically worse in pairs with such phenomena. To this end, we calculated the IAA and the CF score[5] for each pair and each of the six meta-annotations. We then computed the average IAA and CF score of the pairs in each condition of our meta-annotations. The results are shown in Table 1. We should note that we could conduct this kind of study only on the re-annotated SICK pairs of our CU experiment (Section 3) and not on the original SICK annotations because for those the exact IAAs are not available but only the final majority label. Thus, it would not be possible to quantify our findings over those annotations. However, we did investigate how the pairs that had been differently annotated by the original annotators and our annotators (17% of the cases, as explained above) showed these linguistic categories and we could retrace some of the findings discussed below: for example, among the pairs that were differently annotated by the original and our annotators there were significantly more pairs containing loose definitions (37% vs. 20%) and hard coreference (32% vs. 26%) than among the pairs that were annotated with the same label by the original and our annotators.

To test for the involved effects, we analyzed the IAA results using generalized additive mixed models (GAMMs) with the *ocat-linking* function for ordered categorical data (Wood, 2011, 2017).

We chose this kind of modelling due to the nature of our dependent variable IAA.[6] The six meta-annotation categories were added as fixed factors with interactions and the pairs were entered as random smoothers. The fixed factors *coreference, loose definitions, atomicity of A, atomicity of B, negation of A, negation of B* and *quantification of A* and *quantification of B* were binary (True or False for each of them as described in 5) (cf. Table 1, top) and the effect *directionality* was a 3-level variable ("easier", "harder" and "equal") (cf. Table 1, bottom). Interaction, main effects and random smoothers were removed if they were not significant at $\alpha = 0.05$ and the model was refitted.

Concerning the inter-annotator agreement, the results showed main effects of *coreference, directionality, loose definitions* and *negation*. For the *coreference* setting, there was statistically lower agreement in pairs with coreference marked as hard than in pairs with easy coreference, with $p < 0.04$. *Directionality* also showed a correlation with the agreement rates, with pairs in the "harder" direction having statistically lower IAA ($p < 0.001$) than pairs in the "easier" and "same" direction and pairs in the "same" direction having statistically lower agreements than pairs in the "easier" direction ($p < 0.001$). A similar observation can be made for the *loose definitions* effect: pairs not containing loose definitions showed a statistically better agreement than pairs with such definitions ($p < 0.02$). The three factors presented so far confirmed our preliminary observations that these phenomena are not random but are quantitatively depicted in the data. As far as negation is concerned, the results were counter-intuitive at first glance: pairs with negation in one of the sentences A or B had statistically higher IAA rates ($p < 0.001$) than pairs with no negation at all. However, after a closer look, this is not so puzzling: the pairs of our dataset containing negation are the kind of clear-cut, textbook types of negation with one sentence negating exactly what the other sentence is stating by the use of "not", "no" or "nobody", as *A = Nobody is holding a hedgehog. B = Someone is holding a hedgehog.*. Thus, this statistical result shows that it might in fact be easier to decide for such straight-forward pairs with clear-cut negation than for pairs that have no negation

---

[6]IAA normally ranges from 0 to 1 or from 0 to 100 but since we have four possible annotation labels (E, C, N, DN) and three annotators per pair there can only be distinct ordered agreements of 0.00, 33.33 or 100%

but contain hard coreference or loose definitions or generally some complex context. There was no main effect of quantification, i.e. there is no statistical difference between the agreement of annotators in pairs with and without quantifiers. This is probably expected given the very small number of quantifiers found in our data. Otherwise, it could indicate that quantifiers are not so hard for humans as they are assumed to be for machines. Last but not least, the effect of atomicity offers grounds for discussion: for one, annotating atomicity is not as clear cut as one could expect, e.g. there is the open question whether sentences with participles should count as atomic or not. In the example *A = A white dog is standing on a hill covered by grass. B = A white dog is standing on a grassy hillside*, it is not clear whether the participle *covered* should count as an additional predicate-argument structure. We decided to annotate such sentences as atomic (we considered non-atomic only sentences containing more than one *main* clause verbs). For another, we expected pairs with atomic sentences to be significantly easier to annotate for the inference relations compared to non-atomic sentences. This turns out not to be the case in our dataset: the atomicity of the sentences does not impact the agreement rates; the slightly higher agreement when A or B are non-atomic (condition False) is not statistically significant ($p > 0.08$). It is necessary to test this factor with more and more diverse data to see if the significance changes. No significant interactions could be established for this model.

To test for the involved effects in the CF scores results, we analyzed our results with a logistic mixed-effects regression model with CF score as dependent variable and the six meta-annotation categories as fixed factors (main effects and interactions) and the pairs as random effects, using the R-packages lme4 (Bates et al., 2015) and lmerTest (Kuznetsova et al., 2017). Then, the random and fixed effects were backward fitted, using the *step()*-function in lmerTest with the default α cut-off levels (0.1 for random effects and 0.05 for fixed effects). The best fitted model showed main effects of *coreference* and *negation*. Pairs involving hard coreference have statistically lower CF scores, i.e. they are considered harder for an automatic system to label. This correlation also shows that *coreference* is indeed an intuitively detectable factor of inference pairs that annotators "caught" by giving such pairs lower CF scores.

Pairs with negation in A or B sentence have statistically higher CF scores, i.e. they are considered easier for an automatic system to label. Both these findings are consistent with our preliminary observations. As we observed in Section 4, high CF scores seem to correlate with pairs that are highly unambiguous. In our case, these are pairs with the kind of clear-cut, textbook negations like *A = A woman is slicing a tomato. B = There is no woman slicing a tomato.* or pairs containing easy entailments, e.g that a kid is a child or that a small boy is a boy. The fact that the CF scores are statistically higher when there is negation or when the coreference is clear, i.e. there is an easy entailment of the previous kind, confirms this observation. Nevertheless, as we noted for the inter-annotator agreement above, negation seems to be an easy case due to its nature in this dataset; it is expected that in more complex data, negation will play a different role. No significant interactions could be established for this model. Note that the small differences in the average CF scores shown in Table 1 result from the actual average scores used by the annotators for each pair ranging from a minimum of 3.54 to a maximum of 8.65.

In a small side experiment we also tested how the CF scores correlate with what is really hard for automatic systems. We chose the best performing system from the SemEval 2014 task (Marelli et al., 2014a) on SICK by Lai and Hockenmaier (2014) and extracted from their test data those pairs that were also included in our subcorpus. These 92 pairs were split into two groups: those where the label given by the automatic system was the same as the label given by our annotators and those where it was different, i.e. the system got it wrong. For each of those groups we calculated the average CF score. Both groups have an average CF between 6.2 and 6.8, which means that for our subcorpus and this NLI system there is no strong correlation between what our annotators considered hard for machines and what is indeed hard.

6 Discussion

The above results allow us to formulate three conclusions. Firstly, when certain linguistic phenomena are involved in NLI pairs, it is harder for humans to annotate the inference relation and the upper limit they can reach seems to be below the perfect 100% agreement that much research has assumed so far. Given this and the fact that our "ultimate goal" is indeed the human-level understanding, the NLI task should try to account for these cases: either create corpora without those phenomena and expect systems to achieve an almost perfect performance (as humans probably would, without these hard cases) or include the phenomena in the corpus but be aware of them and treat them differently in training and evaluation. Additionally, it seems that our findings strongly confirm our preliminary observations and these observations were possible due to the justifications of the annotators. Thus, enhancing similar annotation tasks with justifications (of some sort) might be a suitable way for building high quality corpora and gaining insights into a given task. Such practices might reduce the original benefits of crowd-sourcing annotations, which lie in much data being gathered fast and cheaply: however, for tasks like NLI, having correctly annotated data might be more beneficial than having huge amounts of data.

6.1 Improvement of the NLI process

The experiment was conducted on a small subset of SICK, yet it was enough to show that even a small subset of a simple NLI dataset like SICK, contains linguistic phenomena that can cause much confusion among the annotators and lead to low inter-annotator agreement or even worse, to acceptable agreement rates but annotations that were not intended in the first place. On the one hand, we showed that *coreference*, *directionality* and *loose definitions* have a strong effect on the resulting agreement and thus these factors should be taken into account at different stages of the process. Some of these issues such as coreference can partly be addressed in the guidelines. Guidelines like the ones we proposed for the CU experiment or the ones from corpora such as SNLI fail to show annotators the difference between contradiction and neutrality. The suggestion of assuming a photo sounded promising but was still not able to avoid confusions. Other phenomena like loose definitions could also partly be treated by appropriate guidelines: the annotators could be motivated to judge the pairs strictly or leniently according to the needs of the corpus creators. To this end, they could be given specific examples like the one mentioned above with the dog sprinting/running and be told that in such situations they should assume double entailment, i.e. be lenient, or assume neutrality in the direction

running $\rightarrow$ sprinting, i.e. be strict. They could alternatively be given dictionaries to adhere to. Still, those issues cannot be fully treated by guidelines and other aspects such as directionality can altogether neither be treated by guidelines nor be predicted during the corpus data creation/generation. This highlights the problem that has plagued the RTE task since its inception: the definition of entailment and contradiction in terms of likely human inference leaves a lot of room for interpretation and neither sufficient annotator training nor unambiguous guidelines can prevent that. However, accepting the fact that the task, though very useful, cannot be well-defined should not scare us but instead motivate us to deal with it in a more efficient way. We need to start devising corpora based on the notion of *human* inference which includes some inherent variability, and find appropriate methods to train our systems on such data and measure their performance on them. For example, NLI pairs could be labelled with the information about the specific kind of inference they are dealing with, similarly to what was already proposed by Zaenen et al. (2005). On the other hand, the systems could be adapted to consider these different labels: in the case of directionality, for example, we could post-hoc measure the IAAs of each pair in both directions and find the harder one. This feature can then be exploited by automatic systems to evaluate their performance on "harder" vs. "easier" cases. It can also be considered for the training process itself: pairs in the "easier" direction have a higher IAA, are more reliable and should have a stronger learning effect, e.g. have higher training weights, than pairs in the "harder", less-reliable direction. Moreover, we showed that phenomena that are considered "hard" for machines can be easy for humans, e.g. quantifiers, while other phenomena are not only considered hard for machines but are proven hard for humans too, e.g. coreference. But since our ultimate goal is human level understanding, certain machine weaknesses are to be expected.

6.2 Justifications for better tasks

The preliminary observations which led us to the quantitative experiment and revealed the impact of the discussed phenomena, were facilitated by the justifications of the annotators. Such justifications can firstly reveal, as in our case, whether the guidelines of the task are clear enough or whether there is confusion. In this way the corpus creators can check the quality of the annotation data. We have shown that the commonly used metric of simple inter-annotator agreement or Cohen's Kappa can be hiding crucial aspects of the annotation quality. Secondly, justifications can indicate other aspects of the task that need to be taken into account during the annotation task, similarly as in this experiment. However, the insights gained can also be exploited in the use of the corpus, i.e. in the training process of some supervised method. When the insights gained can be classified and quantified in clear patterns as in our case, these patterns can be used as additional features during training. This is common in active learning scenarios: the goal in active learning is to output annotations for an initially unlabelled corpus, in addition to linguistic insight (e.g., in the form of rules or deduced patterns). During the labeling stage of the learning loop, the user interacts with the algorithm by labeling an unannotated data instance, verifying a given annotation, providing an estimate of her confidence, and providing a justification for the decision. These justifications along with the annotations and the provided confidence are used to update the existing model in the form of updated or new rules and train the algorithm further (e.g. cf. Sevastjanova et al., 2018). Similarly, the produced justifications in such annotation tasks could be integrated in a "static" learning system in the form of additional rules, patterns or weights and thus lead to a more explainable model. Such justifications can be beneficial in annotations where there is a specific label or score to be chosen among other labels/scores, e.g. in NLI, in semantic similarity tasks, in sentiment analysis, in argument annotation, etc.

7 Relevant Work

Most relevant work on annotation focuses on issues of crowd-sourced annotations. Some work compares such annotations with expert-user annotations (Snow et al., 2008; Munro et al., 2010), while others recommend guidelines and other constraints to make the most of such annotations (Kittur et al., 2008; Aker et al., 2012; Sabou et al., 2014; Dligach et al., 2010). Some researchers propose ways to control and improve discrepancies in such data (Hovy et al., 2013; Tibshirani and Manning, 2014) and others try to point out the quality and ethical issues that arise from such practices (Fort et al., 2011). Considerably less research has been done in task-specific annotations. For NLI there is work discussing annotation challenges (de Marneffe et al., 2008; Kalouli et al., 2017b) and other focusing on improving crowd-sourced corpora (Kalouli et al., 2017a, 2018).

8 Conclusions

This work describes an experiment in which we re-annotated a small subset of the SICK corpus, a benchmark for the NLI task, to investigate how guidelines and specific linguistic phenomena influence annotation quality. Particularly, we discuss the benefits of justifications of the annotation decisions. Based on them, we were able to draw conclusions about aspects of NLI that are hard for humans and need special attention. With a quantitative experiment inspired by these justifications, we could measure the influence of these aspects and make proposals for future annotation tasks, in the NLI domain but also generally. Since NLI is defined based on common human understanding, being aware of the linguistic phenomena that make an inference complex for humans is a fundamental step towards a grounded expectation of what machines should do. We leave as future work to trace and quantify similar trends in other NLI data, e.g. in the SNLI corpus which has been largely used for training NLI systems but also seems to suffer from similar problems. Also, we would like to investigate better the category we called 'loose definitions', following the work of Zaenen et al. (2005). In addition, further research should focus on creating better guidelines for NLI, taking into account the findings of this experiment.

Acknowledgments

We would like to thank the Colorado students for their annotations, Bettina Braun and Katharina Zahner for useful feedback on the statistical analysis, as well as the anonymous reviewers for their constructive comments. We gratefully acknowledge the support of DTRA 1-IDTRAl - 16-1-0002/Project 1553695, eTASC - Empirical Evidence for a Theoretical Approach to Semantic Components and the Linguistics Department of the University of Colorado. Any opinions, findings, and conclusions or recommendations expressed in this material are those of the authors and do not necessarily reflect the views of DTRA or the U.S. government.

References

Ahmet Aker, Mahmoud El-Haj, M-Dyaa Albakour, and Udo Kruschwitz. 2012. Assessing crowdsourcing quality through objective tasks. In *Proceedings of the Eighth International Conference on Language Resources and Evaluation (LREC-2012)*, pages 1456–1461, Istanbul, Turkey. European Language Resources Association (ELRA).

Roy Bar-Haim, Ido Dagan, Bill Dolan, Lisa Ferro, and Danilo Giampiccolo. 2006. The Second PASCAL Recognizing Textual Entailment Challenge. *Proceedings of the Second PASCAL Challenges Workshop on Recognising Textual Entailment.*

Douglas Bates, Martin Mchler, Ben Bolker, and Steve Walker. 2015. Fitting linear mixed-effects models using lme4. *Journal of Statistical Software, Articles*, 67(1):1–48.

Luisa Bentivogli, Peter Clark, Ido Dagan, and Danilo Giampiccolo. 2009a. The Sixth PASCAL Recognizing Textual Entailment Challenge. In *Proceedings of the Text Analysis Conference (TAC).*

Luisa Bentivogli, Peter Clark, Ido Dagan, and Danilo Giampiccolo. 2011. The Seventh PASCAL Recognizing Textual Entailment Challenge. In *Proceedings of the Text Analysis Conference (TAC).*

Luisa Bentivogli, Ido Dagan, Hoa Trang Dang, Danilo Giampiccolo, and Bernardo Magnini. 2009b. The Fifth PASCAL Recognizing Textual Entailment Challenge. In *Proceedings of the Text Analysis Conference (TAC).*

Samuel R. Bowman, Gabor Angeli, Christopher Potts, and Christopher D. Manning. 2015. A large annotated corpus for learning natural language inference. In *Proceedings of the 2015 Conference on Empirical Methods in Natural Language Processing*, pages 632–642, Lisbon, Portugal. Association for Computational Linguistics.

Jean Carletta. 1996. Assessing agreement on classification tasks: The kappa statistic. *Comput. Linguist.*, 22(2):249–254.

Cleo Condoravdi, Dick Crouch, Valeria De Paiva, Reinhard Stolle, and Daniel G Bobrow. 2003. Entailment, intensionality and text understanding. In *Proceedings of the HLT-NAACL 2003 workshop on Text meaning-Volume 9*, pages 38–45. Association for Computational Linguistics.

The Fracas Consortium, Robin Cooper, Dick Crouch, Jan Van Eijck, Chris Fox, Josef Van Genabith, Jan Jaspars, Hans Kamp, David Milward, Manfred Pinkal, Massimo Poesio, Steve Pulman, Ted Briscoe, Holger Maier, and Karsten Konrad. 1996. Using the framework.

Ido Dagan, Bill Dolan, Bernardo Magnini, and Dan Roth. 2010. The Fourth PASCAL Recognizing Textual Entailment Challenge. *Journal of Natural Language Engineering.*

Ido Dagan, Oren Glickman, and Bernardo Magnini. 2006. The PASCAL Recognising Textual Entailment Challenge. In *Proceedings of the First International Conference on Machine Learning Challenges: Evaluating Predictive Uncertainty Visual Object Classification, and Recognizing Textual Entailment*, MLCW'05, pages 177–190, Berlin, Heidelberg. Springer-Verlag.

Dmitriy Dligach, Rodney D. Nielsen, and Martha Palmer. 2010. To annotate more accurately or to annotate more. In *Proceedings of the Fourth Linguistic Annotation Workshop*, LAW IV '10, pages 64–72, Stroudsburg, PA, USA. Association for Computational Linguistics.

Christiane Fellbaum. 1998. *WordNet: An Electronic Lexical Database (Language, Speech, and Communication)*. The MIT Press.

Karen Fort, G Adda, and Kevin Cohen. 2011. Amazon Mechanical Turk: Gold Mine or Coal Mine? *Computational Linguistics*, 37.

Danilo Giampiccolo, Bernardo Magnini, Ido Dagan, and Bill Dolan. 2007. The Third PASCAL Recognizing Textual Entailment Challenge. In *Proceedings of the ACL-PASCAL Workshop on Textual Entailment and Paraphrasing*, RTE '07, pages 1–9, Stroudsburg, PA, USA. Association for Computational Linguistics.

Max Glockner, Vered Shwartz, and Yoav Goldberg. 2018. Breaking NLI Systems with Sentences that Require Simple Lexical Inferences. In *Proceedings of the 56th Annual Meeting of the Association for Computational Linguistics (Volume 2: Short Papers)*, pages 650–655. Association for Computational Linguistics.

Yoav Goldberg and Graeme Hirst. 2017. *Neural Network Methods in Natural Language Processing*. Morgan & Claypool Publishers.

Suchin Gururangan, Swabha Swayamdipta, Omer Levy, Roy Schwartz, Samuel Bowman, and Noah A. Smith. 2018. Annotation Artifacts in Natural Language Inference Data. In *Proceedings of the 2018 Conference of the North American Chapter of the Association for Computational Linguistics: Human Language Technologies, Volume 2 (Short Papers)*, pages 107–112. Association for Computational Linguistics.

Dirk Hovy, Taylor Berg-Kirkpatrick, Ashish Vaswani, and Eduard Hovy. 2013. Learning Whom to Trust with MACE. In *Proceedings of the 2013 Conference of the North American Chapter of the Association for Computational Linguistics: Human Language Technologies*, pages 1120–1130, Atlanta, Georgia. Association for Computational Linguistics.

Aikaterini-Lida Kalouli, Valeria de Paiva, and Livy Real. 2017a. Correcting contradictions. In *Proceedings of the Computing Natural Language Inference Workshop.*

Aikaterini-Lida Kalouli, Livy Real, and Valeria De-Paiva. 2018. WordNet for Easy Textual Inferences. In *Proceedings of the Eleventh International Conference on Language Resources and Evaluation (LREC 2018)*, Paris, France. European Language Resources Association (ELRA).

Aikaterini-Lida Kalouli, Livy Real, and Valeria de Paiva. 2017b. Textual inference: getting logic from humans. In *IWCS 2017 — 12th International Conference on Computational Semantics — Short papers*.

Tushar Khot, Ashutosh Sabharwal, and Peter Clark. 2018. SciTail: A Textual Entailment Dataset from Science Question Answering. In *AAAI*.

Aniket Kittur, Ed H. Chi, and Bongwon Suh. 2008. Crowdsourcing User Studies with Mechanical Turk. In *Proceedings of the SIGCHI Conference on Human Factors in Computing Systems*, CHI '08, pages 453–456, New York, NY, USA. ACM.

Alexandra Kuznetsova, Per Brockhoff, and Rune Christensen. 2017. lmerTest Package: Tests in Linear Mixed Effects Models. *Journal of Statistical Software, Articles*, 82(13):1–26.

Alice Lai and Julia Hockenmaier. 2014. Illinois-LH: A Denotational and Distributional Approach to Semantics. In *Proceedings of the 8th International Workshop on Semantic Evaluation (SemEval 2014)*, pages 329–334, Dublin, Ireland. Association for Computational Linguistics and Dublin City University.

Marco Marelli, Luisa Bentivogli, Marco Baroni, Raffaella Bernardi, Stefano Menini, and Roberto Zamparelli. 2014a. Semeval-2014 task 1: Evaluation of compositional distributional semantic models on full sentences through semantic relatedness and textual entailment. In *Proceedings of the 8th international workshop on semantic evaluation (SemEval 2014)*, pages 1–8.

Marco Marelli, Stefano Menini, Marco Baroni, Luisa Bentivogli, Raffaella Bernardi, and Roberto Zamparelli. 2014b. A SICK cure for the evaluation of compositional distributional semantic models. In *Proceedings of the Ninth International Conference on Language Resources and Evaluation (LREC'14)*, pages 216–223, Reykjavik, Iceland. European Language Resources Association (ELRA).

Marie-Catherine de Marneffe, Anna N. Rafferty, and Christopher D. Manning. 2008. Finding contradictions in text. In *Proceedings of ACL-08: HLT*, pages 1039–1047, Columbus, Ohio. Association for Computational Linguistics.

Robert Munro, Steven Bethard, Victor Kuperman, Vicky Tzuyin Lai, Robin Melnick, Christopher Potts, Tyler Schnoebelen, and Harry Tily. 2010. Crowdsourcing and language studies: the new generation of linguistic data. In *Proceedings of the NAACL HLT 2010 Workshop on Creating Speech and Language Data with Amazon's Mechanical Turk*, pages 122–130, Los Angeles. Association for Computational Linguistics.

Aakanksha Naik, Abhilasha Ravichander, Norman Sadeh, Carolyn Rose, and Graham Neubig. 2018. Stress Test Evaluation for Natural Language Inference. In *Proceedings of the 27th International Conference on Computational Linguistics*, pages 2340–2353, Santa Fe, New Mexico, USA. Association for Computational Linguistics.

Nikita Nangia, Adina Williams, Angeliki Lazaridou, and Samuel Bowman. 2017. The RepEval 2017 Shared Task: Multi-Genre Natural Language Inference with Sentence Representations. In *Proceedings of the 2nd Workshop on Evaluating Vector Space Representations for NLP*, pages 1–10, Copenhagen, Denmark. Association for Computational Linguistics.

Adam Poliak, Pushpendre Rastogi, M. Patrick Martin, and Benjamin Van Durme. 2017. Efficient, Compositional, Order-sensitive n-gram Embeddings. In *Proceedings of the 15th Conference of the European Chapter of the Association for Computational Linguistics: Volume 2, Short Papers*, pages 503–508, Valencia, Spain. Association for Computational Linguistics.

Marta Sabou, Kalina Bontcheva, Leon Derczynski, and Arno Scharl. 2014. Corpus Annotation through Crowdsourcing: Towards Best Practice Guidelines". In *Proceedings of the Ninth International Conference on Language Resources and Evaluation*, pages 859–866, Reykjavik, Iceland. European Language Resources Association (ELRA).

Rita Sevastjanova, Mennatallah El-Assady, Annette Hautli-Janisz, Aikaterini-Lida Kalouli, Rebecca Kehlbeck, Oliver Deussen, Daniel A. Keim, and Miriam Butt. 2018. Mixed-Initiative Active Learning for Generating Linguistic Insights in Question Classification. In *3rd Workshop on Data Systems for Interactive Analysis (DSIA) at IEEE VIS*.

Rion Snow, Brendan O'Connor, Daniel Jurafsky, and Andrew Ng. 2008. Cheap and Fast – But is it Good? Evaluating Non-Expert Annotations for Natural Language Tasks. In *Proceedings of the 2008 Conference on Empirical Methods in Natural Language Processing*, pages 254–263, Honolulu, Hawaii. Association for Computational Linguistics.

Julie Tibshirani and Christopher D. Manning. 2014. Robust Logistic Regression using Shift Parameters. In *Proceedings of the 52nd Annual Meeting of the Association for Computational Linguistics (Volume 2: Short Papers)*, pages 124–129, Baltimore, Maryland. Association for Computational Linguistics.

Adina Williams, Nikita Nangia, and Samuel Bowman. 2018. A Broad-Coverage Challenge Corpus for Sentence Understanding through Inference. In

Proceedings of the 2018 Conference of the North American Chapter of the Association for Computational Linguistics: Human Language Technologies, Volume 1 (Long Papers), pages 1112–1122, New Orleans, Louisiana. Association for Computational Linguistics.

Simon N. Wood. 2011. Fast stable restricted maximum likelihood and marginal likelihood estimation of semiparametric generalized linear models. *Journal of the Royal Statistical Society (B)*, 73(1):3–36.

Simon N. Wood. 2017. *Generalized Additive Models: An Introduction with R*, 2 edition. Chapman and Hall/CRC.

Annie Zaenen, Lauri Karttunen, and Richard Crouch. 2005. Local textual inference: Can it be defined or circumscribed? In *Proceedings of the ACL Workshop on Empirical Modeling of Semantic Equivalence and Entailment*, pages 31–36, Ann Arbor, Michigan. Association for Computational Linguistics.

The role of discourse relations in persuasive texts

Ines Rehbein
Leibniz ScienceCampus
IDS Mannheim / ICL Heidelberg
rehbein@cl.uni-heidelberg.de

Abstract

This paper investigates the use of explicitly signalled discourse relations in persuasive texts. We present a corpus study where we control for speaker and topic and show that the distribution of different discourse *connectives* varies considerably across different discourse settings. While this variation can be explained by genre differences, we also observe variation regarding the distribution of discourse *relations* across different settings. This variation cannot be explained by genre differences. We argue that the differences regarding the use of discourse *relations* reflects different strategies of persuasion and that these might be due to audience design.

1 Introduction

This contribution studies the use of discourse connectives in persuasive texts that have been produced in different communicative settings. Discourse connectives are highly ambiguous and polyfunctional and can vary across different dimensions, depending on the medium (spoken vs. written), the discourse situation (monologic vs. dialogic, formal vs. informal), the purpose of communication (informative vs. persuasive), and more. As we are most interested in investigating different strategies of persuasion, we focus on explicit markers of concessive and contrastive discourse relations, used by the speaker to provide a convincing argument that might persuade the hearer.

Work on discourse analysis and argumentation mining has highlighted the important role of discourse connectives for analysing argumentation structure (Felder, 2015; Stab and Gurevych, 2014; Eckle-Kohler et al., 2015). In addition, psycholinguistic studies have shown that explicit coherence marking not only improves sentence comprehension but also results in a more positive evalua-

tion of the text by the reader (Kamalski et al., 2006). This suggests that discourse connectives might play an important role in persuasion strategies.

We take this hypothesis as our starting point and investigate how different dimensions of variation in persuasive texts can impact the linguistic behaviour of an individual speaker. To that end, we present a corpus study where we try to keep as many variables fixed and only vary the situational setting in which the texts were produced. We control for speaker, topic and function (i.e. persuasive texts) but vary the situational setting of text production.

The data we use in our analysis are political articles, interviews and talks produced by Noam Chomsky. Our data covers spoken and written texts and ranges from highly edited to less edited, including monologic as well as dialogic data.

The variation of discourse settings in our data is accompanied by changes regarding the audience in the different discourse situations. For interviews, the audience is rather small, often on a one-on-one basis, but the hearers have the means to interact with the speaker. This is different from the situation for public talks where we usually have a much larger audience that can be directly addressed by the speaker but has limited possibilities to interact with her. In the last setting, the speaker (or rather: the writer) has the least control and no reliable information about his or her recipients. To account for this variation, we propose the use of the audience design model (Bell, 1984) (see §2.1).

In the paper, we first look at the use of discourse connectives along two dimensions of variation and show that there are systematic differences regarding the frequency of different *forms* of discourse connectives (§4). Next, we show that the differences in the distribution of discourse connectives also reflect differences regarding the distribution

Proceedings of the 13th Linguistic Annotation Workshop, pages 144–154
Florence, Italy, August 1, 2019. ©2019 Association for Computational Linguistics

of discourse *relations* in the different situational settings (§5). Finally, we discuss whether the different distribution of discourse relations in each setting reflects different strategies used to pursue a communicative purpose (§6), and how these might relate to audience design.

2 Background

2.1 Discourse connectives in argumentative and persuasive text

In this work, we focus on the use of explicitly marked discourse relations in persuasive text. In particular, we investigate how different dimensions of variation impact a speaker's linguistic behaviour during the production of argumentative texts. The approach we take is a comparative study of discourse connectives in persuasive texts produced by the *same speaker*, but in different *discourse situations.*

Our investigation takes the following two observations as its starting point. First, it has been shown that the use of discourse connectives and the distribution of explicit and implicit discourse relations is genre-dependent (see, e.g., Webber (2009) for written genres or Rehbein et al. (2016) for spoken texts).[1] Second, Eckle-Kohler et al. (2015) show that certain discourse connectives are highly predictive features for distinguishing claims and premises in argumentative texts.[2] This suggests that discourse connectives play a crucial role as strategic devices for persuasion. We follow O'Keefe (1990) and define persuasion as "a successful intentional effort at influencing another's mental state through communication in a circumstance in which the persuadee has some measure of freedom"(O'Keefe, 1990, p.5).

We distinguish *persuasive* from merely *argumentative* texts that rely on the neutral presentation of a complete set of claims and premises and weigh these against each other. In contrast, persuasive texts use additional rhetorical means to achieve their communicatve goal, such as rhetor-

ical questions, emotional and sentiment-loaded language, a high ratio of imagery, repetition, hyperbole, and more. In addition, presentational choices are made that select or focus on certain aspects of a topic or discourse entity, in order to validate the speaker's point of view and to support her communicative goals. This is often refered to as framing (Entman, 1993).

Stab and Gurevych (2014) look at *argumentative* texts and try to automatically identify claims and premises. They find that discourse connectives are often indicative of certain argument components. Tan et al. (2016) investigate persuasion strategies in online discussion forums. They also try to identify argument structure based on discourse connectives and report negative results for this approach, probably due to data sparseness. Felder (2015) shows how concessive and contrastive discourse connectives can be used to identify the central points of conflict in an argument, based on the selection or foregrounding of specific subtopics that are used to frame the discourse. A certain topic can, for example, be discussed against the background of moral or economic arguments, and thus appeal to different groups of people with differing political views (also see the work of Card et al. (2015, 2016) on media frames). In his work, Felder uses discourse connectives as signals for identifying conflicting framing strategies but does not investigate their strategic function in the discourse.

Kamalski et al. (2006) present two psycholinguistic experiments showing that the use of discourse connectives not only has a positive effect on the hearer's comprehension facility but also leads to a more positive evaluation of the text. This observation suggests that discourse connectives might be used as strategic devices in persuasive text.

2.2 Audience design

Work on accomodation (Giles et al., 1991) and audience design (Bell, 1984) has shown that language variation is not only influenced by social variables describing the speaker (e.g. age, gender, social class, etc.) but that speakers also adapt their style depending on who is listening. Bell investigated the speech of radio news broadcasters from different channels that targeted different audiences. He showed that the same broadcasters varied their linguistic style, depending on the

---

[1]Due to space considerations, we refrain from including a discussion on the definition of *register, genre* and *text type* as there is a lack of agreement on the definition of those terms. In the paper, we try to avoid those terms and instead use the term *discourse setting* to refer to the different situational settings of text production.

[2]The authors, however, do not extend their study to discourse relations but, lacking DR annotations, only look at the word forms of discourse connectives. This is not optimal as most connectives are highly ambiguous and can express a number of different discourse relations.

channel. The audience design model has since been applied to many different discourse settings.

Litt (2012) extended the model for what he calls the "imagined audience", accounting for style shifts in situations where the real audience is not known to the speaker and thus the speaker adapts her style to a mental model of a hearer. This is relevant for many broadcasting media, for example for social media platforms such as forums, blogs or microtext messengers. Many studies have described and quantified effects of audience design in social media, looking at power relations, politeness and other variables of style shifts (Bramsen et al., 2011; Gilbert, 2012; Prabhakaran et al., 2012; niculescu mizil et al., 2012; Danescu-Niculescu-Mizil et al., 2013; Pavalanathan and Eisenstein, 2015).

Applying the audience design model of Bell (1984) to our data, we have to account for different types of audiences. In the interview situation, the speaker is talking to one or more adressees who are known to the speaker and who are able to interact with her. In oral talks, the audience is visible to the speaker and can be directly addressed by her. However, the speaker usually has much less information about the hearers, and the audience has very limited means to actively take part in the communication even though there still is a certain amount of interaction through clapping, heckling or booing. This is different from the production situation of written articles where the text author has no knowledge or control about future readers of the text and thus the recipients can be considered as the "imagined audience", a mental model created in the mind of the author.

In the remainder of the paper, we present an annotation study where we apply the audience design model to our data to see how well it can explain the differences in the use of discourse connectives and explicit discourse relations as strategic devices for persuasion.

3 Data

The data we use in our annotation study are articles and talks by and interviews with Noam Chomsky.[3] We created a corpus with 428,679 tokens of articles, 302,672 tokens of talks and 138,866 tokens of interviews. All data has been produced in a time period between 1985 and 2016.

From the larger corpus, we selected a smaller sample for manual annotation with around 20,000 tokens per discourse setting.[4] The smaller dataset was also controlled for topic. All articles in the sample focus on issues related to Gaza/Middle East/Palestine and the texts were selected from a smaller time range, covering the years from 2008 to 2014.

To take a first step towards investigating our hypothesis that discourse connectives are used as strategic devices for persuasion, we first explore how different *forms* of discourse connectives are used in persuasive texts by the same speaker, but produced in different situational settings.

In the next step, we investigate whether variation with regard to discourse connective *form* also reflects variation regarding the choice of discourse *relations* used to persue the communicative goal, or whether the observed variation can be explained simply by the use of *different forms* of discourse connectives that express the *same discourse relation*.

We argue that if we would find differences regarding the use of discourse *relations* in persuasive texts controlled for speaker and topic but produced in different situational settings, these differences could not be easily explained based on genre differences but would need a situational model that also accounts for the hearer/reader, such as the audience design model.

4 Distribution of discourse connectives

We start with an exploration of the distribution of discourse connectives in the three subcorpora. We follow the tradition of Biber's register analysis (Biber 1995) and perform a Principal Component Analysis (PCA),[5] based on the frequency of 22 causal, concessive and contrastive discourse connective *forms*, to identify the main variables of variance. The set we use includes the following connectives: *accordingly, although, because, but, conversely, hence, however, instead, nevertheless, nonetheless, nor, rather, since, so, still, thereby, therefore, though, thus, whereas, while, yet.* We split the different texts in the large corpus in samples of 250 sentences each, count the frequency for each of the forms in the different samples and

---

[3]We collected the data from https://chomsky.info.

[4]The token counts vary slightly as we did not cut off sentences but incuded all additional tokens until the end of the sentence.

[5]We use the FactoMineR library in the statistical software R (https://www.r-project.org).

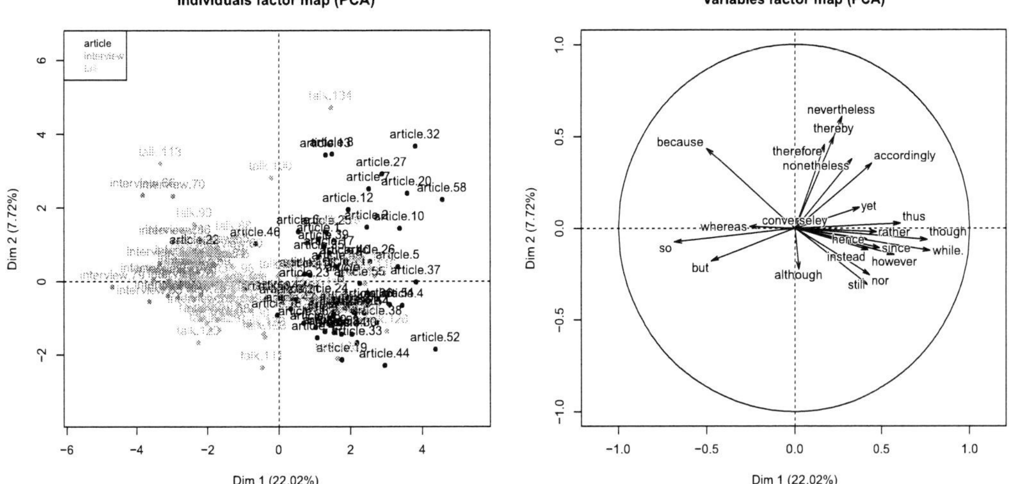

Figure 1: PCA on the larger dataset, showing the distribution of different discourse connective forms in persuasive articles, talks and interviews for the same speaker.

run the PCA on the data.

The PCA, despite having no other information but the frequency for each discourse connective, is able to separate the interviews from the articles along the first dimension. Figure 1 (left) shows how most of the interviews cluster at the left end of the dimension while the articles are positioned at the right end. The talks show a larger variance in the use of discourse connectives, and some talk segments show an overlap with the interviews while in other talks the use of discourse connectives is more similar to the one in the articles.

Figure 1 (right) identifies the discourse connectives most typical for written articles (*though, while, thus, however*) and those that are used in the less edited, dialogic interview data (*because, so, but*).

Our analysis clearly confirms what has been shown before (Webber, 2009; Rehbein et al., 2016), namely that the use of discourse connectives is highly genre-specific. In earlier genre studies, however, the different genres represented texts with different communicative functions, i.e. informative texts versus argumentative texts etc. Therefore, one might assume that the differences in the use of discourse connectives might reflect functional differences.

In our study, we try to eliminate this factor. We control for speaker and –in the smaller subcorpus– also for topic. All texts have a clear persuasive goal, i.e. to convince the audience from a particular political point of view. The main difference between the texts is the *communication setting* in which they were produced. This allows us to investigate the role that discourse connectives play for strategies of persuasion, tailored towards a particular setting and audience.

Given that the texts have the same persuasive function, we assume that the differences we observed reflect differences along two dimensions of variation that are correlated with the situational settings of text production. In a more detailed analysis with more features than just the counts for different connective forms, similar to Biber (1995); Biber and Conrad (2009); Passonneau et al. (2014), we would expect to find the two dimensions displayed in figure 2.

The first dimension distinguishes highly edited texts from less edited ones. Here the articles are positioned on the left end of the dimension, the talks can be located somewhere in the middle and the interviews as the least edited of the three text types are positioned at the right end. The second dimension concerns the interactional dimension of communication and sets monological texts apart from dialogical ones. Here, the articles can be placed at the monological end of the scale while the interviews are clearly dialogical and can thus be positioned at the other end of the dimension. The talks are mostly monological but allow for

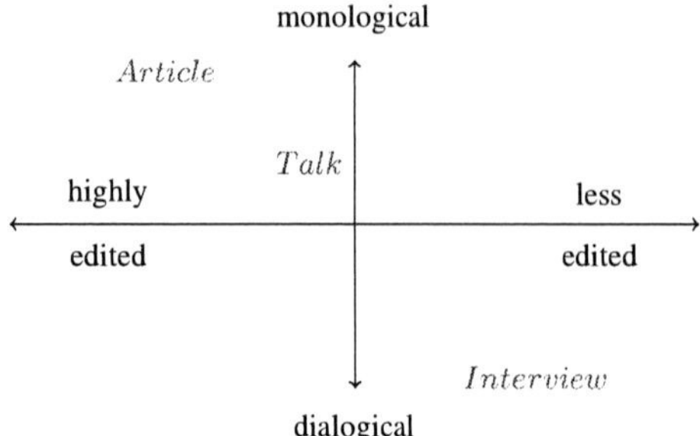

Figure 2: Dimensions of variation for different discourse settings.

LEVEL-1	LEVEL-2	LEVEL-1	LEVEL-2
COMPARISON	Contrast Similarity Concession $+/-\beta, \zeta$	TEMPORAL	Synchronous Asynchronous
CONTINGENCY	Cause $+/-\beta, \zeta$ Condition $+/-\beta, \zeta$ Neg. cond. $+/-\beta, \zeta$ Purpose	EXPANSION	Conjunction Disjunction Equivalence Instantiation Level-of-detail Substitution Exception Manner

Table 1: First two levels of hierarchy in the PDTB3 (level 3 encodes the direction of the relation, if applicable).

some interaction with the audience.

These two dimensions of variation might explain the variance in the distribution of discourse connectives in the data, as the same discourse relations can be expressed via different connectives (or can also be left implicit). We thus hypothesize that the differences we observe will disappear when we look at the level of *discourse relations* instead of discourse connective *forms*. As there is no one-to-one correspondence between discourse connectives and discourse relations and automatic tools are not yet reliable enough, we need to manually disambiguate the relations in the data.

5 Annotation study

We present an annotation study where we annotate all instances of discourse connectives that can express a causal, contrastive or concessive discourse relation. We follow the framework of PDTB3 (Webber et al., 2016), a revised version of the Penn Discourse Treebank scheme (Prasad et al., 2008). The question we would like to answer is: Does the difference in distribution of discourse connectives in the texts shown above reflect differences in the distribution of discourse relations, or are the *same relations* expressed by *different devices* that are more adequate for a given discourse situation?

5.1 Discourse relations in argumentative text

The revised version of the PDTB comprises some changes to the relation hierarchy. Some relations in PDTB2 that were difficult to distinguish even for trained annotators have been merged in PDTB3, and inconsistencies regarding the annotation of the directionality of the relation have been removed. The direction describes the order of the arguments. In the PDTB scheme, Arg1 and Arg2 are determined by position in inter-sentential relations as well as in intra-sentential paratactic structures (e.g. coordinations). In intra-sentential subordinated structures, the subordinated clause is always labelled Arg2, regardless of its position. The new relation hierarchy is shown in table 1.

Additionally, some relations can be marked as either *pragmatic* (epistemic) (β; for implicit beliefs) or as *speech acts* (ζ).[6] These features should be understood as properties of the arguments, not of the relations (Webber et al., 2016). The examples below illustrate the different relation types relevant to our study. We follow the PDTB conventions and mark the first argument in italics and the second argument in boldface. The discourse connective that signals the relation is underlined.

- Concession:
  Although **she was qualified**, *she didn't get the job.*
- Contrast:
  Mary likes to read <u>while</u> **John loves cooking.**
- Cause:
  The street is wet <u>because</u> **it rained last night.**
- Cause + Belief ($+\beta$):
  She must be home <u>because</u> **the light is on.**
- Cause + Speechact ($+\zeta$):
  He's in Denver <u>because</u> **he just called me an hour ago.**

5.2 Discourse connectives versus discourse relations

We manually disambiguate all discourse connective forms in the smaller subcorpus that can express a causal, concessive or contrastive relation. The data includes 20,000 tokens from each discourse setting and was controlled for topic (table 2). The annotation was done by one trained linguist who had previous experience with PDTB-style annotations. As annotation tool, we used

---

[6]For a distinction between, content, epistemic and speech act relations, see Sweetser (1990).

the PDTB Annotator (Lee et al., 2016). We annotated all senses for instances of discourse connectives from a set of 22 word forms (see section 4). This resulted in 1,614 annotated instances (articles: 395, talks: 633, interviews: 586).

As there was only one annotator, we cannot report inter-annotator agreement for this task. However, in a comparable previous study on annotating PDTB-style discourse relations on English, the same annotator showed an IAA of 84.6% (percentage agreement) and a Fleiss' κ of 0.797 (Rehbein et al., 2016).

Table 3 shows the distribution of causal, concessive and contrastive senses for the different discourse settings (see table 7 in the appendix for a complete list of all senses in PDTB3 (Webber et al., 2016)). We decided to normalise raw counts per sentence, as discourse relations mostly operate on the sentence or clause-level.[7]

The talks have the highest amount of signalled causal and concessive discourse relations in our corpus. The number of concessive relations, however, is smaller than in the article and interview subcorpora. In contrast to the use of discourse connective *forms*, the distribution of discourse *relations* found in the data cannot be explained with regard to the two dimensions of variation we discussed above (monologic–dialogic and less edited–highly edited).

However, when looking at more fine-grained sense distinctions, also taking the PDTB level three senses into account that encode the direction of the relation, we make an interesting observation (table 4). We can see that the higher number of causal relations in the talks reflects a more frequent use of RESULT-type relations while the distribution of REASON-type relations in the three discourse settings is fairly similar. If we look at concessive relations, we see that the higher frequency in the talks is caused only by Arg2-as-

---

[7]Results for a normalisation based on clauses were not significantly different from a sentence-based normalisation.

	token	sent	clause	annotations
article	20,020	822	2,062	395
interview	20,009	1,083	2,559	633
talk	20,011	1,123	2,623	586
total	60,040	3,028	7,244	1,614

Table 2: Subcorpus used in the annotation study (annotations lists the number of annotated relations for each discourse setting).

LEVEL-2	article	interview	talk
raw counts			
Cause	41	73	101
Contrast	51	67	49
Concession	47	58	86
total	**139**	**198**	**236**
normalised per sentence			
Cause	5.0	6.7	**9.0**
Contrast	6.2	**6.2**	4.4
Concession	5.7	5.3	**7.7**
total	**16.9**	**18.2**	**21.0**

Table 3: Distribution of causal, concessive and contrastive discourse relations (raw counts per discourse setting, and normalised counts per sentence)

LEVEL-2	LEVEL-3	article	interv.	talk
Cause	Reason	2.43	2.12	2.49
	Result	2.55	4.43	**6.50**
	Result $+\beta$	0.12	0.18	0.00
Concession	Arg1-denier	**0.85**	0.55	0.18
	Arg2-denier	4.87	4.71	**7.48**

Table 4: Amount of level-3 causal and concessive discourse relations (normalised per sentence; β: belief)

denier relations while instances of Arg1-as-denier are more frequent in the article subcorpus. We also found one instance of Concession where we were not able to annotate the direction (see example below). As the example is from the interviews part of the corpus, we assume that it might be a performance error and exclude it from the analysis.

(1)   They can also be supplemented by various forms of direct action , *such as what is now called " BDS , "* though **that is only one of many tactical options**.

To get a different perspective, we go back to the more coarse-grained level-2 senses but this time also include the SPEECHACT features (ζ) (table 5). Here we can see that the crucial difference between the talks and the other two discourse settings regarding the CONCESSION relation can be traced back to the presence or absence of the ζ feature. SPEECHACT-type relations hardly ever occur in the articles and interviews but are quite frequent in the political talks, thus showing that it is not only difference between *oral* and *written* that triggers the use of speechact relations.

LEVEL-2	FEATURES	article	interview	talk
Concession	- ζ	5.2	4.9	5.6
	+ ζ	0.5	0.4	**2.0**

Table 5: Amount of concessive discourse relations with/without SPEECHACT (normalised per sentence; ζ: speech act)

6   Discussion

So far, we have shown that persuasive texts produced by the same speaker in different situational settings do vary with regard to the distribution of discourse connective *forms* in the texts, and that this might reflect differences along the dimension of editedness and the degree of interaction in the texts.

Next, we have shown that the variation with regard to discourse connective forms in persuasive texts controlled for topic and speaker but produced in different discourse settings is not only due to stilistic choices made by the speaker. Instead, we also found variation on the level of discourse relations, with causal result and concessive speechact relations being used far more often in the talks than in the other two discourse settings.

This variation cannot be easily explained with regard to genre differences as looking at the distribution of discourse relations should abstract away the stilistic differences between different connective forms (e.g. formal–informal, highly edited–less edited). As we assume that that function of the texts is the same (*persuasive text*), we hypothesize that the variation in the distribution of discourse relations in each communicative setting reflects the use of different persuasive strategies employed to persue the communicative goal.

6.1   Causal relations

Let us start by looking at the causal relations. While the frequency of REASON relations was more or less equal in all three subcorpora, we observed a substantially higher amount of RESULT relations in the talks. Examples (2), (3) show typical examples for REASON and RESULT relations in the talk subcorpus.

(2)   *He was removed from office soon after* <u>because</u> **he was considered too soft-hearted.** REASON

(3)   *For US leaders, aggression means resistance.* <u>So,</u> **anyone who resists the United States is guilty of aggression.** RESULT

The first example describes an event in the real world (*removed from office*) and presents the cause for this event (*being too soft-harted*). It can thus be categorised as a consequence–cause relation. Example (3), however, does not describe an event

but rather presents two claims, with the first claim providing the pragmatic justification for the second one. Please note that instances like (3) are not annotated as implicit beliefs. The reason for this becomes clear when modifying example (3), as shown below:

(4)   *For US leaders, aggression means resistance.* <u>So I believe</u>, **anyone who resists the United States is guilty of aggression.**

The meaning of (4) is different from (3) where the subject of consciousness holding the belief expressed in Arg2 are the US leaders while in the modified example the subject of consciousness is the speaker.[8]

Looking at more examples, one striking feature is the frequent use of the first person plural pronoun (*we*; examples (5)–(7) below) in the talks.

(5)   *The countries we wanted to sell it to did n't have dollars* <u>so</u> **we had to provide them with dollars.** RESULT

(6)   *And that makes sense if we own the world* <u>so</u> **any active resistance is aggression against us.** RESULT

(7)   *We did it* <u>so therefore</u> **it's efforts to do good.** RESULT

To check whether first person pronouns in general are more frequent in the talk subcorpus, we counted the number of occurrences of *I* and *we* for each discourse setting. Table 6 shows that, as expected, the written texts have the lowest number of first person pronouns. First person pronouns are considered a marker of involvement and are often used to discriminate spoken from written registers (Biber, 1995, p.225). Here, however, they not only distinguish the written from the spoken texts but also set apart the talks from the interviews. While in the latter both *I* and *we* are used with high frequency, in the talks we observe a significantly higher number of first person plural usage.

6.2   Concession and SpeechAct

Another difference between the three discourse settings concerns the substantially higher number

---

[8]The two claims in (3) are presented as facts in the world with the second one following from the first, and not as epistemic beliefs. We therefore annotate them as *content* relations in the sense of Sweetser (1990).

1.ps.pron	article	interview	talk
we	43	86	143
I	13	79	49
all tokens	20,020	20,009	20,011

Table 6: Frequency of 1. person pronouns *I, we* in the three discourse settings.

of SPEECHACT relations in the talks. This can not be ascribed to the medium, i.e. spoken language, as this relation type is not only rare in the written articles but also hardly ever occurs in the interviews. Below are typical examples for CONCESSION + SPEECHACT in the corpus.

(8) *I hope I don't have to describe it to you,* <u>but</u> **it killed several million people , destroyed three countries**.

(9) *I won't go through the rest of the history* <u>but</u> **it continues pretty much like that**.

(10) *I won't run through the whole story* <u>but</u> **the basic facts are clear**.

Again, we observe a high number of first person pronouns, here mostly the singular form *I*. All of these examples anchor the speech act in the *here-and-now* by referring to the discourse situation and also by referencing a common ground shared between speaker and audience. By doing so, the speaker presumes that the hearers agree with his point of view even without giving further details on the topic under discussion (examples (8)–(10)).

This communicative strategy requires that the *Ground* (Langacker, 1990), i.e. the immediate circumstances of the speech event such as time and space, are shared between speaker and audience. This explains why this strategy cannot be used in written articles where the speaker only has access to an imagined audience at best, and no interaction is possible. In the interview setting, however, the increased level of interaction might interfere with the speaker's construction of the shared common ground.

6.3 Political talks as oral narratives

Based on the results of our annotation study, we hypothesize that the differences in the distribution of discourse relations reflect the use of different strategies of persuasion in the different communicative settings. We suggest that it might make sense to consider persuasive political talks as oral narratives in the sense of Labov and Waletzky

(1967), with the function of "transfer[ing] experience from one person to another through oral narratives of personal experience" (Labov, 2010). This fits well with the high number of personal pronouns in the talks which not only reflect a high amount of involvement but also give credibility to the narrative. Furthermore, the use of first person pronouns helps to create an impression of intimacy between speaker and audience and also lends the narrative authenticity (Malti-Douglas, 1988, p.93).

These ideas, however, are highly speculative and need to be tested empirically on a larger basis and including more than one speaker.

7 Conclusions

We presented an annotation study where we investigated the use of discourse connectives and discourse relations in persuasive texts. The texts in our corpus are controlled for speaker and topic but produced in different communicative settings. We observed a substantial variation in the use of discourse connective *forms* and *relations*. While the first can be easily explained by genre differences, we argue that the second variation concerning the use of discourse relations might reflect different strategies of persuasion, and that models of audience design might prove useful for understanding this variation.

Acknowledgments

I would like to thank the reviewers for their helpful comments. This research has been conducted within the Leibniz Science Campus "Empirical Linguistics and Computational Modeling", funded by the Leibniz Association under grant no. SAS-2015-IDS-LWC and by the Ministry of Science, Research, and Art (MWK) of the state of Baden-Württemberg.

References

Allan Bell. 1984. Language style as audience design. *Language in society*, 13(2):145–204.

Doublas Biber and Susan Conrad. 2009. *Register, genre, and style*. Cambridge: Cambridge University Press.

Douglas Biber. 1995. *Variation across speech and writing*. Publisher: Cambridge University Press.

Philip Bramsen, Martha Escobar-Molano, Ami Patel, and Rafael Alonso. 2011. Extracting social power relationships from natural language. In *The 49th Annual Meeting of the Association for Computational Linguistics: Human Language Technologies*, HLT 2011, pages 773–782.

Dallas Card, Amber E. Boydstun, Justin H. Gross, Philip Resnik, and Noah A. Smith. 2015. The media frames corpus: Annotations of frames across issues. In *Proceedings of the 53rd Annual Meeting of the Association for Computational Linguistics and the 7th International Joint Conference on Natural Language Processing of the Asian Federation of Natural Language Processing*, ACL 2015, pages 438–444, Beijing, China.

Dallas Card, Justin H. Gross, Amber E. Boydstun, and Noah A. Smith. 2016. Analyzing framing through the casts of characters in the news. In *Proceedings of the 2016 Conference on Empirical Methods in Natural Language Processing*, EMNLP 2016, pages 1410–1420, Austin, Texas, USA.

Cristian Danescu-Niculescu-Mizil, Moritz Sudhof, Dan Jurafsky, Jure Leskovec, and Christopher Potts. 2013. A computational approach to politeness with application to social factors. In *The 51st Annual Meeting of the Association for Computational Linguistics*, ACL 2013, pages 250–259.

Judith Eckle-Kohler, Roland Kluge, and Iryna Gurevych. 2015. On the role of discourse markers for discriminating claims and premises in argumentative discourse. In *Proceedings of the 2015 Conference on Empirical Methods in Natural Language Processing, EMNLP 2015, Lisbon, Portugal, September 17-21, 2015*, pages 2236–2242.

Robert M. Entman. 1993. Framing: Toward clarification of a fractured paradigm. *Communication*, 43(4):51–58.

Ekkehard Felder. 2015. Lexik und grammatik der agonalität in der linguistischen diskursanalyse. In Heidrun Kmper and Ingo Warnke, editors, *Diskurs – interdisziplinär. Zugänge, Gegenstände, Perspektiven*, pages 87–121. Berlin/Boston: de Gruyter.

Eric Gilbert. 2012. Phrases that signal workplace hierarchy. In *Proceedings of the ACM 2012 Conference on Computer Supported Cooperative Work*, CSCW '12, pages 1037–1046.

Howard Giles, Justine Coupland, and Nikolas Coupland. 1991. *Contexts of Accommodation: Developments in Applied Sociolinguistics*. Cambridge: Cambridge University Press.

Judith Kamalski, Leo Lentz, and Ted Sanders. 2006. Effects of coherence marking on the comprehension and appraisal of discourse. In *Cognitive Science Conference*.

William Labov. 2010. Oral narratives of personal experience. In *Cambridge Encyclopedia of the Language Sciences*. Cambridge: Cambridge University Press.

William Labov and Joshua Waletzky. 1967. Narrative analysis: oral versions of personal experience. In *Essays on the Verbal and Visual Arts: Proceedings of the 1966 Annual Spring Meeting of the American Ethnological Society*, pages 12–44. University of Washington Press, Seattle.

Ronald Langacker. 1990. Subjectification. *Cognitive Linguistics*, 1:5–38.

Alan Lee, Rashmi Prasad, Bonnie L. Webber, and Aravind K. Joshi. 2016. Annotating discourse relations with the PDTB annotator. In *The 26th International Conference on Computational Linguistics, Proceedings of the Conference System Demonstrations*, COLING 2016, pages 121–125.

Eden Litt. 2012. Knock, knock. who's there? the imagined audience. *Journal of Broadcasting & Electronic Media*, 56:330–345.

Fedwa Malti-Douglas. 1988. *Blindness and Autobiography: Al-Ayyam of Taha Husayn*. Princeton University Press.

Cristian Danescu niculescu mizil, Lillian Lee, Bo Pang, and Jon Kleinberg. 2012. Echoes of power: Language effects and power differences in social interaction. In *The 21st International Conference on World Wide Web*, WWW 2012, pages 699–708.

Daniel J. O'Keefe. 1990. *Persuasion: Theory and research*. Newbury Park, CA: Sage.

Rebecca J. Passonneau, Nancy Ide, Songqiao Su, and Jesse Stuart. 2014. Biber redux: Reconsidering dimensions of variation in american english. In *The 25th International Conference on Computational Linguistics*, COLING 2014, pages 565–576.

Umashanthi Pavalanathan and Jacob Eisenstein. 2015. Audience-modulated variation in online social media. *American Speech*, 90(2):187–213.

Vinodkumar Prabhakaran, Owen Rambow, and Mona Diab. 2012. Predicting overt display of power in written dialogs. In *The 2012 Conference of the North American Chapter of the Association for Computational Linguistics: Human Language Technologies*, NAACL 2012, pages 518–522.

R. Prasad, N. Dinesh, A. Lee, E. Miltsakaki, L. Robaldo, A.K. Joshi, and B.L. Webber. 2008. The penn discourse treebank 2.0. In *Proceedings of the 6 International Conference on Language Resources and Evaluation*, LREC'08. European Language Resources Association.

Ines Rehbein, Merel Scholman, and Vera Demberg. 2016. Annotating discourse relations in spoken language: A comparison of the PDTB and CCR frameworks. In *Proceedings of the Tenth International Conference on Language Resources and Evaluation LREC 2016, Portorož, Slovenia, May 23-28, 2016*.

Christian Stab and Iryna Gurevych. 2014. Identifying argumentative discourse structures in persuasive essays. In *Conference on Empirical Methods in Natural Language Processing*, EMNLP 2014, pages 46–56.

Eve Sweetser. 1990. *From Etymology to Pragmatics.* Cambridge University Press, Cambridge.

Chenhao Tan, Vlad Niculae, Cristian Danescu-Niculescu-Mizil, and Lillian Lee. 2016. Winning arguments: Interaction dynamics and persuasion strategies in good-faith online discussions. In *The 25th International Conference on World Wide Web*, WWW 2016, pages 613–624.

Bonnie L. Webber. 2009. Genre distinctions for discourse in the penn treebank. In *ACL 2009, Proceedings of the 47th Annual Meeting of the Association for Computational Linguistics and the 4th International Joint Conference on Natural Language Processing of the AFNLP, 2-7 August 2009, Singapore*, pages 674–682.

Bonnie L. Webber, Rashmi Prasad, Alan Lee, and Aravind K. Joshi. 2016. A discourse-annotated corpus of conjoined vps. In *The 10th Linguistic Annotation Workshop*, LAW 2016.

A   Appendices

LEVEL-1	LEVEL-2	LEVEL-3
TEMPORAL	SYNCHRONOUS	–
	ASYNCHRONOUS	Precedence SUCCESSION
COMPARISON	CONTRAST	–
	SIMILARITY	–
	CONCESSION +/-β, ζ	Arg1-as-denier Arg1-as-denier
CONTINGENCY	Cause +/-β, ζ	Reason Result
	CONDITION +/- ζ	Arg1-as-cond Arg2-as-cond
	NEGATIVE CONDITION +/-ζ	Arg1-as-negcond Arg2-as-negcond
	PURPOSE	Arg1-as-goal Arg1-as-goal
EXPANSION	CONJUNCTION	–
	DISJUNCTION	–
	EQUIVALENCE	–
	INSTANTIATION	–
	LEVEL-OF-DETAIL	Arg1-as-detail Arg2-as-detail
	SUBSTITUTION	Arg1-as-subst Arg2-as-subst
	EXCEPTION	Arg1-as-excpt Arg2-as-excpt
	MANNER	Arg1-as-manner Arg2-as-manner

Table 7: Sense hierarchy in the PDTB3 (level 3 encodes the direction of the relation, if applicable).

One format to rule them all –
The `emtsv` pipeline for Hungarian

Balázs Indig[1,2], Bálint Sass[1], Eszter Simon[1],
Iván Mittelholcz[1], Noémi Vadász[1], and Márton Makrai[1]

[1]Research Institute for Linguistics, Hungarian Academy of Sciences
[1]`lastname.firstname@nytud.mta.hu`
[2]Centre for Digital Humanities, Eötvös Loránd University
[2]`lastname.firstname@btk.elte.hu`

Abstract

We present a more efficient version of
the `e-magyar` NLP pipeline for Hungarian called `emtsv`. It integrates Hungarian
NLP tools in a framework whose individual
modules can be developed or replaced independently and allows new ones to be added.
The design also allows convenient investigation and manual correction of the data flow
from one module to another. The improvements we publish include effective communication between the modules and support of the
use of individual modules both in the chain
and standing alone. Our goals are accomplished using extended `tsv` (tab separated values) files, a simple, uniform, generic and self-
documenting input/output format. Our vision
is maintaining the system for a long time and
making it easier for external developers to fit
their own modules into the system, thus sharing existing competencies in the field of processing Hungarian, a mid-resourced language.
The source code is available under LGPL 3.0
license[1].

1 Introduction

The `e-magyar` processing system (Váradi et al.,
2018) integrates the state-of-the-art Hungarian
NLP tools into a single, easy-to-use, maintained,
and updated system. It has been designed to facilitate both research and application-oriented processing with the important goal of the system being fully open for research purposes, thus encouraging future expansion, but also being easy for
the non-NLP audience to use, and to become a
good experimental tool, delivering the best performance available, regarding both processing speed
and correctness.

Since its publication, the system has become
popular and widely used in the Hungarian NLP

community. Attempts have also been made to analyze large corpora with it, such as the Hungarian Webcorpus (Halácsy et al., 2004) and the Hungarian Gigaword Corpus (Oravecz et al., 2014).
This work led to the discovery of previously unknown errors and weaknesses, which were taken
into account in our developments. In this article,
we present our work with two aspects emphasized:
the unified communication format and the architecture design.

In the first version of `e-magyar`, the intermodular communication format was the internal `xml` format of GATE (Cunningham et al.,
2011), into which the Hungarian system was integrated. However, user experience showed that
most users do not know or want to use the GATE
system for their work: users with linguistic interest found it inconvenient, while for those with a
technical background, it was unnecessarily cumbersome. In many cases, GATE introduces unnecessary complexity regarding installation, debugging, the format, and resource demand, due to the
`xml`-based *standoff* annotation (see Section 3),
which in many cases undermines stability. Therefore, we voted for the development of a new, standard and GATE-independent inter-modular communication format opening the way to use existing devices as separate modules or with transparent inter-modular messages. The format also simplifies the manual modification of inter-modular
content. Available tools, even those independent
of their programming language, become easier to
integrate into the system.

Another focus of the development was on
rethinking the architecture design. Modules
which were available before the creation of
`e-magyar` were written in various programming
languages, following different linguistic annotations, and lacking a modularized and transparent
structure. In contrast, our principles are unifor-

---

[1]`https://github.com/dlt-rilmta/emtsv`

155

Proceedings of the 13th Linguistic Annotation Workshop, pages 155–165
Florence, Italy, August 1, 2019. ©2019 Association for Computational Linguistics

mity, interoperability, comparability, and the interchangeability of individual modules (e.g. when a new candidate performs better).

In this article, we show how we converted the tools of the previous `e-magyar` version following the UNIX toolbox philosophy: "each does one thing and each does it very well". Restructured modules are supposed to be able to both operate independently of each other or interacting, as needed. Also sections of the pipeline can be run, i.e. users can enter or exit at any point and can modify the data manually, as long as they adhere to format requirements, which are natural and programming language agnostic by design from the beginning.

Design properties of other processing chains were kept in mind during the development of `emtsv` for the sake of comparability. Other systems mostly take strictly a single natural language as their starting point, but then they are extended to be multilingual or even intended to be universal afterwards. Some of them go with changed needs, which now favor scalable cloud-based technologies – dubbed *microservices* – that do not require end user installation: the chain is provided as a service, sometimes without source code.

In parallel with the development, the potential use of `emtsv` was also contemplated. For instance, `emtsv` could be profitable for pre-annotating tasks in corpus building. Thanks to the high performance of the modules, pre-analyzing the text could shorten and ease the otherwise expensive and protracted human annotation. Furthermore, the modular architecture of the toolchain allows us to exit at a certain point of the analysis, carry out some manual correction in the data, and then enter the chain again putting the data back to `emtsv`. Let us take an imaginable workflow as an illustrative example. Firstly, the output of tokenization and tagging is corrected manually for a revised, finer input for the dependency parser, the second step of the workflow. Therefore, the effect of occurrent errors from the tokenizer or the part of speech (POS) tagger could be eliminated. It is worth to mention, that since the dependency parser allocates ID numbers to each token, modifications in tokenization (inserting, deleting, splitting, or joining tokens) do not cause complications in token numbering. At the end of the workflow, the output of the dependency parser is converted into the CoNLL-U format[2], which is edible for widely-used annotation and visualization tools, e.g. allowing to carry out further corrections in the dependency graph in a drag-and-drop manner.

In Section 2, we present the currently available language processing systems similar to `emtsv` for the sake of comparison. Section 3 describes our extended `tsv` format, Section 4 gives an overview of the architecture, while Section 5 presents the individual modules. Section 6 summarizes the paper and Section 7 presents future work.

2   Related Work

As an NLP pipeline primarily for Hungarian, `emtsv` can be compared to `Magyarlánc` (Zsibrita et al., 2013), currently in version 3.0, and the `hun*` toolchain[3]. Though there are overlaps between the modules of the compared chains, here we focus on the structure of the chain as a whole, which is, to some extent, independent of the individual modules.

`Magyarlánc` provides a Java-based, tightly coupled chain, using the latest international state-of-the-art modules. It is suitable for annotating a large amount of Hungarian text with detailed and proper linguistic analysis, but the modification of the system (e.g. adding possible new modules or replacing existing ones) is cumbersome.

The most relevant modules of the `hun*` toolchain are the `HunToken`[4] sentence and word tokenizer (written in Flex and Shell), the `HunMorph` morphological analyzer (Trón et al., 2005) (w. in OCaml), the `HunPOS` POS tagger (Halácsy et al., 2006) (w. in OCaml), the `HunNER` named entity recognizer (Varga and Simon, 2007) (w. in Python), and the `HunTag` sequential tagger (Recski and Varga, 2009) (w. in Python). The `hun*` chain and `emtsv` share several properties: the loosely coupled architecture, the `tsv` format, the heterogenity of programming languages applied for the development of the modules, and the open source availability. However, `hun*` only works with Latin-2 character encoding and its direct development has discontinued.

There are several examples of systems similar to `Magyarlánc` on the international scene, which usually suffer from similar shortcomings

---

[2] `http://universaldependencies.org/format`

[3] `https://hlt.bme.hu/en/resources/hun-toolchain`

[4] `https://github.com/zseder/huntoken`

mentioned above. At the same time, they have merits like being language independent (or at least supporting many natural languages), fast or able to process large amounts of data. Currently we do not intend to compete with all of these aspects, but focus on producing the best results for Hungarian the most efficiently, and creating a format that is close to standards and easy to convert to other ones. We want to give full control to the user by creating a loosely coupled system. The point here is to involve the community in the development: for transparent operation, systems not only need to be open-source but also need to be accepted and maintained by the NLP community, which is more difficult to achieve.

In the remainder of this section, we highlight a few existing language-independent analyzers to present some of their disadvantageous properties which tend to be common with the tools not included.

`UDPipe` (Straka and Straková, 2017) was written in C++ roughly at the same time as `e-magyar` with the goal of analyzing general texts. Training data follows the Universal Dependencies and Morphology (UD)[5] annotation scheme and format. Although it has bindings for many programming languages, and is truly efficient, it does not allow for easy extension and development of the applied pipeline, despite that its source code is free[6]. This is a shortcoming if developers want to introduce their own modules, such as a custom morphological analyzer.

The Python-based `spaCy`[7] started similarly, originally consisting of closed-end modules, but since version 2.0, it has become more and more open in architecture in order to support more natural languages. Although `spaCy` and `emtsv` are similar in their direction of development, their current status is too far to allow comparison: `emtsv` is more loosely coupled.

Another strategy is followed by `WebSty`[8] and `Weblicht`[9]. These pipelines try to integrate existing tools including even language-dependent ones to better support individual languages. Their only criterion is that the tools have to support the UD format. The principle of this approach is scalability in great computer clusters: running in the cloud asynchronously orchestrated by a task scheduler on demand. The entire system is accessible via a web-based API, where tasks can be specified with data files. The source code of the software is not available for running a local instance, and modules cannot be developed by external developers.

In `emtsv`, we try to eliminate the architectural drawbacks of previous systems described above and, at the same time, reserve their advantageous features.

3 Uniform Data Format

The classic structure of `e-magyar` (Sass et al., 2017) heavily relies on the features inherited from the original tools, depending on their input and output formats. In that system, GATE is the layer of architecture that creates a common, unified data format, thus providing interoperability between the individual modules, that are agnostic of each other. This idea is suitable as long as the user wants to work within the GATE ecosystem.

The common format is GATE `xml`, which is not a standard and easy-to-implement solution, as no DTD or Schema file is available that describes the format. These are dispensable as long as files are produced and processed solely by GATE: the format can be regarded as internal. In a GATE `xml` file, annotation follows the complete text separately. In a typical scenario of processing this format, one must constantly jump between the two parts of the `xml` file, so the entire text and annotation should be kept in memory e.g. by building a tree with DOM strategy. This requirement at best slows down the processing of large `xml` files, whereas it makes impossible to process the data as stream. In addition, the cumbersome deployment of the GATE system in itself greatly increased the complexity of the pipeline for users, developers, and service providers, whether or not they really needed the added functionality provided by GATE.

This motivated us to design an inline (i.e. in the sense that annotation should be locally available at the element which is annotated), streamable, simple, customisable, self-documenting and easy-to-use format that can be easily converted into other formats. We support conversion without data loss to standard formats such as CoNLL-X (Buchholz and Marsi, 2006), CoNLL-U, or even GATE `xml`. The newly chosen format specifica-

---

[5] `http://universaldependencies.org`
[6] `https://github.com/ufal/udpipe`
[7] `https://spacy.io`
[8] `http://ws.clarin-pl.eu/websty.shtml`
[9] `https://weblicht.sfs.uni-tuebingen.de`

```
form       lemma   xpostag
#This is a comment.
A          a       [/Det|Art.Def]
kutyák     kutya   [/N][Pl][Nom]
ugatnak    ugat    [/V][Prs.NDef.3Pl]
.          .       [Punct]

A          a       [/Det|Art.Def]
...
```

Table 1: An illustration of the format, a three-column `tsv` file with a header (resembling CoNLL-U column names): word forms, lemmas, and explicit morphological analysis. 'The dog-s bark-[3Pl]. The…'. Comments may occur only at the beginning of sentences.

tion allows adaptation to needs as they emerge (we will see that this is achieved by the flexible definition of `tsv` columns), mainly consisting of recommendations (e.g. free text and JSON are preferred as data), and as few constraints as possible.

We use `tsv` files with a header (Table 1), which can even be loaded into spreadsheet editors. Adhering to the classical vertical format, each row specifies a token, and columns (fields, cells) contain annotations for the token. We introduced two additions to the simple `tsv` following the CoNLL-U format: (i) sentence boundaries are marked with empty lines, and (ii) it is possible to insert comments in the forms of lines starting with a hashmark (#) before each sentence, which will be copied to the output. Although the sentence block comment was possible – switchable, not allowed by default – for optional comparability with the CoNLL-U format, its use is not recommended because of the combination of the free column order and hashmark as control character[10]. We recognize the legitimacy of the line starting hashmark in CoNLL-U due to (i) the fixed order of columns and (ii) the constraint for for the first column to be a positive integer number (more precisely mark the number of token in the sentence). However, we prefer the locality property in our format which allows to process individual tokens, without needing to know their context – where it is useful – compared to sentence leading comments or fixed column order.

The role of the header is particularly important:

it determines the operation of the whole system. Modules identify the location of their input data required for processing by strictly defined column names in the header (regardless of the order of the columns), and similarly, they place their output in new columns (with strictly defined names), leaving all other columns unchanged. A consequence is that modules are not allowed to change the number and content of input rows. (If users are about to create a module that will change the number of rows in the future, e.g. by splitting a token to more, they have to be very careful about the contents of the fields in the new rows and the integrity of the complete data, especially in the case of sequential tags.)

Newly created columns are simply placed after the existing columns in the current implementation. This can be taken as our recommendation, but not a mandatory restriction, as columns are identified by name. This way the text remains readable for the human eye, and logically related pieces of annotation are stored close to each other. It is an important property that developers can add any number of extra columns: there is space for expansion with additional information on demand. Column naming and content conventions have to be established by agreement between the producing and processing modules. The recommended field content is free text or the standard JSON format[11], which enables passing bound structures without ad-hoc formats or special characters (like they are used to represent lists of key-value pairs in CoNLL-U). In addition, the JSON format is suitable to represent alternative analyses or ambiguous annotation, e.g. as a (weighted) list of possible tags.

4 Architecture

The described `tsv` format is simple, easy to manage, supported by several existing tools, and enables users to write additional modules. It was our primary goal to facilitate the easy development and integration of additional modules into the system. Furthermore, besides the traditional command-line interface (CLI) and the format-agnostic Python library interface, we have also created a REST API whose use is independent of programming languages.

---

[10]Hashmark as every character, however rare, will have its occurrences in a large corpus: using it as special will lead to error on the long run. Collision of occurrences as literals and as special characters in the original corpus often results in unexpected errors that take a long time to debug, limits and slows down the operation and later the extensibility of the system.

[11]Although the spacing between the structuring elements in JSON can be selected to be tab, it is prohibited in `emtsv` because of its tab separated layout.

With the help of traditional UNIX pipelines, CLI provides a useful tool for advanced users. The CLI can be used even on large texts without knowing the internal operation of the modules. The Python library can be integrated into larger software systems by IT/NLP users. Finally, the REST API opens up the possibility of using the system according to modern cloud-based trends, even for completely non-NLP users and business circles: with its help, emtsv can be made available as a scalable service in the cloud for a wide range of end-users, without a need for installation on the end-user side.

According to the modern requirements, the emtsv system is also available as a Docker image[12]. This image can be used like a 'standalone executable' with 'batteries included' as it features the CLI interface and the REST API as well. Its advantage over the traditional installation is that the whole system is packed together with all its dependencies pre-configured and can be deployed with a single command. Therefore it is easy to use on any machine running Docker in a form comparable to highly integrated pipelines. The deployed image can instantly be used with HTTP requests from local or remote computers, from the command line or from any software.

Individual modules are combined together by our newly developed xtsv framework, which handles tsv as a communication format in a general way. This allows both the communication via the format described in Section 3 (i.e. the choice of the input columns, attaching the output columns, and reserving the rest), the creation of REST APIs, and the dynamic format-check (Section 5) regardless of the specific content of the modules. Extra modules can be added to the system with the following parameters specified in a declarative fashion: the unique name of the module, – that distincts it from alternative instances of the same tool with a different model or parameter setting –, the actual tool that performs the function of the module, the names of the input and output columns, and the specification of models and other parameters when needed as the parameters of the tool. If one wants to use a module with other pre-trained models (e.g. the Named Entity tagger trained on financial reports or on encyclopedic text), alternative instances of the same module can also be created within the xtsv framework. xtsv dy-

namically creates and runs the desired chain as described above. Although the described interfaces (CLI, REST API, Python library) have been implemented in Python to meet the user requirements, the modules can be implemented in other programming languages based on the specification, even in a heterogeneous fashion like in the case of UNIX pipelines.

The description of emtsv so far can be summarized as follows: a loosely coupled architecture, the possibility of adding new modules written in any programming language, the standard tsv format, the three API types (CLI, Python package, REST API, the latter optionally running in the user's cloud), scalability, the openly available source code, and a pipeline adhering to the UNIX philosophy. These enable users being on different levels of programming skills and coming from different backgrounds to combine rule-based and statistical systems, to manually correct the output of any modules then to feed it to any of the next modules, to compare the output of alternative modules as a part of the same pipeline for the same input, to interpret errors, and to retrain the models if needed. This wide spectrum of features exceeds the capabilities of the previously presented tool chains applicable for Hungarian (see Section 2).

The following section describes the role of each of the available modules in the chain, as well as the minimum requirements for new modules, which enable the chain to be expanded with new modules or the modification of existing ones within the framework.

5 Modules

Module management means that the fields required by the given module need to be available by the time of running the module. This can be controlled by the header available already at the time of assembling the pipeline, indicating an error early, even in the case of a dynamically defined pipeline. Recall that each module specifies the needed and produced columns. For example, it is known at the time of chain assembly, on the basis of the specified fields, that the POS tagger needs the form and anas (i.e. analyses) columns, or that dependency parsing must be preceded by POS tagging but not by NP chunking, as shown in Figure 1.

The organization of modules is based on the

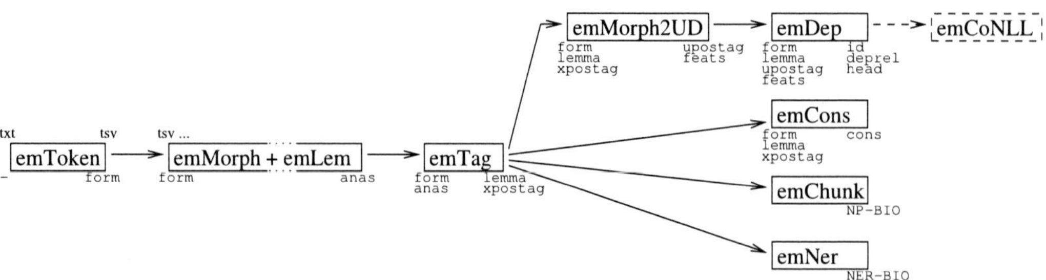

Figure 1: The current processing chain of `emtsv`, with input and output fields.

previous version of `e-magyar`, however we split logically independent functions into separate modules, even if they were built into one module previously. Thus, the tasks of each module can be more clearly specified, which makes their testing and development simpler. For a unified handling of modules in `xtsv` (see Section 4), modules originally written in Java were wrapped into Python modules. The names of these wrappers have been given the uniform ending `py`. In Python wrappers, Java is uniformly called by the Pyjnius package[13]. The Python wrapper communicates with the original Java module through Java-native types, which cuts down the original input and output handling code, so eliminating the differences between the original input and output formats in favor of `emtsv`. The additional changes made to the individual modules are described in the subsections below. Module names are prefixed with em: e for electronic and m for *magyar* 'Hungarian'.

5.1 `emToken`

Although tokenization rules themselves remain unchanged, we revised the tokenizer for the new pipeline significantly. `emToken` (Mittelholcz, 2017), the tokenizer in `e-magyar`, consists of several submodules with different functionalities such as checking illegal characters, sentence segmentation, abbreviation processing, and word tokenization itself. So far, these submodules were compiled into a single monolithic binary file. In the new version, each submodule is compiled into a binary file that can be run separately, reading from standard input and writing to standard output. These submodules are linked together by a Python script. For the new structure, the test system for the `emToken` was also redesigned. These

refactoring steps enabled us an organic integration within the `emtsv` framework.

Detokenization is currently not supported, but `emToken` returns the spaces besides the tokens properly, so future work can modify the module to insert original (possibly spacial) spaces in a separate column to make detokenization possible. An alternative would be to record the word offset (the index of the starting character) in a column, from which it can be seen whether consecutive tokens were originally separated by a space or not.

5.2 `emMorph` and `emLem`

We fixed some bugs that affect the morphological analyzer `emMorph` (Novák et al., 2016) and its interaction with the lemmatizer `emLem`. The output of the morphological analysis, i.e. the string representing individual steps of the underlying transducer, is regarded as an internal format, as it is not used directly but is transformed into a more readable form of the morphemic sequence. The post-processing is executed by the `emLem` module. The original Java implementation of `emLem` has been replaced by a new Python code[14] to improve simplicity and code transparency. Bugs uncovered during rewriting have been fixed.

The module containing `emMorph+emLem` has been supplemented with a special REST API, which allows the user to easily access the analyses of individual word forms through the browser, by pasting each word form into a special URL. This demo interface[15] runs in the cloud, where quick access to `emMorph` is provided.

The output of the extended `emMorph` module is a specially formatted JSON file with fields for both human and machine use (see Figure 2). Each

---

[13]`https://github.com/kivy/pyjnius`

[14]`https://github.com/ppke-nlpg/emmorphpy`

[15]`https://emmorph.herokuapp.com/`

```
{
  "bokrot": [
    {
lemma     "bokor"
morphana  "bokor[/N]=bokr+ot[Acc]=ot"
readable  "bokor[/N]=bokr + ot[Acc]"
tag       "[/N][Acc]"
twolevel  "b:b o:o k:k :o r:r :[/N] o:o t:t :[Acc]"
    },
    ...
  ]
}
```

Figure 2: An example of the JSON output of the morphological analyzer and the lemmatizer. The example *bokrot* is the accusative form of the epenthetic stem *bok(o)r* 'bush'.

analysis contains four fields: the `lemma`; the morphemic sequence in two formats: one intended for machine use (`morphana`) and one for human reading (`readable`); the bare tag of the strict morphosyntactic category without phonological-orthographic content (`tag`); and the two-level output of the morphological analyzer (`twolevel`) for debugging purposes. The `readable` field omits redundant surface forms, i.e. those that coincide with the deep form. The REST API is capable to return multiple words at once, when called using the HTTP POST method. The advantage of the standard JSON format is that it protects against errors caused by unexpected characters in large corpora. For the sake of fitting into `tsv`, the use of a tab outside the string is prohibited in the generated JSON.

5.3 `emTag`

The `emTag` POS tagger is based on PurePOS (Orosz and Novák, 2013). It requires an inconvenient, non-standard input format[16], that is exposed to errors caused by unexpected characters. The new format described in Section 3 makes possible to eliminate errors caused by unexpected characters in large corpora.

Now alternative morphological analyzes can be separately provided for the Java-based PurePOS as native Java data structures with the input text (even from within a Java program). The PurePOS–Python interface contains the add-ons required for `emtsv`. PurePOS can be used in three ways with the Python interface: alone with pre-analyzed input, with its built-in statistical morphological analyzer, or using the `emMorph+emLem` rule-based morphological analyzer.

5.4 `emChunk` and `emNER`

The configuration of the `HunTag3` (Endrédy and Indig, 2015) sequential tagger, which served as the basis of the `xtsv` framework, has been slightly modified to meet the requirements of the new `emtsv` format: features are now reached by column names not by column numbers. In addition, `HunTag3` has undergone a number of internal transformations, resulting in the standardized management of the input and output formats, completely separate from the rest of the computation.

5.5 `emMorph2UD`

The original converter (`DepTool`), that converted the output of `emTag` to linearized attribute–value pairs for the `emDep` dependency parser (see Section 5.6) is replaced by `emMorph2UD`, a new converter. There are two main reasons for this improvement. Firstly, looking more closely at `DepTool`, it turned out that it did not handle certain morphological features: the content of the input morphological tags were often lost. Secondly, the tags generated by `DepTool` had a specific format that could be used only within the toolchain between the two modules.

As UD is a cross-linguistically consistent grammatical annotation scheme, it is reasonable to provide the output in that formalism beside the tags of `emMorph`. Therefore, `emMorph2UD` converts the morphological tags emitted by `emTag` to UD[17]. Formerly in `e-magyar`, the model behind `emDep` was trained on POS tags and morphosyntactic features converted by `DepTool`. Consequently, the model had to be replaced with one trained on Szeged Treebank with UD tags (Vincze et al., 2017).

The `emMorph2UD` module can be used both for inter-modular communication in `emtsv` between `emTag` and `emDep` using the formalism of UD, and as an output format with UD morphological tags. For a detailed description and precise evaluation of `emMorph2UD`[18], see Vadász and Simon (2019).

5.6 `emDep` and `emCons`

We also detached the Bohnet dependency parser (Bohnet and Nivre, 2012) and the Berkeley con-

---

[16]`https://github.com/ppke-nlpg/purepos`

[17]Only UD version 1 has been elaborated for Hungarian, therefore here we mean UDv1 under UD.

[18]For an exhaustive description of annotation schemes for Hungarian morphology with converters, see `https://github.com/dlt-rilmta/panmorph`.

stituent parser (Durrett and Klein, 2015) from `Magyarlánc` 3.0, so the parsers now work with a smaller resource footprint. The model of `emDep` has been replaced (see Section 5.5): its input is now the set of POS tags and morphological attribute–value pairs, converted from the output of `emMorph` to conform the UD annotation scheme. The output of `emDep`, i.e. the syntactical annotation, did not change.

5.7 `emCoNLL`

To satify the need of a standard well-proven format, the output can be converted to the CoNLL-U format with the help of the module `emCoNLL`. By this, the output of `emtsv` is suitable for tools dealing with CoNLL-U format, such as processing, annotation or visualizaton tools[19].

Since the fields UPOS, HEAD and DEPREL are not allowed to be left unspecified in the CoNLL-U format, `emCoNLL` depends on the dependency parser, thus only the output of `emDep` can be used as an input of `emCoNLL`. In addition, CoNLL-U supports only one extra field (MISC) for a further annotation layer, however, there might be several competing modules for that one field (`emMorph`, `emLem`, `emChunk` and `emNer`). This problem is solved by leaving this extra column empty, thus only mandatory fields arc filled during the conversion. This module serves as a good example for splicing a simple and useful additional module to the end of the toolchain.

6 Summary

In this article, we introduced `emtsv`, the new version of the `e-magyar` language processing pipeline that has undergone a major transformation. `emtsv` is not only competing, but at several points exceeds its competitors. Its main characteristics are the uniform communication format, the easy interoperability of the modules thanks to this format, the free source code, the loosely coupled modules (open for new modules, be they rule-based or statistic), and the scalability. It can run as service through a REST API, as a pipeline in CLI, or can be integrated into larger systems as a Python library API and available as Docker image as well. Developers can plug in their own modules. Modules can be individually upgraded, compared, rewritten, retrained, or customized. Consequently,

---

[19]`https://universaldependencies.org/tools.html`

`emtsv` is now the Hungarian NLP pipeline with the broadest functionality.

7 Future Work

Bootstrapping a human-annotated corpus Starting with a large free corpus, we plan to pre-process raw text with `emtsv`, and improve the output module-by-module by semi-manually correcting the output of the nth module and then passing the improved version to module $n + 1$ (this could not be done in the former version of `e-magyar`). Free availability of the corpus used for this process is important in order to that the research community can experiment with new methods by changing tools and data. The process will provide a good opportunity to test the system in detail, to detect errors, and to turn to computational linguistic research proper, i.e. to justify linguistic theories.

Over-tokenizers In the time of pre-trained deep language models (aka contextualized word representations, such as Peters et al. (2018)), a system with symbolic inter-modular communication may seem anachronous, but we believe `emtsv` as a pre-processing tool can help state-of-the-art systems, especially in handling less frequent or out-of-vocabulary words. Our approach belongs to subword-level modelling (Botha and Blunsom, 2014), specifically the simple but effective engineering solution of splitting rare or unknown words to their components (going against our own `xtsv` recommendation of no token splitting introduced in Section 3). Though unsupervised statistical segmentation (e.g. Morfessor (Creutz and Lagus, 2005) or byte-pair encoding (Sennrich et al., 2016)) is widely used, segmentation to meaningful parts (Lazaridou et al., 2013; Avraham and Goldberg, 2017) offers the exploitation of additional linguistic knowledge. Splitting off inflectional suffixes have already hugely reduced word perplexity (Nemeskey, 2017). We plan to extend this line of work to compositional compounds, especially noun+noun compounds like *szín-tan* 'color-theory', compositional derivational suffixes e.g. *szeker-estül*, lit. chariot-along.with.one's 'along with one's chariot', and compositional preverbal prefixes e.g. *agyon-tápol*, 'over-nurture'. The planned modules can work by assigning probability scores to composition candidates based on gold constructions with similar constituents, where similarity is measured in the word embedding space.

Universal guesser We store all possible morphological analyzes to be able to fine-tune them before disambiguating, but these analyzes apply only for the tokens recognized by the fixed lexicon of the rule-based morphological analyzer (`emMorph`). These analyzes also lack weights, which is desired by the latter procesing steps. In order to treat each module equally, we plan to create a *Universal guesser module* (harmonised with `emMorph`) that is able to analyze OOV tokens – with rules or statistical machine-learning – as well and set the appropriate weights for each analyzis (e.g. by using the same training material used by the POS-tagger module (`emTag`) currently). Stripping out this task from the POS-tagger – where it currently resides – creates the possibility to fine-tune analyzes for all tokens prior to POS-tagging if needed. Also it enables us to substitute the guesser module – or the POS-tagger – with others (e.g. Morfessor and Lemmy[20]) and find the one with the best performance by testing it in real-life conditions.

Phrases and verb constructions Our plans include creating new modules for `emNer` trained on texts in different domains, as well as new models for chunking (i.e. annotating all types of phrases in the sentence), and even enhancing `emDep` based on lessons learned from Mazsola (Sass, 2008).

Load-balancing Currently, every module runs in one instance. A rather technical follow-up development would be to run bottleneck modules in multiple copies: paralleling increases performance. For example, if the disambiguator processes 10 sentences while the syntactic parser finishes with 2 sentences, then it is worth starting the syntactic parser in 5 instances and process sentences in parallel. This technology is called load-balancing and it is popular both within the Python and the Docker world.

A multilingual chain The new `xtsv` framework is actually completely language and module independent. We may create a multilingual analyzer whose pipeline can start with a language identifier. In order to do so, we need modules for other natural languages. It is important for these toolsets not to be monolithic like `Magyarlánc`, but separated into modules – by their logical role

---

[20]`https://github.com/sorenlind/lemmy`

in the pipeline – that can be given to a tsv-wrapper and combined freely in `xtsv`.

Acknowledgements

Work supported by the MARCELL project of EU CEF. Márton Makrai was partially supported by project fund 2018-1.2.1-NKP-00008: Exploring the Mathematical Foundations of Artificial Intelligence and National Research, Development and Innovation Office (NKFIH) grant #120145 Recognizing Word Structure with Deep Learning.

References

Oded Avraham and Yoav Goldberg. 2017. The interplay of semantics and morphology in word embeddings. In *Proceedings of the 15th Conference of the European Chapter of the Association for Computational Linguistics: Volume 2, Short Papers*, pages 422–426, Valencia, Spain. Association for Computational Linguistics.

Bernd Bohnet and Joakim Nivre. 2012. A Transition-based System for Joint Part-of-speech Tagging and Labeled Non-projective Dependency Parsing. In *Proceedings of the 2012 Joint Conference on Empirical Methods in Natural Language Processing and Computational Natural Language Learning*, EMNLP-CoNLL '12, pages 1455–1465, Stroudsburg, PA, USA. Association for Computational Linguistics.

Jan A Botha and Phil Blunsom. 2014. Compositional morphology for word representations and language modelling. In *Proceedings of the31st International Conference on Machine Learning*, pages 1899–1907, Beijing, China.

Sabine Buchholz and Erwin Marsi. 2006. CoNLL-X Shared Task on Multilingual Dependency Parsing. In *Proceedings of the Tenth Conference on Computational Natural Language Learning (CoNLL-X)*, pages 149–164, New York City. Association for Computational Linguistics.

Mathias Creutz and Krista Lagus. 2005. Unsupervised morpheme segmentation and morphology induction from text corpora using Morfessor 1.0. Technical Report A81, Helsinki University of Technology.

Hamish Cunningham, Diana Maynard, Kalina Bontcheva, Valentin Tablan, Niraj Aswani, Ian Roberts, Genevieve Gorrell, Adam Funk, Angus Roberts, Danica Damljanovic, Thomas Heitz, Mark A. Greenwood, Horacio Saggion, Johann Petrak, Yaoyong Li, and Wim Peters. 2011. *Text Processing with GATE (Version 6)*. GATE (April 15, 2011).

Greg Durrett and Dan Klein. 2015. Neural CRF Parsing. In *Proceedings of the 53rd Annual Meeting *of the Association for Computational Linguistics and the 7th International Joint Conference on Natural Language Processing (Volume 1: Long Papers)*, pages 302–312. Association for Computational Linguistics.

István Endrédy and Balázs Indig. 2015. HunTag3: a General-purpose, Modular Sequential Tagger – Chunking Phrases in English and Maximal NPs and NER for Hungarian. In *7th Language & Technology Conference, Human Language Technologies as a Challenge for Computer Science and Linguistics (LTC '15)*, pages 213–218, Poznań, Poland. Poznań: Uniwersytet im. Adama Mickiewicza w Poznaniu.

Péter Halácsy, András Kornai, László Németh, András Rung, István Szakadát, and Viktor Trón. 2004. Creating open language resources for Hungarian. In *Proceedings of the Fourth International Conference on Language Resources and Evaluation (LREC 2004)*, pages 203–210. ELRA.

Péter Halácsy, András Kornai, Csaba Oravecz, Viktor Trón, and Dániel Varga. 2006. Using a morphological analyzer in high precision POS tagging of Hungarian. In *Proceedings of the Fifth International Conference on Language Resources and Evaluation (LREC'06)*, Genoa, Italy. European Language Resources Association (ELRA).

Angeliki Lazaridou, Marco Marelli, Roberto Zamparelli, and Marco Baroni. 2013. Compositionally derived representations of morphologically complex words in distributional semantics. In *Proceedings of the 51st Annual Meeting of the Association for Computational Linguistics (Volume 1: Long Papers)*, pages 1517–1526, Sofia, Bulgaria. Association for Computational Linguistics.

Iván Mittelholcz. 2017. emToken: Unicode-képes tokenizáló magyar nyelvre [Unicode-able tokenizer for Hungarian]. In *XIII. Magyar Számítógépes Nyelvészeti Konferencia [13th Conference on Hungarian Computational Linguistics]*, pages 61–69, Szeged.

Dávid Márk Nemeskey. 2017. emLam – a Hungarian Language Modeling baseline. In *XIII. Magyar Számítógépes Nyelvészeti Konferencia [13th Conference on Hungarian Computational Linguistics]*, pages 91–102, Szeged.

Attila Novák, Borbála Siklósi, and Csaba Oravecz. 2016. A New Integrated Open-source Morphological Analyzer for Hungarian. In *Proceedings of the Tenth International Conference on Language Resources and Evaluation (LREC 2016)*, Paris, France. European Language Resources Association (ELRA).

Csaba Oravecz, Tamás Váradi, and Bálint Sass. 2014. The Hungarian Gigaword Corpus. In *Proceedings of the Ninth International Conference on Language Resources and Evaluation (LREC-2014)*. European Language Resources Association (ELRA).

György Orosz and Attila Novák. 2013. PurePos 2.0: a Hybrid Tool for Morphological Disambiguation. In *Proceedings of the International Conference Recent Advances in Natural Language Processing RANLP 2013*, pages 539–545, Hissar, Bulgaria. INCOMA Ltd. Shoumen, BULGARIA.

Matthew Peters, Mark Neumann, Mohit Iyyer, Matt Gardner, Christopher Clark, Kenton Lee, and Luke Zettlemoyer. 2018. Deep contextualized word representations. In *Proceedings of the 2018 Conference of the North American Chapter of the Association for Computational Linguistics: Human Language Technologies, Volume 1 (Long Papers)*, pages 2227–2237. Association for Computational Linguistics.

Gábor Recski and Dániel Varga. 2009. A Hungarian NP Chunker. *The Odd Yearbook. ELTE SEAS Undergraduate Papers in Linguistics*, pages 87–93.

Bálint Sass. 2008. The verb argument browser. In *Text, Speech and Dialogue*, pages 187–192, Berlin, Heidelberg. Springer Berlin Heidelberg.

Bálint Sass, Márton Miháltz, and Péter Kundráth. 2017. Az e-magyar rendszer GATE környezetbe integrált magyar szövegfeldolgozó eszközlánca [The e-magyar Hungarian text processing system embedded into the GATE framework]. In *XIII. Magyar Számítógépes Nyelvészeti Konferencia [13th Conference on Hungarian Computational Linguistics]*, pages 79–90.

Rico Sennrich, Barry Haddow, and Alexandra Birch. 2016. Neural machine translation of rare words with subword units. In *Proceedings of the 54th Annual Meeting of the Association for Computational Linguistics (Volume 1: Long Papers)*, pages 1715–1725, Berlin, Germany. Association for Computational Linguistics.

Milan Straka and Jana Straková. 2017. Tokenizing, POS Tagging, Lemmatizing and Parsing UD 2.0 with UDPipe. In *Proceedings of the CoNLL 2017 Shared Task: Multilingual Parsing from Raw Text to Universal Dependencies*, pages 88–99, Vancouver, Canada. Association for Computational Linguistics.

Viktor Trón, György Gyepesi, Péter Halácsky, András Kornai, László Németh, and Dániel Varga. 2005. Hunmorph: Open source word analysis. In *Proceedings of the ACL Workshop on Software*, pages 77–85. Association for Computational Linguistics, Ann Arbor, Michigan.

Noémi Vadász and Eszter Simon. 2019. Konverterek magyar morfológiai címkekészletek között. [Converters between Hungarian Morphological Tagsets]. In *XV. Magyar Számítógépes Nyelvészeti Konferencia [15th Conference on Hungarian Computational Linguistics]*, pages 99–111, Szeged.

Dániel Varga and Eszter Simon. 2007. Hungarian named entity recognition with a maximum entropy approach. *Acta Cybernetica*, 18:293–301.

Veronika Vincze, Katalin Simkó, Zsolt Szántó, and Richárd Farkas. 2017. Universal dependencies and morphology for Hungarian - and on the price of universality. In *Proceedings of the 15th Conference of the European Chapter of the Association for Computational Linguistics: Volume 1, Long Papers*, pages 356–365, Valencia, Spain. Association for Computational Linguistics.

Tamás Váradi, Eszter Simon, Bálint Sass, Iván Mittelholcz, Attila Novák, Balázs Indig, Richárd Farkas, and Veronika Vincze. 2018. E-magyar – A Digital Language Processing System. In *Proceedings of the Eleventh International Conference on Language Resources and Evaluation (LREC 2018)*, Miyazaki, Japan. European Language Resources Association (ELRA).

János Zsibrita, Richárd Farkas, and Veronika Vincze. 2013. A Toolkit for Morphological and Dependency Parsing of Hungarian. In *International Conference on Recent Advances in Natural Language Processing*, pages 763–771, Shoumen, Bulgária. INCOMA Ltd.

Turkish Treebanking: Unifying and Constructing Efforts

Utku Türk[‡], Furkan Atmaca[‡], Şaziye Betül Özateş[*], Abdullatif Köksal[*],
Balkız Öztürk[‡], Tunga Güngör[*], Arzucan Özgür[*]
[‡]Department of Linguistics
[*]Department of Computer Engineering
Boğaziçi University
Bebek, 34342 İstanbul, Turkey
`utku.turk,furkan.atmaca,saziye.bilgin,abdullatif.koksal,`
`balkiz.ozturk,gungort,arzucan.ozgur@boun.edu.tr`

Abstract

In this paper, we present the re-annotation of
the Turkish PUD Treebank and the first annotation of the Turkish National Corpus Universal Dependency (henceforth TNC-UD) Treebank as part of our efforts for unifying and
extending the Turkish universal dependency
treebanks. In accordance with the Universal Dependencies' guidelines and the necessi-
ties of Turkish grammar, both treebanks, the
Turkish PUD Treebank and TNC-UD, were revised with regards to their syntactic relations.
The TNC-UD is planned to have 10,000 sentences. In this paper, we present the first 500
sentences along with the re-annotation of the
PUD Treebank. Moreover, this paper also offers the parsing results of a graph-based neural
parser on the previous and re-annotated PUD,
as well as the TNC-UD. In light of the comparisons, even though we observe a slight decrease in the attachment scores of the Turkish
PUD treebank, we demonstrate that the annotation of the TNC-UD improves the parsing
accuracy of Turkish. In addition to the treebanks, we have also constructed a custom annotation software with advanced filtering and
morphological editing options. Both of the
treebanks, including a full edit-history and the
annotation guidelines, as well as the custom
software are publicly available online under an
open license.

1 Introduction

The Universal Dependency (UD) project has
proven itself to be an indispensable part of the natural language processing (NLP) framework. The
treebanks built within the scope of the project constitute a great portion of the contribution made
by the UD Project to NLP applications. However, within the UD Project, there is a signifi-

cant mismatch regarding the volume of the treebanks available for each language. Turkish is one
of the under-resourced languages; even though
previous treebanks (Sulubacak et al., 2016a) do
exist together with works on Turkish morphology (Çöltekin, 2016, 2015), the limited number of
Turkish resources poses a challenge for those who
wish to conduct NLP studies.

The main contribution of this paper is making
up for the scarcity of NLP resources in Turkish by
annotating a new corpus that has not been introduced to the UD project before, namely the TNC
(Aksan et al., 2012). The current version of the
annotated treebank only contains 500 sentences;
however, we are currently working to an additional
9,500 sentences to the corpus. The syntactic relations of the sentences in the treebank were manually annotated following the Stanford Dependency
(SD) scheme (de Marneffe et al., 2014) as well as
the UD guidelines. Moreover, the morphological
analyses of the sentences were automatically created by the Turku Neural Parser Pipeline (Kanerva
et al., 2018) trained on the re-annotated version of
the Turkish IMST-UD Treebank that we are currently working on.

As a second contribution, we manually re-
annotated the Turkish PUD treebank for consistency in the annotation. As we do not fully agree
with the annotation scheme of previous Turkish
treebanks, we had incorporated a more strict view
of the SD scheme and tried to balance the six di-
rectives of Manning's Law (Nivre et al., 2017).
Our objective is to unify the annotation schemes
and the level of granularity in terms of linguistic depth within the Turkish treebanks in the UD
Project. The linguistic decisions and departures
from the previous work related to Turkish tree-

166

Proceedings of the 13th Linguistic Annotation Workshop, pages 166–177
Florence, Italy, August 1, 2019. ©2019 Association for Computational Linguistics

banks will also be exemplified in this paper.

As a third contribution, we present an open source desktop application for the annotation process. Our proposed annotation tool integrates a tabular view, a hierarchical tree structure which can also be read in a linear fashion, and advanced morphological editing and filtering features. The tabular aspect of the annotation tool enables a keyboard-driven process for annotators; thus, helping with speed and ergonomy related problems by getting rid of the excessive use of the mouse. The linearity and the hierarchical view are inspired by the CoNLL-U Viewer, which helps linguists in visualizing the data.

2 Related Work

Within the last decade of the 20th century, treebanks and annotated corpora started to hold an extremely important place for NLP tools, applications, and scientific research within the framework of NLP. Even though creating such corpora that are structurally consistent and big enough to help NLP processes was incredibly tedious and time-consuming, it was believed to be worth pursuing by many.

Emulating the first efforts to create an annotated treebank from a corpus in English and in other languages (Marcus et al., 1993; Böhmová et al., 2003; Taylor et al., 2003), Oflazer et al. (2003) and Atalay et al. (2003) introduced the first Turkish treebank, the METU-Sabancı Treebank (MST), consisting of 5,635 sentences. A majority of the sentences in this treebank were drawn from either newspaper articles or novels, making up 42% and 13% of the corpus, respectively. Even though it may seem that the register of the treebank is overwhelmingly newspaper oriented, no other Turkish treebank matched it in size.

The other important aspect of MST was the fact that it became the originating point for the first Turkish UD treebank, IMST-UD. Firstly, Sulubacak et al. (2016b) revisited the syntactic and morphological decisions made in MST, and re-annotated the treebank from the ground up. Unlike Atalay et al. (2003), Sulubacak et al. (2016b) provided the necessary information regarding the annotation process, such as the number of annotators, their background, and the decision making mechanism for the ITU-METU-Sabancı Treebank (IMST). However, their work still lacked inter-annotator agreement scores and a description of

the process behind finding solutions to disagreements, which makes up one of the most important aspects of building an annotated treebank.

After the creation of IMST, Sulubacak et al. (2016a) automatically converted it into the first Turkish treebank in a UD release, resulting in unparalleled success with respect to the attachment scores. They also provide a thorough description of mappings and the automation process. However, the treebank was not post-edited by a human. Until the very recent edits, the treebank had very problematic consistency issues as well as a faulty representation, i.e. punctuations as roots, reversed head-dependent relations etc., caused by the automated nature of the conversion into the UD framework. Even though four different updates were made to the IMST-UD and most of the problems are now resolved, there are still vital divergences from the SD scheme and UD guidelines, such as a non-satisfactory distinction between core and non-core dependencies, the inner structure of embedded clauses, and multiword expressions that include the morphologically ambiguous -*ki* marker (Çöltekin, 2016).

Apart from this line of work, Turkish also has two other annotated treebanks within the UD framework: the Grammar-Book Treebank (Çöltekin, 2015) and the Turkish PUD Treebank[1]. Even though it offers a grand resource containing 2,803 sentences, we excluded the Grammar-Book Treebank in our research for consistency related reasons. The sentences in the Grammar-Book Treebank are unnatural with regards to grammaticality. In other words, the sentences in the treebank are either perfectly good sentences that are engineered to be grammatical, short, and concise or they are fragments of sentences that cannot stand alone and are unlikely to be uttered in isolation.

As for the Turkish PUD Treebank, it was published as a part of the CoNLL 2017 Shared Task on Multilingual Parsing from Raw Text to Universal Dependencies (Zeman et al., 2017). It consists of 1,000 sentences that were parallel annotated for 18 languages, 14 of them used in the shared task. One of the biggest contributions of this treebank is that it allows researchers in the NLP framework to reach a solid common ground in terms of items. Moreover, it allowed researchers to get rid of problems such as hidden semantic or individ-

---

[1] `universaldependencies.org/treebanks/tr_pud/`

ual sentence related confounds. However, unlike languages like English which are manually annotated in native UD, the Turkish PUD Treebank was not annotated manually in native UD style. The process is fairly similar to the creation of the IMST-UD, which involves non-UD style annotation followed by automatic conversion into the UD style. This automatic conversion includes Universal POS, features, and relations. Moreover, much like the IMST-UD, the Turkish PUD Treebank also lacks crucial information like annotator information, inter-annotator agreement, annotation process, and any post-editing process.

In contrast to most of the other annotated treebanks in the UD Project, Turkish treebanks yield an inconsistent picture with regards to their underlying annotations. Furthermore, they lack explanatory information about the annotation process and none were annotated in the native UD style. Thus, it is almost impossible to consider the Turkish treebanks in the UD Project as one unified and structured treebank.

Considering the development of Turkish treebanks in the UD Project, the next most logical step was to first investigate the automatic conversion process and re-annotate the treebanks. We are currently working on re-annotating IMST-UD. The main problems which we yet encountered in the process of re-annotation of IMST-UD can be grouped into three important group: the analyses of embedded clauses, the discussion of core and non-core arguments, and the newly introduced dependency types. Due to the nature of automatic conversion, IMST-UD lacked the necessary linguistic depth with regards to embedded structure. Instead of a hierarchical representation of inner argument and event structure, they were represented as simple nominal phrases. This was due to the nature of the nominalization phenomenon that is present in almost all Turkic and Altaic languages. Moreover, the IMST-UD was criticized for not differentiating between core elements that are non-canonically case-marked and adjuncts using the same case markers. Turkish makes use of cases except the accusative case to mark the core dependents of the predicate. Different than `obl`, when these dependents are left out of the sentence, sentences either gain a totally different meaning or become ungrammatical to native speakers of Turkish. Lastly, we included eight new syntactic relations that are used in UD v2.0, but not used in the IMST-UD. The details of these issues will be explained thoroughly in future work.

Due to the lack of a coherent picture in Turkish treebanks, Turkish NLP tools and applications have remained scarce and stagnant. TRmorph, ITU Treebank Annotation Tool, and the annotation tool of Atalay et al. (2003) are some of the few available tools in this field (Çöltekin, 2014; Eryiğit, 2007; Çöltekin, 2010).

With these reasons in mind, we decided to unify the approach towards the Turkish treebanks within the UD framework. With this initiative, we aimed to create a more consistent picture of Turkish for NLP tools and applications and enhance the use of Turkish in various NLP tasks. As aforementioned, we re-annotated the Turkish PUD Treebank and introduced the first steps to the creation of a new treebank: the TNC-UD.

3 Re-annotating Turkish PUD Treebank

Even though the Turkish PUD Treebank offers a much cleaner picture than the IMST-UD, it is not without its erroneous annotation. However, before addressing the errors, we will discuss the changes that we implemented for the sake of consistency in the two Turkish treebanks.

The consistency related changes mostly include the simplification of the language specific syntactic relation tags that are used in the Turkish PUD Treebank, but not in IMST-UD. We believe that in cases like Example 1, the syntactic relation of `obl` is a sufficient annotation in terms of linguistic adequacy. Such cases include changes from `obl:tmod`, `acl:relcl`, `det:predet`, `flat:name` syntactic relations to `obl`, `acl`, `det`, `flat`, respectively.

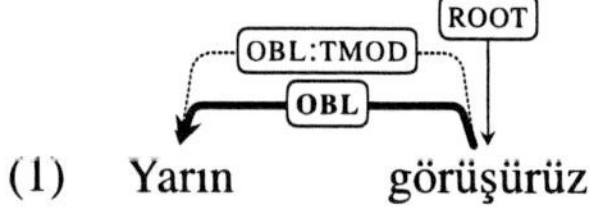

(1) Yarın   görüşürüz

Yarın   gör-üş-ür-üz
tomorrow see-RCP-AOR-3SG.PL

'See you tomorrow'

Having tackled the consistency related issues, we can turn our focus to the linguistically driven

---

[1]In all dependency trees in this paper, the dotted lines show the syntactic relations used in the previous treebank, the bold ones indicate the re-annotated ones in the updated treebank, and the fine lines represent unaltered dependencies.

changes. Table 1 shows the most frequently applied changes, excluding the changes made for reasons solely driven out of consistency.

Turkish PUD Treebank	Boğaziçi PUD Treebank	Number of Alterations
COMPOUND	NMOD:POSS	1331
NMOD:POSS	NSUBJ	192
FIXED	COMPOUND:LVC	168

Table 1: The number of alterations that we made for the most frequent changes.

As is evident in Table 1, the change from the syntactic relation compound to nmod:poss is overwhelmingly high. It makes up 28% of the total changes. Apart from the most changed three syntactic relations the rest was not even close to these changes in number.

It is no surprise that compounds are in the spotlight in these changes. Compounds have always been a controversial topic in Turkish (Hayasi, 1996; Swift, 1963; Göksel, 2009; Göksel and Haznedar, 2007; Göksel and Kerslake, 2005; Öztürk and Erguvanlı-Taylan, 2016). Within the UD guidelines and SD scheme, compounds are treated as head-level (X^0) constructions, which is different than Noun+Noun (NN) constructions that have syntactic reflex in the phrasal level and from compounds that are lexicalized with time. However, the Turkish PUD Treebank does not distinguish between these constructions. As seen in Example 2, the existence of a syntactic reflex, possessive marker, on *alan-ı-ydı* indicates the phrasal level of construction. Since possessive marker in Turkish introduces a transitivity relation, we can conclude that apart from lexicalized NN-*(s)I(n)* constructions, are not head-level constructions. This is why, in the re-annotation process, we have carried out a great number of alterations from the syntactic relation compound to nmod:poss.

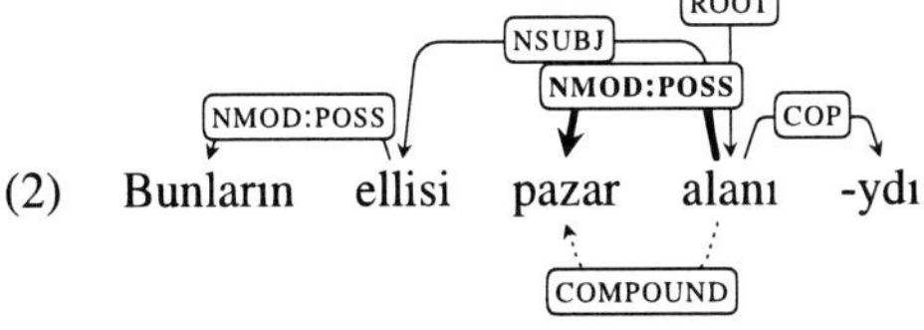

(2) Bunların ellisi pazar alanı -ydı

Bun-lar-ın elli-si pazar alan-ı-ydı
this-PL fifty-POSS market place-POSS-COP

'50 of these were marketplaces'

Following the discussion of compounds, the light verb constructions were also problematic

in the Turkish PUD Treebank as seen in Example 3. They were annotated as fixed, instead of compound:lvc which is highly used in IMST-UD as well as in treebanks of other languages like Persian and Armenian (Seraji et al., 2016; Yavrumyan et al., 2017). The analysis follows from the fact that even though light verbs are grammaticalized expressions, they do still have an internal structure, which separates them from being fixed according to the UD guidelines.

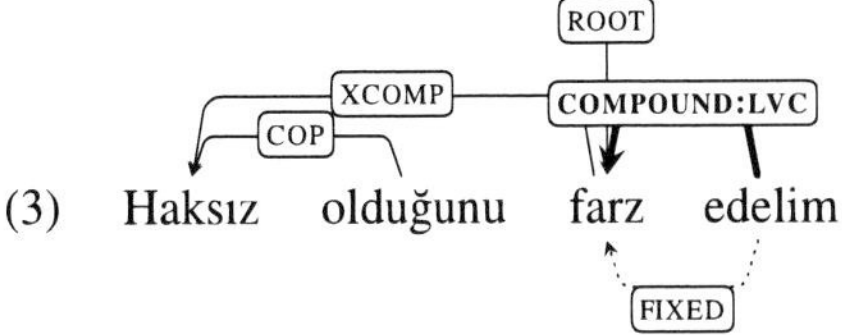

(3) Haksız olduğunu farz edelim

Haksız ol-duğ-un-u farz ed-elim
wrongful be-NMLZ-POSS-ACC presume do-OPT

'Let's just say he's wrong.'

The second most frequent alteration overlaps with the issues that have been addressed in the re-annotation of the IMST-UD. The sentence given in Example 4 is an example of the lack of the inner structure of an embedded sentence. Even though it is marked with genitive case, which is the canonical way of marking nmod:poss in Turkish, *senin de* is not just a possessive nominal modifier; instead, it is the subject of the embedded clause.

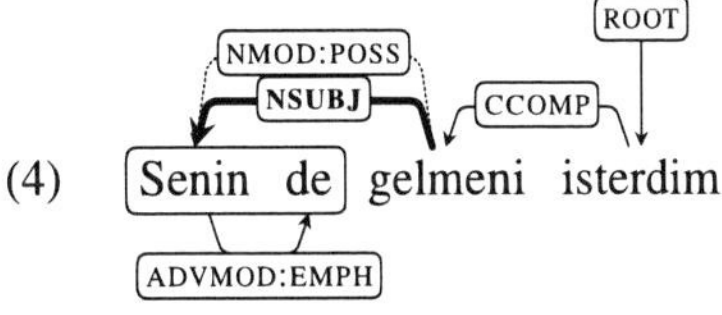

(4) Senin de gelmeni isterdim

Sen-in de gel-me-ni
you-GEN too come-NMLZ-POSS
iste-r-di-m.
want-AOR-PST-1SG

'I would have wanted you come, as well.'

4 Turkish National Corpus UD Treebank

In the current version of the planned treebank, the sentences are drawn from the Turkish National Corpus (TNC) (Aksan et al., 2012). The reason why we selected our sentences from TNC is based on our preference for freely available corpora. TNC is free to use for research purposes and it includes 5 million words of written texts across a variety of genres.

Even though the original TNC corpus has 22 main registers, we only included sentences from 5 different registers: essays, broadsheet national newspapers, instructional texts, popular culture articles, and biographical texts. Each register contributes to the total treebank with 2,000 sentences, which corresponds to 25% of the treebank. Sentences were drawn randomly from these registers with the help of those who regulate the corpus.

The motivation for the selection of these text types was based on the linguistic variety and the integrity of the texts with regards to grammaticality so that it does not hinder the annotation process. The selection of registers includes sentences with an evenly distributed variety of length (from essays to instructional texts), formality (from newspapers to popular culture articles), and literary quality (from biographical texts to newspapers).

We also obtained 5,000 sentences from non-academic texts about natural sciences, humanities, social sciences, medicine, and engineering. These sentences will only be used in case of exclusions from the original 10,000 sentences. In case of such an exclusion, sentences from the non-academic text pool will be randomly selected and annotated in order to reach the target of 10,000 sentences.

5 Annotating the Treebanks

For the re-annotation of the Turkish PUD Treebank and the annotation of the TNC-UD, we used a team of two annotators who are linguists and have comprehensive knowledge of Turkish grammar and general linguistics, as well as grammatical theories. Supporting the team of annotators, we have a senior linguist who leads the discussion whenever there is a disagreement between the two annotators. In addition to the three linguists, a team of four computer scientists with considerable experience in NLP research monitored the process of manual annotation.

As a first step, we created a guideline of annotation in the native UD style and SD scheme. We used the already existing guidelines as a basis (de Marneffe et al., 2014) and focused on optimizing them, especially the guidelines that were created for Turkish. The guidelines were created after every detail was discussed by the entire group of three linguists and four computer scientists. The guidelines were then exemplified with possible sentences. These guidelines are made available together with the other relevant data, corpus, and the software.

Due to time and resource restrictions, we were unable to employ full double annotation. Instead, after each annotator completed his/her own part, the sentences were run through an adjudication process within the group of linguists. When a disagreement occurred, the team discussed it thoroughly before applying the last judgment consistently for all the similar examples. Double annotation was performed for a set of 300 randomly selected sentences. Table 2 shows the kappa measures of inter-annotator agreement for finding the correct heads (κ_{Head}) and the correct dependency label of the syntactic relations (κ_{Label}).

Annotator Pair	κ_{Head}	κ_{Label}
1-2	0.9966	0.8873

Table 2: The Kappa measures of inter-annotator agreement with regards to head-dependent relation and dependency tags.

6 Released Data and Software

With the release of the treebank, we also release the full history of the annotation of TNC-UD, as well as the full history of the re-annotation of the Turkish PUD Treebank. Furthermore, we plan to provide statistical figures about the changes we have employed. We believe that the full transparency and the full replicability of the results are extremely important.

As well as the data and the history of change, the release of the treebank also includes our improvements on the UD Guidelines for Turkish. These guidelines include the necessary explanations and sentences accompanied with theoretical discussion. Being able to trace back our decisions will enable us and other researchers to accommodate according to the new findings in both linguistics and NLP fields in the future.

Finally, we release a desktop annotation tool that is designed for linguists with the aim of advanced morphological editing, ease of use, and decluttering the working environment. Our annotation tool is an open-source desktop application written in Python3 with PyQt5 library. The main objective of the tool is to create a comfortable, fast, and intuitive environment for annotators. As shown in Figure 1, its tabular view enables annotators wander freely only using their

ID	FORM	LEMMA	UPOS	XPOS	FEATS	HEAD	DEPREL	MISC
+ 1	Ancak	ancak	CCONJ	Conj	_	4	conj	_
+ 2	bu	bu	DET	Det	_	3	det	_
+ 3	kuşkular	kuşku	NOUN	Noun	Case=Nom|Number=Plur|Person=3	4	nsubj	_
- 4-5	yersizdir	_	_	_	_	_	_	SpaceAfter=No
+ 4	yersiz	yersiz	ADJ	NAdj	Case=Nom|Number=Sing|Person=3	0	root	_
+ 5	dir	i	AUX	Zero	Aspect=Perf|Mood=Gen|Number=Sing|Person=3|Tense=Pres	4	cop	_
+ 6	.	.	PUNCT	Punc	_	4	punct	_

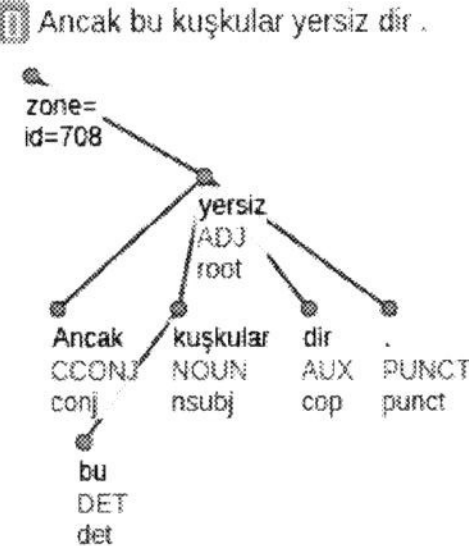

Figure 1: A screenshot of our annotation tool that integrates a tabular view with a hierarchical, but linearly readable tree. The plus and minus symbols on the left enable annotators to easily edit multiword expressions.

keyboard, which eliminates the hustle of using a mouse and the possible wrist injuries in the long hours of manual annotation.

Another important aspect of our tool is its ability to declutter the working environment. Annotators can change the information that is visible at a time with the check boxes above. It also facilitates the validation process since it checks the validity of the trees at every click of the Next and Prev buttons. If an erroneous annotation is detected, such as having two roots, one node having two parents, typos inside the tabs, and the like, it immediately gives an error and informs the annotator about the error.

Besides these, the main objective behind our tool is offering an easy way to edit multiword expressions in agglutinative languages like Turkish. In an automated conversion process, languages like Turkish may face a large number of erroneous tags with respect to multiword expressions. Editing those tags is extremely tedious since there is no way of keeping up with the dependencies and their heads. Our annotation tool enables annotators to easily split a word into two and also easily join them by pressing the plus and minus buttons. Upon such edits, every dependency relation and their ID's are automatically updated. Thus, these

abilities of our tool make it one of the first tools that is shaped according to the needs of the Turkish language.

Lastly, we have ported the CoNLL-U viewer to our annotation tool by changing the related methods in the UDAPI library (Popel et al., 2017). Its hierarchical, yet linearly readable approach is intuitive to many linguists who work in the annotation processes.

7 Experiments

To see the effect of re-annotation on the parsing accuracy, we trained a state-of-the-art graph-based neural parser (Dozat et al., 2017) on the previous and re-annotated versions of the PUD and TNC-UD treebanks. Due to the insufficient amount of data, we use the 5-fold cross-validation technique on the Turkish PUD treebank where each sub-part includes 200 sentences. So the training data size is 600 sentences, and the sizes of the development and test sets is 200 sentences in each fold. To evaluate the TNC-UD Treebank, we trained a model where the TNC-UD Treebank is used as an additional training data for the re-annotated version of the PUD Treebank and then the trained model is evaluated on the test set of the PUD Treebank. We again use the 5-fold cross-validation technique to evaluate this setting. Both projective and non-projective dependencies are included in the training and test phases.

In the evaluation of the dependency parser, we used the word-based unlabeled attachment score (UAS) metric, which is measured as the percentage of words that are attached to the correct head, and the labeled attachment score (LAS) metric, which is defined as the percentage of words that are attached to the correct head with the correct dependency type.

In all of the tables that show the results of the experiments performed, the attachment scores of the parser on both the previous version and the re-annotated version of the treebanks are given. Although comparing these scores is not a correct approach, since the test data sets that the models are evaluated on are annotated differently, observing the parsing accuracies of the previous and the re-annotated versions of the treebanks together gives a better idea to understand the current state of the parsing success of Turkish.

Table 3 shows the attachment scores of the parser on the previous and re-annotated versions of the Turkish PUD Treebank test data set. The re-annotated version of the Turkish PUD Treebank is named as BPUD.

Treebank	UAS	LAS
PUD	**79.83**	**74.31**
BPUD	78.70	70.01

Table 3: UAS and LAS scores of the parser on the previous and re-annotated versions of the Turkish PUD Treebank test data set when the parser is trained only with the training data set of the Turkish PUD Treebank.

From the results, we observe a decrease in the parsing accuracy in terms of the attachment scores. Although the decline in the UAS score is not large, the difference between the LAS scores of the two versions is four percent.

In order to understand whether these results are because of the insufficient amount of training data, we performed additional experiments by including the training set of the corresponding version (i.e., the previous version and the re-annotated version) of the Turkish IMST-UD Treebank to the training data of the PUD Treebank using the 5-fold cross-validation technique. In this setting, the training data set consists of 600 sentence PUD training set and 3685 sentence IMST-UD training set. The development set includes 200 sentence PUD devel-

opment set and 975 sentence IMST-UD development set in each fold. The test set remains the same as in the previous experiment.

Table 4 depicts the UAS and LAS scores of the parser when both IMST-UD and PUD are included in the training phase.

Treebank	UAS	LAS
Previous version of IMST-UD & PUD	**82.41**	**77.47**
Updated version IMST-UD & PUD	81.77	73.68

Table 4: UAS and LAS scores of the parser on the previous and re-annotated versions of the Turkish PUD Treebank test data set when the parser is trained on the training data sets of the Turkish PUD Treebank and the IMST-UD Treebank.

We see that when we increase the size of the training data, the gap between the attachment scores gets smaller between the previous and re-annotated versions of the Turkish PUD Treebank.

The differences in the attachment scores of the previous and the re-annotated versions might result from the annotation scheme adopted in this study. In the re-annotation process, our main aim is to ensure consistent and linguistically correct annotations that follow the UD guidelines. By doing this, we enhanced and elaborated the annotations of the treebanks that have previously rough and incorrect annotations. So, when there is not sufficient amount of training data, the task of learning the syntactic relations between the words of a sentence is harder on the re-annotated versions of the treebanks. The experimental results suggest that, these more accurate annotations of the treebanks will lead to better and more consistent parsing accuracies when more annotated data is available.

We also made an experiment to see the impact of the TNC-UD Treebank on the parsing accuracy of the parser. Table 5 shows the attachment scores when the parser is trained on the PUD and TNC-UD treebanks.

Treebank	UAS	LAS
BPUD & TNC-UD	**79.79**	**71.22**
BPUD	78.70	70.01

Table 5: UAS and LAS scores of the parser on the re-annotated version of the Turkish PUD Treebank test data set when the parser is trained with the training data set of the Turkish PUD Treebank and the TNC-UD Treebank.

Even though the current version of the TNC-

UD Treebank includes only 500 annotated sentences, the parsing performance of the parser has increased more than 1 point in terms of the attachment scores.

The experiment results suggest that the final version of the TNC-UD Treebank which will consist of 10,000 annotated sentences together with the other linguistically corrected Turkish treebanks will greatly improve the syntactic parsing of Turkish texts.

8 Conclusion and Future Work

In this work, we have presented the re-annotation of the Turkish PUD Treebank and the first steps of annotating the TNC-UD Treebank, a new freely available treebank for Turkish. We believe that we have unified the annotation style of the Turkish treebanks in the UD framework. Moreover, we plan to annotate a total of 10,000 sentences in the native UD style, following the SD scheme (de Marneffe et al., 2014). The TNC-UD Treebank consists of four sections, with texts from different registers: essays, broadsheet national newspapers, instructional texts, popular culture articles, and biographical texts.

In the TNC-UD Treebank, morphological analyses has been provided with a deep learning-based parser pipeline (Kanerva et al., 2018) trained on the re-annotated version of the Turkish IMST-UD Treebank. In the syntactic analyses, we have used a team of two linguists for manual annotation. The inter-annotator agreement was 99% and 88% for finding correct heads and correct dependency label of the syntactic relations, respectively. This level of high agreement shows that both annotators followed the pre-prepared guidelines and examples with SD scheme strictly.

The annotated treebanks, the detailed history of changes made in the annotation process, and our new guidelines are available at `https://github.com/ boun-tabi/UD_TURKISH-BPUD`. Moreover, our desktop annotation tool is available at `https://github.com/boun-tabi/BoAT`

Our current goal is to complete the annotation of the TNC-UD Treebank. We believe that 10,000 sentences manually annotated in the native UD style would enable NLP applications even more and help researchers to create a more robust environment for statistical learning.

One other future goal of this work is to enhance the annotation of the TNC-UD Treebank. Such annotation could include human-validated morphological analyses, prosodic information of the sentence, and detailed semantic analysis.

Acknowledgments

This work was supported by the Scientific and Technological Research Council of Turkey (TÜBİTAK) under grant number 117E971 and as a graduate scholarship.

References

Yeşim Aksan, Mustafa Aksan, Ahmet Koltuksuz, Taner Sezer, Ümit Mersinli, Umut Ufuk Demirhan, Hakan Yılmazer, Gülsüm Atasoy, Seda Öz, İpek Yıldız, and Özlem Kurtoğlu. 2012. Construction of the Turkish National Corpus (TNC). In *Proceedings of the Eighth International Conference on Language Resources and Evaluation (LREC-2012)*, pages 3223–3227, Istanbul, Turkey. European Language Resources Association (ELRA).

Nart Bedin Atalay, Kemal Oflazer, and Bilge Say. 2003. The annotation process in the Turkish treebank. In *Proceedings of 4th International Workshop on Linguistically Interpreted Corpora (LINC-03) at EACL 2003*.

Alena Böhmová, Jan Hajič, Eva Hajičová, and Barbora Hladká. 2003. The Prague dependency treebank. In *Treebanks*, pages 103–127. Springer.

Çağrı Çöltekin. 2010. A freely available morphological analyzer for Turkish. In *Proceedings of the 7th International Conference on Language Resources and Evaluation (LREC 2010)*, pages 820–827.

Çağrı Çöltekin. 2014. A set of open source tools for Turkish natural language processing. In *Proceedings of the Ninth International Conference on Language Resources and Evaluation (LREC'14)*, pages 1079–1086. European Language Resources Association (ELRA).

Çağrı Çöltekin. 2015. A grammar-book treebank of Turkish. In *Proceedings of the 14th workshop on Treebanks and Linguistic Theories (TLT 14)*, pages 35–49.

Çağrı Çöltekin. 2016. (When) do we need inflectional groups? In *Proceedings of The First International Conference on Turkic Computational Linguistics*.

Timothy Dozat, Peng Qi, and Christopher D. Manning. 2017. Stanford's Graph-based Neural Dependency Parser at the CoNLL 2017 Shared Task. *Proceedings of the CoNLL 2017 Shared Task: Multilingual Parsing from Raw Text to Universal Dependencies*, pages 20–30.

Gülşen Eryiğit. 2007. ITU Treebank Annotation Tool. In *Proceedings of the ACL workshop on Linguistic Annotation (LAW 2007)*, Prague.

Aslı Göksel. 2009. Compounds in Turkish. *Lingue e linguaggio*, 8(2):213–236.

Aslı Göksel and Belma Haznedar. 2007. Remarks on compounding in Turkish. *MorboComp Project, University of Bologna.*

Aslı Göksel and Celia Kerslake. 2005. *Turkish: A Comprehensive Grammar.* Comprehensive grammars. Routledge.

Tooru Hayasi. 1996. The dual status of possessive compounds in modern Turkish. *Symbolae Turcologicae. Studies in honor of Lars Johanson on the occasion of his sixtieth birthday*, 6:119–29.

Jenna Kanerva, Filip Ginter, Niko Miekka, Akseli Leino, and Tapio Salakoski. 2018. Turku neural parser pipeline: An end-to-end system for the conll 2018 shared task. In *Proceedings of the CoNLL 2018 Shared Task: Multilingual Parsing from Raw Text to Universal Dependencies*, pages 133–142.

Mitchell Marcus, Beatrice Santorini, and Mary Marcinkiewicz. 1993. Building a Large Annotated Corpus of English: the Penn Treebank. *Computational Linguistics*, 19:330–331.

Marie-Catherine de Marneffe, Timothy Dozat, Natalia Silveira, Katri Haverinen, Filip Ginter, Joakim Nivre, and Christopher D. Manning. 2014. Universal Stanford Dependencies: A cross-linguistic typology. *In Proceedings of the Ninth International Conference on Language Resources and Evaluation (LREC-2014)*, pages 4585–4592.

Joakim Nivre, Daniel Zeman, Filip Ginter, and Francis M. Tyers. 2017. Tutorial on Universal Dependencies. Presented at European Chapter of the Association for Computational Linguistics, Valencia [Accessed: 2019 04 08].

Kemal Oflazer, Bilge Say, Dilek Zeynep Hakkani-Tür, and Gökhan Tür. 2003. Building a Turkish Treebank. In *Treebanks, Building and Using Parsed Corpora*, pages 261–277.

Balkız Öztürk and Eser Erguvanlı-Taylan. 2016. Possessive constructions in Turkish. *Lingua*, 182:88–108.

Martin Popel, Zdeněk Žabokrtský, and Martin Vojtek. 2017. Udapi: Universal API for Universal Dependencies. In *Proceedings of the NoDaLiDa 2017 Workshop on Universal Dependencies (UDW 2017)*, pages 96–101, Gothenburg, Sweden. Association for Computational Linguistics.

Mojgan Seraji, Filip Ginter, and Joakim Nivre. 2016. Universal Dependencies for Persian. In *LREC*.

Umut Sulubacak, Memduh Gökırmak, and Francis M. Tyers. 2016a. Universal Dependencies for Turkish. *Proceedings of the 26th International Conference on Computational Linguistics (COLING-16)*, pages 3444–3454.

Umut Sulubacak, Tugba Pamay, and Gülşen Eryiğit. 2016b. IMST: A Revisited Turkish Dependency Treebank. In *In Proceedings of 1st International Conference on Turkic Computational Linguistics, TurCLing*, pages 1–6.

Lloyd Balderston Swift. 1963. *A reference grammar of Modern Turkish*, volume 19. Indiana University.

Ann Taylor, Mitchell Marcus, and Beatrice Santorini. 2003. The Penn treebank: an overview. In *Treebanks*, pages 5–22. Springer.

Marat M. Yavrumyan, Hrant H. Khachatrian, Anna S. Danielyan, and Gor D. Arakelyan. 2017. ArmTDP: Eastern Armenian Treebank and Dependency Parser. In *XI International Conference on Armenian Linguistics, Abstracts*.

Daniel Zeman, Filip Ginter, Jan Hajič, Joakim Nivre, Martin Popel, Milan Straka, and et al. 2017. CoNLL 2017 Shared Task: Multilingual Parsing from Raw Text to Universal Dependencies. In *Proceedings of the CoNLL 2017 Shared Task: Multilingual Parsing from Raw Text to Universal Dependencies*, pages 1–20. Association for Computational Linguistics.

A The Proposed Guidelines for Turkish in the UD Project

For the syntactic analyses and for the annotations, we have accepted most of the already-existing definitions and explanations for the syntactic relations for Turkish in the UD website[2]. Even though, the page itself is in UD version 1.0, the links to the explanations of the syntactic relations are in UD version 2.0. For our analyses, we have edited and/or introduced a total of eight syntactic relations: `advcl`, `advmod`, `compound`, `iobj`, `nmod:poss`, `nsubj`, `obj`, and `obl`. Markdown versions of these guidelines are also available in our github page provided in the paper. In this appendix, we will only include the parts that are different from the original guidelines on the website.

advcl

In the explanation of `advcl`, we have included different examples using different morphological inflections to form adverbial clauses. We also included some inflected reduplications as `advcl` as in Example (5).

---

[2]`https://universaldependencies.org/tr/dep/index.html`

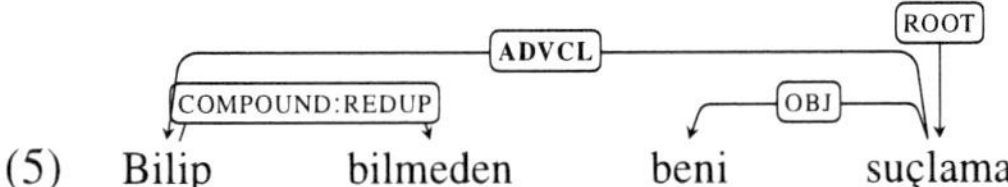

(5) Bilip   bilmeden   beni   suçlama

Bil-ip   bil-me-den   ben-i   suçla-ma.
know-CVB know-NEG-ABL I-ACC blame-NEG

'Don't blame me without knowing anything'

advmod

In addition to the explanation and examples, we also included comparative structures with *daha* as in Example (6), adverbs that are formed with a suffix from nouns as in Example (7), and some reduplications as in Example (8).

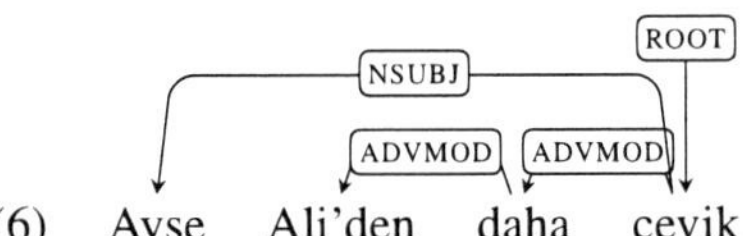

(6) Ayşe   Ali'den   daha   çevik

Ayşe Ali-den daha çevik.
Ayşe Ali-ABL more agile

'Ayşe is more agile than Ali.'

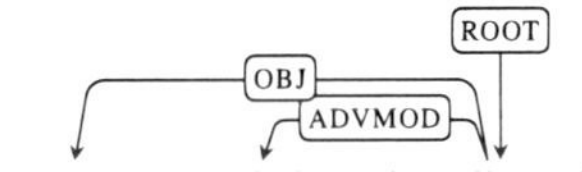

(7) Resmi   ilgiyle   inceliyordu

Resm-i   ilgi-yle   incel-iyor-du.
picture-ACC attention-COM inspect-PROG-PST

'She was inspecting the picture'

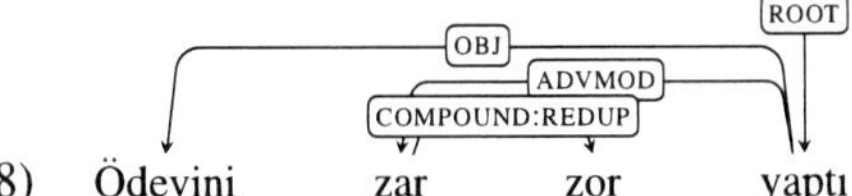

(8) Ödevini   zar   zor   yaptı

Ödev-in-i   zar   zor   yap-tı.
homework-POSS-ACC REDUP difficult do-PST

'She struggled doing her homework'

compound

In the guideline of compounds we have examplified the basic use of the tag as in Example (9). We resort to already-existing guidelines for its use with numbers, and we also used compound:redup and compound:lvc. However, we have specified the use of the subtype for light verbs, which is compound:lvc, and we have limited its use to light verbs that are made up of *et-* and *ol-*. For the rest of the light verbs, we have used compound syntactic tag as in Example

(10). We also excluded compounds that have syntactic reflex of *-(s)I(n)* from the compound tag, instead we have used nmod:poss as in Example (11).

(9) çelik   yelek

çelik yelek
'steel vest'

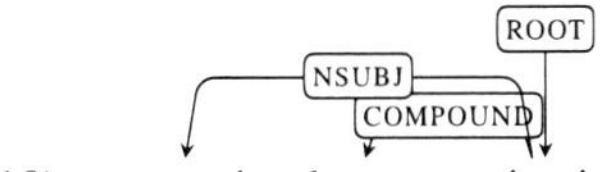

(10) annesi   hapse   girmiş

Anne-si   haps-e   gir-miş.
mom-POSS prison–DAT enter–EVD

'His mom was put in jail.'

(11) kapı   kolu

kapı kolu
'door handle'

iobj

iobj is a core nominal argument of the verb apart from the object and subject as in Example (12). Sentences cannot have a iobj without having first obj.

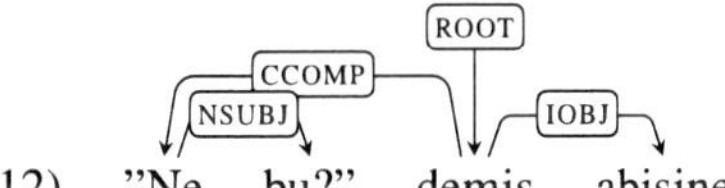

(12) "Ne   bu?"   demiş   abisine

"Ne bu?" de-miş   abi-si-ne.
what this   say-EVD big.brother-POSS-DAT

'"What is this," he asked to his big brother.'

It is important not to mistake every dative case marked nominal with iobj since dative case can be provided semantically and lexically. In those cases, it should be obl and obj, respectively.

nmod:poss

In our analyses, we also extended the use of NMOD:POSS so that it includes 'X out of Y' constructions for Turkish as in Example (13).

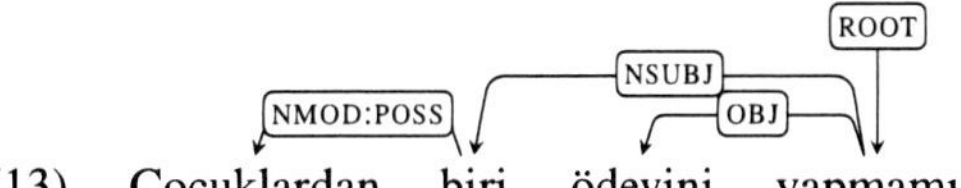

(13) Çocuklardan   biri   ödevini   yapmamış

Çocuk-lar-dan bir-i   ödev-in-i
kid-PL-ABL   one-POSS homework-POSS-ACC
yap-ma-mış.
do-NEG-EVD

'One of the kids did not do his homework'

nsubj

In addition to the already-existing guidelines, we also specified that the subject of an embedded clause should also be marked with the `nsubj` syntactic tag as in Example (14).

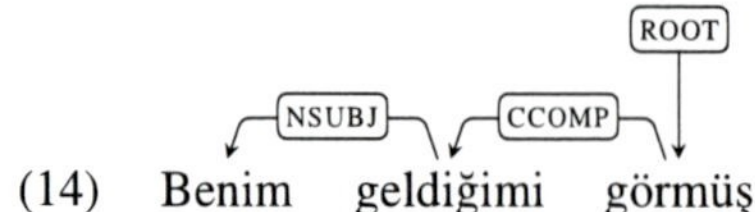

(14) Benim geldiğimi görmüş

    Ben-im gel-diğ-im-i   gör-müş.
    I-GEN   come-NMLZ-POSS-ACC see-EVD

    'He saw that I have arrived.'

obj

The direct object of a verb is the noun phrase that denotes the entity acted upon.

In Turkish, direct objects typically take either nominative (unmarked), or accusative cases. However, any other case except for genitive can be utilized as well. There are two criteria we use when we decide whether a non-canonically marked object is an `obj` or an `obl`:

- Is the case predictable solely from the semantic denotation of the case?

- Does the verb determine the use of the case?

Here, the canonically (marked or unmarked) marked objects:

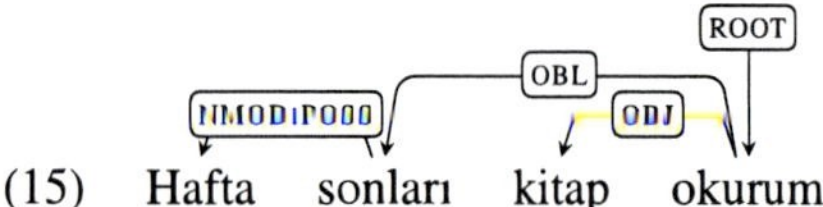

(15) Hafta sonları kitap okurum

    Hafta son-lar-ı   kitap oku-r-um.
    week end-PL-POSS book read-AOR-1SG

    'I read books during weekends.'

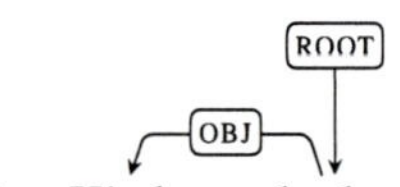

(16) Kitabı okudum

    Kitab-ı   oku-du-m.
    book-ACC read-PST-1SG

    'I read the book'.

We also utilized the already-existing analyses for partitives and non-case marked noun-phrases. However, we included other non-canonically marked objects as well.

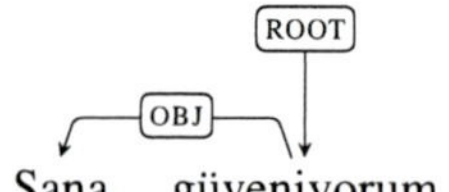

(17) Sana güveniyorum

    San-a   güven-iyor-um.
    you-DAT trust-PROG-1SG

    'I trust you.'

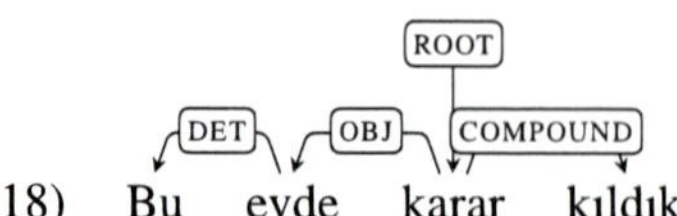

(18) Bu evde karar kıldık

    Bu ev-de   karar   kıl-dı-k.
    this house-LOC decision do-PST-1PL

    'We have decided on this house.'

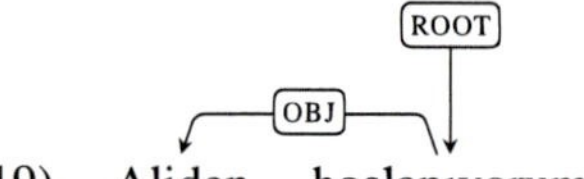

(19) Aliden hoşlanıyorum

    Ali-den hoşlan-ıyor-um.
    Ali-ABL like-PROG-1SG

    'I like Ali.'

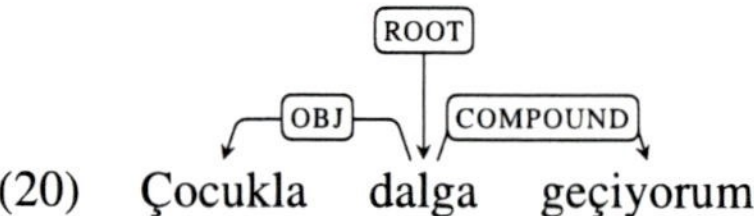

(20) Çocukla dalga geçiyorum

    Çocuk-la dalga geç-iyor-um.
    kid-COM wave pass-PROG-1SG

    'I am kidding the kid.'

Every case marked noun phrase above is a core element in the sentence and the sentences would be ungrammatical if they were to be left out, thus making them `obj`. This phenomenon is not limited to these verbs only. Many more verbs can utilize non-cannonical object marking in Turkish.

obl

In our syntactic analysis, `obl` relation is used for oblique nominal adjuncts of verbs, adjectives or adverbs. Note that we have used [obj] relation for canonically (accusative and nominative) non-canonically (non-accusative and non-nominative) marked obligatory arguments that are not subjects (objects), and we have used [iobj] relation for core arguments necessitated by the Turkish Grammar.

In the examples below, *kitabı* is always the object. However, the other elements that are marked with other cases are adjuncts of the verb and they are not obligatory, which makes them `obl`.

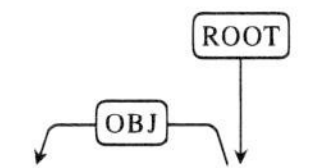

(21)   Kitabı   okudum

Kitab-ı   oku-du-m.
book-ACC read-PST-1SG

'I read the book.'

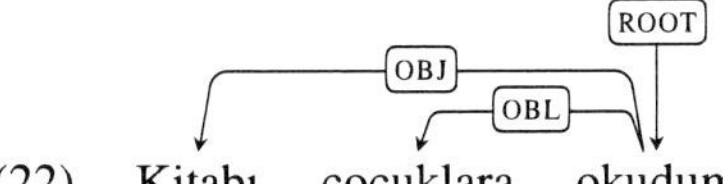

(22)   Kitabı   çocuklara   okudum

Kitab-ı   çocuk-lar-a oku-du-m.
book-ACC kid-PL-DAT read-PST-1SG

'I read the book to the children.'

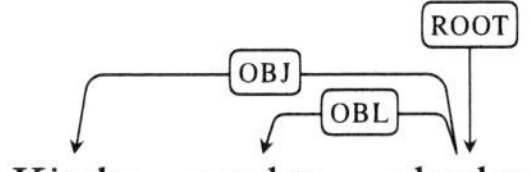

(23)   Kitabı   uçakta   okudum

Kitab-ı   uçak-ta   oku-du-m.
book-ACC plane-LOC read-PST-1SG

'I read the book on the plane.'

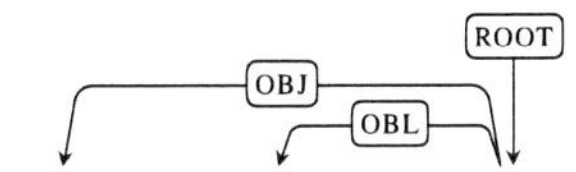

(24)   Kitabı   meraktan   okudum

Kitab-ı   merak-tan   oku-du-m.
book-ACC curiosity-ABL read-PST-1SG

'I read the book out of curiosity.'

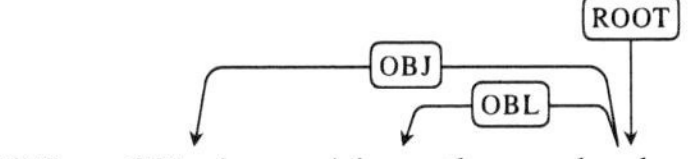

(25)   Kitabı   Ahmetle   okudum

Kitab-ı   Ahmet-le   oku-du-m.
book-ACC PROPN-COM read-PST-1SG

'I read the book with glasses.'

A Dataset for Semantic Role Labelling of Hindi-English Code-Mixed Tweets

Riya Pal and **Dipti Misra Sharma**
Kohli Center on Intelligent Systems (KCIS)
International Institute of Information Technology, Hyderabad (IIIT-Hyderabad)
Gachibowli, Hyderabad, Telangana - 500032, India
`riya.pal@research.iiit.ac.in`
`dipti@iiit.ac.in`

Abstract

We present a data set of 1460 Hindi-English code-mixed tweets consisting of 20,949 tokens labelled with Proposition Bank labels marking their semantic roles. We created verb frames for complex predicates present in the corpus and formulated mappings from Paninian dependency labels to Proposition Bank labels. With the help of these mappings and the dependency tree, we propose a baseline rule based system for Semantic Role Labelling of Hindi-English code-mixed data. We obtain an accuracy of 96.74% for Argument Identification and are able to further classify 73.93% of the labels correctly. While there is relevant ongoing research on Semantic Role Labelling (SRL) and on building tools for code-mixed social media data, this is the first attempt at labelling semantic roles in Hindi-English code-mixed data, to the best of our knowledge.

1 Introduction

In recent times, social media has gained a lot of popularity and serves as a medium for people across the globe to communicate and express their opinions. Forums like Facebook and Twitter are used excessively for this purpose. Increasing availability of such resources online provide a large corpus and subsequently the need for linguistic analysis and tools for automated understanding of this data. Code-mixing is a phenomenon observed largely in social media text. It refers to *"the embedding of linguistic units such as phrases, words and morphemes of one language into an utterance of another language "*(Myers-Scotton, 1993). It is usually an intra-sentential phenomenon observed in multilingual societies in colloquial as well as online usage.

Benchmark NLP tools are majorly based on monolingual corpora which strictly follow the patterns and conform to the rules of the given language in terms of structure, syntax, morphology and so on. However, social media data deviate from these rules. Hence, numerous technologies perform poorly on social media data irrespective of it being monolingual or a mixture of languages (Solorio and Liu, 2008; Çetinoğlu et al., 2016; Bhat et al., 2018). Code-mixed data in particular introduces further variation in the morphology and syntax of the language which leads to poor performance of standard NLP tools. Following are a few instances of Hindi-English code-mixed tweets from the corpus:

T1: *"Lagta hai aaj Sri has not spoken to msd"*
Translation: "It looks like Sri has not spoken to MSD today"

T2: *"Lalu Yadav claimed that Yadav quota ke hisab se Umesh Yadav ko ye wkt mil jana chahiye tha"*
Translation: "Lalu Yadav claimed that according to the Yadav quota, Umesh Yadav should have taken a wicket"

In the above two examples we observe how the two languages are mixed in each utterance. Each tweet has tokens from both English and Hindi. T2 in particular shows a problem common to social media data. The token *'wkt'* doesn't correspond to any word. This may be a typo made by the user or simply a shorthand way of writing adopted by many users online. Here 'wkt' could mean "waqta" which means 'time' in Hindi, or "wicket" in the domain of cricket. As we have the context of the whole tweet and world knowledge about Umesh Yadav who is an Indian cricketer, we are able to disambiguate the usage of the token 'wkt', though this may not always be the case.

In this paper, we present a data set of Hindi-English code-mixed tweets labelled with semantic roles. These labels provide us with information of

Proceedings of the 13th Linguistic Annotation Workshop, pages 178–188
Florence, Italy, August 1, 2019. ©2019 Association for Computational Linguistics

the role played by an argument with respect to a verb in a given sentence. We seek to gain semantic information irrespective of the syntactic variation a sentence or an utterance may have. Semantic Role Labelling for code-mixed data will aid in better understanding of these texts and further the research of any understanding based tasks such as information retrieval (Surdeanu et al., 2003; Moschitti et al., 2003), document classification (Bastianelli et al., 2013), questioning answering systems (Shen and Lapata, 2007) and so on.

A Proposition Bank (Propbank) is a corpus of annotated semantic predicate-argument labels (Palmer et al., 2005). This is done with the help of verb frame files and the Proposition Bank tagset. The frame files contain the semantic roles needed for each verb and all the possible context variations of each verb (sense of the verb). To annotate, one must first identify the 'sense id' (Roleset id) of the verb present according to its usage, and then mark the corresponding labels present in its frame file. We follow exactly this process for the manual annotation of our corpus.

The structure of this paper is as follows. Section 2 talks about relevant work in the domains of Semantic Role Labelling and code-mixed data. We discuss our annotation scheme in section 3. In section 4, we propose a baseline rule based system for manual annotation of the data using dependency label information. Section 5 talks about the results and working of our baseline system. We analyse cases of high errors in classification and explore reasons for the same. In Section 6 we shed light on future scope and conclude the paper.

2 Background and Related Work

The release of large corpora with semantic annotations like the FrameNet (Lowe, 1997; Baker et al., 1998) and Propbank (Kingsbury and Palmer, 2002) have enabled the training and testing of classifiers for automated annotation models. Gildea and Jurafsky (2002) initiated the work on 2001 release of the English Propbank with statistical classifiers and linguistic features. Since then, Propbanks have been created for different languages (Xue and Palmer, 2009; Palmer et al., 2008; Bhatt et al., 2009; Duran and Aluísio, 2012) and several advances have been made towards automating the process of Semantic Role Labelling (Punyakanok et al., 2008; Kshirsagar et al., 2015) using neural networks (FitzGerald et al., 2015; Zhou and Xu,

2015), deep learning methods (He et al., 2018b; Tan et al., 2018), joint prediction of predicates and its arguments (Toutanova et al., 2008; He et al., 2018a; Swayamdipta et al., 2018).

Bali et. al (2014) analysed social media, Facebook in particular, and looking at the extent of Hindi-English code-mixed data available online, emphasise the need to develop NLP tools for code-mixed social media data. Vyas et al.(2014) worked on building a POS tagger for Hindi-English code-mixed data and noted the difficulty posed by transliteration of Hindi tokens onto roman script. Barman et al. (2014) addressed the problem of language identification on Bengali-Hindi-English Facebook comments. Sharma et al. (2016) built a shallow parsing pipeline for Hindi-English code-mixed data. Gupta et al. (2014) introduced the concept of Mixed-Script Information Retrieval and the problems posed by transliterated content such as spelling variations etc. There has been a surge of data set creation for code-mixed data (Bhat et al., 2017; Gupta et al., 2016) and application based tools such as question classification (Raghavi et al., 2015), named-entity recognition (Singh et al., 2018), sentiment analysis (Prabhu et al., 2016; Ghosh et al., 2017) and so on.

3 Data Creation

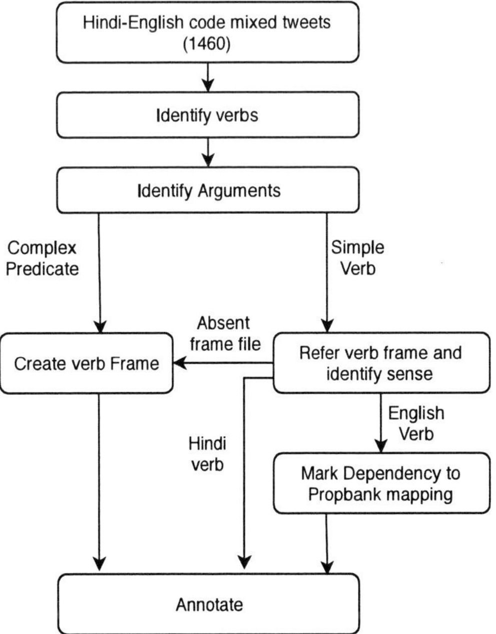

Figure 1: Data Creation workflow for gold annotation of the data

We built our corpus on syntactic information obtained from dependency labels. This allows us to annotate explicitly on the syntactic tree which enables consistency between Propbank structure and dependency structure. Dependency labels provide us with rich syntactic-semantic relations which facilitates mapping between dependency labels and Propbank labels. This would largely reduce annotation effort (Vaidya et al., 2011). We explore this in the working of our baseline model (Section 4). We present a Hindi-English code-mixed Twitter data set comprising 1460 tweets labelled with semantic roles according to the Hindi Propbank tagset. We use the corpus used by (Bhat et al., 2018) in which tweets are labelled with Paninian Dependency labels. Our corpus consists of simple verb constructions, in both Hindi and English, and also complex predicates which have been dealt with separately. These can be within the same language or across the two languages. Figure 1 shows the workflow for the gold annotation of the data.

3.1 Tagset

Label	Description
ARGA	Causer
ARG0	Agent or Experiencer or Doer
ARG1	Theme or Patient
ARG2	Benificiary
ARG2_ATTR	Attribute or Quality
ARG2_LOC	Physical Location
ARG2_GOL	Destination or Goal
ARG2_SOU	Source
ARG3	Instrument
ARGM_DIR	Direction
ARGM_LOC	Location
ARGM_MNR	Manner
ARGM_EXT	Extent or Comparison
ARGM_TMP	Temporal
ARGM_REC	Reciprocal
ARGM_PRP	Purpose
ARGM_CAU	Cause or Reason
ARGM_DIS	Discourse
ARGM_ADV	Adverb
ARGM_NEG	Negative
ARGM_PRX	Complex Predicate

Table 1: Hindi PropBank Tagset

The Propbank adds an additional layer of semantic information on top of the syntactic information present. The Hindi Propbank was built as a part of the "multi-representational and multi-layered" resource creation project for Hindi and Urdu (Bhatt et al., 2009) aimed at simultaneous development of the Propbank, Dependency Treebank and Phrase Structure Treebank. The Hindi Propbank is built on dependency structures unlike Propbanks for other languages such as English, Chinese, Arabic which are built on phrase structure trees (Kingsbury and Palmer, 2002). As we also use dependency structures to annotate Hindi-English code-mixed data, we use the Hindi Propbank tag set (see Table 1) (Palmer et al., 2005) to annotate our data and co-relate the dependency labels with semantic labels.

3.2 Frame File Creation

Frame files are used as guidance for Propbank annotation. Frame file creation is done in two steps:

1. A human expert builds a 'frame file' which marks all the arguments a verb may take across its syntactic variations, depending on the context of its usage.

2. This frame file is used to annotate roles for any occurrence of the said verb to maintain consistency.

Bonial et al (2014) present a lexicon of frame-sets for English Propbank annotation. Vaidya et al. (2013) present Hindi Propbank frame files for simple verb constructions as well as for nominal-verb constructions. As Hindi Propbank is built on syntactic information from Dependency Treebank and we build our model on dependency labelled Hindi English code-mixed data, we use these frame files extensively for annotation of our corpus. We also refer to the English frame files to label the roles for simple English verbs in the corpus.

Frame file for *baca*	
Roleset id: *baca.01*: to remain	
ARG1	Thing left
Roleset id: *baca.02*: to avoid	
ARG0	person avoiding
ARG1	Thing avoided

Table 2: Frame file for the hindi verb *'baca'*. (Vaidya et al., 2013)

Table 2 shows a frame file for the Hindi verb *'baca'*. The rolesets in the frame file give us the senses of the predicate and the different arguments it may take depending on the context in which it is used. In certain cases, we had to create new frame files for novel occurrences of verbs and absence of the relevant frame file. We also created frame files for inter-language complex predicate formations and noted the dependency label to Propbank label mapping.

3.2.1 Absent Verbs

Existing frame files for both Propbanks - Hindi, and English - have been created keeping formal data sets in mind, such as news articles. Hence, the verbs and the senses of the verbs covered, don't necessarily represent all domains. Social media in particular allows its users to use colloquial terms and usage of predicates, some of which have not been taken care of by the existing frame files. To overcome this, we create the gold frame files for **14** such unique predicates in our corpus. (One such example is the verb 'born' shown in Table 3) Some of these include verbs for which a specific sense is not defined. For example, the English verb 'click' in the context of clicking pictures.

Frame file for *born*
Roleset id: *born.01*: Brought to life by birth
ARG1	Entity born

Table 3: Frame file created for the English verb *'born'*. There were 6 instances of this predicate in our corpus.

3.2.2 Complex Predicates

Complex Predicates (CP), also known as 'Light verb constructions' or 'Conjunct Verb Constructions' are seen in both Hindi and English (Butt, 2010). Ahmed et al.(2012) classified the complex predicates present in Hindi into 3 categories: noun-verb constructions, verb - verb constructions and causatives.

Hindi	209
English	21
Intra-language CP	230
Code-mixed CP	232
Total	462

Table 4: Distribution of unique Complex Predicates in the corpus

These constructions occur frequently in our corpus as well. There has been emphasis on the cre-

ation of lexical resources for annotation of complex predicates for English (Hwang et al., 2010) and Hindi (Vaidya et al., 2013) in the form of frame files. In our corpus, we observe complex predicate formations within the same language (intra-language) as well as between the two languages (inter-language or code-mixed). We have **462** unique complex predicates in our corpus. Table 4 gives the distribution of these in our data.

Most of these complex predicates are noun-verb constructions, also known as light verb constructions. Light verbs in Hindi are highly productive and can entirely change the meaning of the predicate. For instance, *'hona'* (to be) and *'karna'* (to do) are two Hindi light verbs. When used with an English noun, say 'save', they give rise to two different complex predicates with distinct meanings and structures: *'Save hona'* means to be saved and *'save karna'* would imply the act of saving something. Hence, we cannot leverage frame files from either language to obtain the argument structure for such constructions and thus built new frame-files for each unique combination encountered. An example from the corpus is as follows:

T3: *"Me in logon ko apny crush ki picture send tw kar dun but but but I cant trust them"*
Translation: "I can send my crush's picture to these people, but I can't trust them"

Frame file for *send_karna*	
Roleset id: *send_karna.01*: To Give	
ARG0	Entity sending (Sender)
ARG1	Entity sent
ARG2	Entity sent to

Table 5: Frame file created for the Complex Predicate *send karna*.

The complex predicate construction observed here (T3) is 'send_karna', which is an inter-language, or code-mixed predicate. We created a frame file (Table 5) for the same which helps us to annotate this predicate for subsequent occurrences in the corpus. The given sentence would be labelled for *'send_karna'* as follows:

T4: *"(Me)*[ARG0]*(in logon ko)* [ARG2]*(apny crush ki picture)*[ARG1]*send tw kar dun but but but I cant trust them"*

Translation: "(I) `[ARG0]` can send (my crush's picture) `[ARG1]` to (these people) `[ARG2]`, but I can't trust them"

3.3 Annotation

The annotation process is done in a series of steps as described in Figure 1. The first step is to identify all the verbs present in the sentence. We will use the following sentence as an example:

*"Yar **end karo** match I have to **sleep**"*

Translation: Hey, end the match, I have to sleep.

Here we can detect two verb constructions. One is a complex predicate *'end karna'* and the other is a simple English verb construction for *'sleep'*. We refer to the frame files for both to identify the arguments in the given sentence. Since *'end karna'* is a complex predicate containing an English nominal and a Hindi light verb, we create its frame file (Table 6). These constructions are easily detectable with the help of special label `pof` or "part-of" used in the Dependency Treebank. The second verb in the sentence is *'sleep'* for which the frame file is already present (Table 7 (Bonial et al., 2014)).

Frame file for *end_karna*	
Roleset id: *end_karna.01*: To Stop	
`ARG0`	Entity ending (Ender)
`ARG1`	Entity ended

Table 6: Frame file created for the Complex Predicate *'end_karna'* as discussed in Section 3.2.2.

Frame file for *sleep*	
Roleset id: *sleep.01*: To Sleep, Slumber	
`ARG0`	Sleeper
`ARG1`	Cognate entity
Roleset id: *sleep.02*: Engage in sexual relations	
`ARG0`	Agentive partner
`ARG1`	Prepositional Partner

Table 7: Frame file for the simple English verb *'sleep'*.

The token for complex predicate is marked with the label `'ARGM_PRX'` according to the Propbank tagset. In the frame file for the verb 'sleep', given in Table 7, we can see possible rolesets or senses

the predicate can take. Looking at the context in our sentence, we choose 'Roleset id: sleep.01'. With the help of frame files, we are able to identify and annotate the numbered arguments of the predicates. Next, we label the modifier arguments as described in Table 1.

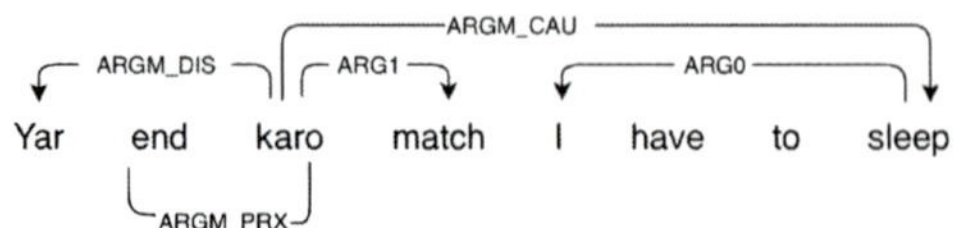

Figure 2: Sentence marked with Propbank labels

In the given sentence, the token *"Yar"* is a term used frequently in colloquial Hindi. It is used to refer to someone or call someone informally. The right label for it is `ARGM_DIS` (Discourse, according to Table 1). The reason for 'ending' the match was the action of 'sleeping'. Hence, we mark it with `ARGM_CAU` (Cause). Figure 2 shows the final sentence annotated with all the semantic roles. Since we are using code-mixed tweets which are annotated with Hindi dependency labels (Bhat et al., 2018), we also note the mappings from dependency labels to Propbank labels for all verb occurrences in the corpus. This mapping would help in automatic annotation of semantic roles of verbs from their syntactic dependents (Vaidya et al., 2011).

Total tokens	20, 949
Unique Hindi Simple Verbs	613
Unique English Simple Verbs	512
Complex Predicates	622

Table 8: Data Distribution 3.2.2

Table 8 shows the statistics of the corpus after annotation of 1460 tweets in the Hindi-English code-mixed tweets.

3.3.1 Pronoun Dropping

Pronoun dropping refers to the linguistic phenomenon of dropping or omitting pronouns wherein it is inferable from prior discourse context. It is observed widely across languages though the conditions may vary from language to language. Bhatia et al.(2010) emphasise the motivation and importance of introducing empty categories in the Hindi Dependency Treebank. This doesn't include empty categories for pronoun dropping but includes empty categories for dropped nouns, conjunctions, verbs etc. Empty categories were introduced in the Hindi Propbank to include core arguments missing from the predicate-argument structure after addition of the empty categories in the Hindi Dependency Treebank (Vaidya et al., 2012).

T5: *"Tore my calendar kyunki woh khana nai laya"*

Translation: "(I) tore my calendar because he/she didn't bring food."

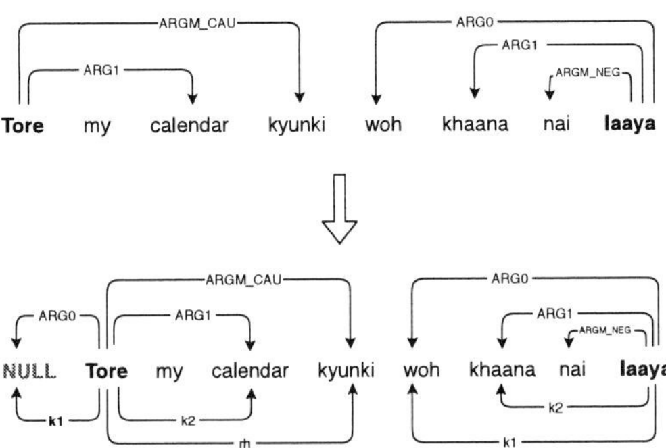

Figure 3: Tweet T5 marked with Propbank labels before and after 'NULL' insertion to account for pro-drop along with dependency relation labels.

Although English is not a pro-drop language, pronoun dropping is observed largely in Hindi-English code-mixed data. The sentence above (T5) is such an example from the corpus. We incorporate this in our data by inserting 'NULL' arguments and labelling them with Propbank labels - ARG0, ARG1, ARG2, as appropriate. Table 9 shows the frame file for the verb 'tear'. Figure 3 shows the semantic roles associated with tweet T5 before and after the empty category insertion to account for pronoun dropping.

Frame file for *tear*	
Roleset id: *tear.01*: To pull apart	
ARG0	Tearer (**dmrel**: k1)
ARG1	Thing torn (drel: k2)

Table 9: Part of the Frame file for the simple English verb *'tear'*. This is the relevant roleset chosen according to the Tweet above (T5). We note the dependency role (drel) associated with the Propbank labels. In case of an empty category insertion, we assign a dummy dependency relation label ('dmrel') as appropriate.

3.3.2 Special Constructions

Code-mixed language refers to the usage of linguistic units of one language in a sentence of another language. One fairly common preliminary step while annotating code-mixed data is Language Identification (Vyas et al., 2014; Sharma et al., 2016). The tokens present in the corpus are marked 'hi', for Hindi, or 'en', for English, or 'ne' for Named Entities. This assumes that code-mixing doesn't occur at sub-lexical levels. However, in our corpus, we came across a few cases where new lexical items are formed by mixing the two languages and modifying the morphology of the individual languages. One way of doing this is to add affixes from one language to a word of the other language. These constructions are used widely in day to day usage. We treat these cases as 'Special Constructions'.

Frame file for *beztify*	
Roleset id: *beztify.01*: To insult	
ARG0	Entity insulting someone
ARG1	Entity insulted

Table 10: Frame file for the *'hinglish'* word *"beztify"*.

When these words of morphological modification play the role of predicates, we need to assign arguments and semantic roles accordingly. To deal with this, we create frame files for such cases. Table 10 shows the frame file for one such construction from our corpus - **beztify**.

'bezti' is a Hindi noun which translates to 'insult' in English. The speaker here uses the English suffix "-fy" to use the word as a verb, thus making it *"beztify"* which translates to "to insult someone" in English.

4 Rule-based Approach

Semantic Role Labelling adds a layer of semantic information on top of the syntactic information. We use Paninian dependency labelled (karaka relations) Hindi-English code-mixed data (Bhat et al., 2018) for creating our corpus and labelling the data. Vaidya et al (2011) analysed the relation between dependency labels and Propbank labels for Hindi. They also proposed mappings between Hindi dependency labels to Propbank labels as shown in Table 11 and Table 12 for numbered arguments and some modifier arguments respectively.

Research shows that English Propbank data is similar to English Dependency Treebank labelled with Paninan dependency labels. (Vaidya et al., 2009). We use these mappings (Table 11, Table 12) to create a rule based model for automatic annotation of semantic roles.

Dependency label	Propbank label
k1 (karta); k4a (experiencer)	ARG0
k2 (karma)	ARG1
k4 (beneficiary)	ARG2
k1s (attribute)	ARG2_ATTR
k5 (source)	ARG2_SOU
k2p (goal)	ARG2_GOL
k3 (instrument)	ARG3

Table 11: Mappings from Dependency label to Propbank Numbered arguments

We first identify the predicates present in the sentence. Simple verb constructions are easily identified by their part of speech tag ('VM') and complex predicates are detected by the dependency label 'pof' as mentioned in Section 3.2.2.

The labelling is done in two steps. The first step is **Argument Identification**. Here, our model labels all the tokens in the sentence as "Argument" or "Not an Argument" with the help of the dependency tree structure. To achieve this, we mark all direct dependents of the identified predicates as their Arguments barring those tokens which are marked as auxiliary verbs, post-positions, symbols (emojis in social media text) or those which show coordination or subordination (diel. 'ccof'). There can be certain cases in social media text where emojis may act as arguments of a predicate. However, we focus only on lexical items for the time being and plan to incorporate this as a part of our future work.

Dependency label	Propbank label
sent-adv (epistemic adv)	ARGM_ADV
rh (cause/reason)	ARGM_CAU
rd (direction)	ARGM_DIR
rad (discourse)	ARGM_DIS
k7p (location)	ARGM_LOC
adv (manner adv)	ARGM_MNR
rt (purpose)	ARGM_PRP
k7t (time)	ARGM_TMP

Table 12: Mappings from Dependency label to Propbank Modifier labels.

The second step is **Argument Classification** wherein we assign the identified arguments with Propbank labels according to the aforementioned mappings. We add more rules to the mappings for modifier labels as mentioned in Table 13. For the rare cases where no such mapping has been proposed, we train the model to label arguments as the most frequently occurring corresponding label in the gold data set.

Dependency label	Propbank label
k7a (according to)	ARGM_ADV
lwg__neg (negation)	ARGM_NEG
k*u (similarity/comparison)	ARGM_EXT

Table 13: Additional mappings from Dependency label to Propbank Modifier labels.

5   Results and Analysis

We obtain an overall accuracy of **96.74%** (overall F1 score of 95.41) for Argument Identification and **73.93%** for Argument Classification. The precision, recall and F1 scores for Argument Identification are given in Table 14. We also compute our scores separately for Numbered arguments and Modifier arguments.

	Dist.	P	R	F1
Overall	100.00	93.22	97.69	95.41
Numbered	61.09	98.81	90.22	94.32
Modifier	38.91	79.50	94.41	87.5

Table 14: Accuracy scores achieved for identification of Numbered and Modifier arguments by our rule based model along with their distribution in the data set.

Figure 4 shows us a sentence from the corpus where a token is labelled as [ARG0] by our model whereas the gold label is [ARG1]. This is a very common error seen across the corpus.

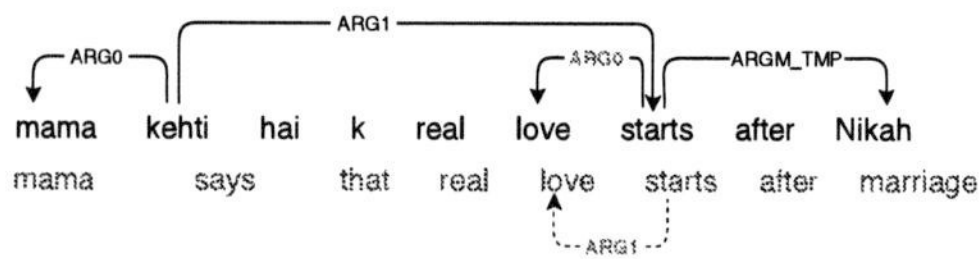

Figure 4: Tweet showing mis-classification between 'ARG0' (given by model, solid line) and 'ARG1' (Gold label, dotted line)

In the example shown, the dependency label given to the token *'love'* is 'k1'. Here, 'love' isn't really the agent of the verb 'start'. The Propbank label [ARG0] denotes the agent of the verb, the argument which causes the action, whereas [ARG1] denotes the argument which is affected or changed by the action. Paninian dependency labels don't account into unaccusativity and hence, k1 maps to both [ARG0] and [ARG1], subject to context (Vaidya et al., 2009, 2011).

Label	Dist.	P	R	F1
ARG0	15.65	81.79	93.83	65.21
ARG1	33.14	92.61	48.56	63.71
ARG2	4.62	75.91	31.04	44.06
ARG2_ATTR	5.63	76.95	86.76	81.56
ARG2_GOL	0.54	90.90	25.64	40.0
ARG2_SOU	0.57	80.00	68.29	73.68
ARG3	0.17	81.81	75.00	78.26
ARGM_DIR	0.07	50.0	80.0	61.53
ARGM_LOC	3.68	50.77	98.50	67.0
ARGM_MNR	7.83	51.52	89.26	65.33
ARGM_EXT	0.28	50.0	95.0	65.51
ARGM_TMP	8.19	97.61	89.73	93.51
ARGM_PRP	1.28	88.77	93.54	91.09
ARGM_CAU	1.71	96.19	81.45	88.21
ARGM_DIS	2.44	98.23	94.35	96.25
ARGM_ADV	0.43	72.31	82.92	77.25
ARGM_NEG	4.36	92.85	94.62	93.73
ARGM_PRX	8.58	97.47	99.35	98.41

Table 15: Precision, Recall and F-scores achieved for all labels with our rule based model. Also shows overall distribution of the labels in our data set.

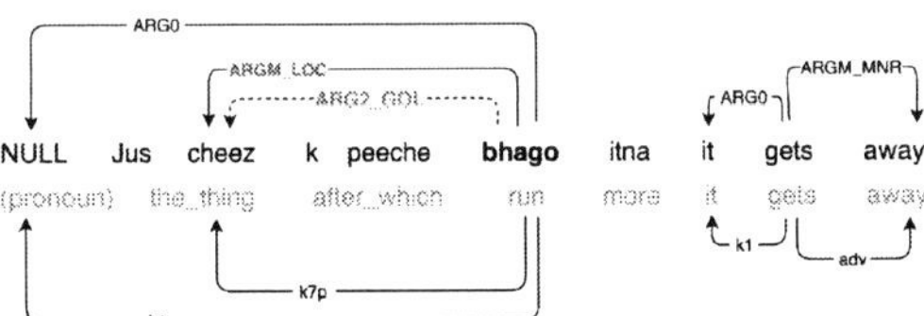

Figure 5: Tweet showing 'ARG2_GOL' (Gold label, dotted line) mis-labelled as 'ARGM_LOC' (given by model, solid line), and the dependency labels of the tokens.

The precision, recall and F1 scores for the various labels obtained in the Argument Classification step are given in Table 15. We see that [ARG2] and [ARG2_GOL] have a significantly low F1 score, although the precision values are decent. ARG2 is most commonly mis-labelled as ARG2_ATTR in our data which results in the low recall score.

Frame file for *BAga*		
Roleset id:*BAga.02*: To run towards something		
ARG0	entity running (drel: k1)	
ARG1	destination (drel: k2p)	

Table 16: Part of the Frame file for the simple Hindi verb 'BAga'. This is the relevant roleset chosen according to the Tweet in figure 5.

Figure 5 shows an example where a token is labelled as [ARGM_LOC] because of the dependency label 'k7p' (Table 12). However, according to the frame file of the verb "Bhaaga" (to run) given in Table 16, the token must be given the label [ARG2_GOL]. We also do a NULL insertion for the dropped pronoun in this tweet as described in section 3.3.1. The mis-classification for [ARG2_GOL] occurs largely due to the ambiguity between the dependency labels 'k2p' and 'k7p' which then lowers the precision value of [ARGM_LOC] as well.

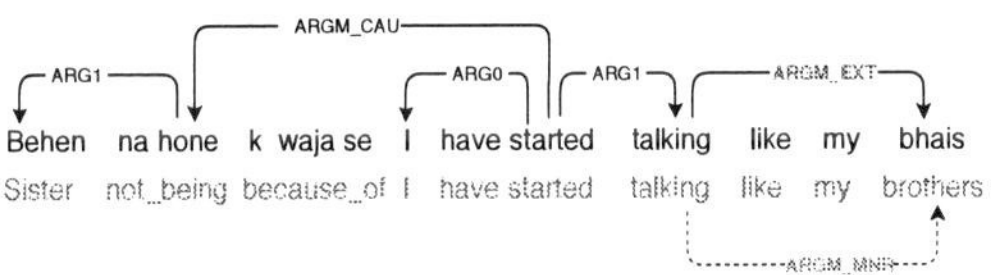

Figure 6: Tweet showing mis-classification between 'ARGM_EXT' (given by model, solid line) and 'ARGM_MNR' (Gold label, dotted line)

Another common error observed is between [ARGM_EXT] and [ARGM_MNR] as seen in Figure 6. The dependency label given to the token *'bhais'* (brothers) is 'k1u' which is used to mark similarities or comparisons. The Propbank label for comparisons is usually [ARGM_EXT]. However, here we are comparing the manner of talking of the speaker with his/her brother(s), and hence the appropriate Propbank label would be [ARGM_MNR]. A similar case can be seen for mis-classification between [ARGM_MNR] and [ARGM_ADV] labels. The former is meant for describing the manner in which the action is carried out and the latter describes the action. Sometimes, the model isn't able to distinguish between them. These cases explain the lower accuracy scores for the labels - 'ARGM_EXT' , 'ARGM_MNR' and 'ARGM_ADV'.

6 Conclusion and Future Work

We present a data set of Hindi-English code-mixed data marked with semantic roles. We take into account nuances of both languages such as complex predicate constructions, pronoun dropping and address issues specific to social media data such as typos, colloquial word usage, as well. We also present a baseline model which maps the correlation between dependency labels and Propbank labels as has been observed with both languages separately and note that the co-relation remains largely consistent. This will aid in faster annotation of such data henceforth. The data set is available online[1].

We plan to further expand this data set and try learning based approaches for code-mixed Semantic Role Labelling and also analyse and compare them with models for monolingual data sets.

References

Tafseer Ahmed, Miriam Butt, Annette Hautli, and Sebastian Sulger. 2012. A reference dependency bank for analyzing complex predicates. In *LREC*.

Collin F Baker, Charles J Fillmore, and John B Lowe. 1998. The berkeley framenet project. In *Proceedings of the 17th international conference on Computational linguistics-Volume 1*, pages 86–90. Association for Computational Linguistics.

Kalika Bali, Jatin Sharma, Monojit Choudhury, and Yogarshi Vyas. 2014. " i am borrowing ya mixing?" an analysis of english-hindi code mixing in facebook. In *Proceedings of the First Workshop on Computational Approaches to Code Switching*, pages 116–126.

Utsab Barman, Amitava Das, Joachim Wagner, and Jennifer Foster. 2014. Code mixing: A challenge for language identification in the language of social media. In *Proceedings of the first workshop on computational approaches to code switching*, pages 13–23.

Emanuele Bastianelli, Giuseppe Castellucci, Danilo Croce, and Roberto Basili. 2013. Textual inference and meaning representation in human robot interaction. In *Proceedings of the Joint Symposium on Semantic Processing. Textual Inference and Structures in Corpora*, pages 65–69.

Irshad Ahmad Bhat, Riyaz Ahmad Bhat, Manish Shrivastava, and Dipti Misra Sharma. 2017. Joining hands: Exploiting monolingual treebanks for parsing of code-mixing data. *arXiv preprint arXiv:1703.10772*.

Irshad Ahmad Bhat, Riyaz Ahmad Bhat, Manish Shrivastava, and Dipti Misra Sharma. 2018. Universal dependency parsing for hindi-english code-switching. *arXiv preprint arXiv:1804.05868*.

Archna Bhatia, Rajesh Bhatt, Bhuvana Narasimhan, Martha Palmer, Owen Rambow, Dipti Misra Sharma, Michael Tepper, Ashwini Vaidya, and Fei Xia. 2010. Empty categories in a hindi treebank. In *LREC*.

Rajesh Bhatt, Bhuvana Narasimhan, Martha Palmer, Owen Rambow, Dipti Sharma, and Fei Xia. 2009. A multi-representational and multi-layered treebank for hindi/urdu. In *Proceedings of the Third Linguistic Annotation Workshop (LAW III)*, pages 186–189.

Claire Bonial, Julia Bonn, Kathryn Conger, Jena D Hwang, and Martha Palmer. 2014. Propbank: Semantics of new predicate types. In *LREC*, pages 3013–3019.

Miriam Butt. 2010. The light verb jungle: Still hacking away. *Complex predicates in cross-linguistic perspective*, pages 48–78.

Özlem Çetinoğlu, Sarah Schulz, and Ngoc Thang Vu. 2016. Challenges of computational processing of code-switching. *arXiv preprint arXiv:1610.02213*.

Magali Sanches Duran and Sandra Maria Aluísio. 2012. Propbank-br: a brazilian treebank annotated with semantic role labels. In *LREC*, pages 1862–1867.

Nicholas FitzGerald, Oscar Täckström, Kuzman Ganchev, and Dipanjan Das. 2015. Semantic role labeling with neural network factors. In *Proceedings of the 2015 Conference on Empirical Methods in Natural Language Processing*, pages 960–970.

Souvick Ghosh, Satanu Ghosh, and Dipankar Das. 2017. Sentiment identification in code-mixed social media text. *arXiv preprint arXiv:1707.01184*.

Daniel Gildea and Daniel Jurafsky. 2002. Automatic labeling of semantic roles. *Computational linguistics*, 28(3):245–288.

Parth Gupta, Kalika Bali, Rafael E Banchs, Monojit Choudhury, and Paolo Rosso. 2014. Query expansion for mixed-script information retrieval. In *Proceedings of the 37th international ACM SIGIR conference on Research & development in information retrieval*, pages 677–686. ACM.

Sakshi Gupta, Piyush Bansal, and Radhika Mamidi. 2016. Resource creation for hindi-english code mixed social media text. In *The 4th International Workshop on Natural Language Processing for Social Media in the 25th International Joint Conference on Artificial Intelligence*.

Luheng He, Kenton Lee, Omer Levy, and Luke Zettlemoyer. 2018a. Jointly predicting predicates and arguments in neural semantic role labeling. *arXiv preprint arXiv:1805.04787*.

---

[1] https://github.com/riyapal/Hi-En-SRL

Shexia He, Zuchao Li, Hai Zhao, and Hongxiao Bai. 2018b. Syntax for semantic role labeling, to be, or not to be. In *Proceedings of the 56th Annual Meeting of the Association for Computational Linguistics (Volume 1: Long Papers)*, volume 1, pages 2061–2071.

Jena D Hwang, Archna Bhatia, Clare Bonial, Aous Mansouri, Ashwini Vaidya, Nianwen Xue, and Martha Palmer. 2010. Propbank annotation of multilingual light verb constructions. In *Proceedings of the Fourth Linguistic Annotation Workshop*, pages 82–90. Association for Computational Linguistics.

Paul Kingsbury and Martha Palmer. 2002. From treebank to propbank. In *LREC*, pages 1989–1993. Citeseer.

Meghana Kshirsagar, Sam Thomson, Nathan Schneider, Jaime Carbonell, Noah A Smith, and Chris Dyer. 2015. Frame-semantic role labeling with heterogeneous annotations. In *Proceedings of the 53rd Annual Meeting of the Association for Computational Linguistics and the 7th International Joint Conference on Natural Language Processing (Volume 2: Short Papers)*, volume 2, pages 218–224.

John B Lowe. 1997. A frame-semantic approach to semantic annotation. *Tagging Text with Lexical Semantics: Why, What, and How?*

Alessandro Moschitti, Paul Morarescu, Sanda M Harabagiu, et al. 2003. Open domain information extraction via automatic semantic labeling. In *FLAIRS conference*, volume 3, pages 397–401.

Carol Myers-Scotton. 1993. Dueling languages: Grammatical structure in code-switching. claredon.

Martha Palmer, Olga Babko-Malaya, Ann Bies, Mona T Diab, Mohamed Maamouri, Aous Mansouri, and Wajdi Zaghouani. 2008. A pilot arabic propbank. In *LREC*.

Martha Palmer, Daniel Gildea, and Paul Kingsbury. 2005. The proposition bank: An annotated corpus of semantic roles. *Computational linguistics*, 31(1):71–106.

Ameya Prabhu, Aditya Joshi, Manish Shrivastava, and Vasudeva Varma. 2016. Towards sub-word level compositions for sentiment analysis of hindi-english code mixed text. *arXiv preprint arXiv:1611.00472*.

Vasin Punyakanok, Dan Roth, and Wen-tau Yih. 2008. The importance of syntactic parsing and inference in semantic role labeling. *Computational Linguistics*, 34(2):257–287.

Khyathi Chandu Raghavi, Manoj Kumar Chinnakotla, and Manish Shrivastava. 2015. Answer ka type kya he?: Learning to classify questions in code-mixed language. In *Proceedings of the 24th International Conference on World Wide Web*, pages 853–858. ACM.

Arnav Sharma, Sakshi Gupta, Raveesh Motlani, Piyush Bansal, Manish Srivastava, Radhika Mamidi, and Dipti M Sharma. 2016. Shallow parsing pipeline for hindi-english code-mixed social media text. *arXiv preprint arXiv:1604.03136*.

Dan Shen and Mirella Lapata. 2007. Using semantic roles to improve question answering. In *Proceedings of the 2007 joint conference on empirical methods in natural language processing and computational natural language learning (EMNLP-CoNLL)*.

Vinay Singh, Deepanshu Vijay, Syed Sarfaraz Akhtar, and Manish Shrivastava. 2018. Named entity recognition for hindi-english code-mixed social media text. In *Proceedings of the Seventh Named Entities Workshop*, pages 27–35.

Thamar Solorio and Yang Liu. 2008. Part-of-speech tagging for english-spanish code-switched text. In *Proceedings of the Conference on Empirical Methods in Natural Language Processing*, pages 1051–1060. Association for Computational Linguistics.

Mihai Surdeanu, Sanda Harabagiu, John Williams, and Paul Aarseth. 2003. Using predicate-argument structures for information extraction. In *Proceedings of the 41st Annual Meeting of the Association for Computational Linguistics*.

Swabha Swayamdipta, Sam Thomson, Kenton Lee, Luke Zettlemoyer, Chris Dyer, and Noah A Smith. 2018. Syntactic scaffolds for semantic structures. *arXiv preprint arXiv:1808.10485*.

Zhixing Tan, Mingxuan Wang, Jun Xie, Yidong Chen, and Xiaodong Shi. 2018. Deep semantic role labeling with self-attention. In *Thirty-Second AAAI Conference on Artificial Intelligence*.

Kristina Toutanova, Aria Haghighi, and Christopher D Manning. 2008. A global joint model for semantic role labeling. *Computational Linguistics*, 34(2):161–191.

Ashwini Vaidya, Jinho D Choi, Martha Palmer, and Bhuvana Narasimhan. 2011. Analysis of the hindi proposition bank using dependency structure. In *Proceedings of the 5th Linguistic Annotation Workshop*, pages 21–29. Association for Computational Linguistics.

Ashwini Vaidya, Jinho D Choi, Martha Palmer, and Bhuvana Narasimhan. 2012. Empty argument insertion in the hindi propbank. In *LREC*, pages 1522–1526.

Ashwini Vaidya, Samar Husain, Prashanth Mannem, and Dipti Misra Sharma. 2009. A karaka based annotation scheme for english. In *International Conference on Intelligent Text Processing and Computational Linguistics*, pages 41–52. Springer.

Ashwini Vaidya, Martha Palmer, and Bhuvana Narasimhan. 2013. Semantic roles for nominal predicates: Building a lexical resource. In *Proceedings of the 9th Workshop on Multiword Expressions*, pages 126–131.

Yogarshi Vyas, Spandana Gella, Jatin Sharma, Kalika Bali, and Monojit Choudhury. 2014. Pos tagging of english-hindi code-mixed social media content. In *Proceedings of the 2014 Conference on Empirical Methods in Natural Language Processing (EMNLP)*, pages 974–979.

Nianwen Xue and Martha Palmer. 2009. Adding semantic roles to the chinese treebank. *Natural Language Engineering*, 15(1):143–172.

Jie Zhou and Wei Xu. 2015. End-to-end learning of semantic role labeling using recurrent neural networks. In *Proceedings of the 53rd Annual Meeting of the Association for Computational Linguistics and the 7th International Joint Conference on Natural Language Processing (Volume 1: Long Papers)*, volume 1, pages 1127–1137.

A Multi-Platform Annotation Ecosystem for Domain Adaptation

Richard Eckart de Castilho♣, Nancy Ide♠, Jin-Dong Kim♡,
Jan-Christoph Klie♣, Keith Suderman♠
♣Ubiquitous Knowledge Processing (UKP) Lab, Department of Computer Science,
Technische Universität Darmstadt, Darmstadt, Germany
♠Department of Computer Science, Vassar College, Poughkeepsie, New York USA
♡Database Center for Life Science, Research Organization of Information and Systems,
Kashiwa-shi, Chiba, Japan

Abstract

This paper describes an ecosystem consisting of three independent text annotation platforms. To demonstrate their ability to work in concert, we illustrate how to use them to address an interactive domain adaptation task in biomedical entity recognition. The platforms and the approach are in general domain-independent and can be readily applied to other areas of science.

1 Introduction

The rapidly growing appearance rate of biomedical publications has increased interest in applying natural language processing (NLP) and machine learning (ML) technologies to navigate the massive volumes of biomedical literature. In particular, the use of *text annotation* to better automate knowledge extraction and identify relevant information in the literature has become an increasingly major activity over the past decade.

Numerous platforms and frameworks that support text annotation have been developed, including the General Architecture for Text Engineering (GATE (Cunningham et al., 2013)), CLARIN WebLicht (Hinrichs et al., 2010), the Language Applications (LAPPS) Grid (Ide et al., 2014), OpenMinTeD (Labropoulou et al., 2018), and several systems based on the Unstructured Information Management Architecture (UIMA (Ferrucci et al., 2009)), e.g. ARGO (Rak et al., 2013), Apache cTAKES (Savova et al., 2010), DKPro Core (Eckart de Castilho and Gurevych, 2014). However, due to factors such as the often highly domain-specific vocabularies in specialized areas of science, these frameworks are rarely usable out-of-the-box. As a result, scholars interested in mining publications may spend considerable effort to adapt existing annotation tools and resources to their particular domains of research (e.g., tune

them to domain-specific terminology), a process referred to as *domain adaptation*.

Machine-assisted interactive annotation (also known as *human-in-the-loop* annotation) is a recognized means to support domain adaptation, by enabling the rapid creation of benchmark annotation data for specialized domains, which can be used for training or adapting annotation models and evaluating their performance. This process requires several capabilities, including ready access to (1) relevant document repositories, (2) retrainable NLP tools (e.g., named entity recognizers), and (3) sophisticated annotation editors that integrate retraining into the interactive annotation process. However, because all of these capabilities are not available within any single text mining platform, the researcher must use multiple platforms and tools. And although tools and resources may be interoperable within a single platform, combining tools and resources across platforms can demand substantial computational expertise.

One approach to solve this problem would be to develop a monolithic framework that incorporates all of the requisite functionalities. Our solution is instead to interconnect three independently developed platforms, each of which supports some aspect(s) of the domain adaptation process, but none of which provides the entire suite of required tools and resources. This necessitates adaptations to achieve *interoperability* among them–i.e., to be able to exchange data among the platforms without the need for explicit conversion.

In this paper, we describe three platforms that constitute our annotation ecosystem, as background for a demonstration of their ability to work in concert to provide easily usable means to adapt NLP processes to specific domains. Our focus is on the use of the ecosystem to address text mining in the biomedical domain, but the strategies outlined are readily applied to other areas of science.

Proceedings of the 13th Linguistic Annotation Workshop, pages 189–194
Florence, Italy, August 1, 2019. ©2019 Association for Computational Linguistics

2 Platforms

This section briefly introduces the three platforms comprising our ecosystem (Figure 1). Each represents a particular class of systems: a repository for annotated corpora, an NLP services platform, and an interactive annotation platform. These are introduced as platforms and not as tools as they are designed as open and extensible software systems. All are open source software and users can set up their own installations, e.g. for their own project, lab, or community. Some also run a *canonical* instance accessible to any registered user.

PubAnnotation (**Kim and Wang, 2012**) takes on the role of the annotation repository in our ecosystem. It links all contributed annotations through references to canonical texts. It also supports annotation development coupled with *PubDictionaries*, a similarly open repository of dictionaries (term lexicons, etc.) to which users can add by registering their own dictionaries or modifying those already in the repository; as well as *TextAE*, a browser-based visualizer/editor for text annotation. The service-oriented architecture makes it easy for end-users to customize annotation tools by engaging in the annotation process from start to finish. It consists of a collection of web services and web clients that can interact with other systems through REST APIs and a JSON-based data format. The SPARQL standard is supported and allows searching the linked annotations.

The *LAPPS Grid* (**Ide et al., 2014**) acts as the NLP services platform in our ecosystem. It provides a large collection of NLP tools exposed as web services, together with a variety of commonly used resources (e.g., gold standard corpora). The services and resources are made available via a web-based workflow development engine[1], directly via SOAP calls, and programmatically through Java and Python interfaces. All tools and resources in the *LAPPS Grid* are rendered mutually interoperable via transduction to the JSON-LD LAPPS Grid Interchange Format (*LIF* (Verhagen et al., 2016)) and the Web Service Exchange Vocabulary (*WSEV* (Ide et al., 2016)), both designed to capture fundamental properties of existing annotation models in order to serve as a common *pivot* among them.

INCEpTION (**Klie et al., 2018**) contributes interactive annotation functionality to the ecosys-

tem. The platform can be configured for different annotation tasks through a configurable annotation schema supporting span and relation annotation that can carry different kinds of attributes (string, numeric, boolean, etc.). It connects to external document repositories in order to search and import documents for later annotation. Automatic *recommenders* provide annotation suggestions by connecting to external NLP services or by using internal machine learning libraries. To support domain adaptation, the suggestions can be improved as the user interactively reviews and corrects them. Domain-specific vocabularies can be accessed from external SPARQL endpoints or be managed in an internal RDF knowledge base. By supporting common formats and standards for annotation representation and knowledge representation, *INCEpTION* offers a high level of interoperability. Through its remote API, it can be integrated into external workflows. The implementation is internally using the UIMA CAS (Götz and Suhre, 2004) data model.

To create a domain adaptation ecosystem from these three independent platforms, it is necessary to establish *cross-platform interoperability*, i.e., the ability to exchange data consisting of text and associated annotations among them. This means that the data must be mutually *understandable* at the *data level* (model and schema), either directly or via trivial conversion. It must also be possible to appropriately utilize data from the other platforms within the constraints of their respective architectures. In the present paper, we focus on the cross-platform scenario and on the possible actions that can be taken, while a detailed description of the challenges for interoperability among the three platforms at a more technical level and the implemented solutions is provided by Eckart de Castilho et al. (2019).

3 Domain Adaptation for Biomedical Publications

A principal requirement for effective information mining from biomedical texts is the identification of biologically and clinically relevant concepts, e.g., genes and gene products, diseases, and treatments, in the vast body of available data. Domain adaptation for biomedical texts therefore centers around the development and refining of applications for *named entity recognition* (NER), for which numerous freely available tools exist.

---

[1]`http://galaxy.lappsgrid.org`

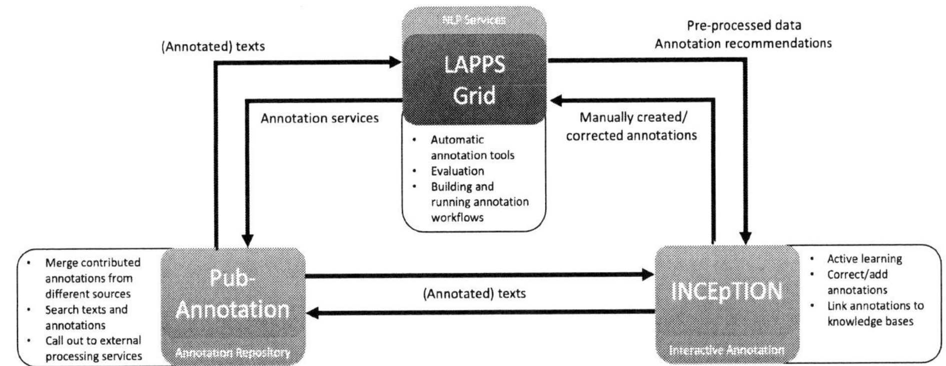

Figure 1: High-level interactions in the tripartite annotation ecosystem

	LAPPS Grid	*PubAnnotation*	*INCEpTION*
BUILD	Build a collection of texts using the *PubAnnotation* datasource or another *LAPPS Grid* datasource	Build a collection of texts from PubMed or PMC	Search an external repository (e.g. *PubAnnotation*) and selectively import relevant texts
ANNOTATE	Perform automatic annotation using one of the *LAPPS Grid*'s NER services	Call out to one of the registered annotation services, e.g. *Pub-Dictionaries* or *LAPPS Grid*'s NER services	Import documents pre-annotated e.g. by *LAPPS Grid* services or *PubAnnotation*
EVALUATE	Compare to another corpus using the *LAPPS Grid* Open Advancement evaluation tools	Compare to another corpus registered in *PubAnnotation*-or- search results using the SPARQL- or keyword-based search interfaces	Compare annotations between users, compute inter-annotator agreement, curate results
REVISE	Edit the annotations using *TextAE* -or- edit dictionary entries externally and re-import to the *LAPPS Grid* for input to dictionary-based NER	Modify/add to the dictionary using *PubDictionaries*-or- edit the annotations using *TextAE*	Edit annotations in *INCEpTION*, optionally assisted by automatic annotation suggestions generated by an embedded ML- or dictionary-based approach, or by calling an external service (e.g., a *LAPPS Grid* NER service)
RE-TRAIN	Re-execute a machine learning algorithm with the newly annotated data, either within the Galaxy history or via direct call to the web service	n/a	When the user makes an edit, automatically retrain embedded approaches or external services if they support it.
REPEAT	Re-execute the appropriate process in the Galaxy history or via direct call to the web service	Re-execute the *PubDictionaries* NER service with revised dictionaries	Re-training and re-processing happens automatically, coupled with updated performance indicators (e.g., F-score)

Table 1: Comparison of supported activities within and across the platforms

Even given the several NER tools and frameworks that have been developed with biomedical entities in mind, including for example the Genia tagger (Tsuruoka et al., 2005), GOST tagger (El-Haj et al., 2018), Termine,[2] the Penn BioTagger[3] (Jin et al., 2006), and OGER++ (Furrer et al., 2019), results are rarely comprehensive and reliable enough to be immediately usable for serious text mining. More importantly, such tools typically cover only very general categories of bioentities, often miss variant bioentity names, and fail to identify newly introduced terms that appear as disciplines progress.

State-of-the-art NER systems employ supervised or semi-supervised machine learning. Supervised learning requires pre-annotated gold standard data from which to learn relevant patterns and features for later annotation of previously unseen data. Semi-supervised learning may also use gold standard annotations, but often relies on information contained in lexicons and ontologies to identify entities in the text. Therefore, adapting

---

[2]http://www.nactem.ac.uk/software/termine/

[3]http://seas.upenn.edu/~strctlrn/BioTagger/BioTagger.html

NER strategies to a new domain or sub-domain may require the manual creation of gold standard data or manual intervention by an expert to correct the output of automatic NER software. The creation and/or augmentation of lexicons and similar supporting resources is also typically necessary in order to provide domain-specific terminology used in semi-supervised settings.

As an example, consider a researcher investigating recent advances in gene interaction research documented in publications from a *document repository* such as PubMed Central. The researcher will typically *build a corpus* by selecting a set of appropriate texts from the repository, but in order to find the desired information, it is necessary to identify mentions of the entities in which he or she is interested. This demands that the researcher *annotates the corpus* by applying an NER text analysis service to identify potential gene mentions in the data. However, even specialized NER tools (Furrer et al., 2019) for the biomedical domain perform at rates of about 0.56 F1-score, at best. At this point, human intervention is required to *revise the annotations* by correcting mis-identified occurrences of gene names as well as annotating gene names that the tagger missed. A sophisticated annotation editor that learns from the user's activity and proposes new annotations or modifications can significantly increase the speed of the correction process. The revised annotations are then used to *re-train a machine learning algorithm* that can be applied to other, unannotated texts; results are evaluated, and the training texts are corrected anew, where necessary, by the human user. The researcher *repeats* this overall cycle as many times as necessary until a satisfactory result is obtained.

Note that there are two human-in-the-loop cycles here: a tight cycle, where a classifier is trained within the annotation editor itself to assist the user, and a larger cycle where a classifier is separately trained and used to annotate the corpus.

The above describes only one possible scenario using the combined functionalities of *PubAnnotation*, the *LAPPS Grid*, and *INCEpTION* to create texts annotated for biomedical entities. The three platforms are mutually interconnectable, and so it is possible to initiate one's corpus building/annotation activity from within any one of them and move to the others as needed, without the need to explicitly export data from one platform and import it to another or convert formats to enable cross-platform communication. Table 1 summarizes the extent to which each platform supports the various steps in the domain adaptation process and how it can interconnect with the other platforms to address a given step. Figure 1 provides a graphic rendering of possible interactions among the platforms.

4 Conclusion

Our goal is to provide an easy-to-use framework to support mining of biomedical publications and, ultimately, scientific publications, by providing an ecosystem that facilitates the rapid development of corpora annotated for phenomena in specific domains and sub-domains. We accomplish this by leveraging the capabilities of three independently developed systems, rather than attempting to develop a single, monolithic system. While monolithic systems tend to be faster to build and are able to better reflect the needs of a particular use case, their maintenance and long-term sustainability is limited by the attention of their developer community. An approach combining the capabilities of multiple platforms reduces the risk of becoming unmaintained. And, even if one platform becomes unavailable or no longer maintained, making them interoperable inherently requires the development of suitable and generic APIs and data formats, which in turn facilitates connecting with new platforms to replace a lost one or expand the overall ecosystem. For users, this means a reduced risk of being locked in to a particular technology and the ability to pick and combine tools best suited for their task from a wider selection.

Acknowledgements

The LAPPS Grid is supported by US National Science Foundation grants NSF-ACI 1147944, NSF-ACI 1147912, NSF-EAGER 181123, and the Andrew K. Mellon Foundation; the LAPPS Grid is also supported by the NSF-funded Jetstream cloud computing environment (Fischer et al., 2015; Towns et al., 2014).

This work was supported by the German Research Foundation under grant No. EC 503/1-1 and GU 798/21-1 (INCEpTION).

PubAnnotation is supported by the Database Integration Coordination Program funded by National Bioscience Database Center (NBDC) of Japan Science and Technology Agency (JST).

References

Richard Eckart de Castilho and Iryna Gurevych. 2014. A broad-coverage collection of portable nlp components for building shareable analysis pipelines. In *Proceedings of the Workshop on Open Infrastructures and Analysis Frameworks for HLT*, pages 1–11, Dublin, Ireland. Association for Computational Linguistics and Dublin City University.

Richard Eckart de Castilho, Nancy Ide, Jin-Dong Kim, Jan-Christoph Klie, and Keith Suderman. 2019. Towards cross-platform interoperability for machine-assisted annotation. page to appear. Genomics Inform.

Hamish Cunningham, Valentin Tablan, Angus Roberts, and Kalina Bontcheva. 2013. Getting More Out of Biomedical Documents with GATE's Full Lifecycle Open Source Text Analytics. *PLoS Computational Biology*, 9(2):e1002854.

Mahmoud El-Haj, Paul Rayson, Scott Piao, and Jo Knight. 2018. Profiling medical journal articles using a gene ontology semantic tagger. In *Proceedings of the Eleventh International Conference on Language Resources and Evaluation (LREC'18)*, pages 4593–4597, Miyazaki, Japan. European Language Resources Association (ELRA).

David Ferrucci, Adam Lally, Karin Verspoor, and Eric Nyberg. 2009. Unstructured information management architecture (UIMA) version 1.0. OASIS Standard.

Jeremy Fischer, Steven Tuecke, Ian Foster, and Craig A. Stewart. 2015. Jetstream: A distributed cloud infrastructure for underresourced higher education communities. In *Proceedings of the 1st Workshop on The Science of Cyberinfrastructure: Research, Experience, Applications and Models*, SCREAM '15, pages 53–61, New York, NY, USA. ACM.

Lenz Furrer, Anna Jancso, Nicola Colic, and Fabio Rinaldi. 2019. Oger++: hybrid multi-type entity recognition. *Journal of Cheminformatics*, 11(1):7.

T. Götz and O. Suhre. 2004. Design and implementation of the UIMA common analysis system. *IBM Systems Journal*, 43(3):476–489.

Marie Hinrichs, Thomas Zastrow, and Erhard Hinrichs. 2010. WebLicht: Web-based LRT Services in a Distributed eScience Infrastructure. In *Proceedings of the Seventh International Conference on Language Resources and Evaluation (LREC'10)*, pages 489–493, Valletta, Malta. European Language Resources Association (ELRA).

Nancy Ide, James Pustejovsky, Christopher Cieri, Eric Nyberg, Di Wang, Keith Suderman, Marc Verhagen, and Jonathan Wright. 2014. The Language Applications Grid. In *Proceedings of the Ninth International Conference on Language Resources and Evaluation (LREC'14)*, pages 22–30, Reykjavik, Iceland. European Language Resources Association (ELRA).

Nancy Ide, Keith Suderman, Marc Verhagen, and James Pustejovsky. 2016. The Language Applications Grid Web Service Exchange Vocabulary. In *Revised Selected Papers of the Second International Workshop on Worldwide Language Service Infrastructure - Volume 9442*, WLSI 2015, pages 18–32, New York, NY, USA. Springer-Verlag New York, Inc.

Yang Jin, Ryan T McDonald, Kevin Lerman, Mark A Mandel, Steven Carroll, Mark Y Liberman, Fernando C Pereira, Raymond S Winters, and Peter S White. 2006. Automated recognition of malignancy mentions in biomedical literature. *BMC Bioinformatics*, 7(492).

Jin-Dong Kim and Yue Wang. 2012. Pubannotation - a persistent and sharable corpus and annotation repository. In *BioNLP: Proceedings of the 2012 Workshop on Biomedical Natural Language Processing*, pages 202–205, Montréal, Canada. Association for Computational Linguistics.

Jan-Christoph Klie, Michael Bugert, Beto Boullosa, Richard Eckart de Castilho, and Iryna Gurevych. 2018. The inception platform: Machine-assisted and knowledge-oriented interactive annotation. In *Proceedings of the 27th International Conference on Computational Linguistics: System Demonstrations*, pages 5–9. Association for Computational Linguistics.

Penny Labropoulou, Dimitris Galanis, Antonis Lempesis, Mark Greenwood, Petr Knoth,

Richard Eckart de Castilho, Stavros Sachtouris, Byron Georgantopoulos, Stefania Martziou, Lucas Anastasiou, Katerina Gkirtzou, Natalia Manola, and Stelios Piperidis. 2018. Openminted: A platform facilitating text mining of scholarly content. In *Proceedings of the Eleventh International Conference on Language Resources and Evaluation (LREC'18)*, Paris, France. European Language Resources Association (ELRA).

Rafal Rak, Andrew Rowley, Jacob Carter, and Sophia Ananiadou. 2013. Development and analysis of nlp pipelines in argo. In *Proceedings of the 51st Annual Meeting of the Association for Computational Linguistics: System Demonstrations*, pages 115–120, Sofia, Bulgaria. Association for Computational Linguistics.

Guergana K. Savova, James J. Masanz, Philip V. Ogren, Jiaping Zheng, Sunghwan Sohn, Karin C. Kipper-Schuler, and Christopher G. Chute. 2010. Mayo clinical text analysis and knowledge extraction system (cTAKES): architecture, component evaluation and applications. *Journal of the American Medical Informatics Association*, 17(5):507–513.

J. Towns, T. Cockerill, M. Dahan, I. Foster, K. Gaither, A. Grimshaw, V. Hazlewood, S. Lathrop, D. Lifka, G. D. Peterson, R. Roskies, J. R. Scott, and N. Wilkins-Diehr. 2014. Xsede: Accelerating scientific discovery. *Computing in Science Engineering*, 16(5):62–74.

Yoshimasa Tsuruoka, Yuka Tateishi, Jin-Dong Kim, Tomoko Ohta, John McNaught, Sophia Ananiadou, and Jun'ichi Tsujii. 2005. Developing a robust part-of-speech tagger for biomedical text. In *Advances in Informatics - 10th Panhellenic Conference on Informatics (PCI 2005), LNCS 3746*, pages 382–392.

Marc Verhagen, Keith Suderman, Di Wang, Nancy Ide, Chunqi Shi, Jonathan Wright, and James Pustejovsky. 2016. The LAPPS Interchange Format. In *Selected Papers of the Second International Workshop on Worldwide Language Service Infrastructure - Volume 9442*, WLSI 2015, pages 33–47, New York, NY, USA. Springer-Verlag New York, Inc.

A New Annotation Scheme for the Sejong Part-of-speech Tagged Corpus

Jungyeul Park
Department of Linguistics
University at Buffalo
jungyeul@buffalo.edu

Francis Tyers
Department of Linguistics
Indiana University
ftyers@indiana.edu

Abstract

In this paper we present a new annotation scheme for the Sejong part-of-speech tagged corpus based on Universal Dependencies style annotation. By using a new annotation scheme, we can produce Sejong-style morphological analysis and part-of-speech tagging results which have been the *de facto* standard for Korean language processing. We also explore the possibility of doing named-entity recognition and semantic-role labelling for Korean using the new annotation scheme.

1 Introduction

In 1998 the Ministry of Culture and Tourism of Korea launched the 21st Century Sejong Project to promote Korean language information processing. The project is named after Sejong the Great who conceived and led the invention of *hangul*, the Korean alphabet. The corpus was released in 2003 and was continually updated until 2011, producing the largest corpus of Korean to date. It includes the several types of texts: historical, contemporary, and parallel texts. The section of contemporary corpora contains both oral and written texts. In this paper we focus on the contemporary written text which is annotated for morphology. This is referred to as the Sejong part-of-speech tagged corpus.

The contents of the Sejong POS-tagged corpus represent a variety of sources: newswire text, magazine articles on various subjects and topics, several book excerpts, and crawled texts from the internet. The current version of the morphologically annotated POS-tagged corpus consists of 279 files with over 802K sentences and 9.2M *eojeols*.[1] The current annotation scheme in the Sejong corpus is exclusively based on the *eojeol* concept. The corpus uses the Sejong tagset that contains 44

---

[1] An *eojeol* is a word separated by blank spaces.

프랑스의	프랑스/NNP+의/JKG	*peurangseu-ui*	'France-GEN'
세계적인	세계/NNG+적/XSN+이/VCP+ㄴ/ETM	*segye-jeok-i-n*	'world class-REL'
의상	의상/NNG	*uisang*	'fashion'
디자이너	디자이너/NNG	*dijaineo*	'designer'
엠마누엘	엠마누엘/NNP	*emmanuel*	'Emanuel'
웅가로가	웅가로/NNP+가/JKS	*unggaro-ga*	'Ungaro-NOM'
실내	실내/NNG	*silnae*	'interior'
장식용	장식용/NNG	*jangsikyong*	'decoration'
직물	직물/NNG	*jikmul*	'textile'
디자이너로	디자이너/NNG+로/JKB	*dijaineo-ro*	'designer-AJT'
나섰다.	나서/VV+었/EP+다/EF+./SF	*naseo-eoss-da.*	'become-PAST-IND-.'

Figure 1: Examples in the Sejong POS tagged corpus: 'The world class French fashion designer Emanuel Ungaro became a designer of interior textile decorations.' (See Table 1 for POS tag information in the Sejong corpus)

POS tags for the entire annotated corpus. Figure 1 shows an example of the annotation in the Sejong POS-tagged corpus.

As the Sejong corpus is the largest annotated corpus of Korean and as it uses a segmentation scheme based on eojeols, most Korean language processing systems have subsequently been developed using this as their basic segmentation scheme. There are many language processing systems based on the eojeol-segmentation schemes, for example: POS tagging (Hong, 2009; Na, 2015; Park et al., 2016) and dependency parsing (Oh, 2009; Oh and Cha, 2010; Park et al., 2013).

There are, however, different segmentation granularity levels — that is, ways to tokenise words in sentences — for Korean which have been independently proposed in previous work as basic units.

This paper explores the Sejong POS-tagged corpus to define a new annotation method for end-to-end morphological analysis and POS tagging. Many upstream applications for Korean language processing are based on a segmentation scheme in which all morphemes are separated. For example Choi et al. (2012) and Park et al. (2016) present work on phrase-structure parsing, and work on statistical machine translation (SMT) is presented by

Proceedings of the 13th Linguistic Annotation Workshop, pages 195–202
Florence, Italy, August 1, 2019. ©2019 Association for Computational Linguistics

Park et al. (2016, 2017), etc. This is done in order to avoid data sparsity, because longer segmentation granularity can combine words in an exponential way.

We propose a new approach to annotation using a morphologically separated word based on the approach for annotating multiword tokens (MWT) in the CoNLL-U format.[2] Using the new annotation scheme, we can also explore tasks beyond POS tagging such as named-entity recognition (NER) and semantic role labelling (SRL). While there are a number of papers looking at NER for Korean (Chung et al., 2003; Yun, 2007), and SRL (Kim et al., 2014)[3], these tasks have hardly been discussed in previous literature on Korean language processing. It has been considered to be difficult to deal with using the current annotation scheme of the Sejong POS corpus because of the limitations of the current eojeol-based annotation and the agglutinative characteristics of the language. For example, for NER, having postpositions attached to the last word in the phrase they modify can make it more difficult to identify the named entity. The annotation scheme we propose (see Figure 3) is also different from the current annotation scheme in Universal Dependencies for Korean morphology, which represents combined morphemes for eojoels (see Figure 4).

2 CoNLL-U Format for Korean

We use CoNLL-U style Universal Dependency (UD) annotation for Korean morphology. We first review the current approaches to annotating Korean in UD and their potential limitations. The CoNLL-U format is a revised version of the previous CoNLL-X format, which contains ten fields from word index to dependency relation to the head. This paper concerns only the morphological annotation: word form, lemma, universal POS tag and language-specific POS tag (Sejong POS tag). The other fields will be annotated either by an underscore which represents not being available or dummy information so that it is well-formed for input into applications that process the CoNLL-U format such as UDPipe (Straka and Straková, 2017).

<hr>

[2] http://universaldependencies.org/format.html

[3] There is also Penn Korean PropBank (https://catalog.ldc.upenn.edu/LDC2006T03)

Sejong POS (S)	description	Universal POS (U)
NNG, NNP, NNB, NR, XR	noun related	NOUN
NNP	proper noun	PROPN
NP	pronoun	PRON
MAG	adverb	ADV
MAJ	conjunctive adverb	CONJ
MM	determiner	DET
VV, VX, VCN, VCP	verb related	VERB
VA	adjective	ADJ
EP, EF, EC, ETN, ETM	verbal endings	PART
JKS, JKC, JKG, JKO, JKB, JKV, JKQ, JX, JC	postpositions (case markers)	ADP
XPN, XSN, XSA, XSV	suffixes	PART
IC	interjection	INTJ
SF, SP, SE, SO, SS	punctuation marks	PUNCT
SW	special characters	X
SH, SL	foreign characters	X
SN	number	NUM
NA, NF, NV	unknown words	X

Table 1: POS tags in the Sejong corpus and their 1-to-1 mapping to Universal POS tags

2.1 Universal POS tags and their mapping

To facilitate future research and to standardize best practices, (Petrov et al., 2012) proposed a tagset of Universal POS categories. The current Universal POS tag mapping for Sejong POS tags is based on a handful of POS patterns of eojeols. However, combinations of words in Korean are very productive and exponential. Therefore, the number of POS patterns of the word does not converge even though the number of words increases. For example, the Sejong treebank contains about 450K words and almost 5K POS patterns. We also test with the Sejong morphologically analysed corpus which contains 9.2M eojeols. The number of POS patterns does not converge and it increases up to over 50K. The wide range of POS patterns is mainly due to the fine-grained morphological analysis, which shows all possible segmentations divided into lexical and functional morphemes. These various POS patterns might indicate useful morpho-syntactic information for Korean. To benefit from the detailed annotation scheme in the Sejong treebank, (Oh et al., 2011) predicted function labels (phrase-level tags) using POS patterns that improve dependency parsing results. Table 1 shows the summary of the Sejong POS tagset and its detailed mapping to the Universal POS tags. Note that we convert the XR (non-autonomous lexical root) into the NOUN because they are mostly considered nouns or a part of a noun:e.g., *minju*/XR ('democracy').

2.2 MWTs in UD

Multiword token (MWT) annotation has been accommodated in the CoNLL-U format, in which MWTs are indexed with ranges from the first token in the word to the last token in the word, e.g. 1-2. These have a value in the word form field, but have an underscore in all the remaining fields. This

	word form	lemma	
verbal ending	ㄴ	은	
	ㄹ지	을지	
case marker	가	이	('NOM')
	를	을	('ACC')
	는	은	('AUX')

Table 2: Suffix normalisation examples

multiword token is then followed by a sequence of words (or morphemes). For example, a Spanish MWT *vámonos* ('let's go') from the sentence *vámonos al mar* ('let's go to the sea') is represented in the CoNLL-U format as in Figure 2a.[4] *Vámonos* which is the first-person plural present imperative of *ir* ('go') consists of *vamos* and *nos* in MWT-style annotation. In this way, we annotate the Korean eojeol as MWTs. Figure 2b shows that *naseossda* ('became') in Korean can also be represented as MWTs, and all morphemes including a verb stem and inflectional-modal suffixes are separated. Sag et al. (2002) defined the various kinds of MWTs, and Salehi et al. (2016) presented an approach to determine MWT types even with no explicit prior knowledge of MWT patterns in a given language. (Çöltekin, 2016) describes a set of heuristics for determining when to annotate individual morphemes as features or separate syntactic words in Turkish. The two main criteria are (1) does the word enter into a labelled syntactic relation with another word in the sentence (e.g. obviating the need for a special relation for derivation); and (2) does the addition of the morpheme entail possible feature class (e.g. two different values for the `Number` feature in the same syntactic word).

3   A New Annotation Scheme

This section describes a new annotation scheme for Korean. We propose a conversion method for the existing UD-style annotation of the Sejong POS tagged corpus to the new scheme.

3.1   Conversion scheme

The conversion is straightforward. For one-morpheme words, we convert them into word index, word form, lemma, universal POS tag and

(a) *vámonos* ('let's go')

(b) *naseossda* ('became')

Figure 2: Examples of MWTs in UD

Sejong POS tag. For multiple-morpheme words, we convert them as described in §2.2: word index ranges and word form followed by lines of morpheme form, lemma, universal POS tag and Sejong POS tag. For the lemma of suffixes, we use the Penn Korean treebank-style (Han et al., 2002) suffix normalisation as described in Table 2. The whole conversion table is provided in Appendix A. Figure 3 shows an example of the proposed CoNLL-U format for the Sejong POS tagged corpus. As previously proposed for Korean Universal Dependencies, we separate punctuation marks from the word in order to tokenize them, which is the only difference from the original Sejong corpus which is exclusively based on the eojeol (that is, punctuation is attached to the word that precedes it). One of the main problems in the Sejong POS tagged corpus is ambiguous annotation of symbols usually tagged with SF, SP, SE, SO, SS, SW. For example, the full stop in *naseo*/VV + *eoss*/EP + *da*/EF + ./SF ('became') and the decimal point in 3/SN + ./SF + 14/SN ('3.14') are not distinguished from each other. We identify symbols whether they are punctuation marks using heuristic rules, and tokenize them. Appendix B details and discusses the tokenisation problem, and how we can further process other symbols.

3.2   Experiments and Results

For our experiments, we automatically convert the Sejong POS-tagged corpus into CoNLL-U style annotation with MWE annotation for eojeols. We evaluate tokenisation, morphological analysis, and POS tagging results using UDPipe (Straka and Straková, 2017). We use the proposed corpus division of the Sejong POS tagged corpus for experiments as described in Appendix C. We obtain 99.88% f_1 score for segmentation and 94.75% accuracy for POS tagging for language specific POS tags (Sejong tag sets). Previously, Na (2015) obtained 97.90% and 94.57% for segmentation and POS tagging respectively using the same Sejong corpus. While we outperform the previous results

---

[4]The example copied from `http://universaldependencies.org/format.html`

```
# sent_id = BTAA0001-00000012
# text = 프랑스의 세계적인 의상 디자이너 엠마누엘 웅가로가 실내 장식용 직물 디자이너로 나섰다.
1-2     프랑스의     -        -       -      -    -              peurangseu-ui ('France-GEN')
1       프랑스       프랑스    PROPN   NNP    -                   peurangseu ('France')
2       의          의        ADP     JKG    -                   -ui ('-GEN')
3-6     세계적인     -        -       -      -    -              segye-jeok-i-n ('world class-REL')
3       세계         세계      NOUN    NNG    -                   segye ('world')
4       적          적        PART    XSN    -                   -jeok ('-SUF')
5       이          이        VERB    VCP    -                   -i ('-COP')
6       ㄴ          은        PART    ETM    -                   -n ('-REL')
7       의상         의상      NOUN    NNG    -                   uisang ('fashion')
8       디자이너     디자이너   NOUN    NNG    -                   dijaineo ('designer')
9       엠마누엘     엠마누엘   PROPN   NNP    -                   emmanuel ('Emanuel')
10-11   웅가로가     -        -       -      -    -              unggaro-ga ('Ungaro-NOM')
10      웅가로       웅가로     PROPN   NNP    -                   unggaro ('Ungaro')
11      가          가        ADP     JKS    -                   -ga ('-NOM')
12      실내         실내      NOUN    NNG    -                   silnae ('interior')
13-14   장식용       -        -       -      -    -              jangsikyong ('decoration')
13      장식         장식      NOUN    NNG    -                   jangsik ('decoration')
14      용          용        PART    XSN    -                   -yong ('usage')
15      직물         직물      NOUN    NNG    -                   jikmul ('textile')
16-17   디자이너로   -        -       -      -    -              dijaineo-ro ('designer-AJT')
16      디자이너     디자이너   NOUN    NNG    -                   dijaineo ('designer')
17      로          로        ADP     JKB    -                   -ro ('-AJT')
18-20   나섰다       -        -       -      SpaceAfter=No       naseo-eoss-da ('become-PAST-IND')
18      나서         나서      VERB    VV     -                   naseo ('become')
19      었          었        PART    EP     -                   -eoss ('PAST')
20      다          다        PART    EF     -                   -da ('-IND')
21      .           .         PUNCT   SF     -
```

Figure 3: The proposed CoNLL-U style annotation with multi-word tokens (MWT) for morphological analysis and POS tagging: a glossed example in provided in Figure 1.

including Na (2015), it would not be the fair to make a direct comparison because the previous results used a different size of the Sejong corpus and a different division of the corpus.[5] (Jung et al., 2018) showed 97.08% f_1 score for their results (instead of accuracy). They are measured by the entire sequence of morphemes because of their seq2seq model. Our accuracy is based on a word level measurement.

3.3 Comparison with the current UD annotation

There are currently two Korean treebanks available in UD v2.2: the Google Korean Universal Dependency Treebank (McDonald et al., 2013) and the KAIST Korean Universal Dependency Treebank (Chun et al., 2018). For the lemma and language-specific POS tag fields, they use annotation concatenation using the plus sign as shown in Figure 4. We note that Sejong and KAIST tag sets are used as language-specific POS tags, re-

spectively. However, while the current CoNLL-U style UD annotation for Korean can simulate and yield POS tagging annotation of the Sejong corpus, they cannot deal with NER or SRL tasks as we propose in §4. For example, a word like *peurangseuui* ('of France') is segmented and analysed into *peurangseu*/PROPER NOUN and *ui*/GEN. The current UD annotation for Korean makes the lemma *peurangseu+ui* and makes NNP+JKG language-specific POS tag, from which we can produce Sejong style POS tagging annotation: *peurangseu*/NNP+*ui*/JKG. While a named entity *peurangseu* ('France') should be recognised independently, UD annotation for Korean does not have any way to identify entities by themselves without case markers. In addition, as we described in §2.1 the number of POS patterns of the word which is used in the language-specific POS tag field does not converge. Recall that the language-specific POS tag is the sequence of concatenated POS tags such as NNP+JKG or NNG+XSN+VCP+ETM. The number of these POS patterns is exponential because of the agglutinative nature of words in Korean. However, it can be a serious problem for system implementation if we want to deal with the entire Sejong corpus

---

[5]Previous work often used cross validation or a corpus split without specific corpus-splitting guidelines. This makes it difficult to correctly compare the POS tagging results. For future reference and to be able to reproduce the results, we propose an explicit-split method for the Sejong POS tagged corpus in Appendix C.

1	프랑스의	프랑스+의	PROPN	NNP+JKG	-
2	세계적인	세계+적+이+ㄴ	NOUN	NNG+XSN+VCP+ETM	-
3	의상	의상	NOUN	NNG	-
4	디자이너	디자이너	NOUN	NNG	-
5	엠마누엘	엠마누엘	PROPN	NNP	-
6	웅기로기	웅가로+가	PROPN	NNP+JKS	-
7	실내	실내	NOUN	NNG	-
8	장식용	장식+용	NOUN	NNG+XSN	-
9	직물	직물	NOUN	NNG	-
10	디자이너로	디자이너+로	NOUN	NNG+JKB	-
11	나섰다	나서+었+다	VERB	VV+EP+EF	SpaceAfter=No
12	.	.	PUNCT	SF	

Figure 4: The current CoNLL-U style UD annotation for Korean. It is based on other agglutinative languages such as Finnish and Hungarian in Universal Dependencies. It separates punctuation marks for tokenisation.

which contains over 50K tags and tag combinations.[6]

4 Discussion on Moving Beyond POS Tagging

Named entity recognition and semantic-role labelling for Korean have hardly been explored compared to other NLP tasks mainly because they are difficult to deal with using the current annotation scheme of the Sejong corpus or other Korean language related corpora such the KAIST treebank (Choi et al., 1994) and the Penn Korean treebank (Han et al., 2002). It is an eojeol-based annotation problem of agglutinative language characteristics without the sequence level morpheme's boundary. For example, a named entity *emmanuel unggaro* without a nominative case marker instead of *emmanuel unggaro-ga* ('Emanuel Ungaro-NOM') should be dealt with for NER. Using the proposed annotation scheme, we can deal with these problems directly using sequence labelling algorithms. This section describes possible annotation for NER and SRL using the new annotation scheme for Korean.

Because of the characteristics of agglutinative languages previous work on NER (Chung et al., 2003; Yun, 2007) or SLR (Kim et al., 2014) used the sequence of morphemes which can be viewed as being similar to our approach for morpheme-wise aspects. However, our approach uses CoNLL-U style annotation which can be used for upstream tasks such as dependency parsing, semantic parsing, etc. These tasks usually share the same CoNLL-like format. Figure 5 shows an example of NER annotation for Korean. It contains following labels:

- B-Entity: beginning of the entity

---

[6]It increases the search space and may have out of memory problem.

1-2	프랑스의	-	-	-	-
1	프랑스	프랑스	PROPN	NNP	**B-LOC**
2	의	의	ADP	JKG	-
3-6	세계적인	-	-	-	-
7	의상	의상	NOUN	NNG	-
8	디자이너	디자이너	NOUN	NNG	-
9	엠마누엘	엠마누엘	PROPN	NNP	**B-PER**
10-11	웅가로가	-	-	-	-
10	웅가로	웅가로	PROPN	NNP	**I-PER**
11	가	가	ADP	JKS	-
12	실내	실내	NOUN	NNG	-
...					
18-20	나섰다	-	-	-	SpaceAfter=No
...					

Figure 5: NER annotation example

...					
9	엠마누엘	엠마누엘	PROPN	NNP	**B-arg$_0$**
10-11	웅가로가	-	-	-	-
10	웅가로	웅가로	PROPN	NNP	**I-arg$_0$**
11	가	가	ADP	JKS	**B-case$_0$**
...					
15	직물	직물	NOUN	NNG	**B-arg$_1$**
16-17	디자이너로	-	-	-	-
16	디자이너	디자이너	NOUN	NNG	**I-arg$_1$**
17	로	로	ADP	JKB	**B-case$_1$**
18-20	나섰다	-	-	-	SpaceAfter=No
18	나서	나서	VERB	VV	**Frame**
...					

Figure 6: SRL annotation example

- I-Entity: inside of the entity

where Entity can be Person, Location, Organisation and other user-defined labels. Figure 6 shows an example of SRL annotation for Korean. It contains following labels:

- B-arg$_x$: beginning of the argument x
- I-arg$_x$: inside of the argument x
- B-case$_x$: beginning of the functional morpheme (*e.g.* case marker) of the argument x
- I-case$_x$: inside of the functional morpheme of the argument x
- Frame: predicate

5 Conclusion

In this paper we have explored the Sejong corpus in order to determine best practices for Korean natural-language processing. We have defined a standard corpus division for training and testing and have tested POS tagging and syntactic parsing. In addition we have proposed a new tokenisation scheme and applied it to the corpus.

One of the other advantages of our approach is that it is compatible with universal morphological lattices (More et al., 2018), which can be easily converted. Language resources including the scripts and POS tagging models presented in this paper will be freely available (Appendix §D).

References

Anne Abeillé, Lionel Clément, and François Toussenel. 2003. Building a Treebank for French. In Anne Abeillé, editor, *Treebanks: Building and Using Parsed Corpora*, pages 165–188. Kluwer.

DongHyun Choi, Jungyeul Park, and Key-Sun Choi. 2012. Korean Treebank Transformation for Parser Training. In *Proceedings of the ACL 2012 Joint Workshop on Statistical Parsing and Semantic Processing of Morphologically Rich Languages*, pages 78–88, Jeju, Republic of Korea. Association for Computational Linguistics.

Jinho D. Choi and Martha Palmer. 2011. Statistical Dependency Parsing in Korean: From Corpus Generation To Automatic Parsing. In *Proceedings of the Second Workshop on Statistical Parsing of Morphologically Rich Languages*, pages 1–11, Dublin, Ireland. Association for Computational Linguistics.

Key-Sun Choi, Young S Han, Young G Han, and Oh W Kwon. 1994. KAIST Tree Bank Project for Korean: Present and Future Development. In *Proceedings of the International Workshop on Sharable Natural Language Resources*, pages 7–14, Nara Institute of Science and Technology. Nara Institute of Science and Technology.

Jayeol Chun, Na-Rae Han, Jena D. Hwang, and Jinho D. Choi. 2018. Building Universal Dependency Treebanks in Korean. In *Proceedings of the Eleventh International Conference on Language Resources and Evaluation (LREC 2018)*, Miyazaki, Japan. European Language Resources Association (ELRA).

Euisok Chung, Yi-Gyu Hwang, and Myung-Gil Jang. 2003. Korean Named Entity Recognition using HMM and CoTraining Model. In *Proceedings of the Sixth International Workshop on Information Retrieval with Asian Languages*, pages 161–167, Sapporo, Japan. Association for Computational Linguistics.

Çağrı Çöltekin. 2016. (When) do we need inflectional groups? In *Proceedings of The First International Conference on Turkic Computational Linguistics (TurCLing 2016)*, pages 38–43, Konya, Turkey.

Chung-Hye Han, Na-Rae Han, Eon-Suk Ko, Martha Palmer, and Heejong Yi. 2002. Penn Korean Treebank: Development and Evaluation. In *Proceedings of the 16th Pacific Asia Conference on Language, Information and Computation*, pages 69–78, Jeju, Korea. Pacific Asia Conference on Language, Information and Computation.

Jeen-Pyo Hong. 2009. Korean Part-Of-Speech Tagger using Eojeol Patterns.

Sangkeun Jung, Changki Lee, and Hyunsun Hwang. 2018. End-to-End Korean Part-of-Speech Tagging Using Copying Mechanism. *ACM Transactions on Asian and Low-Resource Language Information Processing (TALLIP)*, 17(3):19:1–19:8.

Young-Bum Kim, Heemoon Chae, Benjamin Snyder, and Yu-Seop Kim. 2014. Training a Korean SRL System with Rich Morphological Features. In *Proceedings of the 52nd Annual Meeting of the Association for Computational Linguistics (Volume 2: Short Papers)*, pages 637–642, Baltimore, Maryland. Association for Computational Linguistics.

Do-Gil Lee and Hae-Chang Rim. 2009. Probabilistic Modeling of Korean Morphology. *IEEE Transactions on Audio Speech and Language Processing*, 17(5):945–955.

Mitchell P. Marcus, Mary Ann Marcinkiewicz, and Beatrice Santorini. 1993. Building a Large Annotated Corpus of English: The Penn Treebank. *Computational linguistics*, 19(2):313–330.

Ryan McDonald, Joakim Nivre, Yvonne Quirmbach-Brundage, Yoav Goldberg, Dipanjan Das, Kuzman Ganchev, Keith Hall, Slav Petrov, Hao Zhang, Oscar Täckström, Claudia Bedini, Núria Bertomeu Castelló, and Jungmee Lee. 2013. Universal Dependency Annotation for Multilingual Parsing. In *Proceedings of the 51st Annual Meeting of the Association for Computational Linguistics (Volume 2: Short Papers)*, pages 92–97, Sofia, Bulgaria. Association for Computational Linguistics.

Amir More, Özlem Çetinoğlu, Çağrı Çöltekin, Nizar Habash, Benoît Sagot, Djamé Seddah, Dima Taji, and Reut Tsarfaty. 2018. CoNLL-UL: Universal Morphological Lattices for Universal Dependency Parsing. In *Proceedings of the Eleventh International Conference on Language Resources and Evaluation (LREC 2018)*, Paris, France. European Language Resources Association (ELRA).

Seung-Hoon Na. 2015. Conditional Random Fields for Korean Morpheme Segmentation and POS Tagging. *ACM Transactions on Asian and Low-Resource Language Information Processing*, 14(3):1–10

Jin-Young Oh. 2009. *Robust Korean Dependency Parsing Using Cascaded Chunking*. Ph.D. thesis, Changwon National University.

Jin-Young Oh and Jeong-Won Cha. 2010. High Speed Korean Dependency Analysis Using Cascaded Chunking. *Korean Simulation Journal*, 19(1):103–111.

Jin-Young Oh, Yo-Sub Han, Jungyeul Park, and Jeong-Won Cha. 2011. Predicting Phrase-Level Tags Using Entropy Inspired Discriminative Models. In *International Conference on Information Science and Applications (ICISA) 2011*, pages 1–5, Jeju, Korea. Information Science and Applications (ICISA).

Jungyeul Park, Loic Dugast, Jeen-Pyo Hong, Chang-Uk Shin, and Jeong-Won Cha. 2017. Building a Better Bitext for Structurally Different Languages through Self-training. In *Proceedings of the First Workshop on Curation and Applications of Parallel and Comparable Corpora*, pages 1–10, Taipei,

Taiwan. Asian Federation of Natural Language Processing.

Jungyeul Park, Jeen-Pyo Hong, and Jeong-Won Cha. 2016. Korean Language Resources for Everyone. In *Proceedings of the 30th Pacific Asia Conference on Language, Information and Computation: Oral Papers (PACLIC 30)*, pages 49–58, Seoul, Korea. Pacific Asia Conference on Language, Information and Computation.

Jungyeul Park, Daisuke Kawahara, Sadao Kurohashi, and Key-Sun Choi. 2013. Towards Fully Lexicalized Dependency Parsing for Korean. In *Proceedings of The 13th International Conference on Parsing Technologies (IWPT 2013)*, Nara, Japan. International Conference on Parsing Technologies (IWPT 2013).

Jungyeul Park, Sejin Nam, Youngsik Kim, Younggyun Hahm, Dosam Hwang, and Key-Sun Choi. 2014. Frame-Semantic Web : a Case Study for Korean. In *Proceedings of ISWC 2014 : International Semantic Web Conference 2014 (Posters and Demonstrations Track)*, pages 257–260, Riva del Garda, Italy. International Semantic Web Conference.

Slav Petrov, Dipanjan Das, and Ryan McDonald. 2012. A Universal Part-of-Speech Tagset. In *Proceedings of the Eighth International Conference on Language Resources and Evaluation (LREC-2012)*, pages 2089–2096, Istanbul, Turkey. European Language Resources Association (ELRA).

Ivan A. Sag, Timothy Baldwin, Francis Bond, Ann A. Copestake, and Dan Flickinger. 2002. Multiword Expressions: A Pain in the Neck for NLP. In *Proceedings of the Third International Conference on Computational Linguistics and Intelligent Text Processing*, CICLing '02, pages 1–15, London, UK, UK. Springer-Verlag.

Bahar Salehi, Paul Cook, and Timothy Baldwin. 2016. Determining the Multiword Expression Inventory of a Surprise Language. In *Proceedings of COLING 2016, the 26th International Conference on Computational Linguistics: Technical Papers*, pages 471–481, Osaka, Japan. The COLING 2016 Organizing Committee.

Djamé Seddah, Reut Tsarfaty, Sandra Kübler, Marie Candito, Jinho D. Choi, Richárd Farkas, Jennifer Foster, Iakes Goenaga, Koldo Gojenola Galletebeitia, Yoav Goldberg, Spence Green, Nizar Habash, Marco Kuhlmann, Wolfgang Maier, Joakim Nivre, Adam Przepiórkowski, Ryan Roth, Wolfgang Seeker, Yannick Versley, Veronika Vincze, Marcin Woliński, Alina Wróblewska, and Eric Villemonte de la Clergerie. 2013. Overview of the SPMRL 2013 Shared Task: A Cross-Framework Evaluation of Parsing Morphologically Rich Languages. In *Proceedings of the Fourth Workshop on Statistical Parsing of Morphologically-Rich Languages*, pages 146–182, Seattle, Washington, USA. Association for Computational Linguistics.

Milan Straka and Jana Straková. 2017. Tokenizing, POS Tagging, Lemmatizing and Parsing UD 2.0 with UDPipe. In *Proceedings of the CoNLL 2017 Shared Task: Multilingual Parsing from Raw Text to Universal Dependencies*, pages 88–99, Vancouver, Canada. Association for Computational Linguistics.

Bo-Hyun Yun. 2007. HMM-Based Korean Named Entity Recognition for Information Extraction. In *Knowledge Science, Engineering and Management*, pages 526–531, Berlin, Heidelberg. Springer Berlin Heidelberg.

A   A Full List of Suffix Conversions

This appendix provides a full list of Penn Korean treebank (KTB)-style suffix conversions. Note that in the the Sejong-style the surface form of the morpheme is used, while in the KTB-style annotation a generic form is used (like a lemma) which is normalised with respect to allomorphy.

Sejong-style 'word form'	KTB-style normalised 'lemma'	Sejong-style 'word form'	KTB-style normalised 'lemma'
아/EC	어/EC	와/JC	과/JC
았/EP	었/EP	나/JC	이나/JC
ㄴ/ETM	은/ETM	와/JKB	과/JKB
ㄹ/ETM	을/ETM	로/JKB	으로/JKB
ㄹ지/EC	을지/EC	를/JKO	을/JKO
아서/EC	어서/EC	가/JKS	이/JKS
아야/EC	어야/EC	는/JX	은/JX
면서/EC	으면서/EC	ㄴ/JX	은/JX
ㄴ다/EF	는다/EF		
ㄴ다고/EC	은다고/EC		
Verbal endings		Case markers	

B   Tokenisation and Rough Entity Detection

Since the annotation scheme in the Sejong corpus is exclusively based on the eojeol, most Korean NLP systems have been developed based on eojeols as their segmentation scheme. Therefore, the problem of tokenisation of Korean has often been ignored in the literature. However, there are also other word segmentation schemes for Korean as described in the Korean Penn treebank (Han et al., 2002). Korean dependency parsing (Choi and Palmer, 2011), Korean FrameNet (Park et al., 2014) and Korean UDs (Chun et al., 2018) have used the Penn treebank-style tokenisation scheme, in which punctuation marks are separated from the word.

For Korean tokenisation, we separate all punctuation marks in the eojeol by identifying whether symbols are punctuation marks or not. Therefore, entities such as numbers with the decimal point (*3.14*), email addresses (*name@email.com*), web address (*http://www.web.info*), dates (*25/9/2017*), etc. can be presented as a single token while punctuation marks are separated from the eojeol. This idea was originally proposed by (Choi et al., 2012)

	train	dev	test
# of sent	604,390	35,870	36,691
# of tok	16,024,170	895,544	907,290

Table 3: Corpus statistics

to improve constituent parsing results by grouping possible entities. The punctuation mark is separated from the word and the corresponding word is annotated with `SpaceAfter=No`. The tokenisation script from the Sejong corpus will be provided through the DOI system.

C Where to Train and Evaluate?

Other languages such as English and French have standard training/development/test divisions, especially for the purposes of parsing. For example, the English Penn treebank (Marcus et al., 1993) uses Sections 02-21 for the training set, Section 22 for the development set, and Section 23 for the test set. The French treebank (Abeillé et al., 2003) also defines its own treebank splits for training and evaluation (Seddah et al., 2013). For POS tagging using the Sejong corpus, (Hong, 2009; Lee and Rim, 2009) used 10-fold cross-validation, and (Na, 2015) used 80-20 training/test data sets. We propose to use common treebank 15 files as a test data set and their nearest files can be used as a development data set for the Korean POS tagging task. Since BGAA001 is in the treebank, BTAA0001 in the POS tagging corpus would be a part of the test data, and its nearest file BTAA0002 is a part of the development data. Table 4 provides the entire list of test and development files. In this way, we have a standard evaluation data set for POS tagging, and a similar type of the development data set for system tuning regardless of a variety of sources in the Sejong corpus. The remaining 249 files can be used as a training data set. Table 3 shows the brief statistics of the split corpus.

D Conversion Tools

We provide scripts to convert the original POS tagged Sejong corpus in XML into the CoNLL-U format (without syntactic annotation) for Korean. We verify the POS tagging format, and remove sentences which contain words with tagging format errors. Note that the script checks only annotation format errors, not analysis errors.

treebank files	pos tagging (test)	pos tagging (dev)
BGAA0001.txt	BTAA0001.txt	BTAA0002.txt
BGAA0164.txt	BTAA0164.txt	BTAA0165.txt
BGAE0200.txt	BTAE0200.txt	BTAE0201.txt
BGBZ0073.txt	BTBZ0073.txt	BTBZ0074.txt
BGEO0077.txt	BTEO0077.txt	BTEO0078.txt
BGEO0292.txt	BTEO0292.txt	BTEO0293.txt
BGEO0320.txt	BTEO0320.txt	BTEO0321.txt
BGGO0098.txt	BTGO0098.txt	BTGO0096.txt
BGGO0358.txt	BTGO0358.txt	BTGO0359.txt
BGHO0107.txt	BTHO0107.txt	BTHO0108.txt
BGHO0127.txt	BTHO0127.txt	BTHO0128.txt
BGHO0409.txt	BTHO0409.txt	BTHO0406.txt
BGHO0411.txt	BTHO0411.txt	BTHO0412.txt
BGHO0431.txt	BTHO0431.txt	BTHO0432.txt
BGHO0437.txt	BTHO0437.txt	BTHO0439.txt

Table 4: A list of test and development files for POS tagging

The script and the POS tagging model is available at `https://github.com/jungyeul/sjmorph`.

A Turkish Dataset for Gender Identification of Twitter Users

Erhan Sezerer
İzmir Institute of Technology,
Computer Engineering,
İzmir, Turkey
erhansezerer@iyte.edu.tr

Ozan Polatbilek
İzmir Institute of Technology,
Computer Engineering,
İzmir, Turkey
ozanpolatbilek
@iyte.edu.tr

Selma Tekir
İzmir Institute of Technology,
Computer Engineering,
İzmir, Turkey
selmatekir@iyte.edu.tr

Abstract

Author profiling is the identification of an author's gender, age, and language from his/her texts. With the increasing trend of using Twitter as a means to express thought, profiling the gender of an author from his/her tweets has become a challenge. Although several datasets in different languages have been released on this problem, there is still a need for multilingualism. In this work, we propose a dataset of tweets of Turkish Twitter users which are labeled with their gender information. The dataset has 3368 users in the training set and 1924 users in the test set where each user has 100 tweets. The dataset is publicly available[1].

1 Introduction

Author profiling is the characterization of an author through some key dimensions such as gender, age, and language. Among these profiling tasks, gender identification is different from authorship attribution problem in that it is a higher level abstraction, unlike authorship attribution where the candidate set of authors is unavailable a priori (Cheng et al., 2011). In gender identification from tweets, the difficulty lies in working with short text messages rather than using traditional text documents. Further, tweets are informal in their nature. Moreover, social media users have a tendency to hide their identity, to fake gender information. Thus, gender identification from the tweets of Twitter users is a challenging problem.

Author profiling is organized as a shared task in the PAN Workshop series as part of the CLEF conferences. The shared task releases a corpus and an evaluation framework to provide a lab environment to participants and measure their performances. In PAN 2013, the problem is stated as to identify age and gender from anonymous texts that

are in English and Spanish (Pardo et al., 2013). A similar corpus construction effort takes place as part of the PAN 2017 task on gender and language variety identification in Twitter. In terms of methodological novelties; varying language use in tweets by the same user, retweet facility, possibility to retrieve tweets by region, validation through other types of data (photo, profile info, etc.) are considered specific to Twitter (Pardo et al., 2017). Also a dataset for Twitter user gender classification is released in Kaggle in 2015 [2].

There are several works focused on this problem. (Daneshvar and Inkpen, 2018) give Latent Semantic Analysis (LSA)-reduced forms of word and character n-grams into Support Vector Machine (SVM) and achieve state-of-the-art performance on PAN 2018 challenge (Pardo et al., 2018) for gender classification from text. Recently, neural network-based models have been proposed to solve this problem. In literature, CNN (Sezerer et al., 2018) or RNN (Takahashi et al., 2018), (Kodiyan et al., 2017) is used on this task. In the PAN 2018 challenge, using both textual and image data, (Takahashi et al., 2018) obtain state-of-the-art performance by proposing a model architecture where they process text through RNN with GRU cells.

Gender classification problem is addressed in Turkish language as well. (Talebi and Köse, 2013) use Naive Bayes, SVM, and K-nearest neighbour classifiers on a dataset composed of Facebook comments of Turkish users.

In this work, we contribute to the problem of author gender identification by sharing a corpus in Turkish for Twitter user gender classification. Although several datasets in different languages have been released on this problem, there is still a need for multilingualism.

---

[1]https://cloud.iyte.edu.tr/index.php/s/5DhqdlUCCdB60qG

[2]https://www.kaggle.com/crowdflower/twitter-user-gender-classification

Proceedings of the 13th Linguistic Annotation Workshop, pages 203–207
Florence, Italy, August 1, 2019. ©2019 Association for Computational Linguistics

In the remaining part of the paper, in Section 2, we explain the construction of the corpus in detail. Then, in Section 3, we present baseline performances on this dataset. Finally, we conclude the paper with some observations and insights regarding Twitter usage.

2 Dataset

We have compiled a corpus of Twitter for gender classification. Users are annotated as "male" or "female" and the corpus is publicly available.

2.1 Data Collection

In order to have a balanced collection with respect to each gender, we used common names from each gender as search filters (Pardo et al., 2017). In the determination of common names, we referred to websites that suggest names to male/female babies and a name database of Turkish Language Agency (Tr. Türk Dil Kurumu). After constructing the name database, we eliminated names that appear on the name list of both genders and also some names that are known as unisex. In the end, the size of the name database was 507 for female, 589 for male.

We used Twitter Web API[3] to search for names in Twitter. From the resulting set of user accounts that are retrieved from search queries, we selected the ones which have 200 tweets and 20 photos at minimum. The motivation behind this is that in order to identify gender, we need active users who have sufficient number of tweets on their own, and photos are taken to supply a different type of data to help annotators in their task. After retrieving those users, they are auto-labeled by their name's gender category.

Furthermore, in the selection of users we considered the presence of retweets. Since a retweet is not written by the original author, it may belong to a gender other than the user's gender. Thus, we selected those users that have at least 200 tweets of which 100 at minimum are not retweets. As a result, out of 12212 users that are collected from Twitter, only 8211 of them meet this criterion and are available to be labeled by annotators. Since we told annotators not to annotate if they are not sure, only 8071 of them are labeled.

---

[3]developer.twitter.com/en/docs/tweets/search/overview

2.2 Dataset Labeling

To guide the annotators, we have created a set of label categories (0-5) to control for correct/incorrect gender attribute, language of tweets, bot/human account, account belonging to a real individual, and account containing inappropriate content. Some label categories have subcategories to have more specific class labels inside each category for prospective Twitter classification tasks.

To guide the annotators, we have created several labels for users where each label corresponds to the type of rejection or acceptation. The labels are:

"0": If the automatically assigned gender is correct.

"1": If annotator thinks that the automatically assigned gender is wrong. Couples' account also fall into this category since both of them may contribute to the tweets.

"2": If the user mostly uses any language other than Turkish.

"3": If the user is a bot, or tweets are auto-generated texts. Here the definition of bot is extended to include "meaningless texts" (some computer viruses cause an account to generate meaningless texts in order to boost a certain hashtag).

"4a": If the user is a parody account or a sharing account like "funny cats", "funny joke each day" etc.

"4b": If the account is a fan page or an account that pretends to be a celebrity (Annotators are told to check whether the user is a real celebrity on the Internet).

"4c": If the user is a celebrity who doesn't tweet on his/her own (some celebrity or business people create a Twitter account and hire a PR (Public Relations) company to tweet on behalf of them).

"4d": If the user is not a human but a corporate identity (there are non-human accounts, such as company, political party, etc. on Twitter).

"5a": If the user is under 18 (An adult is defined as any person over 18 in Turkey, so if a clue like birthday or high/elementary school information is obtained about users being under-aged, user is discarded).

"5b": If the account has content involving nudity, sex, or prostitution (here nudity doesn't only rely on basic nudity but revealing body parts in favor of prostitution or finding partner).

If an LGBT+ person is found, the user is rejected with code 1 and commented as "neither".

The reason behind is that it's not possible to identify their gender or how they identify themselves by just looking at their tweets and profile pictures. Their status on the Twitter is used to detect whether they identify themselves as LGBT+ or not.

For this labeling task, we asked 22 people who are native speakers to help us. The annotators mostly consist of university students and academic personnel. To guide the annotation process, labels with their detailed descriptions are given to annotators and 400 users are assigned to each of them. The annotators are told to read all tweets of the user and they were able to check their status info and profile picture to be more sure about labeling. The annotators are also told not to label a user if they are not sure about their decision. They were given 6 weeks to finish labeling but to not let them feel pressure, that period is extended to 3 months. To control the consistency of annotations, each annotator is provided with randomly selected 20 users with ground-truth labels and a performance of 80% accuracy was expected on this set to accept his/her labels. The reason behind this threshold is that auto-labels turned out to be approximately 66% accurate on the ground-truth data and as (Nguyen et al., 2014) suggest humans can only achieve approximately 90% accuracy on this subject. So we expect from the annotators to surpass the auto-labels and perform close to 90% with a small margin of error to humans. Only one annotator failed to reach this accuracy, and his/her data are re-assigned to another annotator.

2.3 Post Processing

After the annotation phase, we received feedback from annotators that some accounts tweet some auto-generated texts, such as "az önce bir fotoğraf paylaştı" (eng. "Just shared a photo") or "Günlük istatistiğim, Takipçi: " (eng. "Daily statistics, followers:"). Using these feedbacks, we extracted the specified auto-generated texts and deleted those tweets including them from the dataset. After deletion, users who still have more than 100 tweets on their own are kept in the dataset. Lastly, in order to balance gender classes, some users are randomly discarded from females. Resulting ratio of females in the dataset is 0.53 and the total size of the dataset is 5292. We wanted to keep the test dataset size high (training/test dataset size ratio close to 2) thus we randomly partitioned

Label	number of users	ratio
0	5803	0.718
1	427	0.052
2	111	0.013
3	153	0.018
4a	81	0.010
4b	389	0.048
4c	332	0.041
4d	615	0.076
5a	56	0.006
5b	104	0.012

Table 1: Distribution of labels in the dataset before partitioning

the dataset as a training set of 3368 users and the rest as the test users which are 1924 in total. Additionally, to hide the true identity of the users, the user ids are hashed with the MD5 hash algorithm (Rivest, 1992).

2.4 Findings on Behaviour of Turkish Twitter Users

As can be seen from Table ??, we had to reject approximately 30% (1-5b) of the collected data due to non-human activities or other issues stated previously. This rate is quite higher than we expected and most of the rejections were because of non-real-human accounts (3-4d). This indicates that Twitter is getting more like a medium of advertisement. Moreover, this high rate can be attributed to Twitter's search algorithm. As a result of a search query, Twitter returns highly visible accounts that are related to it. Besides company accounts, since celebrities and people who act like a celebrity have more daily interaction than a regular user, they have a high ranking in the result set of queries.

On the other hand, we rejected more than a half of the total collected data due to insufficient number of tweets. Accounts that have less than 100 tweets of their own are discarded. Our experience in creating a dataset from Twitter shows that one needs to sample twice as much as s/he desires.

Additionally, the rate of bots is approximately 2% which shows that each sampling from the Twitter will have at least 2% noise if not eliminated by hand. This is observed among Turkish users only, it needs to be investigated in other languages.

Baseline Method	Accuracy
Random	0.5000
Bag-of-Words	0.7232

Table 2: Baseline Scores for Proposed Dataset

3 Baselines

To determine what to expect from the dataset, we created some baseline scores. Baselines are methods that define a lower bound for prediction performance. The performances of our baseline methods are given in Table ??.

3.1 Random Baseline

Random Baseline is accepted as a reference point and its score is widely stated in each new dataset release. Random baseline score depends on the number of classes. Since there are two classes in this dataset, random assignment of classes will get approximately 50% accuracy.

3.2 Bag-of-Words

As a more advanced baseline, bag-of-words model is selected to obtain a more realistic lower bound. In the implementation of this baseline, we lower-cased all words and tokenized them with NLTK (Loper and Bird, 2002) tool. Then, stop word removal and term frequency calculation are performed on the training dataset. In the frequency calculation; each mention, hashtag, and URL is labeled as <MENTION>, <HASHTAG>, and <URL> respectively. After getting frequencies, we selected the most frequent 1000 words as bag-of-words and represented all documents as a vector of 1000 frequent words. We used SVM (Cortes and Vapnik, 1995) with linear kernel as a classifier and got an accuracy score of 72.32%.

4 Conclusion

In this work, we propose a new dataset for gender classification from tweets of Twitter users. The language of tweets is Turkish and the dataset is annotated by native Turkish speakers. Random subsets of the annotations are cross-checked to validate the performance of each annotator. The dataset has 3368 users in the training set and 1924 users in the test set where each user has 100 tweets. Additionally, we run the traditional bag-of-words approach with a standard classifier and got 72.32% accuracy score as a baseline.

As a result of this dataset construction experience, we also share some insights and evidences about trends of Turkish Twitter users. We have seen that 17.5% of the users were non-real-human accounts, which shows that Twitter is more than a social media platform for some users. Also nearly 2% of the users were bots, which implies that for a random dataset selection from Twitter, there will be at least 2% noise coming from bot accounts.

Acknowledgments

We would like to thank Onur Keklik, Özge Sevgili Ergüven, Damla Yaşar, Berkay Can, Ceren Atik, İskender Ülgen Oğul, Arif Kürşat Karabayır, Ali Verep, Oğuzhan Öztürk, Mustafa Berkay Özkan, Ahmet Şemsettin Özdemirden, Elif Duran, Hasan Para, Emrah İnan, Cenk Tekir, Zuhal Tekir, Onur Tekir, Algın Poyraz Arslan, and Elgun Jabrayilzade for their great contribution on labeling the dataset.

We also would like to thank anonymous reviewers for their helpful comments and reviews.

The Titan V used for this research was donated by the NVIDIA Corporation.

References

Na Cheng, R. Chandramouli, and K.P. Subbalakshmi. 2011. Author gender identification from text. *Digital Investigation*, 8(1):78 – 88.

Corinna Cortes and Vladimir Vapnik. 1995. Support-vector networks. *Mach. Learn.*, 20(3):273–297.

Saman Daneshvar and Diana Inkpen. 2018. Gender identification in twitter using n-grams and LSA: notebook for PAN at CLEF 2018. In *Working Notes of CLEF 2018 - Conference and Labs of the Evaluation Forum, Avignon, France, September 10-14, 2018*.

Don Kodiyan, Florin Hardegger, Stephan Neuhaus, and Mark Cieliebak. 2017. Author profiling with bidirectional rnns using attention with grus. In *CLEF*.

Edward Loper and Steven Bird. 2002. Nltk: The natural language toolkit. In *Proceedings of the ACL-02 Workshop on Effective Tools and Methodologies for Teaching Natural Language Processing and Computational Linguistics - Volume 1*, ETMTNLP '02, pages 63–70, Stroudsburg, PA, USA. Association for Computational Linguistics.

Dong Nguyen, Dolf Trieschnigg, A. Seza Doğruöz, Rilana Gravel, Mariet Theune, Theo Meder, and Franciska De Jong. 2014. Why gender and age prediction from tweets is hard: Lessons from a crowdsourcing experiment. In *Proceedings of COLING*

2014, the 25th International Conference on Computational Linguistics: Technical Papers, pages 1950–1961. Dublin City University and Association for Computational Linguistics.

Francisco M. Rangel Pardo, Paolo Rosso, Manuel Montes y Gómez, Martin Potthast, and Benno Stein. 2018. Overview of the 6th author profiling task at pan 2018: Multimodal gender identification in twitter. In *CLEF*.

Francisco M. Rangel Pardo, Paolo Rosso, Moshe Koppel, Efstathios Stamatatos, and Giacomo Inches. 2013. Overview of the author profiling task at PAN 2013. In *Working Notes for CLEF 2013 Conference , Valencia, Spain, September 23-26, 2013*.

Francisco Manuel Rangel Pardo, Paolo Rosso, Martin Potthast, and Benno Stein. 2017. Overview of the 5th author profiling task at pan 2017: Gender and language variety identification in twitter. In *CLEF*.

R. Rivest. 1992. The md5 message-digest algorithm.

Erhan Sezerer, Ozan Polatbilek, Özge Sevgili, and Selma Tekir. 2018. Gender prediction from tweets with convolutional neural networks: Notebook for PAN at CLEF 2018. In *Working Notes of CLEF 2018 - Conference and Labs of the Evaluation Forum, Avignon, France, September 10-14, 2018*.

Takumi Takahashi, Takuji Tahara, Koki Nagatani, Yasuhide Miura, Tomoki Taniguchi, and Tomoko Ohkuma. 2018. Text and image synergy with feature cross technique for gender identification: Notebook for PAN at CLEF 2018. In *Working Notes of CLEF 2018 - Conference and Labs of the Evaluation Forum, Avignon, France, September 10-14, 2018*.

M. Talebi and C. Köse. 2013. Identifying gender, age and education level by analyzing comments on facebook. In *2013 21st Signal Processing and Communications Applications Conference (SIU)*, pages 1–4.

Comparative judgments are more consistent than binary classification for labelling word complexity

Sian Gooding, Ekaterina Kochmar, Alan Blackwell
Dept of Computer Science and Technology
University of Cambridge
{shg36|ek358|afb21}@cam.ac.uk

Advait Sarkar
Microsoft Research
Cambridge
advait@microsoft.com

Abstract

Lexical simplification systems replace complex words with simple ones based on a model of which words are complex in context. We explore how users can help train complex word identification models through labelling more efficiently and reliably. We show that using an interface where annotators make comparative rather than binary judgments leads to more reliable and consistent labels, and explore whether comparative judgments may provide a faster way for collecting labels.

1 Introduction

In this paper, we address the use of machine learning (ML) for natural language readability assessment concerned with the identification of factors that affect a reader's understanding, reading speed and level of interest (Dale and Chall, 1949). We focus on *lexical simplification*, which aims to adapt text by replacing contextually complex words with more accessible meaning-equivalent alternatives: e.g. replacing *ameliorate* with *improve* in the context like *"They aimed to* **ameliorate** $\rightarrow$ **improve** *the situation."* Lexical simplification can be framed as a two step procedure, where the algorithm needs to first identify which words (or more specifically word senses) in context require simplification, and then replace them with simpler alternatives. The first step is commonly referred to as *complex word identification* (CWI) (Shardlow, 2013).

In supervised ML, algorithms are trained using data that is labelled according to a target concept (Kulesza et al., 2014). In the CWI task, the concept is word complexity in context, which for a human reader may combine multiple factors that a machine tries to learn from the data. Labelling of large data sets is time-consuming and costly, and often carried out using crowd-sourcing platforms such as Amazon Mechanical Turk (Paolacci

et al., 2010). For the CWI task, crowd-source workers have in the past been employed to identify which words within a training dataset are complex: for example, given a sentence *"They aimed to ameliorate the situation"*, the annotators might identify *ameliorate* as complex. Labelled datasets collected this way are then used to train a model that can predict previously unseen words' complexity. Prior work on labelling of CWI datasets has found that annotation of word complexity is challenging, yielding relatively low levels of inter-annotator agreement such as $\alpha = 0.244$ (Paetzold and Specia, 2016) and $\kappa = 0.398$ (Specia et al., 2012).

In this paper, we show that representing the concept of word complexity in a continuous manner results in higher inter-annotator agreement than using binary labels. In particular, we investigate the following hypothesis:

Hypothesis 1 (H1): *Do comparative judgments for CWI lead to higher inter-annotator agreement and higher quality labelled data than binary judgments?*

Furthermore, this paper poses the following questions regarding the general setting of the CWI annotation experiments:

1. Does controlling for the homogeneity of the group of annotators with respect to their age, education level and native language contribute to higher agreement?

2. Can comparative judgments be made in a significantly shorter period of time than binary judgments for word complexity?

2 Background

2.1 Collecting Complex Word Labels

CWI is an essential first step in the lexical simplification pipeline, and has recently received signif-

Proceedings of the 13th Linguistic Annotation Workshop, pages 208–214
Florence, Italy, August 1, 2019. ©2019 Association for Computational Linguistics

icant attention (Shardlow, 2013). However, there are few labelled datasets suitable for CWI training, and those that exist have a number of drawbacks:

- The homogeneity of the annotator group is usually not controlled for, meaning that labels are provided by individuals with various backgrounds, conflating factors such as age, native language and education. We believe that it is important to clearly define and control for such factors, especially since the reading needs of different groups vary substantively;
- The annotation task is often presented as a binary decision, with annotators being asked to label each word as either complex or not. Intuitively, word complexity is expected to be a continuum, meaning that scalar or rank approaches should be more appropriate;
- Perhaps as a consequence of these two factors, the inter-annotator agreement for the labels is very low – lower than would be expected to support consistent empirical results when training ML algorithms (Cohen, 1968; Krippendorff, 2004; Bhowmick et al., 2008).

The first labelled CWI dataset was collected for the 2012 iteration of the SemEval Task 1 (Specia et al., 2012). This dataset was based on the data from McCarthy and Navigli (2007) which focused on word substitutions. The training set was annotated by 4 people while the test set was annotated by 5. In the labelling task, annotators were shown a short input text and a target word in English. For the target word, several possible substitutions were provided and annotators were asked to rank these substitutions according to their simplicity, e.g.:

(1)   **Gold**: *clear, bright, light, well-lit*

Since the original words were provided as the input, this task was primarily focused on ranking substitution candidates rather than the CWI step. The inter-annotator agreement was measured using Cohen's Kappa coefficient by calculating κ for each pair of annotators, and then averaging over all pairs to derive the final score. The κ value was 0.386 for the training and $\kappa{=}0.398$ for the test set. Cohen's suggested interpretation is that values in the range of $0.21{-}0.40$ represent minimal agreement (Cohen, 1968). Specia et al. (2012) report that, while these scores are low, they correctly reflect the highly subjective nature of the annotation task.

A second CWI dataset was collected and annotated for the 2016 SemEval Task 11 (Paetzold and Specia, 2016). Rather than aiming for a measure of word complexity, this task was designed to evaluate systems that would identify if target words in context were complex or not. Labels were collected from 400 non-native annotators aged between 18 and 66, having 45 language backgrounds. Annotators were asked to select words within a sentence that they considered to be complex. The total dataset contained $9,200$ sentences.

Inter-annotator agreement was calculated using Krippendorff's α agreement coefficient (Hayes and Krippendorff, 2007) for each set of 10 sentences, and each sentence was annotated by 20 volunteers. Krippendorff's α is more appropriate than the κ coefficient for multiple annotators as well as binary and ordinal labelling schemes (Antoine et al., 2014). When interpreting the α coefficient, Krippendorff suggests that $\alpha{\geq}0.667$ is the lowest conceivable limit for tentative conclusions (Krippendorff, 2004). F-scores showed significant difference in annotations ($p{<}0.05$) between the age bands. Paetzold and Specia (2016) reported the quantitative differences in the annotation by the different age and language proficiency groups of annotators, however these differences were not further investigated or controlled for.

Finally, the CWI dataset in the CWI 2018 shared task (Yimam et al., 2018) was based on the dataset by Yimam et al. (2017) and contained data representing three different genres: Wikipedia, professionally-written and non-professionally written news. Annotations for this data were collected from 20 annotators using the MTurk platform. To counteract previous low inter-annotator agreement, the annotators were incentivized to maximize agreement. The inter-annotator agreement (IAA) was not reported, meaning that this dataset cannot be directly compared with the other two datasets. However, it is worth noting that nearly 30% of the words were annotated as complex by only a single annotator, while only 1.1% were annotated as complex by all 20 annotators.

Data	IAA Statistic	Interpretation
2012	$\kappa = 0.386, 0.398$	minimal agreement
2016	$\alpha = 0.244$	inconclusive
2018	1% unanimous	idiosyncratic

Table 1: Standard of inter-annotator agreement in previous CWI datasets

In summary, Table 1 shows low values of the

statistical measures for each of the three previous datasets. High inter-annotator agreement is a key requirement for the usability of an annotated corpus, whereas inconsistent or noisy annotation contributes to poor classifier performance (Bhowmick et al., 2008).

2.2 Approaches to Labelling

It is widely understood that machine learning systems are limited by the quality of the labelled training data. One approach to improving the performance of such systems is to treat the human labeller(s) as a source of noise (Frénay and Verleysen, 2014) who can be modelled statistically (Yan et al., 2010) in order to more accurately identify an underlying ground truth. Noise estimation can be improved if multiple labels are obtained for each item in the training set in order to model inconsistency (Ipeirotis et al., 2014), or if a distribution of label values can be used as a basis for rejecting outliers (Brodley and Friedl, 1999). However, these approaches presume that there is a single correct label for each data point. For our task of word complexity, different reports of complexity may be equally valid for different raters, which means that rather than a single underlying ground truth, the concept itself is individually variable.

Several of the human factors elements can be addressed through the use of pairwise comparison, where labellers make relative judgments to compare training items, rather that attempting to characterize each item independently against an abstract conceptual category, for which they are expected to have a stable definition and associated membership criteria. In the context of labelling, comparative judgments are used to compare how well the training items correspond to the required concept. Carterette et al. (2008) demonstrate that this method can facilitate judgments for information retrieval applications. Comparative judgments have also been used in gamified labelling (Bennett et al., 2009), where cooperating players reduce the set of alternative items until agreement is reached.

Recent work has looked into the application of comparative judgments to labelling as opposed to assignment of categorical values and scores on a scale (Simpson et al., 2019; Yang and Chen, 2011; Kingsley and Brown, 2010). Simpson et al. (2019) note that comparative judgments are suitable for abstract linguistic properties, whose na-

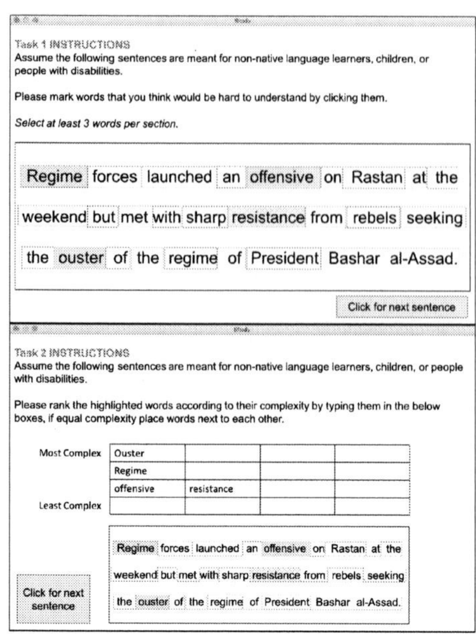

Figure 1: Labelling interfaces used in the study: Task 1 represents the binary annotation task, Task 2 – the ranking annotation task.

ture can cause inconsistencies in the assigned numerical scores. In this work, we assume that word complexity is an instance of such abstract linguistic property. In addition, it has been showed before that comparative labelling allows a total sorting of items and can reduce the time taken to label a dataset (Yang and Chen, 2011; Kingsley and Brown, 2010; Kendall, 1948). In the context of CWI and text simplification systems, the relative nature of word complexity and comparative labels can be utilized to help the systems focus on the most complex words in text (Gooding and Kochmar, 2019).

Finally, such factors as *interface design* (the simplicity of the interface and clarity of the instructions), *representation of target concept*, and *recruitment of annotators* (expertise or knowledge found in specific subgroups) are key to the reliability of annotation (Sarkar et al., 2016).

3 Study

In this paper we aim to study three points of interest: (1) whether controlling for such factors as age, level of education and native language of the annotator group in the task of complex word identification would yield higher inter-annotator agreement than reported in the previous studies; (2) whether modelling the labelling concept as a comparative judgment better represents the concept of word complexity than categorical judgment, thus improving inter-annotator agreement measures; and (3) whether using comparative judgments is a more time-efficient way of labelling complex words. To investigate these, we performed a study using 30 annotators. The entire annotation process took approximately 25 minutes per participant. The participants were selected according to the following criteria: the same first language (English), the same level of educational background (graduate degree) and within a similar age range of 21-30. These initial criteria were motivated by the high availability of native speaking participants. In addition, by restricting the background of the participants, we aimed to show that homogeneity of the group of annotators can lead to higher inter-annotator agreement.

Two alternative interfaces, shown in Figure 1, were designed. We used a within-subjects design, in which each of the 30 annotators labelled 20 sentences (10 sentences per interface). The 20 sentences were extracted from the dataset of Yimam et al. (2017), which was chosen as the most reliable dataset for the task of CWI having yielded the best empirical results to date (Yimam et al., 2018). All sentences used in this study were selected from professionally written news, and were chosen to contain hard, medium and low complexity words as illustrated in Example 2. These words were selected using previous annotations reported for this dataset (Yimam et al., 2017). The proportion of annotators that mark a word as complex indicates the likelihood of the word being complex. We approximate the complexity strength using these measures, where the class boundaries are defined as: *hard* $\in [10, 20]$, *medium* $\in [6, 9]$, *low* $\in [1, 5]$.

(2)   Hard: *politicizing* (14)
       Medium: *warily* (9)
       Low: *trip* (2)

This example shows words of different levels of complexity with the number of annotators that have marked them as complex (Yimam et al., 2017). Note that contrary to the study of Specia et al. (2012), where the annotators were asked to rank synonyms of approximately equal complexity, we ask them to rank words of different complexity. Having clear category differences has been shown to reduce cognitive load, thereby increasing labelling efficiency (Sarkar et al., 2016).

The first interface presented the labelling task as a classification exercise, allowing annotators to choose and label complex words by clicking on them. At least three words had to be selected before moving to the next sentence to ensure annotators' engagement in the task. The second interface presented the labelling task as a ranking exercise where words could be ordered according to their relative complexity. Words were ordered by re-entering them into a table with the position indicating the least to most complex words.

In both experiments, participants were asked to assume that the textual content was intended for a target audience of non-native language learners or people with reduced reading skills. To control for order effects, half the participants performed task 1 first, and half performed task 2 first.

4   Results

For the binary task, 62 distinct words from the 10 sentences were marked as complex by annotators. Two inter-annotator agreement measures are calculated for the binary and ranking tasks – Cohen's Kappa and Krippendorff's Alpha. The Kappa coefficient represents the average of scores across all pairs of raters for consistency with previous CWI studies. The inter-annotator agreement scores as well as the average labelling time per sentence are shown in Table 2.

	Comparative Judgment	*Binary Judgment*
Kappa Coefficient	0.6775	0.3937
Alpha Coefficient	0.6821	0.4960
Avg Time (s)	28.77	38.69

Table 2: Results of the study

Using the Kappa interpretations (Cohen, 1968), the comparative (ranking) labelling task has a *moderate* level of agreement, whereas the agreement in the binary annotation task is *minimal*, showing that the comparative judgment leads to a higher level of agreement than the binary categorisation judgment. At the same time, according to McHugh (2012), since the annotations obtained in our comparative judgment study result in a κ value above 0.60, they can be considered reliable. The α coefficient for the comparative judgment data also reflects this finding as it is above the required 0.667 threshold. This supports our hypothesis H1.

We note that the level of agreement in our binary annotation task is higher than the level of agreement for the previously reported binary annotation tasks ($\alpha = 0.496$ vs $\alpha = 0.244$ in Paetzold and Specia (2016)). We also note that the level of agreement in our comparative judgment annotation task is higher than that in the previously reported studies ($\kappa = 0.6775$ vs $\kappa = 0.398$ in Specia et al. (2012)). We hypothesize that this is due to the more homogeneous group of annotators in our study, though this requires a more thorough investigation of the contributing factors and we leave the more controlled experimentation with various annotator backgrounds to the future.

We also note, that the average time per sentence for the ranking task is 9.92 seconds shorter than that for the binary task. Whilst this is partly expected due to the complex words being preselected, the annotator is still required to read and consider the words within context. These results suggest that ranking is a more efficient mechanism for collecting complex word annotations that results in a higher annotator reliability than traditional approaches. The statistical significance between annotation times was tested using an unpaired t-test and was found to be highly significant (p=0.001). We note that the current setting does not control for the differences in the two user interfaces or take into account the pre-annotation required to identify words in the ranking task, and leave more thorough experimentation on the comparative efficiency of the different approaches to labelling to the future.

5 Discussion and Future Work

This study demonstrates the advantage of annotating datasets using comparative judgments rather than binary classifications, both for efficiency and accuracy. Comparative labels are used relatively rarely in ML research at present, but our results suggest that this may be a more reliable basis for training such models in future, especially where the phenomenon to be modelled relies on human experience (Simpson et al., 2019).

A further advantage of constructing rankings rather than classifications is that we are able to infer additional labels without the need for further annotation, by using a pre-labelled framework (Sarkar et al., 2016). In particular, whereas we only get binary labels for the words in a binary setting, the relative ranking can be extended to the full dataset, thus increasing the size of the labelled data without additional effort. A number of methods for learning total sorting from sparsely annotated data have been proposed in the literature (Simpson and Gurevych, 2018; Marley and Louviere, 2005; Thurstone, 1927).

Our results also show higher agreement coefficients for both binary and relative judgment tasks when compared to previously collected datasets. This supports the case that the concept of word complexity, and thus the level of agreement, is aligned between individuals that share a common background, as for our sample. This emphasizes the importance of considering the annotator group carefully when constructing annotated training corpora, or carrying out labelling experiments. This paper sets the benchmarks for the CWI annotation experiments with a homogeneous group of native speaking annotators using interfaces for collecting comparative and binary judgments. The future steps for this research include: (1) more thorough investigation of effects of annotator group homogeneity on the inter-annotator agreement, and (2) more detailed study of the efficiency of the comparative judgments as opposed to binary judgments.

Finally, although in this work we have focused on the CWI task, our results are potentially applicable to other natural language tasks where specific user experiences like simplicity must be modelled as an ordering so that they can be optimized or personalized.

Acknowledgments

The second author is grateful to Cambridge English for supporting this research via the ALTA Institute.

References

Jean-Yves Antoine, Jeanne Villaneau, and Anas Lefeuvre-Halftermeyer. 2014. Weighted krippendorff's alpha is a more reliable metrics for multicoders ordinal annotations: Experimental studies on emotion, opinion and coreference annotation. *14th Conference of the European Chapter of the Association for Computational Linguistics 2014, EACL 2014.*

Paul N. Bennett, David Maxwell Chickering, and Anton Mityagin. 2009. Learning consensus opinion: mining data from a labeling game. In *Proceedings of the 18th international conference on World wide web*, pages 121–130. ACM.

Plaban Kr Bhowmick, Pabitra Mitra, and Anupam Basu. 2008. An agreement measure for determining inter-annotator reliability of human judgements on affective text. In *Proceedings of the Workshop on Human Judgements in Computational Linguistics*, pages 58–65. Association for Computational Linguistics.

Carla E. Brodley and Mark A. Friedl. 1999. Identifying mislabeled training data. *Journal of Artificial Intelligence Research*, pages 131–167.

Ben Carterette, Paul N. Bennett, David Maxwell Chickering, and Susan T. Dumais. 2008. Here or there preference judgments for relevance. *Lecture Notes in Computer Science (including subseries Lecture Notes in Artificial Intelligence and Lecture Notes in Bioinformatics)*, 4956 LNCS:16–27.

Jacob Cohen. 1968. Weighted kappa: Nominal scale agreement provision for scaled disagreement or partial credit. *Psychological bulletin*, 70(4):213.

Edgar Dale and Jeanne S. Chall. 1949. The concept of readability. *Elementary English*, 26(1):19–26.

Benoit Frénay and Michel Verleysen. 2014. Classification in the presence of label noise: a survey. *IEEE Transactions on Neural Networks and Learning Systems*, 25(5):845–869.

Sian Gooding and Ekaterina Kochmar. 2019. Complex Word Identification as a Sequence Labelling Task. In *Proceedings of the 57th Annual Meeting of the Association for Computational Linguistics (ACL 2019)*. Association for Computational Linguistics.

Andrew F. Hayes and Klaus Krippendorff. 2007. Answering the call for a standard reliability measure for coding data. *Communication methods and measures*, 1(1):77–89.

Panagiotis G. Ipeirotis, Foster Provost, Victor S. Sheng, and Jing Wang. 2014. Repeated labeling using multiple noisy labelers. *Data Mining and Knowledge Discovery*, 28(2):402–441.

Maurice G. Kendall. 1948. *Rank Correlation Methods*. Griffin, Oxford, UK.

David C. Kingsley and Thomas C. Brown. 2010. Preference Uncertainty, Preference Learning, and Paired Comparison Experiments. *Land Economic*, 86:530–544.

Klaus Krippendorff. 2004. Reliability in content analysis: Some common misconceptions and recommendations. *Human communication research*, 30(3):411–433.

Todd Kulesza, Saleema Amershi, Rich Caruana, Danyel Fisher, and Denis Charles. 2014. Structured labeling for facilitating concept evolution in machine learning. *Proceedings of the 32nd annual ACM conference on Human factors in computing systems - CHI '14*, pages 3075–3084.

Anthony A. J. Marley and J. Louviere, Jordan. 2005. Some probabilistic models of best, worst, and best-worst choices. *Journal of Mathematical Psychology*, 49:464–480.

Diana McCarthy and Roberto Navigli. 2007. Semeval-2007 task 10: English lexical substitution task. In *Proceedings of the 4th International Workshop on Semantic Evaluations*, pages 48–53. Association for Computational Linguistics.

Mary L. McHugh. 2012. Interrater reliability: the kappa statistic. *Biochemia medica: Biochemia medica*, 22(3):276–282.

Gustavo Paetzold and Lucia Specia. 2016. SemEval 2016 Task 11: Complex word identification. In *Proceedings of the 10th International Workshop on Semantic Evaluation (SemEval-2016)*, pages 560–569.

Gabriele Paolacci, Jesse Chandler, and Panagiotis G. Ipeirotis. 2010. Running experiments on Amazon Mechanical Turk. *Judgment and Decision Making*, 5(5):411–419.

Advait Sarkar, Cecily Morrison, Jonas F. Dorn, Rishi Bedi, Saskia Steinheimer, Jacques Boisvert, Jessica Burggraaff, Marcus D'Souza, Peter Kontschieder, Samuel Rota Bulò, Lorcan Walsh, Christian P. Kamm, Yordan Zaykov, Abigail Sellen, and Siân Lindley. 2016. Setwise comparison: Consistent, scalable, continuum labels for computer vision. In *Proceedings of the 2016 CHI Conference on Human Factors in Computing Systems*, pages 261–271. ACM.

Matthew Shardlow. 2013. A Comparison of Techniques to Automatically Identify Complex Words. In *Proceedings of the Student Research Workshop at the 51st Annual Meeting of the Association for Computational Linguistics (ACL)*, pages 103–109.

Edwin Simpson, Erik-Lân Do Dinh, Tristan Miller, and Iryna Gurevych. 2019. Predicting Humorousness and Metaphor Novelty with Gaussian Process Preference Learning. In *Proceedings of the 57th Annual Meeting of the Association for Computational Linguistics (ACL 2019)*. Association for Computational Linguistics.

Edwin Simpson and Iryna Gurevych. 2018. Finding Convincing Arguments Using Scalable Bayesian Preference Learning. *Transactions of the Association for Computational Linguistics*, 6:357–371.

Lucia Specia, Sujay Kumar Jauhar, and Rada Mihalcea. 2012. SemEval-2012 Task 1: English Lexical Simplification. In *Proceedings of the First Joint Conference on Lexical and Computational Semantics - Volume 1: Proceedings of the Main Conference and the Shared Task, and Volume 2: Proceedings of the Sixth International Workshop on Semantic Evaluation*, SemEval '12, pages 347–355, Stroudsburg, PA, USA. Association for Computational Linguistics.

Louis L. Thurstone. 1927. A law of comparative judgement. *Psychological Review*, 34:273–286.

Yan Yan, Rómer Rosales, Glenn Fung, Mark Schmidt, Gerardo Hermosillo, Luca Bogoni, Linda Moy, and Jennifer G. Dy. 2010. Modeling annotator expertise: Learning when everybody knows a bit of something. In *International conference on artificial intelligence and statistics*, pages 932 – 939.

Yi-Hsuan Yang and Homer H. Chen. 2011. Ranking-Based Emotion Recognition for Music Organization and Retrieval. *IEEE Transactions on Audio, Speech, and Language Processing*, 19:762–774.

Seid Muhie Yimam, Chris Biemann, Shervin Malmasi, Gustavo Paetzold, Lucia Specia, Sanja Štajner, Anaïs Tack, and Marcos Zampieri. 2018. A Report on the Complex Word Identification Shared Task 2018. In *Proceedings of the 13th Workshop on Innovative Use of NLP for Building Educational Applications*, pages 66–78.

Seid Muhie Yimam, Sanja Štajner, Martin Riedl, and Chris Biemann. 2017. CWIG3G2-Complex Word Identification Task across Three Text Genres and Two User Groups. In *Proceedings of the Eighth International Joint Conference on Natural Language Processing (Volume 2: Short Papers)*, volume 2, pages 401–407.

Continuous Annotation Quality Control, Support for Hierarchically Structured Label Sets and Long-Segment Annotation with WAT-SL 2.0

Christina Lohr,[★] Johannes Kiesel,[°] Stephanie Luther,[★] Johannes Hellrich,[★]
Benno Stein,[°] Udo Hahn[★]

[★] Jena University Language & Information Engineering Lab (JULIE Lab),
Friedrich-Schiller-Universität Jena, Jena, Germany, <firstname.lastname>@uni-jena.de
[°] Faculty of Media,
Bauhaus-Universität Weimar, Weimar, Germany, <firstname.lastname>@uni-weimar.de

Abstract

Today's widely used annotation tools were designed for annotating typically short textual mentions of entities or relations, making their interface cumbersome to use for long(er) stretches of text, e.g, sentences running over several lines in a document. They also lack systematic support for hierarchically structured labels, i.e., one label being conceptually more general than another (e.g., *anamnesis* in relation to *family anamnesis*). Moreover, as a more fundamental shortcoming of today's tools, they provide no continuous quality control mechanisms for the annotation process, an essential feature to intrinsically support iterative cycles in the development of annotation guidelines. We alleviated these problems by developing WAT-SL 2.0, an open-source web-based annotation tool for long-segment labeling, hierarchically structured label sets and built-ins for quality control.

1 Introduction

In the course of large-scale annotation campaigns on medical full-text corpora, we encountered several shortcomings of the current generation of annotation tools. *Labeling long-spanning text segments* (e.g., entire sentences or even paragraphs) is a major issue here that is only insufficiently supported by general purpose open-source annotation tools (Müller and Strube, 2006; Stenetorp et al., 2012; Bontcheva et al., 2013; Rak et al., 2014; Yimam et al., 2014) which typically aim at annotating (much) shorter text spans for entities and relations. This is especially troublesome given the increasing availability of full texts and even books as input for annotation projects.

With annotation schemes becoming more and more conceptually structured, we also faced prob-lems with the lack of systematic support for *hierarchically structured tag labels* where one label is semantically more general than another (e.g., the general tag *anamnesis* in relation to more specific ones like *family anamnesis*).

Finally, and this point addresses a more general design desideratum, we encountered a substantial lack of continuous *quality control* mechanisms in the majority of annotation tools (the WASA tool (AlGhamdi and Diab, 2018) is one of the rare exceptions and shares several design goals with WAT-SL 2.0). This shortcoming requires annotation project managers to reach for external tools for statistical evaluation. As a consequence, shifting back and forth between annotation and evaluation environments slows down the overall progress of the entire annotation project and hampers iterative refinement of annotation guidelines. Yet, a close technical coupling of such test-development cycles within *one* integrated platform is a particularly fruitful strategy in complex annotation campaigns.

As a remedy for these problems, we here present WAT-SL 2.0, an open source *web-based annotation tool for segment labeling*, hierarchically structured label sets and built-ins for quality control that is available under the MIT License.[1] It provides a live view on each annotator's progress on assigned documents and document sets and features Krippendorff's α (Krippendorff, 1970) for agreement statistics. WAT-SL 2.0 is based on WAT-SL, the Web Annotation Tool for Segment Labeling (Kiesel et al., 2017).

WAT-SL 2.0 was successfully employed in an on-going annotation project comprising approxi-

---

[1] https://github.com/webis-de/wat

Proceedings of the 13th Linguistic Annotation Workshop, pages 215–219
Florence, Italy, August 1, 2019. ©2019 Association for Computational Linguistics

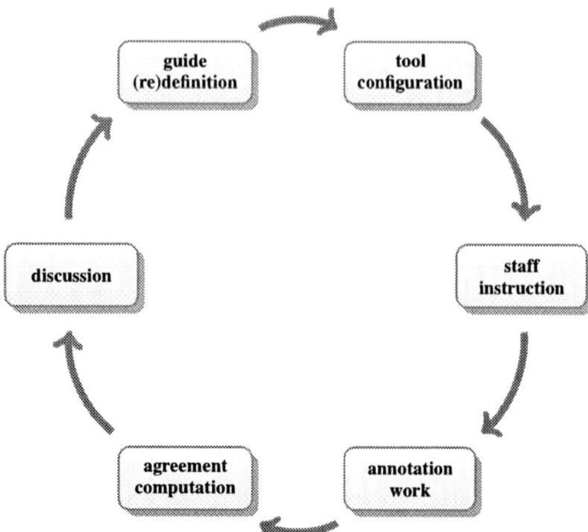

Figure 1: Enhanced annotation life cycle model (based on Pustejovsky and Stubbs (2012)'s four-step model).

mately 1K German clinical reports (Lohr et al., 2018; Hahn et al., 2018). The segment labeling subtask (see Section 4) of this project could not have been accomplished without WAT-SL 2.0's novel features and its new interface functionality.

Annotating large corpora typically requires multiple iterations to refine annotation guidelines and train annotators. This can be illustrated by the enhanced annotation life cycle model in Figure 1. Given a data collection, first an annotation guide has to be (re-)defined. Next annotation tools are configured to support the proper application of these guidelines and annotation staff is trained on them. After that the main annotation process is started and its outcome is evaluated. Finally, the overall process should be discussed by the annotation team and future iterations can be run with changed annotation guidelines and retraining, thus reflecting the experience from earlier cycles.

2 Basic Design of the Annotation Tool

WAT-SL 2.0's basic design follows WAT-SL 1.0 in providing a highly customizable and extensible interface for the annotation of full texts. It is implemented with a JAVA back-end and a Web-based front-end making it highly compatible with different environments and easy to customize. Plain text files are used as input, each line containing one segment for labeling. Results as well as logging information (e.g., time stamps) are stored in key-value files. These easy to process formats made WAT-SL 1.0 already well-suited for large-scale annotation projects and were further extended by us as described in Section 3.3.

The user interface provides annotators not only with a single document view for on-going annotation, but also with an overview page showing their upcoming and finalized tasks, as well as their progress so far—annotators in our clinical annotation project (see Section 4) found this feature particularly favorable to increase their motivation. Last but not least, WAT-SL 2.0 provides two novel administrative views (see next section) showing the progress of all annotators, as well as their agreement on specific documents.

3 Novel Features of the Annotation Tool

WAT-SL 2.0 has more advanced features—both for supporting the annotation process, as well as for servicing quality control concerns—than WAT-SL, its predecessor described by Kiesel et al. (2017), and many other tools widely used in the annotation community, BRAT (Stenetorp et al., 2012), in particular. Its features support both annotators and project managers to allow for faster and easier annotation and monitoring.

3.1 Advanced Annotation Functionality

WAT-SL 2.0 was extended with several features to allow for the large-scale annotation of documents with longer text passages using a large number of different labels.

We added support for hierarchically structured label sets for conceptually more adequate modeling of complex domains, such as clinical activities. Figure 2 shows the drop-down menu used to either directly select a label without sublabels (e.g., *preamble*) or a label with sublabels, such as the selected *anamnesis* tag. Selecting a label with sublabels prompts another drop-down menu to appear providing access to all the sublabels of the selected superlabel (e.g., selecting the superlabel *anamnesis* yields access to its conceptually more specialized sublabels *patient anamnesis* and *family anamnesis*).

Although this feature slightly increases interface complexity for the users, it considerably reduces the visual effort to pinpoint labels in the menu. Moreover, it also avoids excessively long drop-down menus that extend beyond the bottom border of the browser viewport. We successfully applied this design in a task with up to 21 labels in a preliminary annotation iteration and 18 labels (including seven hierarchical sublabels) in the final annotation project (see Section 4).

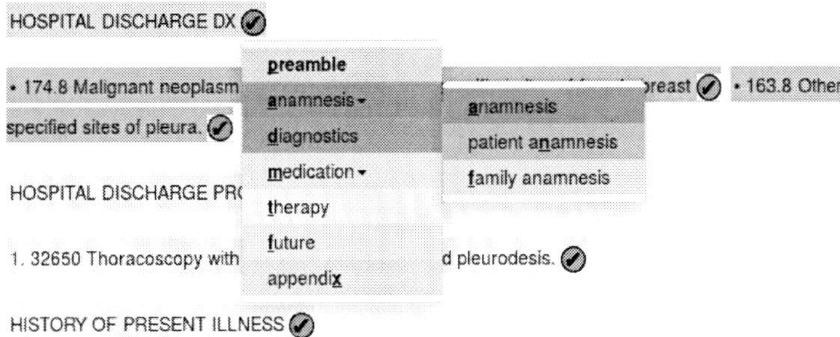

Figure 2: Sublabels of *anamnesis* tag in a secondary drop-down menu shown when the user clicks on the superlabel *anamnesis*; the bold and underlined letters display the shortcuts of the labels.

Following annotator feedback during early iterations of our annotation project, we also introduced keyboard shortcuts for each label, thus increasing both annotation speed and convenience of use. The shortcut key for each label is defined as part of WAT-SL 2.0's configuration file. The annotation drop-down menu provides both a mouse-based option to perform annotations, as well as typographic indicators for the relevant shortcuts as part of individual label names. To further support keyboard-based operation, we also introduced another shortcut (bound to the tabulator key) to select the next segment for annotation. We found these shortcuts to speed up the entire annotation process considerably, especially when labels change infrequently in long stretches of text (see Section 4 for details).

3.2 Annotation Monitoring & Quality Control

We also added advanced features for continuous progress monitoring and quality control. A single administrative interface (see Figure 3 (a)) provides annotator-specific progress reports, i.e., task and segment completion, as well as time spent on each task, and an option to take the role of any single annotator. The latter feature allows inspection and correction (logging provided for correct attribution) of individual segment annotations. We also provide a task-specific progress report for each annotator (see Figure 3 (b)) to support more fine-grained monitoring.

Finally, we added continuous quality monitoring as a task-oriented, yet annotator-agnostic view. As shown in Figure 4, this feature provides data on the progress of each annotation task and inter-annotator agreement values of the tasks completed by all annotators. Krippendorff's α (Krippendorff, 1970) is the metric of choice in WAT-SL 2.0 for measuring the chance-corrected overlap in anno-

tation decisions. Following Artstein and Poesio (2008), we prefer it over a range of alternative measures, like Cohen's κ (Cohen, 1960), which are overly sensitive to individual annotators' decisions when modeling chance agreement.

Based on such kind of statistical evidence, continuous quality monitoring allows annotation project managers to assess the difficulty of tasks, allowing for a swift refinement of annotation guidelines. This feature was implemented by calculating coincidence matrices for each task with DKPRO AGREEMENT (Meyer et al., 2014).

3.3 Export format

WAT-SL 2.0 also provides extended export functions to increase interoperability. In addition to WAT-SL 1.0's key-value export format, we also provide CSV files well-suited as input for machine learning tools. Furthermore, we provide an export option compatible with the widely used BRAT tool, i.e., ANN files similar to the format used in the BioNLP Shared Task.[2] This increased interoperability was vital for our multi-level annotation project described in the next section.

4 Clinical Annotation Project

We employed WAT-SL 2.0 in a large-scale annotation project aiming at the creation of a reference corpus of German clinical language (Hahn et al., 2018). We annotated approximately 1K clinical documents with around 170K text segments (Lohr et al., 2018). This project covers multiple linguistic layers in addition to text segments, such as named entities (e.g., medications, diseases, etc.) and their relations (e.g., drug-drug interactions, temporal relations between clinical episodes, etc.).

---

[2] `http://2011.bionlp-st.org/home/`
`file-formats`

Annotator: **Bob Builder (bob)**

Annotator	Tasks		Segments		Time	Login (new window)
Alice Carroll (alice)	5/6	83%	144/164	88%	0:14:42	Login as Alice Carroll
Bob Builder (bob)	5/6	83%	144/164	88%	0:14:16	Login as Bob Builder
Charlie Brown (charlie)	4/6	67%	82/164	50%	0:08:24	Login as Charlie Brown
Dorothy Gale (dorothy)	5/6	83%	144/164	88%	0:13:24	Login as Dorothy Gale
Frodo Baggins (frodo)	5/6	83%	144/164	88%	0:13:40	Login as Frodo Baggins

(a)

Task	Segments		Time
task-01	21/21	(100.0%)	0:05:08
task-02	64/64	(100.0%)	0:05:06
task-03	26/26	(100.0%)	0:01:54
task-04	18/18	(100.0%)	0:01:28
task-05	15/15	(100.0%)	0:00:40
task-06	0/20	(0.0%)	--

(b)

Figure 3: Project manager's view of progress tracking—(a) by annotator and (b) by task for a single annotator. Columns show the progress in relation to tasks and segments, the time spent and a button to log in as individual annotator (for corrections).

Task	Segments		Annotators		Kripp. Alpha
task-01	168/168	(100%)	8/8	(100%)	0.928
task-02	450/512	(87%)	7/8	(87%)	n.n.
task-03	208/208	(100%)	8/8	(100%)	1.0
task-04	144/144	(100%)	8/8	(100%)	0.741
task-05	120/120	(100%)	8/8	(100%)	0.833
task-06	0/160	(0%)	0/8	(0%)	n.n.

Figure 4: Progress monitoring by tasks and display of Inter-Annotator-Agreement. Columns show the progress in tasks, segments and Krippendorff's α.

Section annotations were performed by up to eight medical students supervised by two annotation managers with a computer science background and further advised by clinical doctors. We iteratively developed and refined guidelines for annotating segments in accordance with existing clinical requirements and standards (see Table 1). We experimented with up to 21 different labels during early exploratory iterations, but finally decided on 18 labels (including 7 hierarchical sublabels) for the final annotation round.

The first three iterations were run with the original version of WAT-SL. However, based on consistent feedback from our annotators, a desire for continuous quality control and faster

Iteration	Doc.	Labels	Ø min / doc	WAT-SL
1	240	6	7:45	1.0
2	400	7	7:47	1.0
3	392	21	9:17	1.0
4	400	19	4:46	2.0
Final	1406	18	3:16	2.0

Table 1: Details for each annotation iteration. The total number of documents is inflated due to multiple annotations (by eight annotators) for agreement calculation.

iterations became obvious. Hence, we decided to implement WAT-SL 2.0. Our interface improvements contributed—probably together with a general training effect—to halving average annotation times per document from approximately 9 minutes to less than 4 minutes. Overall, our improvements clearly increased the general usability of WAT-SL and were vital for the success of our project by increasing annotation quality (effectiveness) and speed (efficiency).

5   Conclusions

We here presented WAT-SL 2.0, a Web-based tool for annotating long texts with (hierarchical) segment labels and built-in facilities for quality measurement. It provides annotators with individual progress overviews, label shortcuts and hierarchically structured label sets which help increase motivation, quality and speed for task completion. Alternative annotation tools (e.g., BRAT (Stenetorp et al., 2012) as a main representative) are mostly ill-suited for applying a large amount of labels to text segments, as they use mouse-based selection of arbitrary text spans (more suited for short-spanning entities and relations) and are thus prone to miss-clicks or lack support for both hierarchical and larger numbers of labels to select.

WAT-SL 2.0's unique elaborated monitoring device includes means for in-depth logging, annotation complexity analysis and continuous quality control. These features allow project managers to make more informed decisions when updating annotation guidelines or evaluating annotators.

We successfully employed WAT-SL 2.0 for the annotation of roughly 1K clinical reports incorporating more than 20 different labels. Furthermore, WAT-SL 2.0 is highly customizable and well-suited for non-clinical annotation tasks as well.

Acknowledgements

This work was partially supported by the Deutsche Forschungsgemeinschaft (DFG) under grants HA 2097/8-1 within the STAKI^{2}B^2 project (Semantic Text Analysis for Quality-controlled Extraction of Clinical Phenotype Information within the Framework of Healthcare Integrated Biobanking) and the German Federal Ministry of Education and Research (BMBF) within the SMITH project under grant 01ZZ1803G.

References

Fahad AlGhamdi and Mona T. Diab. 2018. WASA: a Web application for sequence annotation. In *LREC 2018 — Proceedings of the 11th International Conference on Language Resources and Evaluation. Miyazaki, Japan, May 7-12, 2018*, pages 1073–1077, Paris. European Language Resources Association (ELRA).

Ron Artstein and Massimo Poesio. 2008. Inter-coder agreement for computational linguistics. *Computational Linguistics*, 34(4):555–596.

Kalina Bontcheva, Hamish Cunningham, Ian Roberts, Angus Roberts, Valentin Tablan, Niraj Aswani, and Genevieve Gorrell. 2013. GATE TEAMWARE: a Web-based collaborative text annotation framework. *Language Resources and Evaluation*, 47(4):1007–1029.

Jacob Cohen. 1960. A coefficient of agreement for nominal scales. *Educational and Psychological Measurement*, 20(1):37–46.

Udo Hahn, Franz Matthies, Christina Lohr, and Markus Löffler. 2018. 3000PA: towards a national reference corpus of German clinical language. In *MIE 2018 — Proceedings of the 29th Conference on Medical Informatics in Europe. Building Continents of Knowledge in Oceans of Data: The Future of Co-Created eHealth. Gothenburg, Sweden, 24-26 April 2018*, number 247 in Studies in Health Technology and Informatics, pages 26–30, Amsterdam, Berlin, Washington, D.C. IOS Press.

Johannes Kiesel, Henning Wachsmuth, Khalid Al-Khatib, and Benno Stein. 2017. WAT-SL: a customizable Web annotation tool for segment labeling. In *EACL 2017 — Proceedings of the 15th Conference of the European Chapter of the Association for Computational Linguistics: Software Demonstrations. Valencia, Spain, April 5-6, 2017*, pages 13–16, Stroudsburg/PA. Association for Computational Linguistics (ACL).

Klaus Krippendorff. 1970. Estimating the reliability, systematic error and random error of interval data. *Educational and Psychological Measurement*, 30(1):61–70.

Christina Lohr, Stephanie Luther, Franz Matthies, Luise Modersohn, Danny Ammon, Kutaiba Saleh, Andreas Henkel, Michael Kiehntopf, and Udo Hahn. 2018. CDA-compliant section annotation of German-language discharge summaries: guideline development, annotation campaign, section classification. In *AMIA 2018 — Proceedings of the 2018 Annual Symposium of the American Medical Informatics Association. Data, Technology, and Innovation for Better Health. San Francisco, California, USA, November 3-7, 2018*, pages 770–779.

Christian M. Meyer, Margot Mieskes, Christian Stab, and Iryna Gurevych. 2014. DKPRO AGREEMENT: an open-source JAVA library for measuring inter-rater agreement. In *COLING 2014 — Proceedings of the 25th International Conference on Computational Linguistics: System Demonstrations. Dublin, Ireland, August 25-26, 2014*, pages 105–109. International Committee on Computational Linguistics (ICCL).

Christoph Müller and Michael Strube. 2006. Multi-level annotation of linguistic data with MMAX2. In Sabine Braun, Kurt Kohn, and Joybrato Mukherjee, editors, *Corpus Technology and Language Pedagogy. New Resources, New Tools, New Methods*, number 3 in english corpus linguistics, pages 197–214. Peter Lang, Frankfurt a.M., Germany.

James D. Pustejovsky and Amber Stubbs. 2012. *Natural Language Annotation for Machine Learning. A Guide to Corpus-Building for Applications*. O'Reilly Media, Sebastopol/CA.

Rafal Rak, Jacob Carter, Andrew D. Rowley, Riza Theresa Batista-Navarro, and Sophia Ananiadou. 2014. Interoperability and customisation of annotation schemata in ARGO. In *LREC 2014 — Proceedings of the 9th International Conference on Language Resources and Evaluation. Reykjavik, Iceland, May 26-31, 2014*, pages 3837–3842. European Language Resources Association (ELRA).

Pontus Stenetorp, Sampo Pyysalo, Goran Topić, Tomoko Ohta, Sophia Ananiadou, and Jun'ichi Tsujii. 2012. BRAT: a Web-based tool for NLP-assisted text annotation. In *EACL 2012 — Proceedings of the 13th Conference of the European Chapter of the Association for Computational Linguistics: Demonstrations. Avignon, France, April 25-26, 2012*, pages 102–107, Stroudsburg/PA. Association for Computational Linguistics (ACL).

Seid Muhie Yimam, Richard Eckart de Castilho, Iryna Gurevych, and Chris Biemann. 2014. Automatic annotation suggestions and custom annotation layers in WEBANNO. In *ACL 2014 — Proceedings of the 52nd Annual Meeting of the Association for Computational Linguistics: System Demonstrations. Baltimore, Maryland, USA, June 23-24, 2014*, pages 91–96, Stroudsburg/PA. Association for Computational Linguistics (ACL).

Creation of a corpus with semantic role labels for Hungarian

Attila Novák[1,2], László János Laki[1,2], Borbála Novák[1,2]
Andrea Dömötör[1,3], Noémi Ligeti-Nagy[1,3], Ágnes Kalivoda[1,3]
[1]MTA-PPKE Hungarian Language Technology Research Group,
[2]Pázmány Péter Catholic University, Faculty of Information Technology and Bionics
Práter u. 50/a, 1083 Budapest, Hungary
[3]Pázmány Péter Catholic University, Faculty of Humanities and Social Sciences
Egyetem u. 1, 2087 Piliscsaba, Hungary
`{surname.firstname}@itk.ppke.hu`

Abstract

In this article, an ongoing research is presented, the immediate goal of which is to create a corpus annotated with semantic role labels for Hungarian that can be used to train a parser-based system capable of formulating relevant questions about the text it processes. We briefly describe the objectives of our research, our efforts at eliminating errors in the Hungarian Universal Dependencies corpus, which we use as the base of our annotation effort, at creating a Hungarian verbal argument database annotated with thematic roles, at classifying adjuncts, and at matching verbal argument frames to specific occurrences of verbs and participles in the corpus.

1 Introduction

Recently, state-of-the-art performance in most NLP related tasks has been achieved by end-to-end systems based on neural deep learning networks (see e.g. BERT (Devlin et al., 2018) or GPT-2 (Radford et al., 2019)) surpassing the performance of previous systems employing some sort of grammatical analysis. This has raised doubts as to whether it makes sense to deal with grammatical analysis at all. At the same time, the training of end-to-end systems usually requires a great amount of training material, which is not available in most languages. Therefore, we think it may still make sense put an effort into the implementation of a grammatical analysis framework as long as the output of the system can be directly used to perform tasks relevant to everyday users.

However, we cannot be satisfied with an analysis that relies on completely abstract categories that cannot be clearly translated into terms that can be linked to what that text means in a manner that can also be understood by ordinary people. An essential element of reading comprehension is that we are able to ask meaningful questions about the given text, and this ability is closely related to the ability to answer questions. Therefore, our aim is to create a system that is actually capable of formulating relevant questions about the text it processes. To do this, many distinctions need to be made that are not present in syntactic annotation currently available for Hungarian. This article presents the first phase of this work, which aims to create an annotated corpus where the annotation contains all the features needed to generate questions concerning the text.

2 Shortcomings of the traditional analysis

Since our goal is to create a system that can generate meaningful questions, we have decided that when determining what distinctions need to be made in the annotation should be basically determined by what questions can be asked concerning the particular grammatical construction. For example, in order to be able to formulate questions concerning **noun phrases**, the *Who/What?* distinction is indispensable, so the system must be able to clearly distinguish persons from things. At the same time, we ask *who* or *what* questions concerning NP's that refer to groups or organizations depending on the role they play in the given sentence. For example, a bank is referred to linguistically as a person when sending an invoice letter, but as a thing when it is liquidated. In addition, a more detailed classification is required to generate questions about nominal predicates. Concerning the predicate in the sentence *John is a doctor*, the question *Who is John?* is not very sophisticated. *What is John's occupation?* is a question matching the predicate in the sentence much more precisely. Classifying concepts as occupations, animals, tools, behaviors, etc. also makes for the system possible to generate more specific

Proceedings of the 13th Linguistic Annotation Workshop, pages 220–229
Florence, Italy, August 1, 2019. ©2019 Association for Computational Linguistics

questions related to non-predicative occurrences of noun phrases: e.g. *What animal have you seen in the garden?* vs. *What did you see in the garden?* This is particularly important in the case of coordinated phrases where one can only identify which conjunct is meant in the question if the question is specific enough.

To formulate questions concerning adverbials even at the most basic level, we also need a much more detailed system of distinctions than what is provided by the syntactic annotation present in currently available tree banks. Hungarian NP's headed by a word in inessive case or corresponding English PP's headed by the preposition *in* can have quite a number of different grammatical functions. Thus we ask different questions concerning them: (1) *szeptemberben* 'in September': *mikor?* 'when?', (2) *Londonban* 'in London': *hol?* 'where?', (3) *fájdalmában (felüvöltött)* '(he screamed) in pain': *mitől?* 'what made (him scream)?', (4) *magában (hisz)* '(he believes) in himself': *kiben?* 'in whom?', (5) *bajban* 'in trouble': *milyen helyzetben?* 'in what situation?', (6) *életben (marad)* '(stay) alive' lit. '(stay) in life': no question in general, this is part of a light verb construction.

Generating questions concerning not only nominal but also verbal predicates requires information not provided by currently available annotation for Hungarian. How a question concerning a verbal predicate should be formulated using specific arguments as anchors depends on the thematic roles the arguments play. *What did John do to Frank?* is an adequate question if John is an agent and Frank is a patient. In the same situation, *What happened to Frank?* and *What did John do?* are likewise adequate questions.

Identification of thematic roles of verbal argument slots is also needed in order to be able to distinguish oblique arguments from semantically compositional relations (e.g. locative and oblique uses of *in*: *believe in something* vs. *be somewhere*). We also need to distinguish parts of idioms and light verb constructions from compositional verb-to-argument relations. It is a joke to ask a question concerning a non-compositionally related constituent:

What are you holding? — A meeting.

3   The corpus

As a starting point, we chose the Hungarian sub-corpus (Vincze et al., 2017) of the Universal Dependencies (UD) corpus (Nivre et al., 2016) consisting of 1800 sentences (42000 tokens) of mainly newswire text in order to put the annotation schema we propose in a context that can be interpreted at an international level. The UD corpus contains texts in many languages annotated with morphosyntactic and dependency-based syntactic analysis using unified principles and categories. Our original plan was to supplement or refine the annotation in the Hungarian UD corpus with the information needed to formulate questions. However, it turned out that the annotation in the Hungarian sub-corpus does not correspond to the currently valid UD specification in many respects, and contains many random annotation errors, so fixing these errors turned out to be an inevitable part of our task.

According to the UD 2.0 specification[1], the internal structure of multiword expressions is to be annotated using the `flat`, `fixed` or `compound` dependency relations. The `fixed` relation is used exclusively to annotate fully lexicalized function-word-like structures. In many languages, such as English, multiword names are generally considered to be flat exocentric structures, and the use of `flat` is suggested to annotate the internal structure of these names with all words of the name directly attached to the first word of the name. On the other hand, the UD 2.0 annotation specification explicitly excludes the use of this type of analysis in cases where the name has a regular syntactic structure (eg. in the case of book or movie titles or a large part of names of organizations). Here the generic syntactic dependency structures are to be used. Similarly, endocentric structures should be annotated using the `compound` relation or one of its sub-types[2] (see e.g. Kahane et al. (2017) on the contradiction of applying the flat annotation to languages where names are endocentric). Hungarian noun phrases are always right-headed endocentric structures, so in the case of names that do not have a regular structure and compositional meaning, the `compound` relation is to be used. This ensures,

---

[1]`http://universaldependencies.org/guidelines.html`

[2]`https://universaldependencies.org/u/overview/specific-syntax.html#multiword-expressions`

for example, that case endings always attached to the head of the NP are directly accessible. E.g. the head of an object NP is always in the accusative case in Hungarian. The current annotation for names completely obscures this fact (see e.g. *az Egyesült Államokat* 'the united States[Acc]' in Figure 1)). Therefore, as one of the preprocessing steps, all multiword names, originally erroneously annotated in the corpus as `flat` structures, were automatically converted into `compound` structures (Figure 1). For the time being, the identification and further reannotation of names with a completely regular structure has not been done, as this requires manual intervention.

Structures like *Angela Merkel német kancellár* 'German Chancellor Angela Merkel' were often erroneously annotated as appositive structures in the corpus.[3] We converted these structures introducing the `compound:title_of` relation between the name and the occupation/role.

The UD 2.0 specification prescribes the use of the `obl` relation to attach NP arguments other than subjects, objects or indirect objects even in the case of nonverbal heads. Often, some other relation was used in the corpus even for verbal arguments. We were able to automatically correct most of these annotations in the case of arguments of verbs and participles (Figure 2).

In Hungarian, like in German, verbal particles are detached from the verb in various syntactic constructions, and they are moved to some distinct syntactic position. Nevertheless, these particles are considered part of the verb lemma. The verbal argument database that we created as part of our annotation effort, also contains particle verbs in this form. In the Hungarian UD corpus, on the other hand, verb lemmas did not include the particle in such cases. This needed to be fixed (adding the particle to the verb lemma) in order for the verbal argument frames could be matched to their occurrences in the corpus. Many additional lemmatization errors were fixed, and we also needed to relemmatize participles so that we can match verb argument frames against them.

In Hungarian, demonstrative predeterminers agree in case and number with the head of the NP (*azokat a kutyákat* 'those dogs$_{ACC}$'). These structures were often annotated erroneously, with the demonstrative predeterminer being attached to

the head of the NP using the same dependency label the whole NP was annotated with. We corrected these errors and attached all predeterminers as `det:predet` to the head of the NP (Figure 3).

Further corrections performed automatically included using `nmod:poss` instead of `nmod:att` in possessive structures, (bottom of Figure 2), attaching all postpositions using the `case` relation, and fixing clauses where the subject and the (nominal) predicate were exchanged in the annotation by mistake due to the annotators confusing the focus construction with predication. The latter errors needed to be identified manually, the correction of the identified structures was then performed automatically (Figure 4).

4 The argument frame database

All stems of verbs and participles occurring in the Hungarian UD corpus were collected, and they were clustered using agglomerative clustering like in (Siklósi, 2016) based on their vector representation in a word-embedding model constructed from a morphosyntactically annotated corpus (Novák and Novák, 2018). This process effectively clustered verbs having similar distributional patterns (and argument frames). Each verb in the list was supplemented with its surface argument frames from a Hungarian verb-frame dictionary (Sass et al., 2010). Using this initial representation as a source of inspiration, we have described the possible argument frames of each verb manually. Our description contains the thematic role, the surface features (case ending, postposition, possessive suffix, etc.), possible optionality and, if applicable, lexical/semantic constraints of each argument. Clustering helped us to streamline the process and simplified the task of annotators. Annotating verbs with similar argument frames in a batch together instead of having to process them in some random order made it possible for us to use an inheritance mechanism and improved consistency.

The main point in describing the argument frames of verbs was to provide as much information as possible to make it possible to ask the best, most accurate questions. With that in mind, our set of thematic roles is based on widely known thematic role hierarchies. However, it differs from them in minute details, just like they differ from each other. The description of verbs is intended to cover every possible meaning (argument frame).

---

[3] In appositive structures, like *a bátyámmal, Péterrel* 'with my brother, Peter' there is case agreement between parts of the phrase. This is not the case in these structures.

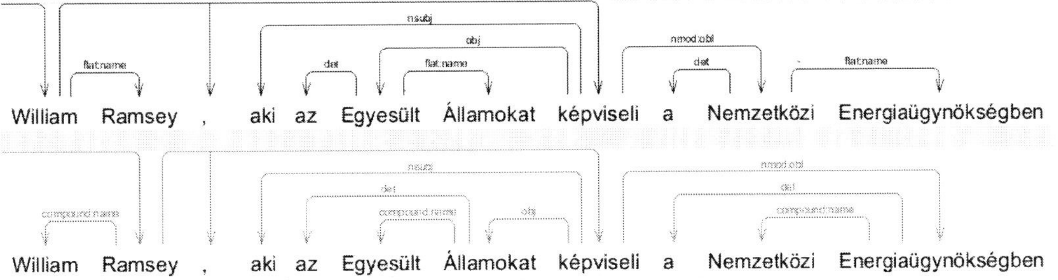

Figure 1: Fixing the annotation of multiword names: 'William Ramsey representing the United States at the International Atomic Energy Agency'

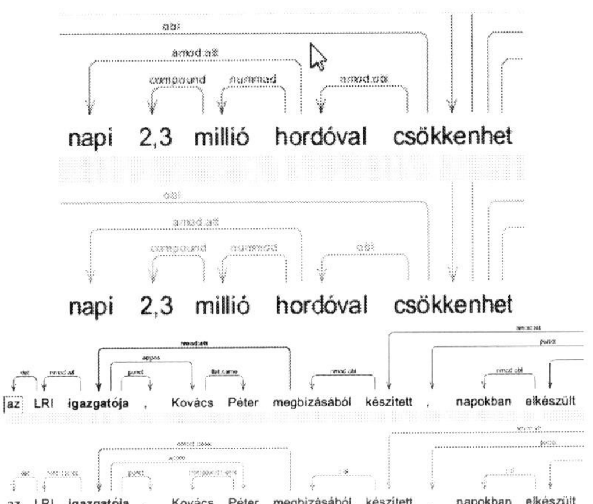

Figure 2: Using the `obl` relation for arguments of verbs and participles: '... may decrease by 2.3 million barrels a day' – 'a recently completed [report] commissioned by Péter Kovács, director of LRI'

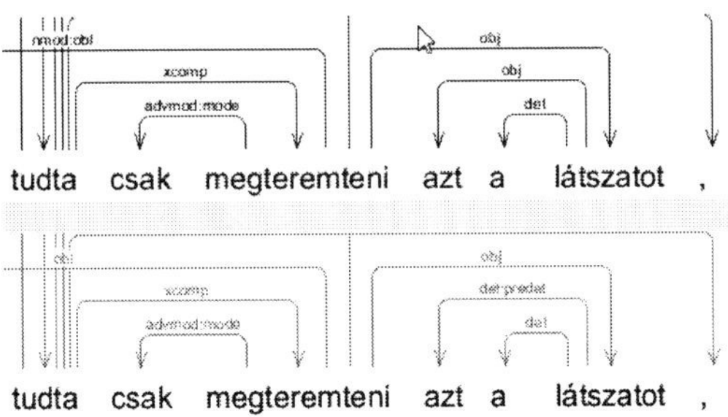

Figure 3: Correction of erroneously annotated predeterminers: '... was the only way he could create that impression'

Since verbs with similar meanings and argument frames were already grouped in the database, it was possible to specify common argument frames for groups of verbs. These frames are inherited automatically by verbs belonging to the same group. In addition, each verb can have its own argument frame which does not apply to the whole group.

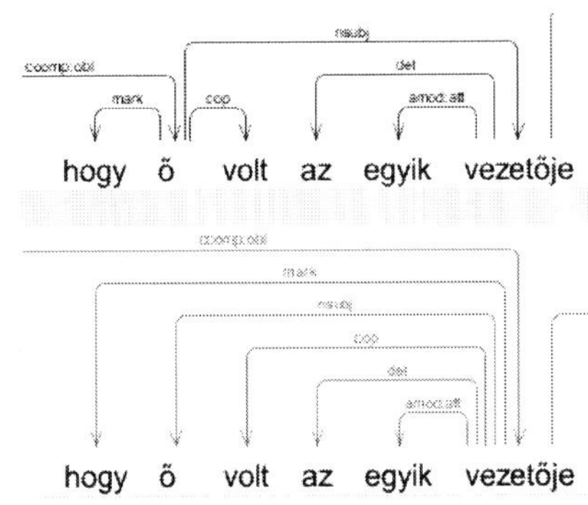

Figure 4: Correction of an exchanged subject and predicate: 'that he (*ő*) was one of the leaders (*vezetője*) of...'

This frame can be added to the record of the specific verb.

The required and optional arguments of each verb are represented either by their thematic roles or lexically, supplemented with the required case-endings or postpositions. The identification of the thematic roles is based on the question that can be asked about the given argument or about the verb with the given argument as an anchor. For example, the question concerning the agent is *what is A doing?*, the question concerning the patient is *what is happening to P?*.

Some roles also represent a kind of semantic category, such as CONT which refers to the content of communication, or ACT which denotes an action (usually expressed as an infinitive `xcomp`). Arguments not having a specific thematic role that could not be used as an anchor when we want to ask a question about the predicate were marked using the semantically neutral theme (TH) thematic role.

The fixed components of idiomatic or semicompositional verbal structures are not labeled by thematic roles but they are specified lexically.

These structures were supplemented with their own argument frame descriptions (thus interpreted as autonomous units) where this solution seemed to be justified. For example, the description of *sor kerül* 'to take place' (lit. 'turn comes') is not part of the description of the word *kerül* 'to come', but we have assigned an argument frame to the whole phrase as a unit. The thematic roles assigned to the verbs and verbal structures are summarized in Table 1.

Since verbs of movement imply the applicability of specific types of questions (e.g. *How did X get to Y?*), in addition to the roles listed in the table, a special annotation was applied to moving actors: for example moving agents are marked as AGMV. Our basic assumption was that a verb can not have more than one argument having the same thematic role. However, in some cases – where it is necessary – the co-actor is marked with the `co-` prefix. For example, *sétál valakivel* 'to walk with someone' is represented with AG_coAG-vAl (-vAl stands for the instrumental case-ending).

The argument frames described above could also obtain some special semantic classification which may help in the further refinement of the possible questions. The categories used for this are as follows:

perception (e.g. *to see*)
emotion (e.g. *to be glad*)
sound (e.g. *to resound*)
situation (e.g. *to be pressed for time*)
beginning (e.g. *to be established*)
cognitive (e.g. *to agree*)
communication (e.g. *to inform*)
mathematical (e.g. *to add*)
nonverbal communication (e.g. *to nod*)
self-propelled motion (e.g. *to step*)
financial (e.g. *to transfer*)
destruction (of patient, e.g. *to dry up*)
natural (e.g. *to rain*)
transformation/change (e.g. *to speed up*)
behavior (e.g. *to flirt*)
relation (e.g. *to support*)

Finally, the argument frames also have a polarity value indicating that the given event is positive, negative or neutral for the patient or experiencer.

Figure 5 shows the description of the verbs *sodródik* 'to drift', *hull* 'to fall' and *zuhan* 'to drop/plummet' in the argument frame database. In the first line of the extract, the PATMV_(PATH) frame including an optional PATH argument that can in turn be expanded as any combination of SRC, DST and VIA arguments, as well as the neutral polarity marked with @. refer to each verb below them. Round brackets in the descriptions indicate optionality, square brackets contain a list of examples defining a semantic category.

At the time of writing this paper, the argument frame database contains 1604 verbs with 5994 different argument frames, including the thematic role of each argument. Although frames containing optional arguments (e.g. olvas AG_ (HOW)_(PAT-t)_(REC-nAk)_(TH-ról)_(LOC-bAn) 'somebody reads (somehow) (something) (to somebody) (about something) (somewhere)') appear as many seemingly different frames in practice, we obtained these numbers by counting the frames containing optional arguments and possible thematic role variants only once.

5 Identifying the role of adjuncts

An important task is to provide a fine-grained description regarding the role of nominals with case-ending, traditionally referred to as adjuncts. If we approach the question from the case-endings, we could say that the nominal having an inessive case-ending indicates some kind of location and answers the question *Where?*. However, if the question is e.g. *Where did Mary graduate?*, it is a joke to say *In her dream*. The case-endings answering the questions *Hol?* 'Where?', *Hová?* 'Where to?' and *Honnan?* 'From where?'[4] are not always used to specify the location, the source or the destination. Depending on the lemma, the suffixed forms may express various temporal relations, modality, etc. For most lexical items that can refer to locations, only one set of the suffixes (e.g. only the inessive *-bAn* 'in', illative *-bA* 'into', and the elative *-bÓl* 'from inside' can be used to express location, source and destination), the rest of the suffixes can only be used as markers of specific oblique arguments of verbs. E.g. while for settlements outside Hungary, the locative relation is always expressed using inessive (e.g. *Londonban* 'in London'), for most Hungarian settlements, the superessive is used (e.g. *Budapesten* 'in Budapest',

---

[4]In Hungarian, locative/lative/delative case-endings are as follows: the inessive *-bAn* 'in', the adessive *-nÁl* 'at', the superessive *-On* 'on'; the illative *-bA* 'into', the allative *-hOz* 'to', the sublative *-rA* 'onto'; the elative *-bÓl* 'from inside', the ablative *-tÓl* 'from', the delative *-rÓl* 'from the top of'.

```
PATMV_(PATH)
@.
sodródik[IGE] +CHAR_ár-vAl 'drift[V] +CHAR_tide~with'
hull[IGE] +AG_térd-rA_(CHAR~előtt) +hó +PAT~[haj|könny]-A +PAT@-pusztulás
    'fall[V] +AG~to~one's~knees +snow +PAT's~hair|tears (die:)+PAT@-decay'
zuhan[IGE] +EXP_álom-bA@.biotünet 'drop/plummet[V] (fall asleep:)+EXP_into~dream'
```

Figure 5: An extract from the argument frame database.

Table 1: Thematic roles used in the description of argument frames

Annotation	Name	Question regarding the verb	Example
AG	agent	What is AG doing?	**John** has climbed the tree.
CHAR	characterized	What is characteristic of CHAR?	**Expertise** is an advantage.
ATTR	attribute	–	Expertise is **an advantage**.
EXP	experiencer	How does EXP feel? What has EXP perceived?	**John** loves Mary. **John** has seen a swallow.
PAT	patient	What happened to PAT?	John kissed **Mary**.
PATDST	patient-destination	What happened to PATDST? Where did PAT get to?	He painted **the wall** green.
TH	theme	–	John relies **on his intuition**.
ST	stimulus	What effect has ST (on EXP)?	John loves **Mary**. John got frightened of **his shadow**.
CONT	information content	–	John presented **the plan** to Joe.
REC	recipient	–	John presented the plan **to Joe**. **Mary** received a letter.
RES	result	How did RES come into being?	Mary baked **a cake**.
INS	instrument	What is AG using INS for?	John travels to work **by scooter**.
CAU	causer	What did CAU cause? What was the consequence of CAU?	John was late **because of an accident**.
MOT	motivation	–	John is studying to be **an engineer**.
LOC	location	What happened in/at/on... LOC?	John kissed Mary **in the cinema**.
SRC	source, starting point	–	John came **out of the room**. Mary received a letter **from John**.
DST	destination	How did AG/PAT get to DST?	John went **into the room**.
HOW	mode	–	John **deftly** climbed the tree.
ASPECT	aspect	–	John is doing well **financially**.
ACT	action	–	John wants **to work** from home.

lit. 'on Budapest'). On the other hand, as oblique arguments of the verbs *hisz* 'believe' and *múlik* 'depend', all nouns take the inessive 'in' and the superessive 'on' suffixes, respectively. Lemmas can thus be be classified concerning what functional/semantic relation is expressed by the combination of the lemma and each case ending. We identified such classes and defined templates that describe the semantic role of each suffixed form in the template. For all words (lemmas) belonging to the specific class, the template yields the semantics of each suffixed form.

The task can also be formulated as a classification of adverbs. There are, of course, adverbs of place such as *a sarkon* 'at the corner' or *bankban* 'in a bank', and adverbs of time such as *télen* 'in winter', *decemberben* 'in December'. However, we also find adverbs of duration, e.g. *5 hónapra*

'for five months' or a category that we could term as 'adverbs of garment' such as *kabátban* 'wearing a coat'. 31 main categories have been identified, some of which can be divided into several subcategories. Together with the subcategories, we have divided the adjuncts having locative case-endings into 51 classes. To illustrate some of the subcategories, in Table 2, we present lemmas which, when combined with a subset of the locative suffixes, function as adverbs of place. When combined with other locative suffixes, they cannot function as heads of adjunct phrases. In these cases, they can only depend on some head word selecting that specific suffix as the marker of a specific oblique argument.

The first two columns of the table show the main category (in this case, *loc*) and its subcategories (*all, ine, city-sup,* etc.). This is followed by an

category		example	-bAn (inessive)	-nÁl (adessive)	-On (superessive)
loc	all	*szekrény* 'wardrobe'	where	where	where
loc	ade	*Microsoft*	in what	where	on what
loc	ine	*állam* 'state'	where	at what	on what
loc	sup	*címoldal* 'title page'	in what	at what	where
loc	ine-sup	*könyv* 'book'	where	at what	where
loc	city-ine	*Altenkirchen*	where	where	on which city
loc	city-sup	*Budapest*	in which city	where	where
loc	country	*Afganisztán* 'Afghanistan'	where	where	on which country

Table 2: Examples of lexical items that function as heads of locative adverbial phrases when combined with a specific subset of locative case suffixes (cells marked with *where*). With other suffixes, they can only function as oblique arguments of some predicate.

example lemma belonging to the given subcategory, and the best applicable questions for each of the case-endings *-bAn*, *-nÁl* and *-On*, respectively. The questions indicate what role the suffixed word form plays in a sentence.

6 Automatic identification of semi-compositional structures

When identifying idiomatic and semi-compositional verbal constructions, we focused on the behavior of phrases with regard to the relevant question that can be asked about the given phrase. In the case of *döntést hoz* 'to make a decision' (lit. 'to bring a decision'), *What does A bring?* is not an acceptable question. Similarly, *Where does A bring P?* is incorrect regarding the phrase *szóba hoz* 'to mention' (lit. 'to bring into word').

We have implemented an algorithm for collecting such phrases from a parallel corpus. First, we generated word alignments in the English-Hungarian parallel subcorpus of the OpenSubtitles corpus consisting of 644.5 million tokens (Lison and Tiedemann, 2016) using the fast align tool (Dyer et al., 2013). To alleviate data sparseness problems due to the rich morphology of Hungarian, to improve alignment quality and to facilitate the subsequent light verb construction and idiom identification process, we used a morphosyntactically annotated version of the corpus. The English side was annotated using Stanford tagger (Toutanova et al., 2003) and the morpha lemmatizer (Minnen et al., 2001), while the Hungarian side using the PurePos tagger (Orosz and Novák, 2013) and the Hungarian Humor morphological analyzer (Novák et al., 2016). We further postprocessed the output of the tagger/lemmatizer tool combos, to generate an annotation in which each word is represented by one or two tokens on the Hungarian as well as on the English side. The first token is the lemma with the main POS tag attached to it, while the other optional token consists of possible extra morphosyntactic tags (such as tense, case, etc.) if present. We extracted at most 7-token-long parallel phrases from the word-aligned corpus using the phrase extraction algorithm using the grow-diag-final heuristic implemented in the Moses SMT toolkit (Koehn et al., 2007). Of the pairs of phrases extracted, we only kept pairs containing exactly one verb both on the English and on the Hungarian side. For each Hungarian verb from these phrase pairs, we collected all the nouns on the Hungarian side that were aligned with the verb on the English side. For example, in *döntést hoz* 'to make a decision' (lit. 'to bring a decision'), the Hungarian verb is *hoz* 'to bring'. If it is aligned with the verb *decide* on the English side, the noun *döntés* 'decision' is also aligned with this verb, as it does not appear as a separate word on the English side. Note that even if the English translation is *make a decision*, *döntés* on the Hungarian side is also usually aligned with *make* as well as with *decision*, because *make* only corresponds to *hoz* 'bring' only in this and a few other similar light verb constructions. In contrast, e.g. in the case of the compositional *táskát hoz* phrase 'to bring a bag', *bring* and *bag* are both present on the English side, so these are only aligned with their Hungarian equivalents. Finally, we have normalized and sorted the list of nouns collected for the Hungarian verbs, based on their frequency and their homogeneity regarding the given verb. We cut off the end of the resulting list (where only phrases having a compositional meaning were gathered). The algorithm generated 6531 candidate expressions for 309 verbs.

Originally, we planned to evaluate the algorithm using a list of light verb constructions[5] (LVC's) (Vincze, 2011) created from the syntacti-

---

[5]The list contains 1524 items.

cally annotated monolingual Szeged Dependency Treebank (Vincze et al., 2010) and the English-Hungarian SzegedParalell corpus. However, we found that it would be a mistake to consider the original list gold standard. Only 83.6% of the expressions on the Szeged list met our criteria. For the rest, we found that there is nothing odd about asking a question concerning the nominal part of the supposed light verb construction. Finally, we manually evaluated the union of the original list and the entries returned by our algorithm (7538 items altogether). The original list had a recall of 32.2% of the true positives on the union of lists. The precision and recall values for our algorithm turned out to be P=28.6%, and R=84.2%. As a result, we managed to extend the list of Hungarian LVC's and verbal idioms significantly compared to the original Szeged list. We extended our lexicon of argument frames with LVC's and idioms on the list we obtained by manually adding other arguments along with their thematic roles.

7 Aligning argument frames to their occurrences in the corpus

The first step of the algorithm aligning the argument frames to their occurrences in the UD corpus is reading the source lexicon files containing the argument frame descriptions and checking them for syntactic errors. It generates the full argument frame description for each verb by applying an inheritance mechanism adding the argument frames belonging to the verb group to those pertaining only to the given verb.

Explicit and implicit constraints on the form of arguments (suffixes, postpositions etc.) implied by the thematic roles in argument frame descriptions are converted into constraints on features and dependency relations applied to the morphological and syntactic annotations in the UD corpus, respectively. We align the argument frames to the verbs and the heads of phrases attached to them in the corpus using these constraints. The thematic roles *location* (LOC), *destination* (DST) and *source* (SRC) cover noun phrases the head of which is marked with the suffixes and postpositions used to denote location, direction and source (*Where?, Where to?, From where?*) and adverbs having such meaning. The argument frames of many verbs contain the thematic role PATH, which can be replaced by any combination of destination, source and location passed by (VIA). For the

sake of readability, case suffixes are represented by their underlying phonological form in the argument frame database. The alignment algorithm converts these descriptions into feature constraints that match the morphosyntactic descriptions in the UD corpus.

Hungarian is a 'pro drop' language, i.e. subject and singular object pronouns generally have an explicit phonological representation in sentences only if they are stressed (e.g. focused or in contrastive topic position). Subjects and objects having no surface realization are recovered in the alignment algorithm by introducing implicit pronouns and assigning the corresponding thematic role to them if the argument frame contains such arguments and there is no explicit subject or object in the given clause. For infinitives, gerunds and participles, verbal argument frames are matched by implicitly binding subjects and objects depending on the type of the construction, while the rest of the arguments are matched in the regular manner. Since objects (NP's marked with accusative case) and infinitives can only occur as arguments, not as adjuncts, frames that do not contain an object/infinitive are discarded if an explicit object/infinitive is attached to the actual verb instance.

The lexically bound nominal element of some of the light verb constructions is an apparently possessive form (annotated as the head of the phrase like in other possessive structures), e.g. *szomszédja nyakára küldte az adóhatóságot* 'he set the tax authority to check up on his neighbour' (lit. 'he sent the tax authority onto his neighbour's neck'). In these constructions, the actual argument that is to be assigned a thematic role is not this semantically empty word, which rather functions like an oblique case ending or postposition, but the possessor (i.e. the neighbor in the previous example). These structures are converted into a form similar to postpositional phrases. The real argument (*his neighbour*) becomes the head in the modified structure, and thus the appropriate thematic role can be directly assigned to it.

When multiple frames match the specific verb instance, the most specific frame is selected: matching light verb or idiomatic constructions are ranked high, otherwise match candidates are ranked by the length of the matching argument list.

Figure 6 shows how the original annotation of a sentence in the original UD corpus was corrected

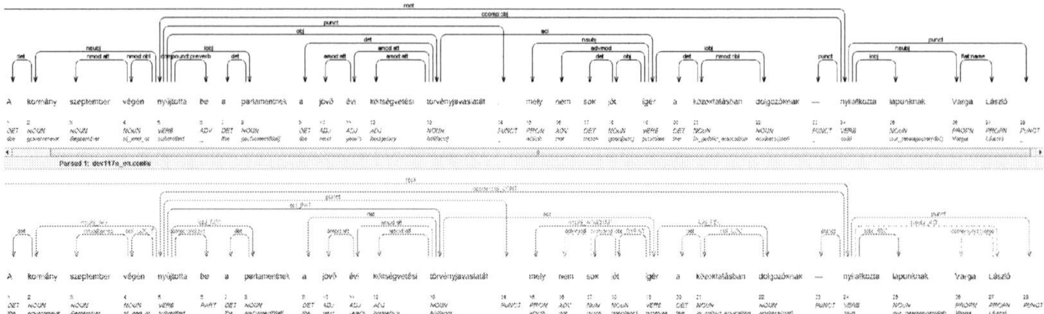

Figure 6: The result of automatic correction and assignment of thematic roles to heads of phrases and clauses attached to verbs in a sentence in the Hungarian UD corpus: 'The government submitted its bill for next year's budget to the parliament at the end of September: it bodes no good for those working in the public education sector, László Varga told our newspaper'

and extended with thematic role labels by the the adjunct and verbal argument frame matching algorithm.

8   Conclusion

Within the scope of the ongoing research presented in this article, we have created a semantically rich corpus annotation for Hungarian using the Hungarian UD subcorpus as a starting point. Our future tasks include integrating the argument frames of nominal predicates and manual checking of the generated thematic role annotation. We may also need to finetune the interaction of lexically-driven automatic adjunct annotation and verbal argument frame alignment, and the ranking of matching argument frames. Furthermore, arguments annotated with thematic roles will need to be semantically further subcategorized to be able to generate the right questions. We have done this, but we have not yet integrated this information with the rest of the annotation. We will also need to extend our corpus (converting and correcting parts of the Szeged Dependency Treebank not included in the Hungarian UD corpus) to provide enough training material for a semantic parser.

Acknowledgments

This research has been implemented with support provided by grants FK 125217 and PD 125216 of the National Research, Development and Innovation Office of Hungary financed under the FK 17 and PD 17 funding schemes as well as by grant ÚNKP-18–3-III-PPKE-26 of the New National Excellence Program of the Ministry of Human Resources. We would like to thank Kinga Fegyó and Ivett Bognár for their participation in creating verbal argument frames and assigning thematic roles.

References

Jacob Devlin, Ming-Wei Chang, Kenton Lee, and Kristina Toutanova. 2018. BERT: Pre-training of deep bidirectional transformers for language understanding. *CoRR*, abs/1810.04805.

Chris Dyer, Victor Chahuneau, and Noah A. Smith. 2013. A simple, fast, and effective reparameterization of IBM Model 2. In *Proceedings of the 2013 Conference of the North American Chapter of the Association for Computational Linguistics: Human Language Technologies*, pages 644–648. Association for Computational Linguistics.

Sylvain Kahane, Marine Courtin, and Kim Gerdes. 2017. Multi-word annotation in syntactic treebanks - propositions for universal dependencies. In *Proceedings of the 16th International Workshop on Treebanks and Linguistic Theories*, pages 181–189, Prague, Czech Republic.

Philipp Koehn, Hieu Hoang, Alexandra Birch, Chris Callison-Burch, Marcello Federico, Nicola Bertoldi, Brooke Cowan, Wade Shen, Christine Moran, Richard Zens, Chris Dyer, Ondrej Bojar, Alexandra Constantin, and Evan Herbst. 2007. Moses: Open source toolkit for statistical machine translation. In *ACL*. The Association for Computer Linguistics.

Pierre Lison and Jörg Tiedemann. 2016. OpenSubtitles2016: Extracting large parallel corpora from movie and TV subtitles. In *Proceedings of the Tenth International Conference on Language Resources and Evaluation (LREC 2016)*, Paris, France. European Language Resources Association (ELRA).

Guido Minnen, John Carroll, and Darren Pearce. 2001.

Applied morphological processing of English. *Nat. Lang. Eng.*, 7(3):207–223.

Joakim Nivre, Marie-Catherine de Marneffe, Filip Ginter, Yoav Goldberg, Jan Hajic, Christopher D. Manning, Ryan McDonald, Slav Petrov, Sampo Pyysalo, Natalia Silveira, Reut Tsarfaty, and Daniel Zeman. 2016. Universal Dependencies v1: A multilingual treebank collection. In *Proceedings of the Tenth International Conference on Language Resources and Evaluation (LREC 2016)*, Paris, France. European Language Resources Association (ELRA).

Attila Novák and Borbála Novák. 2018. POS, ANA and LEM: Word embeddings built from annotated corpora perform better. In *Computational Linguistics and Intelligent Text Processing: 17th International Conference, CICLing 2018*, Hanoi, Vietnam. Springer International Publishing, Cham.

Attila Novák, Borbála Siklósi, and Csaba Oravecz. 2016. A new integrated open-source morphological analyzer for Hungarian. In *Proceedings of the Tenth International Conference on Language Resources and Evaluation (LREC'16)*, Portorož, Slovenia. European Language Resources Association (ELRA).

György Orosz and Attila Novák. 2013. PurePos 2.0: a hybrid tool for morphological disambiguation. In *Proceedings of the International Conference on Recent Advances in Natural Language Processing (RANLP 2013)*, pages 539–545, Hissar, Bulgaria. Incoma Ltd. Shoumen, Bulgaria.

Alec Radford, Jeff Wu, Rewon Child, David Luan, Dario Amodei, and Ilya Sutskever. 2019. Language models are unsupervised multitask learners.

Bálint Sass, Tamás Váradi, Júlia Pajzs, and Margit Kiss. 2010. *Magyar igei szerkezetek: a leggyakoribb vonzatok és szókapcsolatok szótára [Hungarian verbal constructions: a dictionary of the most frequent arguments and phrases]*. A magyar nyelv kézikönyvei. Tinta Könyvkiadó.

Borbála Siklósi. 2016. Using embedding models for lexical categorization in morphologically rich languages. In *Computational Linguistics and Intelligent Text Processing: 17th International Conference, CICLing 2016*, pages 115–126, Konya, Turkey. Springer International Publishing, Cham.

Kristina Toutanova, Dan Klein, Christopher D. Manning, and Yoram Singer. 2003. Feature-rich part-of-speech tagging with a cyclic dependency network. In *NAACL '03: Proceedings of the 2003 Conference of the North American Chapter of the Association for Computational Linguistics on Human Language Technology*, pages 173–180, Morristown, NJ, USA. Association for Computational Linguistics.

Veronika Vincze. 2011. *Semi-Compositional Noun + Verb Constructions: Theoretical Questions and Computational Linguistic Analyses*. Ph.D. thesis.

Veronika Vincze, Richárd Farkas, Zsolt Szántó, and Katalin Ilona Simkó. 2017. Universal Dependencies and morphology for Hungarian – and on the price of universality. In *Proceedings of EACL 2017*, pages 356–365.

Veronika Vincze, Dóra Szauter, Attila Almási, György Móra, Zoltán Alexin, and János Csirik. 2010. Hungarian dependency treebank. In *Proceedings of the Seventh International Conference on Language Resources and Evaluation (LREC'10)*, Valletta, Malta. European Language Resources Association (ELRA).

Toward Dialogue Modeling: A Semantic Annotation Scheme for Questions and Answers

María Andrea Cruz Blandón, Gosse Minnema, Aria Nourbakhsh
Maria Bortichev, Maxime Amblard
LORIA, UMR 7503, Université de Lorraine, CNRS, Inria
Nancy, France
{mariaandrea.cruzblandon, gosseminnema}@gmail.com
aria.nourbakhsh@outlook.com
{maria.boritchev, maxime.amblard}@univ-lorraine.fr

Abstract

The present study proposes an annotation scheme for classifying the content and discourse contribution of question-answer pairs. We propose detailed guidelines for using the scheme and apply them to dialogues in English, Spanish, and Dutch. Finally, we report on initial machine learning experiments for automatic annotation.

1 Introduction

Question-answer pair (QAP) labeling is the problem of characterizing the content and discourse contribution of questions and answers using a small but maximally informative tagset that can be consistently applied by both human annotators and NLP systems. QAP labeling has many potential use cases, for example as a preprocessing step for dialogue modeling systems or for chatbots. The problem is not new: in the NLP literature, different aspects of QAP tagging have been addressed in the context of question answering systems (Li and Roth, 2002), question generation systems (e.g. Graesser et al., 2008), and dialogue act classification (e.g. Allen and Core, 1997; Stolcke et al., 2000).

However, we see several gaps in the literature: existing approaches to QAP classification often do not cover the full range of questions and answers found in human dialogues and are limited in the types of semantic information that they cover. To address these issues, we propose a new annotation scheme that was developed based on corpora of natural conversations in several languages (English, Spanish, and Dutch) and provides several layers of annotations for QAPs. Notably, where applicable, we annotate the semantic role of the questioned constituent in questions and their corresponding answer (e.g. 'Does she live in *Paris or London?*' ⇒ LOCATION), which we believe is an informative, yet easy definable way of globally characterizing the content of a QAP.

Our paper has two main contributions: the annotation scheme itself (section 3) and two ways of applying it to real data. We developed detailed and explicit guidelines for human annotators, and tested these on corpus data (section 4.1). Additionally, we started experimenting with machine learning approaches for automating part of the annotation process (section 4.2).

2 Related Work

Our annotation scheme is related to two existing schemes in particular. The first of these is Freed (1994), which categorizes questions along an *information continuum* that ranges from questions purely asking for factual information to questions that convey, rather than request, (social) information. Within this continuum, questions are divided into classes that are defined based on a combination of formal (syntactic) and functional criteria. Both of these ideas are also used in our scheme: our question types are also distinguished by whether they ask or convey information ('phatic questions' and 'completion suggestions' fall into the latter category) and are defined as combinations of specific forms and functions.

Another related scheme is Stolcke et al. (2000), an adapted version of DAMSL ('Dialog Act Markup in Several Layers', Allen and Core 1997), an annotation scheme for dialogue acts (including QAPs). The scheme includes a set of eight different question types (e.g. *yes/no* questions, *wh*-questions, *rhetorical* questions) that has considerable overlap with our set of question types.

3 Annotation scheme

Annotated information is split between two main 'layers': *question/answer type* and *feature* (se-

Proceedings of the 13th Linguistic Annotation Workshop, pages 230–235
Florence, Italy, August 1, 2019. ©2019 Association for Computational Linguistics

mantic role). Every question or answer is assigned at least a type tag, and depending on the type, a feature tag.

3.1 Questions

The question tagset was designed in a corpus-driven way, starting with two basic types and expanding the tagset based on corpus data. Our starting assumption is that the corpora would contain at least two well-known and well-defined categories of questions: *yes/no* questions and *wh*-questions (Freed, 1994). In our opinion, both of these types are useful *a priori*, because they are each associated with a clear set of syntactic, semantic, and pragmatic characteristics (at least for the languages that are included in this study). Prototypical English *yes/no* questions are characterized by subject-auxiliary inversion and do-support (syntax), express a proposition that could be true or false (semantics), and their answers are expected to either confirm or deny this proposition (pragmatics). On the other hand, a prototypical English *wh*-question contains a fronted constituent that starts with a *wh*-word (syntax), expresses a proposition with missing information (semantics), and expects the answerer to supply this missing information (pragmatics) (Freed, 1994).

Next, we looked for questions in our corpora that did not correspond to either of the two prototypes and extended the scheme to fit them (see table 1 for the final scheme and examples). First, there are questions that are similar to *wh*-questions or *yes/no* questions but have a deviant form (e.g. *wh-in-situ* questions like 'You saw what?', or yes/no questions without inversion such as 'You saw him?'). We decided not to introduce new categories for these on the basis of their semantics and pragmatics.

A second group of questions has the syntactic characteristics of a *yes/no* question or a *wh*-question, but a different pragmatics and/or semantics. For example, the asker of the question suggests a way to complete the utterance of the previous speaker, and the expected answer would confirm or deny this suggestion. This is subtly different from a prototypical *yes/no* question because the asker of the question does not necessarily ask their interlocutor to confirm the truth value of the suggestion (e.g. *A: it includes heat and uhm, I think B: Water?*, SCoSE/Amy, line 746-747[1]). We

---

[1]See section 4.1.2 for information about our corpora.

call these types of questions *completion sugges-tions*.

Tag	Name	Tag	Name
YN	Yes/No question	WH	Wh-question
CS	Completion suggestion	PQ	Phatic question
DQ	Disjunctive question		

Table 1: Question types

The third group of questions appear to be a *yes/no* question or a *wh*-question, respectively, but their context and intonation make clear that the asker is not actually interested in the confirmation or denial of the proposition. Instead, such questions can have various so-called *phatic functions*, i.e. their semantic content is less important than their social and rhetorical functions (Freed, 1994; Senft, 2009). We call this type of questions *phatic questions* (e.g. *right? / oh yeah? / you know?*).[2]

Finally, some questions containing a disjunction (e.g. 'Do you go on Monday or on Tuesday?') are semantically and pragmatically similar to *wh*-questions, but are syntactically closer to *yes/no* questions. This kind of questions, like *yes/no* questions, exhibits subject-auxiliary inversion (at least in English), but does not ask for the confirmation or denial of the proposition that it expresses. Instead, it expects the answerer to provide some missing information with the set of options to choose from. We call this type of questions *disjunctive questions* (sometimes also called *alternative questions* in the literature).

3.2 Features

Wh- and *disjunctive* questions are always 'about' a particular constituent (e.g. 'Which man is running?', 'Do you want *coffee or tea*?'). The *feature*, or semantic role of this constituent provides information about the content of the question and the expected answer (e.g. if the questioned constituent is an AGENT then it is likely that the answer will refer to a person). Detecting semantic roles requires semantically analyzing the sentence, but for *wh*-questions, *wh*-words often provide cues (e.g. 'where' for LOCATION). Our feature annotations follow the feature set (see table 2) and the

---

[2]Note that our use of the term *phatic question* is somewhat broader than the *phatic information* question described in Freed (1994); for example, our definition also includes rethorical questions, while in Freed's scheme, these are not included.

mapping from (English) *wh*-words to features proposed in Boritchev (2017) (adapted from Jurafsky and Martin 2000).

Tag	Name	Tag	Name
TMP	Temporality	OW	Owner
LOC	Location	RE	Reason
AG	Agent	TH	Theme
CH	Characteristic		

Table 2: Features

Tags	Name	Question Type
PA	Positive Answer	YN, CS
NA	Negative Answer	YN, CS
FA	Feature Answer	DQ, WH
PHA	Phatic Answer	YN, CS, DQ, WH, PQ
UA	Uncertainty Answers	YN, CS, DQ, WH, PQ
UT	Unrelated Topic	YN, CS, DQ, WH, PQ
DA	Deny the Assumption	YN, CS, DQ, WH, PQ

Table 3: Answers

3.3 Answers

The main intuition underlying our answer annotation scheme is that question types restrict their answers: for example, *yes/no* questions are prototypically answered by 'yes' or 'no', and *wh*-questions ask for a constituent with a particular feature. Table 3 summarizes our answer types and their corresponding question types. Among these types of answers, there may be overlaps. For example, a 'deny the assumption' answer can be thought of as a negative answer because it is possible that they share the same grammatical and semantic structure. Different factors including the context and prosody are relevant to decide overlapping tags.

Some questions are not followed by answer. We distinguish between two situations. First, there are questions that receive a reply that, while not providing the information asked for in the question, clearly do respond to it. For example, in the QAP *A: 'When will you guys get off?' / B: 'My last exam is like …I don't know'* (SCoSe/Amy, line 243-244), B's response does not answer A's question directly but does engage with it as there is a logical connection between finishing the exams and going on vacation. In such cases, the response is tagged as *unrelated topic (UT)* because it is about a different topic but still responds to the question. By contrast, when there is no response at all, no answer should be annotated.

4 Annotation Experiments

In this section, we discuss our experiments with applying the scheme manually (section 4.1) and using machine learning techniques (section 4.2).

4.1 Manual annotation

We have experimented with applying the scheme on real-world data. Our experiment consists of two parts: writing annotation guidelines to explicitly define the annotation process and annotating 701 questions across three languages, namely, English, Spanish, and Dutch.[3]

4.1.1 Annotation guide

In order to help annotators apply the scheme consistently, we wrote annotation guidelines for English, which include examples and instructions for how to use the annotation software (ELAN 2017, Sloetjes and Wittenburg 2008). The annotation procedure guides the annotator in identifying questions, dealing with transcription errors, determining question types, and adding tags for additional information such as features, complexity, and indirectness.

Some question types have a very specific prototypical syntactic form (e.g. *wh*-questions), whereas other questions can have several different forms (e.g. *phatic* questions). We exploit this by defining a precedence order for question types, which serves as a filter for identifying questions. The precedence order lists question types from the most specific to the most general ones, i.e. from questions with easily identifiable characteristics to those that can have different forms as it is the case for the phatic questions. The precedence order is as follows: (1) *Wh-questions*, (2) *Disjunctive questions*, (3) *Yes/No questions*, (4) *Completion suggestions* (5) *Phatic questions*.

4.1.2 Corpora

We annotated several dialogues from three different corpora in three languages: the *Saarbrücken Corpus of Spoken English (SCoSE)* (Norrick, 2017), a corpus of face-to-face conversations; the *CallFriend* corpus (Spanish) (Canavan and Zipperlen, 1996), a corpus of phone conversations;

---

[3]Our guidelines and annotations are available in our repository at `https://github.com/andrea08/question_answer_annotation`.

Annotators	A_o	κ
Questions	0.73	0.63
Features	0.90	0.67
Answers	0.59	0.49

Table 4: Cohen's Kappa score (κ) and observed agreement (A_o) for gold standard dialogue.

and the *Spoken Dutch Corpus (CGN)* Oostdijk 2001, a corpus of phone conversations. The purpose of annotating these dialogues was to test the annotation scheme on different languages and produce annotated data.

We annotated all questions in a subset of 4,939 utterances from the SCoSE corpus. Of these, 3,578 utterances were used to build the 'gold standard' corpus (used for calculating agreement scores and training machine learning algorithms). The remainder of the corpus was used as a test set in the machine learning algorithms. Furthermore, we annotated questions and answers from 2,618 and 935 utterances of CallFriend and CGN corpora, respectively. We relied primarily on the transcriptions of the corpora; in case of doubt, we made use of the audio recordings as well.

4.1.3 Results

We annotated 701 questions (Q) and 483 answers (A), distributed as follows: 422 (Q) / 289 (A) in the ScoSE corpus; 87 (Q) / 72 (A) in the CGN corpus; and 192 (Q) / 122 (A) in the CallFriend corpus. A descriptive analysis of our annotations shows that *yes/no* questions are the most common type in the three corpora, 40% (Spanish), 42% (English) and 64% (Dutch).

To evaluate the annotations, inter-annotator agreement was calculated based on a subset of the gold standard corpus.[4] Table 4 illustrates the values of observed agreement (A_o) and Cohen's κ (Cohen, 1960) obtained for question, feature and answer annotation. The agreement values obtained for question types were over 0.6 (for all annotators combined). This would generally be considered to be a 'moderate' level of agreement (Landis and Koch, 1977). A large share of our disagreements came from phatic questions; distinguishing these from other question types sometimes relies on subtle pragmatic and semantic con-

textual judgements. Agreement for answer types is lower than for question types because question types restrict answer types and hence question type disagreements can cause answer type disagreements.

In order to improve the annotation guidelines, we systematically examined all of the disagreements, most of which fell into one of four categories: (1) Simple mistakes, such as missing a question or choosing an (obviously) wrong tag. (2) Disagreements as a consequence of a previous disagreement; e.g., *wh*-questions need feature annotations, but *phatic* questions do not. In this case, a disagreement about the question type can cause further disagreement about feature type. (3) Missing instructions in the annotation guidelines for handling particular situations, e.g. annotating utterances containing interruptions. (4) Utterances whose interpretation was ambiguous and depends on subtle intonational or contextual cues for which it is hard to formulate a general rule.

4.2 Machine learning

We also conducted preliminary machine learning experiments for automating the annotation process. For the moment, we focus only on question type classification for English dialogues. So far, the approach that shows the most promising results is a decision tree algorithm (Quinlan, 1986) that takes as input a set of hand-designed features representing formal characteristics of a question, such as its length, the presence of a *wh*-word, and the presence of words such as *really?* or *you know?* Our full feature set is given in Table 5. Note that these features are quite superficial and do not take into account the discourse context of a question. Still, the algorithm achieves an accuracy score of 0.73 and an F1-score of 0.58, outperforming our majority-class baseline algorithm by a wide margin (*acc.* $= 0.47$, $F1 = 0.31$).[5]

Analysing the effect of the features in the predictions of the decision tree, we found that the majority of the mistakes were associated with the length of the questions. From the questions that were misclassified and had a length less than 6 (26 questions), 50% were wrongly predicted as *phatic* questions. Particularly, as with manual annotations, *phatic* questions that contain *wh-words* were source of disagreement and misclassified. Table

---

[4]This subset consists of the 690 utterances jointly annotated by all three annotators.

[5]A global $F1$ score was calculated by macro-averaging the scores for individual classes.

6 shows the confusion matrix for all the question types.

Feature	Description	Value
has_wh	Contains a wh-constituent	True, False
has_or	Contains the word "or"	True, False
has_inversion	Verb before NP (based on shallow parse)	True, False
has_tag	Contains a tag ('isn't it', 'right')	True, False
last_utt_similar	Question shares $\geq$ 50% of its words with the previous utterance	True, False
last_utt_incomplete	Previous utterance is interrupted (marked with special transcription symbol)	True, False
has_cliche	Contains a phatic marker ('you know?', 'really?')	True, False
length	Number of words	Numerical

Table 5: Extracted features for the classification task

	YN	DQ	PQ	CS	WH	Support
YN	74	1	8	3	2	88
DQ	0	3	0	0	0	3
PQ	7	0	15	0	8	30
CS	1	0	0	0	0	1
WH	10	0	9	0	43	62

Table 6: Confusion matrix of decision tree prediction. Testing data set, 184 questions.

Furthermore, we experimented with two neural architectures, a bag-of-words (BOW) classifier and a recurrent neural network (RNN), to test what input representations are most informative. However, so far these models suffer from overfitting and perform worse than the decision tree model (BOW: $acc. = 0.76$, $F1 = 0.44$; RNN: $acc. = 0.54$, $F1 = 0.24$). We expect these models to perform better when more training data is available.

5 Conclusion

This paper introduced a new annotation scheme for question-answer pairs in natural conversation. The scheme defines five question types and seven answer types based on a mix of formal and functional criteria. An annotation guide was developed and multi-lingual corpora were annotated. Inter-annotator agreement scores were moderately high; a qualitative analysis of disagreements led to improvements to the annotation guidelines. Initial machine learning experiments show that a simple decision tree algorithm achieves above-baseline performance, but much work remains to be done for making automatic annotation practically feasible. For future work, we would also like to expand the multilingual component of our work by adding language-specific guidelines, annotating more corpora, and adapting our machine learning algorithms to different languages.

Acknowledgements

This paper was written while the first authors (Cruz Blandón, Minnema, Nourbakhsh) were enrolled in the European Master Program in Language and Communication Technologies (LCT) and were supported by the European Union Erasmus Mundus program.

References

James Allen and Mark Core. 1997. Draft of DAMSL: Dialog act markup in several layers. `https://www.cs.rochester.edu/research/speech/damsl/RevisedManual/`, accessed January 22, 2019.

Maria Boritchev. 2017. Approaching dialogue modeling in a dynamic framework. Master's thesis, Université de Lorraine.

Alexandra Canavan and George Zipperlen. 1996. CALLFRIEND, Spanish-Non-Caribbean Dialect (LDC Catalog Number: LDC96S58).

Jacob Cohen. 1960. A coefficient of agreement for nominal scales. *Educational and Psychological Measurement*, 20(1):37–46.

ELAN (version 5.2). 2017. The Language Archive, Max Planck Institute for Psycholinguistics, Nijmegen, The Netherlands. `https://tla.mpi.nl/tools/tla-tools/elan/`.

Alice F. Freed. 1994. The form and function of questions in informal dyadic conversation. *Journal of Pragmatics*, 21(6):621 – 644.

Art Graesser, Vasile Rus, and Zhiqiang Cai. 2008. Question classification schemes. In *Proceedings of the Workshop on Question Generation*.

Daniel Jurafsky and James H. Martin. 2000. *Speech and Language Processing: An Introduction to Natural Language Processing, Computational Linguistics, and Speech Recognition*, 1st edition. Prentice Hall PTR, Upper Saddle River, NJ, USA.

J. Richard Landis and Gary G. Koch. 1977. The measurement of observer agreement for categorical data. *Biometrics*, 33(1):159–174.

Xin Li and Dan Roth. 2002. Learning question classifiers. In *COLING '02 Proceedings of the 19th international conference on computational linguistics*, pages 1–7.

Neal Norrick. 2017. SCoSE part 1: Complete conversations. English Linguistics, Department of English at Saarland University.

Nelleke Oostdijk. 2001. The design of the Spoken Dutch Corpus. *Language and Computers*, 36:105–112.

J. Ross Quinlan. 1986. Induction of decision trees. *Machine learning*, 1(1):81–106.

Gunter Senft. 2009. Phatic communion. In Gunter Senft, Jan-Ola stman, and Jef Verschueren, editors, *Culture and language use*, pages 226–233. John Benjamins Publishing, Amsterdam/Philadelphia.

Han Sloetjes and Peter Wittenburg. 2008. Annotation by category: ELAN and ISO DCR. In *LREC*.

Andreas Stolcke, Klaus Ries, Noah Coccaro, Elizabeth. Shriberg, Rebecca. Bates, Daniel. Jurafsky, Paul Taylor, Rachel Martin, Carol Van Ess-Dykema, and Marie Meteer. 2000. Dialogue act modeling for automatic tagging and recognition of conversational speech. *Computational linguistics*, 26(3):339–373.

Towards a General Abstract Meaning Representation Corpus for Brazilian Portuguese

Marco Antonio Sobrevilla Cabezudo and Thiago Alexandre Salgueiro Pardo
Interinstitutional Center for Computational Linguistics (NILC)
Institute of Mathematical and Computer Sciences, University of São Paulo
São Carlos/SP, Brazil
`msobrevillac@usp.br, taspardo@icmc.usp.br`

Abstract

Abstract Meaning Representation (AMR) is a recent and prominent semantic representation with good acceptance and several applications in the Natural Language Processing area. For English, there is a large annotated corpus (with approximately 39K sentences) that supports the research with the representation. However, to the best of our knowledge, there is only one restricted corpus for Portuguese, which contains 1,527 sentences. In this context, this paper presents an effort to build a general purpose AMR-annotated corpus for Brazilian Portuguese by translating and adapting AMR English guidelines. Our results show that such approach is feasible, but there are some challenging phenomena to solve. More than this, efforts are necessary to increase the coverage of the corresponding lexical resource that supports the annotation.

1 Introduction

In recent years, there has been renewed interest in the Natural Language Processing (NLP) community in language understanding and dialogue. Thus, the issue of how the semantic content of language should be represented has reentered into the NLP discussion. In this context, several semantic representations, like Universal Networking Language (UNL) (Uchida et al., 1996), the semantic representation used in the Groningen Meaning Bank (Basile et al., 2012), Universal Conceptual Cognitive Annotation (UCCA) (Abend and Rappoport, 2013), and, more recently, the Abstract Meaning Representation (AMR) (Banarescu et al., 2013), have emerged.

Abstract Meaning Representation is a semantic formalism that aims to encode the meaning of a sentence with a simple representation in the form of a directed rooted graph (Banarescu et al., 2013). This representation includes information about se-

mantic roles, named entities, wiki entities, spatial-temporal information, and co-references, among other information. AMR may be represented using logic forms (see (a) in Figure 1), PENMAN notation (see (b) in Figure 1), and graphs (see (c) in Figure 1). AMR has gained relevance in the research community due to its easiness to be read by computers and humans (as it could be represented using graphs or first-order logic, which are representations that are more familiar to computers and humans, respectively), its attempt to abstract away from syntactic idiosyncrasies (making the tasks to focus only on semantic processing) and its wide use of other comprehensive linguistic resources, such as PropBank (Bos, 2016).

In relation to its attempt to abstract away from syntactic idiosyncrasies, it may be seen that AMR annotation in Figure 1 could be generated from the sentences "The boy wants the girl to believe him." and "The boy wants to be believed by the girl.", which are semantically similar, but with different syntactic realizations. Regarding the use of linguistic resources, AMR annotation in Figure 1 shows information provided by PropBank, as the framesets "want-01" and "believe-01", and some semantic roles that they require.

The available AMR-annotated corpora for English are large, containing approximately 39,000 sentences. Some efforts have been performed for using AMR as an interlingua and building corpus for Non-English languages, taking advantage of the alignments and the parallel corpora that exist (Xue et al., 2014; Damonte and Cohen, 2018). Other works tried to adapt the AMR guidelines to other languages (Migueles-Abraira et al., 2018), considering its cross-linguistic potential.

It is unnecessary to stress the importance of corpus creation for other languages. Annotated corpora provide qualitative and reusable data for building or improving existing methods and ap-

Proceedings of the 13th Linguistic Annotation Workshop, pages 236–244
Florence, Italy, August 1, 2019. ©2019 Association for Computational Linguistics

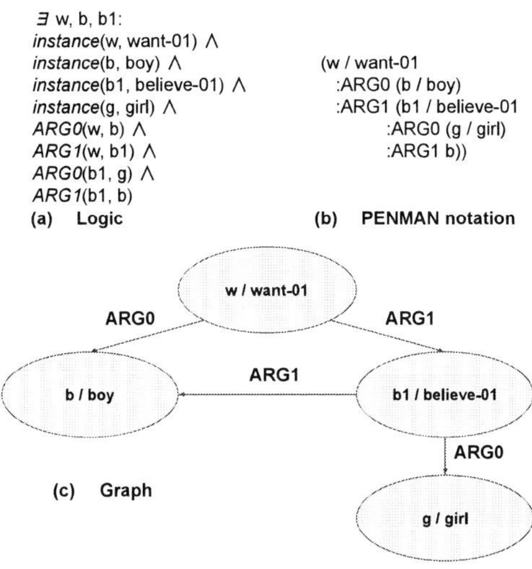

Figure 1: AMR examples

plications, as well as for serving as benchmarks to compare different approaches. In the case of Portuguese language, to the best of our knowledge, there is an unique AMR-annotated corpus, composed by the sentences of the "The Little Prince" book (Anchiêta and Pardo, 2018). The lexical resource they used to annotate some concepts was the Verbo-Brasil (Duran and Aluísio, 2015), which replicates the PropBank experience for Portuguese.

One difficulty related to the above corpus is its unusual writing style (since it is a tale) and its restricted vocabulary, which make the creation or adequacy of general purpose tools a more difficult task. More than this, the corpus is too small, hindering the development or adaptation of methods for tasks that require semantics. In this context, this work intends to show the extension process of the AMR annotation on a general purpose corpus (which covers a wide vocabulary and several domains) using the current AMR guidelines and some adaptations for Portuguese.

This paper is organized as follows. Section 2 briefly introduces some previous work that tried to build AMR corpora for Non-English languages. The corpus in Portuguese is described in Section 3. The annotation methodology and evaluation are described in Section 4 and 5, respectively. The current state of the annotation is reported in Section 6, and, finally, some concluding remarks are presented in Section 7.

2   Related Work

One of the first works that tried to build an AMR-annotated corpus for a Non-English language was proposed by Xue et al. (2014). The main goal of this work was to evaluate the potentiality of AMR to work as an interlingua. In order to achieve this goal, the authors annotated 100 English sentences of the Penn Treebank using AMR and then translated them to Czech and Chinese, which were annotated with AMR as well. Their main finding was that the level of compatibility of AMR between English and Chinese was higher than between English and Czech.

In other research line, Vanderwende et al. (2015) proposed an AMR parser to convert Logic Form representations into AMR for English. The authors also built an AMR-annotated corpus for French, German, Spanish, and Japanese.

Damonte and Cohen (2018) developed an AMR parser for English and used parallel corpora to learn AMR parsers for Italian, Spanish, German, and Chinese. The main results showed that the new parsers overcame structural differences between the languages. The authors also proposed a method to evaluate the parsers that does not need gold standard data in the target languages.

In the case of Spanish, Migueles-Abraira et al. (2018) performed a manual AMR annotation of the book "The Little Prince" using the guidelines of the AMR project. The main goal was to analyze the guidelines and to suggest some adaptions in order to cover the relevant linguistic phenomena in Spanish.

For Portuguese, Anchiêta and Pardo (2018) built the first AMR-annotated corpus taking advantage of the alignments between the book "The Little Prince" for English and Portuguese languages. Thus, the strategy consisted of importing the corresponding AMR annotation for each sentence from the English annotated corpus and revising the annotation to adapt it to Portuguese.

3   The Corpus for Brazilian Portuguese

As mentioned, the AMR-annotated corpus for Brazilian Portuguese was composed by sentences of the "The Little Prince" book (Anchiêta and Pardo, 2018). In order to broaden the annotation to other domains and text genres, our proposal focused on annotating news in several domains.

The news texts were extracted from RSS[1] from *Folha de São Paulo* news agency[2], one of the mainstream agencies in Brazil. The selected news came from different sections/domains: "daily news", "world news", "education", "environment", "sports", "science", "balance and health", "*ilustrada*", "*ilustríssima*", "power", and "technology". Additionally to these sentences, sentences of the PropBank.Br[3] (Duran and Aluísio, 2012) were collected in order to enrich the corpus (PropBank.Br already contains semantic role annotation, which makes the AMR annotation task much easier). It is important to note that PropBank.Br sentences are also from news texts.

The news download interval was from November 25th to November 28th, 2018. Overall, 249 news were collected from different domains, totalizing 7,643 sentences. The news distribution is presented in Table 1.

Section	# News	# Sentences	Avg. tokens by sentence	# Selected sentences
Daily news	48	1,521	22.94	848
World news	43	1,212	24.38	617
Education	13	426	23.72	222
Environment	4	98	25.40	45
Sports	29	875	20.93	531
Science	10	460	23.50	243
Balance and Health	6	159	23.15	88
Ilustrada	27	648	24.10	348
Ilustríssima	7	305	24.41	161
Power	51	1,677	19.93	1,121
Technology	11	262	22.55	149
Total	249	7,643	22.53	4,563

Table 1: News collection statistics

Due to the statistics observed in Table 1 and the difficulty that the task of semantic annotation carries, the scope of the work was focused on annotating only short sentences (but guaranteeing that different domains are covered). In order to define what a short sentence is, the average number of tokens by sentence was calculated and this value was used as threshold. Thus, sentences with a number of tokens below the average (in our case, it was 22.53 tokens) were selected, resulting in 4,563 sentences to be AMR annotated (indicated by the "Selected sentences" column in the table).

In relation to the PropBank.Br sentences (Duran and Aluísio, 2012), the same strategy for selecion was adopted. In total, 3,012 PropBank.Br sentences were added to our corpus.

4 Annotation Methodology

The proposed annotation methodology consisted of two main steps. The first step aimed to independently analyze and think about the sentence structure, while the second step counted with the aid of the AMR Editor tool (Hermjakob, 2013) to produce the AMR annotation in PENMAN format in order to export the annotation.

In relation to the first step, a sequence of actions need to be carried out in order to facilitate the second step. These actions are described as follows:

- To identify the kind of sentence to be analyzed (default, comparative, superlative, coordinate, subordinate, and others). This is useful to determine whether it is necessary to build two or more sub-graphs (in case of coordinate or subordinate sentences) and then to join them using a conjunction (usually coordinate sentences) or a concept of the main sub-graph (in the case of subordinate sentences).

- To identify concepts. Annotators must follow the AMR guidelines[4] in order to define a concept. Thus, they may identify general concepts, concepts from AMR Guidelines or concepts from Verbo-Brasil.

- To identify the main concept from the two previous steps. For example, the main verb could be the main concept in a default sentence.

- To identify the relations among the identified concepts[5].

An example of the execution of the actions is presented in Figure 2. The sentence to be analyzed is "*Ieltsin adotou outras medidas simbólicas para mostrar a perda de poderes do Parlamento.*"("Yeltsin took other symbolic measures to show the loss of Parliament's power."). This is the case of a subordinate sentence. Then, we need to identify the concepts. Thus, some words became general concepts, named-entities or Verbo-Brasil framesets. Then, it was necessary to identify the graph top (in this case, the verb "*adotar*" because

---

[1]RSS stands for "Really Simple Syndication".

[2]Available at `https://www.folha.uol.com.br/`.

[3]PropBank.Br was the basis for the construction of the previously cited Verbo-Brasil.

[4]Available at `https://github.com/amrisi/amr-guidelines/blob/master/amr.md`. Accessed on April 1st, 2019. The adopted version was the 1.2.5.

[5]The relations were extracted from Verbo-Brasil (for core relations) and AMR guidelines (for non-core relations).

it is the main verb of the main sentence "*Ieltsin adotou outras medidas simbólicas*"). Finally, the relations among all concepts were identified.

Similar to the work of Migueles-Abraira et al. (2018), our proposal tried to adapt the AMR guidelines to Brazilian Portuguese, making some modifications on it in order to deal with the specific linguistic phenomena. The general guideline used to annotate a sentence is described as follows:

- To use the framesets of Verbo-Brasil (Duran and Aluísio, 2015) to determine verb senses and the argument structure of verbs.

- To use the 3rd singular person ("*ele*") or the pronoun "that" ("*isso*") in case of NP Ellipsis, clitic or possessive pronouns. Differently from Migueles-Abraira et al. (2018), we propose to use ("*ele*") or "that" ("*isso*") as a default value. We decided to determine this guideline in order to keep some annotation pattern.

- In the case of indeterminate subject, not to use any pronoun.

- In the case of multi-word expression, to identify the one-word synonym of the expression and use it in the annotation, or define a one-word as the join of the words.

- To use the AMR framesets to annotate modal verbs, since Verbo-Brasil does not include that kind of verbs. In order to facilitate the identification of a modal verb, to try to replace by "*poder*" ("can") or "*dever*" ("should") verbs.

- In cases where the difference among two or more senses is subtle, to use the most frequent sense that satisfies the predicted argument structure.

- To use the AMR guidelines and dictionary[6] for the other cases.

The proposed annotation strategy consisted of annotating sentences of shorter size at the beginning and then increasing sentence size up to 22 tokens, according to the annotators' learning. Sentences that had verbs that were not included in the Verbo-Brasil repository were not annotated and the new verbs were put in a list in order to enrich the repository in the future.

Smatch score (Cai and Knight, 2013) was used to calculate the inter-annotator agreement. Unlike the work of Banarescu et al. (2013), which built a gold standard (using the total agreement between the annotators), the way to calculate the inter-annotator agreement consisted in comparing all annotations in an all-against-all configuration, obtaining the average of all inter-annotator agreements. Finally, the annotated versions of the sentences belonging to the agreement sample that were included in the final corpus were chosen by an adjudicator (since that more than one possible annotation exists).

5 Evaluation

In relation to the overview of the annotation process, it is important to know that the annotation team was originally composed of 14 annotators[7] that belong to the areas of Computer Science and Linguistics (all of them focused on Natural Language Processing). These annotators participated in two training sessions. In the first session, the task and the resources to be used were presented. The participants were trained by annotating sentences of PropBank.Br (Duran and Aluísio, 2012) in order to perceive the difficulty of the task. The second session aimed to answer questions about the annotation, show the inter-annotator agreement during the training stage, some common mistakes, and launch the annotation process.

5.1 Inter-annotator Agreement

The results of the inter-annotator agreement are presented in Table 2. During the training stage, the agreement was measured once in each week (with 4-5 sentences to annotate per week). Currently, the annotators are building AMR annotations for more sentences until they reach 100 sentences (as in the original AMR project) in order to have an adequate sample to measure the agreement.

In general, the Smatch was 0.72, with the minimum being 0.70 and the maximum 0.77. These results are similar to the obtained by the work of Banarescu et al. (2013) (between 0.70 and 0.80), although the number of sentences assessed in English was 100 (in our case, there were 34 sentences) and the number of annotators was 4 (we

---

[6]Available at `https://www.isi.edu/~ulf/amr/lib/amr-dict.html`. **Accessed on April 1st, 2019.**

[7]During the annotation process, some of the annotators gave up.

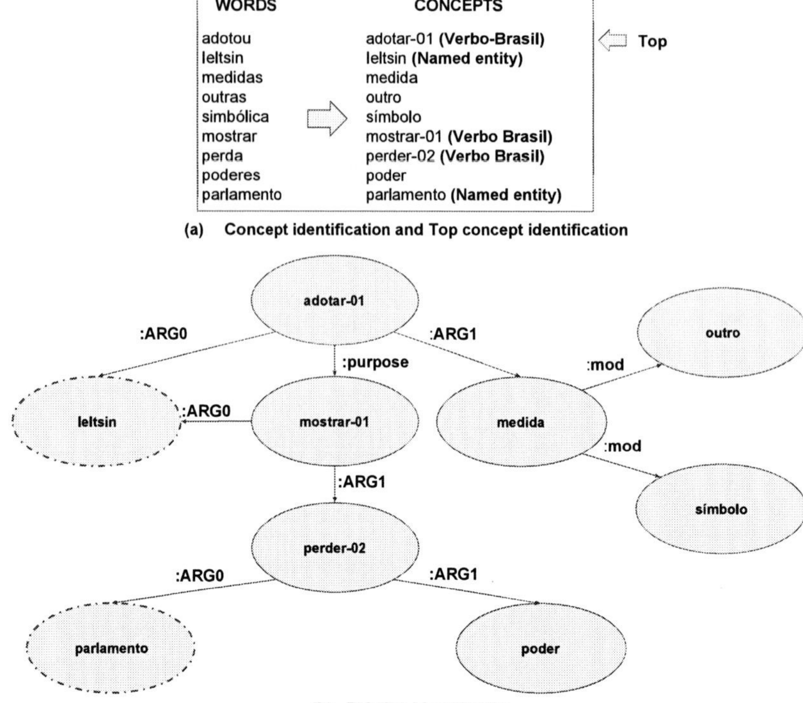

Figure 2: Example of the annotation steps

had from 5 to 7).

Week	# Annotators	# Sentences	Smatch
1	5	5	0.77
2	7	5	0.72
3	5	4	0.73
-	-	20	0.70
Total		34	0.72

Table 2: Annotation agreement

5.2 Disagreement Analysis

It is important to highlight some reasons that led to the occurring disagreements. One of the reasons was the difficulty identifying some kinds of verbs, as modal, copula, light and auxiliary verbs. Additionally, due to the use of English framesets for modal verbs, there were cases where the frameset to be used was difficult to be determined. For example, the sentence "*A quem podemos nos aliar?*" ("Who can we ally with?") was encoded as follows:

(r / **recommend-01**
   :ARG1 (a / aliar-01
     :ARG0 (n / nós)
     :ARG1 (a2 / amr-unknown)))

(p5 / **possible-01**
   :ARG1 (a8 / aliar-01
     :ARG1 (n3 / nós)
     :ARG2 (a9 / amr-unknown)))

As one may see, the modal verb "*poder*" was encoded as "recommend-01" and "possible-01", depending on the interpretation of the annotator. This problem occurred because a modal verb in Portuguese may be translated in different ways to English according to the context.

Another difficulty was the identification of verbs whose modality could not be easy to identify. For example, the verb "*conseguir*" (usually translated to "get") in the sentence "*Ele contou que conseguiu adquirir 20 entradas porque ofereceu Cr$ 5.000 ao bilheteiro.*" ("He said he was able to get 20 tickets because he offered Cr$ 5.000 to the ticket clerk.") was annotated using a Verbo-Brasil frameset (without modal verb) by some annotators and using the AMR frameset (for modal verb) by others. To solve this difficulty, the guidelines (adapted for Portuguese) suggested that they should try to substitute verbs for some modal verbs as "*dever*" or "*poder*". In the previous sentence, the verb "*conseguir*" could be replaced by the verb "*poder*". This way, "*conseguir*" might be identified as a modal verb.

As for the modal verbs, the annotation of auxiliary verbs also presented some difficulties. Some annotators used the Verbo-Brasil framesets and others omitted that verb annotation, being this last one the correct way to annotate. For example, this happens for the verb "*ficar*" in the sentence "*Eles ficaram aguardando o resultado da negociação.*" ("They were waiting for the outcome of the negotiation."), where the verb fulfills an auxiliary function, and, therefore, it should not be considered in the final AMR representation.

Another difficulty was related to the identification of the verb sense in the Verbo-Brasil repository. This identification was problematic in some cases. For example, the verb "*admitir*" in the sentence "*Ele não treinava como devia, o que não admito*" ("He did not train as he should, what I do not admit") was associated to the concept "*admitir-01*" (whose meaning is related to confess or acknowledge as truth) and to the concept *admitir-02* (whose meaning is related to agree, allow, or tolerate). In this case, i.e., when the verb sense is difficult to identify, the suggestion was to select the most frequent sense (usually the first in the sense list) that covers all the arguments in the sentence.

In a similar way, sometimes the identification of the argument labels and the relations between concepts presented challenges to the annotators. For example, the word "*porque*" in the sentence "*Ele contou que conseguiu adquirir 20 entradas porque ofereceu Cr$ 5.000 ao bilheteiro.*" was associated to the relation "*cause*". However, some annotators omitted this relation.

In relation to the reference annotation, we may highlight that the annotators had disagreements in some cases, mainly when they had to choose where the reference should be inserted. For example, in the sentence "*A empresa considera os equipamentos ultrapassados e quer adquirir modelos modernos.*" ("The company considers the equipment to be outdated and wants to acquire modern models.") represented in the two following ways), the concept "*empresa*" ("company") was used as reference for "querer-01" and "adquirir-01" by some annotators and as reference only for "*querer-01*" by others.

```
(e / and
   :op1 (c / considerar-01
      :ARG0 (e2 / empresa)
      :ARG1 (e3 / equipamento)
      :ARG2 (u / ultrapassado))
   :op2 (q / querer-01
      :ARG0 e2
      :ARG1 (a2 / adquirir-01
         :ARG0 e2
         :ARG1 (m / modelo
            :mod (m2 / moderno)))))


(e / and
   :op1 (c6 / considerar-01
      :ARG0 (e / empresa)
      :ARG1 (e12 / equipamento
      :ARG2 (u2 / ultrapassado)))
   :op2 (q / querer-01
      :ARG0 e
      :ARG1 (a12 / adquirir-01
         :ARG1 (m / modelo
            :mod (m2 / moderno)))))
```

In relation to part of speech tags, we remark that there were problems in the annotation of some adjectives and nouns. In the case of adjectives, there were some difficulties to nominalize some adjectives (pertainym adjectives). For example, the adjective "*tributária*" ("tributary") in the expression "*carga tributária*" ("Tax burden") refers to a type of "*carga*" ("charge"), therefore, the concept "*tributo*" ("tribute") should be used instead of "*tributária*". In the case of nouns, there were difficulties to convert some nouns into verbs and to deal with some nouns like executors of some action. For example, the word "*competividade*" ("competitiveness") was encoded using the concept "*competivididade*" (wrong way) and using the concept "*competir-01*" (correct way). Another example is the word "*bilheteiro*" ("ticket clerk"), which was encoded using the concept "*bilheteiro*" by some annotators. However, the correct encoding was to interpret "*bilheteiro*" as "*pessoa que vende bilhetes*" ("person that sells tickets") and, thus, encoding it as follows:

```
(p / pessoa
   :ARG0-of (v / vender-01
      :ARG1 (b / bilhete)
```

Finally, another difficulty was associated to the

use of temporal expressions. For example, the expression *"até agora"* ("until now") was encoded in several ways by the annotators. In this case, this expression was treated as fixed, using the concept *"até-agora"*.

5.3 Common Mistakes

Some of the frequent errors made in the annotation process include the following:

- No lemmatization: there were several cases where some annotators did not use the lemmas to represent the concepts. In this way, this decreased inter-annotator agreement and could harm the annotation quality. For example, the concept *"equipamento"* ("equipment") should be used instead of *"equipamentos"* ("equipments"), and the concept *"ele"* ("he") instead of *"eles"* ("they").

- Specific characters for Portuguese: the AMR Editor tool was developed for annotating English sentences. Thus, this tool does not work well when a sentence to be annotated includes words with characters used in Portuguese like *"â"* or *"ç"*. To solve this problem, it was suggested that annotators omit these characters when using the editor (replacing by one general character like *"a"* and *"c"*) and then restore the correct characters as a post-editing step. However, these errors occurred, impairing the agreement.

- Variable errors or format errors: some annotators opted not to use the AMR Editor tool to build the AMR graphs, resulting in mistakes related to the number of parenthesis of the PENMAN notation and the variable declaration repetition. For example, the concept *"correr"* ("run") was represented by the variable *"c"* and the concept *"coelho"* ("rabbit") was also represented by the same variable, producing an error in the graph representation.

5.4 Annotation Challenges

During the annotation process (after the training stage), several challenges emerged. In what follows, some of these challenges are briefly discussed.

- Expressions or short sentences. Although the length of the sentences (or expressions) were tiny (3-5 words), expressions like *"nada demais?"*, *"De quem é a culpa?"*, *"Não, em hipótese alguma."* were difficult to annotate. In some cases, it happened due to lack of context. In other cases, to identify which concepts should be included in the representation and how these concepts should be related was a hard task. This representation problem may be reflected in the inter-annotator agreement decay down to 0.70 (in comparison with the previous agreement).

- Multi-word expressions (MWE). Expressions like *"toda hora"*, *"todo mundo"*, or *"estar na moda"* in the sentence *"Academias especializadas estão na moda."* were examples of multi-word expressions that annotators could not represent as a 1-word synonym (as the guideline indicates). In these cases, annotators join the words (for example, *"toda-hora"* is described as AMR dictionary suggests) or tried to separate the concepts in the graph. Another problem was the MWE identification. Expressions like *"na moda"* could be difficult to identify as a MWE and bring some challenges into the annotation.

- Particularities of Portuguese. Some expressions are specific for Portuguese or similar languages. For example, we may see a double negation in the sentence *"**Não** temos **nenhuma** intelectualidade pronta."*, which does not naturally occur in English. Thus, annotators omitted one of the negations to preserve the meaning of the sentence.

- Indeterminate subjects. In some cases, the subject was indeterminate and the annotators did not annotate the reference. For example, in the sentence *"bebe-se"*, the particle *"se"* did not show who is the subject, so, it was not marked in the representation.

6 Current State of the Annotation

Currently, the corpus is composed by 299 AMR-annotated sentences (considering the inter-annotator agreement sample), which include 907 concepts and 711 relations (excluding "instance", "name", and "op" relations). It is important to notice that there are 26 verbs (or verb senses) that did not appear in the Verbo-Brasil and it is necessary to analyze them in order to increase the coverage of the repository in the future.

Table 3 and Table 4 show the statistics about the concepts and the top 10 most frequent relations annotated in the corpus. For comparison purposes, Table 4 also shows the top 10 most frequent relations annotated in the AMR-annotated corpus based on "The Little Prince" book for Brazilian Portuguese.

One point to remark in relation to Table 4 is that both corpora keep the same proportion in the first relations (the top 5); then, both show slightly different distributions. In the case of "The Little Prince", relations like "degree" and "poss" are more frequent. One reason to explain this is that tales use intensifiers like "more" or "less" and possessives like "mine" or "his" in their vocabulary. On the other hand, news texts, and the sentences and expressions contained in it, describe facts and usually use numbers to report quantities ("quant" relation). More than this, some expressions collected until now (due to their short size) describe imperatives like *"arranje!"* ("get it"). Thus, the imperative mode is frequent in the corpus. It is expected that, when the news corpus grows, these relation will change a bit.

Concepts	Frequency
General concepts	504
Verbo-Brasil concepts	235
Named entities	66
Modal verbs	20
Amr-unknown	33
Other entities and special frames	49

Table 3: Statistics of concepts in the corpus

Current corpus			"The Little Prince" corpus		
Relation	Freq.	%	Relation	Freq.	%
ARG1	173	24.33	ARG1	1,734	25.88
ARG0	140	19.69	ARG0	1,520	22.69
polarity	70	9.85	mod	678	10.12
mod	69	9.70	ARG2	454	6.78
ARG2	53	7.45	polarity	295	4.40
domain	35	4.92	time	246	3.67
quant	25	3.52	domain	211	3.15
time	23	3.23	degree	194	2.90
manner	20	2.81	manner	187	2.79
mode	17	2.39	poss	162	2.42

Table 4: Ten most frequent relations in the news corpus and in the "The Little Prince" corpus

7   Concluding Remarks

This paper showed the process of the AMR annotation on a general purpose corpus using the current AMR guidelines and some adaptations for Portuguese. In general, most of the guidelines could be translated to Portuguese. However, there were some cases that needed improvements, as the use of modal verbs and multi-word expressions. On the other hand, the adopted PropBank-like lexical resource (Verbo-Brasil) needs to increase its coverage.

As future work, besides extending Verbo-Brasil, we plan to try back-translation strategies to accelerate the annotation process.

More details about the corpus and the related ongoing work may be found at the OPINANDO project webpage[8].

Acknowledgments

The authors are grateful to CAPES and USP Research Office for supporting this work and to the several corpus annotators that have collaborated with this research.

References

Omri Abend and Ari Rappoport. 2013. Ucca: A semantics-based grammatical annotation scheme. In *Proccedings of the 10th International Conference on Computational Semantics*, pages 1–12, Potsdam, Germany. Association for Computer Linguistics.

Rafael Anchiêta and Thiago Pardo. 2018. Towards AMR-BR: A SemBank for Brazilian Portuguese Language. In *Proceedings of the 11th International Conference on Language Resources and Evaluation*, pages 974–979, Miyazaki, Japan. European Language Resources Association (ELRA).

Laura Banarescu, Claire Bonial, Shu Cai, Madalina Georgescu, Kira Griffitt, Ulf Hermjakob, Kevin Knight, Philipp Koehn, Martha Palmer, and Nathan Schneider. 2013. Abstract meaning representation for sembanking. In *Proceedings of the 7th Linguistic Annotation Workshop and Interoperability with Discourse*, pages 178–186, Sofia, Bulgaria. Association for Computational Linguistics.

Valerio Basile, Johan Bos, Kilian Evang, and Noortje Venhuizen. 2012. Developing a large semantically annotated corpus. In *Proceedings of the 8th International Conference on Language Resources and Evaluation*, pages 3196–3200, Istanbul, Turkey. European Language Resource Association (ELRA).

---

[8]Available at `https://sites.google.com/icmc.usp.br/opinando/`

Johan Bos. 2016. Expressive power of abstract meaning representations. *Computational Linguistics*, 42(3):527–535.

Shu Cai and Kevin Knight. 2013. Smatch: an evaluation metric for semantic feature structures. In *Proceedings of the 51st Annual Meeting of the Association for Computational Linguistics (Volume 2: Short Papers)*, pages 748–752, Sofia, Bulgaria. Association for Computational Linguistics.

Marco Damonte and Shay B. Cohen. 2018. Cross-lingual abstract meaning representation parsing. In *Proceedings of the 16th Conference of the North American Chapter of the Association for Computational Linguistics: Human Language Technologies, Volume 1 (Long Papers)*, pages 1146–1155, New Orleans, Louisiana. Association for Computational Linguistics.

Magali Sanches Duran and Sandra Maria Aluísio. 2012. Propbank-br: a brazilian treebank annotated with semantic role labels. In *Proceedings of the 8th International Conference on Language Resources and Evaluation*, pages 1862–1867, Istanbul, Turkey. European Language Resources Association (ELRA).

Magali Sanches Duran and Sandra Maria Aluísio. 2015. Automatic generation of a lexical resource to support semantic role labeling in portuguese. In *Proceedings of the Fourth Joint Conference on Lexical and Computational Semantics*, pages 216–221, Denver, Colorado. Association for Computational Linguistics.

Ulf Hermjakob. 2013. Amr editor: A tool to build abstract meaning representations.

Noelia Migueles-Abraira, Rodrigo Agerri, and Arantza Diaz de Ilarraza. 2018. Annotating abstract meaning representations for spanish. In *Proceedings of the 11th Language Resources and Evaluation Conference*, pages 3074–3078, Miyazaki, Japan. European Language Resource Association (ELRA).

Hiroshi Uchida, M Zhu, and T Della Senta. 1996. UNL: Universal networking language–an electronic language for communication, understanding, and collaboration. *Tokyo: UNU/IAS/UNL Center*.

Lucy Vanderwende, Arul Menezes, and Chris Quirk. 2015. An amr parser for english, french, german, spanish and japanese and a new amr-annotated corpus. In *Proceedings of the 13th Conference of the North American Chapter of the Association for Computational Linguistics: Demonstrations*, pages 26–30, Denver, Colorado. Association for Computational Linguistics.

Nianwen Xue, Ondrej Bojar, Jan Hajic, Martha Palmer, Zdenka Uresova, and Xiuhong Zhang. 2014. Not an interlingua, but close: Comparison of english amrs to chinese and czech. In *Proceedings of the 9th International Conference on Language Resources and Evaluation*, pages 1765–1772, Reykjavik, Iceland. European Language Resources Association (ELRA).

Author Index